If you're wondering why you should buy this new edition of *International Politics,* here are five good reasons

1. Fourteen new readings expose you to **new directions in the field** of international relations while also putting perspective on current world affairs, including the 2008–2009 global financial crisis.

2. A new section—**"The Meaning of Globalization"**—considers the ongoing challenge in defining what global interdependence is.

3. A new section—**"The Critics of Globalization"**—offers different views on the pros and cons of globalization.

4. A new section—**"Future Developments"**—looks at broader political, economic, cultural, environmental, and demographic trends that are on the verge of reshaping world politics.

5. **The Reading Guides on MyPoliSciKit** help you understand the selections in *International Politics* by highlighting key passages and illustrating their application to current events.

PEARSON

Save Time and Improve Results with MyPoliSciKit for *International Politics: Enduring Concepts and Contemporary Issues*

mypoliscikit™

This state-of-the-art online learning companion features book-specific assessment and interactive/ multimedia activities to help students connect concepts and current events and to help instructors follow students' learning.

---

mypoliscikit™ **includes:**

 Assessment   Review each chapter using learning objectives, chapter summaries, practice tests, and more.

 Reading Guides Understand and apply the key ideas in each reading by examining key passages.

 Videos   Analyze recent world affairs by watching streaming video from major news providers.

 Simulations   Play the role of an IR decision-maker and experience how IR concepts work in practice.

 World Politics News Review Look beyond today's headlines in this blog's analysis of world politics.

 Financial Times Newsfeeds Get hourly updates of U.S. and world news to keep up with current events.

 This Week's Current Events Quiz   Master the headlines in this review of the week's most important news.

 Mapping Exercises   Test your geographical knowledge of regions around the world.

Online Administration   With Grade Tracker, instructors can easily follow students' work on the site and their progress on each activity.

Log onto www.mypoliscikit.com today to see a demo, redeem your access code, or purchase a subscription.

Questions? Contact your Pearson Longman representative for more information www.pearsonhighered .com/replocator.

INTERNATIONAL POLITICS

Enduring Concepts and Contemporary Issues

TENTH EDITION

BY
ROBERT J. ART
Brandeis University

ROBERT JERVIS
Columbia University

Longman

Boston • Columbus • Indianapolis • New York • San Francisco • Upper Saddle River
•Amsterdam • Cape Town • Dubai • London • Madrid • Milan • Munich • Paris
Montreal • Toronto • Delhi • Mexico City • São Paulo • Sydney
Hong Kong • Seoul • Singapore • Taipei • Tokyo

Acquisitions Editor: Vikram Mukhija
Associate Editor: Donna Garnier
Editorial Assistant: Toni Magyar
Marketing Manager: Lindsey Prudhomme
Senior Media Producer: Regina Vertiz
Production Manager: Denise Phillip
Project Coordination, Text Design, and Electronic Page Makeup: Electronic Publishing
    Services Inc., NYC
Cover Design Manager: Wendy Ann Fredericks
Cover Designer: Bernadette Skok
Cover Photo: © William Andrew/Photographer's Choice/Getty Images
Text Permissions: Glenview
Manufacturing Manager: Mary Fischer
Printer and Binder: R. R. Donnelley & Sons/Crawfordsville
Cover Printer: R. R. Donnelley & Sons/Crawfordsville

For permission to use copyrighted material, grateful acknowledgment is made to the copyright
holders throughout the text and which are hereby made part of this copyright page.

Library of Congress Cataloging-in-Publication Data

  International politics: enduring concepts and contemporary issues / [edited by]
  Robert J. Art and Robert Jervis. — 10th ed.
      p. cm.
  ISBN-13: 978-0-205-77876-8 (pbk.)
  ISBN-10: 0-205-77876-3 (pbk.)
   1. International relations. 2. World politics—1989– 3. Globalization. I. Art, Robert J.
II. Jervis, Robert, 1940–

JZ1242.I574 2010
327—dc22   2009049562

1 2 3 4 5 6 7 8 9 10—DOC—13 12 11 10

Longman
is an imprint of

www.pearsonhighered.com   ISBN-13: 978-0-205-77876-8
ISBN-10:   0-205-77876-3

BRIEF CONTENTS

DETAILED CONTENTS

PREFACE

The first edition of *International Politics* appeared in 1973, and now, with the tenth edition, *International Politics* celebrates its 37th birthday. We are pleased that this reader has been so well received, and we hope instructors and students find the tenth edition as useful as they have found the previous nine.

NEW TO THIS EDITION

The tenth edition retains the four major parts of the ninth edition, and contains 54 selections, fourteen of which are new, giving this edition 25 percent new material. Three important organizational changes have been made in the tenth edition:

- We have moved material on the global environment and climate change to Part Four under the heading "The Global Commons."
- We have expanded the coverage of globalization in Part Three and subdivided the readings on globalization into two sections—"The Meaning of Globalization" and "The Critics of Globalization."
- We have added a new section to Part Four titled "Future Developments."

In addition to these major organizational changes, we have made the following alterations:

- Part One retains the three major subdivisions, but we have added the "Melian Dialogue" by Thucydides to the first subdivision so as to incorporate Thucydides' reflections on the relationship between might and right in international politics; and we have moved Robert Jervis's essay on "Offense, Defense, and the Security Dilemma" to the subdivision on mitigating anarchy, where it more properly belongs.
- Part Two retains its three major subdivisions, but we have added an expanded version of Bruce Hoffman's essay on terrorism; a new selection by Mary Kaldor on the difference between the wars of the contemporary world and those of the past; and a piece by Henry Sokolski that takes issue with Barry Posen's views about a nuclear-armed Iran.
- Part Three has two new selections on international political economy: an essay by Alan Blinder that puts offshoring (the movement of production and services overseas) in historical perspective, and a selection by Robert Wade that puts the 2008–2009 financial crisis in its historic and international context.

- Part Four has nine new selections: Robert Art on what the rise of China portends for Sino-American relations; Audrey Cronin on how terrorism ends; Alan Kuperman on the nature of humanitarian intervention; Barry Schwartz on how to solve commons problems; Moses Naim on an effective form of multilateralism he terms "minilateralism"; and four readings—the National Intelligence Council's *Global 2025* Report, Barry Posen on emerging multipolarity, Robert Kagan on the return of great power rivalry, and Richard Jackson and Neil Howe on coming demographic realities—that peer into the future to divine the contours of international politics then.

FEATURES

Originally, we put this reader together to help give the field of international relations greater focus and to bring to students the best articles we could find on the key theoretical concepts in the field. This accounts for the "enduring concepts" in the book's subtitle. A few editions after the first, we then added a separate section on contemporary issues because of our view that these enduring concepts have more meaning for students when applied to salient contemporary issues. All subsequent editions have followed this basic philosophy of combining the best scholarship on theoretical perspectives with that on important contemporary problems.

In constructing the first edition, and in putting together all subsequent editions, including this one, we have tried to create a reader that embodies four features:

- A selection of subjects that, while not exhaustively covering the field of international politics, nevertheless encompasses most of the essential topics that all of us teach in our introductory courses.
- Individual readings that are mainly analytical in content, that take issue with one another, and that thereby introduce the student to the fundamental debates and points of view in the field.
- Editors' introductions to each part that summarize the central concepts the student must master, that organize the central themes of each part, and that relate the readings to one another.
- A book that can be used either as the core around which to design an introductory course or as the primary supplement to enrich an assigned text.

Since the first edition, the field of international relations has experienced a dramatic enrichment in the subjects studied and the quality of works published. Political economy came into its own as an important subfield in the 1970s. New and important works in the field of security studies appeared. The literature on cooperation among states flourished in the early 1980s, and important studies about the environment began to appear in the mid-1980s. Feminist, post-modernist, and constructivist critiques of the mainstream made their appearance also. With the end of the Cold War, these new issues came to the fore: human rights, the tension between state sovereignty and the obligations of the international community, the global environment, civil wars, failed states, nation-building, and, most recently, the search for new modes of global governance to deal with the collective action problems that are increasingly pressing upon states. The growing diversity of the field has closely mirrored the actual developments in international relations.

Consequently, as for the previous editions, in fashioning the tenth, we have kept in mind both the new developments in world politics and the literature that has accompanied them. Central to this edition, though, as for the other nine, is our belief that the realm of international politics differs fundamentally from that of domestic politics. Therefore, we have continued to put both the developments and the literature in the context of the patterns that still remain valid for understanding the differences between politics in an anarchic environment and politics that takes place under a government.

ACKNOWLEDGMENTS

In putting together this and previous editions, we received excellent advice from the following colleagues, whom we would like to thank for the time and care they took: Linda S. Adams, Baylor University; David G. Becker, Dartmouth College; Andrew Bennett, Georgetown University; Chelsea Brown, Southern Methodist University; James A. Caporaso, University of Washington; Timothy M. Cole, University of Maine; Jane Cramer, University of Oregon; David Edelstein, Georgetown University; Joseph Foudy, Hunter College; Sonia Gardenas, Trinity College; Robert C. Gray, Franklin & Marshall College; Robert J. Griffiths, University of North Carolina at Greensboro; James Hentz, Virginia Military Institute; David Houghton, University of Central Florida; Benjamin Judkins, University of Utah; Sean Kay, Ohio Wesleyan University; Mary McCarthy, Drake University; Timothy McKeown, University of North Carolina at Chapel Hill; James A. Mitchell, California State University, Northridge; Ronald Mitchell, University of Oregon; Layna Mosley, University of North Carolina at Chapel Hill; Mueni W. Muiu, Winston-Salem State University; Kathy L. Powers, Pennsylvania State University; Philip Schrodt, University of Kansas; Randall Schweller, The Ohio State University; Margaret E. Scranton, University of Arkansas at Little Rock; Roslin Simowitz, University of Texas at Arlington; Veronica Ward, Utah State University; and Ken Wise, Creighton University.

ROBERT J. ART

ROBERT JERVIS

PART 1

Anarchy and Its Consequences

Unlike domestic politics, international politics takes place in an arena that has no central governing body. From this central fact flows important consequences for the behavior of states. In Part 1, we explore three of them: the role that principles and morality can and should play in statecraft; the effects that anarchy has on how states view and relate to one another; and the ways that the harsher edges of anarchy can be mitigated, even if not wholly removed.

POWER AND PRINCIPLE IN STATECRAFT

Citizens, students, and scholars alike often take up the study of international politics because they want their country to behave in as principled a way as possible. But they soon discover that principle and power, morality and statecraft do not easily mix. Why should this be? Is it inevitable? Can and should states seek to do good in the world? Will they endanger themselves and harm others if they try? These are timeless questions, having been asked by observers of international politics in nearly every previous era. They therefore make a good starting point for thinking about the nature of international politics and the choices states face in our era.

In his history of the Peloponnesian War, the Greek historian Thucydides made the first, and perhaps the most famous, statement about the relation between the prerogatives of power and the dictates of morality. In the Melian dialogue, he argued that "the strong do what they have the power to do and the weak accept what they have to accept" (more frequently stated as "the strong do what they can and the weak suffer what they must"). For Thucydides considerations of power reigned supreme in international politics and were the key to understanding why the war between Athens and Sparta began in the first place. At root, he argued: "what made war inevitable was the growth of Athenian power and the fear which this caused in Sparta." Fearing that Athens' power was growing more quickly than its own, Sparta launched a preventive war to stop Athens from becoming too powerful. Herein lies the first written insight that changes in relative power positions among states, in this case "city-states," can be a cause of war. The forcefulness with which he argued for the "power politics" view of international relations makes Thucydides the first "Realist" theorist of international politics.

1

Hans J. Morgenthau, a leading twentieth-century theorist of international relations, also takes the "power politics" position. He argues that universal standards of morality cannot be an invariable guide to statecraft because there is an "ineluctable tension between the moral command and the requirements of successful political action." Rather than base statecraft on morality, Morgenthau argues that state actors must think and act in terms of power and must do whatever it takes to defend the national interests of their state. J. Ann Tickner, commenting on the primacy of power in Morgenthau's writings, explains that what he considers to be a realistic description of international politics is only a picture of the past and therefore not a prediction about the future, and proposes what she considers to be a feminist alternative. A world in which state actors think of power in terms of collective empowerment, not in terms of leverage over one another, could produce more cooperative outcomes and pose fewer conflicts between the dictates of morality and the power of self-interest.

THE CONSEQUENCES OF ANARCHY

Even those who argue that morality should play a large role in statecraft acknowledge that international politics is not like domestic politics. In the latter, there is government; in the former, there is none. As a consequence, no agency exists above the individual states with authority and power to make laws and settle disputes. States can make commitments and treaties, but no sovereign power ensures compliance and punishes deviations. This—the absence of a supreme power—is what is meant by the anarchic environment of international politics. Anarchy is therefore said to constitute a *state of war:* When all else fails, force is the *ultima ratio*—the final and legitimate arbiter of disputes among states.

The state of war does not mean that every nation is constantly at the brink of war or actually at war with other nations. Most countries, though, do feel threatened by some states at some time, and every state has experienced periods of intense insecurity. No two contiguous states, moreover, have had a history of close, friendly relations uninterrupted by severe tension if not outright war. Because a nation cannot look to a supreme body to enforce laws, nor count on other nations for constant aid and support, it must rely on its own efforts, particularly for defense against attack. Coexistence in an anarchic environment thus requires *self-help*. The psychological outlook that self-help breeds is best described by a saying common among British statesmen since Palmerston: "Great Britain has no permanent enemies or permanent friends, she has only permanent interests."

Although states must provide the wherewithal to achieve their own ends, they do not always reach their foreign policy goals. The goals may be grandiose; the means available, meager. The goals may be attainable; the means selected, inappropriate. But even if the goals are realistic and the means both available and appropriate, a state can be frustrated in pursuit of its ends. The reason is simple but fundamental to an understanding of international politics: What one state does will inevitably impinge on some other states—on some beneficially, but on others adversely. What one state desires, another may covet. What one thinks its just due, another may find threatening. Steps that a state takes to achieve its goals may be rendered useless by the countersteps others take. No state, therefore, can afford to disregard the effects its actions will have on other nations' behavior. In this sense state behavior is contingent: What one state does is dependent in part upon what others do. Mutual dependence means that each must take the others into account.

Mutual dependence affects nothing more powerfully than it does security— the measures states take to protect their territory. Like other foreign policy goals, the security of one state is contingent upon the behavior of other states. Herein lies the *security dilemma* to which each state is subject: In its efforts to preserve or enhance its own security, one state can take measures that decrease the security of other states and cause them to take countermeasures that neutralize the actions of the first state and that may even menace it. The first state may feel impelled to take further actions, provoking additional countermeasures . . . and so forth. The security dilemma means that an action–reaction spiral can occur between two states or among several of them, forcing each to spend ever larger sums on arms to be no more secure than before. All will run faster merely to stay where they are.

At the heart of the security dilemma are these two constraints: the inherent difficulty in distinguishing between offensive and defensive postures, and the inability of one state to believe or trust that another state's present pacific intentions will remain so. The capability to defend can also provide the capability to attack. In adding to its arms, state A may know that its aim is defensive, that its intentions are peaceful, and therefore that it has no aggressive designs on state B. In a world where states must look to themselves for protection, however, B will examine A's actions carefully and suspiciously. B may think that A will attack it when A's arms become powerful enough and that A's protestations of friendship are designed to lull it into lowering its guard. But even if B believes A's actions are not directed against it, B cannot assume that A's intentions will remain peaceful. Anarchy makes it impossible for A to bind itself to continuing to respect B's interests in the future. B must allow for the possibility that what A can do to it, A sometime might do. The need to assess capabilities along with intentions, or, the equivalent, to allow for a change in intentions, makes state actors profoundly conservative. They prefer to err on the side of safety, to have too much rather than too little. Because security is the basis of existence and the prerequisite for the achievement of all other goals, state actors must be acutely sensitive to the security actions of others. The security dilemma thus means that state actors cannot risk *not* reacting to the security actions of other states, but that in so reacting they can produce circumstances that leave them worse off than before.

The anarchic environment of international politics, then, allows every state to be the final judge of its own interests, but requires that each provide the means to attain them. Because the absence of a central authority permits wars to occur, security considerations become paramount. Because of the effects of the security dilemma, efforts of state leaders to protect their peoples can lead to severe tension and war even when all parties sincerely desire peace. Two states, or two groups of states, each satisfied with the status quo and seeking only security, may not be able to achieve it. Conflicts and wars with no economic or ideological basis can occur. The outbreak of war, therefore, does not necessarily mean that some or all states seek expansion, or that humans have an innate drive for power. That states go to war when none of them wants to, however, does not imply that they never seek war. The security dilemma may explain some wars; it does not explain all wars. States often do experience conflicts of interest over trade, real estate, ideology, and prestige. For example, when someone asked Francis I what differences led to his constant wars with Charles V, he replied: "None whatever. We agree perfectly. We both want control of Italy!" (Cited in Frederick L. Schuman, *International Politics,* 7th ed., New York, 1953, p. 283.) If states cannot obtain what they want by blackmail, bribery, or threats, they may resort to war. Wars can occur when no one wants them; wars usually do occur when someone wants them.

Realists argue that even under propitious circumstances, international cooperation is difficult to achieve because in anarchy, states are often more concerned with relative advantages than with absolute gains. That is, because international politics is a self-help system in which each state must be prepared to rely on its own resources and strength to further its interests, national leaders often seek to become more powerful than their potential adversaries. Cooperation is then made difficult not only by the fear that others will cheat and fail to live up to their agreements, but also by the perceived need to gain a superior position. The reason is not that state actors are concerned with status, but that they fear that arrangements that benefit all, but provide greater benefits to others than to them, will render their country vulnerable to pressure and coercion in the future.

Kenneth N. Waltz develops the above points more fully by analyzing the differences between hierarchic (domestic) and anarchic (international) political systems. He shows why the distribution of capabilities (the relative power positions of states) in anarchic systems is so important and lays out the ways in which political behavior differs in hierarchic and anarchic systems.

There is broad agreement among realists on the consequences of anarchy for states' behavior, but not total agreement. One brand of realists, who are called the "offensive realists," argue that the consequences of anarchy go far beyond producing security dilemmas and making cooperation hard to come by. They assert that anarchy forces states, and especially the great powers, to become "power maximizers" because the only way to assure the state's security is to be the most powerful state in the system. Offensive realism envisions a "dog-eat-dog" world of international politics in which power and fear dominate great power interactions and in which war, or the threat of war, among the great powers or among their proxies is a constant feature of international relations. John J. Mearsheimer lays out the tenets of this brand of Realism.

In an anarchic condition, however, the question to ask may not be, "Why does war occur?" but rather "Why does war not occur more frequently than it does?" Instead of asking "Why do states not cooperate more to achieve common interests?" we should ask "Given anarchy and the security dilemma, how is it that states are able to cooperate at all?" Anarchy and the security dilemma do not produce their effects automatically, and it is not self-evident that states are power maximizers.

Thus, Alexander Wendt argues that Waltz and other realists have missed the extent to which the unpleasant patterns they describe are "socially constructed"—that is, they stem from the actors' beliefs, perceptions, and interpretations of others' behavior. If national leaders believe that anarchy requires an assertive stance that endangers others, conflict will be generated. But if they think they have more freedom of action and do not take the hostility of others for granted, they may be able to create more peaceful relationships. In this view, structure (anarchy) does not determine state action; agency (human decision) does.

THE MITIGATION OF ANARCHY

Even realists note that conflict and warfare are not constant characteristics of international politics. Most states remain at peace with most others most of the time. State actors have developed a number of ways of coping with anarchy; of gaining more than a modicum of security; of regulating their competition with other states; and of developing patterns that contain, but do not eliminate, the dangers of aggression.

Kenneth A. Oye shows that even if anarchy and the security dilemma inhibit cooperation, they do not prevent it. A number of conditions and national strategies can make it easier for states to achieve common ends. Cooperation is usually easier if there are a small number of actors. Not only can each more carefully observe the others, but all actors know that their impact on the system is great enough so that if they fail to cooperate with others, joint enterprises are likely to fail. Furthermore, when the number of actors is large, there may be mechanisms and institutions that group them together, thereby reproducing some of the advantages of small numbers.

The conditions actors face also influence their fates. The barriers of anarchy are more likely to be overcome when actors have long time horizons, when even successfully exploiting others produces an outcome that is only a little better than mutual cooperation, when being exploited by others is only slightly worse than mutual noncooperation, and when mutual cooperation is much better than unrestricted competition. Under such circumstances, states are particularly likely to undertake contingent strategies such as tit-for-tat. That is, they will cooperate with others if others do likewise and refuse to cooperate if others have refused to cooperate with them.

The conditions that actors face are also affected by how severely the security dilemma, discussed above, operates. Robert Jervis shows that the extent to which states can make themselves more secure without menacing others depends in large part on whether offensive postures can be distinguished from defensive ones and whether the offense is believed to be more efficacious than the defense. In a world where defense is thought to be easier than offense, the security dilemma is mitigated and, consequently, states are more secure and the hard edge of anarchy is softened. The reverse is true if offense is thought to be easier: the security dilemma operates powerfully, and, consequently, states are less secure and the effects of anarchy cut deeply.

Most strikingly, it appears that democracies may never have gone to war against each other. This is not to say, as Woodrow Wilson did, that democracies are inherently peaceful. They seem to fight as many wars as do dictatorships. But, as Michael W. Doyle shows, they do not fight each other. If this is correct—and, of course, both the evidence and the reasons are open to dispute—it implies that anarchy and the security dilemma do not prevent peaceful and even harmonious relations among states that share certain common values and beliefs.

Democracies are relatively recent developments. For a longer period of time, two specific devices—international law and diplomacy—have proved useful in resolving conflicts among states. Although not enforced by a world government, international law can provide norms for behavior and mechanisms for settling disputes. The effectiveness of international law derives from the willingness of states to observe it. Its power extends no further than the disposition of states "to agree to agree." Where less than vital interests are at stake, state actors may accept settlements that are not entirely satisfactory because they think the precedents or principles justify the compromises made. Much of international law reflects a consensus among states on what is of equal benefit to all, as, for example, the rules regulating international communications. Diplomacy, too, can facilitate cooperation and resolve disputes. If diplomacy is skillful, and the legitimate interests of the parties in dispute are taken into account, understandings can often be reached on issues that might otherwise lead to war. These points and others are explored more fully by Stanley Hoffmann and Hans J. Morgenthau.

National leaders use these two traditional tools within a balance-of-power system. Much maligned by President Wilson and his followers and misunderstood by many others, balance of power refers to the way in which stability is achieved through the conflicting efforts of individual states, whether or not any or all of them deliberately pursue that goal. Just as Adam Smith argued that if every individual pursued his or her own self-interest, the interaction of individual egoisms would enhance national wealth, so international relations theorists have argued that even if every state seeks power at the expense of the others, no one state will likely dominate. In both cases a general good can be the unintended product of selfish individual actions. Moreover, even if most states desire only to keep what they have, their own interests dictate that they band together in order to resist any state or coalition of states that threatens to dominate them.

The balance-of-power system is likely to prevent any one state's acquiring hegemony. It will not, however, benefit all states equally nor maintain the peace permanently. Rewards will be unequal because of inequalities in power and expertise. Wars will occur because they are one means by which states can preserve what they have or acquire what they covet. Small states may even be eliminated by their more powerful neighbors. The international system will be unstable, however, only if states flock to what they think is the strongest side. What is called *bandwagoning* or the *domino theory* argues that the international system is precarious because successful aggression will attract many followers, either out of fear or out of a desire to share the spoils of victory. Stephen M. Walt disagrees, drawing on balance-of-power theory and historical evidence to argue that, rather than bandwagoning, under most conditions states balance against emerging threats. They do not throw in their lot with the stronger side. Instead, they join with others to prevent any state from becoming so strong that it could dominate the system.

Power balancing is a strategy followed by individual states acting on their own. Other ways of coping with anarchy, which may supplement or exist alongside this impulse, are more explicitly collective. Regimes and institutions can help overcome anarchy and facilitate cooperation. When states agree on the principles, rules, and norms that should govern behavior, they can often ameliorate the security dilemma and increase the scope for cooperation. Institutions may not only embody common understandings but, as Robert O. Keohane argues, they can also help states work toward mutually desired outcomes by providing a framework for long-run agreements, making it easier for each state to see whether others are living up to their promises, and increasing the costs the state will pay if it cheats. In the final section of this reader we will discuss how institutions can contribute to global governance under current conditions.

POWER AND PRINCIPLE IN STATECRAFT

The Melian Dialogue

THUCYDIDES

Next summer Alcibiades sailed to Argos with twenty ships and seized 300 Argive citizens who were still suspected of being pro-Spartan. These were put by the Athenians into the nearby islands under Athenian control.

The Athenians also made an expedition against the island of Melos. They had thirty of their own ships, six from Chios, and two from Lesbos; 1,200 hoplites, 300 archers, and twenty mounted archers, all from Athens; and about 1,500 hoplites from the allies and the islanders.

The Melians are a colony from Sparta. They had refused to join the Athenian empire like the other islanders, and at first had remained neutral without helping either side; but afterwards, when the Athenians had brought force to bear on them by laying waste their land, they had become open enemies of Athens.

Now the generals Cleomedes, the son of Lycomedes, and Tisias, the son of Tisimachus, encamped with the above force in Melian territory and, before doing any harm to the land, first of all sent representatives to negotiate. The Melians did not invite these representatives to speak before the people, but asked them to make the statement for which they had come in front of the governing body and the few. The Athenian representatives then spoke as follows:

'So we are not to speak before the people, no doubt in case the mass of the people should hear once and for all and without interruption an argument from us which is both persuasive and incontrovertible, and should so be led astray. This, we realize, is your motive in bringing us here to speak before the few. Now suppose that you who sit here should make assurance doubly sure. Suppose that you, too, should

Thucydides, "The Melian Dialogue" from *History of the Peloponnesian War*, translated by Rex Warner. Harmondsworth, England: Penguin Classics, 1954, pp. 400–408. Translation copyright © Rex Warner, 1954. Reproduced by permission of Penguin Books Ltd.

refrain from dealing with every point in detail in a set speech, and should instead interrupt us whenever we say something controversial and deal with that before going on to the next point? Tell us first whether you approve of this suggestion of ours.'

The Council of the Melians replied as follows:

'No one can object to each of us putting forward our own views in a calm atmosphere. That is perfectly reasonable. What is scarcely consistent with such a proposal is the present threat, indeed the certainty, of your making war on us. We see that you have come prepared to judge the argument yourselves, and that the likely end of it all will be either war, if we prove that we are in the right, and so refuse to surrender, or else slavery.'

Athenians: If you are going to spend the time in enumerating your suspicions about the future, or if you have met here for any other reason except to look the facts in the face and on the basis of these facts to consider how you can save your city from destruction, there is no point in our going on with this discussion. If, however, you will do as we suggest, then we will speak on.

Melians: It is natural and understandable that people who are placed as we are should have recourse to all kinds of arguments and different points of view. However, you are right in saying that we are met together here to discuss the safety of our country and, if you will have it so, the discussion shall proceed on the lines that you have laid down.

Athenians: Then we on our side will use no fine phrases saying, for example, that we have a right to our empire because we defeated the Persians, or that we have come against you now because of the injuries you have done us—a great mass of words that nobody would believe. And we ask you on your side not to imagine that you will influence us by saying that you, though a colony of Sparta, have not joined Sparta in the war, or that you have never done us any harm. Instead we recommend that you should try to get what it is possible for you to get, taking into consideration what we both really do think; since you know as well as we do that, when these matters are discussed by practical people, the standard of justice depends on the equality of power to compel and that in fact the strong do what they have the power to do and the weak accept what they have to accept.

Melians: Then in our view (since you force us to leave justice out of account and to confine ourselves to self-interest)—in our view it is at any rate useful that you should not destroy a principle that is to the general good of all men—namely, that in the case of all who fall into danger there should be such a thing as fair play and just dealing, and that such people should be allowed to use and to profit by arguments that fall short of a mathematical accuracy. And this is a principle which affects you as much as anybody, since your own fall would be visited by the most terrible vengeance and would be an example to the world.

Athenians: As for us, even assuming that our empire does come to an end, we are not despondent about what would happen next. One is not so much frightened of being conquered by a power which rules over others, as Sparta does (not that we are concerned with Sparta now), as of what would happen if a ruling power is attacked and defeated by its own subjects. So far as this point is concerned, you can leave it to us to face the risks involved. What we shall do now is to show you that it is for the good of our own empire that we are here and that it is for the preservation of your city that we shall say what we are going to say. We do not want any trouble in bringing you into our empire, and we want you to be spared for the good both of yourselves and of ourselves.

Melians: And how could it be just as good for us to be the slaves as for you to be the masters?

Athenians: You, by giving in, would save yourselves from disaster; we, by not destroying you, would be able to profit from you.

Melians: So you would not agree to our being neutral, friends instead of enemies, but allies of neither side?

Athenians: No, because it is not so much your hostility that injures us; it is rather the case that, if we were on friendly terms with you, our subjects would regard that as a sign of weakness in us, whereas your hatred is evidence of our power.

Melians: Is that your subjects' idea of fair play—that no distinction should be made between people who are quite unconnected with you and people who are mostly your own colonists or else rebels whom you have conquered?

Athenians: So far as right and wrong are concerned they think that there is no difference between the two, that those who still preserve their independence do so because they are strong, and that if we fail to attack them it is because we are afraid. So that by conquering you we shall increase not only the size but the security of our empire. We rule the sea and you are islanders, and weaker islanders too than the others; it is therefore particularly important that you should not escape.

Melians: But do you think there is no security for you in what we suggest? For here again, since you will not let us mention justice, but tell us to give in to your interests, we, too, must tell you what our interests are and, if yours and ours happen to coincide, we must try to persuade you of the fact. Is it not certain that you will make enemies of all states who are at present neutral, when they see what is happening here and naturally conclude that in course of time you will attack them too? Does not this mean that you are strengthening the enemies you have already and are forcing others to become your enemies even against their intentions and their inclinations?

Athenians: As a matter of fact we are not so much frightened of states on the continent. They have their liberty, and this means that it will be a long time before they begin to take precautions against us. We are more concerned about islanders like yourselves, who are still unsubdued, or subjects who have already become embittered by the constraint which our empire imposes on them. These are the people who are most likely to act in a reckless manner and to bring themselves and us, too, into the most obvious danger.

Melians: Then surely, if such hazards are taken by you to keep your empire and by your subjects to escape from it, we who are still free would show ourselves great cowards and weaklings if we failed to face everything that comes rather than submit to slavery.

Athenians: No, not if you are sensible. This is no fair fight, with honour on one side and shame on the other. It is rather a question of saving your lives and not resisting those who are far too strong for you.

Melians: Yet we know that in war fortune sometimes makes the odds more level than could be expected from the difference in numbers of the two sides. And if we surrender, then all our hope is lost at once, whereas, so long as we remain in action, there is still a hope that we may yet stand upright.

Athenians: Hope, that comforter in danger! If one already has solid advantages to fall back upon, one can indulge in hope. It may do harm, but will not destroy one. But hope is by nature an expensive commodity, and those who are risking their all on one cast find out what it means only when they are already ruined; it never fails them in the period when such a knowledge would enable them to take precautions. Do not let this happen to you, you who are weak and whose fate depends on a single movement of the scale. And do not be like those people who, as so commonly happens, miss the chance of saving themselves in a human and practical way, and, when every clear and distinct hope has left them in their adversity, turn to what is blind and vague, to prophecies and oracles and such things which by encouraging hope lead men to ruin.

Melians: It is difficult, and you may be sure that we know it, for us to oppose your power and fortune, unless the terms be equal. Nevertheless we trust that the gods will give us fortune as good as yours, because we are standing for what is right against what is wrong; and as for what we lack in power, we trust that it will be made up for by our alliance with the Spartans, who are bound, if for no other reason, then for honour's sake, and because we are their kinsmen, to come to our help. Our confidence, therefore, is not so entirely irrational as you think.

Athenians: So far as the favour of the gods is concerned, we think we have as much right to that as you have. Our aims and our actions are perfectly consistent with the beliefs men hold about the gods and with the principles which govern their own conduct. Our opinion of the gods and our knowledge of men lead us to conclude that it is a general and necessary law of nature to rule whatever one can. This is not a law that we made ourselves, nor were we the first to act upon it when it was made. We found it already in existence, and we shall leave it to exist for ever among those who come after us. We are merely acting in accordance with it, and we know that you or anybody else with the same power as ours would be acting in precisely the same way. And therefore, so far as the gods are concerned, we see no good reason why we should fear to be at a disadvantage. But with regard to your views about Sparta and your confidence that she, out of a sense of honour, will come to your aid, we must say that we congratulate you on your simplicity but do not envy you your folly. In matters that concern themselves or their own constitution the Spartans are quite remarkably good; as for their relations with others, that is a long story, but it can be expressed shortly and clearly by saying that of all people we know the Spartans are most conspicuous for believing that what they like doing is honourable and what suits their interests is just. And this kind of attitude is not going to be of much help to you in your absurd quest for safety at the moment.

Melians: But this is the very point where we can feel most sure. Their own self-interest will make them refuse to betray their own colonists, the Melians, for that would mean losing the confidence of their friends among the Hellenes and doing good to their enemies.

Athenians: You seem to forget that if one follows one's self-interest one wants to be safe, whereas the path of justice and honour involves one in danger. And, where danger is concerned, the Spartans are not, as a rule, very venturesome.

Melians: But we think that they would even endanger themselves for our sake and count the risk more worth taking than in the case of others, because we are so close to the Peloponnese that they could operate more easily, and because they can depend on us more than on others, since we are of the same race and share the same feelings.

Athenians: Goodwill shown by the party that is asking for help does not mean security for the prospective ally. What is looked for is a positive preponderance of power in action. And the Spartans pay attention to this point even more than others do. Certainly they distrust their own native resources so much that when they attack a neighbour they bring a great army of allies with them. It is hardly likely therefore that, while we are in control of the sea, they will cross over to an island.

Melians: But they still might send others. The Cretan sea is a wide one, and it is harder for those who control it to intercept others than for those who want to slip through to do so safely. And even if they were to fail in this, they would turn against your own land and against those of your allies left unvisited by Brasidas. So, instead of troubling about a country which has nothing to do with you, you will find trouble nearer home, among your allies, and in your own country.

Athenians: It is a possibility, something that has in fact happened before. It may happen in your case, but you are well aware that the Athenians have never yet relinquished a single siege operation through fear of others. But we are somewhat shocked to find that, though you announced your intention of discussing how you could preserve yourselves, in all this talk you have said absolutely nothing which could justify a man in thinking that he could be preserved. Your chief points are concerned with what you hope may happen in the future, while your actual resources are too scanty to give you a chance of survival against the forces that are opposed to you at this moment. You will therefore be showing an extraordinary lack of common sense if, after you have asked us to retire from this meeting, you still fail to reach a conclusion wiser than anything you have mentioned so far. Do not be led astray by a false sense of honour—a thing which often brings men to ruin when they are faced with an obvious danger that somehow affects their pride. For in many cases men have still been able to see the dangers ahead of them, but this thing called dishonour, this word, by its own force of seduction, has drawn them into a state where they have surrendered to an idea, while in fact they have fallen voluntarily into irrevocable disaster, in dishonour that is all the more dishonourable because it has come to them from their own folly rather than their misfortune. You, if you take the right view, will be careful to avoid this. You will see that there is nothing disgraceful in giving way to the greatest city in Hellas when she is offering you such reasonable terms—alliance on a tribute-paying basis and liberty to enjoy your own property. And, when you are allowed to choose between war and safety, you will not be so insensitively arrogant as to make the wrong choice. This is the safe rule—to stand up to one's equals, to behave with deference towards one's superiors, and to treat one's inferiors with moderation. Think it over again, then, when we have withdrawn from the meeting, and let this be a point that constantly recurs to your minds—that you are discussing the fate of your country, that you have only one country, and that its future for good or ill depends on this one single decision which you are going to make.

The Athenians then withdrew from the discussion. The Melians, left to themselves, reached a conclusion which was much the same as they had indicated in their previous replies. Their answer was as follows:

'Our decision, Athenians, is just the same as it was at first. We are not prepared to give up in a short moment the liberty which our city has enjoyed from its foundation for 700 years. We put our trust in the fortune that the gods will send and which has saved us up to now, and in the help of men—that is, of the Spartans; and so we shall try to save ourselves. But we invite you to allow us to be friends of yours and enemies to neither side, to make a treaty which shall be agreeable to both you and us, and so to leave our country.'

The Melians made this reply, and the Athenians, just as they were breaking off the discussion, said:

'Well, at any rate, judging from this decision of yours, you seem to us quite unique in your ability to consider the future as something more certain than what is before your eyes, and to see uncertainties as realities, simply because you would like them to be so. As you have staked most on and trusted most in Spartans, luck, and hopes, so in all these you will find yourselves most completely deluded.'

The Athenian representatives then went back to the army, and the Athenian generals, finding that the Melians would not submit, immediately commenced hostilities and built a wall completely round the city of Melos, dividing the work out among the various states. Later they left behind a garrison of some of their own and some allied troops to blockade the place by land and sea, and with the greater part of their army returned home. The force left behind stayed on and continued with the siege.

About the same time the Argives invaded Phliasia and were ambushed by the Phliasians and the exiles from Argos, losing about eighty men.

Then, too, the Athenians at Pylos captured a great quantity of plunder from Spartan territory. Not even after this did the Spartans renounce the treaty and make war, but they issued a proclamation saying that any of their people who wished to do so were free to make raids on the Athenians. The Corinthians also made some attacks on the Athenians because of private quarrels of their own, but the rest of the Peloponnesians stayed quiet.

Meanwhile the Melians made a night attack and captured the part of the Athenian lines opposite the market-place. They killed some of the troops, and then, after bringing in corn and everything else useful that they could lay their hands on, retired again and made no further move, while the Athenians took measures to make their blockade more efficient in future. So the summer came to an end.

In the following winter the Spartans planned to invade the territory of Argos, but when the sacrifices for crossing the frontier turned out unfavourably, they gave up the expedition. The fact that they had intended to invade made the Argives suspect certain people in their city, some of whom they arrested, though others succeeded in escaping.

About this same time the Melians again captured another part of the Athenian lines where there were only a few of the garrison on guard. As a result of this, another force came out afterwards from Athens under the command of Philocrates, the son of Demeas. Siege operations were now carried on vigorously and, as there was also some treachery from inside, the Melians surrendered unconditionally to the Athenians, who put to death all the men of military age whom they took, and sold the women and children as slaves. Melos itself they took over for themselves, sending out later a colony of 500 men.

Six Principles of Political Realism

HANS J. MORGENTHAU

1. Political realism believes that politics, like society in general, is governed by objective laws that have their roots in human nature. In order to improve society it is first necessary to understand the laws by which society lives. The operation of these laws being impervious to our preferences, men will challenge them only as the risk of failure.

Realism, believing as it does in the objectivity of the laws of politics, must also believe in the possibility of developing a rational theory that reflects, however imperfectly and one-sidedly, these objective laws. It believes also, then, in the possibility of distinguishing in politics between truth and opinion—between what is true objectively and rationally, supported by evidence and illuminated by reason, and what is only a subjective judgment, divorced from the facts as they are and informed by prejudice and wishful thinking.

Human nature, in which the laws of politics have their roots, has not changed since the classical philosophies of China, India, and Greece endeavored to discover these laws. Hence, novelty is not necessarily a virtue in political theory, nor is old age a defect. The fact that a theory of politics, if there be such a theory, has never been heard of before tends to create a presumption against, rather than in favor of, its soundness. Conversely, the fact that a theory of politics was developed hundreds or even thousands of years ago—as was the theory of the balance of power—does not create a presumption that it must be outmoded and obsolete. . . .

For realism, theory consists in ascertaining facts and giving them meaning through reason. It assumes that the character of a foreign policy can be ascertained only through the examination of the political acts performed and of the foreseeable consequences of these acts. Thus we can find out what statesmen have actually done, and from the foreseeable consequences of their acts we can surmise what their objectives might have been.

Yet examination of the facts is not enough. To give meaning to the factual raw material of foreign policy, we must approach political reality with a kind of rational outline, a map that suggests to us the possible meanings of foreign policy. In other words, we put ourselves in the position of a statesman who must meet a certain problem of foreign policy under certain circumstances, and we ask ourselves what the rational alternatives are from which a statesman may choose who must meet this problem under these circumstances (presuming always that he acts in a rational manner), and which of these rational alternatives this particular statesman, acting under these circumstances, is likely to choose. It is the testing of this rational hypothesis against the actual facts and their consequences that gives theoretical meaning to the facts of international politics.

2. The main signpost that helps political realism to find its way through the landscape of international politics is the concept of interest defined in terms of power. This concept provides the link between reason trying to understand international politics and the facts to be understood. It sets politics as an autonomous sphere of action and understanding apart from other spheres, such as economics (understood in terms of interest defined as wealth), ethics, aesthetics, or religion. Without such a concept a theory of politics, international or domestic, would be altogether impossible, for without it we could not distinguish between political and nonpolitical facts, nor could we bring at least a measure of systematic order to the political sphere.

We assume that statesmen think and act in terms of interest defined as power, and the evidence of history bears that assumption out. That assumption allows us to retrace and anticipate, as it were, the steps a statesman—past, present, or future—has taken or will take on the political scene. We look over his shoulder when he writes his dispatches; we listen in on his conversation with other statesmen; we read and anticipate his very thoughts. Thinking in terms of interest defined as power, we think as he does, and as disinterested observers we understand his thoughts and actions perhaps better than he, the actor on the political scene, does himself.

The concept of interest defined as power imposes intellectual discipline upon the observer, infuses rational order into the subject matter of politics, and thus makes the theoretical understanding of politics possible. On the side of the actor, it provides for rational discipline in action and creates that astounding continuity in foreign policy which makes American, British, or Russian foreign policy appear as an intelligible, rational continuum, by and large consistent within itself, regardless of the different motives, preferences, and intellectual and moral qualities of successive statesmen. A realist theory of international politics, then, will guard against two popular fallacies: the concern with motives and the concern with ideological preferences.

To search for the clue to foreign policy exclusively in the motives of statesmen is both futile and deceptive. It is futile because motives are the most illusive of psychological data, distorted as they are, frequently beyond recognition, by the interests and emotions of actor and observer alike. Do we really know what our own motives are? And what do we know of the motives of others?

Yet even if we had access to the real motives of statesmen, that knowledge would help us little in understanding foreign policies, and might well lead us astray. It is true that the knowledge of the statesman's motives may give us one among many clues as to what the direction of his foreign policy might be. It cannot give us, however, the one clue by which to predict his foreign policies. History shows no exact and necessary correlation between the quality of motives and the quality of foreign policy. This is true in both moral and political terms.

We cannot conclude from the good intentions of a statesman that his foreign policies will be either morally praiseworthy or politically successful. Judging his motives, we can say that he will not intentionally pursue policies that are morally wrong, but we can say nothing about the probability of their success. If we want to know the moral and political qualities of his actions, we must know them, not his motives. How often have statesmen been motivated by the desire to improve the world, and ended by making it worse? And how often have they sought one goal and ended by achieving something they neither expected nor desired?. . .

A realist theory of international politics will also avoid the other popular fallacy of equating the foreign policies of a statesman with his philosophic or political sympathies, and of deducing the former from the latter. Statesmen, especially under contemporary conditions, may well make a habit of presenting their foreign policies in terms of their philosophic and political sympathies in order to gain popular support for them. Yet they will distinguish with Lincoln between their "*official duty,*" which is to think and act in terms of the national interest, and their "*personal wish,*" which is to see their own moral values and political principles realized throughout the world. Political realism does not require, nor does it condone, indifference to political ideals and moral principles, but it requires indeed a sharp distinction between the desirable and the possible—between what is desirable everywhere and at all times and what is possible under the concrete circumstances of time and place.

It stands to reason that not all foreign policies have always followed so rational an objective, and unemotional a course. The contingent elements of personality, prejudice, and subjective preference, and of all the weaknesses of intellect and will which flesh is heir to, are bound to deflect foreign policies from their rational course. Especially where foreign policy is conducted under the conditions of democratic control, the need to marshal popular emotions to the support of foreign policy cannot fail to impair the rationality of foreign policy itself. Yet a theory of foreign policy which aims at rationality must for the time being, as it were, abstract from these irrational elements and seek to paint a picture of foreign policy which presents the rational essence to be found in experience, without the contingent deviations from rationality which are also found in experience. . . .

The difference between international politics as it actually is and a rational theory derived from it is like the difference between a photograph and a painted portrait. The photograph shows everything that can be seen by the naked eye; the painted portrait does not show everything that can be seen by the naked eye, but it shows, or at least seeks to show, one thing that the naked eye cannot see: the human essence of the person portrayed.

Political realism contains not only a theoretical but also a normative element. It knows that political reality is replete with contingencies and systemic irrationalities and points to the typical influences they exert upon foreign policy. Yet it shares with all social theory the need, for the sake of theoretical understanding, to stress the rational elements of political reality; for it is these rational elements that make reality intelligible for theory. Political realism presents the theoretical construct of a rational foreign policy which experience can never completely achieve.

At the same time political realism considers a rational foreign policy to be good foreign policy; for only a rational foreign policy minimizes risks and maximizes benefits and, hence, complies both with the moral precept of prudence and the political requirement of success. Political realism wants the photographic picture of the political world to resemble as much as possible its painted portrait. Aware of the inevitable gap between good—that is, rational—foreign policy and foreign policy as it actually is, political realism maintains not only that theory must focus upon the rational elements of political reality, but also that foreign policy ought to be rational in view of its own moral and practical purposes.

Hence, it is no argument against the theory here presented that actual foreign policy does not or cannot live up to it. That argument misunderstands the intention of this book, which is to present not an indiscriminate description of political reality, but a rational theory of international politics. Far from being invalidated by the fact that, for instance, a perfect balance of power policy will scarcely be found in reality, it assumes that reality, being deficient in this respect, must be understood and evaluated as an approximation to an ideal system of balance of power.

3. Realism assumes that its key concept of interest defined as power is an objective category which is universally valid, but it does not endow that concept with a meaning that is fixed once and for all. The idea of interest is indeed of the essence of politics and is unaffected by the circumstances of time and place. Thucydides' statement, born of the experiences of ancient Greece, that "identity of interests is the surest of bonds whether between states or individuals" was taken up in the nineteenth century by Lord Salisbury's remark that "the only bond of union that endures" among nations is "the absence of all clashing interests." It was erected into a general principle of government by George Washington:

> A small knowledge of human nature will convince us, that, with far the greatest part of mankind, interest is the governing principle; and that almost every man is more or less, under its influence. Motives of public virtue may for a time, or in particular instances, actuate men to the observance of a conduct purely disinterested; but they are not of themselves sufficient to produce persevering conformity to the refined dictates and obligations of social duty. Few men are capable of making a continual sacrifice of all views of private interest, or advantage, to the common good. It is vain to exclaim against the depravity of human nature on this account; the fact is so, the experience of every age and nation has proved it and we must in a great measure, change the constitution of man, before we can make it otherwise. No institution, not built on the presumptive truth of these maxims can succeed.[1]

It was echoed and enlarged upon in our century by Max Weber's observation:

> Interests (material and ideal), not ideas, dominate directly the actions of men. Yet the "images of the world" created by these ideas have very often served as switches determining the tracks on which the dynamism of interests kept actions moving.[2]

Yet the kind of interest determining political action in a particular period of history depends upon the political and cultural context within which foreign policy is formulated. The goals that might be pursued by nations in their foreign policy can run the whole gamut of objectives any nation has ever pursued or might possibly pursue.

The same observations apply to the concept of power. Its content and the manner of its use are determined by the political and cultural environment. Power may comprise anything that establishes and maintains the control of man over man. Thus power covers all social relationships which serve that end, from physical violence to the most subtle psychological ties by which one mind controls another. Power covers the domination of man by man, both when it is disciplined by moral ends and controlled by constitutional safeguards, as in Western democracies, and when it is that untamed and barbaric force which finds its laws in nothing but its own strength and its sole justification in its aggrandizement.

Political realism does not assume that the contemporary conditions under which foreign policy operates, with their extreme instability and the ever present threat of large-scale violence, cannot be changed. The balance of power, for instance, is indeed a perennial element of all pluralistic societies, as the authors of *The Federalist* papers well knew; yet it is capable of operating, as it does in the United States, under the conditions of relative stability and peaceful conflict. If the factors that have given rise to these conditions can be duplicated on the international scene, similar conditions of stability and peace will then prevail there, as they have over long stretches of history among certain nations.

What is true of the general character of international relations is also true of the nation state as the ultimate point of reference of contemporary foreign policy. While the realist indeed believes that interest is the perennial standard by which political action must be judged and directed, the contemporary connection between interest and the nation state is a product of history, and is therefore bound to disappear in the course of history. Nothing in the realist position militates against the assumption that the present division of the political world into nation states will be replaced by larger units of a quite different character, more in keeping with the technical potentialities and the moral requirements of the contemporary world.

The realist parts company with other schools of thought before the all-important question of how the contemporary world is to be transformed. The realist is persuaded that this transformation can be achieved only through the workmanlike manipulation of the perennial forces that have shaped the past as they will the future. The realist cannot be persuaded that we can bring about that transformation by confronting a political reality that has its own laws with an abstract ideal that refuses to take those laws into account.

4. Political realism is aware of the moral significance of political action. It is also aware of the ineluctable tension between the moral command and the requirements of successful political action. And it is unwilling to gloss over and obliterate that tension and thus to obfuscate both the moral and the political issue by making it appear as though the stark facts of politics were morally more satisfying than they actually are, and the moral law less exacting than it actually is.

Realism maintains that universal moral principles cannot be applied to the actions of states in their abstract universal formulation, but that they must be filtered through the concrete circumstances of time and place. The individual may say for himself: "*Fiat justitia, pereat mundus* (Let justice be done, even if the world perish)," but the state has no right to say so in the name of those who are in its care. Both individual and state must judge political action by universal moral principles, such as that of liberty. Yet while the individual has a moral right to sacrifice himself in defense of such a moral principle, the state has no right to let its moral disapprobation of the infringement of liberty get in the way of successful political action, itself inspired by the moral principle of national survival. There can be no political morality without prudence; that is, without consideration of the political consequences of seemingly moral action. Realism, then, considers prudence—the weighing of the consequences of alternative political actions—to be the supreme virtue in politics. Ethics in the abstract judges action by its conformity with the moral law; political ethics judges action by its political consequences. Classical and medieval philosophy knew this, and so did Lincoln when he said:

> I do the very best I know how, the very best I can, and I mean to keep doing so until the end. If the end brings me out all right, what is said against me won't amount to anything. If the end brings me out wrong, ten angels swearing I was right would make no difference.

5. Political realism refuses to identify the moral aspirations of a particular nation with the moral laws that govern the universe. As it distinguishes between truth and opinion, so it distinguishes between truth and idolatry. All nations are tempted—and few have been able to resist the temptation for long—to clothe their own particular aspirations and actions in the moral purposes of the universe. To know that nations are subject to the moral law is one thing, while to pretend to know with certainty what is good and evil in the relations among nations is quite another. There is a world of difference between the belief that all nations stand under the judgment of God, inscrutable to the human mind, and the blasphemous conviction that God is always on one's side and that what one wills oneself cannot fail to be willed by God also.

The lighthearted equation between a particular nationalism and the counsels of Providence is morally indefensible, for it is that very sin of pride against which the Greek tragedians and the Biblical prophets have warned rulers and ruled. That equation is also politically pernicious, for it is liable to engender the distortion in judgement which, in the blindness of crusading frenzy, destroys nations and civilizations—in the name of moral principle, ideal, or God himself.

On the other hand, it is exactly the concept of interest defined in terms of power that saves us from both that moral excess and that political folly. For if we look at all nations, our own included, as political entities pursuing their respective interests defined in terms of power, we are able to do justice to all of them. And we are able to do justice to all of them in a dual sense: We are able to judge other nations as we judge our own and, having judged them in this fashion, we are then capable of pursuing policies that respect the interests of other nations, while protecting and promoting those of our own. Moderation in policy cannot fail to reflect the moderation of moral judgment.

6. The difference, then, between political realism and other schools of thought is real, and it is profound. However much the theory of political realism may have been misunderstood and misinterpreted, there is no gainsaying its distinctive intellectual and moral attitude to matters political.

Intellectually, the political realist maintains the autonomy of the political sphere, as the economist, the lawyer, the moralist maintain theirs. He thinks in terms of interest defined as power, as the economist thinks in terms of interest defined as wealth; the lawyer, of the conformity of action with legal rules; the moralist, of the conformity of action with moral principles. The economist asks, "How does this policy affect the wealth of society, or a segment of it?" The lawyer asks: "Is this policy in accord with the rules of law?" The moralist asks: "Is this policy in accord with moral principles?" And the political realist asks: "How does this policy affect the power of the nation?" (Or of the federal government, of Congress, of the party, of agriculture, as the case may be.)

The political realist is not unaware of the existence and relevance of standards of thought other than political ones. As political realist, he cannot but subordinate these other standards to those of politics. And he parts company with other schools when they impose standards of thought appropriate to other spheres upon the political sphere. . . .

This realist defense of the autonomy of the political sphere against its subversion by other modes of thought does not imply disregard for the existence and importance of these other modes of thought. It rather implies that each should be assigned its proper sphere and function. Political realism is based upon a pluralistic conception of human nature. Real man is a composite of "economic man," "political man," "moral man," "religious man," etc. A man who was nothing but "political man" would be a beast, for he would be completely lacking in moral restraints. A man who was nothing but "moral man" would be a fool, for he would be completely lacking in prudence. A man who was nothing but "religious man" would be a saint, for he would be completely lacking in worldly desires.

Recognizing that these different facets of human nature exist, political realism also recognizes that in order to understand one of them one has to deal with it on its own terms. That is to say, if I want to understand "religious man," I must for the time being abstract from the other aspects of human nature and deal with its religious aspect as if it were the only one. Furthermore, I must apply to the religious sphere the standards of thought appropriate to it, always remaining aware of the existence of other standards and their actual influence upon the religious qualities of man. What is true of this facet of human nature is true of all the others. No modern economist, for instance, would conceive of his science and its relations to other sciences of man in any other way. It is exactly through such a process of emancipation from other standards of thought, and the development of one appropriate to its subject matter, that economics has developed as an autonomous theory of the economic activities of man. To contribute to a similar development in the field of politics is indeed the purpose of political realism.

It is in the nature of things that a theory of politics which is based upon such principles will not meet with unanimous approval—nor does, for that matter, such a foreign policy. For theory and policy alike run counter to two trends in our culture which are not able to reconcile themselves to the assumptions and results of a rational, objective theory of politics. One of these trends disparages the role of power in society on grounds that stem from the experience and philosophy of the nineteenth century; we shall address ourselves to this tendency later in greater detail. The other trend, opposed to the realist theory and practice of politics, stems from the very relationship that exists, and must exist, between the human mind and the political sphere. . . . The human mind in its day-by-day operations cannot bear to look the truth of politics straight in the face. It must disguise, distort, belittle, and embellish the truth—the more so, the more the individual is actively involved in the processes of politics, and particularly in those of international politics. For only by deceiving himself about the nature of politics and the role he plays on the political scene is man able to live contentedly as a political animal with himself and his fellow men.

Thus it is inevitable that a theory which tries to understand international politics as it actually is and as it ought to be in view of its intrinsic nature, rather than as people would like to see it, must overcome a psychological resistance that most other branches of learning need not face.

NOTES

1. *The Writings of George Washington,* edited by John C. Fitzpatrick (Washington: United States Printing Office, 1931–44), Vol. X, p. 363.
2. Marianne Weber, *Max Weber* (Tuebingen: J. C. B. Mohr, 1926), pp. 347–8. See also Max Weber, *Gesammelte Aufsätze zur Religionssociology* (Tuebingen: J. C. B. Mohr, 1920), p. 252.

A Critique of Morgenthau's Principles of Political Realism

J. ANN TICKNER

It is not in giving life but in risking life that man is raised above the animal: that is why superiority has been accorded in humanity not to the sex that brings forth but to that which kills.

SIMONE DE BEAUVOIR[1]

International politics is a man's world, a world of power and conflict in which warfare is a privileged activity. Traditionally, diplomacy, military service and the science of international politics have been largely male domains. In the past women have rarely been included in the ranks of professional diplomats or the military; of the relatively few women who specialize in the academic discipline of international relations, few are security specialists. Women political scientists who do study international relations tend to focus on areas such as international political economy, North–South relations and matters of distributive justice.

Today, in the United States, where women are entering the military and the foreign service in greater numbers than ever before, they are rarely to be found in positions of military leadership or at the top of the foreign policy establishment.[2] One notable exception, Jeane Kirkpatrick, who was U.S. ambassador to the United Nations in the early 1980s, has described herself as "a mouse in a man's world"; for, in spite of her authoritative and forceful public style and strong conservative credentials, Kirkpatrick maintains that she failed to win the respect or attention of her male colleagues on matters of foreign policy.[3]

Kirkpatrick's story could serve to illustrate the discrimination that women often encounter when they rise to high political office. However, the doubts as to whether a woman would be strong enough to press the nuclear button (an issue raised when a tearful Patricia Schroeder was pictured sobbing on her husband's shoulder as she bowed out of the 1988 U.S. presidential race), suggest that there may be an even more fundamental barrier to women's entry into the highest ranks of the military or of foreign policy making. Nuclear strategy, with its vocabulary of power, threat, force and deterrence, has a distinctly masculine ring;[4] moreover women are stereo-

From J. Ann Tickner, "A Critique of Morgenthau's Principles of Political Realism" in *Gender and International Relations*, eds. Rebecca Grant and Kathleen Newland. Published by Indiana University Press. Reprinted by permission of Kathleen Newland. Portions of the text and some footnotes have been omitted.

typically judged to be lacking in qualities which these terms evoke. It has also been suggested that, although more women are entering the world of public policy, they are more comfortable dealing with domestic issues such as social welfare that are more compatible with their nurturing skills. Yet the large number of women in the ranks of the peace movement suggests that women are not uninterested in issues of war and peace, although their frequent dissent from national security policy has often branded them as naive, uninformed or even unpatriotic.

In this Chapter I propose to explore the question of why international politics is perceived as a man's world and why women remain so underrepresented in the higher echelons of the foreign policy establishment, the military and the academic discipline of international relations. Since I believe that there is something about this field that renders it particularly inhospitable and unattractive to women, I intend to focus on the nature of the discipline itself rather than on possible strategies to remove barriers to women's access to high policy positions. As I have already suggested, the issues that are given priority in foreign policy are issues with which men have had a special affinity. Moreover, if it is primarily men who are describing these issues and constructing theories to explain the workings of the international system, might we not expect to find a masculine perspective in the academic discipline also? If this were so then it could be argued that the exclusion of women has operated not only at the level of discrimination but also through a process of self-selection which begins with the way in which we are taught about international relations.

In order to investigate this claim that the discipline of international relations, as it has traditionally been defined by realism, is based on a masculine world view, I propose to examine the six principles of political realism formulated by Hans J. Morgenthau in his classic work *Politics Among Nations*. I shall use some ideas from feminist theory to show that the way in which Morgenthau describes and explains international politics, and the prescriptions that ensue are embedded in a masculine perspective. Then I shall suggest some ways in which feminist theory might help us begin to conceptualize a worldview from a feminine perspective and to formulate a feminist epistemology of international relations. Drawing on these observations I shall conclude with a reformulation of Morgenthau's six principles. Male critics of contemporary realism have already raised many of the same questions about realism that I shall address. However, in undertaking this exercise, I hope to make a link between a growing critical perspective on international relations theory and feminist writers interested in global issues. Adding a feminist perspective to its discourse could also help to make the field of international relations more accessible to women scholars and practitioners.

HANS J. MORGENTHAU'S PRINCIPLES OF POLITICAL REALISM: A MASCULINE PERSPECTIVE?

I have chosen to focus on Hans J. Morgenthau's six principles of political realism because they represent one of the most important statements of contemporary realism from which several generations of scholars and practitioners of international relations in the United States have been nourished. Although Morgenthau has frequently been criticized for his lack of scientific rigour and ambiguous use of language, these six principles have significantly framed the way in which the majority of international relations scholars and practitioners in the West have thought about international politics since 1945.[5]

Morgenthau's principles of political realism can be summarized as follows:

1. Politics, like society in general, is governed by objective laws that have their roots in human nature, which is unchanging: therefore it is possible to develop a rational theory that reflects these objective laws.

2. The main signpost of political realism is the concept of interest defined in terms of power which infuses rational order into the subject matter of politics, and thus makes the theoretical understanding of politics possible. Political realism stresses the rational, objective and unemotional.

3. Realism assumes that interest defined as power is an objective category which is universally valid but not with a meaning that is fixed once and for all. Power is the control of man over man.

4. Political realism is aware of the moral significance of political action. It is also aware of the tension between the moral command and the requirements of successful political action.

5. Political realism refuses to identify the moral aspirations of a particular nation with the moral laws that govern the universe. It is the concept of interest defined in terms of power that saves us from moral excess and political folly.

6. The political realist maintains the autonomy of the political sphere; he asks "How does this policy affect the power of the nation?" Political realism is based on a pluralistic conception of human nature. A man who was nothing but "political man" would be a beast, for he would be completely lacking in moral restraints. But, in order to develop an autonomous theory of political behaviour, "political man" must be abstracted from other aspects of human nature.[6]

I am not going to argue that Morgenthau is incorrect in his portrayal of the international system. I do believe, however, that it is a partial description of international politics because it is based on assumptions about human nature that are partial and that privilege masculinity. First, it is necessary to define masculinity and femininity. According to almost all feminist theorists, masculinity and femininity refer to a set of socially constructed categories, which vary in time and place, rather than to biological determinants. In the West, conceptual dichotomies such as objectivity vs. subjectivity, reason vs. emotion, mind vs. body, culture vs. nature, self vs. other or autonomy vs. relatedness, knowing vs. being and public vs. private have typically been used to describe male/female differences by feminists and non-feminists alike.[7] In the United States, psychological tests conducted across different socioeconomic groups confirm that individuals perceive these dichotomies as masculine and feminine and also that the characteristics associated with masculinity are more highly valued by men and women alike.[8] It is important to stress, however, that these characteristics are stereotypical; they do not necessarily describe individual men or women, who can exhibit characteristics and modes of thought associated with the opposite sex.

Using a vocabulary that contains many of the words associated with masculinity as I have identified it, Morgenthau asserts that it is possible to develop a rational (and unemotional) theory of international politics based on objective laws that have their roots in human nature. Since Morgenthau wrote the first edition of *Politics Among Nations* in 1948, this search for an objective science of international politics based on the model of the natural sciences has been an important part of the realist and neorealist agenda. In her feminist critique of the natural sciences, Evelyn Fox Keller points out that most scientific communities share the "assumption that the universe they study is directly accessible, represented by concepts and shaped not by language but only by the demands of logic and experiment."[9] The laws of nature, according to this view of science, are "beyond the relativity of language." Like most feminists, Keller rejects this view of science which, she asserts, imposes a coercive, hierarchical and conformist pattern on scientific inquiry. Feminists in general are sceptical about the possibility of finding a universal and objective foundation for knowledge, which Morgenthau claims is possible. Most share the belief that knowledge is socially constructed: since it is language that transmits knowledge, the use of language and its claims to objectivity must continually be questioned.

Keller argues that objectivity, as it is usually defined in our culture, is associated with masculinity. She identifies it as "a network of interactions between gender development, a belief system that equates objectivity with masculinity, and a set of cultural values that simultaneously (and cojointly) elevates what is defined as scientific and what is defined as masculine."[10] Keller links the separation of self from other, an important stage of masculine gender development, with this notion of objectivity. Translated into scientific inquiry this becomes the striving for the separation of subject and object, an important goal of modern science and one which, Keller asserts, is based on the need for control; hence objectivity becomes associated with power and domination.

The need for control has been an important motivating force for modern realism. To begin his search for an objective, rational theory of international politics, which could impose order on a chaotic and conflictual world, Morgenthau constructs an abstraction which he calls political man, a beast completely lacking in moral restraints. Morgenthau is deeply aware that real men, like real states, are both moral and bestial but, because states do not live up to the universal moral laws that govern the universe, those who behave morally in international politics are doomed to failure because of the immoral actions of others. To solve this tension Morgenthau postulates a realm of international politics in which the amoral behaviour of political man is not only permissible but prudent. It is a Hobbesian world, separate and distinct from the world of domestic order. In it, states may act like beasts, for survival depends on a maximization of power and a willingness to fight.

Having long argued that the personal is political, most feminist theory would reject the validity of constructing an autonomous political sphere around which boundaries of permissible modes of conduct have been drawn. As Keller maintains, "the demarcation between public and private not only defines and defends the boundaries of the political but also helps form its content and style."[11] Morgenthau's political man is a social construct based on a partial representation of human nature. One might well ask where the women were in Hobbes's state of nature; presumably they must have been involved in reproduction and childrearing, rather than warfare, if life was to go on for more than one generation.[12] Morgenthau's emphasis on the conflictual aspects of the international system contributes to a tendency, shared by other realists, to de-emphasize elements of cooperation and regeneration which are also aspects of international relations.[13]

Morgenthau's construction of an amoral realm of international power politics is an attempt to resolve what he sees as a fundamental tension between the moral laws that govern the universe and the requirements of successful political action in a world where states use morality as a cloak to justify the pursuit of their own national interests. Morgenthau's universalistic morality postulates the highest form of morality as an abstract ideal, similar to the Golden Rule, to which states seldom adhere: the morality of states, by contrast, is an instrumental morality guided by self-interest.

Morgenthau's hierarchical ordering of morality contains parallels with the work of psychologist Lawrence Kohlberg. Based on a study of the moral development of 84 American boys, Kohlberg concludes that the highest stage of human moral development (which he calls stage 6) is the ability to recognize abstract universal principles of justice; lower on the scale (stage 2) is an instrumental morality concerned with serving one's own interests while recognizing that others have interests too. Between these two is an interpersonal morality which is contextual and characterized by sensitivity to the needs of others (stage 3).[14]

In her critique of Kohlberg's stages of moral development, Carol Gilligan argues that they are based on a masculine conception of morality. On Kohlberg's scale women rarely rise above the third or contextual stage. Gilligan claims that this is not a sign of inferiority but of difference. Since women are socialized into a mode of thinking which is contextual and narrative, rather than formal and abstract, they tend to see issues in contextual rather than in abstract terms.[15] In international relations the tendency to think about morality either in terms of abstract, universal and unattainable standards or as purely instrumental, as Morgenthau does, detracts from our ability to tolerate cultural differences and to seek potential for building community in spite of these differences.

Using examples from feminist literature I have suggested that Morgenthau's attempt to construct an objective, universal theory of international politics is rooted in assumptions about human nature and morality that, in modern Western culture, are associated with masculinity. Further evidence that Morgenthau's principles are not the basis for a universalistic and objective theory is contained in his frequent references to the failure of what he calls the "legalistic–moralistic" or idealist approach to world politics which he claims was largely responsible for both the world wars. Having laid the blame for the Second World War on the misguided morality of appeasement, Morgenthau's *realpolitik* prescriptions for successful political action appear as prescriptions for avoiding the mistakes of the 1930s rather than as prescriptions with timeless applicability.

If Morgenthau's world view is embedded in the traumas of the Second World War, are his prescriptions still valid as we move further away from this event? I share with other critics of realism the view that, in a rapidly changing world, we must begin to search for modes of behaviour different from those prescribed by Morgenthau. Given that any war between the major powers is likely to be nuclear, increasing security by increasing power could be suicidal.[16] Moreover, the nation state, the primary constitutive element of the international system for Morgenthau and other realists, is no longer able to deal with an increasingly pluralistic array of problems ranging from economic interdependence to environmental degradation. Could feminist theory make a contribution to international relations theory by constructing an alternative, feminist perspective on international politics that might help us to search for more appropriate solutions?

A FEMINIST PERSPECTIVE ON INTERNATIONAL RELATIONS?

If the way in which we describe reality has an effect on the ways we perceive and act upon our environment, new perspectives might lead us to consider alternative courses of action. With this in mind I shall first examine two important concepts in international relations, power and security, from a feminist perspective and then discuss some feminist approaches to conflict resolution.

Morgenthau's definition of power, the control of man over man, is typical of the way power is usually defined in international relations. Nancy Hartsock argues that this type of power-as-domination has always been associated with masculinity, since the exercise of power has generally been a masculine activity: rarely have women exercised legitimized power in the public domain. When women write about power they stress energy, capacity and potential, says Hartsock. She notes that women theorists, even when they have little else in common, offer similar definitions of power which differ substantially from the understanding of power as domination.[17]

Hannah Arendt, frequently cited by feminists writing about power, defines power as the human ability to act in concert, or to take action in connection with others who share similar concerns.[18] This definition of power is similar to that of psychologist David McClelland's portrayal of female power, which he describes as shared rather than assertive.[19] Jane Jaquette argues that, since women have had less access to the instruments of coercion, they have been more apt to rely on power as persuasion; she compares women's domestic activities to coalition building.[20]

All of these writers are portraying power as a relationship of mutual enablement. Tying her definition of female power to international relations, Jaquette sees similarities between female strategies of persuasion and strategies of small states operating from a position of weakness in the international system. There are also examples of states' behaviour that contain elements of the female strategy of coalition building. One such example is the Southern African Development Coordination Conference (SADCC), which is designed to build regional infrastructure based on mutual cooperation and collective self-reliance in order to decrease dependence on the South

African economy. Another is the European Community, which has had considerable success in building mutual cooperation in an area of the world whose history would not predict such a course of events.[21] It is rare, however, that cooperative outcomes in international relations are described in these terms, although Karl Deutsch's notion of pluralistic security communities might be one such example where power is associated with building community.[22] I am not denying that power as domination is a pervasive reality in international relations. However, there are also instances of cooperation in interstate relations, which tend to be obscured when power is seen solely as domination. Thinking about power in this multidimensional sense may help us to think constructively about the potential for cooperation as well as conflict, an aspect of international relations generally played down by realism.

Redefining national security is another way in which feminist theory could contribute to new thinking about international relations.[23] Traditionally in the West, the concept of national security has been tied to military strength and its role in the physical protection of the nation state from external threats. Morgenthau's notion of defending the national interest in terms of power is consistent with this definition. But this traditional definition of national security is partial at best in today's world.[24] The technologically advanced states are highly interdependent, and rely on weapons whose effects would be equally devastating to winners and losers alike. For them to defend national security by relying on war as the last resort no longer appears very useful. Moreover, if one thinks of security in North–South rather than East–West terms, for a large portion of the world's population security has as much to do with the satisfaction of basic material needs as with military threats. According to Johan Galtung's notion of structural violence, to suffer a lower life expectancy by virtue of one's place of birth is a form of violence whose effects can be as devastating as war.[25]

Basic needs satisfaction has a great deal to do with women, but only recently have women's roles as providers of basic needs, and in development more generally, become visible as important components in development strategies.[26] Traditionally the development literature has focused on aspects of the development process that are in the public sphere, are technologically complex and are usually undertaken by men. Thinking about the role of women in development and the way in which we can define development and basic needs satisfaction to be inclusive of women's roles and needs are topics that deserve higher priority on the international agenda. Typically, however, this is an area about which traditional international relations theory, with the priority it gives to order over justice, has had very little to say.

A further threat to national security, more broadly defined, which has also been missing from the agenda of traditional international relations, concerns the environment. Carolyn Merchant argues that a mechanistic view of nature, contained in modern science, has helped to guide an industrial and technological development which has resulted in environmental damage that has now become a matter of global concern. In the introduction to her book *The Death of Nature*, Merchant suggests that, "Women and nature have an age-old association—an affiliation that has persisted throughout culture, language, and history."[27] Hence she maintains that the ecology movement, which is growing up in response to environmental threats, and the women's movement are deeply interconnected. Both stress living in equilibrium with nature rather than dominating it, both see nature as a living non-hierarchical entity in which each part is mutually dependent on the whole. Ecologists, as well as many feminists, are now suggesting that only such a fundamental change of world view will allow the human species to survive the damage it is inflicting on the environment.

Thinking about military, economic and environmental security in interdependent terms suggests the need for new methods of conflict resolution that seek to achieve mutually beneficial, rather than zero sum, outcomes. One such method comes from Sara Ruddick's work on "maternal thinking."[28] Ruddick describes maternal thinking as focused on the preservation of life and the growth of children. To foster a domestic environment conducive to these goals, tranquility must be preserved by avoiding conflict where possible, engaging in it non-violently and restoring community when it is over. In such an environment the ends for which disputes are fought are subordinate to the means by which they are resolved. This method of conflict resolution involves making contextual judgements rather than appealing to absolute standards and thus has much in common with Gilligan's definition of female morality.

While non-violent resolution of conflict in the domestic sphere is a widely accepted norm, passive resistance in the public realm is regarded as deviant. But, as Ruddick argues, the peaceful resolution of conflict by mothers does not usually extend to the children of one's enemies, an important reason why women have been ready to support men's wars.[29] The question for Ruddick then becomes how to get maternal thinking, a mode of thinking which she believes can be found in men as well as women, out into the public realm. Ruddick believes that finding a common humanity among one's opponents has become a condition of survival in the nuclear age when the notion of winners and losers has become questionable.[30] Portraying the adversary as less than human has all too often been a technique of the nation state to command loyalty and to increase its legitimacy in the eyes of its citizens. Such behaviour in an age of weapons of mass destruction may be self-defeating.

We might also look to Gilligan's work for a feminist perspective on conflict resolution. Reporting on a study of playground behaviour of American boys and girls, Gilligan argues that girls are less able to tolerate high levels of conflict, and more likely than boys to play games that involve taking turns and in which the success of one does not depend on the failure of another.[31] While Gilligan's study does not take into account attitudes toward other groups (racial, ethnic, economic or national), it does suggest the validity of investigating whether girls are socialized to use different modes of problem solving when dealing with conflict, and whether such behaviour might be useful in thinking about international conflict resolution.

TOWARD A FEMINIST EPISTEMOLOGY OF INTERNATIONAL RELATIONS

I am deeply aware that there is no *one* feminist approach but many, which come out of various disciplines and intellectual traditions. Yet there are common themes in the different feminist literatures that I have reviewed which could help us to begin to formulate a feminist epistemology of international relations. Morgenthau encourages us to try to stand back from the world and to think about theory build-ing in terms of constructing a rational outline or map that has universal applica-tions. In contrast, the feminist literature reviewed here emphasizes connection and contingency. Keller argues for a form of knowledge, which she calls "dynamic objectivity," "that grants to the world around us its independent integrity, but does so in a way that remains cognizant of, indeed relies on, our connectivity with that world."[32] Keller illustrates this mode of thinking in her study of Barbara McClintock, whose work on genetic transposition won her a Nobel prize after many years of marginalization by the scientific community.[33] McClintock, Keller argues, was a scientist with a respect for complexity, diversity and individual difference whose methodology allowed her data to speak rather than imposing explanations on it.

Keller's portrayal of McClintock's science contains parallels with what Sandra Harding calls an African world view.[34] Harding tells us that the Western liberal notion of rational economic man, an individualist and a welfare maximizer, similar to the image of rational political man on which realism has based its theoretical investigations, does not make any sense in the African world view where the individual is seen as part of the social order acting within that order rather than upon it. Harding believes that this view of human behaviour has much in common with a feminist perspective. If we combine this view of human behaviour with Merchant's holistic perspective which stresses the interconnectedness of all things, including nature, it may help us to begin to think from a more global perspective. Such a perspective appreciates cultural diver-sity but at the same time recognizes a growing interdependence, which makes anachronistic the exclusionary thinking fostered by the nation state system.

Keller's dynamic objectivity, Harding's African world view and Merchant's ecological thinking all point us in the direction of an appreciation of the "other" as a subject whose views are as legitimate as our own, a way of thinking that has been sadly lacking in the history of international relations. Just as Keller cautions us against the construction of a feminist science which could perpetuate similar exclusionary atti-tudes, Harding warns us against schema that contrast people by race, gender or class and that originate within projects of social domination. Feminist thinkers generally dislike dichotomization and the distancing of subject from object that goes with abstract thinking, both of which, they believe, encourage a we/they attitude character-istic of international relations. Instead, feminist literature urges us to construct episte-mologies that value ambiguity and difference. These qualities could stand us in good stead as we begin to build a human or ungendered theory of international relations which contains elements of both masculine and feminine modes of thought.

MORGENTHAU'S PRINCIPLES OF POLITICAL REALISM: A FEMINIST REFORMULATION

The first part of this paper used feminist theory to develop a critique of Morgenthau's principles of political realism in order to demonstrate how the theory and practice of international relations may exhibit a masculine bias. The second part suggested some contributions that feminist theory might make to reconceptualizing some important elements in international relations and to thinking about a feminist epistemology. Drawing on these observations, this conclusion will present a feminist reformulation of Morgenthau's six principles of political realism, outlined earlier in this paper, which might help us to begin to think differently about international relations. I shall not use the term realism since feminists believe that there are multiple realities: a truly realistic picture of international politics must recognize elements of cooperation as well as conflict, morality as well as *realpolitik*, and the strivings for justice as well as order.[35] This reformulation may help us to think in these multidimensional terms.

1. A feminist perspective believes that objectivity, as it is culturally defined, is associated with masculinity. Therefore, supposedly "objective" laws of human nature are based on a partial, masculine view of human nature. Human nature is both masculine and feminine; it contains elements of social reproduction and development as well as political domination. Dynamic objectivity offers us a more connected view of objectivity with less potential for domination.

2. A feminist perspective believes that the national interest is multidimensional and contextually contingent. Therefore, it cannot be defined solely in terms of power. In the contemporary world the national interest demands cooperative rather than zero sum solutions to a set of interdependent global problems which include nuclear war, economic well-being and environmental degradation.

3. Power cannot be infused with meaning that is universally valid. Power as domination and control privileges masculinity and ignores the possibility of collective empowerment, another aspect of power often associated with femininity.

4. A feminist perspective rejects the possibility of separating moral command from political action. All political action has moral significance. The realist agenda for maximizing order through power and control gives priority to the moral command of order over those of justice and the satisfaction of basic needs necessary to ensure social reproduction.

5. While recognizing that the moral aspirations of particular nations cannot be equated with universal moral principles, a feminist perspective seeks to find common moral elements in human aspirations which could become the basis for de-escalating international conflict and building international community.

6. A feminist perspective denies the autonomy of the political. Since autonomy is associated with masculinity in Western culture, disciplinary efforts to construct a world view which does not rest on a pluralistic conception of human nature are partial and masculine. Building boundaries around a narrowly defined political realm defines political in a way that excludes the concerns and contributions of women.

To construct this feminist alternative is not to deny the validity of Morgenthau's work. But adding a feminist perspective to the epistemology of international relations is a stage through which we must pass if we are to think about constructing an ungendered or human science of international politics which is sensitive to, but goes beyond, both masculine and feminine perspectives. Such inclusionary thinking, as Simone de Beauvoir tells us, values the bringing forth of life as much as the risking of life; it is becoming imperative in a world in which the technology of war and a fragile natural environment threaten human existence. An ungendered, or human, discourse becomes possible only when women are adequately represented in the discipline and when there is equal respect for the contributions of women and men alike.

NOTES

An earlier version of this paper was presented at a symposium on Gender and International Relations at the London School of Economics in June 1988. I would like to thank the editors of *Millennium,* who organized this symposium, for encouraging me to undertake this rewriting. I am also grateful to Hayward Alker Jr. and Susan Okin for their careful reading of the manuscript and helpful suggestions.

1. Quoted in Sandra Harding, *The Science Question in Feminism* (Ithaca, N.Y.: Cornell University Press, 1986), p. 148.
2. In 1987 only 4.8 per cent of the top career Foreign Service employees were women. Statement of Patricia Schroeder before the Committee on Foreign Affairs, U.S. House of Representatives, p. 4; *Women's Perspectives on U.S. Foreign Policy: A Compilation of Views* (Washington, D.C.: U.S. Government Printing Office, 1988). For an analysis of women's roles in the American military, see Cynthia Enloe, *Does Khaki Become You? The Militarisation of Women's Lives* (London: Pluto Press, 1983).
3. Edward P. Crapol (ed.), *Women and American Foreign Policy* (Westport, Conn.: Greenwood Press, 1987), p. 167.
4. For an analysis of the role of masculine language in shaping strategic thinking see Carol Cohn, "Sex and Death in the Rational World of Defense Intellectuals," *Signs: Journal of Women in Culture and Society* (Vol. 12, No. 4, Summer 1987).
5. The claim for the dominance of the realist paradigm is supported by John A. Vasquez, "Colouring It Morgenthau: New Evidence for an Old Thesis on Quantitative International Studies," *British Journal of International Studies* (Vol. 3, No. 5, October 1979), pp. 210–28. For a critique of Morgenthau's ambiguous use of language see Inis L. Claude Jr., *Power and International Relations* (New York: Random House, 1962), especially pp. 25–37.
6. These are drawn from Hans Morgenthau, *Politics Among Nations: The Struggle for Power and Peace,* 5th revised edition (New York: Alfred Knopf, 1973), pp. 4–15. I am aware that these principles embody only a partial statement of Morgenthau's very rich study of international politics, a study which deserves a much more detailed analysis than I can give here.
7. This list is a composite of the male/female dichotomies which appear in Evelyn Fox Keller's *Reflections on Gender and Science* (New Haven, Conn.: Yale University Press, 1985) and Harding, *op. cit.*
8. Inge K. Broverman, Susan R. Vogel, Donald M. Broverman, Frank E. Clarkson and Paul S. Rosenkranz, "Sex-role Stereotypes: A Current Appraisal," *Journal of Social Issues* (Vol. 28, No. 2, 1972), pp. 59–78. Replication of this research in the 1980s confirms that these perceptions still hold.
9. Keller, *op. cit.,* p. 130.
10. *Ibid.,* p. 89.
11. *Ibid.,* p. 9.
12. Sara Ann Ketchum, "Female Culture, Woman Culture and Conceptual Change: Toward a Philosophy of Women's Studies," *Social Theory and Practice* (Vol. 6, No. 2, Summer 1980).

13. Others have questioned whether Hobbes's state of nature provides an accurate description of the international system. See, for example. Charles Beitz, *Political Theory and International Relations* (Princeton, N.J.: Princeton University Press, 1979), pp. 35–50; and Stanley Hoffmann, *Duties Beyond Borders* (Syracuse, N.Y.: Syracuse University Press, 1981), chap. 1.

14. Kohlberg's stages of moral development are described and discussed in Robert Kegan, *The Evolving Self: Problem and Process in Human Development* (Cambridge, Mass.: Harvard University Press, 1982), chap. 2.

15. Carol Gilligan, *In a Different Voice: Psychological Theory and Women's Development* (Cambridge, Mass.: Harvard University Press, 1982). See chap. 1 for Gilligan's critique of Kohlberg.

16. There is evidence that, toward the end of his life, Morgenthau himself was aware that his own prescriptions were becoming anachronistic. In a seminar presentation in 1978 he suggested that power politics as the guiding principle for the conduct of international relations had become fatally defective. For a description of this seminar presentation see Francis Anthony Boyle, *World Politics and International Law* (Durham, N.C.: Duke University Press, 1985), pp. 70–4.

17. Nancy C. M. Hartsock, *Money, Sex and Power: Toward a Feminist Historical Materialism* (Boston: Northeastern University Press, 1983), p. 210.

18. Hannah Arendt, *On Violence* (New York: Harcourt, Brace and World, 1969), p. 44. Arendt's definition of power, as it relates to international relations, is discussed more extensively in Jean Bethke Elshtain's "Reflections on War and Political Discourse: Realism, Just War, and Feminism in a Nuclear Age," *Political Theory* (Vol. 13, No. 1, February 1985), pp. 39–57.

19. David McClelland, "Power and the Feminine Role," in David McClelland, *Power: The Inner Experience* (New York: Wiley, 1975).

20. Jane S. Jaquette, "Power as Ideology: A Feminist Analysis," in Judith H. Stiehm (ed.), *Women's Views of the Political World of Men* (Dobbs Ferry, N.Y.: Transnational Publishers, 1984).

21. These examples are cited by Christine Sylvester, "The Emperor's Theories and Transformations: Looking at the Field through Feminist Lenses," in Dennis Pirages and Christine Sylvester (eds.), *Transformations in the Global Political Economy* (Basingstoke: Macmillan, 1989).

22. Karl W. Deutsch et al., *Political Community and the North Atlantic Area* (Princeton, N.J.: Princeton University Press, 1957).

23. New thinking is a term that is also being used in the Soviet Union to describe foreign policy reformulations under Gorbachev. There are indications that the Soviets are beginning to conceptualize security in the multidimensional terms described here. See Margot Light, *The Soviet Theory of International Relations* (New York: St. Martin's Press, 1988), chap. 10.

24. This is the argument made by Edward Azar and Chung-in Moon, "Third World National Security: Toward a New Conceptual Framework," *International Interactions* (Vol. 11, No. 2, 1984), pp. 103–35.

25. Johan Galtung, "Violence, Peace, and Peace Research," in Galtung, *Essays in Peace Research*, Vol. I (Copenhagen: Christian Ejlers, 1975).

26. See, for example, Gita Sen and Caren Grown, *Development, Crises and Alternative Visions: Third World Women's Perspectives* (New York: Monthly Review Press, 1987). This is an example of a growing literature on women and development which deserves more attention from the international relations community.

27. Carolyn Merchant, *The Death of Nature: Women, Ecology and the Scientific Revolution* (New York: Harper and Row, 1982), p. xv.

28. Sara Ruddick, "Maternal Thinking" and "Preservative Love and Military Destruction: Some Reflections on Mothering and Peace," in Joyce Treblicot, *Mothering: Essays in Feminist Theory* (Totowa, N.J.: Rowman and Allenhead, 1984).

29. For a more extensive analysis of this issue see Jean Bethke Elshtain, *Women and War* (New York: Basic Books, 1987).

30. This type of conflict resolution contains similarities with the problem solving approach of Edward Azar, John Burton and Herbert Kelman. See, for example, Edward E. Azar and John W. Burton, *International Conflict Resolution: Theory and Practice* (Brighton: Wheatsheaf, 1986) and Herbert C. Kelman, "Interactive Problem Solving: A Social-Psychological Approach to Conflict Resolution," in W. Klassen (ed.), *Dialogue Toward Inter-Faith Understanding* (Tantur/Jerusalem: Ecumenical Institute for Theoretical Research, 1986), pp. 293–314.

31. Gilligan, *op. cit.*, pp. 9–10.

32. Keller, *op. cit.*, p. 117.

33. Evelyn Fox Keller, *A Feeling for the Organism: The Life and Work of Barbara McClintock* (New York: Freeman, 1983).

34. Harding, *op. cit.*, chap. 7.

35. "Utopia and reality are . . . the two facets of political science. Sound political thought and sound political life will be found only where both have their place": E. H. Carr, *The Twenty Years Crisis: 1919–1939* (New York: Harper and Row, 1964), p. 10.

Exercises for Power and Principle in Statecraft

Apply what you learned in this chapter by using the online resources on MyPoliSciKit (www.mypoliscikit.com).

 Practice Tests

Videos:
- "Chamberlain's Appeasement"
- "Churchill's Iron Curtain Speech"

 Simulation: "Why Study International Relations?"

 Reading Guides:
- Thucydides, "The Melian Dialogue"
- Hans J. Morgenthau, "Six Principles of Political Realism"
- J. Ann Tickner, "A Critique of Morgenthau's Principles of Political Realism"

THE CONSEQUENCE OF ANARCHY

The Anarchic Structure of World Politics

KENNETH N. WALTZ

POLITICAL STRUCTURES

Only through some sort of systems theory can international politics be understood. To be a success, such a theory has to show how international politics can be conceived of as a domain distinct from the economic, social, and other international domains that one may conceive of. To mark international-political systems off from other international systems, and to distinguish systems-level from unit-level forces, requires showing how political structures are generated and how they affect, and are affected by, the units of the system. How can we conceive of international politics as a distinct system? What is it that intervenes between interacting units and the results that their acts and interactions produce? To answer these questions, this chapter first examines the concept of social structure and then defines structure as a concept appropriate for national and for international politics.

A system is composed of a structure and of interacting units. The structure is the system-wide component that makes it possible to think of the system as a whole. The problem is . . . to contrive a definition of structure free of the attributes and the interactions of units. Definitions of structure must leave aside, or abstract from, the characteristics of units, their behavior, and their interactions. Why must those obviously important matters be omitted? They must be omitted so that we can distinguish between variables at the level of the units and variables at the level of the system. The problem is to develop theoretically useful concepts to replace

...e vague and varying systemic notions that are customarily employed—notions such as environment, situation, context, and milieu. Structure is a useful concept if it gives clear and fixed meaning to such vague and varying terms.

We know what we have to omit from any definition of structure if the definition is to be useful theoretically. Abstracting from the attributes of units means leaving aside questions about the kinds of political leaders, social and economic institutions, and ideological commitments states may have. Abstracting from relations means leaving aside questions about the cultural, economic, political, and military interactions of states. To say what is to be left out does not indicate what is to be put in. The negative point is important nevertheless because the instruction to omit attributes is often violated and the instruction to omit interactions almost always goes unobserved. But if attributes and interactions are omitted, what is left? The question is answered by considering the double meaning of the term "relation." As S. F. Nadel points out, ordinary language obscures a distinction that is important in theory. "Relation" is used to mean both the interaction of units and the positions they occupy vis-à-vis each other.[1] To define a structure requires ignoring how units relate with one another (how they interact) and concentrating on how they stand in relation to one another (how they are arranged or positioned). Interactions, as I have insisted, take place at the level of the units. How units stand in relation to one another, the way they are arranged or positioned, is not a property of the units. The arrangement of units is a property of the system.

By leaving aside the personality of actors, their behavior, and their interactions, one arrives at a purely positional picture of society. Three propositions follow from this. First, structures may endure while personality, behavior, and interactions vary widely. Structure is sharply distinguished from actions and interactions. Second, a structural definition applies to realms of widely different substance so long as the arrangement of parts is similar.[2] Third, because this is so, theories developed for one realm may with some modification be applicable to other realms as well. . . .

The concept of structure is based on the fact that units differently juxtaposed and combined behave differently and in interacting produce different outcomes. I first want to show how internal political structure can be defined. In a book on international-political theory, domestic political structure has to be examined in order to draw a distinction between expectations about behavior and outcomes in the internal and external realms. Moreover, considering domestic political structure now will make the elusive international-political structure easier to catch later on.

Structure defines the arrangement, or the ordering, of the parts of a system. Structure is not a collection of political institutions but rather the arrangement of them. How is the arrangement defined? The constitution of a state describes some parts of the arrangement, but political structures as they develop are not identical with formal constitutions. In defining structures, the first question to answer is this: What is the principle by which the parts are arranged?

Domestic politics is hierarchically ordered. The units—institutions and agencies—stand vis-à-vis each other in relations of super- and subordination. The ordering principle of a system gives the first, and basic, bit of information about how the parts of a realm are related to each other. In a polity the hierarchy of offices is by no means completely articulated, nor are all ambiguities about relations of super- and subordination removed. Nevertheless, political actors are formally differentiated according to the degrees of their authority, and their distinct functions are specified. By "specified" I do not mean that the law of the land fully describes the duties that different agencies perform, but only that broad agreement prevails on the tasks that various parts of a government are to undertake and on the extent of the power they legitimately wield. Thus Congress supplies the military forces; the President commands them. Congress makes the laws; the executive branch enforces them; agencies administer laws; judges interpret them. Such specification of roles and differentiation of functions is found in any state, the more fully so as the state is more highly developed. The specification of functions of formally differentiated parts gives the second bit of structural information. This second part of the definition adds some content to the structure, but only enough to say more fully how the units stand in relation to one another. The roles and the functions of the British Prime Minister and Parliament, for example, differ from those of the American President and Congress. When offices are juxtaposed and functions are combined in different ways, different behaviors and outcomes result, as I shall shortly show.

The placement of units in relation to one another is not fully defined by a system's ordering principle and by the formal differentiation of its parts. The standing of the units also changes with changes in their relative capabilities. In the performance of their functions, agencies may gain capabilities or lose them. The relation of Prime Minister to Parliament and of President to Congress depends on, and varies with, their relative capabilities. The third part of the definition of structure acknowledges that even while specified functions remain unchanged, units come to stand in different relation to each other through changes in relative capability.

A domestic political structure is thus defined: first, according to the principle by which it is ordered; second, by specification of the functions of formally differentiated units; and third, by the distribution of capabilities across those units. Structure is a highly abstract notion, but the definition of structure does not abstract from everything. To do so would be to leave everything aside and to include nothing at all. The three-part definition of structure includes only what is required to show how the units of the system are positioned or arranged. Everything else is omitted. Concern for tradition and culture, analysis of the character and personality of political actors, consideration of the conflictive and accommodative processes of politics, description of the making and execution of policy—all such matters are left aside. Their omission does not imply their unimportance. They are omitted because we want to figure out the expected effects of structure on process and of process on structure. That can be done only if structure and process are distinctly defined.

I defined domestic political structures first by the principle according to which they are organized or ordered, second by the differentiation of units and the specification of their functions, and third by the distribution of capabilities across units. Let us see how the three terms of the definition apply to international politics.

1. Ordering Principles

Structural questions are questions about the arrangement of the parts of a system. The parts of domestic political systems stand in relations of super- and subordination. Some are entitled to command; others are required to obey. Domestic systems are centralized and hierarchic. The parts of international-political systems stand in relations of coordination. Formally, each is the equal of all the others. None is entitled to command; none is required to obey. International systems are decentralized and anarchic. The ordering principles of the two structures are distinctly different, indeed, contrary to each other. Domestic political structures have governmental institutions and offices as their concrete counterparts. International politics, in contrast, has been called "politics in the absence of government."[3] International organizations do exist, and in ever-growing numbers. Supranational agents able to act effectively, however, either themselves acquire some of the attributes and capabilities of states, as did the medieval papacy in the era of Innocent III, or they soon reveal their inability to act in important ways except with the support, or at least the acquiescence, of the principal states concerned with the matters at hand. Whatever elements of authority emerge internationally are barely once removed from the capability that provides the foundation for the appearance of those elements. Authority quickly reduces to a particular expression of capability. In the absence of agents with system-wide authority, formal relations of super and subordination fail to develop.

The first term of a structural definition states the principle by which the system is ordered. Structure is an organizational concept. The prominent characteristic of international politics, however, seems to be the lack of order and of organization. How can one think of international politics as being any kind of an order at all? The anarchy of politics internationally is often referred to. If structure is an organizational concept, the terms "structure" and "anarchy" seem to be in contradiction. If international politics is "politics in the absence of government," what are we in the presence of? In looking for international structure, one is brought face to face with the invisible, an uncomfortable position to be in.

The problem is this: how to conceive of an order without an orderer and of organizational effects where formal organization is lacking. Because these are difficult questions, I shall answer them through analogy with microeconomic theory. Reasoning by analogy is helpful where one can move from a domain for which theory is well developed to one where it is not. Reasoning by analogy is permissible where different domains are structurally similar.

Classical economic theory, developed by Adam Smith and his followers, is microtheory. Political scientists tend to think that microtheory is theory about small-scale matters, a usage that ill accords with its established meaning. The term "micro" in economic theory indicates the way in which the theory is constructed rather than the scope of the matters it pertains to. Microeconomic theory describes how an order is spontaneously formed from the self-interested acts and interactions of individual units—in this case, persons and firms. The theory then turns upon the two central concepts of the economic units and of the market. Economic units and economic markets are concepts, not descriptive realities or concrete entities. This must be emphasized since from the early eighteenth century to the present, from the sociologist Auguste Comte to the psychologist George Katona, economic theory has been faulted because its assumptions fail to correspond with realities.[4] Unrealistically, economic theorists conceive of an economy operating in isolation from its society and polity. Unrealistically, economists assume that the economic world is the world of the world. Unrealistically, economists think of the acting unit, the famous "economic man," as a single-minded profit maximizer. They single out one aspect of man and leave aside the wondrous variety of human life. As any moderately sensible economist knows, "economic man" does not exist. Anyone who asks businessmen how they make their decisions will find that the assumption that men are economic maximizers grossly distorts their characters. The assumption that men behave as economic men, which is known to be false as a descriptive statement, turns out to be useful in the construction of theory.

Markets are the second major concept invented by microeconomic theorists. Two general questions must be asked about markets: How are they formed? How do they work? The answer to the first question is this: The market of a decentralized economy is individualist in origin, spontaneously generated, and unintended. The market arises out of the activities of separate units—persons and firms—whose aims and efforts are directed not toward creating an order but rather toward fulfilling their own internally defined interests by whatever means they can muster. The individual unit acts for itself. From the coaction of like units emerges a structure that affects and constrains all of them. Once formed, a market becomes a force in itself, and a force that the constitutive units acting singly or in small numbers cannot control. Instead, in lesser or greater degree as market conditions vary, the creators become the creatures of the market that their activity gave rise to. Adam Smith's great achievement was to show how self-interested, greed-driven actions may produce good social outcomes if only political and social conditions permit free competition. If a laissez-faire economy is harmonious, it is so because the intentions of actors do not correspond with the outcomes their actions produce. What intervenes between the actors and the objects of their action in order to thwart their purposes? To account for the unexpectedly favorable outcomes of selfish acts, the concept of a market is brought into play. Each unit seeks its own good; the result of a number of units simultaneously doing so transcends the motives and the aims of the separate units. Each would like to work less hard and price his product higher. Taken together, all have to work harder and price their products lower. Each firm seeks to increase its profit; the result of many firms doing so drives the profit rate downward. Each man seeks his own end, and, in doing so, produces a result that was no part of his intention. Out of the mean ambition of its members, the greater good of society is produced.

The market is a cause interposed between the economic actors and the results they produce. It conditions their calculations, their behaviors, and their interactions. It is not an agent in the sense of A being the agent that produces outcome X. Rather it is a structural cause. A market constrains the units that comprise it from taking certain actions and disposes them toward taking others. The market, created by self-directed interacting economic units, selects behaviors according to their consequences. The market rewards some with high profits and assigns others to bankruptcy. Since a market is not an institution or an agent in any concrete or palpable sense, such statements become impressive only if they can be reliably inferred from a theory as part of a set of more elaborate expectations. They can be. Microeconomic theory explains how an economy operates and why certain effects are to be expected. . . .

International-political systems, like economic markets, are formed by the co-action of self-regarding units. International structures are defined in terms of the primary political units of an era, be they city states, empires, or nations. Structures emerge from the coexistence of states. No state intends to participate in the formation of a structure by which it and others will be constrained. International-political systems, like economic markets, are individualist in origin, spontaneously generated, and unintended. In both systems, structures are formed by the coaction of their units. Whether those units live, prosper, or die depends on their own efforts. Both systems are formed and maintained on a principle of self-help that applies to the units. . . .

In a microtheory, whether of international politics or of economics, the motivation of the actors is assumed rather than realistically described. I assume that states seek to ensure their survival. The assumption is a radical simplification made for the sake of constructing theory. The question to ask of the assumption, as ever, is not whether it is true but whether it is the most sensible and useful one that can be made. Whether it is a useful assumption depends on whether a theory based on the assumption can be contrived, a theory from which important consequences not otherwise obvious can be inferred. Whether it is a sensible assumption can be directly discussed.

Beyond the survival motive, the aims of states may be endlessly varied; they may range from the ambition to conquer the world to the desire merely to be left alone. Survival is a prerequisite to achieving any goals that states may have, other than the goal of promoting their own disappearance as political entities. The survival motive is taken as the ground of action in a world where the security of states is not assured, rather than as a realistic description of the impulse that lies behind every act of state. The assumption allows for the fact that no state always acts exclusively to ensure its survival. It allows for the fact that some states may persistently seek goals that they value more highly than survival; they may, for example, prefer amalgamation with other states to their own survival in form. It allows for the fact that in pursuit of its security no state will act with perfect knowledge and wisdom— if indeed we could know what those terms might mean. . . .

Actors may perceive the structure that constrains them and understand how it serves to reward some kinds of behavior and to penalize others. But then again they either may not see it or, seeing it, may for any of many reasons fail to conform their actions to the patterns that are most often rewarded and least often punished. To say that "the structure selects" means simply that those who conform to accepted and successful practices more often rise to the top and are likelier to stay there. The game one has to win is defined by the structure that determines the kind of player who is likely to prosper. . . .

2. The Character of the Units

The second term in the definition of domestic political structure specifies the functions performed by differentiated units. Hierarchy entails relations of super- and subordination among a system's parts, and that implies their differentiation. In defining domestic political structure the second term, like the first and third, is needed because each term points to a possible source of structural variation. The states that are the units of international-political systems are not formally differentiated by the functions they perform. Anarchy entails relations of coordination among a system's units, and that implies their sameness. The second term is not needed in defining international-political structure, because, so long as anarchy endures, states remain like units. International structures vary only through a change of organizing principle or, failing that, through variations in the capabilities of units. Nevertheless I shall discuss these like units here, because it is by their interactions that international-politics structures are generated.

Two questions arise: Why should states be taken as the units of the system? Given a wide variety of states, how can one call them "like units"? Questioning the choice of states as the primary units of international-political systems became popular in the 1960s and 1970s as it was at the turn of the century. Once one understands what is logically involved, the issue is easily resolved. Those who question the state-centric view do so for two main reasons. First, states are not the only actors of importance on the international scene. Second, states are declining in importance, and other actors are gaining, or so it is said. Neither reason is cogent, as the following discussion shows.

States are not and never have been the only international actors. But then structures are defined not by all of the actors that flourish within them but by the major ones. In defining a system's structure one chooses one or some of the infinitely many objects comprising the system and defines its structure in terms of them. For international-political systems, as for any system, one must first decide which units to take as being the parts of the system. Here the economic analogy will help again. The structure of a market is defined by the number of firms competing. If many roughly equal firms contend, a condition of perfect competition is approximated. If a few firms dominate the market, competition is said to be oligopolistic even though many smaller firms may also be in the field. But we are told that definitions of this sort cannot be applied to international politics because of the interpenetration of states, because of their inability to control the environment of their action, and because rising multinational corporations and other nonstate actors are difficult to regulate and may rival some states in influence. The importance of nonstate actors and the extent of transnational activities are obvious. The conclusion that the state-centric conception of international politics is made obsolete by them does not follow. That economists and economically minded politics scientists have thought that it does is ironic. The irony lies in the fact that all of the reasons given for scrapping the state-centric concept can be related more strongly and applied to firms. Firms competing with numerous others have no hope of controlling their market, and oligopolistic firms constantly struggle with imperfect success to do so. Firms interpenetrate, merge, and buy each up at a merry pace. Moreover, firms are constantly threatened and regulated by, shall we say, "non-firm" actors. Some governments encourage concentration; others work to prevent it. The market structure of parts of an economy may move from a wider to a narrower competition or may move in the opposite direction, but whatever the extent and the frequency of change, market structures, generated by the interaction of firms, are defined in terms of them.

Just as economists define markets in terms of firms, so I define international-political structures in terms of states. If Charles P. Kindleberger were right in saying that "the nation-state is just about through as an economic unit,"[5] then the structure of international politics would have to be redefined. That would be necessary because economic capabilities cannot be separated from the other capabilities of states. The distinction frequently drawn between matters of high and low politics is misplaced. States use economic means for military and political ends; and military and political means for the achievement of economic interests.

An amended version of Kindleberger's statement may hold: Some states may be nearly washed up as economic entities, and others not. That poses no problem for international-political theory since international politics is mostly about inequalities anyway. So long as the major states are the major actors, the structure of international politics is defined in terms of them. That theoretical statement is of course borne out in practice. States set the scene in which they, along with non-state actors, state their dramas or carry on their humdrum affairs. Though they may choose to interfere little in the affairs of nonstate actors for long periods of time, states nevertheless set the terms of intercourse, whether by passively permitting informal rules to develop or by actively intervening to change rules that no longer suit them. When the crunch comes, states remake the rules by which other actors operate. Indeed, one may be struck by the ability of weak states to impede the operation of strong international corporations and by the attention the latter pay to the wishes of the former. . . .

States are the units whose interactions form the structure of international-political systems. They will long remain so. The death rate among states is remarkably low. Few states die; many firms do. . . . To call states "like units" is to say that each state is like all other states in being an autonomous political unit. It is another way of saying that states are sovereign. But sovereignty is also a bothersome concept. Many believe, as the anthropologist M. G. Smith has said, that "in a system of sovereign states no state is sovereign."[6] The error lies in identifying the sovereignty of states with their ability to do as they wish. To say that states are sovereign is not to say that they can do as they please, that they are free of others' influence, that they are able to get what they want. Sovereign states may be hardpressed all around, constrained to act in ways they would like to avoid, and able to do hardly anything just as they would like to. The sovereignty of states has never entailed their insulation from the effects of other states' actions. To be sovereign and to be dependent are not contradictory conditions. Sovereign states have seldom led free and easy lives. What then is sovereignty? To say that a state is sovereign means that it decides for itself how it will cope with its internal and external problems, including whether or not to seek assistance from others and in doing so to limit its freedom by making commitments to them. States develop their own strategies, chart their own courses, make their own decisions about how to meet whatever needs they experience and whatever desires they develop. It is no more contradictory to say that sovereign states are always constrained and often tightly so than it is to say that free individuals often make decisions under the heavy pressure of events.

Each state, like every other state, is a sovereign political entity. And yet the differences across states, from Costa Rica to the Soviet Union, from Gambia to the United States, are immense. States are alike, and they are also different. So are corporations, apples, universities, and people. Whenever we put two or more objects in the same category, we are saying that they are alike not in all respects but in some. No two objects in this world are identical, yet they can often be usefully compared and combined. "You can't add apples and oranges" is an old saying that seems to be especially popular among salesmen who do not want you to compare their wares with others. But we all know that the trick of adding dissimilar objects is to express the result in terms of a category that comprises them. Three apples plus four oranges equals seven pieces of fruit. The only interesting question is whether the category that classifies objects according to their common qualities is useful. One can add up a large number of widely varied objects and say that one has eight million things, but seldom need one do that.

States vary widely in size, wealth, power, and form. And yet variations in these and in other respects are variations among like units. In what way are they like units? How can they be placed in a single category? States are alike in the tasks that they face, though not in their abilities to perform them. The differences are of capability, not of function. States perform or try to perform tasks, most of which are common to all of them; the ends they aspire to are similar. Each state duplicates the activities of other states at least to a considerable extent. Each state has its agencies for making, executing, and interpreting laws and regulations, for raising revenues, and for defending itself. Each state supplies out of its own resources and by its own means most of the food, clothing, housing, transportation, and amenities consumed and used by its citizens. All states, except the smallest ones, do much more of their business at home than abroad. One has to be impressed with the functional similarity of states and, now more than ever before, with the similar lines their development follows. From the rich to the poor states, from the old to the new ones, nearly all of them take a larger hand in matters of economic regulation, of education, health, and housing, of culture and the arts, and so on almost endlessly. The increase of the activities of states is a strong and strikingly uniform international trend. The functions of states are similar, and distinctions among them arise principally from their varied capabilities. International politics consists of like units duplicating one another's activities.

3. The Distribution of Capabilities

The parts of a hierarchic system are related to one another in ways that are determined both by their functional differentiation and by the extent of their capabilities.

The units of an anarchic system are functionally undifferentiated. The units of such an order are then distinguished primarily by their greater or lesser capabilities for performing similar tasks. This states formally what students of international politics have long noticed. The great powers of an era have always been marked off from others by practitioners and theorists alike. Students of national government make such distinctions as that between parliamentary and presidential systems; governmental systems differ in form. Students of international politics make distinctions between international-political systems only according to the number of their great powers. The structure of a system changes with changes in the distribution of capabilities across the system's units. And changes in structure change expectations about how the units of the system will behave and about the outcomes their interactions will produce. Domestically, the differentiated parts of a system may perform similar tasks. We know from observing the American government that executives sometimes legislate and legislatures sometimes execute. Internationally, like units sometimes perform different tasks . . . but two problems should be considered.

The first problem is this: Capability tells us something about units. Defining structure partly in terms of the distribution of capabilities seems to violate my instruction to keep unit attributes out of structural definitions. As I remarked earlier, structure is a highly but not entirely abstract concept. The maximum of abstraction allows a minimum of content, and that minimum is what is needed to enable one to say how the units stand in relation to one another. States are differently placed by their power. And yet one may wonder why only *capability* is included in the third part of the definition, and not such characteristics as ideology, form of government, peacefulness, bellicosity, or whatever. The answer is this: Power is estimated by comparing the capabilities of a number of units. Although capabilities are attributes of units, the distribution of capabilities across units is not. The distribution of capabilities is not a unit attribute, but rather a system-wide concept. . . .

The second problem is this: Though relations defined in terms of interactions must be excluded from structural definitions, relations defined in terms of grouping of states do seem to tell us something about how states are placed in the system. Why not specify how states stand in relation to one another by considering the alliances they form? Would doing so not be comparable to defining national political structures partly in terms of how presidents and prime ministers are related to other political agents? It would not be. Nationally as internationally, structural definitions deal with the relation of agents and agencies in terms of the organization of realms and not in terms of the accommodations and conflicts that may occur within them or the groupings that may now and then form. Parts of a government may draw together or pull apart, may oppose each other or cooperate in greater or lesser degree. These are the relations that form and dissolve within a system rather than structural alterations that mark a change from one system to another. This is made clear by the example that runs nicely parallel to the case of alliances. Distinguishing systems of political parties according to their number is common. A multiparty system changes if, say, eight parties become two, but not if two groupings of the eight form merely for the occasion of fighting an election. By the same logic, an international-political system in which three or more great powers have split into two alliances remains a multipolar system—structurally distinct from a bipolar system, a system in which no third power is able to challenge the top two. . . .

In defining international-political structures we take states with whatever traditions, habits, objectives, desires, and forms of government they may have. We do not ask whether states are revolutionary or legitimate, authoritarian or democratic, ideological or pragmatic. We abstract from every attribute of states except their capabilities. Nor in thinking about structure do we ask about the relations of states—their feelings of friendship and hostility, their diplomatic exchanges, the alliances they form, and the extent of the contacts and exchanges among them. We ask what range of expectations arises merely from looking at the type of order that prevails among them and at the distribution of capabilities within that order. We abstract from any particular qualities of states and from all of their concrete connections. What emerges is a positional picture, a general description of the ordered overall arrangement of a society written in terms of the placement of units rather than in terms of their qualities. . . .

ANARCHIC STRUCTURES AND BALANCES OF POWER

[We must now] examine the characteristics of anarchy and the expectations about outcomes associated with anarchic realms. . . . [This] is best accomplished by drawing some comparisons between behavior and outcomes in anarchic and hierarchic realms.

4. Violence at Home and Abroad

The state among states, it is often said, conducts its affairs in the brooding shadow of violence. Because some states may at any time use force, all states must be prepared to do so—or live at the mercy of their militarily more vigorous neighbors. Among states, the state of nature is a state of war. This is meant not in the sense that war constantly occurs but in the sense that, with each state deciding for itself whether or not to use force, war may at any time break out. Whether in the family, the community, or the world at large, contact without at least occasional conflict is inconceivable; and the hope that in the absence of an agent to manage or to manipulate conflicting parties the use of force will always be avoided cannot be realistically entertained. Among men as among states, anarchy, or the absence of government, is associated with the occurrence of violence.

The threat of violence and the recurrent use of force are said to distinguish international from national affairs. But in the history of the world surely most rulers have had to bear in mind that their subjects might use force to resist or overthrow them. If the absence of government is associated with the threat of violence, so also is its presence. A haphazard list of national tragedies illustrates the point all too well. The most destructive wars of the hundred years following the defeat of Napoleon took place not among states but *within* them. Estimates of deaths in China's Taiping Rebellion, which began in 1851 and lasted 13 years, range as high as 20 million. In the American Civil War some 600 thousand people lost their lives. In more recent history, forced collectivation and Stalin's purges eliminated 5 million Russians, and Hitler exterminated 6 million Jews. In some Latin American countries, coups d'états and rebellions have been normal features of national life. Between 1948 and 1957, for example, 200 thousand Colombians were killed in civil strife. In the middle 1970s most inhabitants of Idi Amin's Uganda must have felt their lives becoming nasty, brutish, and short, quite as in Thomas Hobbes's state of nature. If such cases constitute aberrations, they are uncomfortably common ones. We easily lose sight of the fact that struggles to achieve and maintain power, to establish order, and to contrive a kind of justice within states may be bloodier than wars among them.

If anarchy is identified with chaos, destruction, and death, then the distinction between anarchy and government does not tell us much. Which is more precarious: the life of a state among states, or of a government in relation to its subjects? The answer varies with time and place. Among some states at some times, the actual or expected occurrence of violence is low. Within some states at some times, the actual or expected occurrence of violence is high. The use of force, or the constant fear of its use, are not sufficient grounds for distinguishing international from domestic affairs. If the possible and the actual use of force mark both national and international orders, then no durable distinction between the two realms can be drawn in terms of the use or the nonuse of force. No human order is proof against violence.

To discover qualitative differences between internal and external affairs one must look for a criterion other than the occurrence of violence. The distinction between international and national realms of politics is not found in the use or the nonuse of force but in their different structures. But if the dangers of being violently attacked are greater, say, in taking an evening stroll through downtown Detroit than they are in picnicking along the French and German border, what practical difference does the difference of structure make? Nationally as internationally, contact generates conflict and at times issues in violence. The difference between national and international politics lies not in the use of force but in the different modes of organization for doing something about it. A government, ruling by some standard of legitimacy, arrogates to itself the right to use force—that is, to apply a variety of sanctions to control the use of force by its subjects. If some use private force, others may appeal to the government. A government has no monopoly on the use of force, as is all too evident. An effective government, however, has a monopoly on the *legitimate* use of force, and legitimate here means that public agents are organized to prevent and to counter the private use of force. Citizens need not prepare to defend themselves. Public agencies do that. A national system is not one of self-help. The international system is.

5. Interdependence and Integration

The political significance of interdependence varies depending on whether a realm is organized, with relations of authority specified and established, or remains formally unorganized. Insofar as a realm is formally organized, its units are free to specialize, to pursue their own interests without concern for developing the means of maintaining their identity and preserving their security in the presence of others. They are free to specialize because they have no reason to fear the increased interdependence that goes with specialization. If those who specialize most benefit most, then competition in specialization ensues. Goods are manufactured, grain is produced, law and order are maintained, commerce is conducted, and financial services are provided by people who ever more narrowly specialize. In simple economic terms, the cobbler depends on the tailor for his pants and the tailor on the cobbler for his shoes, and each would be ill-clad without the services of the other. In simple political terms, Kansas depends on Washington for protection and regulation and Washington depends on Kansas for beef and wheat. In saying that in such situations interdependence is close, one need not maintain that the one part could not learn to live without the other. One need only say that the cost of breaking the interdependent relation would be high. Persons and institutions depend heavily on one another because of the different tasks they perform and the different goods they produce and exchange. The parts of a polity bind themselves together by their differences.[7]

Differences between national and international structures are reflected in the ways the units of each system define their ends and develop the means for reaching them. In anarchic realms, like units coact. In hierarchic realms, unlike units interact. In an anarchic realm, the units are functionally similar and tend to remain so. Like units work to maintain a measure of independence and may even strive for autarchy. In a hierarchic realm, the units are differentiated, and they tend to increase the extent of their specialization. Differentiated units become closely interdependent, the more closely so as their specialization proceeds. Because of the difference of structure, interdependence within and interdependence among nations are two distinct concepts. So as to follow the logicians' admonition to keep a single meaning for a given term throughout one's discourse, I shall use "integration" to describe the condition within nations and "interdependence" to describe the condition among them.

Although states are like units functionally, they differ vastly in their capabilities. Out of such differences something of a division of labor develops. The division of labor across nations, however, is slight in comparison with the highly articulated division of labor within them. Integration draws the parts of a nation closely together. Interdependence among nations leaves them loosely connected. Although the integration of nations is often talked about, it seldom takes place. Nations could mutually enrich themselves by further dividing not just the labor that goes into the production of goods but also some of the other tasks they perform, such as political management and military defense. Why does their integration not take place? The structure of international politics limits the cooperation of states in two ways.

In a self-help system each of the units spends a portion of its effort, not in forwarding its own good, but in providing the means of protecting itself against others. Specialization in a system of divided labor works to everyone's advantage, though not equally so. Inequality in the expected distribution of the increased product works strongly against extension of the division of labor internationally. When faced with the possibility of cooperating for mutual gain, states that feel insecure must ask how the gain will be divided. They are compelled to ask not "Will both of us gain?" but "Who will gain more?" If an expected gain is to be divided, say, in the ratio of two to one, one state may use its disproportionate gain to implement a policy intended to damage or destroy the other. Even the prospect of large absolute gains for both parties does not elicit their cooperation so long as each fears how the other will use its increased capabilities. Notice that the impediments to collaboration may not lie in the character and the immediate intention of either party. Instead, the condition of insecurity—at the least, the uncertainty of each about the other's future intentions and actions—works against their cooperation. . . .

A state worries about a division of possible gains that may favor others more than itself. That is the first way in which the structure of international politics limits the cooperation of states. A state also worries lest it become dependent on others through cooperative endeavors and exchanges of goods and services. That is the second way in which the structure of international politics limits the cooperation of states. The more a state specializes, the more it relies on others to supply the materials and goods that it is not producing. The larger a state's imports and exports, the more it depends on others. The world's well-being would be increased if an ever more elaborate division of labor were developed, but states would thereby place themselves in situations of ever closer interdependence. Some states may not resist that. For small and ill-endowed states the costs of doing so are excessively high. But states that can resist becoming ever more enmeshed with others ordinarily do so in either or both of two ways. States that are heavily dependent, or closely interdependent, worry about securing that which they depend on. The high interdependence of states means that the states in question experience, or are subject to, the common vulnerability that high interdependence entails. Like other organizations, states seek to control what they depend on or to lessen the extent of their dependency. This simple thought explains quite a bit of the behavior of states: their imperial thrusts to widen the scope of their control and their autarchic strivings toward greater self-sufficiency.

Structures encourage certain behaviors and penalize those who do not respond to the encouragement. Nationally, many lament the extreme development of the division of labor, a development that results in the allocation of ever narrower tasks to individuals. And yet specialization proceeds, and its extent is a measure of the development of societies. In a formally organized realm a premium is put on each unit's being able to specialize in order to increase its value to others in a system of divided labor. The domestic imperative is "specialize"! Internationally, many lament the resources states spend unproductively for their own defense and the opportunities they miss to enhance the welfare of their people through cooperation with other states. And yet the ways of states change little. In an unorganized realm each unit's incentive is to put itself in a position to be able to take care of itself since no one else can be counted on to do so. The international imperative is "take care of yourself"! Some leaders of nations may understand that the well-being of all of them would increase through their participation in a fuller division of labor. But to act on the idea would be to act on a domestic imperative, an imperative that does not run internationally. What one might want to do in the absence of structural constraints is different from what one is encouraged to do in their presence. States do not willingly place themselves in situations of increased dependence. In a self-help system, considerations of security subordinate economic gain to political interest. . . .

6. Structures and Strategies

That motives and outcomes may well be disjoined should now be easily seen. Structures cause nations to have consequences they were not intended to have. Surely most of the actors will notice that, and at least some of them will be able to figure out why. They may develop a pretty good sense of just how structures work their effects. Will they not then be able to achieve their original ends by appropriately adjusting their strategies? Unfortunately, they often cannot. To show why this is so I shall give only a few examples; once the point is made, the reader will easily think of others.

If shortage of a commodity is expected, all are collectively better off if they buy less of it in order to moderate price increases and to distribute shortages equitably. But because some will be better off if they lay in extra supplies quickly, all have a strong incentive to do so. If one expects others to make a run on a bank, one's prudent course is to run faster then they do even while knowing that if few others run, the bank will remain solvent, and if many run, it will fail. In such cases, pursuit of individual interest produces collective results that nobody wants, yet individuals by behaving differently will hurt themselves without altering outcomes. These two much used examples establish the main point. Some courses of action I cannot sensibly follow unless we are pretty sure that many others will as well. . . .

We may well notice that our behavior produces unwanted outcomes, but we are also likely to see that such instances as these are examples of what Alfred E. Kahn describes as "large" changes that are brought about by the accumulation of "small" decisions. In such situations people are victims of the "tyranny of small decisions," a phrase suggesting that "if one hundred consumers choose option x, and this causes the market to make decision X (where X equals $100x$), it is not necessarily true that those same consumers would have voted for that outcome if that large decision had ever been presented for their explicit consideration."[8] If the market does not present the large question for decision, then individuals are doomed to making decisions that are sensible within their narrow contexts even though they know all the while that in making such decisions they are bringing about a result that most of them do not want. Either that or they organize to overcome some of the effects of the market by changing its structure—for example, by bringing consumer units roughly up to the size of the units that are making producers' decisions. This nicely makes the point: So long as one leaves the structure unaffected it is not possible for changes in the intentions and the actions of particular actors to produce desirable outcomes or to avoid undesirable ones. . . .The only remedies for strong structural effects are structural changes.

Structural constraints cannot be wished away, although many fail to understand this. In every age and place, the units of self-help systems—nations, corporations, or whatever—are told that the greater good, along with their own, requires them to act for the sake of the system and not for their own narrowly defined advantage. In the 1950s, as fear of the world's destruction in nuclear war grew, some concluded that the alternative to world destruction was world disarmament. In the 1970s, with the rapid growth of population, poverty, and pollution, some concluded, as one political scientist put it, that "states must meet the needs of the political ecosystem in its global dimensions or court annihilation."[9] The international interest must be served; and if that means anything at all, it means that national interests are subordinate to it. The problems are found at the global level. Solutions to the problems continue to depend on national policies. What are the conditions that would make nations more or less willing to obey the injunctions that are so often laid on them? How can they resolve the tension between pursuing their own interests and acting for the sake of the system? No one has shown how that can be done, although many wring their hands and plead for rational behavior. The very problem, however, is that rational behavior, given structural constraints, does not lead to the wanted results. With each country constrained to take care of itself, no one can take care of the system.[10]

A strong sense of peril and doom may lead to a clear definition of ends that must be achieved. Their achievement is not thereby made possible. The possibility of effective action depends on the ability to provide necessary means. It depends even more so on the existence of conditions that permit nations and other organizations to follow appropriate policies and strategies. World-shaking problems cry for global solutions, but there is no global agency to provide them. Necessities do not create possibilities. Wishing that final causes were efficient ones does not make them so.

Great tasks can be accomplished only by agents of great capability. That is why states, and especially the major ones, are called on to do what is necessary for the world's survival. But states have to do whatever they think necessary for their own preservation, since no one can be relied on to do it for them. Why the advice to place the international interest above national interests is meaningless can be explained precisely in terms of the distinction between micro- and macrotheories. . . .

Some have hoped that changes in the awareness and purpose, in the organization and ideology of states would change the quality of international life. Over the centuries states have changed in many ways, but the quality of international life has remained much the same. States may seek reasonable and worthy ends, but they cannot figure out how to reach them. The problem is not in their stupidity or ill will, although one does not want to claim that those qualities are lacking. The depth of the difficulty is not understood until one realizes that intelligence and goodwill cannot discover and act on adequate programs. Early in this century Winston Churchill observed that the British-German naval race promised disaster *and* that Britain had no realistic choice other than to run it. States facing global problems are like individual consumers trapped by the "tyranny of small decisions." States, like consumers, can get out of the trap only by changing the structure of their field of activity. The message bears repeating: The only remedy for a strong structural effect is a structural change.

7. The Virtues of Anarchy

To achieve their objectives and maintain their security, units in a condition of anarchy—be they people, corporations, states, or whatever—must rely on the means they can generate and the arrangements they can make for themselves. Self-help is necessarily the principle of action in an anarchic order. A self-help situation is one of high risk—of bankruptcy in the economic realm and of war in a world of free states. It is also one in which organizational costs are low. Within an economy or within an international order, risks may be avoided or lessened by moving from a situation of coordinate action to one of super- and subordination, that is, by erecting agencies with effective authority and extending a system of rules. Government emerges where the functions of regulation and management themselves become distinct and specialized tasks. The costs of maintaining a hierarchic order are frequently ignored by those who deplore its absence. Organizations have at least two aims: to get something done and to maintain themselves as organizations. Many of their activities are directed toward the second purpose. The leaders of organizations, and political leaders preeminently, are not masters of the matters their organizations deal with. They have become leaders not by being experts on one thing or another but by excelling in the organizational arts—in maintaining control of a group's members, in eliciting predictable and satisfactory efforts from them, in holding a group together. In making political decisions, the first and most important concern is not to achieve the aims the members of an organization may have but to secure the continuity and health of the organization itself.[11]

Along with the advantages of hierarchic orders go the costs. In hierarchic orders, moreover, the means of control become an object of struggle. Substantive issues become entwined with efforts to influence or control the controllers. The hierarchic ordering of politics adds one to the already numerous objects of struggle, and the object added is at a new order of magnitude.

If the risks of war are unbearably high, can they be reduced by organizing to manage the affairs of nations? At a minimum, management requires controlling the military forces that are at the disposal of states. Within nations, organizations have to work to maintain themselves. As organizations, nations, in working to maintain themselves, sometimes have to use force against dissident elements and areas. As hierarchical systems, governments nationally or globally are disrupted by the defection of major parts. In a society of states with little coherence, attempts at world government would founder on the inability of an emerging central authority to mobilize the resources needed to create and maintain the unity of the system by regulating and managing its parts. The prospect of world government would be an invitation to prepare for world civil war. . . . States cannot entrust managerial powers to a central agency unless that agency is able to protect its client states. The more powerful the clients and the more the power of each of them appears as a threat to the others, the greater the power lodged in the center must be. The greater the power of the center, the stronger the incentive for states to engage in a struggle to control it.

States, like people, are insecure in proportion to the extent of their freedom. If freedom is wanted, insecurity must be accepted. Organizations that establish relations of authority and control may increase insecurity as they decrease freedom. If might does not make right, whether among people or states, then some institution or agency has intervened to lift them out of nature's realm. The more influential the agency, the stronger the desire to control it becomes. In contrast, units in an anarchic order act for their own sakes and not for the sake of preserving an organization and furthering their fortunes within it. Force is used for one's own interest. In the absence of organization, people or states are free to leave one another alone. Even when they do not do so, they are better able, in the absence of the politics of the organization, to concentrate on the politics of the problem and to aim for a minimum agreement that will permit their separate existence rather than a maximum agreement for the sake of maintaining unity. If might decides, then bloody struggles over right can more easily be avoided.

Nationally, the force of a government is exercised in the name of right and justice. Internationally, the force of a state is employed for the sake of its own protection and advantage. Rebels challenge a government's claim to authority; they question the rightfulness of its rule. Wars among states cannot settle questions of authority and right; they can only determine the allocation of gains and losses among contenders and settle for a time the question of who is the stronger. Nationally, relations of authority are established. Internationally, only relations of strength result. Nationally, private force used against a government threatens the political system. Force used by a state—a public body—is, from the international perspective, the private use of force; but there is no government to overthrow and no governmental apparatus to capture. Short of a drive toward world hegemony, the private use of force does not threaten the system of international politics, only some of its members. War pits some states against others in a struggle among similarly constituted entities. The power of the strong may deter the weak from asserting their claims, not because the weak recognize a kind of rightfulness of rule on the part of the strong, but simply because it is not sensible to tangle with them. Conversely, the weak may enjoy considerable freedom of action if they are so far removed in their capabilities from the strong that the latter are not much bothered by their actions or much concerned by marginal increases in their capabilities.

National politics is the realm of authority, of administration, and of law. International politics is the realm of power, of struggle, and of accommodation. The international realm is preeminently a political one. The national realm is variously described as being hierarchic, vertical, centralized, heterogeneous, directed, and contrived; the international realm, as being anarchic, horizontal, decentralized, homogeneous, undirected, and mutually adaptive. The more centralized the order, the nearer to the top the locus of decisions ascends. Internationally, decisions are made at the bottom level, there being scarcely any other. In the vertical–horizontal dichotomy, international structures assume the prone position. Adjustments are made internationally, but they are made without a formal or authoritative adjuster. Adjustment and accommodation proceed by mutual adaptation.[12] Action and reaction, and reaction to the reaction, proceed by a piecemeal process. The parties feel each other out, so to speak, and define a situation simultaneously with its development. Among coordinate units, adjustment is achieved and accommodations arrived at by the exchange of "considerations," in a condition, as Chester Barnard put it, "in which the duty of command and the desire to obey are essentially absent."[13] Where the contest is over considerations, the parties seek to maintain or improve their positions by maneuvering, by bargaining, or by fighting. The manner and intensity of the competition is determined by the desires and the abilities of parties that are at once separate and interacting.

Whether or not by force, each state plots the course it thinks will best serve its interests. If force is used by one state or its use is expected, the recourse of other states is to use force or be prepared to use it singly or in combination. No appeal can be made to a higher entity clothed with the authority and equipped with the ability to act on its own initiative. Under such conditions the possibility that force will be used by one or another of the parties looms always as a threat in the background. In politics force is said to be the *ultima ratio.* In international politics force serves, not only as the *ultima ratio,* but indeed as the first and constant one. To limit force to being the *ultima ratio* of politics implies, in the words of Ortega y Gasset, "the previous submission of force to methods of reason."[14] The constant possibility that force will be used limits manipulations, moderates demands, and serves as an incentive for the settlement of disputes. One who knows that pressing too hard may lead to war has strong reason to consider whether possible gains are worth the risks entailed. The threat of force internationally is comparable to the role of the strike in labor and management bargaining. "The few strikes that take place are in a sense," as Livernash has said, "the cost of the strike option which produces settlements in the large mass of negotiations."[15] Even if workers seldom strike, their doing so is always a possibility. The possibility of industrial dispute, leading to long and costly strikes encourages labor and management to face difficult issues, to try to understand each other's problems, and to work hard to find accommodations. The possibility that conflicts among nations may lead to long and costly wars has similarly sobering effects.

8. Anarchy and Hierarchy

I have described anarchies and hierarchies as though every political order were of one type or the other. Many, and I suppose most, political scientists who write of structures allow for a greater, and sometimes for a bewildering, variety of types. Anarchy is seen as one end of a continuum whose other end is marked by the presence of a legitimate and competent government. International politics is then described as being flecked with particles of government and alloyed with elements of community—supranational organizations whether universal or regional, alliances, multinational corporations, networks of trade, and whatnot. International-political systems are thought of as being more or less anarchic.

Those who view the world as a modified anarchy do so, it seems, for two reasons. First, anarchy is taken to mean not just the absence of government but also the presence of disorder and chaos. Since world politics, although not reliably peaceful, falls short of unrelieved chaos, students are inclined to see a lessening of anarchy in each outbreak of peace. Since world politics, although not formally organized, is not entirely without institutions and orderly procedures, students are inclined to see a lessening of anarchy when alliances form, when transactions across national borders increase, and when international agencies multiply. Such views confuse structure with process, and I have drawn attention to that error often enough.

Second, the two simple categories of anarchy and hierarchy do not seem to accommodate the infinite social variety our senses record. Why insist on reducing the types of structure to two instead of allowing for a greater variety? Anarchies are ordered by the juxtaposition of similar units, but those similar units are not identical. Some specialization by function develops among them. Hierarchies are ordered by the social division of labor among units specializing in different tasks, but the resemblance of units does not vanish. Much duplication of effort continues. All societies are organized segmentally or hierarchically in greater or lesser degree. Why not, then, define additional social types according to the mixture of organizing principles they embody? One might conceive of some societies approaching the purely anarchic, of others approaching the purely hierarchic, and of still others reflecting specified mixes of the two organizational types. In anarchies the exact likeness of units and the determination of relations by capability alone would describe a realm wholly of politics and power with none of the interaction of units guided by administration and conditioned by authority. In hierarchies the complete differentiation of parts and the full specification of their functions would produce a realm wholly of authority and administration with none of the interaction of parts affected by politics and power. Although such pure orders do not exist, to distinguish realms by their organizing principles is nevertheless proper and important.

Increasing the number of categories would bring the classification of societies closer to reality. But that would be to move away from a theory claiming explanatory power to a less theoretical system promising greater descriptive accuracy. One who wishes to explain rather than to describe should resist moving in that direction if resistance is reasonable. Is it? What does one gain by insisting on two types when admitting three or four would still be to simplify boldly? One gains clarity and economy of concepts. A new concept should be introduced only to cover matters that existing concepts do not reach. If some societies are neither anarchic or hierarchic, if their structures are defined by some third ordering principle, then we would have to define a third system.[16] All societies are mixed. Elements in them represent both of the ordering principles. That does not mean that some societies are ordered according to a third principle. Usually one can easily identify the principle by which a society is ordered. The appearance of anarchic sectors within hierarchies does not alter and should not obscure the ordering principle of the larger system, for those sectors are anarchic only within limits. The attributes and behavior of the units populating those sectors within the larger system differ, moreover, from what they should be and how they would behave outside of it. Firms in oligopolistic markets again are perfect examples of this. They struggle against one another, but because they need not prepare to defend themselves physically, they can afford to specialize and to participate more fully in the division of economic labor than states can. Nor do the states that populate an anarchic world find it impossible to work with one another, to make agreements limiting their arms, and to cooperate in establishing organizations. Hierarchic elements within international structures limit and restrain the exercise of sovereignty but only in ways strongly conditioned by the anarchy of the larger system. The anarchy of that order strongly affects the likelihood of cooperation, the extent of arms agreements, and the jurisdiction of international organizations. . . .

NOTES

1. S. F. Nadel, *The Theory of Social Structure* (Glencoe, Ill.: Free Press, 1957), pp. 8–11.
2. Ibid., pp. 104–9.
3. William T. R. Fox, "The Uses of International Relations Theory," in William T. R. Fox, ed., *Theoretical Aspects of International Relations* (Notre Dame, Ind.: University of Notre Dame Press, 1959), p. 35.
4. Marriet Martineau, *The Positive Philosophy of Auguste Comte: Freely Translated and Condensed,* 3rd ed. (London: Kegan Paul, Trench, Trubner, 1983), Vol. 2, pp. 51–53; George Katona, "Rational Behavior and Economic Behavior," *Psychological Review* 60 (September 1953).
5. Charles P. Kindleberger, *American Business Abroad* (New Haven, Ct.: Yale University Press, 1969), p. 207.
6. Smith should know better. Translated into terms that he has himself so effectively used, to say that states are sovereign is to say that they are segments of a plural society. See his "A Structural Approach to Comparative Politics" in David Easton, ed., *Varieties of Politics Theories* (Englewood Cliffs, N.J.: Prentice Hall, 1966), p. 122; cf. his "On Segmentary Lineage Systems," *Journal of the Royal Anthropological Society of Great Britain and Ireland* 86 (July–December 1956).
7. Émile Durkheim, *The Division of Labor in Society,* trans. George Simpson (New York: Free Press, 1964), p. 212.
8. Alfred E. Kahn, "The Tyranny of Small Decision: Market Failure, Imperfections and Limits of Econometrics," in Bruce M. Russett, ed., *Economic Theories of International Relations* (Chicago, Ill.: Markham, 1966), p. 23.
9. Richard W. Sterling, *Macropolitics: International Relations in a Global Society* (New York: Knopf, 1974), p. 336.
10. Put differently, states face a "prisoners' dilemma." If each of two parties follows his own interest, both end up worse off than if each acted to achieve joint interests. For thorough examination of the logic of such situations, see Glenn H. Snyder and Paul Diesing, *Conflict among Nations* (Princeton, N.J.: Princeton University Press, 1977); for brief and suggestive international applications, see Robert Jervis, "Cooperation under the Security Dilemma," *World Politics* 30 (January 1978).
11. Cf. Paul Diesing, *Reason in Society* (Urbana, Ill.: University of Illinois Press, 1962), pp. 198–204; Anthony Downs, *Inside Bureaucracy* (Boston: Little, Brown, 1967), pp. 262–70.

12. Cf. Chester I. Barnard, "On Planning for World Government," in Chester I. Barnard, ed., *Organization and Management* (Cambridge, Mass.: Harvard University Press, 1948), pp. 148–52; Michael Polanyi, "The Growth of Thought in Society," *Economica* 8 (November 1941), pp. 428–56.
13. Barnard, "On Planning," pp. 150–51.
14. Quoted in Chalmers A. Johnson, *Revolutionary Change* (Boston: Little, Brown, 1966), p. 13.
15. E. R. Livernash, "The Relation of Power to the Structure and Process of Collective Bargaining," in Bruce M. Russett, ed., *Economic Theories of International Politics* (Chicago, Ill.: Markham, 1963), p. 430.
16. Émile Durkheim's depiction of solidary and mechanical societies still provides the best explication of the two ordering principles, and his logic in limiting the types of society to two continues to be compelling despite the efforts of his many critics to overthrow it (see esp. *The Division of Labor in Society*).

Anarchy and the Struggle for Power

JOHN J. MEARSHEIMER

Great powers, I argue, are always searching for opportunities to gain power over their rivals, with hegemony as their final goal. This perspective does not allow for status quo powers, except for the unusual state that achieves preponderance. Instead, the system is populated with great powers that have revisionist intentions at their core. This chapter presents a theory that explains this competition for power. Specifically, I attempt to show that there is a compelling logic behind my claim that great powers seek to maximize their share of world power. . . .

WHY STATES PURSUE POWER

My explanation for why great powers vie with each other for power and strive for hegemony is derived from five assumptions about the international system. None of these assumptions alone mandates that states behave competitively. Taken together, however, they depict a world in which states have considerable reason to think and sometimes behave aggressively. In particular, the system encourages states to look for opportunities to maximize their power vis-à-vis other states. . . .

The first assumption is that the international system is anarchic, which does not mean that it is chaotic or riven by disorder. It is easy to draw that conclusion, since realism depicts a world characterized by security competition and war. By itself, however, the realist notion of anarchy has nothing to do with conflict; it is an ordering principle, which says that the system comprises independent states that have no central authority above them. Sovereignty, in other words, inheres in states because there is no higher ruling body in the international system. There is no "government over governments."

The second assumption is that great powers inherently possess some offensive military capability, which gives them the wherewithal to hurt and possibly destroy each other. States are potentially dangerous to each other, although some states have more military might than others and are therefore more dangerous. A state's military power is usually identified with the particular weaponry at its disposal, although even if there were no weapons, the individuals in those states could still

From *The Tragedy of Great Power Politics* by John Mearsheimer, pp. 29–40, 46–53. Copyright © 2001 by John J. Mearsheimer. Used by permission of W. W. Norton & Company, Inc.

use their feet and hands to attack the population of another state. After all, for every neck, there are two hands to choke it.

The third assumption is that states can never be certain about other states' intentions. Specifically, no state can be sure that another state will not use its offensive military capability to attack the first state. This is not to say that states necessarily have hostile intentions. Indeed, all of the states in the system may be reliably benign, but it is impossible to be sure of that judgment because intentions are impossible to divine with 100 percent certainty. There are many possible causes of aggression, and no state can be sure that another state is not motivated by one of them. Furthermore, intentions can change quickly, so a state's intentions can be benign one day and hostile the next. Uncertainty about intentions is unavoidable, which means that states can never be sure that other states do not have offensive intentions to go along with their offensive capabilities.

The fourth assumption is that survival is the primary goal of great powers. Specifically, states seek to maintain their territorial integrity and the autonomy of their domestic political order. Survival dominates other motives because, once a state is conquered, it is unlikely to be in a position to pursue other aims. . . . States can and do pursue other goals, of course, but security is their most important objective.

The fifth assumption is that great powers are rational actors. They are aware of their external environment and they think strategically about how to survive in it. In particular, they consider the preferences of other states and how their own behavior is likely to affect the behavior of those other states, and how the behavior of those other states is likely to affect their own strategy for survival. Moreover, states pay attention to the long term as well as the immediate consequences of their actions.

As emphasized, none of these assumptions alone dictates that great powers as a general rule *should* behave aggressively toward each other. There is surely the possibility that some state might have hostile intentions, but the only assumption dealing with a specific motive that is common to all states says that their principal objective is to survive, which by itself is a rather harmless goal. Nevertheless, when the five assumptions are married together, they create powerful incentives for great powers to think and act offensively with regard to each other. In particular, three general patterns of behavior result: fear, self-help, and power maximization.

STATE BEHAVIOR

Great powers fear each other. They regard each other with suspicion, and they worry that war might be in the offing. They anticipate danger. There is little room for trust among states. For sure, the level of fear varies across time and space, but it cannot be reduced to a trivial level. From the perspective of any one great power, all other great powers are potential enemies. This point is illustrated by the reaction of the United Kingdom and France to German reunification at the end of the Cold War. Despite the fact that these three states had been close allies for almost forty-five years, both the United Kingdom and France immediately began worrying about the potential dangers of a united Germany.

The basis of this fear is that in a world where great powers have the capability to attack each other and might have the motive to do so, any state bent on survival must be at least suspicious of other states and reluctant to trust them. Add to this the "911" problem—the absence of a central authority to which a threatened state can turn for help—and states have even greater incentive to fear each other. Moreover, there is no mechanism, other than the possible self-interest of third parties, for punishing an aggressor. Because it is sometimes difficult to deter potential aggressors, states have ample reason not to trust other states and to be prepared for war with them.

The possible consequences of falling victim to aggression further amplify the importance of fear as a motivating force in world politics. Great powers do not compete with each other as if international politics were merely an economic marketplace. Political competition among states is a much more dangerous business than mere economic intercourse; the former can lead to war, and war often means mass killing on the battlefield as well as mass murder of civilians. In extreme cases, war can even lead to the destruction of states. The horrible consequences of war sometimes cause states to view each other not just as competitors, but as potentially deadly enemies. Political antagonism, in short, tends to be intense, because the stakes are great.

States in the international system also aim to guarantee their own survival. Because other states are potential threats, and because there is no higher authority to come to their rescue when they dial 911, states cannot depend on others for their own security. Each state tends to see itself as vulnerable and alone, and therefore it aims to provide for its own survival. In international politics, God helps those who help themselves. This emphasis on self-help does not preclude states from forming alliances. But alliances are only temporary marriages of convenience: today's alliance partner might be tomorrow's enemy, and today's enemy might be tomorrow's alliance partner. For example, the United States fought with China and the Soviet Union against Germany and Japan in World War II, but soon thereafter flip-flopped enemies and partners and allied with West Germany and Japan against China and the Soviet Union during the Cold War.

States operating in a self-help world almost always act according to their own self-interest and do not subordinate their interests to the interests of other states, or to the interests of the so-called international community. The reason is simple: it pays to be selfish in a self-help world. This is true in the short term as well as in the long term, because if a state loses in the short run, it might not be around for the long haul.

Apprehensive about the ultimate intentions of other states, and aware that they operate in a self-help system, states quickly understand that the best way to ensure their survival is to be the most powerful state in the system. The stronger a state is relative to its potential rivals, the less likely it is that any of those rivals will attack it and threaten its survival. Weaker states will be reluctant to pick fights with more powerful states because the weaker states are likely to suffer military defeat. Indeed, the bigger the gap in power between any two states, the less likely it is that the weaker will attack the stronger. Neither Canada nor Mexico, for example, would countenance attacking the United States, which is far more powerful than its neighbors. The ideal situation is to be the hegemon in the system. . . .Survival would then be almost guaranteed.

Consequently, states pay close attention to how power is distributed among them, and they make a special effort to maximize their share of world power. Specifically, they look for opportunities to alter the balance of power by acquiring additional increments of power at the expense of potential rivals. States employ a variety of means—economic, diplomatic, and military—to shift the balance of power in their favor, even if doing so makes other states suspicious or even hostile. Because one state's gain in power is another state's loss, great powers tend to have a zero-sum mentality when dealing with each other. The trick, of course, is to be the winner in this competition and to dominate the other states in the system. Thus, the claim that states maximize relative power is tantamount to arguing that states are disposed to think offensively toward other states, even though their ultimate motive is simply to survive. In short, great powers have aggressive intentions.

Even when a great power achieves a distinct military advantage over its rivals, it continues looking for chances to gain more power. The pursuit of power stops only when hegemony is achieved. The idea that a great power might feel secure without dominating the system, provided it has an "appropriate amount" of power, is not persuasive, for two reasons. First, it is difficult to assess how much relative power one state must have over its rivals before it is secure. Is twice as much power an appropriate threshold? Or is three times as much power the magic number? The root of the problem is that power calculations alone do not determine which side wins a war. Clever strategies, for example, sometimes allow less powerful states to defeat more powerful foes.

Second, determining how much power is enough becomes even more complicated when great powers contemplate how power will be distributed among them ten or twenty years down the road. The capabilities of individual states vary over time, sometimes markedly, and it is often difficult to predict the direction and scope of change in the balance of power. Remember, few in the West anticipated the collapse of the Soviet Union before it happened. In fact, during the first half of the Cold War, many in the West feared that the Soviet economy would eventually generate greater wealth than the American economy, which would cause a marked power shift against the United States and its allies. What the future holds for China and Russia and what the balance of power will look like in 2020 is difficult to foresee.

Given the difficulty of determining how much power is enough for today and tomorrow, great powers recognize that the best way to ensure their security is to achieve hegemony now, thus eliminating any possibility of a challenge by another great power. Only a misguided state would pass up an opportunity to be the hegemon in the system because it thought it already had sufficient power to survive. But even if a great power does not have the wherewithal to achieve hegemony (and that is usually the case), it will still act offensively to amass as much power as it can, because states are almost always better off with more rather than less power. In short, states do not become status quo powers until they completely dominate the system.

All states are influenced by this logic, which means that not only do they look for opportunities to take advantage of one another, they also work to ensure that other states do not take advantage of them. After all, rival states are driven by the same logic, and most states are likely to recognize their own motives at play in the actions of other states. In short, states ultimately pay attention to defense as well as offense. They think about conquest themselves, and they work to check aggressor states from gaining power at their expense. This inexorably leads to a world of constant security competition, where states are willing to lie, cheat, and use brute force if it helps them gain advantage over their rivals. Peace, if one defines that concept as a state of tranquility or mutual concord, is not likely to break out in this world. . . .

It should be apparent from this discussion that saying that states are power maximizers is tantamount to saying that they care about relative power, not absolute power. There is an important distinction here, because states concerned about relative power behave differently than do states interested in absolute power. States that maximize relative power are concerned primarily with the distribution of material capabilities. In particular, they try to gain as large a power advantage as possible over potential rivals, because power is the best means to survival in a dangerous world. Thus, states motivated by relative power concerns are likely to forgo large gains in their own power, if such gains give rival states even greater power, for smaller national gains that nevertheless provide them with a power advantage over their rivals. States that maximize absolute power, on the other hand, care only about the size of their own gains, not those of other states. They are not motivated by balance-of-power logic but instead are concerned with amassing power without regard to how much power other states control. They would jump at the opportunity for large gains, even if a rival gained more in the deal. Power, according to this logic, is not a means to an end (survival), but an end in itself.

CALCULATED AGGRESSION

There is obviously little room for status quo powers in a world where states are inclined to look for opportunities to gain more power. Nevertheless, great powers cannot always act on their offensive intentions, because behavior is influenced not only by what states want, but also by their capacity to realize these desires. Every state might want to be king of the hill, but not every state has the wherewithal to compete for that lofty position, much less achieve it. Much depends on how military might is distributed among the great powers. A great power that has a marked power advantage over its rivals is likely to behave more aggressively, because it has the capability as well as the incentive to do so.

By contrast, great powers facing powerful opponents will be less inclined to consider offensive action and more concerned with defending the existing balance of power from threats by their more powerful opponents. Let there be an opportunity for those weaker states to revise the balance in their own favor, however, and they will take advantage of it.

In short, great powers are not mindless aggressors so bent on gaining power that they charge headlong into losing wars or pursue Pyrrhic victories. On the contrary, before great powers take offensive actions, they think carefully about the balance of power and about how other states will react to their moves. They weigh the costs and risks of offense against the likely benefits. If the benefits do not outweigh the risks, they sit tight and wait for a more propitious moment. Nor do states start arms races that are unlikely to improve their overall position. . . .States sometimes limit defense spending either because spending more would bring no strategic advantage or because spending more would weaken the economy and undermine the state's power in the long run. To paraphrase Clint Eastwood, a state has to know its limitations to survive in the international system.

Nevertheless, great powers miscalculate from time to time because they invariably make important decisions on the basis of imperfect information. States hardly ever have complete information about any situation they confront. There are two dimensions to this problem. Potential adversaries have incentives to misrepresent their own strength or weakness, and to conceal their true aims. For example, a weaker state trying to deter a stronger state is likely to exaggerate its own power to discourage the potential aggressor from attacking. On the other hand, a state bent on aggression is likely to emphasize its peaceful goals while exaggerating its military weakness, so that the potential victim does not build up its own arms and thus leaves itself vulnerable to attack. Probably no national leader was better at practicing this kind of deception than Adolf Hitler.

But even if disinformation was not a problem, great powers are often unsure about how their own military forces, as well as the adversary's, will perform on the battlefield. For example, it is sometimes difficult to determine in advance how new weapons and untested combat units will perform in the face of enemy fire. Peacetime maneuvers and war games are helpful but imperfect indicators of what is likely to happen in actual combat. Fighting wars is a complicated business in which it is often difficult to predict outcomes. . . .

Great powers are also sometimes unsure about the resolve of opposing states as well as allies. For example, Germany believed that if it went to war against France and Russia in the summer of 1914, the United Kingdom would probably stay out of the fight. Saddam Hussein expected the United States to stand aside when he invaded Kuwait in August 1990. Both aggressors guessed wrong, but each had good reason to think that its initial judgment was correct. In the 1930s, Adolf Hitler believed that his great-power rivals would be easy to exploit and isolate because each had little interest in fighting Germany and instead was determined to get someone else to assume that burden. He guessed right. In short, great powers constantly find themselves confronting situations in which they have to make important decisions with incomplete information. Not surprisingly, they sometimes make faulty judgments and end up doing themselves serious harm.

Some defensive realists go so far as to suggest that the constraints of the international system are so powerful that offense rarely succeeds, and that aggressive great powers invariably end up being punished. . . .They emphasize that (1) threatened states balance against aggressors and ultimately crush them, and (2) there is an offense-defense balance that is usually heavily tilted toward the defense, thus making conquest especially difficult. Great powers, therefore, should be content with the existing balance of power and not try to change it by force. . . .

There is no question that systemic factors constrain aggression, especially balancing by threatened states. But defensive realists exaggerate those restraining forces. Indeed, the historical record provides little support for their claim that offense rarely succeeds. One study estimates that there were 63 wars between 1815 and 1980, and the initiator won 39 times, which translates into about a 60 percent success rate. . . .In short, the historical record shows that offense sometimes succeeds and sometimes does not. The trick for a sophisticated power maximizer is to figure out when to raise and when to fold.

HEGEMONY'S LIMITS

Great powers, as I have emphasized, strive to gain power over their rivals and hopefully become hegemons. Once a state achieves that exalted position, it becomes a status quo power. More needs to be said, however, about the meaning of hegemony.

A hegemon is a state that is so powerful that it dominates all the other states in the system. No other state has the military wherewithal to put up a serious fight against it. In essence, a hegemon is the only great power in the system. A state that is substantially more powerful than the other great powers in the system is not a hegemon, because it faces, by definition, other great powers. The United Kingdom in the mid-nineteenth century, for example, is sometimes called a hegemon. But it was not a hegemon, because there were four other great powers in Europe at the time—Austria, France, Prussia, and Russia—and the United Kingdom did not dominate them in any meaningful way. In fact, during that period, the United Kingdom considered France to be a serious threat to the balance of power. Europe in the nineteenth century was multipolar, not unipolar.

Hegemony means domination of the system, which is usually interpreted to mean the entire world. It is possible, however, to apply the concept of a system more narrowly and use it to describe particular regions, such as Europe, Northeast Asia, and the Western Hemisphere. Thus, one can distinguish between *global hegemons,* which dominate the world, and *regional hegemons,* which dominate distinct geographical areas. The United States has been a regional hegemon in the Western Hemisphere for at least the past one hundred years. No other state in the Americas has sufficient military might to challenge it, which is why the United States is widely recognized as the only great power in its region. . . .

POWER AND FEAR

That great powers fear each other is a central aspect of life in the international system. But as noted, the level of fear varies from case to case. For example, the Soviet Union worried much less about Germany in 1930 than it did in 1939. How much states fear each other matters greatly, because the amount of fear between them largely determines the severity of their security competition, as well as the probability that they will fight a war. The more profound the fear is, the more intense is the security competition, and the more likely is war. The logic is straightforward: a scared state will look especially hard for ways to enhance its security, and it will be disposed to pursue risky policies to achieve that end. Therefore, it is important to understand what causes states to fear each other more or less intensely.

Fear among great powers derives from the fact that they invariably have some offensive military capability that they can use against each other, and the fact that one can never be certain that other states do not intend to use that power against oneself. Moreover, because states operate in an anarchic system, there is no night watchman to whom they can turn for help if another great power attacks them. Although anarchy and uncertainty about other states' intentions create an irreducible level of fear among states that leads to power-maximizing behavior, they cannot account for why sometimes that level of fear is greater than at other times. The reason is that anarchy and the difficulty of discerning state intentions are constant facts of life, and constants cannot explain variation. The capability that states have to threaten each other, however, varies from case to case, and it is the key factor that drives fear levels up and down. Specifically, the more power a state possesses, the more fear it generates among its rivals. Germany, for example, was much more powerful at the end of the 1930s than it was at the decade's beginning, which is why the Soviets became increasingly fearful of Germany over the course of that decade. . . .

THE HIERARCHY OF STATE GOALS

Survival is the number one goal of great powers, according to my theory. In practice, however, states pursue non-security goals as well. For example, great powers invariably seek greater economic prosperity to enhance the welfare of their citizenry. They sometimes seek to promote a particular ideology abroad, as happened during the Cold War when the United States tried to spread democracy around the world and the Soviet Union tried to sell communism. National unification is another goal that sometimes motivates states, as it did with Prussia and Italy in the nineteenth century and Germany after the Cold War. Great powers also occasionally try to foster human rights around the globe. States might pursue any of these, as well as a number of other non-security goals.

Offensive realism certainly recognizes that great powers might pursue these non-security goals, but it has little to say about them, save for one important point: states can pursue them as long as the requisite behavior does not conflict with balance-of-power logic, which is often the case. Indeed, the pursuit of these non-security goals sometimes complements the hunt for relative power. For example, Nazi Germany expanded into eastern Europe for both ideological and realist reasons, and the superpowers competed with each other during the Cold War for similar reasons. Furthermore, greater economic prosperity invariably means greater wealth, which has significant implications for security, because wealth is the foundation of military power. Wealthy states can afford powerful military forces, which enhance a state's prospects for survival. . . .

Sometimes the pursuit of non-security goals has hardly any effect on the balance of power, one way or the other. Human rights interventions usually fit this description, because they tend to be small-scale operations that cost little and do not detract from a great power's prospects for survival. For better or for worse, states are rarely willing to expend blood and treasure to protect foreign populations from gross abuses, including genocide. For instance, despite claims that American foreign policy is infused with moralism, Somalia (1992–93) is the only instance during the past one hundred years in which U.S. soldiers were killed in action on a humanitarian mission. And in that case, the loss of a mere eighteen soldiers in an infamous firefight in October 1993 so traumatized American policymakers that they immediately pulled all U.S. troops out of Somalia and then refused to intervene in Rwanda in the spring of 1994, when ethnic Hutu went on a genocidal rampage against their Tutsi neighbors. Stopping that genocide would have been relatively easy and it would have had virtually no effect on the position of the United States in the balance of power. Yet nothing was done. In short, although realism does not prescribe human rights interventions, it does not necessarily proscribe them.

But sometimes the pursuit of non-security goals conflicts with balance-of-power logic, in which case states usually act according to the dictates of realism. For example, despite the U.S. commitment to spreading democracy across the globe, it helped overthrow democratically elected governments and embraced a number of authoritarian regimes during the Cold War, when American policymakers felt that these actions would help contain the Soviet Union. In World War II, the liberal democracies put aside their antipathy for communism and formed an alliance with the Soviet Union against Nazi Germany. "I can't take communism," Franklin Roosevelt emphasized, but to defeat Hitler "I would hold hands with the Devil." In the same way, Stalin repeatedly demonstrated that when his ideological preferences clashed with power considerations, the latter won out. To take the most blatant example of his realism, the Soviet Union formed a non-aggression pact with Nazi Germany in August 1939—the infamous Molotov-Ribbentrop Pact—in hopes that the agreement would at least temporarily satisfy Hitler's territorial ambitions in eastern Europe and turn the Wehrmacht toward France and the United Kingdom. When great powers confront a serious threat, in short, they pay little attention to ideology as they search for alliance partners.

Security also trumps wealth when those two goals conflict, because "defence," as Adam Smith wrote in *The Wealth of Nations*, "is of much more importance than opulence." Smith provides a good illustration of how states behave when forced to choose between wealth and relative power. In 1651, England put into effect the famous Navigation Act, protectionist legislation designed to damage Holland's commerce and ultimately cripple the Dutch economy. The legislation mandated that all goods imported into England be carried either in English ships or ships owned by the country that originally produced the goods. Since the Dutch produced few goods themselves, this measure would badly damage their shipping, the central ingredient in their economic success. Of course, the Navigation Act would hurt England's economy as well, mainly because it would rob England of the benefits of free trade. "The act of navigation," Smith wrote, "is not favorable to foreign commerce, or to the growth of that opulence that can arise from it." Nevertheless, Smith considered the legislation "the wisest of all the commercial regulations of England" because it did more damage to the Dutch economy than to the English economy, and in the mid-seventeenth century Holland was "the only naval power which could endanger the security of England." . . .

COOPERATION AMONG STATES

One might conclude from the preceding discussion that my theory does not allow for any cooperation among the great powers. But this conclusion would be wrong. States can cooperate, although cooperation is sometimes difficult to achieve and always difficult to sustain. Two factors inhibit cooperation: considerations about relative gains and concern about cheating. Ultimately, great powers live in a fundamentally competitive world where they view each other as real, or at least potential, enemies, and they therefore look to gain power at each other's expense.

Any two states contemplating cooperation must consider how profits or gains will be distributed between them. They can think about the division in terms of either absolute or relative gains (recall the distinction made earlier between pursuing either absolute power or relative power; the concept here is the same). With absolute gains, each side is concerned with maximizing its own profits and cares little about how much the other side gains or loses in the deal. Each side cares about the other only to the extent that the other side's behavior affects its own prospects for achieving maximum profits. With relative gains, on the other hand, each side considers not only its own individual gain, but also how well it fares compared to the other side.

Because great powers care deeply about the balance of power, their thinking focuses on relative gains when they consider cooperating with other states. For sure, each state tries to maximize its absolute gains; still, it is more important for a state to make sure that it does no worse, and perhaps better, than the other state in any agreement. Cooperation is more difficult to achieve, however, when states are attuned to relative gains rather than absolute gains. This is because states concerned about absolute gains have to make sure that if the pie is expanding, they are getting at least some portion of the increase, whereas states that worry about relative gains must pay careful attention to how the pie is divided, which complicates cooperative efforts.

Concerns about cheating also hinder cooperation. Great powers are often reluctant to enter into cooperative agreements for fear that the other side will cheat on the agreement and gain a significant advantage. This concern is especially acute in the military realm, causing a "special peril of defection," because the nature of military weaponry allows for rapid shifts in the balance of power. Such a development could create a window of opportunity for the state that cheats to inflict a decisive defeat on its victim.

These barriers to cooperation notwithstanding, great powers do cooperate in a realist world. Balance-of-power logic often causes great powers to form alliances and cooperate against common enemies. The United Kingdom, France, and Russia, for example, were allies against Germany before and during World War I. States sometimes cooperate to gang up on a third state, as Germany and the Soviet Union did against Poland in 1939. More recently, Serbia and Croatia agreed to conquer and divide Bosnia between them, although the United States and its European allies prevented them from executing their agreement. Rivals as well as allies cooperate. After all, deals can be struck that roughly reflect the distribution of power and satisfy concerns about cheating. The various arms control agreements signed by the superpowers during the Cold War illustrate this point.

The bottom line, however, is that cooperation takes place in a world that is competitive at its core—one where states have powerful incentives to take advantage of other states. This point is graphically highlighted by the state of European politics in the forty years before World War I. The great powers cooperated frequently during this period, but that did not stop them from going to war on August 1, 1914. The United States and the Soviet Union also cooperated considerably during World War II, but that cooperation did not prevent the outbreak of the Cold War shortly after Germany and Japan were defeated. Perhaps most amazingly, there was significant economic and military cooperation between Nazi Germany and the Soviet Union during the two years before the Wehrmacht attacked the Red Army. No amount of cooperation can eliminate the dominating logic of security competition. Genuine peace, or a world in which states do not compete for power, is not likely as long as the state system remains anarchic.

Anarchy Is What States Make of It

ALEXANDER WENDT

Classical realists such as Thomas Hobbes, Reinhold Niebuhr, and Hans J. Morgen-thau attributed egoism and power politics primarily to human nature, whereas structural realists or neorealists emphasize anarchy. The difference stems in part from different interpretations of anarchy's causal powers. Kenneth Waltz's work is important for both. In *Man, the State, and War,* he defines anarchy as a condition of possibility for or "permissive" cause of war, arguing that "wars occur because there is nothing to prevent them."[1] It is the human nature or domestic politics of predator states, however, that provide the initial impetus or "efficient" cause of conflict which forces other states to respond in kind. . . .But . . .In Waltz's *Theory of International Politics* . . . the logic of anarchy seems by itself to constitute self-help and power politics as necessary features of world politics.[2] . . .

Waltz defines political structure in three dimensions: ordering principles (in this case, anarchy), principles of differentiation (which here drop out), and the distribution of capabilities.[3] By itself, this definition predicts little about state behavior. It does not predict whether two states will be friends or foes, will recognize each other's sovereignty, will have dynastic ties, will be revisionist or status quo powers, and so on. These factors, which are fundamentally intersubjective, affect states' security interests and thus the character of their interaction under anarchy. . . . Put more generally, without assumptions about the structure of identities and interests in the system, Waltz's definition of structure cannot predict the content or dynamics of anarchy. Self-help is one such intersubjective structure and, as such, does the decisive explanatory work in the theory. The question is whether self-help is a logical or contingent feature of anarchy. In this section, I develop the concept of a "structure of identity and interest" and show that no particular one follows logically from anarchy.

A fundamental principle of constructivist social theory is that people act toward objects, including other actors, on the basis of the meanings that the objects have for them. States act differently toward enemies than they do toward friends because enemies are threatening and friends are not. Anarchy and the distribution of power are insufficient to tell us which is which. U.S. military power has

From Alexander Wendt, "Anarchy Is What States Make of It: The Social Construction of Power Politics," *International Organization,* Vol. 46, No. 2 (Spring 1992), pp. 391–425. © 1992 by the World Peace Foundation and the Massachusetts Institute of Technology. Reprinted by permission of MIT Press Journals. Portions of the text and some footnotes have been omitted.

a different significance for Canada than for Cuba, despite their similar "structural" positions, just as British missiles have a different significance for the United States than do Soviet missiles. The distribution of power may always affect states' calculations, but how it does so depends on the intersubjective understandings and expectations, on the "distribution of knowledge," that constitute their conceptions of self and other.[4] If society "forgets" what a university is, the powers and practices of professor and student cease to exist; if the United States and Soviet Union decide that they are no longer enemies, "the Cold War is over." It is collective meanings that constitute the structures which organize our actions.

Actors acquire identities—relatively stable, role-specific understandings and expectations about self—by participating in such collective meanings. Identities are inherently relational: "Identity, with its appropriate attachments of psychological reality, is always identity within a specific, socially constructed world," Peter Berger argues.[5] Each person has many identities linked to institutional roles, such as brother, son, teacher, and citizen. Similarly, a state may have multiple identities as "sovereign," "leader of the free world," "imperial power," and so on. The commitment to and the salience of particular identities vary, but each identity is an inherently social definition of the actor grounded in the theories which actors collectively hold about themselves and one another and which constitute the structure of the social world.

Identities are the basis of interests. Actors do not have a "portfolio" of interests that they carry around independent of social context; instead, they define their interests on the process of defining situations. . . . Sometimes situations are unprecedented in our experience, and in these cases we have to construct their meaning, and thus our interests, by analogy or invent them de novo. More often they have routine qualities in which we assign meanings on the basis of institutionally defined roles. When we say that professors have an "interest" in teaching, research, or going on leave, we are saying that to function in the role identity of "professor," they have to define certain situations as calling for certain actions. This does not mean that they will necessarily do so (expectations and competence do not equal performance), but if they do not, they will not get tenure. The absence or failure of roles makes defining situations and interests more difficult, and identity confusion may result. This seems to be happening today in the United States and the former Soviet Union: Without the cold war's mutual attributions of threat and hostility to define their identities, these states seem unsure of what their "interests" should be.

An institution is a relatively stable set or "structure" of identities and interests. Such structures are often codified in formal rules and norms, but these have motivational force only in virtue of actors' socialization to and participation in collective knowledge. Institutions are fundamentally cognitive entities that do not exist apart from actors' ideas about how the world works. This does not mean that institutions are not real or objective, that they are "nothing but" beliefs. As collective knowledge, they are experienced as having an existence "over and above the individuals who happen to embody them at the moment."[6] In this way, institutions come to confront individuals as more or less coercive social facts, but they are still a function of what actors collectively "know." Identities and such collective cognitions do not exist apart from each other; they are "mutually constitutive." On this view, institutionalization is a process of internalizing new identities and interests, not something occurring outside them and affecting only behavior; socialization is a cognitive process, not just a behavioral one. Conceived in this way, institutions may be cooperative or conflictual, a point sometimes lost in scholarship on international regimes, which tends to equate institutions with cooperation. There are important differences between conflictual and cooperative institutions to be sure, but all relatively stable self-other relations—even those of "enemies"—are defined intersubjectively.

Self-help is an institution, one of various structures of identity and interest that may exist under anarchy. Processes of identity formation under anarchy are concerned first and foremost with preservation or "security" of the self. Concepts of security therefore differ in the extent to which and the manner in which the self is identified cognitively with the other, and, I want to suggest, it is upon this cognitive variation that the meaning of anarchy and the distribution of power depends. Let me illustrate with a standard continuum of security systems.

At one end is the "competitive" security system, in which states identify negatively with each other's security so that ego's gain is seen as alter's loss. Negative identification under anarchy constitutes systems of "realist" power politics: risk-averse actors that infer intentions from capabilities and worry about relative gains and losses. At the limit—in the Hobbesian war of all against all—collective action is nearly impossible in such a system because each actor must constantly fear being stabbed in the back.

In the middle is the "individualistic" security system, in which states are indifferent to the relationship between their own and others' security. This constitutes "neoliberal" systems: States are still self-regarding about their security but are concerned primarily with absolute gains rather than relative gains. One's position in the distribution of power is less important, and collective action is more possible (though still subject to free riding because states continue to be "egoists").

Competitive and individualistic systems are both "self-help" forms of anarchy in the sense that states do not positively identify the security of self with that of others but instead treat security as the individual responsibility of each. Given the lack of a positive cognitive identification on the basis of which to build security regimes, power politics within such systems will necessarily consist of efforts to manipulate others to satisfy self-regarding interests.

This contrasts with the "cooperative" security system, in which states identify positively with one another so that the security of each is perceived as the responsibility of all. This is not self-help in any interesting sense, since the "self" in terms of which interests are defined is the community; national interests are international interests. In practice, of course, the extent to which states identify with the community varies from the limited form found in "concerts" to the full-blown form seen in "collective security" arrangements. Depending on how well developed the collective self is, it will produce security practices that are in varying degrees altruistic or prosocial. This makes collective action less dependent on the presence of active threats and less prone to free riding. Moreover, it restructures efforts to advance one's objectives, or "power politics," in terms of shared norms rather than relative power.

On this view, the tendency in international relations scholarship to view power and institutions as two opposing explanations of foreign policy is therefore misleading, since anarchy and the distribution of power only have meaning for state action in virtue of the understandings and expectations that constitute institutional identities and interests. Self-help is one such institution, constituting one kind of anarchy but not the only kind. Waltz's three-part definition of structure therefore seems underspecified. In order to go from structure to action, we need to add a fourth: the intersubjectively constituted structure of identities and interests in the system.

This has an important implication for the way in which we conceive of states in the state of nature before their first encounter with each other. Because states do not have conceptions of self and other, and thus security interests, apart from or prior to interaction, we assume too much about the state of nature if we concur with Waltz that, in virtue of anarchy, "international political systems, like economic markets, are formed by the coaction of self-regarding units."[7] We also assume too much if we argue that, in virtue of anarchy, states in the state of nature necessarily face a "stag hunt" or "security dilemma."[8] These claims presuppose a history of interaction in which actors have acquired "selfish" identities and interests; before interaction (and still in abstraction from first- and second-image factors) they would have no experience upon which to base such definitions of self and other. To assume otherwise is to attribute to states in the state of nature qualities that they can only possess in society. Self-help is an institution, not a constitutive feature of anarchy.

What, then, *is* a constitutive feature of the state of nature before interaction? Two things are left if we strip away those properties of the self which presuppose interaction with others. The first is the material substrate of agency, including its zintrinsic capabilities. For human beings, this is the body; for states, it is an organizational apparatus of governance. In effect, I am suggesting for rhetorical purposes that the raw material out of which members of the state system are constituted is created by domestic society before states enter the constitutive process of international society, although this process implies neither stable territoriality nor sovereignty, which are internationally negotiated terms of individuality (as discussed further below). The second is a desire to preserve this material substrate, to survive. This does not entail "self-regardingness," however, since actors do not have a self prior to interaction with another; how they view the meaning and requirements of this survival therefore depends on the processes by which conceptions of self evolve.

This may all seem very arcane, but there is an important issue at stake: Are the foreign policy identities and interests of states exogenous or endogenous to the state system? The former is the answer of an individualistic or undersocialized systemic theory for which rationalism is appropriate; the latter is the answer of a fully socialized systemic theory. Waltz seems to offer the latter and proposes two mechanisms, competition and socialization, by which structure conditions state action.[9] The content of his argument about this conditioning, however, presupposes a self-help system that is not itself a constitutive feature of anarchy. As James Morrow points out, Waltz's two mechanisms condition behavior, not identity and interest. . . .[10]

If self-help is not a constitutive feature of anarchy, it must emerge causally from processes in which anarchy plays only a permissive role. This reflects a second principle of constructivism: that the meanings in terms of which action is organized arise out of interaction. . . .

Consider two actors—ego and alter—encountering each other for the first time.[11] Each wants to survive and has certain material capabilities, but neither actor has biological or domestic imperatives for power, glory, or conquest . . . and there is no history of security or insecurity between the two. What should they do? Realists would probably argue that each should act on the basis of worst-case assumptions about the other's intentions, justifying such an attitude as prudent in view of the possibility of death from making a mistake. Such a possibility always exists, even in civil society; however, society would be impossible if people made decisions purely on the basis of worst-case possibilities. Instead, most decisions are and should be made on the basis of probabilities, and these are produced by interaction, by what actors *do*.

In the beginning is ego's gesture, which may consist, for example, of an advance, a retreat, a brandishing of arms, a laying down of arms, or an attack. For ego, this gesture represents the basis on which it is prepared to respond to alter. This basis is unknown to alter, however, and so it must make an inference or "attribution" about ego's intentions and, in particular, given that this is anarchy, about whether ego is a threat. The content of this inference will largely depend on two considerations. The first is the gesture's and ego's physical qualities, which are in part contrived by ego and which include the direction of movement, noise, numbers, and immediate consequences of the gesture. The second consideration concerns what alter would intend by such qualities were it to make such a gesture itself. Alter may make an attributional "error" in its inference about ego's intent, but there is also no reason for it to assume a priori—before the gesture—that ego is threatening, since it is only through a process of signaling and interpreting that the costs and probabilities of being wrong can be determined. Social threats are constructed, not natural.

Consider an example. Would we assume, a priori, that we were about to be attacked if we are ever contacted by members of an alien civilization? I think not. We would be highly alert, of course, but whether we placed our military forces on alert or launched an attack would depend on how we interpreted the import of their first gesture for our security—if only to avoid making an immediate enemy out of what may be a dangerous adversary. The possibility of error, in other words, does not force us to act on the assumption that the aliens are threatening: Action depends on the probabilities we assign, and these are in key part a function of what the aliens do; prior to their gesture, we have no systemic basis for assigning probabilities. If their first gesture is to appear with a thousand spaceships and destroy New York, we will define the situation as threatening and respond accordingly. But if they appear with one spaceship, saying what seems to be "we come in peace," we will feel "reassured" and will probably respond with a gesture intended to reassure them, even if this gesture is not necessarily interpreted by them as such.

This process of signaling, interpreting, and responding completes a "social act" and begins the process of creating intersubjective meanings. It advances the same way. The first social act creates expectations on both sides about each other's future behavior: potentially mistaken and certainly tentative, but expectations nonetheless. Based on this tentative knowledge, ego makes a new gesture, again signifying the basis on which it will respond to alter, and again alter responds, adding to the pool of knowledge each has about the other, and so on over time. The mechanism here is reinforcement; interaction rewards actors for holding certain ideas about each other and discourages them from holding others. If repeated long enough, these "reciprocal typifications" will create relatively stable concepts of self and other regarding the issue at stake in the interaction.[12]

Competitive systems of interaction are prone to security "dilemmas," in which the efforts of actors to enhance their security unilaterally threatens the security of the others, perpetuating distrust and alienation. The forms of identity and interest that constitute such dilemmas, however, are themselves ongoing effects of, not exogenous to, the interaction; identities are produced in and through "situated activity."[13] We do not *begin* our relationship with the aliens in a security dilemma; security dilemmas are not given by anarchy or nature. . . .

The mirror theory of identity formation is a crude account of how the process of creating identities and interests might work, but it does not tell us why a system of states—such as, arguably, our own—would have ended up with self-regarding and not collective identities. In this section, I examine an efficient cause, predation, which, in conjunction with anarchy as a permissive cause, may generate a self-help system. In so doing, however, I show the key role that the structure of identities and interests plays in mediating anarchy's explanatory role.

The predator argument is straightforward and compelling. For whatever reasons—biology, domestic politics, or systemic victimization—some states may become predisposed toward aggression. The aggressive behavior of these predators or "bad apples" forces other states to engage in competitive power politics, to meet fire with fire, since failure to do so may degrade or destroy them. One predator will best a hundred pacifists because anarchy provides no guarantees. This argument is powerful in part because it is so weak: Rather than making the strong assumption that all states are inherently power-seeking (a purely reductionist theory of power politics), it assumes that just one is power-seeking and that the others have to follow suit because anarchy permits the one to exploit them.

In making this argument, it is important to reiterate that the possibility of predation does not in itself force states to anticipate it a priori with competitive power politics of their own. The possibility of predation does not mean that "war may at any moment occur"; it may in fact be extremely unlikely. Once a predator emerges, however, it may condition identity and interest formation in the following manner.

In an anarchy of two, if ego is predatory, alter must either define its security in self-help terms or pay the price. . . . The timing of the emergence of predation relative to the history of identity formation in the community is therefore crucial to anarchy's explanatory role as a permissive cause. Predation will always lead victims to defend themselves, but whether defense will be collective or not depends on the history of interaction within the potential collective as much as on the ambitions of the predator. Will the disappearance of the Soviet threat renew old insecurities among the members of the North Atlantic Treaty Organization? Perhaps, but not if they have reasons independent of that threat for identifying their security with one another. Identities and interests are relationship-specific, not intrinsic attributes of a "portfolio"; states may be competitive in some relationships and solidary in others . . .

The source of predation also matters. If it stems from unit-level causes that are immune to systemic impacts (causes such as human nature or domestic politics taken in isolation), then it functions in a manner analogous to a "genetic trait" in the constructed world of the state system. Even if successful, this trait does not select for other predators in an evolutionary sense so much as it teaches other states to respond in kind, but since traits cannot be unlearned, the other states will continue competitive behavior until the predator is either destroyed or transformed from within. However, in the more likely event that predation stems at least in part from prior systemic interaction—perhaps as a result of being victimized in the past (one thinks here of Nazi Germany or the Soviet Union)—then it is more a response to a learned identity and, as such, might be transformed by future social interaction in the form of appeasement, reassurances that security needs will be met, systemic effects on domestic politics, and so on. In this case, in other words, there is more hope that process can transform a bad apple into a good one. . . .

This raises anew the question of exactly how much and what kind of role human nature and domestic politics play in world politics. The greater and more destructive this role, the more significant predation will be, and the less amenable anarchy will be to formation of collective identities. Classical realists, of course, assumed that human nature was possessed by an inherent lust for power or glory. My argument suggests that assumptions such as this were made for a reason: An unchanging Hobbesian man provides the powerful efficient cause necessary for a relentless pessimism about world politics that anarchic structure alone, or even structure plus intermittent predation, cannot supply. . . .

Assuming for now that systemic theories of identity formation in world politics are worth pursuing, let me conclude by suggesting that the realist-rationalist alliance "reifies" self-help in the sense of treating it as something separate from the practices by which it is produced and sustained. Peter Berger and

Thomas Luckmann define reification as follows: "[It] is the apprehension of the products of human activity *as if* they were something else than human products—such as facts of nature, results of cosmic laws, or manifestations of divine will. Reification implies that man is capable of forgetting his own authorship of the human world, and further, that the dialectic between man, the producer, and his products is lost to consciousness. The reified world is . . . experienced by man as a strange facticity, an *opus alienum* over which he has no control rather than as the *opus proprium* of his own productive activity."[14] By denying or bracketing states' collective authorship of their identities and interests, in other words, the realist–rationalist alliance denies or brackets the fact that competitive power politics help create a very "problem of order" they are supposed to solve—that realism is a self-fulfilling prophecy. Far from being exogenously given, the intersubjective knowledge that constitutes competitive identities and interests is constructed every day by processes of "social will formation."[15] It is what states have made of themselves.

NOTES

1. Kenneth Waltz, *Man, the State, and War* (New York: Columbia University Press, 1959), p. 232.
2. Kenneth Waltz, *Theory of International Politics* (Boston: Addison-Wesley, 1979).
3. Waltz, *Theory of International Politics*, pp. 79–101.
4. The phrase "distribution of knowledge" is Barry Barnes's, as discussed in his work *The Nature of Power* (Cambridge: Polity Press, 1988); see also Peter Berger and Thomas Luckmann, *The Social Construction of Reality* (New York: Anchor Books, 1966).
5. Berger, "Identity as a Problem in the Sociology of Knowledge," *European Journal of Sociology*, 7, 1 (1966), 111.
6. Berger and Luckmann, p. 58.
7. Waltz, *Theory of International Politics*, p. 91.
8. See Waltz, *Man, the State, and War;* and Robert Jervis, "Cooperation Under the Security Dilemma," *World Politics* 30 (January 1978), 167–214.
9. Waltz, *Theory of International Politics*, pp. 74–77.
10. See James Morrow, "Social Choice and System Structure in World Politics," *World Politics* 41 (October 1988), 89.
11. This situation is not entirely metaphorical in world politics, since throughout history states have "discovered" each other, generating an instant anarchy as it were. A systematic empirical study of first contacts would be interesting.
12. On "reciprocal typifications," see Berger and Luckmann, pp. 54–58.
13. See C. Norman Alexander and Mary Glenn Wiley, "Situated Activity and Identity Formation," in Morris Rosenberg and Ralph Turner, eds., *Social Psychology: Sociological Perspectives* (New York: Basic Books, 1981), pp. 269–89.
14. See Berger and Luckmann, p. 89.
15. See Richard Ashley, "Social Will and International Anarchy," in Hayward Alker and Richard Ashley, eds., *After Realism*, work in progress, Massachusetts Institute of Technology, Cambridge, and Arizona State University, Tempe, 1992.

Exercises for the Consequences of Anarchy

Apply what you learned in this chapter by using the online resources on MyPoliSciKit (www.mypoliscikit.com).

 Practice Tests

 Videos:
■ "The Cuban Missile Crisis"
■ "The Iran-Iraq War"

 Simulation: "The Prisoner's Dilemma: You Are a Presidential Adviser"

Reading Guides:
■ Kenneth N. Waltz, "The Anarchic Structure of World Politics"
■ John J. Mearsheimer, "Anarchy and the Struggle for Power"
■ Alexander Wendt, "Anarchy Is What States Make of It"

THE MITIGATION OF ANARCHY

The Conditions for Cooperation in World Politics

KENNETH A. OYE

I. INTRODUCTION

Nations dwell in perpetual anarchy, for no central authority imposes limits on the pursuit of sovereign interests. This common condition gives rise to diverse outcomes. Relations among states are marked by war and concert, arms races and arms control, trade wars and tariff truces, financial panics and rescues, competitive devaluation and monetary stabilization. At times, the absence of centralized international authority precludes attainment of common goals. Because, as states, they cannot cede ultimate control over their conduct to a supranational sovereign, they cannot guarantee that they will adhere to their promises. The possibility of a breach of promise can impede cooperation even when cooperation would leave all better off. Yet, at other times, states do realize common goals through cooperation under anarchy. Despite the absence of any ultimate international authority, governments often bind themselves to mutually advantageous courses of action. And, though no international sovereign stands ready to enforce the terms of agreement, states can realize common interests through tacit cooperation, formal bilateral and multi-lateral negotiation, and the creation of international regimes. The question is: if international relations can approximate both a Hobbesian state of nature and a Lockean evil society, why does cooperation emerge in some cases and not in others?

[Scholars] address both explanatory and prescriptive aspects of this perennial question. *First, what circumstances favor the emergence of cooperation under*

From "Explaining Cooperation under Anarchy: Hypothesis and Strategies" by Kenneth A. Oye from *World Politics*, pp. 1–22. Reprinted by permission of Johns Hopkins University Press. Portions of the text and some footnotes have been omitted.

anarchy? Given the lack of a central authority to guarantee adherence to agreements, what features of situations encourage or permit states to bind themselves to mutually beneficial courses of action? What features of situations preclude cooperation? *Second, what strategies can states adopt to foster the emergence of cooperation by altering the circumstances they confront?* Governments need not necessarily accept circumstances as given. To what extent are situational impediments to cooperation subject to willful modification? Through what higher order strategies can states create the preconditions for cooperation?. . .

I submit that three circumstantial dimensions serve both as proximate explanations of cooperation and as targets of longer-term strategies to promote cooperation. Each of the three major sections of this piece defines a dimension, explains how that dimension accounts for the incidence of cooperation and conflict in the absence of centralized authority, and examines associated strategies for enhancing the prospects for cooperation.

In the section entitled "Payoff Structure: Mutual and Conflicting Preferences," I discuss how payoffs affect the prospects for cooperation and present strategies to improve the prospects for cooperation by altering payoffs. Orthodox game theorists identify optimal strategies *given* ordinally defined classes of games, and their familiar insights provide the starting point for the discussion. Recent works in security studies, institutional microeconomics, and international political economy suggest strategies to *alter* payoff structures and thereby improve the prospects for cooperation.[1]

In the next section, entitled "Shadow of the Future: Single-play and Iterated Games," I discuss how the prospect of continuing interaction affects the likelihood of cooperation; examine how strategies of reciprocity can provide direct paths to cooperative outcomes under iterated conditions; and suggest strategies to lengthen the shadow of the future.[2] In addition, this section shows that recognition and control capabilities—the ability to distinguish between cooperation and defection by others and to respond in kind—can affect the power of reciprocity, and suggests strategies to improve recognition capabilities.

In the third section, "Number of Players: Two-Person and N-Person Games," I explain why cooperation becomes more difficult as the number of actors increases; present strategies for promoting cooperation in N-actor situations; and offer strategies for promoting cooperation by reducing the number of actors necessary to the realization of common interests. Game theorists and oligopoly theorists have long noted that cooperation becomes more difficult as numbers increase, and their insights provide a starting point for discussion. Recent work in political economy focuses on two strategies for promoting cooperation in thorny N-person situations: functionalist analysts of regimes suggest strategies for increasing the likelihood and robustness of cooperation *given* large numbers of actors,[3] analysts of *ad hoc* bargaining in international political economy suggest strategies of bilateral and regional decomposition to *reduce* the number of actors necessary to the realization of some mutual interests, at the expense of the magnitude of gains from cooperation. . . .[4]

II. PAYOFF STRUCTURE: MUTUAL AND CONFLICTING PREFERENCES

The structure of payoffs in a given round of play—the benefits of mutual cooperation (CC) relative to mutual defection (DD) and the benefits of unilateral defection (DC) relative to unrequited cooperation (CD)—is fundamental to the analysis of cooperation. The argument proceeds in three stages. First, how does payoff structure affect the significance of cooperation? More narrowly, when is cooperation, defined in terms of conscious policy coordination, necessary to the realization of mutual interests? Second, how does payoff structure affect the likelihood and robustness of cooperation? Third, through what strategies can states increase the long-term prospects for cooperation by altering payoff structures?

Before turning to these questions, consider briefly some tangible and intangible determinants of payoff structures. The security and political economy literatures examine the effects of military force structure and doctrine, economic ideology, the size of currency reserves, macroeconomic circumstance, and a host of other factors on national assessments of national interests. In "Cooperation under the Security Dilemma," Robert Jervis has explained how the diffusion of offensive military technology and strategies can increase rewards from defection and thereby reduce the prospects for cooperation. In "International Regimes, Transactions, and Chance: Embedded Liberalism in the Postwar Economic Order," John Ruggie has demonstrated how the diffusion of liberal economic ideas increased the perceived benefits of mutual economic openness over mutual closure (CC-DD), and diminished the perceived rewards from asymmetric defection relative to asymmetric cooperation (DC-CD). In "Firms and Tariff Regime Change," Timothy McKeown has shown how downturns in the business cycle alter national tastes for protection and thereby decrease the perceived benefits of mutual openness relative to mutual closure and increase the perceived rewards of asymmetric defection. . . .[5]

A. Payoff Structure and Cooperation

How does payoff structure determine the significance of cooperation? More narrowly, when is *cooperation,* defined in terms of conscious policy coordination, *necessary* to the realization of *mutual benefits?* For a *mutual benefit* to exist, actors must prefer mutual cooperation (CC) to mutual defection (DD). For coordination to be *necessary* to the realization of the mutual benefit, actors must prefer unilateral defection (DC) to unrequited cooperation (CD). These preference orderings are consistent with the familiar games of Prisoners' Dilemma, Stag Hunt, and Chicken. Indeed, these games have attracted a disproportionate share of scholarly attention precisely because cooperation is desirable but not automatic. In these cases, the capacity of states to cooperate under anarchy, to bind themselves to mutually beneficial courses of action without resort to any ultimate central authority, is vital to the realization of a common good. . . .

In the class of games—including Prisoners' Dilemma, Stag Hunt, and Chicken—where cooperation is necessary to the realization of mutual benefits, how does payoff structure affect the likelihood and robustness of cooperation in these situations? Cooperation will be less likely in Prisoners' Dilemma than in Stag Hunt or Chicken. To understand why, consider each of these games in conjunction with the illustrative stories from which they derive their names.

Prisoners' Dilemma: Two prisoners are suspected of a major crime. The authorities possess evidence to secure conviction on only a minor charge. If neither prisoner squeals, both will draw a light sentence on the minor charge (CC). If one prisoner squeals and the other stonewalls, the rat will go free (DC) and the sucker will draw a very heavy sentence (CD). If both squeal, both will draw a moderate sentence (DD). Each prisoner's preference ordering is: DC > CC > DD > CD. If the prisoners expect to "play" only one time, each prisoner will be better off squealing than stonewalling, no matter what his partner chooses to do (DC > CC and DD > CD). The temptation of the rat payoff and fear of the sucker payoff will drive single-play Prisoners' Dilemmas toward mutual defection. Unfortunately, if both prisoners act on this reasoning, they will draw a moderate sentence on the major charge, while cooperation could have led to a light sentence on the minor charge (CC > DD). In single-play Prisoners' Dilemmas, individually rational actions produce a collectively suboptimal outcome.

Stag Hunt: A group of hunters surround a stag. If all cooperate to trap the stag, all will eat well (CC). If one person defects to chase a passing rabbit, the stag will escape. The defector will eat lightly (DC) and none of the others will eat at all (CD). If all chase rabbits, all will have some chance of catching a rabbit and eating lightly (DD). Each hunter's preference ordering is: CC > DC > DD > CD. The mutual interest in plentiful venison (CC) relative to all other outcomes militates strongly against defection. However, because a rabbit in the hand (DC) is better than a stag in the bush (CD), cooperation will be assured only if each hunter believes that all hunters will cooperate. In single-play Stag Hunt, the temptation to defect to protect against the defection of others is balanced by the strong universal preference for stag over rabbit.

Chicken: Two drivers race down the center of a road from opposite directions. If one swerves and the other does not, then the first will suffer the stigma of being known as a chicken (CD) while the second will enjoy being known as a hero (DC). If neither swerves, both will suffer grievously in the ensuing collision (DD). If both swerve, damage to the reputation of each will be limited (CC). Each driver's preference ordering is: DC > CC > CD > DD. If each believes that the other will swerve, then each will be tempted to defect by continuing down the center of the road. Better to be a live hero than a live chicken. If both succumb to this temptation, however, defection will result in collision. The fear that the other driver may not swerve decreases the appeal of continuing down the center of the road. In single-play Chicken, the temptations of unilateral defection are balanced by fear of mutual defection.

In games that are not repeated, only ordinally defined preferences matter. Under single-play conditions, interval-level payoffs in ordinally defined categories of games cannot (in theory) affect the likelihood of cooperation. In the illustrations above, discussions of dominant strategies do not hinge on the magnitude of differences among the payoffs. Yet the magnitude of differences between CC and DD and between DC and CD can be large or small, if not precisely measurable, and can increase or decrease. Changes in the magnitude of differences in the value placed on outcomes can influence the prospects for cooperation through two paths.

First, changes in the value attached to outcomes can transform situations from one ordinally defined class of game into another. For example, in "Cooperation under the Security Dilemma," Robert Jervis described how difficult Prisoners' Dilemmas may evolve into less challenging Stag Hunts if the gains from mutual cooperation (CC) increase relative to the gains from exploitation (DC). He related the structure of payoffs to traditional concepts of offensive and defensive dominance, and offensive and defensive dominance to technological and doctrinal shifts. Ernst Haas, Mary Pat Williams, and Don Babai have emphasized the importance of cognitive congruence as a determinant of technological cooperation. The diffusion of common conceptions of the nature and effects of technology enhanced perceived gains from cooperation and diminished perceived gains from defection, and may have transformed some Prisoners' Dilemmas into Harmony.[6]

Second, under iterated conditions, the magnitude of differences among payoffs *within* a given class of games can be an important determinant of cooperation. The more substantial the gains from mutual cooperation (CC-DD) and the less substantial the gains from unilateral defection (DC-CD), the greater the likelihood of cooperation. In iterated situations, the magnitude of the difference between CC and DD and between DC and CD in present and future rounds of play affects the likelihood of cooperation in the present. This point is developed at length in the section on the shadow of the future.

B. Strategies to Alter Payoff Structure

If payoff structure affects the likelihood of cooperation, to what extent can states alter situations by modifying payoff structures, and thereby increase the long-term likelihood of cooperation? Many of the tangible and intangible determinants of payoff structure, discussed at the outset of this section, are subject to willful modification through unilateral, bilateral, and multilateral strategies. In "Cooperation under the Security Dilemma," Robert Jervis has offered specific suggestions for altering payoff structures through unilateral strategies. Procurement policy can affect the prospects for cooperation. If one superpower favors procurement of defensive over offensive weapons, it can reduce its own gains from exploitation through surprise attack (DC) and reduce its adversary's fear of exploitation (CD). Members of alliances have often resorted to the device of deploying troops on troubled frontiers to increase the likelihood of cooperation. A state's use of troops as hostages is designed to diminish the payoff from its own defection—to reduce its gains from exploitation (DC)—and thereby render defensive defection by its partner less likely. Publicizing an agreement diminishes payoffs associated with defection from the agreement, and thereby lessens gains from exploitation. These observations in international relations are paralleled by recent developments in microeconomics. Oliver Williamson has identified unilateral and bilateral techniques used by firms to facilitate interfirm cooperation by diminishing gains from exploitation. He distinguishes between specific and nonspecific costs associated with adherence to agreements. Specific costs, such as specialized training, machine tools, and construction, cannot be recovered in the event of the breakdown of an agreement. When parties to an agreement incur high specific costs, repudiation of commitments will entail substantial losses. Firms can thus reduce their gains from exploitation through the technique of acquiring dedicated assets that serve as hostages to continuing cooperation. Nonspecific assets, such as general-purpose trucks and airplanes, are salvageable if agreements break down; firms can reduce their fear of being exploited by maximizing the use of nonspecific assets, but such assets cannot diminish gains from exploitation by serving as hostages.[7] Unilateral strategies can improve the prospects of cooperation by reducing both the costs of being exploited (CD) and the gains from exploitation (DC). The new literature on interfirm cooperation indirectly raises an old question on the costs of unilateral strategies to promote cooperation in international relations.

In many instances, unilateral actions that limit one's gains from exploitation may have the effect of increasing one's vulnerability to exploitation by others. For example, a state could limit gains from defection from liberal international economic norms by permitting the expansion of sectors of comparative advantage and by permitting liquidation of inefficient sectors. Because a specialized economy is a hostage to international economic cooperation, this strategy would unquestionably increase the credibility of the nation's commitment to liberalism. It also has the effect, however, of increasing the nation's vulnerability to protection by others. In the troops-as-hostage example, the government that stations troops may promote cooperation by diminishing an ally's fear of abandonment, but in so doing it raises its own fears of exploitation by the ally. . . .

Unilateral strategies do not exhaust the range of options that states may use to alter payoff structures. Bilateral strategies—most significantly strategies of issue linkage—can be used to alter payoff structures by combining dissimilar games. Because resort to issue linkage generally assumes iteration, analysis of how issue linkage can be used to alter payoffs is presented in the section on the shadow of the future. Furthermore, bilateral "instructional" strategies can aim at altering another country's understanding of cause-and-effect relationships, and result in altered perceptions of interest. For example, American negotiators in SALT I sought to instruct their Soviet counterparts on the logic of mutual assured destruction.[8]

Multilateral strategies, centering on the formation of international regimes, can be used to alter payoff structures in two ways. First, norms generated by regimes may be internalized by states, and thereby alter payoff structure. Second, information generated by regimes may alter states' understanding of their interests. As Ernst Haas argues, new regimes may gather and distribute information that can highlight cause-and-effect relationships not previously understood. Changing perceptions of means-ends hierarchies can, in turn, result in changing perceptions of interest.[9]

III. THE SHADOW OF THE FUTURE:
SINGLE-PLAY AND ITERATED GAMES

The distinction between cases in which similar transactions among parties are unlikely to be repeated and cases in which the expectation of future interaction can influence decisions in the present is fundamental to the emergence of cooperation among egotists. As the previous section suggests, states confronting strategic situations that resemble single-play Prisoners' Dilemma and, to a lesser extent, single-play Stag Hunt and Chicken, are constantly tempted by immediate gains from unilateral defection, and fearful of immediate losses from unrequited cooperation. How does continuing interaction affect prospects for cooperation? The argument proceeds in four stages. First, why do iterated conditions improve the prospects for cooperation in Prisoners' Dilemma and Stag Hunt while diminishing the prospects for cooperation in Chicken? Second, how do strategies of reciprocity improve the prospects for cooperation under iterated conditions? Third, why does the effectiveness of reciprocity hinge on conditions of play—the ability of actors to distinguish reliably between cooperation and defection by others and to respond in kind? Fourth, through what strategies can states improve conditions of play and lengthen the shadow of the future?

Before turning to these questions, consider the attributes of iterated situations. First, states must expect to continue dealing with each other. This condition is, in practice, not particularly restrictive. With the possible exception of global thermonuclear war, international politics is characterized by the expectation of future interaction. Second, payoff structures must not change substantially over time. In other words, each round of play should not alter the structure of the game in the future. This condition is, in practice, quite restrictive. For example, states considering surprise attack when offense is dominant are in a situation that has many of the characteristics of a single-play game: Attack alters options and payoffs in future rounds of interaction. Conversely, nations considering increases or decreases in their military budgets are in a situation that has many of the characteristics of an iterated game: Spending options and associated marginal increases or decreases in military strength are likely to remain fairly stable over future rounds of interaction. In international monetary affairs, governments considering or fearing devaluation under a gold-exchange standard are in a situation that has many of the characteristics of a single-play game: Devaluation may diminish the value of another state's foreign currency reserves on a one-time basis, while reductions in holdings of reserves would diminish possible losses on a one-time basis. Conversely, governments considering intervention under a floating system with minimal reserves are in a situation that has many of the characteristics of an iterated game: Depreciation or appreciation of a currency would not produce substantial one-time losses or gains. Third, the size of the discount rate applied to the future affects the iterativeness of games. If a government places little value on future payoffs, its situation has many of the characteristics of a single-play game. If it places a high value on future payoffs, its situation may have many of the characteristics of an iterated game. For example, political leaders in their final term are likely to discount the future more substantially than political leaders running for, or certain of, reelection.

A. The Shadow of the Future and Cooperation

How does the shadow of the future affect the likelihood of cooperation? Under single-play conditions without a sovereign, adherence to agreements is often irrational. Consider the single-play Prisoners' Dilemma. Each prisoner is better off squealing, whether or not his partner decides to squeal. In the absence of continuing interaction, defection would emerge as the dominant strategy. Because the prisoners can neither turn to a central authority for enforcement of an agreement to cooperate nor rely on the anticipation of retaliation to deter present defection, cooperation will be unlikely under single-play conditions. If the prisoners expect to be placed in similar situations in the future, the prospects for cooperation improve. Experimental evidence suggests that under iterated Prisoners' Dilemma the incidence of cooperation rises substantially.[10] Even in the absence of centralized authority, tacit agreements to cooperate through mutual stonewalling are frequently reached and maintained. Under iterated Prisoners' Dilemma, a potential defector compares the immediate gain from squealing with the possible sacrifice of future gains that may result from squealing. In single-play Stag Hunt, each hunter is tempted to defect in order to defend himself against the possibility of defection by others. A reputation for reliability, for resisting temptation, reduces the likelihood of defection. If the hunters are a permanent group, and expect to hunt together again, the immediate gains from unilateral defection relative to unrequited cooperation must be balanced against the cost of diminished cooperation in the future. In both Prisoners' Dilemma and Stag Hunt, defection in the present *decreases* the likelihood of cooperation in the future. In both, therefore, iteration improves the prospects for cooperation. In Chicken, iteration may decrease the prospects for cooperation. Under single-play conditions, the temptation of unilateral defection is balanced by the fear of the collision that follows from mutual defection. How does iteration affect this balance? If the game is repeated indefinitely, then each driver may refrain from swerving in the present to coerce the other driver into swerving in the future. Each driver may seek to acquire a reputation for not swerving to cause the other driver to swerve. In iterated Chicken, one driver's defection in the present may decrease the likelihood of the other driver's defection in the future.

B. Strategies of Reciprocity and Conditions of Play

It is at this juncture that strategy enters the explanation. Although the expectation of continuing interaction has varying effects on the likelihood of cooperation in the illustrations above, an iterated environment permits resort to strategies of reciprocity that may improve the prospects of cooperation in Chicken as well as in Prisoners' Dilemma and Stag Hunt. Robert Axelrod argues that strategies of reciprocity have the effect of promoting cooperation by establishing a direct connection between an actor's present behavior and anticipated future benefits. Tit-for-tat, or conditional cooperation, can increase the likelihood of joint cooperation by shaping the future consequences of present cooperation or defection.

In iterated Prisoners' Dilemma and Stag Hunt, reciprocity underscores the future consequences of present cooperation and defection. The argument presented above—that iteration enhances the prospects for cooperation in these games—rests on the assumption that defection in the present will decrease the likelihood of cooperation in the future. Adoption of an implicit or explicit strategy of matching stonewalling with stonewalling, squealing with squealing, rabbit chasing with rabbit chasing, and cooperative hunting with cooperative hunting validates the assumption. In iterated Chicken, a strategy of reciprocity can offset the perverse effects of reputational considerations on the prospects for cooperation. Recall that in iterated Chicken, each driver may refrain from swerving in the present to coerce the other driver into swerving in the future. Adoption of an implicit or explicit strategy of tit-for-tat in iterated games of Chicken alters the failure stream of benefits associated with present defection. If a strategy of reciprocity is credible, then the mutual losses associated with future collisions can encourage present swerving. In all three games, a promise to respond to present cooperation with future cooperation and a threat to respond to present defection with future defection can improve the prospects for cooperation.

The effectiveness of strategies of reciprocity hinges on conditions of play—the ability of actors to distinguish reliably between cooperation and defection by others and to respond in kind. In the illustrations provided above, the meaning of "defect" and "cooperate" is unambiguous. Dichotomous choices—between squeal and stonewall, chase the rabbit or capture the stag, continue down the road or swerve—limit the likelihood of misperception. Further, the actions of all are transparent. Given the definitions of the situations, prisoners, hunters, and drivers can reliably detect defection and cooperation by other actors. Finally, the definition of the actors eliminates the possibility of control problems. Unitary prisoners, hunters, and drivers do not suffer from factional, organizational, or bureaucratic dysfunctions that might hinder implementation of strategies of reciprocity.

In international relations, conditions of play can limit the effectiveness of reciprocity. The definition of cooperation and defection may be ambiguous. For example, the Soviet Union and the United States hold to markedly different definitions of "defection" from the terms of détente as presented in the Basic Principles Agreement;[11] the European Community and the United States differ over whether domestic sectoral policies comprise indirect export subsidies. Further, actions may not be transparent. For example, governments may not be able to detect one another's violations of arms control agreements or indirect export subsidies. If defection cannot be reliably detected, the effect of present cooperation on possible future reprisals will erode. Together, ambiguous definitions and a lack of transparency can limit the ability of states to recognize cooperation and defection by others.

Because reciprocity requires flexibility, control is as important as recognition. Internal factional, organizational, and bureaucratic dysfunctions may limit the ability of nations to implement tit-for-tat strategies. It may be easier to sell one unvarying line of policy than to sell a strategy of shifting between lines of policy in response to the actions of others. For example, arms suppliers and defense planners tend to resist the cancellation of weapons systems even if the cancellation is a response to the actions of a rival. Import-competing industries tend to resist the removal of barriers to imports, even if trade liberalization is in response to liberalization by another state. At times, national decision makers may be unable to implement strategies of reciprocity. On other occasions, they must invest heavily in selling reciprocity. For these reasons, national decision makers may display a bias against conditional strategies: The domestic costs of pursuing such strategies may partially offset the value of the discounted stream of future benefits that conditional policies are expected to yield. . . .

C. Strategies to Improve Recognition and Lengthen the Shadow of the Future

To what extent can governments promote cooperation by creating favorable conditions of play and by lengthening the shadow of the future? The literature on international regimes offers several techniques for creating favorable conditions of play. Explicit codification of norms can limit definitional ambiguity. The very act of clarifying standards of conduct, of defining cooperative and uncooperative behavior, can permit more effective resort to strategies of reciprocity. Further, provisions for surveillance—for example, mechanisms for verification in arms control agreements or for sharing information on the nature and effects of domestic sectoral policies—can increase transparency. In practice, the goal of enhancing recognition capabilities is often central to negotiations under anarchy.

The game-theoretic and institutional microeconomic literatures offer several approaches to increasing the iterative character of situations. Thomas Schelling and Robert Axelrod suggest tactics of decomposition over time to lengthen the shadow of the future.[12] For example, the temptation to defect in a deal promising thirty billion dollars for a billion barrels of oil may be reduced if the deal is sliced up into a series of payments and deliveries. Cooperation in arms reduction or in territorial disengagement may be difficult if the reduction or disengagement must be achieved in one jump. If a reduction or disengagement can be sliced up into increments, the problem of cooperation may be rendered more tractable. Finally, strategies of issue linkage can be used to alter payoff structures and to interject elements of iterativeness into single-play situations. Relations among states are rarely limited to one single-play issue of overriding importance. When nations confront a single-play game on one issue, present defection may be deterred by threats of retaliation on other iterated issues. In international monetary affairs, for instance, a government fearing one-time reserve losses if another state devalues its currency may link devaluation to an iterated trade game. By establishing a direct connection between present behavior in a single-play game and future benefits in an iterated game, tacit or explicit cross-issue linkage can lengthen the shadow of the future. . . .

IV. NUMBER OF PLAYERS: TWO-PERSON AND N-PERSON GAMES

Up to now, I have discussed the effects of payoff structure and the shadow of the future on the prospects of cooperation in terms of two-person situations. What happens to the prospects for cooperation as the number of significant actors rises?

In this section, I explain why the prospects for cooperation diminish as the number of players increases; examine the function of international regimes as a response to the problems created by large numbers; and offer strategies to improve the prospects for cooperation by altering situations to diminish the number of significant players.

The numbers problem is central to many areas of the social sciences. Mancur Olson's theory of collective action focuses on N-person versions of Prisoners' Dilemma. The optimism of our earlier discussions of cooperation under iterated Prisoners' Dilemma gives way to the pessimism of analyses of cooperation in the provision of public goods. Applications of Olsonian theory to problems ranging from cartelization to the provision of public goods in alliances underscore the significance of "free-riding" as an impediment to cooperation.[13] In international relations, the numbers problem has been central to two debates. The longstanding controversy over the stability of bipolar versus multipolar systems reduces to a debate over the impact of the number of significant actors on international conflict.[14] A more recent controversy, between proponents of the theory of hegemonic stability and advocates of international regimes, reduces to a debate over the effects of large numbers on the robustness of cooperation.[15]

A. Number of Players and Cooperation

How do numbers affect the likelihood of cooperation? There are at least three important channels of influence.[16] First, cooperation requires recognition of opportunities for the advancement of mutual interests, as well as policy coordination once these opportunities have been identified. As the number of players increases, transactions and information costs rise. In simple terms, the complexity of N-person situations militates against identification and realization of common interests. Avoiding nuclear war during the Cuban missile crisis called for cooperation by the Soviet Union and the United States. The transaction and information costs in this particularly harrowing crisis, though substantial, did not preclude cooperation. By contrast, the problem of identifying significant actors, defining interests, and negotiating agreements that embodied mutual interests in the N-actor case of 1914 was far more difficult. These secondary costs associated with attaining cooperative outcomes in N-actor cases erode the difference between CC and DD. More significantly, the intrinsic difficulty of anticipating the behavior of other players and of weighing the value of the future goes up with the number of players. The complexity of solving N-person games, even in the purely deductive sense, has stunted the development of formal work on the problem. This complexity is even greater in real situations, and operates against multilateral cooperation.

Second, as the number of players increases, the likelihood of autonomous defection and of recognition and control problems increases. Cooperative behavior rests on calculations of expected utility—merging discount rates, payoff structures, and anticipated behavior of other players. Discount rates and approaches to calculation are likely to vary across actors, and the prospects for mutual cooperation may decline as the number of players and probable heterogeneity of actors increases. The chances of including a state that discounts the future heavily, that is too weak (domestically) to detect, react, or implement a strategy of reciprocity, that cannot distinguish reliably between cooperation and defection by other states, or that departs from even minimal standards of rationality increase with the number of states in a game. For example, many pessimistic analyses of the consequences of nuclear proliferation focus on how breakdowns of deterrence may become more likely as the number of countries with nuclear weapons increases.

Third, as the number of players increases, the feasibility of sanctioning defectors diminishes. Strategies of reciprocity become more difficult to implement without triggering a collapse of cooperation. In two-person games, tit-for-tat works well because the costs of defection are focused on only one other party. If defection imposes costs on all parties in an N-person game, however, the power of strategies of reciprocity is undermined. The infeasibility of sanctioning defectors creates the possibility of free-riding. What happens if we increase the number of actors in the iterated Prisoners' Dilemma from 2 to 20? Confession by any one of them could lead to the conviction of all on the major charge; therefore, the threat to retaliate against defection in the present with defection in the future will impose costs on all prisoners, and could lead to wholesale defection in subsequent rounds. For example, under the 1914 system of alliances, retaliation against one member of the alliance was the equivalent of retaliation against all. In N-person games, a strategy of conditional defection can have the effect of spreading, rather than containing, defection.

B. Strategies of Institutionalization and Decomposition

Given a large number of players, what strategies can states use to increase the likelihood of cooperation? Regime creation can increase the likelihood of cooperation in N-person games. First, conventions provide rules of thumb that can diminish transaction and information costs. Second, collective enforcement mechanisms both decrease the likelihood of autonomous defection and permit selective punishment of violators of norms. These two functions of international regimes directly address problems created by large numbers of players. For example, Japan and the members of NATO profess a mutual interest in limiting flows of militarily useful goods and technology to the Soviet Union. Obviously, all suppliers of militarily useful goods and technology must cooperate to deny the Soviet Union access to such items. Although governments differ in their assessment of the military value of some goods and technologies, there is consensus on a rather lengthy list of prohibited items. By facilitating agreement of the prohibited list, the Coordinating Committee on the Consultative Group of NATO (CoCom) provides a relatively clear definition of what exports would constitute defection. By defining the scope of defection, the CoCom list forestalls the necessity of retaliation against nations that ship technology or goods that do not fall within the consensual definition of defection. Generally, cooperation is a prerequisite of regime creation. The creation of rules of thumb and mechanisms of collective enforcement and the maintenance and administration of regimes can demand an extraordinary degree of cooperation. This problem may limit the range of situations susceptible to modification through regimist strategies.

What strategies can reduce the number of significant players in a game and thereby render cooperation more likely? When governments are unable to cooperate on a global scale, they often turn to discriminatory strategies to encourage bilateral or regional cooperation. Tactics of decomposition across actors can, at times, improve the prospects for cooperation. Both the possibilities and the limits of strategies to reduce the number of players are evident in the discussions that follow. First, reductions in the number of actors can usually be purchased at the expense of the magnitude of gains from cooperation. The benefits of regional openness are smaller than the gains from global openness. A bilateral clearing arrangement is less economically efficient than a multilateral clearing arrangement. Strategies to reduce the number of players in a game generally diminish the gains from cooperation while they increase the likelihood and robustness of cooperation. Second, strategies to reduce the number of players generally impose substantial costs on third parties. These externalities may motivate third parties to undermine the limited area of cooperation or may serve as an impetus for a third party to enlarge the zone of cooperation. In the 1930s, for example, wholesale resort to discriminatory trading policies facilitated creation of exclusive zones of commercial openness. When confronted by a shrinking market share, Great Britain adopted a less liberal and more discriminatory commercial policy in order to secure preferential access to its empire and to undermine preferential agreements between other countries. As the American market share diminished, the United States adopted a more liberal and more discriminatory commercial policy to increase its access to export markets. It is not possible, however, to reduce the number of players in all situations. For example, compare the example of limited commercial openness with the example of a limited strategic embargo. To reduce the number of actors in a trade war, market access can simply be offered to only one country and withheld from others. By contrast, defection by only one supplier can permit the target of a strategic embargo to obtain a critical technology. These problems may limit the range of situations susceptible to modification through strategies that reduce the number of players in games.

NOTES

1. For examples, see Robert Jervis, "Cooperation under the Security Dilemma," *World Politics* 30 (January 1978), pp. 167–214; Oliver E. Williamson, "Credible Commitments: Using Hostages to Support Exchange," *American Economic Review* (September 1983), pp. 519–40; John Gerard Ruggie, "International Regimes, Transactions, and Change: Embedded Liberalism in the Postwar Economic Order," in Stephen D. Krasner, ed., *International Regimes* (Ithaca, N.Y.: Cornell University Press, 1983).

2. For orthodox game-theoretic analyses of the importance of iteration, see R. Duncan Luce and Howard Raiffa, *Games and Decisions* (New York: Wiley, 1957), Appendix 8, and David M. Kreps, Paul Milgram, John Roberts, and Robert Wilson, "Rational Cooperation in Finitely-Repeated Prisoner's Dilemma," *Journal of Economic Theory* 27 (August 1982),

pp. 245–52. For the results of laboratory experiments, see Robert Radlow, "An Experimental Study of Cooperation in the Prisoners' Dilemma Game," *Journal of Conflict Resolution* 9 (June 1965), pp. 221–27. On the importance of indefinite iteration to the emergence of cooperation in business transactions, see Robert Telsor, "A Theory of Self-Enforcing Agreements," *Journal of Business* 53 (January 1980), pp. 27–44.

3. See Robert O. Keohane, *After Hegemony: Cooperation and Discord in the World Political Economy* (Princeton, N.J.: Princeton University Press, 1984), and Krasner (fn. 1).

4. See John A. C. Conybeare, "International Organization and the Theory of Property Rights," *International Organization* 34 (Summer 1980), pp. 307–34, and Kenneth A. Oye, "Belief Systems, Bargaining, and Breakdown: International Political Economy 1929–1936," Ph.D. diss. (Harvard University, 1983), chap. 3.

5. See Jervis (fn. 1); Ruggie (fn. 1); Timothy J. McKeown, "Firms and Tariff Regime Change: Explaining the Demand for Protection," *World Politics* 36 (January 1984), pp. 215–33. On the effects of *ambiguity* of preferences on the prospects of cooperation, see the concluding sections of Jervis (fn. 1).

6. Haas, Williams, and Babai, *Scientists and World Order: The Uses of Technical Knowledge in International Organizations* (Berkeley: University of California Press, 1977).

7. Williamson (fn. 1).

8. See John Newhouse, *Cold Dawn: The Story of SALT I* (New York: Holt, Rinehart & Winston, 1973).

9. See Haas, "Words Can Hurt You; Or Who Said What to Whom About Regimes," in Krasner (fn. 1).

10. See Anatol Rapoport and Albert Chammah, *Prisoners' Dilemma* (Ann Arbor: University of Michigan Press, 1965), and subsequent essays in *Journal of Conflict Resolution.*

11. See Alexander L. George, *Managing U.S.–Soviet Rivalry: Problems of Crisis Prevention* (Boulder, Colo.: Westview, 1983).

12. Schelling, *Strategy of Conflict* (Cambridge, Mass.: Harvard University Press, 1960), pp. 43–46.

13. See Mancur Olson, Jr., *The Logic of Collective Action: Public Goods and the Theory of Groups* (Cambridge, Mass.: Harvard University Press, 1965), and Mancur Olson and Richard Zeckhauser, "An Economic Theory of Alliances," *Review of Economics and Statistics* 48 (August 1966), pp. 266–79. For a recent elegant summary and extension of the large literature on dilemmas of collective action, see Russell Hardin, *Collective Action* (Baltimore: Johns Hopkins University Press, 1982).

14. See Kenneth N. Waltz, "The Stability of a Bipolar World," *Daedalus* 93 (Summer 1964), and Richard N. Rosecrance, "Bipolarity, Multipolarity, and the Future," *Journal of Conflict Resolution* (September 1966), pp. 314–27.

15. On hegemony, see Robert Gilpin, *U.S. Power and the Multinational Corporation* (New York: Basic Books, 1975), pp. 258–59. On duopoly, see Timothy McKeown, "Hegemonic Stability Theory and 19th-Century Tariff Levels in Europe," *International Organization* 37 (Winter 1983), pp. 73–91.

16. See Keohane (fn. 3), chap. 6, for extensions of these points.

Offense, Defense, and the Security Dilemma

ROBERT JERVIS

Another approach starts with the central point of the security dilemma—that an increase in one state's security decreases the security of others—and examines the conditions under which this proposition holds. Two crucial variables are involved: whether defensive weapons and policies can be distinguished from offensive ones, and whether the defense or the offense has the advantage. The definitions are not always clear, and many cases are difficult to judge, but these two variables shed a great deal of light on the question of whether status-quo powers will adopt compatible security policies. All the variables discussed so far leave the heart of the problem untouched. But when defensive weapons differ from offensive ones, it is possible for a state to make itself more secure without making others less secure. And when the defense has the advantage over the offense, a large increase in one state's security only slightly decreases the security of the others, and status-quo powers can all enjoy a high level of security and largely escape from the state of nature.

OFFENSE–DEFENSE BALANCE

When we say that the offense has the advantage, we simply mean that it is easier to destroy the other's army and take its territory than it is to defend one's own. When the defense has the advantage, it is easier to protect and to hold than it is to move forward, destroy, and take. If effective defenses can be erected quickly, an attacker may be able to keep territory he has taken in an initial victory. Thus, the dominance of the defense made it very hard for Britain and France to push Germany out of France in World War I. But when superior defenses are difficult for an aggressor to improvise on the battlefield and must be constructed during peacetime, they provide no direct assistance to him.

The security dilemma is at its most vicious when commitments, strategy, or technology dictate that the only route to security lies through expansion. Status-quo powers must then act like aggressors: the fact that they would gladly agree to

From "Cooperation Under the Security Dilemma" from *World Politics*, Vol. 30, No. 2 (January 1978), pp. 186–214 by Robert Jervis. Reprinted with permission of Johns Hopkins University Press. Portions of the text and some footnotes have been omitted.

the opportunity for expansion in return for guarantees for their security has implications for their behavior. Even if expansion is not sought as a goal in itself, there will be quick and drastic changes in the distribution of territory and influence. Conversely, when the defense has the advantage, status-quo states can make themselves more secure without gravely endangering others.[1] Indeed, if the defense has enough of an advantage and if the states are of roughly equal size, not only will the security dilemma cease to inhibit status-quo states from cooperating, but aggression will be next to impossible, thus rendering international anarchy relatively unimportant. If states cannot conquer each other, then the lack of sovereignty, although it presents problems of collective goods in a number of areas, no longer forces states to devote their primary attention to self-preservation. Although, if force were not usable, there would be fewer restraints on the use of nonmilitary instruments, these are rarely powerful enough to threaten the vital interests of a major state.

Two questions of the offense-defense balance can be separated. First, does the state have to spend more or less than one dollar on defensive forces to offset each dollar spent by the other side on forces that could be used to attack? If the state has one dollar to spend on increasing its security, should it put it into offensive or defensive forces? Second, with a given inventory of forces, is it better to attack or to defend? Is there an incentive to strike first or to absorb the other's blow? These two aspects are often linked: If each dollar spent on offense can overcome each dollar spent on defense, and if both sides have the same defense budgets, then both are likely to build offensive forces and find it attractive to attack rather than to wait for the adversary to strike.

These aspects affect the security dilemma in different ways. The first has its greatest impact on arms races. If the defense has the advantage, and if the status-quo powers have reasonable subjective security requirements, they can probably avoid an arms race. Although an increase in one side's arms and security will still decrease the other's security, the former's increase will be larger than the latter's decrease. So if one side increases its arms, the other can bring its security back up to its previous level by adding a smaller amount to its forces. And if the first side reacts to this change, its increase will also be smaller than the stimulus that produced it. Thus a stable equilibrium will be reached. Shifting from dynamics to statics, each side can be quite secure with forces roughly equal to those of the other. Indeed, if the defense is much more potent than the offense, each side can be willing to have forces much smaller than the other's, and can be indifferent to a wide range of the other's defense policies.

The second aspect—whether it is better to attack or to defend—influences short-run stability. When the offense has the advantage, a state's reaction to international tension will increase the chances of war. The incentives for preemption and the "reciprocal fear of surprise attack" in this situation have been made clear by analyses of the dangers that exist when two countries have first-strike capabilities.[2] There is no way for the state to increase its security without menacing, or even attacking, the other. Even Bismarck, who once called preventive war "committing suicide from fear of death," said that "no government, if it regards war as inevitable even if it does not want it, would be so foolish as to leave to the enemy the choice of time and occasion and to wait for the moment which is most convenient for the enemy."[3] In another arena, the same dilemma applies to the policeman in a dark alley confronting a suspected criminal who appears to be holding a weapon. Though racism may indeed be present, the security dilemma can account for many of the tragic shootings of innocent people in the ghettos.

Beliefs about the course of a war in which the offense has the advantage further deepen the security dilemma. When there are incentives to strike first, a successful attack will usually so weaken the other side that victory will be relatively quick, bloodless, and decisive. It is in these periods when conquest is possible and attractive that states consolidate power internally—for instance, by destroying the feudal barons—and expand externally. There are several consequences that decrease the chance of cooperation among status-quo states. First, war will be profitable for the winner. The costs will be low and the benefits high. Of course, losers will suffer; the fear of losing could induce states to try to form stable cooperative arrangements, but the temptation of victory will make this particularly difficult. Second, because wars are expected to be both frequent and short, there will be incentives for high levels of arms, and quick and strong reaction to the other's increases in arms. The state cannot afford to wait until there is unambiguous evidence that the other is building new weapons. Even large states that have faith in their economic strength cannot wait, because the war will be over before their products can reach the army. Third, when wars are quick, states will have to recruit allies in advance.[4] Without the opportunity for bargaining and realignments during the opening stages of hostilities, peacetime diplomacy loses a degree of the fluidity that facilitates balance-of-power policies. Because alliances must be secured during peacetime, the international system is more likely to become bipolar. It is hard to say whether war therefore becomes more or less likely, but this bipolarity increases tension between the two camps and makes it harder for status-quo states to gain the benefits of cooperation. Fourth, if wars are frequent, statesmen's perceptual thresholds will be adjusted accordingly and they will be quick to perceive ambiguous evidence as indicating that others are aggressive. Thus, there will be more cases of status-quo powers arming against each other in the incorrect belief that the other is hostile.

When the defense has the advantage, all the foregoing is reversed. The state that fears attack does not preempt—since that would be a wasteful use of its military resources—but rather prepares to receive an attack. Doing so does not decrease the security of others, and several states can do it simultaneously; the situation will therefore be stable, and status-quo powers will be able to cooperate. When Herman Kahn argues that ultimatums "are vastly too dangerous to give because. . .they are quite likely to touch off a pre-emptive strike,"[5] he incorrectly assumes that it is always advantageous to strike first.

More is involved than short-run dynamics. When the defense is dominant, wars are likely to become stalemates and can be won only at enormous cost. Relatively small and weak states can hold off larger and stronger ones, or can deter attack by raising the costs of conquest to an unacceptable level. States then approach equality in what they can do to each other. Like the .45-caliber pistol in the American West, fortifications were the "great equalizer" in some periods. Changes in the status quo are less frequent and cooperation is more common wherever the security dilemma is thereby reduced.

Many of these arguments can be illustrated by the major powers' policies in the periods preceding the two world wars. Bismarck's wars surprised statesmen by showing that the offense had the advantage, and by being quick, relatively cheap, and quite decisive. Falling into a common error, observers projected this pattern into the future.[6] The resulting expectations had several effects. First, states sought semi-permanent allies. In the early stages of the Franco-Prussian War, Napoleon III had thought that there would be plenty of time to recruit Austria to his side. Now, others were not going to repeat this mistake. Second, defense budgets were high and reacted quite sharply to increases on the other side. It is not surprising that Richardson's theory of arms races fits this period well. Third, most decision makers thought that the next European war would not cost much blood and treasure.[7] That is one reason why war was generally seen as inevitable and why mass opinion was so bellicose. Fourth, once war seemed likely, there were strong pressures to preempt. Both sides believed that whoever moved first could penetrate the other deep enough to disrupt mobilization and thus gain an insurmountable advantage. (There was no such belief about the use of naval forces. Although Churchill made an ill-advised speech saying that if German ships "do not come out and fight in time of war they will be dug out like rats in a hole,"[8] everyone knew that submarines, mines and coastal fortifications made this impossible. So at the start of the war each navy prepared to defend itself rather than attack, and the short-run destabilizing forces that launched the armies toward each other did not operate.)[9] Furthermore, each side knew that the other saw the situation the same way, thus increasing the perceived danger that the other would attack, and giving each added reasons to precipitate a war if conditions seemed favorable. In the long and the short run, there were thus both offensive and defensive incentives to strike. This situation casts light on the common question about German motives in 1914: "Did Germany unleash the war deliberately to become a world power or did she support Austria merely to defend a weakening ally," thereby protecting her own position?[10] To some extent, this question is misleading. Because of the perceived advantage of the offense, war was seen as the best route both to gaining expansion and to avoiding drastic loss of influence. There seemed to be no way for Germany merely to retain and safeguard her existing position.

Of course the war showed these beliefs to have been wrong on all points. Trenches and machine guns gave the defense an overwhelming advantage. The fighting became deadlocked and produced horrendous casualties. It made no sense for the combatants to bleed themselves to death. If they had known the power of the defense beforehand, they would have rushed for their own trenches rather than for the enemy's territory. Each side could have done this without increasing the other's incentives to strike. War might have broken out anyway; but at least the pressures of time and the fear of allowing the other to get the first blow would not have contributed to this end. And, had both sides known the costs of the war, they would have negotiated much more seriously. The obvious question is why the states did not seek a negotiated settlement as soon as the shape of the war became clear. Schlieffen had said that if his plan failed, peace should be sought.[11] The answer is complex, uncertain, and largely outside of the scope of our concerns. But part of the reason was the hope and sometimes the expectation that break-throughs could be made and the dominance of the offensive restored. Without that hope, the political and psychological pressures to fight to a decisive victory might have been overcome.

The politics of the interwar period were shaped by the memories of the previous conflict and the belief that any future war would resemble it. Political and military lessons reinforced each other in ameliorating the security dilemma. Because it was believed that the First World War had been a mistake that could have been avoided by skillful conciliation, both Britain and, to a lesser extent, France were highly sensitive to the possibility that interwar Germany was not a real threat to peace, and alert to the danger that reacting quickly and strongly to her arms could create unnecessary conflict. And because Britain and France expected the defense to continue to dominate, they concluded that it was safe to adopt a more relaxed and nonthreatening military posture.[12] Britain also felt less need to maintain tight alliance bonds. The Allies' military posture then constituted only a slight danger to Germany; had the latter been content with the status quo, it would have been easy for both sides to have felt secure behind their lines of fortifications. Of course the Germans were not content, so it is not surprising that they devoted their money and attention to finding ways out of a defense-dominated stalemate. *Blitzkrieg* tactics were necessary if they were to use force to change the status quo.

The initial stages of the war on the Western Front also contrasted with the First World War. Only with the new air arm were there any incentives to strike first, and these forces were too weak to carry out the grandiose plans that had been both dreamed and feared. The armies, still the main instrument, rushed to defensive positions. Perhaps the allies could have successfully attacked while the Germans were occupied in Poland.[13] But belief in the defense was so great that this was never seriously contemplated. Three months after the start of the war, the French Prime Minister summed up the view held by almost everyone but Hitler: on the Western Front there is "deadlock. Two Forces of equal strength and the one that attacks seeing such enormous casualties that it cannot move without endangering the continuation of the war or of the aftermath."[14] The Allies were caught in a dilemma they never fully recognized, let alone solved. On the one hand, they had very high war aims; although unconditional surrender had not yet been adopted, the British had decided from the start that the removal of Hitler was a necessary condition for peace.[15] On the other hand, there were no realistic plans or instruments for allowing the Allies to impose their will on the other side. The British Chief of the Imperial General Staff noted, "The French have no intention of carrying out an offensive for years, if at all"; the British were only slightly bolder.[16] So the Allies looked to a long war that would wear the Germans down, cause civilian suffering through shortages, and eventually undermine Hitler. There was little analysis to support this view—and indeed it probably was not supportable—but as long as the defense was dominant and the numbers on each side relatively equal, what else could the Allies do?

To summarize, the security dilemma was much less powerful after World War I than it had been before. In the later period, the expected power of the defense allowed status-quo states to pursue compatible security policies and avoid arms races. Furthermore, high tension and fear of war did not set off short-run dynamics by which each state, trying to increase its security, inadvertently acted to make war more likely. The expected high costs of war, however, led the Allies to believe that no sane German leader would run the risks entailed in an attempt to dominate the Continent, and discouraged them from risking war themselves.

Technology and Geography

Technology and geography are the two main factors that determine whether the offense or the defense has the advantage. As Brodie notes, "On the tactical level, as a rule, few physical factors favor the attacker but many favor the defender. The defender usually has the advantage of cover. He characteristically fires from behind some form of shelter while his opponent crosses open ground."[17] Anything that increases the amount of ground the attacker has to cross, or impedes his progress across it, or makes him more vulnerable while crossing, increases the advantage accruing to the defense. When states are separated by barriers that produce these effects, the security dilemma is eased, since both can have forces adequate for defense without being able to attack. Impenetrable barriers would actually prevent war; in reality, decision makers have to settle for a good deal less. Buffer zones slow the attacker's progress; they thereby give the defender time to prepare, increase problems of logistics, and reduce the number of soldiers available for the final assault. At the end of the nineteenth century, Arthur Balfour noted Afghanistan's "non-conducting" qualities. "So long as it possesses few roads, and no railroads, it will be impossible for Russia to make effective use of her great numerical superiority at any point immediately vital to the Empire." The Russians valued buffers for the same reasons; it is not surprising that when Persia was being divided into Russian and British spheres of influence some years later, the Russians sought assurances that the British would refrain from building potentially menacing railroads in their sphere. Indeed, since railroad construction radically altered the abilities of countries to defend themselves and to attack others, many diplomatic notes and much intelligence activity in the late nineteenth century centered on this subject.[18]

Oceans, large rivers, and mountain ranges serve the same function as buffer zones. Being hard to cross, they allow defense against superior numbers. The defender has merely to stay on his side of the barrier and so can utilize all the men he can bring up to it. The attacker's men, however, can cross only a few at a time, and they are very vulnerable when doing so. If all states were self-sufficient islands, anarchy would be much less of a problem. A small investment in shore defenses and a small army would be sufficient to repel invasion. Only very weak states would be vulnerable, and only very large ones could menace others. As noted above, the

United States, and to a lesser extent Great Britain, have partly been able to escape from the state of nature because their geographical positions approximated this ideal.

Although geography cannot be changed to conform to borders, borders can and do change to conform to geography. Borders across which an attack is easy tend to be unstable. States living within them are likely to expand or be absorbed. Frequent wars are almost inevitable since attacking will often seem the best way to protect what one has. This process will stop, or at least slow down, when the state's borders reach—by expansion or contraction—a line of natural obstacles. Security without attack will then be possible. Furthermore, these lines constitute salient solutions to bargaining problems and, to the extent that they are barriers to migration, are likely to divide ethnic groups, thereby raising the costs and lowering the incentives for conquest.

Attachment to one's state and its land reinforce one quasi-geographical aid to the defense. Conquest usually becomes more difficult the deeper the attacker pushes into the other's territory. Nationalism spurs the defenders to fight harder; advancing not only lengthens the attacker's supply lines, but takes him through unfamiliar and often devastated lands that require troops for garrison duty. These stabilizing dynamics will not operate, however, if the defender's war matériel is situated near its borders, or if the people do not care about their state, but only about being on the winning side. In such cases, positive feedback will be at work and initial defeats will be insurmountable.[19]

Imitating geography, men have tried to create barriers. Treaties may provide for demilitarized zones on both sides of the border, although such zones will rarely be deep enough to provide more than warning. Even this was not possible in Europe, but the Russians adopted a gauge for their railroads that was broader than that of the neighboring states, thereby complicating the logistics problems of any attacker—including Russia.

Perhaps the most ambitious and at least temporarily successful attempts to construct a system that would aid the defenses of both sides were the interwar naval treaties, as they affected Japanese-American relations. As mentioned earlier, the problem was that the United States could not defend the Philippines without denying Japan the ability to protect her home islands.[20] (In 1941 this dilemma became insoluble when Japan sought to extend her control to Malaya and the Dutch East Indies. If the Philippines had been invulnerable, they could have provided a secure base from which the United States could interdict Japanese shipping between the homeland and the areas she was trying to conquer.) In the 1920s and early 1930s each side would have been willing to grant the other security for its possessions in return for a reciprocal grant, and the Washington Naval Conference agreements were designed to approach this goal. As a Japanese diplomat later put it, their country's "fundamental principle" was to have "a strength insufficient for attack and adequate for defense."[21] Thus Japan agreed in 1922 to accept a navy only three-fifths as large as that of the United States, and the United States agreed not to fortify its Pacific islands.[22] (Japan had earlier been forced to agree not to fortify the islands she had taken from Germany in World War I.) Japan's navy would not be large enough to defeat America's anywhere other than close to the home islands. Although the Japanese could still take the Philippines, not only would they be unable to move farther, but they might be weakened enough by their efforts to be vulnerable to counterattack. Japan, however, gained security. An American attack was rendered more difficult because the American bases were unprotected and because, until 1930, Japan was allowed unlimited numbers of cruisers, destroyers, and submarines that could weaken the American fleet as it made its way across the ocean.[23]

The other major determinant of the offense-defense balance is technology. When weapons are highly vulnerable, they must be employed before they are attacked. Others can remain quite invulnerable in their bases. The former character-istics are embodied in unprotected missiles and many kinds of bombers. (It should be noted that it is not vulnerability *per se* that is crucial, but the location of the vul-nerability. Bombers and missiles that are easy to destroy only after having been launched toward their targets do not create destabilizing dynamics.) Incentives to strike first are usually absent for naval forces that are threatened by a naval attack. Like missiles in hardened silos, they are usually well protected when in their bases. Both sides can then simultaneously be prepared to defend themselves successfully.

In ground warfare under some conditions, forts, trenches, and small groups of men in prepared positions can hold off large numbers of attackers. Less frequently, a few attackers can storm the defenses. By and large, it is a contest between fortifi-cations and supporting light weapons on the one hand, and mobility and heavier weapons that clear the way for the attack on the other. As the erroneous views held before the two world wars show, there is no simple way to determine which is dom-inant. "[T]hese oscillations are not smooth and predictable like those of a swinging pendulum. They are uneven in both extent and time. Some occur in the course of a single battle or campaign, others in the course of a war, still others during a series of wars." Longer-term oscillations can also be detected:

> The early Gothic age, from the twelfth to the late thirteenth century, with its wonderful cathedrals and fortified places, was a period during which the attackers in Europe gen-erally met serious and increasing difficulties, because the improvement in the strength of fortresses outran the advance in the power of destruction. Later, with the spread of firearms at the end of the fifteenth century, old fortresses lost their power to resist. An age ensued during which the offense possessed, apart from short-term setbacks, new advantages. Then, during the seventeenth century, especially after about 1660, and until at least the outbreak of the War of the Austrian Succession in 1740, the defense regained much of the ground it had lost since the great medieval fortresses had proved unable to meet the bombardment of the new and more numerous artillery.[24]

Another scholar has continued the argument: "The offensive gained an advan-tage with new forms of heavy mobile artillery in the nineteenth century, but the stalemate of World War I created the impression that the defense again had an advantage; the German invasion in World War II, however, indicated the offensive superiority of highly mechanized armies in the field."[25]

The situation today with respect to conventional weapons is unclear. Until recently it was believed that tanks and tactical air power gave the attacker an advan-tage. The initial analyses of the 1973 Arab-Israeli war indicated that new anti-tank and anti-aircraft weapons have restored the primacy of the defense. These weapons are cheap, easy to use, and can destroy a high proportion of the attacking vehicles and planes that are sighted. It then would make sense for a status-quo power to buy lots of $20,000 missiles rather than buy a few half-million dollar fighter-bombers. Defense would be possible even against a large and well-equipped force; states that care primarily about self-protection would not need to engage in arms races. But further examinations of the new technologies and the history of the October War cast doubt on these optimistic conclusions and leave us unable to render any firm judgment.[26]

Concerning nuclear weapons, it is generally agreed that defense is impossible—a triumph not of the offense, but of deterrence. Attack makes no sense, not because it can be beaten off, but because the attacker will be destroyed in turn. In terms of the questions under consideration here, the result is the equivalent of the primacy of the defense. First, security is relatively cheap. Less than one percent of the G.N.P. is devoted to deterring a direct attack on the United States; most of it is spent on acquiring redundant systems to provide a lot of insurance against the worst conceivable contingencies. Second, both sides can simultaneously gain security in the form of second-strike capability. Third, and related to the foregoing, second-strike capability can be maintained in the face of wide variations in the other side's military posture. There is no purely military reason why each side has to react quickly and strongly to the other's increases in arms. Any spending that the other devotes to trying to achieve first-strike capability can be neutralized by the state's spending much smaller sums on protecting its second-strike capability. Fourth, there are no incentives to strike first in a crisis.

Important problems remain, of course. Both sides have interests that go well beyond defense of the homeland. The protection of these interests creates conflicts even if neither side desires expansion. Furthermore, the shift from defense to deterrence has greatly increased the importance and perceptions of resolve. Security now rests on each side's belief that the other would prefer to run high risks of total destruction rather than sacrifice its vital interests. Aspects of the security dilemma thus appear in a new form. Are weapons procurements used as an index of resolve? Must they be so used? If one side fails to respond to the other's buildup, will it appear weak and thereby invite predation? Can both sides simultaneously have images of high resolve or is there a zero-sum element involved? Although these problems are real, they are not as severe as those in the prenuclear era: There are many indices of resolve, and states do not so much judge images of resolve in the abstract as ask how likely it is that the other will stand firm in a particular dispute. Since states are most likely to stand firm on matters which concern them most, it is quite possible for both to demonstrate their resolve to protect their own security simultaneously.

OFFENSE–DEFENSE DIFFERENTIATION

The other major variable that affects how strongly the security dilemma operates is whether weapons and policies that protect the state also provide the capability for attack. If they do not, the basic postulate of the security dilemma no longer applies.

A state can increase its own security without decreasing that of others. The advantage of the defense can only ameliorate the security dilemma. A differentiation between offensive and defensive stances comes close to abolishing it. Such differentiation does not mean, however, that all security problems will be abolished. If the offense has the advantage, conquest and aggression will still be possible. And if the offense's advantage is great enough, status-quo powers may find it too expensive to protect themselves by defensive forces and decide to procure offensive weapons even though this will menace others. Furthermore, states will still have to worry that even if the other's military posture shows that it is peaceful now, it may develop aggressive intentions in the future.

Assuming that the defense is at least as potent as the offense, the differentiation between them allows status-quo states to behave in ways that are clearly different from those of aggressors. Three beneficial consequences follow. First, status-quo powers can identify each other, thus laying the foundations for cooperation. Conflicts growing out of the mistaken belief that the other side is expansionist will be less frequent. Second, status-quo states will obtain advance warning when others plan aggression. Before a state can attack, it has to develop and deploy offensive weapons. If procurement of these weapons cannot be disguised and takes a fair amount of time, as it almost always does, a status-quo state will have the time to take countermeasures. It need not maintain a high level of defensive arms as long as its potential adversaries are adopting a peaceful posture. (Although being so armed should not, with the one important exception noted below, alarm other status-quo powers.) States do, in fact, pay special attention to actions that they believe would not be taken by a status-quo state because they feel that states exhibiting such behavior are aggressive. Thus the seizure or development of transportation facilities will alarm others more if these facilities have no commercial value, and therefore can only be wanted for military reasons. In 1906, the British rejected a Russian protest about their activities in a district of Persia by claiming that this area was "only of [strategic] importance [to the Russians] if they wished to attack the Indian frontier, or to put pressure upon us by making us think that they intend to attack it."[27]

The same inferences are drawn when a state acquires more weapons than observers feel are needed for defense. Thus, the Japanese spokesman at the 1930 London naval conference said that his country was alarmed by the American refusal to give Japan a 70 percent ratio (in place of a 60 percent ratio) in heavy cruisers: "As long as America held that ten percent advantage, it was possible for her to attack. So when America insisted on sixty percent instead of seventy percent, the idea would exist that they were trying to keep that possibility, and the Japanese people could not accept that."[28] Similarly, when Mussolini told Chamberlain in January 1939 that Hitler's arms program was motivated by defensive considerations, the Prime Minister replied that "German military forces were now so strong as to make it impossible for any Power or combination of Powers to attack her successfully. She could not want any further armaments for defensive purposes; what then did she want them for?"[29]

Of course these inferences can be wrong—as they are especially likely to be because states underestimate the degree to which they menace others.[30] And when they are wrong, the security dilemma is deepened. Because the state thinks it has received notice that the other is aggressive, its own arms building will be less restrained and the chances of cooperation will be decreased. But the dangers of incorrect inferences should not obscure the main point: When offensive and defensive postures are different, much of the uncertainty about the other's intentions that contributes to the security dilemma is removed.

The third beneficial consequence of a difference between offensive and defensive weapons is that if all states support the status quo, an obvious arms control agreement is a ban on weapons that are useful for attacking. As President Roosevelt put it in his message to the Geneva Disarmament Conference in 1933: "If all nations will agree wholly to eliminate from possession and use the weapons which make possible a successful attack, defenses automatically will become impregnable, and the frontiers and independence of every nation will become secure."[31] The fact that such treaties have been rare—the Washington naval agreements discussed above and the anti-ABM treaty can be cited as examples—shows either that states are not always willing to guarantee the security of others, or that it is hard to distinguish offensive from defensive weapons.

Is such a distinction possible? Salvador de Madariaga, the Spanish statesman active in the disarmament negotiations of the interwar years, thought not: "A weapon is either offensive or defensive according to which end of it you are looking at." The French Foreign Minister agreed (although French policy did not always follow this view): "Every arm can be employed offensively or defensively in turn. . . . The only way to discover whether arms are intended for purely defensive purposes or are held in a spirit of aggression is in all cases to enquire into the intentions of the country concerned." Some evidence for the validity of this argument is provided by the fact that much time in these unsuccessful negotiations was devoted to separating offensive from defensive weapons. Indeed, no simple and unambiguous definition is possible and in many cases no judgment can be reached. Before the American entry into World War I, Woodrow Wilson wanted to arm merchantmen only with guns in the back of the ship so they could not initiate a fight, but this expedient cannot be applied to more common forms of armaments.[32]

There are several problems. Even when a differentiation is possible, a status-quo power will want offensive arms under any of three conditions: (1) If the offense has a great advantage over the defense, protection through defensive forces will be too expensive. (2) Status-quo states may need offensive weapons to regain territory lost in the opening stages of war. It might be possible, however, for a state to wait to procure these weapons until war seems likely, and they might be needed only in relatively small numbers, unless the aggressor was able to construct strong defenses quickly in the occupied areas. (3) The state may feel that it must be prepared to take the offensive either because the other side will make peace only if it loses territory or because the state has commitments to attack if the other makes war on a third party. As noted above, status-quo states with extensive commitments are often forced to behave like aggressors. Even when they lack such commitments, status-quo states must worry about the possibility that if they are able to hold off an attack, they will still not be able to end the war unless they move into the other's territory to damage its military forces and inflict pain. Many American naval officers after the Civil War, for example, believed that "only by destroying the commerce of the opponent could the United States bring him to terms."[33]

A further complication is introduced by the fact that aggressors as well as status-quo powers require defensive forces as a prelude to acquiring offensive ones, to protect one frontier while attacking another, or for insurance in case the war goes badly. Criminals as well as policemen can use bulletproof vests. Hitler as well as Maginot built a line of forts. Indeed, Churchill reports that in 1936 the German Foreign Minister said: "As soon as our fortifications are constructed [on our western borders] and the countries in Central Europe realize that France cannot enter German territory, all these countries will begin to feel very differently about their foreign policies, and a new constellation will develop."[34] So a state may not necessarily be reassured if its neighbor constructs strong defenses.

More central difficulties are created by the fact that whether a weapon is offensive or defensive often depends on the particular situation—for instance, the geographical setting and the way in which the weapon is used. "Tanks. . . . spearheaded the fateful German thrust through the Ardennes in 1940, but if the French had disposed of a properly concentrated armored reserve, it would have provided the best means for their cutting off the penetration and turning into a disaster for the Germans what became instead an overwhelming victory."[35] Anti-aircraft weapons seem obviously defensive—to be used, they must wait for the other side to come to them. But the Egyptian attack on Israel in 1973 would have been impossible without effective air defenses that covered the battlefield. Nevertheless, some distinctions are possible. Sir John Simon, then the British Foreign Secretary, in response to the views cited earlier, stated that just because a fine line could not be drawn, "that was no reason for saying that there were not stretches of territory on either side which all practical men and women knew to be well on this or that side of the line." Although there are almost no weapons and strategies that are useful only for attacking, there are some that are almost exclusively defensive. Aggressors could want them for protection, but a state that relied mostly on them could not menace others. More frequently, we cannot "determine the absolute character of a weapon, but [we can] make a comparison. . .[and] discover whether or not the offensive potentialities predominate, whether a weapon is more useful in attack or in defense."[36]

The essence of defense is keeping the other side out of your territory. A purely defensive weapon is one that can do this without being able to penetrate the enemy's land. Thus a committee of military experts in an interwar disarmament conference declared that armaments "incapable of mobility by means of self- contained power," or movable only after long delay, were "only capable of being used for the defense of a State's territory."[37] The most obvious examples are fortifications. They can shelter attacking forces, especially when they are built right along the frontier,[38] but they cannot occupy enemy territory. A state with only a strong line of forts, fixed guns, and a small army to man them would not be much of a menace. Anything else that can serve only as a barrier against attacking troops is similarly defensive. In this category are systems that provide warning of an attack, the Russian's adoption of a different railroad gauge, and nuclear land mines that can seal off invasion routes.

If total immobility clearly defines a system that is defensive only, limited mobility is unfortunately ambiguous. As noted above, short-range fighter aircraft and anti-aircraft missiles can be used to cover an attack. And, unlike forts, they can advance with the troops. Still, their inability to reach deep into enemy territory does make them more useful for the defense than for the offense. Thus, the United States and Israel would have been more alarmed in the early 1970s had the Russians provided the Egyptians with long-range instead of short-range aircraft. Naval forces are particularly difficult to classify in these terms, but those that are very short-legged can be used only for coastal defense.

Any forces that for various reasons fight well only when on their own soil in effect lack mobility and therefore are defensive. The most extreme example would be passive resistance. Noncooperation can thwart an aggressor, but it is very hard for large numbers of people to cross the border and stage a sit-in on another's territory. Morocco's recent march on the Spanish Sahara approached this tactic, but its success depended on special circumstances. Similarly, guerrilla warfare is defensive to the extent to which it requires civilian support that is likely to be forthcoming only in opposition to a foreign invasion. Indeed, if guerrilla warfare were easily exportable and if it took ten defenders to destroy each guerrilla, then this weapon would not only be one which could be used as easily to attack the other's territory as to defend one's own, but one in which the offense had the advantage: so the security dilemma would operate especially strongly.

If guerrillas are unable to fight on foreign soil, other kinds of armies may be unwilling to do so. An army imbued with the idea that only defensive wars were just would fight less effectively, if at all, if the goal were conquest. Citizen militias may lack both the ability and the will for aggression. The weapons employed, the short term of service, the time required for mobilization, and the spirit of repelling attacks on the homeland, all lend themselves much more to defense than to attacks on foreign territory.[39]

Less idealistic motives can produce the same result. A leading student of medieval warfare has described the armies of that period as follows: "Assembled with difficulty, insubordinate, unable to maneuver, ready to melt away from its standard the moment that its short period of service was over, a feudal force presented an assemblage of unsoldierlike qualities such as have seldom been known to coexist. Primarily intended to defend its own borders from the Magyar, the Northman, or the Saracen . . ., the institution was utterly unadapted to take the offensive."[40] Some political groupings can be similarly described. International coalitions are more readily held together by fear than by hope of gain. Thus Castlereagh was not being entirely self-serving when in 1816 he argued that the Quadruple Alliance "could only have owed its origin to a sense of common danger; in its very nature it must be conservative; it cannot threaten either the security or the liberties of other States."[41] It is no accident that most of the major campaigns of expansion have been waged by one dominant nation (for example, Napoleon's France and Hitler's Germany), and that coalitions among relative equals are usually found defending the status quo. Most gains from conquest are too uncertain and raise too many questions of future squabbles among the victors to hold an alliance together for long. Although defensive coalitions are by no means easy to maintain—conflicting national objectives and the free-rider problem partly explain why three of them dissolved before Napoleon was defeated—the common interest of seeing that no state dominates provides a strong incentive for solidarity.

Weapons that are particularly effective in reducing fortifications and barriers are of great value to the offense. This is not to deny that a defensive power will want some of those weapons if the other side has them: Brodie is certainly correct to argue that while their tanks allowed the Germans to conquer France, properly used French tanks could have halted the attack. But France would not have needed these weapons if Germany had not acquired them, whereas even if France had no tanks, Germany could not have foregone them since they provided the only chance of breaking through the French lines. Mobile heavy artillery is, similarly, especially useful in destroying fortifications. The defender, while needing artillery to fight off attacking troops or to counterattack, can usually use lighter guns since they do not need to penetrate such massive obstacles. So it is not surprising that one of the few things that most nations at the interwar disarmament conferences were able to agree on was that heavy tanks and mobile heavy guns were particularly valuable to a state planning an attack.[42]

Weapons and strategies that depend for their effectiveness on surprise are almost always offensive. That fact was recognized by some of the delegates to the interwar disarmament conferences and is the principle behind the common national ban on concealed weapons. An earlier representative of this widespread view was the mid-nineteenth-century Philadelphia newspaper that argued: "As a measure of defense, knives, dirks, and sword canes are entirely useless. They are fit only for attack, and all such attacks are of murderous character. Whoever carries such a weapon has prepared himself for homicide."[43]

It is, of course, not always possible to distinguish between forces that are most effective for holding territory and forces optimally designed for taking it. Such a distinction could not have been made for the strategies and weapons in Europe during most of the period between the Franco-Prussian War and World War I. Neither naval forces nor tactical air forces can be readily classified in these terms. But the point here is that when such a distinction is possible, the central characteristic of the security dilemma no longer holds, and one of the most troublesome consequences of anarchy is removed.

Offense-Defense Differentiation and Strategic Nuclear Weapons

In the interwar period, most statesmen held the reasonable position that weapons that threatened civilians were offensive.[44] But when neither side can protect its civilians, a counter-city posture is defensive because the state can credibly threaten to retaliate only in response to an attack on itself or its closest allies. The costs of this strike are so high that the state could not threaten to use it for the less-than-vital interest of compelling the other to abandon an established position.

In the context of deterrence, offensive weapons are those that provide defense. In the now familiar reversal of common sense, the state that could take its population out of hostage, either by active or passive defense or by destroying the other's strategic weapons on the ground, would be able to alter the status quo. The desire to prevent such a situation was one of the rationales for the anti-ABM agreements; it explains why some arms controllers opposed building ABMs to protect cities, but favored sites that covered ICBM fields. Similarly, many analysts wanted to limit warhead accuracy and favored multiple re-entry vehicles (MRVs), but opposed multiple independently targetable re-entry vehicles (MIRVs). The former are more useful than single warheads for penetrating city defenses, and ensure that the state has a second-strike capability. MIRVs enhance counterforce capabilities. . . .

What is most important for the argument here is that land-based ICBMs are both offensive and defensive, but when both sides rely on Polaris-type systems (SLBMs), offense and defense use different weapons. ICBMs can be used either to destroy the other's cities in retaliation or to initiate hostilities by attacking the other's strategic missiles. Some measures—for instance, hardening of missile sites and warning systems—are purely defensive, since they do not make a first strike easier. Others are predominantly offensive—for instance, passive or active city defenses, and highly accurate warheads. But ICBMs themselves are useful for both purposes. And because states seek a high level of insurance, the desire for protection as well as the contemplation of a counterforce strike can explain the acquisition of extremely large numbers of missiles. So it is very difficult to infer the other's intentions from its military posture. Each side's efforts to increase its own security by procuring more missiles decreases, to an extent determined by the relative efficacy of the offense and the defense, the other side's security. That is not the case when both sides use SLBMs. The point is not that sea-based systems are less vulnerable than land-based ones (this bears on the offense-defense ratio) but that SLBMs are defensive, retaliatory weapons. . . . SLBMs are not the main instrument of attack against other SLBMs. The hardest problem confronting a state that wants to take its cities out of hostage is to locate the other's SLBMs, a job that requires not SLBMs but anti-submarine weapons. A state might use SLBMs to attack the other's submarines (although other weapons would probably be more efficient), but without anti-submarine warfare (ASW) capability the task cannot be performed. A status-quo state that wanted to forego offensive capability could simply forego ASW research and procurement. . . .

When both sides rely on ICBMs, one side's missiles can attack the other's, and so the state cannot be indifferent to the other's building program. But because one side's SLBMs do not menace the other's, each side can build as many as it wants and the other need not respond. Each side's decision on the size of its force depends on technical questions, its judgment about how much destruction is enough to deter, and the amount of insurance it is willing to pay for—and these considerations are independent of the size of the other's strategic force. Thus the crucial nexus in the arms race is severed. . . .

FOUR WORLDS

The two variables we have been discussing—whether the offense or the defense has the advantage, and whether offensive postures can be distinguished from defensive ones—can be combined to yield four possible worlds.

The first world is the worst for status-quo states. These is no way to get security without menacing others, and security through defense is terribly difficult to obtain. Because offensive and defensive postures are the same, status-quo states acquire the same kind of arms that are sought by aggressors. And because the offense has the advantage over the defense, attacking is the best route to protecting what you have; status-quo states will therefore behave like aggressors. The situation will be unstable. Arms races are likely. Incentives to strike first will turn crises into wars. Decisive victories and conquests will be common. States will grow and shrink rapidly, and it will be hard for any state to maintain its size and influence without trying to increase them. Cooperation among status-quo powers will be extremely hard to achieve.

There are no cases that totally fit this picture, but it bears more than a passing resemblance to Europe before World War I. Britain and Germany, although in many respects natural allies, ended up as enemies. Of course much of the explanation lies in Germany's ill-chosen policy. And from the perspective of our theory, the powers' ability to avoid war in a series of earlier crises cannot be easily explained. Nevertheless, much of the behavior in this period was the product of technology and beliefs that magnified the security dilemma. Decision makers thought that the offense had a big advantage and saw little difference between offensive and defensive military postures. The era was characterized by arms races. And once war seemed likely, mobilization races created powerful incentives to strike first.

In the nuclear era, the first world would be one in which each side relied on vulnerable weapons that were aimed at similar forces and each side understood the situation. In this case, the incentives to strike first would be very high—so high that status-quo powers as well as aggressors would be sorely tempted to preempt. And since the forces could be used to change the status quo as well as to preserve it, there would be no way for both sides to increase their security simultaneously. Now the familiar logic of deterrence leads both sides to see the dangers in this world. Indeed, the new understanding of this situation was one reason why vulnerable bombers and missiles were replaced. Ironically, the 1950s would have been more hazardous if the decision makers had been aware of the dangers of their posture and had therefore felt greater pressure to strike first.

In the second world, the security dilemma operates because offensive and defensive postures cannot be distinguished; but it does not operate as strongly as in the first world because the defense has the advantage, and so an increment in one side's strength increases its security more than it decreases the other's. So, if both sides have reasonable subjective security requirements, are of roughly equal power, and the variables discussed earlier are favorable, it is quite likely that status-quo states can adopt compatible security policies. Although a state will not be able to judge the other's intentions from the kinds of weapons it procures, the level of arms

TABLE 1 ■

	Offense has the Advantage	Defense has the Advantage
Offensive posture not distinguishable from defensive one	1 Doubly dangerous	2 Security dilemma, but security requirements may be compatible
Offensive posture not distinguishable from defensive one	3 No security dilemma, but aggression possible Status-quo states can follow different policy than aggressors Warning given	4 Doubly stable

spending will give important evidence. Of course a state that seeks a high level of arms might be not an aggressor but merely an insecure state, which if conciliated will reduce its arms, and if confronted will reply in kind. To assume that the apparently excessive level of arms indicates aggressiveness could therefore lead to a response that would deepen the dilemma and create needless conflict. But empathy and skillful statesmanship can reduce this danger. Furthermore, the advantageous position of the defense means that a status-quo state can often maintain a high degree of security with a level of arms lower than that of its expected adversary. Such a state demonstrates that it lacks the ability or desire to alter the status quo, at least at the present time. The strength of the defense also allows states to react slowly and with restraint when they fear that others are menacing them. So, although status-quo powers will to some extent be threatening to others, that extent will be limited.

This world is the one that comes closest to matching most periods in history. Attacking is usually harder than defending because of the strength of fortifications and obstacles. But purely defensive postures are rarely possible because fortifications are usually supplemented by armies and mobile guns which can support an attack. In the nuclear era, this world would be one in which both sides relied on relatively invulnerable ICBMs and believed that limited nuclear war was impossible. Assuming no MIRVs, it would take more than one attacking missile to destroy one of the adversary's. Preemption is therefore unattractive. If both sides have large inventories, they can ignore all but drastic increases on the other side. A world of either ICBMs or SLBMs in which both sides adopted the policy of limited nuclear war would probably fit in this category too. The means of preserving the status quo would also be the means of changing it, as we discussed earlier. And the defense usually would have the advantage, because compellence is more difficult than deterrence. Although a state might succeed in changing the status quo on issues that matter much more to it than to others, status-quo powers could deter major provocations under most circumstances.

In the third world there may be no security dilemma, but there are security problems. Because states can procure defensive systems that do not threaten others, the dilemma need not operate. But because the offense has the advantage, aggression is possible, and perhaps easy. If the offense has less of an advantage, stability and cooperation are likely because the status-quo states will procure defensive forces. They need not react to others who are similarly armed, but can wait for the warning they would receive if others started to deploy offensive weapons. But each state will have to watch the others carefully, and there is room for false suspicions. The costliness of the defense and the allure of the offense can lead to unnecessary mistrust, hostility, and war, unless some of the variables discussed earlier are operating to restrain defection.

A hypothetical nuclear world that would fit this description would be one in which both sides relied on SLBMs, but in which ASW techniques were very effective. Offense and defense would be different, but the former would have the advantage. This situation is not likely to occur; but if it did, a status-quo state could show its lack of desire to exploit the other by refraining from threatening its submarines. The desire to have more protecting you than merely the other side's fear of retaliation is a strong one, however, and a state that knows that it would not expand even if its cities were safe is likely to believe that the other would not feel threatened by its ASW program. It is easy to see how such a world could become unstable, and how spirals of tensions and conflict could develop.

The fourth world is doubly safe. The differentiation between offensive and defensive systems permits a way out of the security dilemma; the advantage of the defense disposes of the problems discussed in the previous paragraphs. There is no reason for a status-quo power to be tempted to procure offensive forces, and aggressors give notice of their intentions by the posture they adopt. Indeed, if the advantage of the defense is great enough, there are no security problems. The loss of the ultimate form of the power to alter the status quo would allow greater scope for the exercise of nonmilitary means and probably would tend to freeze the distribution of values.

This world would have existed in the first decade of the twentieth century if the decision makers had understood the available technology. In that case, the European powers would have followed different policies both in the long run and in the summer of 1914. Even Germany, facing powerful enemies on both sides, could have made herself secure by developing strong defenses. France could also have made her frontier almost impregnable. Furthermore, when crises arose, no one would have had incentives to strike first. There would have been no competitive mobilization races reducing the time available for negotiations.

In the nuclear era, this world would be one in which the superpowers relied on SLBMs, ASW technology was not up to its task, and limited nuclear options were not taken seriously. . . . Because the problem of violence below the nuclear threshold would remain, on issues other than defense of the homeland, there would still be security dilemmas and security problems. But the world would nevertheless be safer than it has usually been.

NOTES

1. Thus, when Wolfers argues that a status-quo state that settles for rough equality of power with its adversary, rather than seeking preponderance, may be able to convince the other to reciprocate by showing that it wants only to protect itself, not menace the other, he assumes that the defense has an advantage. See Arnold Wolfers, *Discord and Collaboration* (Baltimore: Johns Hopkins Press, 1962), p. 126.

2. Thomas Schelling, *The Strategy of Conflict* (New York: Oxford University Press, 1963), chap. 9.

3. Quoted in Fritz Fischer, *War of Illusions* (New York: Norton, 1975), pp. 377, 461.

4. George Quester, *Offense and Defense in the International System* (New York: John Wiley, 1977), p. 105.

5. Herman Kahn, *On Thermonuclear War* (Princeton, N.J.: Princeton University Press, 1960), p. 211 (also see p. 144).

6. For a general discussion of such mistaken learning from the past, see Jervis, *Perception and Misperception in International Relations* (Princeton, N.J.: Princeton University Press, 1976), chap. 6. The important and still not completely understood question of why this belief formed and was maintained throughout the war is examined in Bernard Brodie, *War and Politics* (New York: Macmillan, 1973), pp. 262–70; Brodie, "Technological Change, Strategic Doctrine, and Political Outcomes," in Klaus Knorr, ed., *Historical Dimensions of National Security Problems* (Lawrence: University Press of Kansas, 1976), pp. 290–92; and Douglas Porch, "The French Army and the Spirit of the Offensive, 1900–14," in Brian Bond and Ian Roy, eds., *War and Society* (New York: Holmes & Meier, 1975), pp. 117–43.

7. Some were not so optimistic. Grey's remark is well-known: "The lamps are going out all over Europe; we shall not see them lit again in our life-time." The German Prime Minister, Bethmann Hollweg, also feared the consequences of the war. But the controlling view was that it would certainly pay for the winner.

8. Quoted in Martin Gilbert, *Winston S. Churchill*, III, *The Challenge of War, 1914–1916* (Boston: Houghton Mifflin, 1971), p. 84.

9. Quester (fn. 4), pp. 98–99. Robert Art, *The Influence of Foreign Policy on Seapower*, II (Beverly Hills: Sage Professional Papers in International Studies Series, 1973), pp. 14–18, 26–28.

10. Konrad Jarausch, "The Illusion of Limited War: Chancellor Bethmann Hollweg's Calculated Risk, July 1914," *Central European History*, II (March 1969): p. 50.

11. Brodie, *War and Politics* (New York: Macmillan, 1973), p. 58.

12. President Roosevelt and the American delegates to the League of Nations Disarmament Conference maintained that the tank and the mobile heavy artillery had reestablished the dominance of the offensive, thus making disarmament more urgent (Marion Boggs, *Attempts to Define and Limit "Aggressive" Armament in Diplomacy and Strategy* [Columbia: University of Missouri Studies, XVI, No. 1, 1941]: pp. 31, 108), but this was a minority position and may not even have been believed by the Americans. The reduced prestige and influence of the military, and the high pressures to cut government spending throughout this period also contributed to the lowering of defense budgets.

13. Jon Kimche, *The Unfought Battle* (New York: Stein, 1968); Nicholas William Bethell, *The War Hitler Won: The Fall of Poland, September 1939* (New York: Holt, 1972); Alan Alexandroff and Richard Rosecrance, "Deterrence in 1939," *World Politics*, XXIX (April 1977): pp. 404–24.

14. Roderick Macleod and Denis Kelly, eds., *Time Unguarded: The Ironside Diaries, 1937–1940* (New York: McKay, 1962), p. 173.

15. For a short time, as France was falling, the British Cabinet did discuss reaching a negotiated peace with Hitler. The official history downplays this, but it is covered in P. M. H. Bell, *A Certain Eventuality* (Farnborough, England: Saxon House, 1974), pp. 40–48.

16. MacLeod and Kelly (fn. 14), 174. In flat contradiction to common sense and almost everything they believed about modern warfare, the Allies planned an expedition to Scandinavia to cut the supply of iron ore to Germany and to aid Finland against the Russians. But the dominant mood was the one described above.

17. Brodie (fn. 11), p. 179.

18. Arthur Balfour, "Memorandum," Committee on Imperial Defence, April 30, 1903, pp. 2–3; see the telegrams by Sir Arthur Nicolson, in G. P. Gooch and Harold Temperley, eds., *British Documents on the Origins of the War*, Vol. 4 (London: H.M.S.O., 1929), pp. 429, 524. These barriers do not prevent the passage of long-range aircraft; but even in the air, distance usually aids the defender.

19. See, for example, the discussion of warfare among Chinese warlords in Hsi-Sheng Chi, "The Chinese Warlord System as an International System," in Morton Kaplan, ed., *New Approaches to International Relations* (New York: St. Martin's, 1968), pp. 405–25.

20. Some American decision makers, including military officers, thought that the best way out of the dilemma was to abandon the Philippines.

21. Quoted in Elting Morrison, *Turmoil and Tradition: A Study of the Life and Times of Henry L. Stimson* (Boston: Houghton Mifflin, 1960), p. 326.

22. The U.S. "refused to consider limitations on Hawaiian defenses, since these works posed no threat to Japan." William Braisted, *The United States Navy in the Pacific, 1909–1922* (Austin: University of Texas Press, 1971), p. 612.

23. That is part of the reason why the Japanese admirals strongly objected when the civilian leaders decided to accept a seven-to-ten ratio in lighter craft in 1930. Stephen Pelz, *Race to Pearl Harbor* (Cambridge, Mass.: Harvard University Press, 1974), p. 3.

24. John Nef, *War and Human Progress* (New York: Norton, 1963), p. 185. Also see *ibid.*, pp. 237, 242–43, and 323; C. W. Oman, *The Art of War in the Middle Ages* (Ithaca, N.Y.: Cornell University Press, 1953), pp. 70–72; John Beeler, *Warfare in Feudal Europe, 730–1200* (Ithaca, N.Y.: Cornell University Press, 1971), pp. 212–14; Michael Howard, *War in European History* (London: Oxford University Press, 1976), pp. 33–37.

25. Quincy Wright, *A Study of War* (abridged ed.; Chicago: University of Chicago Press, 1964), p. 142. Also see pp. 63–70, 74–75. There are important exceptions to these generalizations—the American Civil War, for instance, falls in the middle of the period Wright says is dominated by the offense.

26. Geoffrey Kemp, Robert Pfaltzgraff, and Uri Ra'anan, eds., *The Other Arms Race* (Lexington, Mass.: D.C. Heath, 1975); James Foster, "The Future of Conventional Arms Control," *Policy Sciences*, No. 8 (Spring 1977): pp. 1–19.

27. Richard Challener, *Admirals, Generals, and American Foreign Policy, 1898–1914* (Princeton, N.J.: Princeton University Press, 1973); Grey to Nicolson, in Gooch and Temperley (fn. 18), p. 414.

28. Quoted in James Crowley, *Japan's Quest for Autonomy* (Princeton, N.J.: Princeton University Press, 1966), p. 49. American naval officers agreed with the Japanese that a ten-to-six ratio would endanger Japan's supremacy in her home waters.

29. E. L. Woodward and R. Butler, ed., *Documents on British Foreign Policy, 1919–1939.* 3d ser. III (London: H.M.S.O., 1950), p. 526.

30. Jervis (fn. 6), pp. 69–72, 352–55.

31. Quoted in Merze Tate, *The United States and Armaments* (Cambridge, Mass.: Harvard University Press, 1948), p. 108.

32. Boggs (fn. 12), pp. 15, 40.

33. Kenneth Hagan, *American Gunboat Diplomacy and the Old Navy, 1877–1899* (Westport, Conn.: Greenwood Press, 1973), p. 20.

34. Winston Churchill, *The Gathering Storm* (Boston: Houghton, 1948), p. 206.

35. Brodie, *War and Politics* (fn. 6), p. 325.

36. Boggs (fn. 12), pp. 42, 83. For a good argument about the possible differentiation between offensive and defensive weapons in the 1930s, see Basil Liddell Hart, "Aggression and the Problem of Weapons," *English Review,* 55 (July 1932): pp. 71–78.

37. Quoted in Boggs (fn. 12), p. 39.

38. On these grounds, the Germans claimed in 1932 that the French forts were offensive (*ibid.,* p. 49). Similarly, fortified forward naval bases can be necessary for launching an attack; see Braisted (fn. 22), p. 643.

39. The French made this argument in the interwar period; see Richard Challener, *The French Theory of the Nation in Arms* (New York: Columbia University Press, 1955), pp. 181–82. The Germans disagreed; see Boggs (fn. 12), pp. 44–45.

40. Oman (fn. 24), pp. 57–58.

41. Quoted in Charles Webster, *The Foreign Policy of Castlereagh,* II, *1815–1822* (London: G. Bell and Sons, 1963), p. 510.

42. Boggs (fn. 12), pp. 14–15, 47–48, 60.

43. Quoted in Philip Jordan, *Frontier Law and Order* (Lincoln: University of Nebraska Press, 1970), p. 7; also see pp. 16–17.

44. Boggs (fn. 12), pp. 20, 28.

Kant, Liberal Legacies, and Foreign Affairs

MICHAEL W. DOYLE

I

What difference do liberal principles and institutions make to the conduct of the foreign affairs of liberal states? A thicket of conflicting judgments suggests that the legacies of liberalism have not been clearly appreciated. For many citizens of liberal states, liberal principles and institutions have so fully absorbed domestic politics that their influence on foreign affairs tends to be either overlooked altogether or, when perceived, exaggerated. Liberalism becomes either unselfconsciously patriotic or inherently "peace-loving." For many scholars and diplomats, the relations among independent states appear to differ so significantly from domestic politics that influences of liberal principles and domestic liberal institutions are denied or denigrated. They judge that international relations are governed by perceptions of national security and the balance of power; liberal principles and institutions, when they do intrude, confuse and disrupt the pursuit of balance-of-power politics.

Although liberalism is misinterpreted from both these points of view, a crucial aspect of the liberal legacy is captured by each. Liberalism is a distinct ideology and set of institutions that has shaped the perceptions of and capacities for foreign relations of political societies that range from social welfare or social democratic to laissez faire. It defines much of the content of the liberal patriot's nationalism. Liberalism does appear to disrupt the pursuit of balance-of-power politics. Thus its foreign relations cannot be adequately explained (or prescribed) by a sole reliance on the balance of power. But liberalism is not inherently "peace-loving"; nor is it consistently restrained or peaceful in intent. Furthermore, liberal practice may reduce the probability that states will successfully exercise the consistent restraint and peaceful intentions that a world peace may well require in the nuclear age. Yet the peaceful intent and restraint that liberalism does manifest in limited aspects of its foreign affairs announces the possibility of a world peace this side of the grave or of world conquest. It has strengthened the prospects for a world peace established by the steady expansion of a separate peace among liberal societies. . . .

From Michael W. Doyle, "Kant, Liberal Legacies, and Foreign Affairs, Part 1," *Philosophy & Public Affairs*, Vol. 12, No. 3 (Summer 1983), pp. 205-232. Reproduced with permission of Blackwell Publishing Ltd.

II

Liberalism has been identified with an essential principle—the importance of the freedom of the individual. Above all, this is a belief in the importance of moral freedom, of the right to be treated and a duty to treat others as ethical subjects, and not as objects or means only. This principle has generated rights and institutions.

A commitment to a threefold set of rights forms the foundation of liberalism. Liberalism calls for freedom from arbitrary authority, often called "negative freedom," which includes freedom of conscience, a free press and free speech, equality under the law, and the right to hold, and therefore to exchange, property without fear of arbitrary seizure. Liberalism also calls for those rights necessary to protect and promote the capacity and opportunity for freedom, the "positive freedoms." Such social and economic rights as equality of opportunity in education and rights to health care and employment, necessary for effective self-expression and participation, are thus among liberal rights. A third liberal right, democratic participation or representation, is necessary to guarantee the other two. To ensure that morally autonomous individuals remain free in those areas of social action where public authority is needed, public legislation has to express the will of the citizens making laws for their own community.

These three sets of rights, taken together, seem to meet the challenge that Kant identified:

> To organize a group of rational beings who demand general laws for their survival, but of whom each inclines toward exempting himself, and to establish their constitution in such a way that, in spite of the fact their private attitudes are opposed, these private attitudes mutually impede each other in such a manner that [their] public behavior is the same as if they did not have such evil attitudes.[1]

But the dilemma within liberalism is how to reconcile the three sets of liberal rights. The right to private property, for example, can conflict with equality of opportunity and both rights can be violated by democratic legislation. During the 180 years since Kant wrote, the liberal tradition has evolved two high roads to individual freedom and social order; one is laissez-faire, or "conservative," liberalism and the other is social welfare, or social democratic, or "liberal," liberalism. Both reconcile these conflicting rights (though in differing ways) by successfully organizing free individuals into a political order.

The political order of laissez-faire and social welfare liberals is marked by a shared commitment to four essential institutions. First, citizens possess juridical equality and other fundamental civil rights such as freedom of religion and the press. Second, the effective sovereigns of the state are representative legislatures deriving their authority from the consent of the electorate and exercising their authority free from all restraint apart from the requirement that basic civic rights be preserved. Most pertinently for the impact of liberalism on foreign affairs, the state is subject to neither the external authority of other states nor to the internal authority of special prerogatives held, for example, by monarchs or military castes over foreign policy. Third, the economy rests on a recognition of the rights of private property including the ownership of means of production. Property is justi-fied by individual acquisition (for example, by labor) or by social agreement or social utility. This excludes state socialism or state capitalism, but it need not exclude market socialism or various forms of the mixed economy. Fourth, economic decisions are predominantly shaped by the forces of supply and demand, domesti-cally and internationally, and are free from strict control by bureaucracies. . . .

III

In foreign affairs liberalism has shown, as it has in the domestic realm, serious weak-nesses. But unlike liberalism's domestic realm, its foreign affairs have experienced startling but less than fully appreciated successes. Together they shape an unrecog-nized dilemma, for both these successes and weaknesses in large part spring from the same cause: the international implications of liberal principles and institutions.

The basic postulate of liberal international theory holds that states have the right to be free from foreign intervention. Since morally autonomous citizens hold rights to liberty, the states that democratically represent them have the right to exercise political independence. Mutual respect for these rights then becomes the touchstone of international liberal theory. When states respect each other's rights, individuals are free to establish private international ties without state interfer-ence. Profitable exchange between merchants and educational exchanges among scholars then create a web of mutual advantages and commitments that bolsters sentiments of public respect.

These conventions of mutual respect have formed a cooperative foundation for relations among liberal democracies of a remarkably effective kind. *Even though liberal states have become involved in numerous wars with nonliberal states, consti-tutionally secure liberal states have yet to engage in war with one another.*[2] No one should argue that such wars are impossible; but preliminary evidence does appear to indicate that there exists a significant predisposition against warfare between liberal states. Indeed, threats of war also have been regarded as illegitimate. A liberal zone of peace, a pacific union, has been maintained and has expanded despite numerous particular conflicts of economic and strategic interest. . . .

Statistically, war between any two states (in any single year or other short period of time) is a low probability event. War between any two adjacent states, considered over a long period of time, may be somewhat more probable. The apparent absence of war among the more clearly liberal states, whether adjacent or not, for almost two hundred years thus has some significance. Politically more significant, perhaps, is that, when states are forced to decide, by the pressure of an impinging world war, on which side of a world contest they will fight, liberal states wind up all on the same side, despite the real complexity of the historical, economic, and political factors that affect their foreign policies. And historically, we should recall that medieval and early modern Europe were the warring cock-pits of states, wherein France and England and the Low Countries engaged in near constant strife. Then in the late eighteenth century there began to emerge liberal regimes. At first hesitant and confused, and later clear and confident as liberal regimes gained deeper domestic foundations and longer international experience, a pacific union of these liberal states became established.

The realist model of international relations, which provides a plausible explanation of the general insecurity of states, offers little guidance in explaining the pacification of the liberal world. Realism, in its classical formation, holds that the state is and should be formally sovereign, effectively unbounded by individual rights nationally and thus capable of determining its own scope of authority. (This determination can be made democratically, oligarchically, or autocratically.) Internationally, the sovereign state exists in an anarchical society in which it is radically independent, neither bounded nor protected by international "law" or treaties or duties, and hence, insecure. Hobbes, one of the seventeenth-century founders of the realist approach, drew the international implications of realism when he argued that the existence of international anarchy, the very independence of states, best accounts for the competition, the fear, and the temptation toward preventive war that characterize international relations. Politics among nations is not a continuous combat, but it is in this view a "state of war . . . a tract of time, wherein the will to contend by battle is sufficiently known."[3] . . .

Finding that all states, including liberal states, do engage in war, the realist concludes that the effects of differing domestic regimes (whether liberal or not) are overridden by the international anarchy under which all states live.[4] . . . But the ends that shape the international state of war are decreed for the realist by the anarchy of the international order and the fundamental quest for power that directs the policy of all states, irrespective of differences in their domestic regimes. As Rousseau argued, international peace therefore depends on the abolition of international relations either by the achievement of a world state or by a radical isolationism (Corsica). Realists judge neither to be possible.

Recent additions to game theory specify some of the circumstances under which prudence could lead to peace. Experience; geography; expectations of cooperation and belief patterns; and the differing payoffs to cooperation (peace) or conflict associated with various types of military technology all appear to influence the calculus.[5] But when it comes to acquiring the techniques of peaceable interaction, nations appear to be slow, or at least erratic, learners. The balance of power (more below) is regarded as a primary lesson in the realist primer, but centuries of experience did not prevent either France (Louis XIV, Napoleon I) or Germany (Wilhelm II, Hitler) from attempting to conquer Europe, twice each. Yet some, very new, black African states appear to have achieved a twenty-year-old system of impressively effective standards of mutual toleration. These standards are not completely effective (as in Tanzania's invasion of Uganda); but they have confounded expectations of a scramble to redivide Africa.[6] Geography—"insular security" and "continental insecurity"—may affect foreign policy attitudes; but it does not appear to determine behavior, as the bellicose records of England and Japan suggest. Beliefs, expectations, and attitudes of leaders and masses should influence strategic behavior. . . . Nevertheless, it would be difficult to determine if liberal leaders have had more peaceable attitudes than leaders who lead nonliberal states. But even if one did make that discovery, he also would have to account for why these peaceable attitudes only appear to be effective in relations with other liberals (since wars with nonliberals have not been uniformly defensive). . . .

Second, at the level of social determinants, some might argue that relations among any group of states with similar social structures or with compatible values would be peaceful. But again, the evidence for feudal societies, communist societies, fascist societies, or socialist societies does not support this conclusion. Feudal warfare was frequent and very much a sport of the monarchs and nobility. There have not been enough truly totalitarian, fascist powers (nor have they lasted long enough) to test fairly their pacific compatibility; but fascist powers in the wider sense of nationalist, capitalist, military dictatorships fought each other in the 1930s. Communist powers have engaged in wars more recently in East Asia. And we have not had enough socialist societies to consider the relevance of socialist pacification. The more abstract category of pluralism does not suffice. Certainly Germany was pluralist when it engaged in war with liberal states in 1914; Japan as well in 1941. But they were not liberal.

And third, at the level of interstate relations, neither specific regional attributes nor historic alliances or friendships can account for the wide reach of the liberal peace. The peace extends as far as, and no further than, the relations among liberal states, not including nonliberal states in an otherwise liberal region (such as the north Atlantic in the 1930s) nor excluding liberal states in a nonliberal region (such as Central America or Africa).

At this level, Raymond Aron has identified three types of interstate peace: empire, hegemony, and equilibrium.[7] An empire generally succeeds in creating an internal peace, but this is not an explanation of peace among independent liberal states. Hegemony can create peace by over-awing potential rivals. Although far from perfect and certainly precarious, United States hegemony, as Aron notes, might account for the interstate peace in South America in the postwar period during the height of the Cold War conflict. However, the liberal peace cannot be attributed merely to effective international policing by a predominant hegemon—Britain in the nineteenth century, the United States in the postwar period. Even though a hegemon might well have an interest in enforcing a peace for the sake of commerce or investments or as a means of enhancing its prestige or security, hegemons such as seventeenth-century France were not peace-enforcing police, and the liberal peace persisted in the interwar period when international society lacked a predominant hegemonic power. Moreover, this explanation overestimates hegemonic control in both periods. Neither England nor the United States was able to prevent direct challenges to its interests (colonial competition in the nineteenth century, Middle East diplomacy and conflicts over trading with the enemy in the postwar period). Where then was the capacity to prevent all armed conflicts between liberal regimes, many of which were remote and others strategically or economically insignificant? Liberal hegemony and leadership are important, but they are not sufficient to explain a liberal peace. . . .

Finally, some realists might suggest that the liberal peace simply reflects the absence of deep conflicts of interest among liberal states. Wars occur outside the liberal zone because conflicts of interest are deeper there. But this argument does nothing more than raise the question of why liberal states have fewer or less fundamental conflicts of interest with other liberal states than liberal states have with nonliberal, or nonliberal states have with other nonliberals. We must therefore examine the workings of liberalism among its own kind—a special pacification of the "state of war" resting on liberalism and nothing either more specific or more general.

IV

Most liberal theorists have offered inadequate guidance in understanding the exceptional nature of liberal pacification. Some have argued that democratic states would be inherently peaceful simply and solely because in these states citizens rule the polity and bear the costs of wars. Unlike monarchs, citizens are not able to indulge their aggressive passions and have the consequences suffered by someone else. Other liberals have argued that laissez-faire capitalism contains an inherent tendency toward rationalism, and that, since war is irrational, liberal capitalisms will be pacifistic. Others still, such as Montesquieu, claim that "commerce is the cure for the most destructive prejudices," and "Peace is the natural effect of trade."[8] While these developments can help account for the liberal peace, they do not explain the fact that liberal states are peaceful only in relations with other liberal states. France and England fought expansionist, colonial wars throughout the nineteenth century (in the 1830s and 1840s against Algeria and China); the United States fought a similar war with Mexico in 1848 and intervened again in 1914 under president Wilson. Liberal states are as aggressive and war prone as any other form of government or society in their relations with nonliberal states.

Immanuel Kant offers the best guidance. "Perpetual Peace," written in 1795, predicts the ever-widening pacification of the liberal pacific union, explains that pacification, and at the same time suggests why liberal states are not pacific in their relations with nonliberal states. . . .

Kant shows how republics, once established, lead to peaceful relations. He argues that once the aggressive interests of absolutist monarchies are tamed and once the habit of respect for individual rights is engrained by republican government, wars would appear as the disaster to the people's welfare that he and the other liberals thought them to be. The fundamental reason is this:

> If the consent of the citizens is required in order to decide that war should be declared (and in this constitution it cannot but be the case), nothing is more natural than that they would be very cautious in commencing such a poor game, decreeing for themselves all the calamities of war. Among the latter would be: having to fight, having to pay the costs of war from their own resources, having painfully to repair the devastation war leaves behind, and, to fill up the measure of evils, load themselves with a heavy

national debt that would embitter peace itself and that can never be liquidated on account of constant wars in the future. But, on the other hand, in a constitution which is not republican, and under which the subjects are not citizens, a declaration of war is the easiest thing in the world to decide upon, because war does not require of the ruler, who is the proprietor and not a member of the state, the least sacrifice of the pleasure of his table, the chase, his country houses, his court functions, and the like. He may, therefore, resolve on war as on a pleasure party for the most trivial reasons, and with perfect indifference leave the justification which decency requires to the diplomatic corps who are ever ready to provide it.[9]

One could add to Kant's list another source of pacification specific to liberal constitutions. The regular rotation of office in liberal democratic polities is a nontrivial device that helps ensure that personal animosities among heads of government provide no lasting, escalating source of tension.

These domestic republican restraints do not end war. If they did, liberal states would not be warlike, which is far from the case. They do introduce Kant's "caution" in place of monarchical caprice. Liberal wars are only fought for popular, liberal purposes. To see how this removes the occasion of wars among liberal states and not wars between liberal and nonliberal states, we need to shift our attention from constitutional law to international law, Kant's second source.

Complementing the constitutional guarantee of caution, *international law* adds a second source—a guarantee of respect. The separation of nations that asocial sociability encourages is reinforced by the development of separate languages and religions. These further guarantee a world of separate states—an essential condition needed to avoid a "global, soul-less despotism." Yet, at the same time, they also morally integrate liberal states "as culture progresses and men gradually come closer together toward a greater agreement on principles for peace and understanding."[10] As republics emerge (the first source) and as culture progresses, an understanding of the legitimate rights of all citizens and of all republics comes into play; and this, now that caution characterizes policy, sets up the moral foundations for the liberal peace. Correspondingly, international law highlights the importance of Kantian publicity. Domestically, publicity helps ensure that the officials of republics act according to the principles they profess to hold just and according to the interests of the electors they claim to represent. Internationally, free speech and the effective communication of accurate conceptions of the political life of foreign peoples is essential to establish and preserve the understanding on which the guarantee of respect depends. In short, domestically just republics, which rest on consent, presume foreign republics to be also consensual, just, and therefore deserving of accommodation. The experience of cooperation helps engender further cooperative behavior when the consequences of state policy are unclear but (potentially) mutually beneficial.[11]

Lastly, *cosmopolitan law* adds material incentives to moral commitments. The cosmopolitan right to hospitality permits the "spirit of commerce" sooner or later to take hold of every nation, thus impelling states to promote peace and to try to avert war.

Liberal economic theory holds that these cosmopolitan ties derive from a cooperative international division of labor and free trade according to comparative advantage. Each economy is said to be better off than it would have been under autarky; each thus acquires an incentive to avoid policies that would lead the other to break these economic ties. Since keeping open markets rests upon the assumption that the next set of transactions will also be determined by prices rather than coercion, a sense of mutual security is vital to avoid security-motivated searches for economic autarky. Thus, avoiding a challenge to another liberal state's security or even enhancing each other's security by means of alliance naturally follows economic interdependence.

A further cosmopolitan source of liberal peace is that the international market removes difficult decisions of production and distribution from the direct sphere of state policy. A foreign state thus does not appear directly responsible for these outcomes; states can stand aside from, and to some degree above, these contentious market rivalries and be ready to step in to resolve crises. Furthermore, the interdependence of commerce and the connections of state officials help create crosscutting transnational ties that serve as lobbies for mutual accommodation. According to modern liberal scholars, international financiers and transnational, bureaucratic, and domestic organizations create interests in favor of accommodation and have ensured by their variety that no single conflict sours an entire relationship.[12]

No one of these constitutional, international or cosmopolitan sources is alone sufficient, but together (and only where together) they plausibly connect the characteristics of liberal politics and economies with sustained liberal peace. Liberal states have not escaped from the realists' "security dilemma," the insecurity caused by anarchy in the world political system considered as a whole. But the effects of international anarchy have been tamed in the relations among states of a similarly liberal character. Alliances of purely mutual strategic interest among liberal and nonliberal states have been broken, economic ties between liberal and nonliberal states have proven fragile, but the political bond of liberal rights and interests has proven a remarkably firm foundation for mutual nonaggression. A separate peace exists among liberal states.

NOTES

1. Immanuel Kant, "Perpetual Peace" (1795), in *The Philosophy of Kant*, ed. Carl J. Friedrich (New York: Modern Library, 1949), p. 453.
2. There appear to be some exceptions to the tendency for liberal states not to engage in a war with each other. Peru and Ecuador, for example, entered into conflict. But for each, the war came within one to three years after the establishment of a liberal regime, that is, before the pacifying effects of liberalism could become deeply ingrained. The Palestinians and the Israelis clashed frequently along the Lebanese border, which Lebanon could not hold secure from either belligerent. But at the beginning of the 1967 War, Lebanon seems to have sent a flight of its own jets into

Israel. The jets were repulsed. Alone among Israel's Arab neighbors, Lebanon engaged in no further hostilities with Israel. Israel's recent attack on the territory of Lebanon was an attack on a country that had already been occupied by Syria (and the P.L.O.). Whether Israel actually will withdraw (if Syria withdraws) and restore an independent Lebanon is yet to be determined.

3. Thomas Hobbes, *Leviathan* (New York: Penguin, 1980), I, chap. 13, 62, p. 186.

4. Kenneth N. Waltz, *Man, the State, and War* (New York: Columbia University Press, 1954, 1959), pp. 120–23; and see his *Theory of International Politics* (Reading, Mass.: Addison-Wesley, 1979). The classic sources of this form of Realism are Hobbes and, more particularly, Rousseau's "Essay on St. Pierre's Peace Project" and his "State of War" in *A Lasting Peace* (London: Constable, 1917), E. H. Carr's *The Twenty Year's Crisis: 1919–1939* (London: Macmillan & Co., 1951), and the works of Hans Morgenthau.

5. Jervis, "Cooperation under the Security Dilemma," *World Politics* 30, no. 1 (January 1978), pp. 172–86.

6. Robert H. Jackson and Carl G. Rosberg, "Why West Africa's Weak States Persist," *World Politics* 35, No. 1 (October 1962).

7. Raymond Aron, *Peace and War* (New York: Praeger, 1968), pp. 151–54.

8. The incompatibility of democracy and war is forcefully asserted by Paine in *The Rights of Man*. The connection between liberal capitalism, democracy, and peace is argued by, among others, Joseph Schumpeter in *Imperialism and Social Classes* (New York: Meridian, 1955); and Montesquieu, *Spirit of the Laws* I, bk. 20, chap. 1. This literature is surveyed and analyzed by Albert Hirschman, "Rival Interpretations of Market Society: Civilizing, Destructive, or Feeble?" *Journal of Economic Literature* 20 (December 1982).

9. Immanuel Kant, "Perpetual Peace," in *The Enlightenment*, ed. Peter Gay (New York: Simon & Schuster, 1974), pp. 790–92.

10. Kant, *The Philosophy of Kant*, p. 454. These factors also have a bearing on Karl Deutsch's "compatibility of values" and "predictability of behavior."

11. A highly stylized version of this effect can be found in the realist's "Prisoners' Dilemma" game. There, a failure of mutual trust and the incentives to enhance one's own position produce a noncooperative solution that makes both parties worse off. Contrarily, cooperation, a commitment to avoid exploiting the other party, produces joint gains. The significance of the game in this context is the character of its participants. The "prisoners" are presumed to be felonious, unrelated apart from their partnership in crime, and lacking in mutual trust—competitive nation-states in an anarchic world. A similar game between fraternal or sororal twins—Kant's republics—would be likely to lead to different results. See Robert Jervis, "Hypotheses on Misperception,"*World Politics* 20, No. 3 (April 1968), for an exposition of the role of presumptions; and "Cooperation under the Security Dilemma," *World Politics* 30, No. 2 (January 1978), for the factors realists see as mitigating the security dilemma caused by anarchy.

    Also, expectations (including theory and history) can influence behavior, making liberal states expect (and fulfill) pacific policies toward each other. These effects are explored at a theoretical level in R. Dacey, "Some Implications of 'Theory Absorption' for Economic Theory and the Economics Information," in *Philosophical Dimensions of Economics*, ed. J. Pitt (Dordrecht, Holland: D. Reidel, 1980).

12. Karl Polanyi, *The Great Transformation* (Boston: Beacon Press, 1944), chaps. 1–2 and Samuel Huntington and Z. Brzezinski, *Political Power: USA/USSR* (New York: Viking Press, 1963, 1964), chap. 9. And see Richard Neustadt, *Alliance Politics* (New York: Columbia University Press, 1970) for a detailed case study of interliberal politics.

TABLE 1 ■ WARS INVOLVING LIBERAL REGIMES

Period	Liberal Regimes and the Pacific Union (by Date "Liberal")[a]	Total Number
18th century	Swiss Cantons[b]	3
	French Republic 1790–1795 the United States[b] 1776–	
1800–1850	Swiss Confederation, the United States	8
	France 1830–1849	
	Belgium 1830–	
	Great Britain 1832–	
	Netherlands 1848–	
	Piedmont 1848–	
	Denmark 1849–	
1850–1900	Switzerland, the United States, Belgium, Great Britain, Netherlands	13
	Piedmont 1861, Italy 1861–	
	Denmark 1866	
	Sweden 1864–	
	Greece 1864–	
	Canada 1867–	
	France 1871–	
	Argentina 1880–	
	Chile 1891–	
1900–1945	Switzerland, the United States, Great Britain, Sweden, Canada Greece 1911, 1928–1936	29
	Italy 1922	
	Belgium 1940	
	Netherlands 1940	
	Argentina 1943	
	France 1940	
	Chile 1924, 1932	
	Australia 1901–	
	Norway 1905–1940	
	New Zealand 1907–	
	Colombia 1910–1949	
	Denmark 1914–1940	
	Poland 1917–1935	
	Latvia 1922–1934	
	Germany 1918–1932	
	Austria 1918–1934	
	Estonia 1919–1934	
	Finland 1919–	
	Uruguay 1919–	
	Costa Rica 1919–	
	Czechoslovakia 1920–1939	
	Ireland 1920–	

(Continued)

TABLE 1 ■ (Continued)

Period	Liberal Regimes and the Pacific Union (by Date "Liberal")	Total Number
1945[c]	Mexico 1928–	49
	Lebanon 1944–	
	Switzerland, the United States, Great Britain, Sweden, Canada, Australia, New Zealand, Finland, Ireland, Mexico	
	Uruguay 1973	
	Chile 1973	
	Lebanon 1975	
	Costa Rica 1948, 1953–	
	Iceland 1944–	
	France 1945–	
	Denmark 1945–	
	Norway 1945–	
	Austria 1945–	
	Brazil 1945–1954, 1955–1964	
	Belgium 1946–	
	Luxemburg 1946–	
	Netherlands 1946–	
	Italy 1946–	
	Philippines 1946–1972	
	India 1947–1975, 1977–	
	Sri Lanka 1948–1961, 1963–1977, 1978–	
	Ecuador 1948–1963, 1979–	
	Israel 1949–	
	West Germany 1949–	
	Peru 1950–1962, 1963–1968, 1980–	
	El Salvador 1950–1961	
	Turkey 1950–1960, 1966–1971	
	Japan 1951–	
	Bolivia 1956–1969	
	Colombia 1958–	
	Venezuela 1959–	
	Nigeria 1961–1964, 1979–	
	Jamaica 1962–	
	Trinidad 1962–	
	Senegal 1963–	
	Malaysia 1963–	
	South Korea 1963–1972	
	Botswana 1966–	
	Singapore 1965–	
	Greece 1975–	
	Portugal 1976–	
	Spain 1978–	
	Dominican Republic 1978–	

[a] I have drawn up this approximate list of "Liberal Regimes" according to the four institutions described as essential: market and private property economies; politics that are extremely sovereign; citizens who possess juridical rights; and "republican" (whether republican or monarchical), representative, government. This latter includes the requirement that the legislative branch have an effective role in public policy and be formally and competitively, either potentially or actually, elected. Furthermore, I have taken into account whether male suffrage is wide (that is, 30 percent) or open to "achievement" by inhabitants (for example, to poll-tax payers or householders) of the national or metropolitan territory. Female suffrage is granted within a generation of its being demanded; and representative government is internally sovereign (for example, including and especially over military and foreign affairs) as well as stable (in existence for at least three years).

[b] There are domestic variations within these liberal regimes. For example, Switzerland was liberal only in certain cantons; the United States was liberal only north of the Mason-Dixon line until 1865, when it became liberal throughout. These lists also exclude ancient "republics," since none appear to fit Kant's criteria. See Stephen Holmes, "Aristippus in and out of Athens," American Political Science Review 73, No. 1 (March 1979).

[c] Selected list, excludes liberal regimes with populations less than one million.

Sources: Arthur Banks and W. Overstreet, eds., The Political Handbook of the World, 1980 (New York: McGraw-Hill, 1980); Foreign and Commonwealth Office, A Year Book of the Commonwealth 1980 (London: HMSO, 1980); Europa Yearbook 1981 (London: Europe, 1981); W. L. Langer, An Encyclopedia of World History (Boston: Houghton-Mifflin, 1968); Department of State, Country Reports on Human Rights Practices (Washington, D.C.: U.S. Government Printing Office, 1981); and Freedom at Issue, No. 54 (January–February 1980).

TABLE 2 ■ INTERNATIONAL WARS LISTED CHRONOLOGICALLY

British-Maharattan (1817–1818)	Franco-Mexican (1862–1867)
Greek (1821–1828)	Ecuadorian-Colombian (1863)
Franco-Spanish (1823)	Second Polish (1863–1864)
First Anglo-Burmese (1823–1826)	Spanish-Santo Dominican (1863–1865)
Japanese (1825–1830)	Second Schleswig-Holstein (1864)
Russo-Persian (1826–1828)	Lopez (1864–1870)
Russo-Turkish (1828–1829)	Spanish-Chilean (1865–1866)
First Polish (1831)	Seven Weeks (1866)
First Syrian (1831–1832)	Ten Years (1868–1878)
Texan (1835–1836)	Franco-Prussian (1870–1871)
First British-Afghan (1838–1842)	Dutch-Achinese (1873–1878)
Second Syrian (1839–1840)	Balkan (1875–1877)
Franco-Algerian (1839–1847)	Russo-Turkish (1877–1878)
Peruvian-Bolivian (1841)	Bosnian (1878)
First British-Sikh (1845–1846)	Second British-Afghan (1878–1880)
Mexican-American (1846–1848)	Pacific (1879–1880)
Austro-Sardinian (1848–1849)	British-Zulu (1879)
First Schleswig-Holstein (1848–1849)	Franco-Indochinese (1882–1884)
Hungarian (1848–1849)	Mahdist (1882–1885)
Second British-Sikh (1848–1849)	Sino-French (1884–1885)
Roman Republic (1849)	Central American (1885)
La Plata (1851–1852)	Serbo-Bulgarian (1885)
First Turco-Montenegran (1852–1853)	Sino-Japanese (1894–1895)
Crimean (1853–1856)	Franco-Madagascan (1894–1895)
Sepoy (1857–1859)	Cuban (1895–1896)
Second Turco-Montenegran (1858–1859)	Italo-Ethiopian (1895–1896)
Italian Unification (1859)	First Philippine (1896–1898)

(Continued)

TABLE 2 ■ (Continued)

Spanish-Moroccan (1859–1860)	Greco-Turkish (1897)
Italo-Roman (1860)	Spanish-American (1898)
Italo-Sicilian (1860–1861)	Second Philippine (1899–1902)
Boer (1899–1902)	Palestine (1948–1949)
Boxer Rebellion (1900)	Hyderabad (1948)
Ilinden (1903)	Madagascan (1947–1948)
Russo-Japanese (1904–1905)	First Kashmir (1947–1949)
Central American (1906)	Korean (1950–1953)
Central American (1907)	Algerian (1954–1962)
Spanish-Moroccan (1909–1910)	Russo-Hungarian (1956)
Italo-Turkish (1911–1912)	Sinai (1956)
First Balkan (1912–1913)	Tibetan (1956–1959)
Second Balkan (1913)	Sino-Indian (1962)
World War I (1914–1918)	Vietnamese (1965–1975)
Russian Nationalities (1917–1921)	Second Kashmir (1965)
Russo-Polish (1919–1920)	Six Day (1967)
Hungarian-Allies (1919)	Israeli-Egyptian (1969–1970)
Greco-Turkish (1919–1922)	Football (1969)
Riffian (1921–1926)	Bangladesh (1971)
Druze (1925–1927)	Philippine-MNLF (1972–)
Sino-Soviet (1929)	Yom Kippur (1973)
Manchurian (1931–1933)	Turco-Cypriot (1974)
Chaco (1932–1935)	Ethiopian-Eritrean (1974–)
Italo-Ethiopian (1935–1936)	Vietnamese-Cambodian (1975–)
Sino-Japanese (1937–1941)	Timor (1975–)
Changkufeng (1938)	Saharan (1975–)
Nomohan (1939)	Ogaden (1976–)
World War II (1939–1945)	Ugandan-Tanzanian (1978–1979)
Russo-Finnish (1939–1940)	Sino-Vietnamese (1979)
Franco-Thai (1940–1941)	Russo-Afghan (1979–1989)
Indonesian (1945–1946)	Irani-Iraqi (1980–1988)
Indochinese (1945–1954)	

* Table 2 is from Melvin Small and J. David Singer, *Resort to Arms: International and Civil Wars, 1816–1980,* pp. 79–80. Copyright 1982 by Sage Publications Inc Books. Reproduced with permission of Sage Publications Inc Books in the format Textbook via Copyright Clearance Center. This is a partial list of international wars fought between 1816 and 1980. In Appendices A and B of *Resort to Arms,* Small and Singer identify a total of 575 wars in this period, but approximately 159 of them appear to be largely domestic or civil wars.

This definition of war excludes covert interventions, some of which have been directed by liberal regimes against other liberal regimes. One example is the United States' effort to destabilize the Chilean election and Allende's government. Nonetheless, it is significant . . . that such interventions are not pursued publicly as acknowledged policy. The covert destabilization campaign against Chile is recounted in U.S. Congress, Senate, Select Committee to Study Governmental Operations with Respect to Intelligence Activities, *Covert Action in Chile,* 1963–73, 94th Congress, 1st Session (Washington, D.C.: U.S. Government Printing Office, 1975).

Alliances: Balancing and Bandwagoning

STEPHEN M. WALT

When confronted by a significant external threat, states may either balance or bandwagon. Balancing is defined as allying with others against the prevailing threat; bandwagoning refers to alignment with the source of danger. Thus two distinct hypotheses about how states will select their alliance partners can be identified on the basis of whether the states ally against or with the principal external threat.[1]

These two hypotheses depict very different worlds. If balancing is more common than bandwagoning, then states are more secure, because aggressors will face combined opposition. But if bandwagoning is the dominant tendency, then security is scarce, because successful aggressors will attract additional allies, enhancing their power while reducing that of their opponents. . . .

BALANCING BEHAVIOR

The belief that states form alliances in order to prevent stronger powers from dominating them lies at the heart of traditional balance-of-power theory. According to this view, states join alliances to protect themselves from states or coalitions whose superior resources could pose a threat. States choose to balance for two main reasons.

First, they place their survival at risk if they fail to curb a potential hegemon before it becomes too strong. To ally with the dominant power means placing one's trust in its continued benevolence. The safer strategy is to join with those who cannot readily dominate their allies, in order to avoid being dominated by those who can. As Winston Churchill explained Britain's traditional alliance policy: "For four hundred years the foreign policy of England has been to oppose the strongest, most aggressive, most dominating power on the Continent. . . . [I]t would have been easy . . . and tempting to join with the stronger and share the fruits of his conquest. However, we always took the harder course, joined with the less strong powers, . . . and thus defeated the Continental military tyrant whoever he was."[2] More recently,

Henry Kissinger advocated a rapprochement with China, because he believed that in a triangular relationship, it was better to align with the weaker side.

Second, joining the weaker side increases the new member's influence within the alliance, because the weaker side has greater need for assistance. Allying with the strong side, by contrast, gives the new member little influence (because it adds relatively less to the coalition) and leaves it vulnerable to the whims of its partners. Joining the weaker side should be the preferred choice.

BANDWAGONING BEHAVIOR

The belief that states will balance is unsurprising, given the many familiar examples of states joining together to resist a threatening state or coalition. Yet, despite the powerful evidence that history provides in support of the balancing hypothesis, the belief that the opposite response is more likely is widespread. According to one scholar: "In international politics, nothing succeeds like success. Momentum accrues to the gainer and accelerates his movement. The appearance of irreversibility in his gains enfeebles one side and stimulates the other all the more. The bandwagon collects those on the sidelines."[3]

The bandwagoning hypothesis is especially popular with statesmen seeking to justify overseas involvements or increased military budgets. For example, German admiral Alfred von Tirpitz's famous risk theory rested on this type of logic. By building a great battle fleet, Tirpitz argued, Germany could force England into neutrality or alliance with her by posing a threat to England's vital maritime supremacy.

Bandwagoning beliefs have also been a recurring theme throughout the Cold War. Soviet efforts to intimidate both Norway and Turkey into not joining NATO reveal the Soviet conviction that states will accommodate readily to threats, although these moves merely encouraged Norway and Turkey to align more closely with the West.[4] Soviet officials made a similar error in believing that the growth of Soviet military power in the 1960s and 1970s would lead to a permanent shift in the correlation of forces against the West. Instead, it contributed to a Sino-American rapprochement in the 1970s and the largest peacetime increase in U.S. military power in the 1980s.

American officials have been equally fond of bandwagoning notions. According to NSC–68, the classified study that helped justify a major U.S. military buildup in the 1950s: "In the absence of an affirmative decision [to increase U.S. military capabilities] . . . our friends will become more than a liability to us, they will become a positive increment to Soviet power."[5] President John F. Kennedy once claimed that "if the United States were to falter, the whole world . . . would inevitably begin to move toward the Communist bloc."[6] And though Henry Kissinger often argued that the United States should form balancing alliances to contain the Soviet Union, he apparently believed that U.S. allies were likely to bandwagon. As he put it, "If leaders around the world . . . assume that the U.S. lacked either the forces or the will . . . they will accommodate themselves to what they will regard as the dominant trend."[7] Ronald Reagan's claim, "If we cannot defend ourselves [in Central America] . . . then we cannot expect to prevail elsewhere. . . . [O]ur credibility will collapse and our alliances will crumble," reveals the same logic in a familiar role—that of justifying overseas intervention.[8]

Balancing and bandwagoning are usually framed solely in terms of capabilities. Balancing is alignment with the weaker side, bandwagoning with the stronger. This conception should be revised, however, to account for the other factors that statesmen consider when deciding with whom to ally. Although power is an important part of the equation, it is not the only one. It is more accurate to say that states tend to ally with or against the foreign power that poses the greatest threat. For example, states may balance by allying with other strong states if a weaker power is more dangerous for other reasons. Thus the coalitions that defeated Germany in World War I and World War II were vastly superior in total resources, but they came together when it became clear that the aggressive aims of the Wilhelmines and Nazis posed the greater danger. Because balancing and bandwagoning are more accurately viewed as a response to threats, it is important to consider other factors that will affect the level of threat that states may pose: aggregate power, geographic proximity, offensive power, and aggressive intentions. . . .

By defining the basic hypotheses in terms of threats rather than power alone, we gain a more complete picture of the factors that statesmen will consider when making alliance choices. One cannot determine a priori, however, which sources of threat will be most important in any given case; one can say only that all of them are likely to play a role. And the greater the threat, the greater the probability that the vulnerable state will seek an alliance.

THE IMPLICATIONS OF BALANCING AND BANDWAGONING

The two general hypotheses of balancing and bandwagoning paint starkly contrasting pictures of international politics. Resolving the question of which hypothesis is more accurate is especially important, because each implies very different policy prescriptions. What sort of world does each depict, and what policies are implied?

If balancing is the dominant tendency, then threatening states will provoke others to align against them. Because those who seek to dominate others will attract widespread opposition, status quo states can take a relatively sanguine view of threats. Credibility is less important in a balancing world, because one's allies will resist threatening states out of their own self-interest, not because they expect others to do it for them. Thus the fear of allies defecting will decline. Moreover, if balancing is the norm and if statesmen understand this tendency, aggression will be discouraged because those who contemplate it will anticipate resistance.

In a balancing world, policies that convey restraint and benevolence are best. Strong states may be valued as allies because they have much to offer their partners, but they must take particular care to avoid appearing aggressive. Foreign and defense policies that minimize the threat one poses to others make the most sense in such a world.

A bandwagoning world, by contrast, is much more competitive. If states tend to ally with those who seem most dangerous, then great powers will be rewarded if they appear both strong and potentially aggressive. International rivalries will be more intense, because a single defeat may signal the decline of one side and the ascendancy of the other. This situation is especially alarming in a bandwagoning world, because additional defections and a further decline in position are to be expected. Moreover, if statesmen believe that bandwagoning is widespread, they will be more inclined to use force. This tendency is true for both aggressors and status quo powers. The former will use force because they will assume that others will be unlikely to balance against them and because they can attract more allies through belligerence or brinkmanship. The latter will follow suit because they will fear the gains their opponents will make by appearing powerful and resolute.[9]

Finally, misperceiving the relative propensity to balance or bandwagon is dangerous, because the policies that are appropriate for one situation will backfire in the other. If statesmen follow the balancing prescription in a bandwagoning world, their moderate responses and relaxed view of threats will encourage their allies to defect, leaving them isolated against an overwhelming coalition. Conversely, following the bandwagoning prescription in a world of balancers (employing power and threats frequently) will lead others to oppose you more and more vigorously.[10]

These concerns are not merely theoretical. In the 1930s, France failed to recognize that her allies in the Little Entente were prone to bandwagon, a tendency that French military and diplomatic policies reinforced. As noted earlier, Soviet attempts to intimidate Turkey and Norway after World War II reveal the opposite error; they merely provoked a greater U.S. commitment to these regions and cemented their entry into NATO. Likewise, the self-encircling bellicosity of Wilhelmine Germany and Imperial Japan reflected the assumption, prevalent in both states, that bandwagoning was the dominant tendency in international affairs.

WHEN DO STATES BALANCE? WHEN DO THEY BANDWAGON?

These examples highlight the importance of identifying whether states are more likely to balance or bandwagon and which sources of threat have the greatest impact on the decision. . . . In general, we should expect balancing behavior to be much more common than bandwagoning, and we should expect bandwagoning to occur only under certain identifiable conditions.

Although many statesmen fear that potential allies will align with the strongest side, this fear receives little support from most of international history. For example, every attempt to achieve hegemony in Europe since the Thirty Years' War has been thwarted by a defensive coalition formed precisely for the purpose of defeating the potential hegemon. Other examples are equally telling. Although isolated cases of bandwagoning do occur, the great powers have shown a remarkable tendency to ignore other temptations and follow the balancing prescription when necessary.

This tendency should not surprise us. Balancing should be preferred for the simple reason that no statesman can be completely sure of what another will do.

Bandwagoning is dangerous because it increases the resources available to a threatening power and requires placing trust in its continued forbearance. Because perceptions are unreliable and intentions can change, it is safer to balance against potential threats than to rely on the hope that a state will remain benevolently disposed.

But if balancing is to be expected, bandwagoning remains a possibility. Several factors may affect the relative propensity for states to select this course.

Strong versus Weak States

In general, the weaker the state, the more likely it is to bandwagon rather than balance. This situation occurs because weak states add little to the strength of a defensive coalition but incur the wrath of the more threatening states nonetheless. Because weak states can do little to affect the outcome (and may suffer grievously in the process), they must choose the winning side. Only when their decision can affect the outcome is it rational for them to join the weaker alliance. By contrast, strong states can turn a losing coalition into a winning one. And because their decision may mean the difference between victory and defeat, they are likely to be amply rewarded for their contribution.

Weak states are also likely to be especially sensitive to proximate power. Where great powers have both global interests and global capabilities, weak states will be concerned primarily with events in their immediate vicinity. Moreover, weak states can be expected to balance when threatened by states with roughly equal capabilities but they will be tempted to bandwagon when threatened by a great power. Obviously, when the great power is capable of rapid and effective action (i.e., when its offensive capabilities are especially strong), this temptation will be even greater.

The Availability of Allies

States will also be tempted to bandwagon when allies are simply unavailable. This statement is not simply tautological, because states may balance by mobilizing their own resources instead of relying on allied support. They are more likely to do so, however, when they are confident that allied assistance will be available. Thus a further prerequisite for balancing behavior is an effective system of diplomatic communication. The ability to communicate enables potential allies to recognize their shared interests and coordinate their responses. If weak states see no possibility of outside assistance, however, they may be forced to accommodate the most imminent threat. Thus the first Shah of Iran saw the British withdrawal from Kandahar in 1881 as a signal to bandwagon with Russia. As he told the British representative, all he had received from Great Britain was "good advice and honeyed words—nothing else."[11] Finland's policy of partial alignment with the Soviet Union suggests the same lesson. When Finland joined forces with Nazi Germany during World War II, it alienated the potential allies (the United States and Great Britain) that might otherwise have helped protect it from Soviet pressure after the war.

Of course, excessive confidence in allied support will encourage weak states to free-ride, relying on the efforts of others to provide security. Free-riding is the optimal policy for a weak state, because its efforts will contribute little in any case. Among the great powers, the belief that allies are readily available encourages buck-passing; states that are threatened strive to pass to others the burdens of standing up to the aggressor. Neither response is a form of bandwagoning, but both suggest that effective balancing behavior is more likely to occur when members of an alliance are not convinced that their partners are unconditionally loyal.

Taken together, these factors help explain the formation of spheres of influence surrounding the great powers. Although strong neighbors of strong states are likely to balance, small and weak neighbors of the great powers may be more inclined to bandwagon. Because they will be the first victims of expansion, because they lack the capabilities to stand alone, and because a defensive alliance may operate too slowly to do them much good, accommodating a threatening great power may be tempting.

Peace and War

Finally, the context in which alliance choices are made will affect decisions to balance or bandwagon. States are more likely to balance in peacetime or in the early stages of a war, as they seek to deter or defeat the powers posing the greatest threat. But once the outcome appears certain, some will be tempted to defect from the losing side at an opportune moment. Thus both Rumania and Bulgaria allied with Nazi Germany initially and then abandoned Germany for the Allies, as the tides of war ebbed and flowed across Europe in World War II.

The restoration of peace, however, restores the incentive to balance. As many observers have noted, victorious coalitions are likely to disintegrate with the conclusion of peace. Prominent examples include Austria and Prussia after their war with Denmark in 1864, Britain and France after World War I, the Soviet Union and the United States after World War II, and China and Vietnam after the U.S. withdrawal from Vietnam. This recurring pattern provides further support for the proposition that balancing is the dominant tendency in international politics and that bandwagoning is the opportunistic exception.

SUMMARY OF HYPOTHESES ON BALANCING AND BANDWAGONING

Hypotheses on Balancing

1. *General form:* States facing an external threat will align with others to oppose the states posing the threat.
2. The greater the threatening state's aggregate power, the greater the tendency for others to align against it.

3. The nearer a powerful state, the greater the tendency for those nearby to align against it. Therefore, neighboring states are less likely to be allies than are states separated by at least one other power.
4. The greater a state's offensive capabilities, the greater the tendency for others to align against it. Therefore, states with offensively oriented military capabilities are likely to provoke other states to form defensive coalitions.
5. The more aggressive a state's perceived intentions, the more likely others are to align against that state.
6. Alliances formed during wartime will disintegrate when the enemy is defeated.

Hypotheses on Bandwagoning

The hypotheses on bandwagoning are the opposite of those on balancing.

1. *General form:* States facing an external threat will ally with the most threatening power.
2. The greater a state's aggregate capabilities, the greater the tendency for others to align with it.
3. The nearer a powerful state, the greater the tendency for those nearby to align with it.
4. The greater a state's offensive capabilities, the greater the tendency for others to align with it.
5. The more aggressive a state's perceived intentions, the less likely other states are to align against it.
6. Alliances formed to oppose a threat will disintegrate when the threat becomes serious.

Hypotheses on the Conditions Favoring Balancing or Bandwagoning

1. Balancing is more common than bandwagoning.
2. The stronger the state, the greater its tendency to balance. Weak states will balance against other weak states but may bandwagon when threatened by great powers.
3. The greater the probability of allied support, the greater the tendency to balance. When adequate allied support is certain, however, the tendency for free-riding or buck-passing increases.
4. The more unalterably aggressive a state is perceived to be, the greater the tendency for others to balance against it.
5. In wartime, the closer one side is to victory, the greater the tendency for others to bandwagon with it.

NOTES

1. My use of the terms *balancing* and *bandwagoning* follows that of Kenneth Waltz (who credits it to Stephen Van Evera) in his *Theory of International Politics* (Reading, Mass., 1979). Arnold Wolfers uses a similar terminology in his essay "The Balance of Power in Theory and Practice," in *Discord and Collaboration: Essays on International Politics* (Baltimore, Md., 1962), pp. 122–24.

2. Winston S. Churchill, *The Second World War,* vol. 1: *The Gathering Storm* (Boston, 1948), pp. 207–8.

3. W. Scott Thompson, "The Communist International System," *Orbis* 20, no. 4 (1977).

4 For the effects of the Soviet pressure on Turkey, see George Lenczowski, *The Middle East in World Affairs,* 4th ed. (Ithaca, 1980), pp. 134–38; and Bruce R. Kuniholm, *The Origins of the Cold War in the Near East* (Princeton, N.J., 1980), pp. 355–78. For the Norwegian response to Soviet pressure, see Herbert Feis, *From Trust to Terror: The Onset of the Cold War, 1945–50* (New York, 1970), p. 381; and Geir Lundestad, *America, Scandinavia, and the Cold War: 1945–1949* (New York, 1980), pp. 308–9.

5. NSC–68 ("United States Objectives and Programs for National Security"), reprinted in Gaddis and Etzold, *Containment,* p. 404. Similar passages can be found on pp. 389, 414, and 434.

6. Quoted in Seyom Brown, *The Faces of Power: Constancy and Change in United States Foreign Policy from Truman to Johnson* (New York, 1968), p. 217.

7. Quoted in U.S. House Committee on Foreign Affairs, *The Soviet Union and the Third World: Watershed in Great Power Policy?* 97th Cong., 1st sess., 1977, pp. 157–58.

8. *New York Times,* April 28, 1983, p. A12. In the same speech, Reagan also said: "If Central America were to fall, what would the consequences be for our position in Asia and Europe and for alliances such as NATO? . . . Which ally, which friend would trust us then?"

9. It is worth noting that Napoleon and Hitler underestimated the costs of aggression by assuming that their potential enemies would bandwagon. After Munich, for example, Hitler dismissed the possibility of opposition by claiming that British and French states-men were "little worms." Napoleon apparently believed that England could not "rea-sonably make war on us unaided" and assumed that the Peace of Amiens guaranteed that England had abandoned its opposition to France. Because Hitler and Napoleon believed in a bandwagoning world, they were excessively eager to go to war.

10. This situation is analogous to Robert Jervis's distinction between the deterrence model and the spiral model. The former calls for opposition to a suspected aggressor, the latter for appeasement. Balancing and bandwagoning are the alliance equivalents of deterring and appeasing. See Robert Jervis, *Perception and Misperception in International Politics* (Princeton, N.J., 1976), chap. 3.

11. Quoted in C. J. Lowe, *The Reluctant Imperialists* (New York, 1967), p. 85.

The Future of Diplomacy

HANS J. MORGENTHAU

FOUR TASKS OF DIPLOMACY

. . . Diplomacy [is] an element of national power. The importance of diplomacy for the preservation of international peace is but a particular aspect of that general function. For a diplomacy that ends in war has failed in its primary objective: the promotion of the national interest by peaceful means. This has always been so and is particularly so in view of the destructive potentialities of total war.

Taken in its widest meaning, comprising the whole range of foreign policy, the task of diplomacy is fourfold: (1) Diplomacy must determine its objectives in the light of the power actually and potentially available for the pursuit of these objectives. (2) Diplomacy must assess the objectives of other nations and the power actually and potentially available for the pursuit of these objectives. (3) Diplomacy must determine to what extent these different objectives are compatible with each other. (4) Diplomacy must employ the means suited to the pursuit of its objectives. Failure in any one of these tasks may jeopardize the success of foreign policy and with it the peace of the world.

A nation that sets itself goals which it has not the power to attain may have to face the risk of war on two counts. Such a nation is likely to dissipate its strength and not to be strong enough at all points of friction to deter a hostile nation from challenging it beyond endurance. The failure of its foreign policy may force the nation to retrace its steps and to redefine its objectives in view of its actual strength. Yet it is more likely that, under the pressure of an inflamed public opinion, such a nation will go forward on the road toward an unattainable goal, strain all its resources to achieve it, and finally, confounding the national interest with that goal, seek in war the solution to a problem that cannot be solved by peaceful means.

A nation will also invite war if its diplomacy wrongly assesses the objectives of other nations and the power at their disposal. . . . A nation that mistakes a policy of imperialism for a policy of the status quo will be unprepared to meet the threat to its own existence which the other nation's policy entails. Its weakness will invite attack and may make war inevitable. A nation that mistakes a policy of the status quo for a policy of imperialism will evoke through its disproportionate reaction the very danger of war which it is trying to avoid. For as A mistakes B's policy for imperialism, so B might mistake A's defensive reaction for imperialism. Thus both nations, each intent upon forestalling imaginary aggression from the other side, will rush to arms. Similarly, the confusion of one type of imperialism with another may call for disproportionate reaction and thus evoke the risk of war.

As for the assessment of the power of other nations, either to overrate or to underrate it may be equally fatal to the cause of peace. By overrating the power of B, A may prefer to yield to B's demands until, finally, A is forced to fight for its very existence under the most unfavorable conditions. By underrating the power of B, A may become overconfident in its assumed superiority. A may advance demands and impose conditions upon B which the latter is supposedly too weak to resist. Unsuspecting B's actual power of resistance, A may be faced with the alternative of either retreating and conceding defeat or of advancing and risking war.

A nation that seeks to pursue an intelligent and peaceful foreign policy cannot cease comparing its own objectives and the objectives of other nations in the light of their compatibility. If they are compatible, no problem arises. If they are not compatible, nation A must determine whether its objectives are so vital to itself that they must be pursued despite that incompatibility with the objectives of B. If it is found that A's vital interests can be safeguarded without the attainment of these objectives, they ought to be abandoned. On the other hand, if A finds that these objectives are essential for its vital interests, A must then ask itself whether B's objectives, incompatible with its own, are essential for B's vital interests. If the answer seems to be in the negative, A must try to induce B to abandon its objectives, offering B equivalents not vital to A. In other words, through diplomatic bargaining, the give and take of compromise, a way must be sought by which the interests of A and B can be reconciled.

Finally, if the incompatible objectives of A and B should prove to be vital to either side, a way might still be sought in which the vital interests of A and B might be redefined, reconciled, and their objectives thus made compatible with each other. Here, however—even provided that both sides pursue intelligent and peaceful policies—A and B are moving dangerously close to the brink of war.

It is the final task of an intelligent diplomacy, intent upon preserving peace, to choose the appropriate means for pursuing its objectives. The means at the disposal of diplomacy are three: persuasion, compromise, and threat of force. No diplomacy relying only upon the threat of force can claim to be both intelligent and peaceful. No diplomacy that would stake everything on persuasion and compromise deserves to be called intelligent. Rarely, if ever, in the conduct of the foreign policy of a great power is there justification for using only one method to the exclusion of the others. Generally, the diplomatic representative of a great power, in order to be able to serve both the interests of his country and the interests of peace, must at the same time use persuasion, hold out the advantages of a compromise, and impress the other side with the military strength of his country.

The art of diplomacy consists in putting the right emphasis at any particular moment on each of these three means at its disposal. A diplomacy that has been successfully discharged in its other functions may well fail in advancing the national interest and preserving peace if it stresses persuasion when the give and take of compromise is primarily required by the circumstances of the case. A diplomacy that puts most of its eggs in the basket of compromise when the military might of the nation should be predominantly displayed, or stresses military might when the political situation calls for persuasion and compromise, will likewise fail. . . .

The Promise of Diplomacy: Its Nine Rules[1]

Diplomacy could revive if it would part with [the] vices, which in recent years have well-nigh destroyed its usefulness, and if it would restore the techniques which have controlled the mutual relations of nations since time immemorial. By doing so, however, diplomacy would realize only one of the preconditions for the preservation of peace. The contribution of a revived diplomacy to the cause of peace would depend upon the methods and purposes of its use. . . .

We have already formulated the four main tasks with which a foreign policy must cope successfully in order to be able to promote the national interest and preserve peace. It remains for us now to reformulate those tasks in the light of the special problems with which contemporary world politics confront diplomacy. . . .

The main reason for [the] threatening aspect of contemporary world politics [lies] in the character of modern war, which has changed profoundly under the impact of nationalistic universalism° and modern technology. The effects of modern technology cannot be undone. The only variable that remains subject to deliberate manipulation is the new moral force of nationalistic universalism. The attempt to reverse the trend toward war through the techniques of a revived diplomacy must start with this phenomenon. That means, in negative terms, that a revived diplomacy will have a chance to preserve peace only when it is not used as the instrument of a political religion aiming at universal dominion.

Four Fundamental Rules

Diplomacy Must Be Divested of the Crusading Spirit   This is the first of the rules that diplomacy can neglect only at the risk of war. In the words of William Graham Sumner:

> If you want war, nourish a doctrine. Doctrines are the most frightful tyrants to which men ever are subject, because doctrines get inside of a man's own reason and betray him against himself. Civilised men have done their fiercest fighting for doctrines. The reconquest of the Holy Sepulcher, "the balance of power," "no universal dominion," "trade follows the flag," "he who holds the land will hold the sea," "the throne and the altar," the revolution, the faith—these are the things for which men have given their lives. . . . Now when any doctrine arrives at that degree of authority, the name of it is a club which any demagogue may swing over you at any time and apropos of anything. In order to describe a doctrine, we must have recourse to theological language. A doctrine is an article of faith. It is something which you are bound to believe, not because you have some rational grounds for believing it is true, but because you belong to such and

---

°[Editors' Note: By this term Professor Morgenthau refers to the injection of ideology into international politics and to each nation's claim that its own ethical code would serve as the basis of international conduct for all nations.]

such a church or denomination. . . . A policy in a state we can understand; for instance, it was the policy of the United States at the end of the eighteenth century to get the free navigation of the Mississippi to its mouth, even at the expense of war with Spain. That policy had reason and justice in it; it was founded in our interests; it had positive form and definite scope. A doctrine is an abstract principle; it is necessarily absolute in its scope and abstruse in its terms; it is metaphysical assertion. It is never true, because it is absolute, and the affairs of men are all conditioned and relative. . . . Now to turn back to politics, just think what an abomination in statecraft an abstract doctrine must be. Any politician or editor can, at any moment, put a new extension on it. The people acquiesce in the doctrine and applaud it because they hear the politicians and editors repeat it, and the politicians and editors repeat it because they think it is popular. So it grows. . . . It may mean anything or nothing, at any moment, and no one knows how it will be. You accede to it now, within the vague limits of what you suppose it to be; therefore, you will have to accede to it tomorrow when the same name is made to cover something which you never have heard or thought of. If you allow a political catchword to go on and grow, you will awaken some day to find it standing over you, the arbiter of your destiny, against which you are powerless, as men are powerless against delusions. . . . What can be more contrary to sound statesmanship and common sense than to put forth an abstract assertion which has no definite relation to any interest of ours now at stake, but which has in it any number of possibilities of producing complications which we cannot foresee, but which are sure to be embarrassing when they arise![2]

The Wars of Religion have shown that the attempt to impose one's own religion as the only true one upon the rest of the world is as futile as it is costly. A century of almost unprecedented bloodshed, devastation, and barbarization was needed to convince the contestants that the two religions could live together in mutual toleration. The two political religions of our time have taken the place of the two great Christian denominations of the sixteenth and seventeenth centuries. Will the political religions of our time need the lesson of the Thirty Years' War, or will they rid themselves in time of the universalistic aspirations that inevitably issue in inconclusive war?

Upon the answer to that question depends the cause of peace. For only if it is answered in the affirmative can a moral consensus, emerging from shared convictions and common values, develop—a moral consensus within which a peace-preserving diplomacy will have a chance to grow. Only then will diplomacy have a chance to face the concrete political problems that require peaceful solution. If the objectives of foreign policy are not to be defined in terms of a world-embracing political religion, how are they to be defined? This is a fundamental problem to be solved once the crusading aspirations of nationalistic universalism have been discarded.

The Objectives of Foreign Policy Must Be Defined in Terms of the National Interest and Must Be Supported with Adequate Power This is the second rule of a peace-preserving diplomacy. The national interest of a peace-loving nation can only be defined in terms of national security, and national security must be defined as integrity of the national territory and of its institutions. National security, then, is the irreducible minimum that diplomacy must defend with adequate power without compromise. But diplomacy must ever be alive to the radical transformation that national security has undergone under the impact of the nuclear age. Until the advent of that age, a nation could use its diplomacy to purchase its security at the expense of another nation. Today, short of a radical change in the atomic balance of power in favor of a particular nation, diplomacy, in order to make one nation secure from nuclear destruction, must make them all secure. With the national interest defined in such restrictive and transcendent terms, diplomacy must observe the third of its rules.

Diplomacy Must Look at the Political Scene from the Point of View of Other Nations   "Nothing is so fatal to a nation as an extreme of self-partiality, and the total want of consideration of what others will naturally hope or fear."[3] What are the national interests of other nations in terms of national security and are they compatible with one's own? The definition of the national interest in terms of national security is easier, and the interests of the two opposing nations are more likely to be compatible in a bipolar system than in any other system of the balance of power. The bipolar system, as we have seen, is more unsafe from the point of view of peace than any other, when both blocs are in competitive contact throughout the world and the ambition of both is fired by the crusading zeal of a universal mission. ". . . Vicinity, or nearness of situation, constitutes nations natural enemies."[4]

Yet once they have defined their national interests in terms of national security, they can draw back from their outlying positions, located close to, or within, the sphere of national security of the other side, and retreat into their respective spheres, each self-contained within its orbit. Those outlying positions add nothing to national security; they are but liabilities, positions that cannot be held in case of war. Each bloc will be the more secure the wider it makes the distance that separates both spheres of national security. Each side can draw a line far distant from each other, making it understood that to touch or even to approach it means war. What then about the interjacent spaces, stretching between the two lines of demarcation? Here the fourth rule of diplomacy applies.

Nations Must Be Willing to Compromise on All Issues that Are Not Vital to Them

> All government, indeed every human benefit and enjoyment, every virtue and every prudent act, is founded on compromise and barter. We balance inconveniences; we give and take; we remit some rights, that we may enjoy others; and we choose rather to be happy citizens than subtle disputants. As we must give away some natural liberties, for the advantages to be derived from the communion and fellowship of a great empire. But, in all fair dealings, the thing bought must bear some proportion to the purchase paid. None will barter away the immediate jewel of his soul.[5]

Here diplomacy meets its most difficult task. For minds not beclouded by the crusading zeal of a political religion and capable of viewing the national interests of both sides with objectivity, the delimitation of these vital interests should not prove too difficult. Compromise on secondary issues is a different matter. Here the task is not to separate and define interests that by their very nature already tend toward separation and definition, but to keep in balance interests that touch each other at many points and may be intertwined beyond the possibility of separation. It is an immense task to allow the other side a certain influence in those interjacent spaces without allowing them to be absorbed into the orbit of the other side. It is hardly a less immense task to keep the other side's influence as small as possible in the regions close to one's own security zone without absorbing those regions into one's own orbit. For the performance of these tasks, no formula stands ready for automatic application. It is only through a continuous process of adaptation, supported both by firmness and self-restraint, that compromise on secondary issues can be made to work. It is, however, possible to indicate a priori what approaches will facilitate or hamper the success of policies of compromise.

First of all, it is worth noting to what extent the success of compromise—that is, compliance with the fourth rule—depends upon compliance with the other three rules, which in turn are similarly interdependent. As the compliance with the second rule depends upon the realization of the first, so the third rule must await its realization from compliance with the second. A nation can only take a rational view of its national interests after it has parted company with the crusading spirit of a political creed. A nation is able to consider the national interests of the other side with objectivity only after it has become secure in what it considers its own national interests. Compromise on any issue, however minor, is impossible so long as both sides are not secure in their national interests. Thus nations cannot hope to comply with the fourth rule if they are not willing to comply with the other three. Both morality and expediency require compliance with these four fundamental rules.

Compliance makes compromise possible, but it does not assure its success. To give compromise, made possible through compliance with the first three rules, a chance to succeed, five other rules must be observed.

Five Prerequisites of Compromise

Give up the Shadow of Worthless Rights for the Substance of Real Advantage   A diplomacy that thinks in legalistic and propagandistic terms is particularly tempted to insist upon the letter of the law, as it interprets the law, and to lose sight of the consequences such insistence may have for its own nation and for humanity. Since there are rights to be defended, this kind of diplomacy thinks that the issue cannot be compromised. Yet the choice that confronts the diplomat is not between legality and illegality, but between political wisdom and political folly. "The question with me," said Edmund Burke, "is not whether you have a right to render your people miserable, but whether it is not your interest to make them happy. It is not what a lawyer tells me I *may* do, but what humanity, reason and justice tell me I ought to do."[6]

Never Put Yourself in a Position from Which You Cannot Retreat Without Losing Face and from Which You Cannot Advance Without Grave Risks   The violation of this rule often results from disregard for the preceding one. A diplomacy that confounds the shadow of legal right with the actuality of political advantage is likely to find itself in a position where it may have a legal right, but no political business, to be. In other words, a nation may identify itself with a position, which it may or may not have a right to hold, regardless of the political consequences. And again compromise becomes a difficult matter. A nation cannot retreat from that position without incurring a serious loss of prestige. It cannot advance from that position without exposing itself to political risks, perhaps even the risk of war. That heedless rush into untenable positions and, more particularly, the stubborn refusal to extricate oneself from them in time is the earmark of incompetent diplomacy. Its classic examples are the policy of Napoleon III on the eve of the Franco-Prussian War of 1870 and the policies of Austria and Germany on the eve of the First World War. These examples also show how closely the risk of war is allied with the violation of this rule.

Never Allow a Weak Ally to Make Decisions for You   Strong nations that are oblivious to the preceding rules are particularly susceptible to violating this one. They lose their freedom of action by identifying their own national interests completely with those of the weak ally. Secure in the support of its powerful friend, the weak ally can choose the objectives and methods of its foreign policy to suit itself. The powerful nation then finds that it must support interests not its own and that it is unable to compromise on issues that are vital not to itself, but only to its ally.

The classic example of the violation of this rule is to be found in the way in which Turkey forced the hand of Great Britain and France on the eve of the Crimean War in 1853. The Concert of Europe had virtually agreed upon a compromise settling the conflict between Russia and Turkey, when Turkey, knowing that the Western powers would support it in a war with Russia, did its best to provoke that war and thus involved Great Britain and France in it against their will. Thus Turkey went far in deciding the issue of war and peace for Great Britain and France according to its own national interests. Great Britain and France had to accept that decision even though their national interests did not require war with Russia and they had almost succeeded in preventing its outbreak. They had surrendered their freedom of action to a weak ally, which used its control over their policies for its own purposes.

The Armed Forces Are the Instrument of Foreign Policy, Not Its Master   No successful and no peaceful foreign policy is possible without observance of this rule. No nation can pursue a policy of compromise with the military determining the ends and means of foreign policy. The armed forces are instruments of war; foreign policy is an instrument of peace. It is true that the ultimate objectives of the conduct of war and of the conduct of foreign policy are identical: Both serve the national interest. Both, however, differ fundamentally in their immediate objective, in the means they employ, and in the modes of thought they bring to bear upon their respective tasks.

The objective of war is simple and unconditional: to break the will of the enemy. Its methods are equally simple and unconditional: to bring the greatest amount of violence to bear upon the most vulnerable spot in the enemy's armor. Consequently, the military leader must think in absolute terms. He lives in the present and in the immediate future. The sole question before him is how to win victories as cheaply and quickly as possible and how to avoid defeat.

The objective of foreign policy is relative and conditional: to bend, not to break, the will of the other side as far as necessary in order to safeguard one's own vital interests without hurting those of the other side. The methods of foreign policy are relative and conditional: not to advance by destroying the obstacles in one's way, but to retreat before them, to circumvent them, to maneuver around them, to soften and dissolve them slowly by means of persuasion, negotiation, and pressure. In consequence, the mind of the diplomat is complicated and subtle. It sees the issue in hand as a moment in history, and beyond the victory of tomorrow it anticipates the incalculable possibilities of the future. In the words of Bolingbroke:

> Here let me only say, that the glory of taking towns, and winning battles, is to be measured by the utility that results from those victories. Victories that bring honour to the arms, may bring shame to the councils, of a nation. To win a battle, to take a town, is the glory of a general, and of an army. . . . But the glow of a nation is to proportion the ends she proposes, to her interest and her strength; the means she employs to the ends she proposes, and the vigour she exerts to both.[7]

To surrender the conduct of foreign affairs to the military, then, is to destroy the possibility of compromise and thus surrender the cause of peace. The military mind knows how to operate between the absolutes of victory and defeat. It knows nothing of that patient intricate and subtle maneuvering of diplomacy, whose main purpose is to avoid the absolutes of victory and defeat and meet the other side on the middle ground of negotiated compromise. A foreign policy conducted by military men according to the rules of the military art can only end in war, for "what we prepare for is what we shall get."[8]

For nations conscious of the potentialities of modern war, peace must be the goal of their foreign policies. Foreign policy must be conducted in such a way as to make the preservation of peace possible and not make the outbreak of war inevitable. In a society of sovereign nations, military force is a necessary instrument of foreign policy. Yet the instrument of foreign policy should not become the master of foreign policy. As war is fought in order to make peace possible, foreign policy should be conducted in order to make peace permanent. For the performance of both tasks, the subordination of the military under the civilian authorities which are constitutionally responsible for the conduct of foreign affairs is an indispensable prerequisite.

The Government Is the Leader of Public Opinion, Not Its Slave   Those responsible for the conduct of foreign policy will not be able to comply with the foregoing principles of diplomacy if they do not keep this principle constantly in mind. As has been pointed out above in greater detail, the rational requirements of good foreign policy cannot from the outset count upon the support of a public opinion whose preferences are emotional rather than rational. This is bound to be particularly true of a foreign policy whose goal is compromise, and which, therefore, must concede some of the objectives of the other side and give up some of its own. Especially when foreign policy is conducted under conditions of democratic control and is inspired by the crusading zeal of a political religion, statesmen are always tempted to sacrifice the requirements of good foreign policy to the applause of the masses. On the other hand, the statesmen who would defend the integrity of these requirements against even the slightest contamination with popular passion would seal his own doom as a political leader and, with it, the doom of his foreign policy, for he would lose the popular support which put and keeps him in power.

The statesman, then, is allowed neither to surrender to popular passions nor disregard them. He must strike a prudent balance between adapting himself to them and marshaling them to the support of his policies. In one word, he must lead. He must perform that highest feat of statesmanship: trimming his sails to the winds of popular passion while using them to carry the ship to the port of good foreign policy, on however roundabout and zigzag a course.

CONCLUSION

The road to international peace which we have outlined cannot compete in inspirational qualities with the simple and fascinating formulae that for a century and a half have fired the imagination of a war-weary world. There is something spectacular in the radial simplicity of a formula that with one sweep seems to dispose of the problem of war once and for all. This has been the promise of such solutions as free trade, arbitration, disarmament, collective security, universal socialism, international government, and the world state. There is nothing spectacular, fascinating, or inspiring, at least for the people at large, in the business of diplomacy.

We have made the point, however, that these solutions, insofar as they deal with the real problem and not merely with some of its symptoms, presuppose the existence of an integrated international society, which actually does not exist. To bring into existence such an international society and keep it in being, the accommodating techniques of diplomacy are required. As the integration of domestic society and its peace develop from the unspectacular and almost unnoticed day-by-day operations of the techniques of accommodation and change, so the ultimate ideal of international life—that is, to transcend itself in a supranational society— must await its realization from the techniques of persuasion, negotiation, and pressure, which are the traditional instruments of diplomacy.

The reader who has followed us to this point may well ask: But has not diplomacy failed in preventing war in the past? To that legitimate question two answers can be given.

Diplomacy has failed many times, and it has succeeded many times, in its peace-preserving task. It has failed sometimes because nobody wanted it to succeed. We have seen how different in their objectives and methods the limited wars of the past have been from the total war of our time. When war was the normal activity of kings, the task of diplomacy was not to prevent it, but to bring it about at the most propitious moment.

On the other hand, when nations have used diplomacy for the purpose of preventing war, they have often succeeded. The outstanding example of a successful war-preventing diplomacy in modern times is the Congress of Berlin of 1878. By the peaceful means of an accommodating diplomacy, that Congress settled, or at least made susceptible of settlement, the issues that had separated Great Britain and Russia since the end of the Napoleonic Wars. During the better part of the nineteenth century, the conflict between Great Britain and Russia over the Balkans, the Dardanelles, and the Eastern Mediterranean hung like a suspended sword over the peace of the world. Yet, during the fifty years following the Crimean War, though hostilities between Great Britain and Russia threatened to break out time and again, they never actually did break out. The main credit for the preservation of peace must go to the techniques of an accommodating diplomacy which culminated in the Congress of Berlin. When British Prime Minister Disraeli returned from that Congress to London, he declared with pride that he was bringing home "peace . . . with honor." In fact, he had brought peace for later generations, too; for a century there has been no war between Great Britain and Russia.

We have, however, recognized the precariousness of peace in a society of sovereign nations. The continuing success of diplomacy in preserving peace depends, as we have seen, upon extraordinary moral and intellectual qualities that all the leading participants must possess. A mistake in the evaluation of one of the elements of national power, made by one or the other of the leading statesmen, may spell the difference between peace and war. So may an accident spoiling a plan or a power calculation.

Diplomacy is the best means of preserving peace which a society of sovereign nations has to offer, but, especially under the conditions of contemporary world politics and of contemporary war, it is not good enough. It is only when nations have surrendered to a higher authority the means of destruction which modern technology has put in their hands—when they have given up their sovereignty—that international peace can be made as secure as domestic peace. Diplomacy can make peace more secure than it is today, and the world state can make peace more secure than it would be if nations were to abide by the rules of diplomacy. Yet, as there can be no permanent peace without a world state, there can be no world state without the peace-preserving and community-building processes of diplomacy. For the world state to be more than a dim vision, the accommodating processes of diplomacy, mitigating and minimizing conflicts, must be revived. Whatever one's conception of the ultimate state of international affairs may be, in the recognition of that need and in the demand that it be met all men of good will can join.

NOTES

1. We by no means intend to give here an exhaustive account of rules of diplomacy. We propose to discuss only those which seem to have a special bearing upon the contemporary situation.
2. "War." *Essays of William Graham Sumner* (New Haven, Conn.: Yale University Press, 1934), Vol. I, pp. 169 ff.
3. Edmund Burke, "Remarks on the Policy of the Allies with Respect to France" (1793), *Works*, Vol. IV (Boston: Little, Brown and Company, 1889), p. 447.
4. *The Federalist,* No. 6.
5. Edmund Burke, "Speech on the Conciliation with America," *loc. cit.*, Vol. II, p. 169.
6. "Speech on Conciliation with the Colonies" (1775), *The Works of Edmund Burke*, Vol.II (Boston: Little, Brown and Company, 1865), p. 140.
7. *Bolingbroke's Defense of the Treaty of Utrecht* (Cambridge: Cambridge University Press, 1932), p. 95.
8. William Graham Sumner, *op. cit.*, p. 173.

The Uses and Limits of International Law

STANLEY HOFFMANN

The student of international law who examines its functions in the present international system and in the foreign policy of states will, unless he takes refuge in the comforting seclusion from reality that the pure theory of law once provided, be reduced to one of three attitudes. He will become a cynic, if he chooses to stress, like Giraudoux in *Tiger at the Gates,* the way in which legal claims are shaped to support any position a state deems useful or necessary on nonlegal grounds, or if he gets fascinated by the combination of cacophony and silence that characterizes international law as a system of world public order. He will become a hypocrite, if he chooses to rationalize either the conflicting interpretations and uses of law by states as a somehow converging effort destined to lead to some such system endowed with sufficient stability and solidity, or else if he endorses one particular construction (that of his own statesmen) as a privileged and enlightened contribution to the achievement of such a system. He will be overcome by consternation, if he reflects upon the gap between, on the one hand, the ideal of a world in which traditional self-help will be at least moderated by procedures and rules made even more indispensable by the proliferation both of states and of lethal weapons, and, on the other hand, the realities of inexpiable conflicts, sacred egoisms, and mutual recriminations. . . .

1. Some of the functions of international law constitute *assets both for the policy maker and from the viewpoint of world order,* i.e., of providing the international milieu with a framework of predictability and with procedures for the transaction of interstate business.

    (a) International law is an instrument of *communication*. To present one's claims in legal terms means, 1, to signal to one's partner or opponent which "basic conduct norms" (to use Professor Scheinman's expression) one considers relevant or essential, and 2, to indicate which procedures one intends to follow and would like the other side to follow. At a time when both the size of a highly heterogeneous international milieu and the

Reprinted by permission from *International Law and Political Crisis* edited by Lawrence Scheinman and David Wilkinson, eds., pp. xi–xix. Copyright © 1968 by Little, Brown and Company (Inc.). Portions of the text and all footnotes have been omitted.

imperatives of prudence in the resort to force make communication essential and often turn international relations into a psychological contest, international law provides a kind of common language that does not amount to a common code of legitimacy yet can serve as a joint frame of reference. (One must however remember, 1, that communication is no guarantee against misperception, and 2, that what is being communicated may well determine the other side's response to the message: If "we" communicate to "them" an understanding of the situation that threatens their basic values or goals—like our interpretation of the war in South Vietnam as a case of aggression—there will be no joint frame of reference at all, and in fact the competition may become fiercer.)

(b) International law affords means of *channeling conflict*—of diverting inevitable tensions and clashes from the resort to force. Whenever there have been strong independent reasons for avoiding armed conflict—in an international system in which the superpowers in particular have excellent reasons for "managing" their confrontations, either by keeping them nonviolent, or by using proxies—international law has provided statesmen both with alibis for shunning force and with alternatives to violence. . . . In Berlin, both the Soviets and the West shaped their moves in such a way as to leave to the other side full responsibility for a first use of force, and to avoid the kind of frontal collision with the other side's legal claim that could have obliged the opponent to resort to force in order not to lose power or face. Thus, today as in earlier periods, law can indeed . . . serve as an alternative to confrontation whenever states are eager or forced to look for an alternative.

2. International law also plays various useful roles in the policy process, which however do not ipso facto contribute to world order. Here, we are concerned with *law as a tool of policy* in the competition of state visions, objectives, and tactics.

(a) The establishment of a network of rights and obligations, or the resort to legal arguments can be useful for the *protection or enhancement of a position:* if one wants to give oneself a full range of means with which to buttress a threatened status quo (cf. the present position of the West in Berlin; this is also what treaties of alliance frequently are for); if one wants to enhance one's power in a way that is demonstrably authorized by principles in international law (cf. Nasser's claim when he nationalized the Suez Canal, and Sukarno's invocation of the principle of self-determination against Malaysia); if one wants to restore a political position badly battered by an adversary's move, so that the resort to legal arguments becomes part of a strategy of restoring the status quo ante (Western position during the Berlin blockade; Kennedy's strategy during the Cuban missile crisis; Western powers' attempts during the first phase of the Suez crisis; Soviet tactics in the U.N. General Assembly debates on the financing of peace-keeping operations).

(b) In all those instances, policy makers use law as a way of putting pressure on an opponent by *mobilizing international support* behind the legal rules invoked: law serves as a focal point, as the tool for "internationalizing" a national interest and as the cement of a political coalition. States that may have political misgivings about pledging direct support to a certain power whose interests only partly coincide with theirs, or because they do not want to antagonize another power thereby, may find it both easier and useful to rally to the defense of a legal principle in whose maintenance or promotion they may have a stake.

(c) A policy maker who ignores international law leaves the field of political-competition-through-legal-manipulation open to his opponents or rivals. International law provides one of the numerous *chessboards* on which state contests occur.

3. Obviously, this indicates not only that to the statesmen international law provides an instrument rather than a guide for action, but also that this tool is often *not used,* when resort to it would hamper the state's interest as defined by the policy maker.

(a) One of the reasons why international law often serves as a technique of political mobilization is the appeal of reciprocity: "You must support my invocation of the rule against him, because if you let the rule be violated at my expense, someday it may be breached at yours; and we both have an interest in its preservation." But *reciprocity cuts both ways:* My using a certain legal argument to buttress my case against him may encourage him, now or later, to resort to the same argument against me; I may therefore be unwise to play on a chessboard in which, given the solemn and abstract nature of legal rights and obligations, I may not be able to make the kind of distinction between my (good) case and your (bad) one that can best be made by resort to ad hoc, political and circumstantial evidence that is irrelevant or ruled out in legal argumentation. Thus . . . during the Cuban crisis, when the United States tried to distinguish between Soviet missiles in Cuba and American ones in Turkey in order to build its case and get support, America's use of the OAS [Organization of American States] Charter as the legal basis for its "quarantine" established a dangerous precedent which the Soviets could use some day, against the U.S. or its allies, on behalf of the Warsaw Pact. And in the tragicomedy of the battle over Article 19 of the U.N. Charter, one reason why the U.S. finally climbed down from its high legal horse and gave up the attempt to deprive the Soviets of their right to vote, unless they paid their share, was the growing awareness of the peril which the principle of the exercise of the U.N. taxing power by the General Assembly could constitute some day for the United States if it lost control of the Assembly.

(b) One of the things that international law "communicates" is the solemnity of a commitment: a treaty, or a provision of the Charter, serves as a kind of tripwire or burglar alarm. When it fails to deter, the victim and third parties have a fateful choice between upholding the legal principle by all means, at the cost of a possible escalation in violence, and choosing to settle the dispute more peacefully, at the cost of *fuzzing the legal issue.* For excellent political reasons, the latter course is frequently adopted . . . in the form of dropping any reference to the legal principle at stake. . . .

(c) The very *ambiguity* of international law, which in many essential areas displays either gaping holes or conflicting principles, allows policy makers in an emergency to act as if international law were irrelevant—as if it were neither a restraint nor a guide. . . .

However, precisely because there is a legal chessboard for state competition, the fact that international law does not, in a crisis, really restrict one's freedom of action, does not mean that one will forgo legal rationalizations of the moves selected. Here we come to the last set of considerations about the role of law:

4. The resort to legal arguments by policy makers may be *detrimental to world order and thereby counterproductive for the state* that used such arguments.

(a) In the legal vacuum or confusion which prevails in areas as vital to states as internal war or the use of force, each state tries to justify its conduct with legal rationalizations. The result is a kind of *escalation of claims and counterclaims*, whose consequence, in turn, is both a further devaluation of international law and a "credibility gap" at the expense of those states who have debased the currency. America's rather indiscriminate resort to highly debatable legal arguments to support its Vietnam policy is a case in point. The unsubtle reduction of international law to a mere storehouse of convenient *ex post* justifications (as in the case of British intervention at Suez, or American interventions in Santo Domingo and Vietnam) undermines the very pretense of contributing to world order with which these states have tried to justify their unilateral acts.

(b) Much of contemporary international law authorizes states to *increase their power*. In this connection, Nasser's nationalization of the Suez Canal Company was probably quite legal, and those who accept the rather tortured argument put forth by the State Department legal advisers to justify the Cuban "quarantine" have concluded that this partial blockade was authorized by the OAS Charter and not in contradiction with the U.N. Charter. Yet it is obvious that a full exploitation by all states of all permissions granted by international law would be a perfect recipe for chaos.

(c) *Attempts to enforce or to strengthen international law*, far from consolidating a system of desirable restraints on state (mis)behavior, may actually *backfire* if the political conditions are not ripe. This is the central lesson of the long story of the financing of U.N. peace-keeping operations. American self-intoxication with the importance of the rule of law, fed by misleading analogies between the U.N. Charter and the U.S. Constitution, resulted ultimately in a weakening of the influence of the World Court (which largely followed America's line of reasoning), and in an overplaying of America's hand during the "non-session" of the General Assembly in the fall of 1964 and winter of 1965.

These are sobering considerations. But what they tell us is not, as so many political scientists seem to believe, that international law is, at best, a farce, and, at worst, even a potential danger; what they tell us is that *the nature of the international system condemns international law to all the weaknesses and perversions that it is so easy to deride.* International law is merely a magnifying mirror that reflects faithfully and cruelly the essence and the logic of international politics. In a fragmented world, there is no "global perspective" from which anyone can authoritatively assess, endorse, or reject the separate national efforts at making international law serve national interests above all. Like the somber universe of Albert Camus' Caligula, this is a judgeless world where no one is innocent. . . .

The permanent plight of international law is that, now as before, it shows on its body of rules all the scars inflicted by the international state of war. The tragedy of contemporary international law is that of a double divorce: first, between the old liberal dream of a world rule of law, and the realities of an international system of multiple minidramas that always threaten to become major catastrophes; second, between the old dream and the new requirements of moderation which in the circumstances of the present system suggest a *down-playing* of formal law in the realm of peace-and-war issues, and an *upgrading* of more flexible techniques, until the system has become less fierce. The interest of international law for the political scientist is that there is no better way of grasping the continuing differences between order within a national society and the fragile order of international affairs than to study how and when states use legal language, symbols, and documents, and with what results. . . .

International Institutions:
Can Interdependence Work?

ROBERT O. KEOHANE

To analyze world politics in the [current era] is to discuss international institutions: the rules that govern elements of world politics and the organizations that help implement those rules. . . . Under what conditions should China be admitted to the World Trade Organization (WTO)? How many billions of dollars does the International Monetary Fund (IMF) need at its disposal to remain an effective "lender of last resort" for countries such as Indonesia, Korea, and Thailand that were threatened in 1997 with financial collapse? Will the tentative Kyoto Protocol on Climate Change be renegotiated, ratified, and implemented effectively? Can future United Nations peacekeeping practices—in contrast to the UN fiascoes in Bosnia and Somalia—be made more effective?

These questions help illustrate the growing importance of international institutions for maintaining world order. . . . Superpowers need general rules because they seek to influence events around the world. Even an unchallenged superpower such as the United States would be unable to achieve its goals through the bilateral exercise of influence: the costs of such massive "arm-twisting" would be too great.

International institutions are increasingly important, but they are not always successful. Ineffective institutions such as the United Nations Industrial Development Organization or the Organization of African Unity exist alongside effectual ones such as the Montreal Protocol on Substances that Deplete the Ozone Layer and the European Union. In recent years, we have gained insight into what makes some institutions more capable than others—how such institutions best promote cooperation among states and what mechanics of bargaining they use. But our knowledge is incomplete, and as the world moves toward new forms of global regulation and governance, the increasing impact of international institutions has raised new questions about how these institutions themselves are governed.

From Robert O. Keohane, "International Institutions: Can Interdependence Work?" *Foreign Policy*, issue #110 (Spring 1998), pp. 82–94. © 1998 by the Carnegie Endowment for International Peace. Reprinted with permission. www.foreignpolicy.com

THEORY AND REALITY, 1919–89

Academic "scribblers" did not always have to pay much attention to international institutions. The 1919 Versailles Treaty constituted an attempt to construct an institution for multilateral diplomacy—the League of Nations. But the rejection of the League Covenant by the U.S. Senate ensured that until World War II the most important negotiations in world politics—from the secret German-Russian deals of the 1920s to the 1938 Munich conference—took place on an ad hoc basis. Only after the United Nations was founded in 1945, with strong support from the United States and a multiplicity of specialized agencies performing different tasks, did international institutions begin to command substantial international attention. . . .

[After 1945], however, even the most powerful states [came to] rely increasingly on international institutions. . . . From the late 1960s onward, the Treaty on the Non-Proliferation of Nuclear Weapons was the chief vehicle for efforts to prevent the dangerous spread of nuclear weapons. NATO was not only the most successful multilateral alliance in history but also the most highly institutionalized, with a secretary-general, a permanent staff, and elaborate rules governing relations among members. From its founding in 1947 through the Uruguay Round that concluded in 1993, the General Agreement on Tariffs and Trade (GATT) presided over a series of trade rounds that have reduced import tariffs among industrialized countries by up to 90 percent, boosting international trade. After a shaky start in the 1940s, the IMF had—by the 1960s—become the centerpiece of efforts by the major capitalist democracies to regulate their monetary affairs. When that function atrophied with the onset of flexible exchange rates in the 1970s, it became their leading agent for financing and promoting economic development in Africa, Asia, and Latin America. The sheer number of inter-governmental organizations also rose dramatically— from about 30 in 1910 to 70 in 1940 to more than 1,000 by 1981.

The exchange rate and oil crises of the early 1970s helped bring perceptions in line with reality. Suddenly, both top policymakers and academic observers in the United States realized that global issues required systematic policy coordination and that such coordination required institutions. In 1974, then secretary of state Henry Kissinger, who had paid little attention to international institutions, helped establish the International Energy Agency to enable Western countries to deal cooperatively with the threat of future oil embargoes like the 1973 OPEC embargo of the Netherlands and United States. And the Ford administration sought to construct a new international monetary regime based on flexible rather than pegged exchange rates. Confronted with complex interdependence and the efforts of states to manage it, political scientists began to redefine the study of international institutions, broadening it to encompass what they called "international regimes"—structures of rules and norms that could be more or less informal. The international trade regime, for example, did not have strong formal rules or integrated, centralized management; rather, it provided a set of interlocking institutions, including regular meetings of the GATT contracting parties, formal dispute settlement arrangements, and delegation of technical tasks to a secretariat, which gradually developed a body of case law and practice. . . .

In the 1980s, research on international regimes moved from attempts to describe the phenomena of interdependence and international regimes to closer analysis of the conditions under which countries cooperate. How does cooperation occur among sovereign states and how do international institutions affect it? From the standpoint of political realism, both the reliance placed by states on certain international institutions and the explosion in their numbers were puzzling. Why should international institutions exist at all in a world dominated by sovereign states? This question seemed unanswerable if institutions were seen as opposed to, or above, the state but not if they were viewed as devices to help states accomplish their objectives.

The new research on international institutions broke decisively with legalism— the view that law can be effective regardless of political conditions—as well as with the idealism associated with the field's origins. Instead, scholars adopted the assumptions of realism, accepting that relative state power and competing interests were key factors in world politics, but at the same time drawing new conclusions about the influence of institutions on the process. Institutions create the capability for states to cooperate in mutually beneficial ways by reducing the costs of making and enforcing agreements—what economists refer to as "transaction costs." They rarely engage in centralized enforcement of agreements, but they do reinforce practices of reciprocity, which provide incentives for governments to keep their own commitments to ensure that others do so as well. Even powerful states have an interest, most of the time, in following the rules of well-established international institutions, since general conformity to rules makes the behavior of other states more predictable.

This scholarship drew heavily on the twin concepts of uncertainty and credibility. Theorists increasingly recognized that the preferences of states amount to "private information"—that absent full transparency, states are uncertain about what their partners and rivals value at any given time. They naturally respond to uncertainty by being less willing to enter into agreements, since they are unsure how their partners will later interpret the terms of such agreements. International institutions can reduce this uncertainty by promoting negotiations in which transparency is encouraged; by dealing with a series of issues over many years and under similar rules, thus encouraging honesty in order to preserve future reputation; and by systematically monitoring the compliance of governments with their commitments.

Even if a government genuinely desires an international agreement, it may be unable to persuade its partners that it will, in the future, be willing and able to implement it. Successful international negotiations may therefore require changes in domestic institutions. For instance, without "fast-track" authority on trade, the United States' negotiating partners have no assurance that Congress will refrain from adding new provisions to trade agreements as a condition for their ratification. Hence, other states are reluctant to enter into trade negotiations with the United States since they may be confronted, at the end of tortuous negotiations, with a redesigned agreement less favorable to them than the draft they initialed.

By the same token, without fast-track authority, no promise by the U.S. government to abide by negotiated terms has much credibility, due to the president's lack of control over Congress.

In short, this new school of thought argued that, rather than imposing themselves on states, international institutions should respond to the demand by states for cooperative ways to fulfill their own purposes. By reducing uncertainty and the costs of making and enforcing agreements, international institutions help states achieve collective gains.

YESTERDAY'S CONTROVERSIES: 1989–95

This new institutionalism was not without its critics, who focused their attacks on three perceived shortcomings: First, they claimed that international institutions are fundamentally insignificant since states wield the only real power in world politics. They emphasized the weakness of efforts by the UN or League of Nations to achieve collective security against aggression by great powers, and they pointed to the dominant role of major contributors in international economic organizations. Hence, any effects of these international institutions were attributed more to the efforts of their great power backers than to the institutions themselves.

This argument was overstated. Of course, great powers such as the United States exercise enormous influence within international institutions. But the policies that emerge from these institutions are different from those that the United States would have adopted unilaterally. . . . Where agreement by many states is necessary for policy to be effective, even the United States finds it useful to compromise on substance to obtain the institutional seal of approval. Therefore, the decision-making procedures and general rules of international institutions matter. They affect both the substance of policy and the degree to which other states accept it.

The second counterargument focused on "anarchy": the absence of a world government or effective international legal system to which victims of injustice can appeal. As a result of anarchy, critics argued, states prefer relative gains (i.e., doing better than other states) to absolute gains. They seek to protect their power and status and will resist even mutually beneficial cooperation if their partners are likely to benefit more than they are. For instance, throughout the American-Soviet arms race, both sides focused on their relative positions—who was ahead or threatening to gain a decisive advantage—rather than on their own levels of armaments. Similar dynamics appear on certain economic issues, such as the fierce Euro-American competition (i.e., Airbus Industrie versus Boeing) in the production of large passenger jets.

Scholarly disputes about the "relative gains question" were intense but short-lived. It turned out that the question needed to be reframed: not, "do states seek relative or absolute gains?" but "under what conditions do they forego even mutually beneficial cooperation to preserve their relative power and status?" When there are only two major players, and one side's gains may decisively change power relationships, relative gains loom large: in arms races, for example, or monopolistic competition (as between Airbus and Boeing). Most issues of potential cooperation, however, from trade liberalization to climate change, involve multilateral negotiations that make relative gains hard to calculate and entail little risk of decisive power shifts for one side over another. Therefore, states can be expected most of the time to seek to enhance their own welfare without being worried that others will also make advances. So the relative gains argument merely highlights the difficulties of cooperation where there is tough bilateral competition; it does not by any means undermine prospects for cooperation in general.

The third objection to theories of cooperation was less radical but more enduring. Theorists of cooperation had recognized that cooperation is not harmonious: it emerges out of discord and takes place through tough bargaining. Nevertheless, they claimed that the potential joint gains from such cooperation explained the dramatic increases in the number and scope of cooperative multilateral institutions. Critics pointed out, however, that bargaining problems could produce obstacles to achieving joint gains. For instance, whether the Kyoto Protocol will lead to a global agreement is questionable in part because developing countries refused to accept binding limits on their emissions and the U.S. Senate declared its unwillingness to ratify any agreement not containing such commitments by developing countries. Both sides staked out tough bargaining positions, hindering efforts at credible compromise. As a result of these bargaining problems, the fact that possible deals could produce joint gains does not assure that cooperative solutions will be reached. The tactics of political actors and the information they have available about one another are both key aspects of a process that does not necessarily lead to cooperation. Institutions may help provide "focal points," on which competing actors may agree, but new issues often lack such institutions. In this case, both the pace and the extent of cooperation become more problematic.

TODAY'S DEBATES

The general problem of bargaining raises specific issues about how institutions affect international negotiations, which always involve a mixture of discord and potential cooperation. Thinking about bargaining leads to concerns about subjectivity, since bargaining depends so heavily on the beliefs of the parties involved. And the most fundamental question scholars wish to answer concerns effectiveness: What structures, processes, and practices make international institutions more or less capable of affecting policies—and outcomes—in desired ways?

The impact of institutional arrangements on bargaining remains puzzling. We understand from observation, from game theory, and from explorations of bargaining in a variety of contexts that outcomes depend on more than the resources available to the actors or the pay-offs they receive. Institutions affect bargaining patterns in complex and nuanced ways. Who, for example, has authority over the agenda? In the 1980s, Jacques Delors used his authority as head of the European Commission to structure the agenda of the European Community, thus leading to the Single European Act and the Maastricht Treaty. What voting or consensus arrangements are used and who interprets ambiguities? At the Kyoto Conference, agreement on a rule of "consensus" did not prevent the conference chair from ignoring objections as he gaveled through provision after provision in the final session. Can disgruntled participants block implementation of formally ratified agreements? In the GATT, until 1993, losers could prevent the findings of dispute resolution panels from being implemented; but in the WTO, panel recommendations take effect unless there is a consensus not to implement them. Asking such questions systematically about international institutions may well yield significant new insights in future years.

Institutional maneuvers take place within a larger ideological context that helps define which purposes such institutions pursue and which practices they find acceptable. The Mandates System of the League of Nations depended in part on specific institutional arrangements, but more fundamental was the shared understanding that continued European rule over non-European peoples was acceptable. No system of rule by Europeans over non-Europeans could remain legitimate after the collapse of that consensus during the 15 years following World War II. . . .

The procedures and rules of international institutions create informational structures. They determine what principles are acceptable as the basis for reducing conflicts and whether governmental actions are legitimate or illegitimate. Consequently, they help shape actors' expectations. For instance, trade conflicts are increasingly ritualized in a process of protesting in the WTO—promising tough action on behalf of one's own industries, engaging in quasi-judicial dispute resolution procedures, claiming victory if possible, or complaining about defeat when necessary. There is much sound and fury, but regularly institutionalized processes usually relegate conflict to the realm of dramatic expression. Institutions thereby create differentiated information. "Insiders" can interpret the language directed toward "outsiders" and use their own understandings to interpret, or manipulate, others' beliefs.

Finally, students of international institutions continue to try to understand why some institutions are so much more effective than others. Variation in the coherence of institutional policy or members' conformity with institutional rules is partially accounted for by the degree of common interests and the distribution of power among members. Institutions whose members share social values and have similar political systems—such as NATO or the European Union—are likely to be stronger than those such as the Organization for Security and Cooperation in Europe or the Association of South East Asian Nations, whose more diverse membership does not necessarily have the same kind of deep common interests. Additionally, the character of domestic politics, . . . has a substantial impact on international institutions. The distribution of power is also important. Institutions dominated by a small number of members—for example, the IMF, with its weighted voting system—can typically take more decisive action than those where influence is more widely diffused, such as the UN General Assembly.

OVERCOMING THE DEMOCRATIC DEFICIT

Even as scholars pursue these areas of inquiry, they are in danger of overlooking a major normative issue: the "democratic deficit" that exists in many of the world's most important international institutions. As illustrated most recently by the far-reaching interventions of the IMF in East Asia, the globalization of the world economy and the expanding role of international institutions are creating a powerful form of global regulation. Major international institutions are increasingly laying down rules and guidelines that governments, if they wish to attract foreign investment and generate growth, must follow. But these international institutions are managed by technocrats and supervised by high governmental officials. That is, they are run by élites. Only in the most attenuated sense is democratic control exercised over major international organizations. Key negotiations in the WTO are made in closed sessions. The IMF negotiates in secret with potential borrowers, and it has only begun in the last few months to provide the conditions it imposes on recipients. . . .

Admittedly, democracy does not always work well. American politicians regularly engage in diatribes against international institutions, playing on the dismay of a vocal segment of their electorates at the excessive number of foreigners in the United Nations. More seriously, an argument can be made that the IMF, like central banks, can only be effective if it is insulated from direct democratic control. Ever since 1787, however, practitioners and theorists have explored how authoritative decision making can be combined with accountability to publics and indirect democratic control. The U.S. Constitution is based on such a theory—the idea that popular sovereignty, though essential, is best exercised indirectly, through rather elaborate institutions. An issue that scholars should now explore is how to devise international institutions that are not only competent and effective but also accountable, at least ultimately, to democratic publics.

One possible response is to say that all is well, since international institutions are responsible to governments—which, in turn, are accountable in democracies to their own people. International regulation simply adds another link to the chain of delegation. But long chains of delegation, in which the public affects action only at several removes, reduce actual public authority. If the terms of multilateral cooperation are to reflect the interests of broader democratic publics rather than just those of narrow élites, traditional patterns of delegation will have to be supplemented by other means of ensuring greater accountability to public opinion.

One promising approach would be to seek to invigorate transnational society in the form of networks among individuals and nongovernmental organizations. The growth of such networks—of scientists, professionals in various fields, and human rights and environmental activists—has been aided greatly by the fax machine and the Internet and by institutional arrangements that incorporate these networks into decision making. For example, natural and social scientists developed the scientific consensus underlying the Kyoto Protocol through the Intergovernmental Panel on Climate Change (IPCC) whose scientific work was organized by scientists who did not have to answer to any governments. The Kyoto Protocol was negotiated, but governments opposed to effective action on climate change could not hope to renegotiate the scientific guidelines set by the IPCC. . . .

Therefore, the future accountability of international institutions to their publics may rest only partly on delegation through formal democratic institutions. Its other pillar may be voluntary pluralism under conditions of maximum transparency. International policies may increasingly be monitored by loose groupings of scientists or other professionals, or by issue advocacy networks such as Amnesty International and Greenpeace, whose members, scattered around the world, will be linked even more closely by modern information technology. Accountability will be enhanced not only by chains of official responsibility, but by the requirement of transparency. Official actions, negotiated among state representatives in international organizations, will be subjected to scrutiny by transnational networks.

Such transparency, however, represents nongovernmental organizations and networks more than ordinary people, who may be as excluded from élite networks as they are from government circles. That is, transnational civil society may be a necessary but insufficient condition for democratic accountability. Democracies should insist that, wherever feasible, international organizations maintain sufficient transparency for transnational networks of advocacy groups, domestic legislators, and democratic publics to evaluate their actions. But proponents of democratic accountability should also seek counterparts to the mechanisms of control embedded in national democratic institutions. Governors of the Federal Reserve Board are, after all, nominated by the president and confirmed by the Senate, even if they exercise great authority during their terms of office. If Madison, Hamilton, and Jay could invent indirect mechanisms of popular control in the *Federalist Papers* two centuries ago, it should not be beyond our competence to devise comparable mechanisms at the global level in the twenty-first century.

Exercises for the Mitigation of Anarchy

Apply what you learned in this chapter by using the online resources on MyPoliSciKit (www.mypoliscikit.com).

    Practice Tests

    Videos:
- "Conventional Forces in Europe"
- "International Diplomacy at the United Nations"

    Simulation: "Using Theory: You Are the New Prime Minister"

Reading Guides:
- Kenneth A. Oye, "The Conditions for Cooperation in World Politics"
- Robert Jervis, "Offense, Defense, and the Security Dilemma"
- Michael W. Doyle, "Kant, Liberal Legacies, and Foreign Affairs"
- Stephen M. Walt, "Alliances: Balancing and Bandwagoning"
- Hans J. Morgenthau, "The Future of Diplomacy"
- Stanley Hoffmann, "The Uses and Limits of International Law"
- Robert O. Keohane, "International Institutions: Can Interdependence Work?"

2 The Uses of Force

With the end of both the Cold War and the Soviet Union, the nightmare of an all-out nuclear war between the superpowers that so dominated world politics since 1945 ended. It is not likely that a new danger of the same magnitude will arise, at least for the economically developed democracies of North America, Japan, and Western Europe. Indeed, for the first time since the formation of these nation-states, the citizens of these countries may live out their lives without worrying that they or their children will have to die or kill in a major war.

This fact, however, does not mean that we should no longer be concerned with how states use force. Even if the optimistic prediction is correct, we still need to understand previous eras in which warfare played such a large role. We cannot understand the course of the Cold War without studying the role nuclear weapons played in it. Moreover, an understanding of the role that nuclear weapons played in that era is central for determining the role they will play in this era. This is true for no other reason than that national leaders' views of the present are heavily influenced by their reading of the past. Furthermore, even within the developed rich world, where a great-power war is unlikely, military power still remains useful to the conduct of statecraft. If it were not, these states would have already disarmed. They have not because the use of force must always be available, even if it is not always necessary. For much of the rest of the world, unfortunately, circumstances are different. Threats to the security of states remain real, and war among them has not been abolished. For all states, then—those likely to enjoy peace and those that will have to endure war—what has changed is not so much the utility of military power as how it can be usefully employed. Most obviously, the attacks of September 11, 2001, and the subsequent American "global war on terror" have shown the potency of an old form of force that has been given new life by modern technologies. People have been killed by terrorism from time immemorial, but now attacks can do much greater damage, not only by killing more people but by disrupting entire societies. The new forms of force call for new understandings and new countermeasures, many of them subject to fierce debate.

THE POLITICAL USES OF FORCE

The use of force almost always represents the partial failure of a policy. The exception, of course, is the case in which fighting is valued for its own sake—when it is believed that war brings out heroic values and purifies individuals and cultures, or when fighting is seen as entertainment. Changes in states' values and the increased destructiveness of war, however, have led state actors to view armed conflicts as the last resort. Threats are a second choice to diplomatic maneuvers; actual use of force follows only if the threats fail.

Because of the high costs of violence, its use is tempered by restraints and bargaining. As bloody as most wars are, they could always be bloodier. Brutalities are limited in part by the combatants' shared interests, if not by their scruples. Even if two states differ enough to go to war, it does not necessarily follow that they have no common interests. Only when everything that is good for one side is bad for the other (a "zero-sum" situation) do the opponents gain nothing by bargaining. In most cases, however, certain outcomes are clearly bad for both sides; therefore, even though they are at war, each side shares an interest in avoiding them.

The shared nature of the interest, as Thomas C. Schelling points out, stems from the fact that it is easier to destroy than to create. Force can be used to take— or to bargain. If you can take what you want, you do not need your adversary's cooperation and do not have to bargain with him. A country may use force to seize disputed territory just as a robber may kill you to get your wallet. Most of the things people and nations want, however, cannot be taken in this way. A nation not only wants to take territory, it wants to govern and exploit it. A nation may want others to stop menacing it; it may even want others to adopt its values. Brute force alone cannot achieve these goals. A nation that wants to stop others from menacing it may not want to fight them in order to remove the threat. A nation that wants others to adopt its values cannot impose them solely through conquest. Where the cooperation of an adversary is needed, bargaining will ensue. The robber does not need the cooperation of his victim if he kills him to get his wallet. However, the thief who must obtain the combination of a safe from the hostage who carries it only in his head does need such cooperation. The thief may use force to demonstrate that the hostage can lose his life if he does not surrender the combination. But the thief no more wishes to kill the hostage and lose the combination than the hostage wishes to die. The hostage may trade the combination for his life. The bargain may be unequal or unfair, but it is still a bargain.

The mutual avoidance of certain outcomes explains why past wars have not been as bloody as they could have been; but an analysis of why wars were not more destructive should not blind us to the factors that made them as destructive as they were. By 1914, for example, all the statesmen of Europe believed a war inevitable, and all were ready to exploit it. None, however, imagined the staggering losses that their respective nations would inflict and bear in the field, or the extent to which noncombatants would be attacked. Yet by the second year of World War I, the same men were accepting the deaths of hundreds or thousands for a few yards' gain in the front lines; and by the end of the war, they were planning large-scale aerial gas attacks on each other's major cities. The German bombing of Guernica in 1937 and Rotterdam in 1940 shocked statesmen and citizens alike, but by the middle of World War II both were accepting as routine the total destruction of German and Japanese cities.

Three factors largely account for the increasing destructiveness of the wars of the last two centuries. First was the steady technological improvement in weaponry. Weapons such as machine guns, submarines, poison gas, and aircraft made it feasible to maim or kill large numbers of people quickly. The rapidity of destruction that is possible with nuclear weapons is only the most recent, albeit biggest, advance. Second was the growth in the capacity, and thus the need, of states to field ever larger numbers of forces. As states became more industrialized and centralized, they acquired the wealth and developed the administrative apparatus to move men on a grand scale. Concomitant with the increase in military potential was the necessity to realize this potential. As soon as one state expanded the forces at its disposal, all other states had to follow suit. Thus, when Prussia instituted universal conscription and the general-staff system, and then demonstrated their advantages with swift victories over Austria and France, the rest of the Continent quickly adopted its methods. An increase in the potential power of states led to an increase in their standing power.

Third was the gradual "democratization" of war: the expansion of the battlefield and hence the indiscriminate mass killing of noncombatants. Everyone, citizens and soldiers alike, began fighting and dying. World War II, with its extensive use of airpower, marked not the debut but the zenith of this mass killing. As war changed from the province of the princes to the burden of the masses, the distinction between combatants and noncombatants increasingly blurred. Most wars of the eighteenth century did impinge upon the citizenry, but mainly financially; few civilians died in them. With the widespread use of conscription in the nineteenth and twentieth centuries, however, more citizens became soldiers. With the advent of industrialization and with the increasing division of labor, the citizens who did not fight remained behind to produce weapons. Now, a nation not only had to conquer its enemy's armies, but also had to destroy the industrial plant that supplied their weapons. Gradually, the total energy of a country was diverted into waging wars, and as the costs of wars increased, so did the justifications given for them and the benefits claimed to derive from them. The greater the sacrifices asked, the larger the victory spoils demanded. Because wars became literally wars of, by, and for the people, governments depended increasingly on the support of their citizens. As wars became democratized, so too did they become popularized and propagandized.

The readings in the first section explore how force has been and can be used in a changing world. Robert J. Art notes that the threat and use of force has four distinct functions and shows how their relative importance varies from one situation to another. Thomas C. Schelling examines the differences between the uses of conventional and nuclear weapons and the links between force and foreign policy goals. Terrorism has never been absent from world politics, and Bruce Hoffman discusses its changing forms and purposes, and distinguishes terrorism from guerrilla warfare and criminal activity.

THE POLITICAL UTILITY OF FORCE TODAY

It is a mistake to examine the possible use of force in a vacuum. As Clausewitz stressed, force is an instrument for reaching political goals. Its utility, as well as the likelihood of its use, depends not only on the costs and perceived benefits of fighting but on the general political context, the values statesmen and citizens hold, the alternative policy instruments available, and the objectives sought.

Realism, represented in many of the readings in Part 1, stresses the importance of military power. The three readings in this section demonstrate the continuing relevance of force to political outcomes. Robert J. Art argues that military power is fungible—that is, it can be used to reach a number of goals, even for a state such as the United States that lacks strong state enemies. Robert A. Pape examines the political logic of suicide terrorism, surveys the universe of cases of this unfortunate phenomenon from 1980 to 2001, and argues that "it pays" because it has forced liberal democracies to compromise. Mary Kaldor shows that a new form of war took shape in the last decades of the twentieth century and that the wars of this type center on identity politics (i.e., which group will control a state) rather than the traditional geopolitical and ideological reasons for war. Wars within states, not among states, is the new reality of war.

NUCLEAR DETERRENCE AND NUCLEAR SPREAD

During the Cold War, nuclear weapons, it was argued, helped make competition between the two superpowers safer than it would otherwise have been. That is, nuclear weapons made the two superpowers scared, not safe, and this restrained them. Each had to worry that if it pushed the other too far, matters could get out of hand and escalate to nuclear war. Each learned, especially after the Cuban missile crisis of 1962, not to push the other to the point where it faced the choice of upping the ante and risking loss of control, or backing down and risking humiliation. Rules of the road between the two superpowers gradually developed, and their subsequent competition proved safer in the last 28 years of the Cold War than it had been in the first 15.

How relevant for today is the superpower experience with nuclear weapons? Will states that experience intense political conflicts with one another be deterred from pushing one another too far? Or will they be less restrained than were the superpowers and find themselves in the horror of escalating to the use of nuclear weapons? How valid a model is the U.S.–Soviet experience for dyadic conflicts today? In 1980 Kenneth N. Waltz argued that the logic of nuclear deterrence will apply to new nuclear states just as it did for the superpowers during the Cold War. Mutual possession of nuclear weapons by two hostile states will cause both of them to restrain their ambitions and rein in their military. A test of the validity of the Waltz argument may well occur in the next few years. What will happen if Iran acquires nuclear weapons? Will Iran become a more adventuresome and aggressive state? Will Iran and Israel come to blows? Will an American nuclear umbrella extended over the Arab states of the Middle East operate in the same ways that the U.S. nuclear umbrella over Western Europe and Japan operated vis-á-vis the Soviet Union during the Cold War? Henry Sokolski argues that a nuclear Iran will be a more dangerous Iran. Barry R. Posen discusses the dilemmas posed by Iran's pursuit of nuclear capability, with particular attention to how Iranian behavior might change and how the United States and states in the region might respond.

THE POLITICAL US
OF FORCE

The Four Functions of Force

ROBERT J. ART

In view of what is likely to be before us, it is vital to think carefully and precisely about the uses and limits of military power. That is the purpose of this essay. It is intended as a backdrop for policy debates, not a prescription of specific policies. It consciously eschews elaborate detail on the requisite military forces for scenarios *a . . . n* and focuses instead on what military power has and has not done, can and cannot do. Every model of how the world works has policy implications. But not every policy is based on a clear view of how the world works. What, then, are the uses to which military power can be put? How have nuclear weapons affected these uses? And what is the future of force in a world of nuclear parity and increasing economic interdependence?

WHAT ARE THE USES OF FORCE?

The goals that states pursue range widely and vary considerably from case to case. Military power is more useful for realizing some goals than others, though it is generally considered of some use by most states for all of the goals that they hold. If we attempt, however, to be descriptively accurate, to enumerate all of the purposes for which states use force, we shall simply end up with a bewildering list. Descriptive accuracy is not a virtue *per se* for analysis. In fact, descriptive accuracy is generally bought at the cost of analytical utility. (A concept that is descriptively accurate is usually analytically useless.) Therefore, rather than compile an exhaustive list of such purposes, I have selected four categories that themselves analytically exhaust the functions that force can serve: defense, deterrence, compellence, and "swaggering."

From "To What Ends Military Power" by Robert J. Art, in *International Security*, Vol. 4 (Spring 1980), pp. 4–35. Portions of the text and the footnotes have been omitted.

all four functions are necessarily well or equally served by a given military ture. In fact, usually only the great powers have the wherewithal to develop ilitary forces that can serve more than two functions at once. Even then, this is achieved only vis-à-vis smaller powers, not vis-à-vis the other great ones. The measure of the capabilities of a state's military forces must be made relative to those of another state, not with reference to some absolute scale. A state that can compel another state can also defend against it and usually deter it. A state that can defend against another state cannot thereby automatically deter or compel it. A state can deter another state without having the ability to either defend against or compel it. A state that can swagger vis-à-vis another may or may not be able to perform any of the other three functions relative to it. Where feasible, defense is the goal that all states aim for first. If defense is not possible, deterrence is generally the next priority. Swaggering is the function most difficult to pin down analytically; deterrence, the one whose achievement is the most difficult to demonstrate; compellence, the easiest to demonstrate but among the hardest to achieve. The following discussion develops these points more fully.

The *defensive* use of force is the deployment of military power so as to be able to do two things—to ward off an attack and to minimize damage to oneself if attacked. For defensive purposes, a state will direct its forces against those of a potential or actual attacker, but not against his unarmed population. For defensive purposes, a state can deploy its forces in place prior to an attack, use them after an attack has occurred to repel it, or strike first if it believes that an attack upon it is imminent or inevitable. The defensive use of force can thus involve both peaceful and physical employment and both repellent (second) strikes and offensive (first) strikes. If a state strikes first when it believes an attack upon it is imminent, it is launching a preemptive blow. If it strikes first when it believes an attack is inevitable but not momentary, it is launching a preventive blow. Preemptive and preventive blows are undertaken when a state calculates, first, that others plan to attack it and, second, that to delay in striking offensively is against its interests. A state preempts in order to wrest the advantage of the first strike from an opponent. A state launches a preventive attack because it believes that others will attack it when the balance of forces turns in their favor and therefore attacks while the balance of forces is in its favor. In both cases it is better to strike first than to be struck first. The major distinction between preemption and prevention is the calculation about when an opponent's attack will occur. For preemption, it is a matter of hours, days, or even a few weeks at the most; for prevention, months or even a few years. In the case of preemption, the state has almost no control over the timing of its attack; in the case of prevention, the state can in a more leisurely way contemplate the timing of its attack. For both cases, it is the belief in the certainty of war that governs the offensive, defensive attack. For both cases, the maxim, "the best defense is a good offense," makes good sense.

The *deterrent* use of force is the deployment of military power so as to be able to prevent an adversary from doing something that one does not want him to do and that he might otherwise be tempted to do by threatening him with unacceptable punishment if he does it. Deterrence is thus the threat of retaliation. Its purpose is to prevent something undesirable from happening. The threat of punishment is directed at the adversary's population and/or industrial infrastructure. The effectiveness of the threat depends upon a state's ability to convince a potential adversary that it has both the will and power to punish him severely if he undertakes the undesirable action in question. Deterrence therefore employs force peacefully. It is the threat to resort to force in order to punish that is the essence of deterrence. If the threat has to be carried out, deterrence by definition has failed. A deterrent threat is made precisely with the intent that it will not have to be carried out. Threats are made to prevent actions from being undertaken. If the threat has to be implemented, the action has already been undertaken. Hence deterrence can be judged successful only if the retaliatory threats have not been implemented.

Deterrence and defense are alike in that both are intended to protect the state or its closest allies from physical attacks. The purpose of both is dissuasion—persuading others *not* to undertake actions harmful to oneself. The defensive use of force dissuades by convincing an adversary that he cannot conquer one's military forces. The deterrent use of force dissuades by convincing the adversary that his population and territory will suffer terrible damage if he initiates the undesirable action. Defense dissuades by presenting an unvanquishable military force. Deterrence dissuades by presenting the certainty of retaliatory devastation.

Defense is possible without deterrence, and deterrence is possible without defense. A state can have the military wherewithal to repel an invasion without also being able to threaten devastation to the invader's population or territory. Similarly, a state can have the wherewithal credibly to threaten an adversary with such devastation and yet be unable to repel his invading force. Defense, therefore, does not necessarily buy deterrence, nor deterrence defense. A state that can defend itself from attack, moreover, will have little need to develop the wherewithal to deter. If physical attacks can be repelled or if the damage from them drastically minimized, the incentive to develop a retaliatory capability is low. A state that cannot defend itself, however, will try to develop an effective deterrent if that be possible. No state will leave its population and territory open to attack if it has the means to redress the situation. Whether a given state can defend or deter or do both vis-à-vis another depends upon two factors: (1) the quantitative balance of forces between it and its adversary; and (2) the qualitative balance of forces, that is, whether the extant military technology favors the offense or the defense. These two factors are situation-specific and therefore require careful analysis of the case at hand.

The *compellent* use of force is the deployment of military power so as to be able either to stop an adversary from doing something that he has already undertaken or to get him to do something that he has not yet undertaken. Compellence, in Schelling's words, "involves initiating an action . . . that can cease, or become harmless, only if the opponent responds." Compellence can employ force either physically or peacefully. A state can start actually harming another with physical destruction until the latter abides by the former's wishes. Or, a state can take actions against another that do not cause physical harm but that require the latter to pay some type of significant price until it changes its behavior. America's bombing of North Vietnam in early 1965 was an example of physical compellence; Tirpitz's building of a German fleet aimed against England's in the two decades before World War I, an example of peaceful compellence. In the first case, the United States started bombing North Vietnam in order to compel it to stop assisting the Vietcong forces in South Vietnam. In the latter case, Germany built a battlefleet that in an engagement threatened to cripple England's in order to compel her to make a general political settlement advantageous to Germany. In both cases, one state initiated some type of action against another precisely so as to be able to stop it, to bargain it away for the appropriate response from the "put upon" state.

The distinction between compellence and deterrence is one between the active and passive use of force. The success of a deterrent threat is measured by its not having to be used. The success of a compellent action is measured by how closely and quickly the adversary conforms to one's stipulated wishes. In the case of successful deterrence, one is trying to demonstrate a negative, to show why something did not happen. It can never be clear whether one's actions were crucial to, or irrelevant to, why another state chose *not* to do something. In the case of successful compellence, the clear sequence of actions and reactions lends a compelling plausibility to the centrality of one's actions. Figure 1 illustrates the distinction. In successful compellence, state B can claim that its pressure deflected state A from its course of action. In successful deterrence, state B has no change in state A's behavior to point to, but instead must resort to claiming that its threats were responsible for the continuity in A's behavior. State A may have changed its behavior for reasons other than state B's compellent action. State A may have continued with its same behavior for reasons other than state B's deterrent threat. "Proving" the

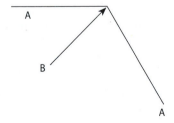

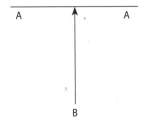

COMPELLENCE

(1) A is doing something that B cannot tolerate
(2) B initiates action against A in order to get him to stop his intolerable actions
(3) A stops his intolerable actions and B stops his (or both cease simultaneously)

DETERRENCE

(1) A is presently not doing anything that B finds intolerable
(2) B tells A that if A changes his behavior and does something intolerable, B will punish him
(3) A continues not to do anything B finds intolerable

FIGURE 1 ■

importance of B's influence on A for either case is not easy, but it is more plausible to claim that B influenced A when there is a change in A's behavior than when there is not. Explaining why something did not happen is more difficult than explaining why something did.

Compellence may be easier to demonstrate than deterrence, but it is harder to achieve. Schelling argues that compellent actions tend to be vaguer in their objectives than deterrent threats and for that reason more difficult to attain. If an adversary has a hard time understanding what it is that one wished him to do, his compliance with one's wishes is made more difficult. There is, however, no inherent reason why a compellent action must be vaguer than a deterrent threat with regard to how clearly the adversary understands what is wanted from him. "Do not attack me" is not any clearer in its ultimate meaning than "stop attacking my friend." A state can be as confused or as clear about what it wishes to prevent as it can be about what it wishes to stop. The clarity, or lack of it, of the objectives of compellent actions and deterrent threats does not vary according to whether the given action is compellent or deterrent in nature, but rather according to a welter of particularities associated with the given action. Some objectives, for example, are inherently clearer and hence easier to perceive than others. Some statesmen communicate more clearly than others. Some states have more power to bring to bear for a given objective than others. It is the specifics of a given situation, not any intrinsic difference between compellence and deterrence, that determines the clarity with which an objective is perceived.

We must, therefore, look elsewhere for the reason as to why compellence is comparatively harder to achieve than deterrence. It lies, not in what one asks another to do, but in *how* one asks. With deterrence, state B asks something of state A in this fashion: "Do not take action *X;* for if you do, I will bash you over the head with this club." With compellence, state B asks something of state A in this fashion: "I am now going to bash you over the head with this club and will continue to do so until you do what I want." In the former case, state A can easily deny with great plausibility any intention of having planned to take action *X*. In the latter case, state A cannot deny either that it is engaged in a given course of action or that it is being subjected to pressure by state B. If they are to be successful, compellent actions require a state to alter its behavior in a manner quite visible to all in response to an equally visible forceful initiative taken by another state. In contrast to compellent actions, deterrent threats are both easier to appear to have ignored or easier to acquiesce to without great loss of face. In contrast to deterrent threats, compellent actions more directly engage the prestige and the passions of the put-upon state. Less prestige is lost in not doing something than in clearly altering behavior due to pressure from another. In the case of compellence, a state has publicly committed its prestige and resources to a given line of conduct that it is now asked to give up. This is not so for deterrence. Thus, compellence is intrinsically harder to attain than deterrence, not because its objectives are vaguer, but because it demands mere humiliation from the compelled state.

The fourth purpose to which military power can be put is the most difficult to be precise about. *Swaggering* is in part a residual category, the deployment of military power for purposes other than defense, deterrence, or compellence. Force is not aimed directly at dissuading another state from attacking, at repelling attacks, nor at compelling it to do something specific. The objectives for swaggering are more diffuse, ill-defined, and problematic than that. Swaggering almost always involves only the peaceful use of force and is expressed usually in one of two ways: displaying one's military might at military exercises and national demonstrations and buying or building the era's most prestigious weapons. The swagger use of force is the most egoistic: It aims to enhance the national pride of a people or to satisfy the personal ambitions of its ruler. A state or statesman swaggers in order to look and feel more powerful and important, to be taken seriously by others in the councils of international decision making, to enhance the nation's image in the eyes of others. If its image is enhanced, the nation's defense, deterrent, and compellent capabilities may also be enhanced; but swaggering is not undertaken solely or even primarily for these specific purposes. Swaggering is pursued because it offers to bring prestige "on the cheap." Swaggering is pursued because of the fundamental yearning of states and statesmen for respect and prestige. Swaggering is more something to be enjoyed for itself than to be employed for a specific, consciously thought-out end.

And yet, the instrumental role of swaggering cannot be totally discounted because of the fundamental relation between force and foreign policy that it obtains in an anarchic environment. Because there is a connection between the military might that a nation is thought to possess and the success that it achieves in attaining its objectives, the enhancement of a state's stature in the eyes of others can always be justified on *realpolitik* lines. If swaggering causes other states to take one's interests more seriously into account, then the general interests of the state will benefit. Even in its instrumental role, however, swaggering is undertaken less for any given end than for all ends. The swaggering function of military power is thus at one and the same time the most comprehensive and the most diffuse, the most versatile in its effects and the least focused in its immediate aims, the most instrumental in the long run and the least instrumental in the short run, easy to justify on hardheaded grounds and often undertaken on emotional grounds. Swaggering mixes the rational and irrational more than the other three functions of military power and, for that reason, remains both pervasive in international relations and elusive to describe.

Defense, deterrence, compellence, and swaggering—these are the four general purposes for which force can be employed. Discriminating among them analytically, however, is easier than applying them in practice. This is due to two factors. First, we need to know the motives behind an act in order to judge its purpose; but the problem is that motives cannot be readily inferred from actions because several motives can be served by the same action. But neither can one readily infer the motives of a state from what it publicly or officially proclaims them to be. Such statements should not necessarily be taken at face value because of the role that bluff and dissimulation play in statecraft. Such statements are also often concocted with domestic political, not foreign audiences in mind, or else are deliberate exercises in studied ambiguity. Motives are important in order to interpret actions, but neither actions nor words always clearly delineate motives.

It is, moreover, especially difficult to distinguish defensive from compellent actions and deterrent from swaggering ones unless we know the reasons for which they were undertaken. Peaceful defensive preparations often look largely the same as peaceful compellent ones. Defensive attacks are nearly indistinguishable from compellent ones. Is he who attacks first the defender or the compeller? Deterrence and swaggering both involve the acquisition and display of an era's prestigious weapons. Are such weapons acquired to enhance prestige or to dissuade an attack?

Second, to make matters worse, consider the following example. Germany launched an attack upon France and Russia at the end of July 1914 and thereby began World War I. There are two schools of thought as to why Germany did this. One holds that its motives were aggressive—territorial aggrandizement, economic gain, and elevation to the status of a world empire. Another holds that her motives were preventive and hence defensive. She struck first because she feared encirclement, slow strangulation, and then inevitable attack by her two powerful neighbors, foes whom she felt were daily increasing their military might faster than she was. She struck while she had the chance to win.

It is not simple to decide which school is the more nearly correct because both can marshall evidence to build a powerful case. Assume for the moment, though, that the second is closer to the truth. There are then two possibilities to consider: (1) Germany launched an attack because it *was* the case that her foes were planning to attack her ultimately, and Germany had the evidence to prove it; or (2) Germany felt she had reasonable evidence of her foes' *intent* to attack her eventually, but in fact her evidence was wrong because she misperceived their intent from their actions. If the first was the case, then we must ask this question: How responsible was Germany's diplomacy in the fifteen years before 1914, aggressive and blundering as it was, in breeding hostility in her neighbors? Germany attacked in the knowledge that they would eventually have struck her, but if her fifteen-year diplomatic record was a significant factor in causing them to lay these plans, must we conclude that Germany in 1914 was merely acting defensively? Must we confine our judgment about the defensive or aggressive nature of the act to the month or even the year in which it occurred? If not, how many years back in history do we go in order to make a judgment? If the second was the case, then we must ask this question: If Germany attacked in the belief, mistakenly as it turns out, that she would be attacked, must we conclude that Germany was acting defensively? Must we confine our judgment about the defensive or aggressive nature of the act simply to Germany's beliefs about others' intent, without reference to their actual intent?

It is not easy to answer these questions. Fortunately, we do not have to. Asking them is enough because it illustrates that an assessment of the *legitimacy* of a state's motives in using force is integral to the task of determining what its motives are. One cannot, that is, specify motives without at the same time making judgments about their legitimacy. The root cause of this need lies in the nature of state action. In anarchy every state is a valid judge of the legitimacy of its goals because there is no supranational authority to enforce agreed upon rules. Because of the lack of universal standards, we are forced to examine each case within its given context and to make individual judgments about the meaning of the particulars. When individual judgment is exercised, individuals may well differ. Definitive answers are more likely to be the exception rather than the rule.

Where does all of this leave us? Our four categories tell us what are the four possible purposes for which states can employ military power. The attributes of each alert us to the types of evidence for which to search. But because the context of an action is crucial in order to judge its ultimate purpose, these four categories cannot be applied mindlessly and ahistorically. Each state's purpose in using force in a given instance must fall into one of these four categories. We know *a priori* what the possibilities are. Which one it is, is an exercise in judgment, an exercise that depends as much upon the particulars of the given case as it does upon the general features of the given category . . . (see Table 1).

TABLE 1 ■ THE PURPOSES OF FORCE

Type	Purpose	Mode	Targets	Characteristics
Defensive	Fend off attacks and/or reduce damage of an attack	Peaceful and physical	Primarily military	Defensive preparations can have dissuasion value;
			Secondarily industrial	Defensive preparations can look aggressive; First strikes can be taken for defense.
Deterrent	Prevent adversary from initiating an action	Peaceful	Primarily civilian	Threats of retaliation made as not to have to be carried out;
			Tertiarily military	Second strike preparations can be viewed as first strike preparations.
Compellent	Get adversary to stop doing something or start doing something	Peaceful and physical	All three with no clear ranking	Easy to recognize but hard to achieve; Competent actions can be justified on defensive grounds.
Swaggering	Enhance prestige	Peaceful	None	Difficult to describe because of instrumental and irrational nature; Swaggering can be threatening.

The Diplomacy of Violence

THOMAS C. SCHELLING

The usual distinction between diplomacy and force is not merely in the instruments, words or bullets, but in the relation between adversaries—in the interplay of motives and the role of communication, understandings, compromise, and restraint. Diplomacy is bargaining; it seeks outcomes that, though not ideal for either party, are better for both than some of the alternatives. In diplomacy each party somewhat controls what the other wants, and can get more by compromise, exchange, or collaboration than by taking things in his own hands and ignoring the other's wishes. The bargaining can be polite or rude, entail threats as well as offers, assume a status quo or ignore all rights and privileges, and assume mistrust rather than trust. But whether polite or impolite, constructive or aggressive, respectful or vicious, whether it occurs among friends or antagonists and whether or not there is a basis for trust and goodwill, there must be some common interest, if only in the avoidance of mutual damage, and an awareness of the need to make the other party prefer an outcome acceptable to oneself.

With enough military force a country may not need to bargain. Some things a country wants it can take, and some things it has it can keep, by sheer strength, skill, and ingenuity. It can do this *forcibly*, accommodating only to opposing strength, skill, and ingenuity and without trying to appeal to an enemy's wishes. Forcibly a country can repel and expel, penetrate and occupy, seize, exterminate, disarm and disable, confine, deny access, and directly frustrate intrusion or attack. It can, that is, if it has enough strength. "Enough" depends on how much an opponent has.

There is something else, though, that force can do. It is less military, less heroic, less impersonal, and less unilateral; it is uglier, and has received less attention in Western military strategy. In addition to seizing and holding, disarming and confining, penetrating and obstructing, and all that, military force can be used to *hurt*. In addition to taking and protecting things of value it can destroy value. In addition to weakening an enemy militarily it can cause an enemy plain suffering. . . .

From Thomas C. Schelling, *Arms and Influence*, pp. 1–34. Copyright © 1966 by Yale University. Reprinted by permission of Yale University Press. Portions of the text and some footnotes have been omitted.

THE CONTRAST OF BRUTE FORCE WITH COERCION

There is a difference between taking what you want and making someone give it to you, between fending off assault and making someone afraid to assault you, between holding what people are trying to take and making them afraid to take it, between losing what someone can forcibly take and giving it up to avoid risk or damage. It is the difference between defense and deterrence, between brute force and intimidation, between conquest and blackmail, between action and threats. It is the difference between the unilateral, "undiplomatic" recourse to strength, and coercive diplomacy based on the power to hurt.

The contrasts are several. The purely "military" or "undiplomatic" recourse to forcible action is concerned with enemy strength, not enemy interests; the coercive use of the power to hurt, though, is the very exploitation of enemy wants and fears. And brute strength is usually measured relative to enemy strength, the one directly opposing the other, while the power to hurt is typically not reduced by the enemy's power to hurt in return. Opposing strengths may cancel each other, pain and grief do not. The willingness to hurt, the credibility of a threat, and the ability to exploit the power to hurt will indeed depend on how much the adversary can hurt in return but there is little or nothing about an adversary's pain or grief that directly reduces one's own. Two sides cannot both overcome each other with superior strength; they may both be able to hurt each other. With strength they can dispute objects of value; with sheer violence they can destroy them.

And brute force succeeds when it is used, whereas the power to hurt is most successful when held in reserve. It is the *threat* of damage, or of more damage to come, that can make someone yield or comply. It is *latent* violence that can influence someone's choice—violence that can still be withheld or inflicted or that a victim believes can be withheld or inflicted. The threat of pain tries to structure someone's motives, while brute force tries to overcome his strength. Unhappily, the power to hurt is often communicated by some performance of it. Whether it is sheer terroristic violence to induce an irrational response, or cool premeditated violence to persuade somebody that you mean it and may do it again, it is not the pain and damage itself but its influence on somebody's behavior that matters. It is the expectation of *more* violence that gets the wanted behavior, if the power to hurt can get it at all.

To exploit a capacity for hurting and inflicting damage one needs to know what an adversary treasures and what scares him and one needs the adversary to understand what behavior of his will cause the violence to be inflicted and what will cause it to be withheld. The victim has to know what is wanted, and he may have to be assured of what is not wanted. The pain and suffering have to appear *contingent* on his behavior; it is not the threat alone that is effective—the threat of pain or loss if he fails to comply—but the corresponding assurance, possibly an implicit one, that he can avoid the pain or loss if he does comply. The prospect of certain death may stun him, but it gives him no choice.

Coercion by threat of damage also requires that our interests and our opponent's not be absolutely opposed. If his pain were our greatest delight and our satisfaction his great woe, we would just proceed to hurt and to frustrate each other. It is when his pain gives us little or no satisfaction compared with what he can do for us, and the action or inaction that satisfies us costs him less than the pain we can cause, that there is room for coercion. Coercion requires finding a bargain, arranging for him to be better off doing what we want—worse off not . . . doing what we want—when he takes the threatened penalty into account. . . .

This difference between coercion and brute force is as often in the intent as in the instrument. To hunt down Comanches and to exterminate them was brute force; to raid their villages to make them behave was coercive diplomacy, based on the power to hurt. The pain and loss to the Indians might have looked much the same one way as the other; the difference was one of purpose and effect. If Indians were killed because they were in the way, or somebody wanted their land, or the authorities despaired of making them behave and could not confine them and decided to exterminate them, that was pure unilateral force. If *some* Indians were killed to make *other* Indians behave, that was coercive violence—or intended to be, whether or not it was effective. The Germans at Verdun perceived themselves to be chewing up hundreds of thousands of French soldiers in a gruesome "meatgrinder." If the purpose was to eliminate a military obstacle—the French infantryman, viewed as a military "asset" rather than as a warm human being—the offensive at Verdun was a unilateral exercise of military force. If instead the object was to make the loss of young men—not of impersonal "effectives," but of sons, husbands, fathers and the pride of French manhood—so anguishing as to be unendurable, to make surrender a welcome relief and to spoil the foretaste of an Allied victory, then it was an exercise in coercion, in applied violence, intended to offer relief upon accommodation. And of course, since any use of force tends to be brutal, thoughtless, vengeful, or plain obstinate, the motives themselves can be mixed and confused. The fact that heroism and brutality can be either coercive diplomacy or a contest in pure strength does not promise that the distinction will be made, and the strategies enlightened by the distinction, every time some vicious enterprise gets launched. . . .

War appears to be, or threatens to be, not so much a contest of strength as one of endurance, nerve, obstinacy, and pain. It appears to be, and threatens to be, not so much a contest of military strength as a bargaining process—dirty, extortionate, and often quite reluctant bargaining on one side or both—nevertheless a bargaining process.

The difference cannot quite be expressed as one between the *use* of force and the *threat* of force. The actions involved in forcible accomplishment, on the one hand, and in fulfilling a threat, on the other, can be quite different. Sometimes the most effective direct action inflicts enough cost or pain on the enemy to serve as a threat, sometimes not. The United States threatens the Soviet Union with virtual destruction of its society in the event of a surprise attack on the United States; a hundred million deaths are awesome as pure damage, but they are useless in stopping the Soviet attack—especially if the threat is to do it all afterward anyway. So it is worthwhile to keep the concepts distinct—to distinguish forcible action from the threat of pain—recognizing that some actions serve as both a means of forcible accomplishment and a means of inflicting pure damage; some do not. Hostages tend to entail almost pure pain and damage, as do all forms of reprisal after the fact. Some modes of self-defense may exact so little in blood or treasure as to entail negligible violence; and some forcible actions entail so much violence that their threat can be effective by itself.

The power to hurt, though it can usually accomplish nothing directly, is potentially more versatile than a straightforward capacity for forcible accomplishment. By force alone we cannot even lead a horse to water—we have to drag him—much less make him drink. Any affirmative action, any collaboration, almost anything but physical exclusion, expulsion, or extermination, requires that an opponent or a victim do something, even if only to stop or get out. The threat of pain and damage may make him want to do it, and anything he can do is potentially susceptible to inducement. Brute force can only accomplish what requires no collaboration. The principle is illustrated by a technique of unarmed combat: One can disable a man by various stunning, fracturing, or killing blows, but to take him to jail one has to exploit the man's own efforts. "Come-along" holds are those that threaten pain or disablement, giving relief as long as the victim complies, giving him the option of using his own legs to get to jail. . . .

The fact that violence—pure pain and damage—can be used or threatened to coerce and to deter, to intimidate and to blackmail, to demoralize and to paralyze, in a conscious process of dirty bargaining, does not by any means imply that violence is not often wanton and meaningless or, even when purposive, in danger of getting out of hand. Ancient wars were often quite "total" for the loser, the men being put to death, the women sold as slaves, the boys castrated, the cattle slaughtered, and the buildings leveled, for the sake of revenge, justice, personal gain, or merely custom. If an enemy bombs a city, by design or by carelessness, we usually bomb his if we can. In the excitement and fatigue of warfare, revenge is one of the few satisfactions that can be savored. . . . Pure violence, like fire, can be harnessed to a purpose; that does not mean that behind every holocaust is a shrewd intention successfully fulfilled.

But if the occurrence of violence does not always bespeak a shrewd purpose, the absence of pain and destruction is no sign that violence was idle. Violence is most purposive and most successful when it is threatened and not used. Successful threats are those that do not have to be carried out. . . .

THE STRATEGIC ROLE OF PAIN AND DAMAGE

Pure violence, nonmilitary violence, appears most conspicuously in relations between unequal countries, where there is no substantial military challenge and the outcome of military engagement is not in question: Hitler could make his threats contemptuously and brutally against Austria; he could make them, if he wished, in a more refined way against Denmark. It is noteworthy that it was Hitler, not his generals, who used this kind of language; proud military establishments do not like to think of themselves as extortionists. Their favorite job is to deliver victory, to dispose of opposing military force and to leave most of the civilian violence to politics and diplomacy. But if there is no room for doubt how a contest in strength will come out, it may be possible to bypass the military stage altogether and to proceed at once to the coercive bargaining.

A typical confrontation of unequal forces occurs at the *end* of a war, between victor and vanquished. Where Austria was vulnerable before a shot was fired, France was vulnerable after its military shield had collapsed in 1940. Surrender negotiations are the place where the threat of civil violence can come to the fore. Surrender negotiations are often so one-sided, or the potential violence so unmistakable, that bargaining succeeds and the violence remains in reserve. But the fact that most of the actual damage was done during the military stage of the war, prior to victory and defeat, does not mean that violence was idle in the aftermath, only that it was latent and the threat of it successful. . . .

The Russians crushed Budapest in 1956 and cowed Poland and other neighboring countries. There was a lag of ten years between military victory and this show of violence, but the principle was the one [just] explained. . . . Military victory is often the prelude to violence, not the end of it, and the fact that successful violence is usually held in reserve should not deceive us about the role it plays.

What about pure violence during war itself, the infliction of pain and suffering as a military technique? Is the threat of pain involved only in the political use of victory, or is it a decisive technique of war itself?

Evidently between unequal powers it has been part of warfare. Colonial conquest has often been a matter of "punitive expeditions" rather than genuine military engagements. If the tribesmen escape into the brush you can burn their villages without them until they assent to receive what, in strikingly modern language, used to be known as the Queen's "protection." . . .

Pure hurting, as a military tactic, appeared in some of the military actions against the plains Indians. In 1868, during the war with the Cheyennes, General Sheridan decided that his best hope was to attack the Indians in their winter camps. His reasoning was that the Indians could maraud as they pleased during the seasons when their ponies could subsist on grass, and in the winter hide away in remote places. "To disabuse their minds from the idea that they were secure from punishment, and to strike at a period when they were helpless to move their stock and villages, a winter campaign was projected against the large bands hiding away in the Indian territory."[1]

These were not military engagements; they were punitive attacks on people. They were an effort to subdue by the use of violence, without a futile attempt to draw the enemy's military forces into decisive battle. They were "massive retaliation" on a diminutive scale, with local effects not unlike those of Hiroshima. The Indians themselves totally lacked organization and discipline, and typically could not afford enough ammunitions for target practice and were no military match for the calvary; their own rudimentary strategy was at best one of harassment and reprisal. Half a century of Indian fighting in the West left us a legacy of cavalry tactics; but it is hard to find a serious treatise on American strategy against the Indians or Indian strategy against the whites. The twentieth is not the first century in which "retaliation" has been part of our strategy, but it is the first in which we have systematically recognized it. . . .

Making it "terrible beyond endurance" is what we associate with Algeria and Palestine, the crushing of Budapest, and the tribal warfare in Central Africa. But in the great wars of the last hundred years it was usually military victory, not the hurting of the people, that was decisive; General Sherman's attempt to make war hell for the Southern people did not come to epitomize military strategy for the century to follow. To seek out and destroy the enemy's military force, to achieve a crushing victory over enemy armies, was still the avowed purpose and the central aim of American strategy in both world wars. Military action was seen as an *alternative* to bargaining, not a *process* of bargaining.

The reason is not that civilized countries are so averse to hurting people that they prefer "purely military" wars. (Nor were all of the participants in these wars entirely civilized.) The reason is apparently that the technology and geography of warfare, at least for a war between anything like equal powers during the century ending in World War II, kept coercive violence from being decisive before military victory was achieved. Blockade indeed was aimed at the whole enemy nation, not concentrated on its military forces; the German civilians who died of influenza in the First World War were victims directed at the whole country. It has never been quite clear whether blockade—of the South in the Civil War or of the Central Powers in both world wars, or submarine warfare against Britain—was expected to make war unendurable for the people or just to weaken the enemy forces by denying economic support. Both arguments were made, but there was no need to be clear about the purpose as long as either purpose was regarded as legitimate and either might be served. "Strategic bombing" of enemy homelands was also occasionally rationalized in terms of the pain and privation it could inflict on people and the civil damage it could do to the nation, as an effort to display either to the population or to the enemy leadership that surrender was better than persistence in view of the damage that could be done. It was also rationalized in more "military" terms, as a way of selectively denying war material to the troops or as a way of generally weakening the economy on which the military effort rested.

But terrorism—as violence intended to coerce the enemy rather than to weaken him militarily—blockade and strategic bombing by themselves were not quite up to the job in either world war in Europe. (They might have been sufficient in the war with Japan after straightforward military action had brought American aircraft into range.) Airplanes could not quite make punitive, coercive violence decisive in Europe, at least on a tolerable time schedule, and preclude the need to defeat or to destroy enemy forces as long as they had nothing but conventional explosives and incendiaries to carry. Hitler's V–1 buzz bomb and his V–2 rocket are fairly pure cases of weapons whose purpose was to intimidate, to hurt Britain itself rather than Allied military forces. What the V–2 needed was a punitive payload worth carrying, and the Germans did not have it. Some of the expectations in the 1920s and the 1930s that another major war would be one of pure civilian violence, of shock and terror from the skies, were not borne out by the available technology. The threat of punitive violence kept occupied countries quiescent; but the wars were won in Europe on the basis of brute strength and skill and not by intimidation, not by the threat of civilian violence but by the application of military force. Military victory was still the price of admission. Latent violence against people was reserved for the politics of surrender and occupation.

The great exception was the two atomic bombs on Japanese cities. These were weapons of terror and shock. They hurt, and promised more hurt, and that was their purpose. The few "small" weapons we had were undoubtedly of some direct military value but their enormous advantage was in pure violence. In a military sense the United States could gain a little by destruction of two Japanese industrial cities; in a civilian sense, the Japanese could lose much. The bomb that hit Hiroshima was a threat aimed at all of Japan. The political target of the bomb was not the dead of Hiroshima or the factories they worked in, but the survivors of Tokyo. The two bombs were in the tradition of Sheridan against the Comanches and Sherman in Georgia. Whether in the end those two bombs saved lives or wasted them, Japanese lives or American lives; whether punitive coercive violence is uglier than straightforward military force or more civilized; whether terror is more or less humane than military destruction; we can at least perceive that the bombs on Hiroshima and Nagasaki represented violence against the country itself and not mainly an attack on Japan's material strength. The effect of the bombs, and their purpose, was not mainly the military destruction they accomplished but the pain and the shock and the promise of more.

THE NUCLEAR CONTRIBUTION TO TERROR AND VIOLENCE

Man has, it is said, for the first time in history enough military power to eliminate his species from the earth, weapons against which there is no conceivable defense. War has become, it is said, so destructive and terrible that it ceases to be an instrument of national power. "For the first time in human history," says Max Lerner in a book whose title, *The Age of Overkill,* conveys the point, "men have bottled up a power . . . which they have thus far not dared to use." And Soviet military authorities, whose party dislikes having to accommodate an entire theory of history to a single technological event, have had to re-examine a set of principles that had been given the embarrassing name of "permanently operating factors" in warfare. Indeed, our era is epitomized by words like "the first time in human history," and by the abdication of what was "permanent."

For dramatic impact these statements are splendid. Some of them display a tendency, not at all necessary, to belittle the catastrophe of earlier wars. They may exaggerate the historical novelty of deterrence and the balance of terror.[2] More important, they do not help to identify just what is new about war when so much destructive energy can be packed in warheads at a price that permits advanced countries to have them in large numbers. Nuclear warheads are incomparably more devastating than anything packaged before. What does that imply about war?

It is not true that for the first time in history man has the capability to destroy a large fraction, even the major part, of the human race. Japan was defenseless by August 1945. With a combination of bombing and blockade, eventually invasion, and if necessary the deliberate spread of disease, the United States could probably have exterminated the population of the Japanese islands without nuclear weapons. . . .

It is a grisly thing to talk about. We did not do it and it is not imaginable that we would have done it. We had no reason; if we had had a reason, we would not have the persistence of purpose once the fury of war had been dissipated in victory and we had taken on the task of the executioner. If we and our enemies might do such a thing to each other now, and to others as well, it is not because nuclear weapons have for the first time made it feasible.

Nuclear weapons can do it quickly. . . . To compress a catastrophic war within the span of time that a man can stay awake drastically changes the politics of war, the process of decision, the possibility of central control and restraint, the motivations of people in charge, and the capacity to think and reflect while war is in progress. It *is* imaginable that we might destroy 200,000,000 Russians in a war of the present, though not 80,000,000 Japanese in a war of the past. It is not only imaginable, it is imagined. It is imaginable because it could be done "in a moment, in the twinkling of an eye, at the last trumpet."

This may be why there is so little discussion of how an all-out war might be brought to a close. People do not expect it to be "brought" to a close, but just to come to an end when everything has been spent. It is also why the idea of "limited war" has become so explicit in recent years. Earlier wars, like the World Wars I and II or the Franco-Prussian War, were limited by *termination*, by an ending that occurred before the period of greatest potential violence, by negotiation that brought the *threat* of pain and privation to bear but often precluded the massive *exercise* of civilian violence. With nuclear weapons available, the restraint of violence cannot await the outcome of a contest of military strength; restraint, to occur at all, must occur during war itself.

This is a difference between nuclear weapons and bayonets. It is not in the number of people they can eventually kill but in the speed with which it can be done, in the centralization of decision, in the divorce of the war from political process, and in computerized programs that threaten to take the war out of human hands once it begins.

That nuclear weapons make it *possible* to compress the fury of global war into a few hours does not mean that they make it *inevitable*. We have still to ask whether that is the way a major nuclear war would be fought, or ought to be fought. Nevertheless, that the whole war might go off like one big string of firecrackers makes a critical difference between our conception of nuclear war and the world wars we have experienced. . . .

There is another difference. In the past it has usually been the victors who could do what they pleased to the enemy. War has often been "total war" for the loser. With deadly monotony the Persians, Greeks and Romans "put to death all men of military age, and sold the women and children into slavery," leaving the defeated territory nothing but its name until new settlers arrived sometime later. But the defeated could not do the same to their victors. The boys could be castrated and sold only after the war had been won, and only on the side that lost it. The power to hurt could be brought to bear only after military strength had achieved victory. The same sequence characterized the great wars of this century; for reasons of technology and geography, military force has usually had to penetrate, to exhaust, or to collapse opposing military force—to achieve military victory—before it could be brought to bear on the enemy nation itself. The Allies in

World War I could not inflict coercive pain and suffering directly on the Germans in a decisive way until they could defeat the German army; and the Germans could not coerce the French people with bayonets unless they first beat the Allied troops that stood in their way. With two-dimensional warfare, there is a tendency for troops to confront each other, shielding their own lands while attempting to press into each other. Small penetrations could not do major damage to the people; large penetrations were so destructive of military organization that they usually ended the military phase of the war.

Nuclear weapons make it possible to do monstrous violence to the enemy without first achieving victory. With nuclear weapons and today's means of delivery, one expects to penetrate an enemy homeland without first collapsing his military force. What nuclear weapons have done, or appear to do, is to promote this kind of warfare to first place. Nuclear weapons threaten to make war less military, and are responsible for the lowered status of "military victory" at the present time. *Victory is no longer a prerequisite for hurting the enemy.* And it is no assurance against being terribly hurt. One need not wait until he has won the war before inflicting "unendurable" damages on his enemy. One need not wait until he has lost the war. There was a time when the assurance of victory—false or genuine assurance—could make national leaders not just willing but sometimes enthusiastic about war. Not now.

Not only *can* nuclear weapons hurt the enemy before the war has been won, and perhaps hurt decisively enough to make the military engagement academic, but it is widely assumed that in a major war that is *all* they can do. Major war is often discussed as though it would be only a contest in national destruction. If this is indeed the case—if the destruction of cities and their populations has become, with nuclear weapons, the primary object in an all-out war the sequence of war has been reversed. Instead of destroying enemy forces as a prelude to imposing one's will on the enemy nation, one would have to destroy the nation as a means or a prelude to destroying the enemy forces. If one cannot disable enemy forces without virtually destroying the country, the victor does not even have the option of sparing the conquered nation. He has already destroyed it. Even with blockade and strategic bombing it could be supposed that a country would be defeated before it was destroyed, or would elect surrender before annihilation had gone far. In the Civil War it could be hoped that the South would become too weak to fight before it became too weak to survive. For "all-out" war, nuclear weapons threaten to reverse this sequence.

So nuclear weapons do make a difference, marking an epoch in warfare. The difference is not just in the amount of destruction that can be accomplished but in the role of destruction and in the decision process. Nuclear weapons can change the speed of events, the control of events, the sequence of events, the relation of victor to vanquished, and the relation of homeland to fighting front. Deterrence rests today on the threat of pain and extinction, not just on the threat of military defeat. We may argue about the wisdom of announcing "unconditional surrender" as an aim in the last major war, but seem to expect "unconditional destruction" as a matter of course in another one.

Something like the same destruction always *could* be done. With nuclear weapons there is an expectation that it would be done. . . . What is new is . . . the idea that major war might be just a contest in the killing of countries, or not even a contest but just two parallel exercises in devastation.

That is the difference nuclear weapons make. At least they *may* make the difference. They also may not. If the weapons themselves are vulnerable to attack, or the machines that carry them, a successful surprise might eliminate the opponent's means of retribution. That an enormous explosion can be packaged in a single bomb does not by itself guarantee that the victor will receive deadly punishment. Two gunfighters facing each other in a Western town had an unquestioned capacity to kill one another; that did not guarantee that both would die in a gunfight—only the slower of the two. Less deadly weapons, permitting an injured one to shoot back before he died, might have been more conducive to a restraining balance of terror, or of caution. The very efficiency of nuclear weapons could make them ideal for starting war, if they can suddenly eliminate the enemy's capability to shoot back.

And there is a contrary possibility: that nuclear weapons are not vulnerable to attack and prove not to be terribly effective against each other, posing no need to shoot them quickly for fear they will be destroyed before they are launched, and with no task available but the systematic destruction of the enemy country and no necessary reason to do it fast rather than slowly. Imagine that nuclear destruction had to go slowly—that the bombs could be dropped only one per day. The prospect would look very different, something like the most terroristic guerrilla warfare on a massive scale. It happens that nuclear war does not have to go slowly; but it may also not have to go speedily. The mere existence of nuclear weapons does not itself determine that everything must go off in a blinding flash, any more than that it must go slowly. Nuclear weapons do not simplify things quite that much. . . .

In World Wars I and II one went to work on enemy military forces, not his people, because until the enemy's military forces had been taken care of there was typically not anything decisive that one could do to the enemy nation itself. The Germans did not, in World War I, refrain from bayoneting French citizens by the millions in the hopes that the Allies would abstain from shooting up the German population. They could not get at the French citizens until they had breached the Allied lines. Hitler tried to terrorize London and did not make it. The Allied air forces took the war straight to Hitler's territory, with at least some thought of doing in Germany what Sherman recognized he was doing in Georgia; but with the bombing technology of World War II one could not afford to bypass the troops and go exclusively for enemy populations—not, anyway, in Germany. With nuclear weapons one has that alternative.

To concentrate on the enemy's military installations while deliberately holding in reserve a massive capacity for destroying his cities, for exterminating his people and eliminating his society, on condition that the enemy observe similar restraint with respect to one's own society is not the "conventional approach." In World Wars I and II the first order of business was to destroy enemy armed forces because that was the only promising way to make him surrender. To fight a purely military engagement "all-out" while holding in reserve a decisive capacity for violence, on condition the enemy do likewise, is not the way military operations have traditionally been approached.

. . . In the present era noncombatants appear to be not only deliberate targets but primary targets. . . . In fact, noncombatants appeared to be primary targets at both ends of the scale of warfare; thermonuclear war threatened to be a contest in the destruction of cities and populations; and, at the other end of the scale, insurgency is almost entirely terroristic. We live in an era of dirty war.

Why is this so? Is war properly a military affair among combatants, and is it a depravity peculiar to the twentieth century that we cannot keep it within decent bounds? Or is war inherently dirty?

To answer this question it is useful to distinguish three stages in the involvement of noncombatants—of plain people and their possessions—in the fury of war. These stages are worth distinguishing; but their sequence is merely descriptive of Western Europe during the past three hundred years, not a historical generalization. The first stage is that in which the people may get hurt by inconsiderate combatants. This is the status that people had during the period of "civilized warfare" that the International Committee had in mind.

From about 1648 to the Napoleonic era, war in much of Western Europe was something superimposed on society. It was a contest engaged in by monarchies for stakes that were measured in territories, and, occasionally, money or dynastic claims. The troops were mostly mercenaries and the motivation for war was confined to the aristocratic elite. Monarchs fought for bits of territory, but the residents of disputed terrain were more concerned with protecting their crops and their daughters from marauding troops than with whom they owed allegiance to. They were, as Quincy Wright remarked in his classic *Study of War,* little concerned that the territory in which they lived had a new sovereign.[3] Furthermore, as far as the King of Prussia and the Emperor of Austria were concerned, the loyalty and enthusiasm of the Bohemian farmer were not decisive considerations. It is an exaggeration to refer to European war during this period as a sport of kings, but not a gross exaggeration. And the military logistics of those days confined military operations to a scale that did not require the enthusiasm of a multitude.

Hurting people was not a decisive instrument in warfare. Hurting people or destroying property only reduced the value of things that were being fought over, to the disadvantage of both sides. Furthermore, the monarchs who conducted wars often did not want to discredit the social institutions they shared with their enemies. Bypassing an enemy monarch and taking the war straight to his people would have had revolutionary implications. Destroying the opposing monarchy was often not in the interest of either side; opposing sovereigns had much more in common with each other than with their own subjects, and to discredit the claims of a monarchy might have produced a disastrous backlash. It is not surprising—or, if it is surprising, not altogether astonishing—that on the European continent in that particular era war was fairly well confined to military activity.

One could still, in those days and in that part of the world, be concerned for the rights of noncombatants and hope to devise rules that both sides in the war might observe. The rules might well be observed because both sides had something to gain from preserving social order and not destroying the enemy. Rules might be a nuisance, but if they restricted both sides the disadvantages might cancel out.

This was changed during the Napoleonic wars. In Napoleon's France, people cared about the outcome. The nation was mobilized. The war was a national effort, not just an activity of the elite. It was both political and military genius on the part of Napoleon and his ministers that an entire nation could be mobilized for war. Propaganda became a tool of warfare, and war became vulgarized.

Many writers deplored this popularization of war, this involvement of the democratic masses. In fact, the horrors we attribute to thermonuclear war were already foreseen by many commentators, some before the First World War and more after it, but the new "weapon" to which these terrors were ascribed was people, millions of people, passionately engaged in national wars, spending themselves in a quest for total victory and desperate to avoid total defeat. Today we are impressed that a small number of highly trained pilots can carry enough energy to blast and burn tens of millions of people and the buildings they live in; two or three generations ago there was concern that tens of millions of people using bayonets and barbed wire, machine guns and shrapnel, could create the same kind of destruction and disorder.

That was the second stage in the relation of people to war, the second in Europe since the middle of the seventeenth century. In the first stage people had been neutral but their welfare might be disregarded; in the second stage people were involved because it was *their* war. Some fought, some produced materials of war, some produced food, and some took care of children; but they were all part of a war-making nation. When Hitler attacked Poland in 1939, the Poles had reason to care about the outcome. When Churchill said the British would fight on the beaches, he spoke for the British and not for a mercenary army. The war was about something that mattered. If people would rather fight a dirty war than lose a clean one, the war will be between nations and not just between governments. If people have an influence on whether the war is continued or on the terms of a truce, making the war hurt people serves a purpose. It is a dirty purpose, but war itself is often about something dirty. The Poles and the Norwegians, the Russians and the British, had reason to believe that if they lost the war the consequences would be dirty. This is so evident in modern civil wars—civil wars that involve popular feelings—that we expect them to be bloody and violent. To hope that they would be fought cleanly with no violence to people would be a little like hoping for a clean race riot.

There is another way to put it that helps to bring out the sequence of events. If a modern war were a clean one, the violence would not be ruled out but merely saved for the postwar period. Once the army has been defeated in the clean war, the victorious enemy can be as brutally coercive as he wishes. A clean war would determine which side gets to use its power to hurt coercively after victory, and it is likely to be worth some violence to avoid being the loser.

"Surrender" is the process following military hostilities in which the power to hurt is brought to bear. If surrender negotiations are successful and not followed by overt violence, it is because the capacity to inflict pain and damage was successfully used in the bargaining process. On the losing side, prospective pain and damage were averted by concessions; on the winning side, the capacity for inflicting further harm was traded for concessions. The same is true in a successful kidnapping. It only reminds us that the purpose of pure pain and damage is extortion; it is *latent* violence that can be used to advantage. A well-behaved occupied country is not one in which violence plays no part; it may be one in which latent violence is used so skillfully that it need not be spent in punishment.

This brings us to the third stage in the relation of civilian violence to warfare. If the pain and damage can be inflicted during war itself, they need not wait for the surrender negotiation that succeeds a military decision. If one can coerce people and their governments while war is going on, one does not need to wait until he has achieved victory or risk losing that coercive power by spending it all in a losing war. General Sherman's march through Georgia might have made as much sense, possibly more, had the North been losing the war, just as the German buzz bombs and V–2 rockets can be thought of as coercive instruments to get the war stopped before suffering military defeat.

In the present era, since at least the major East-West powers are capable of massive civilian violence during war itself beyond anything available during the Second World War, the occasion for restraint does not await the achievement of military victory or truce. The principal restraint during the Second World War was a temporal boundary, the date of surrender. In the present era we find the violence dramatically restrained during war itself. The Korean War was furiously "all-out" in the fighting, not only on the peninsular battlefield but in the resources used by both sides. It was "all-out," though, only within some dramatic restraints; no nuclear weapons, no Russians, no Chinese territory, no Japanese territory, no bombing of ships at sea or even airfields on the United Nations side of the line. It was a contest in military strength circumscribed by the threat of unprecedented civilian violence. Korea may or may not be a good model for speculation on limited war in the age of nuclear violence, but it was dramatic evidence that the capacity for violence can be consciously restrained even under the provocation of war that measures its military dead in tens of thousands and that fully preoccupies two of the largest countries in the world.

A consequence of this third stage is that "victory" inadequately expresses what a nation wants from its military forces. Mostly it wants, in these times, the influence that resides in latent force. It wants the bargaining power that comes from its capacity to hurt, not just the direct consequence of successful military action. Even total victory over an enemy provides at best an opportunity for unopposed violence against the enemy population. How to use that opportunity in the national interest, or in some wider interest, can be just as important as the achievement of victory itself; but traditional military science does not tell us how to use that capacity for inflicting pain. And if a nation, victor or potential loser, is going to use its capacity for pure violence to influence the enemy, there may be no need to await the achievement of total victory.

Actually, this third stage can be analyzed into two quite different variants. In one, sheer pain and damage are primary instruments of coercive warfare and may actually be applied, to intimidate or to deter. In the other, pain and destruction *in* war are expected to serve little or no purpose but *prior threats* of sheer violence, even of automatic and uncontrolled violence, are coupled to military force. The difference is in the all-or-none character of deterrence and intimidation. Two acute dilemmas arise. One is the choice of making prospective violence as frightening as possible or hedging with some capacity for reciprocated restraint. The other is the choice of making retaliation as automatic as possible or keeping deliberate control over the fateful decisions. The choices are determined partly by governments, partly by technology. Both variants are characterized by the coercive role of pain and destruction—of threatened (not inflicted) pain and destruction. But in one the threat either succeeds or fails altogether, and any ensuing violence is gratuitous; in the other, progressive pain and damage may actually be used to threaten more. The present era, for countries possessing nuclear weapons, is a complex and uncertain blend of the two. . . .

The power to hurt is nothing new in warfare, but for the United States modern technology has drastically enhanced the strategic importance of pure, unconstructive, unacquisitive pain and damage, whether used against us or in our own defense. This in turn enhances the importance of war and threats of war as techniques of influence, not of destruction; of coercion and deterrence, not of conquest and defense; of bargaining and intimidation. . . .

War no longer looks like just a contest of strength. War and the brink of war are more a contest of nerve and risk-taking, of pain and endurance. Small wars embody the threat of a larger war; they are not just military engagements but "crisis diplomacy." The threat of war has always been somewhere underneath international diplomacy, but for Americans it is now much nearer the surface. Like the threat of a strike in industrial relations, the threat of divorce in a family dispute, or the threat of bolting the party at a political convention, the threat of violence continuously circumscribes international politics. Neither strength nor goodwill procures immunity.

Military strategy can no longer be thought of, as it could for some countries in some eras, as the science of military victory. It is now equally, if not more, the art of coercion, of intimidation and deterrence. The instruments of war are more punitive than acquisitive. Military strategy, whether we like it or not, has become the diplomacy of violence.

NOTES

1. Paul I. Wellman, *Death on the Prairie* (New York: Macmillan, 1934), p. 82.
2. Winston Churchill is often credited with the term, "balance of terror," and the following quotation succinctly expresses the familiar notion of nuclear mutual deterrence. This, though, is from a speech in Commons in November 1934. "The fact remains that when all is said and done as regards defensive methods, pending some new discovery the only direct measure of defense upon a great scale is the certainty of being able to inflict simultaneously upon the enemy as great damage as he can inflict upon ourselves. Do not let us undervalue the efficiency of this procedure. It may well prove in practice—I admit I cannot prove it in theory—capable of giving complete immunity. If two Powers show themselves equally capable of inflicting damage upon each other by some particular process of war, so that neither gains an advantage from its adoption and both suffer the most hideous reciprocal injuries, it is not only possible but it seems probable that neither will employ that means . . ."
3. (Chicago: University of Chicago Press), 1942, p. 296.

What is Terrorism?

BRUCE HOFFMAN

What is terrorism? Few words have so insidiously worked their way into our everyday vocabulary. Like "Internet"—another grossly overused term that has similarly become an indispensable part of the argot of the early twenty-first century—most people have a vague idea or impression of what terrorism is but lack a more precise, concrete, and truly explanatory definition of the word. This imprecision has been abetted partly by the modern media, whose efforts to communicate an often complex and convoluted message in the briefest amount of airtime or print space possible have led to the promiscuous labeling of a range of violent acts as "terrorism." Pick up a newspaper or turn on the television and—even within the same broadcast or on the same page—one can find such disparate acts as the bombing of a building, the assassination of a head of state, the massacre of civilians by a military unit, the poisoning of produce on supermarket shelves, or the deliberate contamination of over-the-counter medication in a drugstore, all described as incidents of terrorism. Indeed, virtually any especially abhorrent act of violence perceived as directed against society—whether it involves the activities of antigovernment dissidents or governments themselves, organized-crime syndicates, common criminals, rioting mobs, people engaged in militant protest, individual psychotics, or lone extortionists—is often labeled "terrorism" . . .

WHY IS TERRORISM SO DIFFICULT TO DEFINE?

Not surprisingly, as the meaning and usage of the word have changed over time to accommodate the political vernacular and discourse of each successive era, terrorism has proved increasingly elusive in the face of attempts to construct one consistent definition. At one time, the terrorists themselves were far more cooperative in this endeavor than they are today. The early practitioners didn't mince their words or hide behind the semantic camouflage of more anodyne labels such as "freedom fighter" or "urban guerrilla." The nineteenth-century anarchists, for example, unabashedly proclaimed themselves to be terrorists and frankly proclaimed their tactics to be

From *Inside Terrorism, Revised and Expanded Edition* by Bruce Hoffman, pp. 1–41. Copyright © 2006 Bruce Hoffman. Reprinted with permission of Columbia University Press. Portions of the text and the footnotes have been omitted.

terrorism. The members of Narodnaya Volya similarly displayed no qualms in using these same words to describe themselves and their deeds. Such frankness did not last, however. Although the Jewish terrorist group of the 1940s known as Lehi (the Hebrew acronym for Lohamei Herut Yisrael, the Freedom Fighters for Israel), but more popularly called the Stern Gang after its founder and first leader, Abraham Stern, would admit to its effective use of terrorist tactics, its members never considered themselves to be terrorists. It is significant, however, that even Lehi, while it may have been far more candid than its latter-day counterparts, chose as the name of the organization not Terrorist Fighters for Israel but the far less pejorative Freedom Fighters for Israel. Similarly, although more than twenty years later the Brazilian revolutionary Carlos Marighela displayed little compunction about openly advocating the use of "terrorist" tactics, he still insisted on depicting himself and his disciples as "urban guerrillas" rather than "urban terrorists." Indeed, it is clear from Marighela's writings that he was well aware of the word's undesirable connotations and strove to displace them with positive resonances. "The words 'aggressor' and 'terrorist,'" Marighela wrote in his famous *Handbook of Urban Guerrilla War* (also known as the "Mini-Manual"), "no longer mean what they did. Instead of arousing fear or censure, they are a call to action. To be called an aggressor or a terrorist in Brazil is now an honour to any citizen, for it means that he is fighting, with a gun in his hand, against the monstrosity of the present dictatorship and the suffering it causes.

This trend toward ever more convoluted semantic obfuscations to sidestep terrorism's pejorative overtones has, if anything, become more entrenched in recent decades. Terrorist organizations almost without exception now regularly select names for themselves that consciously eschew the word "terrorism" in any of its forms. Instead these groups actively seek to evoke images of

- freedom and liberation (e.g., the National Liberation Front, the Popular Front for the Liberation of Palestine, Freedom for the Basque Homeland);
- armies or other military organizational structures (e.g., the National Military Organization, the Popular Liberation Army, the Fifth Battalion of the Liberation Army);
- actual self-defense movements (e.g., the Afrikaner Resistance Movement, the Shankhill Defence Association, the Organization for the Defence of the Free People, the Jewish Defense Organization);
- righteous vengeance (the Organization for the Oppressed on Earth, the Justice Commandos of the Armenian Genocide, the Palestinian Revenge Organization)

—or else deliberately choose names that are decidedly neutral and therefore bereft of all but the most innocuous suggestions or associations (e.g., the Shining Path, Front Line, al-Dawa (the Call), Alfaro Lives—Damn It!, Kach (Thus), al-Gamat al-Islamiya (the Islamic Organization), the Lantaro Youth Movement, and *especially* al Qaeda (the Arabic word for the "base of operation" or "foundation"— meaning the base or foundation from which worldwide Islamic revolution can be waged—or, as other translations have it, the "precept" or "method").

What all these examples suggest is the terrorists clearly do not see or regard themselves as others do. "Above all I am a family man," the archterrorist Carlos, the Jackal, described himself to a French newspaper following his capture in 1994. Similarly, when the infamous KSM—Khalid Sheikh Mohammed, mastermind of the 9/11 attacks whom bin Laden called simply "al Mukhtar" (Arabic for "the brain")—was apprehended in March 2003, a photograph of him with his arms around his two young sons was found next to the bed in which he had been sleeping. Cast perpetually on the defensive and forced to take up arms to protect themselves and their real or imagined constituents only, terrorists perceive themselves as reluctant warriors, driven by desperation—and lacking any viable alternative—to violence against a repressive state, a predatory rival ethnic or nationalist group, or an unresponsive international order. This perceived characteristic of self-denial also distinguishes the terrorist from other types of political extremists as well as from people similarly involved in illegal, violent avocations. A communist or a revolutionary, for example, would likely readily accept and admit that he is in fact a communist or a revolutionary. Indeed, many would doubtless take particular pride in claiming either of those appellations for themselves. Similarly, even a person engaged in illegal, wholly disreputable, or entirely selfish violent activities, such as robbing banks or carrying out contract killings, would probably admit to being a bank robber or a murderer for hire. The terrorist, by contrast, will *never* acknowledge that he is a terrorist and moreover will go to great lengths to evade and obscure any such inference or connection. . . . The terrorist will always argue that it is society or the government or the socioeconomic "system" and its laws that are the *real* "terrorists," and moreover that if it were not for this oppression, he would not have felt the need to defend either himself or the population he claims to represent.

On one point, at least, everyone agrees: "Terrorism" is a pejorative term. It is a word with intrinsically negative connotations that is generally applied to one's enemies and opponents, or to those with whom one disagrees and would otherwise prefer to ignore. "What is called terrorism," Brian Jenkins has written, "thus seems to depend on one's point of view. Use of the term implies a moral judgement; and if one party can successfully attach the label *terrorist* to its opponent, then it has indirectly persuaded others to adopt its moral viewpoint." Hence the decision to call someone or label some organization "terrorist" becomes almost unavoidably subjective, depending largely on whether one sympathizes with or opposes the person/group/cause concerned. If one identifies with the victim of the violence, for example, then the act is terrorism. If, however, one identifies with the perpetrator, the violent act is regarded in a more sympathetic, if not positive (or, at the worst, ambivalent) light, and it is not terrorism. . . .

The opposite approach, in which identification with the victim determines the classification of a violent act as terrorism, is evident in the conclusions of a parliamentary working group of NATO (an organization comprising long-established, status quo Western states). The final report of the 1989 North Atlantic Assembly's Subcommittee on Terrorism states: "Murder, kidnapping, arson and other felonious acts constitute criminal behavior, but many non-Western nations have proved reluctant to condemn as terrorist acts what they consider to be struggles of national liberation." In this reasoning, the defining characteristic of terrorism is the act of violence itself, not the motivations or justification for or reasons behind it. . . .

But this is not an entirely satisfactory solution either, since it fails to differentiate clearly between violence perpetrated by states and by nonstate entities, such as terrorists. Accordingly, it plays into the hands of terrorists and their apologists who would argue that there is no difference between the "low-tech" terrorist pipe bomb placed in the rubbish bin at a crowded market that wantonly and indiscriminately kills or maims everyone within a radius measured in tens of feet and the "high-tech" precision-guided ordnance dropped by air force fighter-bombers from a height of twenty thousand feet or more that achieves the same wanton and indiscriminate effects on the crowded marketplace far below. This rationale thus equates the random violence inflicted on enemy population centers by military forces—such as the Luftwaffe's raids on Warsaw and Coventry, the Allied fire-bombings of Dresden and Tokyo, and the atomic bombs dropped by the United States on Hiroshima and Nagasaki during the Second World War, and indeed the countervalue strategy of the postwar superpowers' strategic nuclear policy, which deliberately targeted the enemy's civilian population—with the violence committed by substate entities labeled "terrorists," since both involve the infliction of death and injury on noncombatants. . . .

It is a familiar argument. Terrorists, as we have seen, deliberately cloak themselves in the terminology of military jargon. They consciously portray themselves as bona fide (freedom) fighters, if not soldiers, who—though they wear no identifying uniform or insignia—are entitled to treatment as prisoners of war (POWs) if captured and therefore should not be prosecuted as common criminals in ordinary courts of law. Terrorists further argue that, because of their numerical inferiority, far more limited firepower, and paucity of resources compared with an established nation-state's massive defense and national security apparatus, they have no choice but to operate clandestinely, emerging from the shadows to carry out dramatic (in other words, bloody and destructive) acts of hit-and-run violence in order to attract attention to, and ensure publicity for, themselves and their cause. The bomb in the rubbish bin, in their view, is merely a circumstantially imposed "poor man's air force": the only means with which the terrorist can challenge—and get the attention of—the more powerful state. "How else can we bring pressure to bear on the world?" one of Arafat's political aides once inquired. "The deaths are regrettable, but they are a fact of war in which innocents have become involved. They are no more innocent than the Palestinian women and children killed by the Israelis and we are ready to carry the war all over the world."

But rationalizations such as these ignore the fact that, even while national armed forces have been responsible for far more death and destruction than terrorists might ever aspire to bring about, there nonetheless is a fundamental qualitative difference between the two types of violence. Even in war there are rules and accepted norms of behavior that prohibit the use of certain types of weapons (for example, hollow-point or "dum-dum" bullets, CS "tear" gas, chemical and biological warfare agents) and proscribe various tactics and outlaw attacks on specific categories of targets. Accordingly, in theory, if not always in practice, the rules of war—as observed from the early seventeenth century when they were first proposed by the Dutch jurist Hugo Grotius and subsequently codified in the famous

Geneva and Hague Conventions on Warfare of the 1860s, 1899, 1907, and 1949—not only grant civilian noncombatants immunity from attack but also

- prohibit taking civilians as hostages;
- impose regulations governing the treatment of captured or surrendered soldiers (POWs);
- outlaw reprisals against either civilians or POWs;
- recognize neutral territory and the rights of citizens of neutral states; and
- uphold the inviolability of diplomats and other accredited representatives.

Even the most cursory review of terrorist tactics and targets over the past quarter century reveals that terrorists have violated all these rules. They not infrequently have

- taken civilians as hostages, and in some instances then brutally executed them (e.g., the former Italian prime minister Aldo Moro and the German industrialist Hans Martin Schleyer, who, respectively, were taken captive and later murdered by the Red Brigades and the Red Army Faction in the 1970s and, more recently, Daniel Pearl, a *Wall Street Journal* reporter, and Nicholas Berg, an American businessmen, who were kidnapped by radical Islamic terrorists in Pakistan and Iraq, respectively, and grotesquely beheaded);
- similarly abused and murdered kidnapped military officers—even when they were serving on UN-sponsored peacekeeping or truce supervisory missions (e.g., the American Marine Lieutenant Colonel William Higgins, the commander of a UN truce-monitoring detachment, who was abducted by Lebanese Shi'a terrorists in 1989 and subsequently hanged);
- undertaken reprisals against wholly innocent civilians, often in countries far removed from the terrorists' ostensible "theater of operation," thus disdaining any concept of neutral states or the rights of citizens of neutral countries (e.g., the brutal 1986 machine-gun and hand-grenade attack on Turkish Jewish worshipers at an Istanbul synagogue carried out by the Palestinian Abu Nidal Organization (ANO) in retaliation for a recent Israeli raid on a guerrilla base in southern Lebanon); and
- repeatedly attacked embassies and other diplomatic installations (e.g., the bombings of the U.S. embassies in Nairobi and Dar es Salaam in 1998 and in Beirut and Kuwait City in 1983 and 1984, and the mass hostage-taking at the Japanese ambassador's residence in Lima, Peru, in 1996–97), as well as deliberately targeting diplomats and other accredited representatives (e.g., the British ambassador to Uruguay, Sir Geoffrey Jackson, who was kidnapped by leftist terrorists in that country in 1971, and the fifty-two American diplomats taken hostage at the Tehran legation in 1979).

Admittedly, the armed forces of established states have also been guilty of violating some of the same rules of war. However, when these transgressions do occur—when civilians are deliberately and wantonly attacked in war or taken hostage and killed by military forces—the term "war crime" is used to describe such acts and, as imperfect and flawed as both international and national judicial remedies may be, steps nonetheless are often taken to hold the perpetrators accountable for the crimes. By comparison, one of the fundamental raisons d'être of international terrorism is a refusal to be bound by such rules of warfare and codes of conduct. International terrorism disdains any concept of delimited areas of combat or demarcated battlefields, much less respect for neutral territory. Accordingly, terrorists have repeatedly taken their often parochial struggles to other, sometimes geographically distant, third-party countries and there deliberately enmeshed people completely unconnected with the terrorists' cause or grievances in violent incidents designed to generate attention and publicity. . . .

If it is impossible to define terrorism, as Laqueur argues, and fruitless to attempt to cobble together a truly comprehensive definition, as Schmid admits, are we to conclude that terrorism is impervious to precise, much less accurate definition? Not entirely. If we cannot define terrorism, then we can at least usefully distinguish it from other types of violence and identify the characteristics that make terrorism the distinct phenomenon of political violence that it is.

DISTINCTIONS AS A PATH TO DEFINITION

Guerrilla warfare and insurgency are good places to start. Terrorism is often confused or equated with, or treated as synonymous with, guerrilla warfare and insurgency. This is not entirely surprising, since guerrillas and insurgents often employ the same tactics (assassination, kidnapping, hit-and-run attack, bombings of public gathering places, hostage-taking, etc.) for the same purposes (to intimidate or coerce, thereby affecting behavior through the arousal of fear) as terrorists. In addition, terrorists as well as guerrillas and insurgents wear neither uniform nor identifying insignia and thus are often indistinguishable from noncombatants. However, despite the inclination to lump terrorists, guerrillas, and insurgents into the same catchall category of "irregulars," there are nonetheless fundamental differences among the three. "Guerrilla," for example, in its most widely accepted usage, is taken to refer to a numerically larger group of armed individuals, who operate as a military unit, attack enemy military forces, and seize and hold territory (even if only ephemerally during daylight hours), while also exercising some form of sovereignty or control over a defined geographical area and its population. "Insurgents" share these same characteristics: however, their strategy and operations transcend hit-and-run attacks to embrace what in the past has variously been called "revolutionary guerrilla warfare," "modern revolutionary warfare," or "people's war" but is today commonly termed "insurgency." Thus, in addition to the irregular military tactics that characterize guerrilla operations, insurgencies typically involve coordinated informational (e.g., propaganda) and psychological warfare efforts designed to mobilize popular support in a struggle against an established national government, imperialist power, or foreign occupying force. Terrorists, however, do not function in the open as armed units, generally do not attempt to seize or hold territory, deliberately avoid engaging enemy military forces in combat, are constrained both numerically and logistically from undertaking concerted mass political mobilization efforts, and exercise no direct control or governance over a populace at either the local or the national level.

It should be emphasized that none of these are pure categories and considerable overlap exists. Established terrorist groups like Hezbollah, FARC (Revolutionary Armed Forces of Colombia), and the LTTE (Liberation Tigers of Tamil Eelam, or Tamil Tigers), for example, are also often described as guerrilla movements because of their size, tactics, and control over territory and populace. Indeed, nearly a third of the thirty-seven groups on the U.S. State Department's "Designated Foreign Terrorist Organizations" list could just as easily be categorized as guerrillas. The ongoing insurgency in Iraq has further contributed to this semantic confusion. The 2003 edition of the State Department's *Global Patterns of Terrorism* specifically cited the challenge of making meaningful distinctions between these categories, lamenting how the "line between insurgency and terrorism has become increasingly blurred as attacks on civilian targets have become more common." Generally, the State Department considers attacks against U.S. and coalition military forces as insurgent operations and incidents such as the August 2003 suicide vehicle-borne bombings of the UN headquarters in Baghdad and the Jordanian embassy in that city, the assassinations of Japanese diplomats, and kidnapping and murder of aid workers and civilian contractors as terrorist attacks. The definitional rule of thumb therefore is that secular Ba'athist Party loyalists and other former regime elements who stage guerrilla-like hit-and-run assaults or carry out attacks using roadside IEDs (improvised explosive devices) are deemed "insurgents," while foreign jihadists and domestic Islamic extremists who belong to groups like al Qaeda in Mesopotamia, led by Abu Musab Zarqawi, and who are responsible for most of the suicide attacks and the videotaped beheading of hostages, are labeled terrorists.

It is also useful to distinguish terrorists from ordinary criminals. Like terrorists, criminals use violence as a means to attain a specific end. However, while the violent act itself may be similar—kidnapping, shooting, and arson, for example—the purpose or motivation clearly is different. Whether the criminal employs violence as a means to obtain money, to acquire material goods, or to kill or injure a specific victim for pay, he is acting primarily for selfish, personal motivations (usually material gain). Moreover, unlike terrorism, the ordinary criminal's violent act is not designed or intended to have consequences or create psychological repercussions beyond the act itself. The criminal may of course use some short-term act of violence to "terrorize" his victim, such as waving a gun in the face of a bank clerk during a robbery in order to ensure the clerk's expeditious compliance. In these instances, however, the bank robber is conveying no "message" (political or otherwise) through his act of violence beyond facilitating the rapid handing over of his "loot." The criminal's act therefore is not meant to have any effect reaching beyond either the incident itself or the immediate victim. Further, the violence is neither conceived nor intended to convey any message to anyone other than the bank clerk himself, whose rapid cooperation is the robber's only objective. Perhaps most fundamentally, the criminal is not concerned with influencing or affecting public opinion; he simply wants to abscond with his money or accomplish his mercenary task in the quickest and easiest way possible so that he may reap his reward and enjoy the fruits of his labors. By contrast, the fundamental aim of the terrorist's violence is ultimately to change "the system"—about which the ordinary criminal, of course, couldn't care less.

The terrorist is also very different from the lunatic assassin, who may use identical tactics (e.g., shooting, bombing) and perhaps even seeks the same objective (e.g., the death of a political figure). However, while the tactics and targets of terrorists and lone assassins are often identical, their purpose is different. Whereas the terrorist's goal is again ineluctably *political* (to change or fundamentally alter a political system through his violent act), the lunatic assassin's goal is more often intrinsically idiosyncratic, completely egocentric and deeply personal. John Hinckley, who tried to kill President Reagan in 1981 to impress the actress Jodie Foster, is a case in point. He acted not from political motivation or ideological conviction but to fulfill some profound personal quest (killing the president to impress his screen idol). Such entirely *apolitical* motivations can in no way be compared to the rationalizations used by the Narodnaya Volya to justify its campaign of tyrannicide against the czar and his minions, nor even to the Irish Republican Army's efforts to assassinate Prime Minister Margaret Thatcher or her successor, John Major, in hopes of dramatically changing British policy toward Northern Ireland. Further, just as one person cannot credibly claim to be a political party, so a lone individual cannot be considered to constitute a terrorist group. In this respect, even though Sirhan Sirhan's assassination of presidential candidate and U.S. senator Robert Kennedy in 1968 had a political motive (to protest against U.S. support for Israel), it is debatable whether the murder should be defined as a terrorist act since Sirhan belonged to no organized political group and there is no evidence that he was directly influenced or inspired by an identifiable political or terrorist movement. Rather, Sirhan acted entirely on his own, out of deep personal frustration and a profound animus.

Finally, the point should be emphasized that, unlike the ordinary criminal or the lunatic assassin, the terrorist is not pursuing purely egocentric goals; he is not driven by the wish to line his own pocket or satisfy some personal need or grievance. The terrorist is fundamentally an *altruist:* he believes that he is serving a "good" cause designed to achieve a greater good for a wider constituency— whether real or imagined—that the terrorist and his organization purport to represent. The criminal, by comparison, serves no cause at all, just his own personal aggrandizement and material satiation. Indeed, a "terrorist without a cause (at least in his own mind)," Konrad Kellen has argued, "is not a terrorist." Yet the possession or identification of a cause is not a sufficient criterion for labeling someone a terrorist. In this key respect, the difference between terrorists and political extremists is clear. Many people, of course, harbor all sorts of radical and extreme beliefs and opinions, and many of them belong to radical or even illegal or proscribed political organizations. However, if they do not use violence in the pursuit of their beliefs, they cannot be considered terrorists. The terrorist is fundamentally a *violent intellectual,* prepared to use and, indeed, committed to using force in the attainment of his goals.

In the past, terrorism was arguably easier to define than it is today. To qualify as terrorism, violence had to be perpetrated by an individual acting at the behest of or on the behalf of some existent organizational entity or movement with at least some conspiratorial structure and identifiable chain of command. This criterion, however, is no longer sufficient. In recent years, a variety of terrorist movements have increasingly adopted a strategy of "leaderless networks" in order to thwart law enforcement and intelligence agency efforts to penetrate them. Craig Rosebraugh, the publicist for a radical environmentalist group calling itself the Earth Liberation Front (ELF), described the movement in a 2001 interview as a deliberately conceived "series of cells across the country with no chain of command and no membership roll . . . only a shared philosophy." It is designed this way, he continued, so that "there's no central leadership where [the authorities] can go and knock off the top guy and [the movement then] will be defunct." Indeed, an ELF recruitment video narrated by Rosebraugh advises "individuals interested in becoming active in the Earth Liberation Front to . . . form your own close-knit autonomous cells made of trustworthy and sincere people. Remember, the ELF and each cell within it are anonymous not only to one another but to the general public." As a senior FBI official conceded, the ELF is "not a group you can put your fingers on" and thus is extremely difficult to infiltrate.

This type of networked adversary is a new and different breed of terrorist entity to which traditional organizational constructs and definitions do not neatly apply. It is populated by individuals who are ideologically motivated, inspired, and animated by a movement or a leader, but who neither formally belong to a specific, identifiable terrorist group nor directly follow orders issued by its leadership and are therefore outside any established chain of command. It is a structure and approach that al Qaeda has also sought to implement. Ayman al-Zawahiri, bin Laden's deputy and al Qaeda's chief theoretician, extolled this strategy in his seminal clarion call to jihad (Arabic for "striving," but also "holy war"), *Knights Under the Prophet's Banner: Meditations on the Jihadist Movement*. The chapter titled "Small Groups Could Frighten the Americans" explains:

> Tracking down Americans and the Jews is not impossible. Killing them with a single bullet, a stab, or a device made up of a popular mix of explosives or hitting them with an iron rod is not impossible. Burning down their property with Molotov cocktails is not difficult. With the available means, small groups could prove to be a frightening horror for the Americans and the Jews.

Whether termed "leaderless resistance," "phantom cell networks," "autonomous leadership units," "autonomous cells," a "network of networks," or "lone wolves," this new conflict paradigm conforms to what John Arquilla and David Ronfeldt call "netwar":

> an emerging mode of conflict (and crime) at societal levels, short of traditional military warfare, in which the protagonists use network forms of organization and related doctrines, strategies, and technologies attuned to the information age. These protagonists are likely to consist of dispersed organizations, small groups, and individuals who communicate, coordinate, and conduct their campaigns in an internetted manner, often without precise central command.

Unlike the hierarchical, pyramidal structure that typified terrorist groups of the past, this new type of organization is looser, flatter, more linear. Although there is a leadership of sorts, its role may be more titular than actual, with less a direct command and control relationship than a mostly inspirational and motivational one. "The organizational structure," Arquilla and Ronfeldt explain,

> is quite flat. There is no single central leader or commander; the network as a whole (but not necessarily each node) has little to no hierarchy. There may be multiple leaders. Decisionmaking and operations are decentralized and depend on consultative consensus-building that allows for local initiative and autonomy. The design is both acephalous (headless) and polycephalous (Hydra-headed)—it has not precise heart or head, although not all nodes may be "created equal."

As part of this "leaderless" strategy, autonomous local terrorist cells plan and execute attacks independently of one another or of any central command authority, but through their individual terrorist efforts seek the eventual attainment of a terrorist organization or movement's wider goals. Although these ad hoc terrorist cells and lone individuals may be less sophisticated and therefore less capable than their more professional, trained counterparts who are members of actual established terrorist groups, these "amateur" terrorists can be just as bloody-minded. A recent FBI strategic planning document, for instance, describes lone wolves as the "most significant domestic terrorism threat" that the United States faces. "They typically draw ideological inspiration from formal terrorist organizations," the 2004–09 plan states, "but operate on the fringes of those movements. Despite their ad hoc nature and generally limited resources, they can mount high-profile, extremely destructive attacks, and their operational planning is often difficult to detect."

CONCLUSION

By distinguishing terrorists from other types of criminals and irregular fighters and terrorism from other forms of crime and irregular warfare, we come to appreciate that terrorism is

- ineluctably political in aims and motives;
- violent—or, equally important, threatens violence;
- designed to have far-reaching psychological repercussions beyond the immediate victim or target;
- conducted *either* by an organization with an identifiable chain of command or conspiratorial cell structure (whose members wear no uniform or identifying insignia) or by individuals or a small collection of individuals directly influenced, motivated, or inspired by the ideological aims or example of some existent terrorist movement and/or its leaders; and
- perpetrated by a subnational group or nonstate entity.

We may therefore now attempt to define terrorism as the deliberate creation and exploitation of fear through violence or the threat of violence in the pursuit of political change. All terrorist acts involve violence or the threat of violence.

Terrorism is specifically designed to have far-reaching psychological effects beyond the immediate victim(s) or object of the terrorist attack. It is meant to instill fear within, and thereby intimidate, a wider "target audience" that might include a rival ethnic or religious group, an entire country, a national government or political party, or public opinion in general. Terrorism is designed to create power where there is none or to consolidate power where there is very little. Through the publicity generated by their violence, terrorists seek to obtain the leverage, influence, and power they otherwise lack to effect political change on either a local or an international scale.

mypoliscikit Exercises for the Political Uses of Force

Apply what you learned in this chapter by using the online resources on MyPoliSciKit (www.mypoliscikit.com).

 Practice Tests

 Videos:
- "The Berlin Blockade"
- "Germany's Anschluss of Austria"

 Simulation: "Foreign Policy: You Are the President"

 Reading Guides:
- Robert J. Art, "The Four Functions of Force"
- Thomas C. Schelling, "The Diplomacy of Violence"
- Bruce Hoffman, "What Is Terrorism?"

THE POLITICAL UTILITY OF FORCE TODAY

The Fungibility of Force

ROBERT J. ART

There are two fundamental reasons why military power remains more essential to statecraft than is commonly thought. First, in an anarchic realm (one without a central government), force is integral to political interaction. Foreign policy cannot be divorced from military power. Second, force is "fungible." It can be used for a wide variety of tasks and across different policy domains; it can be employed for both military and nonmilitary purposes. . . .

POWER ASSETS: COMPARISONS AND CONFUSIONS

. . . I have argued that force is integral to statecraft because international politics is anarchic. By itself, that fact makes force fungible to a degree. Exactly how fungible an instrument is military power, however, and how does it compare in this regard to the other power assets a state wields? In this section, I answer these questions. First, I make a rough comparison as to the fungibility of the main instruments of statecraft. Second, I present a counterargument that force has little fungibility and then critique it.

Comparing Power Assets

Comparing the instruments of statecraft according to their fungibility is a difficult task. We do not have a large body of empirical studies that systematically analyze

From Robert J. Art, "American Foreign Policy and the Fungibility of Force," *Security Studies*, Vol. 5, No. 4 (Summer 1996), pp. 7–42. Reprinted by permission of the publisher (Taylor & Francis Ltd, http://www.tandf.co.uk/journals). Portions of the text have been omitted.

the comparative fungibility of a state's power assets. The few studies we do have, even though they are carefully done, focus on only one or two instruments and are more concerned with looking at assets within specific issue areas than with comparing assets across issue areas. As a consequence, we lack sufficient evidence to compare power assets according to their fungibility. Through a little logic, however, we can provide some ballpark estimates.

Consider what power assets a state owns. They include population—the size, education level, and skills of its citizenry; geography—the size, location, and natural resource endowment of the state; governance—the effectiveness of its political system; values—the norms a state lives by and stands for, the nature of its ideology, and the extent of its appeal to foreigners; wealth—the level, sources, and nature of its productive economy; leadership—the political skill of its leaders and the number of skillful leaders it has; and military power—the nature, size, and composition of its military forces. Of all these assets, wealth and political skill look to be the most versatile, geography and governance the least versatile, because both are more in the nature of givens that set the physical and political context within which the other assets operate; values and population are highly variable, depending, respectively, on the content of the values and on the education and skill of the populace; and military power lies somewhere between wealth and skill on the one hand, and geography and governance on the other hand, but closer to the former than to the latter. In rank order, the three most fungible power assets appear to be wealth, political skill, and military power.

Economic wealth has the highest fungibility. It is the easiest to convert into the most liquid asset of all, namely, money, which in turn can be used to buy many different things—such as a good press, topflight international negotiators, smart lawyers, cutting-edge technology, bargaining power in international organizations, and so on. Wealth is also integral to military power. A rich state can generate more military power than a poor one. A state that is large and rich can, if it so chooses, generate especially large amounts of military power. The old mercantilist insight that wealth generates power (and vice-versa) is still valid.

Political skill is a second power asset that is highly fungible. By definition, skilled political operators are ones who can operate well in different policy realms because they have mastered the techniques of persuasion and influence. They are equally adept at selling free trade agreements, wars, or foreign aid to their citizens. Politically skillful statesmen can roam with ease across different policy realms. Indeed, that is what we commonly mean by a politically skillful leader—one who can lead in many different policy arenas. Thus, wealth and skill are resources that are easily transferable from one policy realm to another and are probably the two most liquid power assets.

Military power is a third fungible asset. It is not as fungible as wealth or skill, but that does not make it illiquid. Military power possesses versatility because force is integral to politics, even when states are at peace. If force is integral to international politics, it must be fungible. It cannot have pervasive effects and yet be severely restricted in its utility. Its pervasive effects, however, can be uniformly strong, uniformly weak, or variable in strength. Which is the case depends on how military power affects the many domains, policy arenas, and disparate issues that come within its field. At the minimum, however, military power is fungible to a degree because its physical use, its threatened use, or simply its mere presence structure expectations and influence the political calculations of actors. The gravitational effects of military power mean that its influence pervades the other policy realms, even if it is not dominant in most of them. Pervasiveness implies fungibility.

In the case of military power, moreover, greater amounts of it increase its fungibility. Up to a reasonable point, more of it is therefore better than less. It is more desirable to be militarily powerful than militarily weak. Militarily powerful states have greater clout in world politics than militarily weak ones. Militarily strong states are less subject to the influence of other states than militarily weak ones. Militarily powerful states can better offer protection to other states, or more seriously threaten them, in order to influence their behavior than can militarily weak ones. Finally, militarily powerful states are more secure than militarily weak ones. To have more clout, to be less subject to the will of others, to be in a stronger position to offer protection or threaten harm, and to be secure in a world where others are insecure—these are political advantages that can be diplomatically exploited, and they can also strengthen the will, resolve, and bargaining stance of the state that has them. Thus, although military power ranks behind wealth and skill in terms of its versatility, it can be a close third behind those two, at least for those great powers that choose to generate large amounts of it and then to exploit it.

Conflating Sufficiency and Fungibility

The view argued here—that military power possesses a relatively high degree of fungibility—is not the conventional wisdom. Rather, the commonly accepted view is that put forward by David Baldwin, who argues that military power is of restricted utility. Baldwin asserts:

> Two of the most important weaknesses in traditional theorizing about international politics have been the tendency to exaggerate the effectiveness of military power resources and the tendency to treat military power as the ultimate measuring rod to which other forms of power should be compared.[1]

Baldwin's view of military power follows from his more general argument that power assets tend to be situationally specific. By that he means: "What functions as a power resource in one policy-contingency framework may be irrelevant in another." If assets are situationally or domain-specific, then they are not easily transferable from one policy realm to another. In fact, as Baldwin argues: "Political power resources. . .tend to be much less liquid than economic resources"; and although power resources vary in their degree of fungibility, "no political power resource begins to approach the degree of fungibility of money."[2]

For Baldwin, two consequences flow from the domain-specific nature of power resources. First, we cannot rely on a gross assessment of a state's overall power assets in order to determine how well it will do in any specific area. Instead, we must assess the strength of the resources that it wields in that specific domain.

Second, the generally low fungibility of political power resources explains what Baldwin calls the "paradox of unrealized power": the fact that a strong state can prevail in one policy area and lose in another. The reason for this, he tells us, is simple: The state at issue has strong assets in the domain where it prevails and weak ones where it does not.

On the face of it, Baldwin's argument is reasonable. It makes intuitive sense to argue, for example, that armies are better at defeating armies than they are at promoting stable exchange rates. It also makes good sense to take the position that the more carefully we assess what specific assets a state can bring to bear on a specific issue, the more fine-tuned our feel will be of what the state can realistically accomplish on that issue. To deny that all power assets are domain-specific to a degree is therefore absurd. Equally absurd, however, are the positions that all assets are domain-specific to the same degree, and that a gross inventory of a state's overall power assets is not a reliable, even if only a rough, guide to how well the state is likely to do in any given domain. Assets are not equal in fungibility, and fine-tuning does not mean dramatically altering assessments.

What does all this mean for the fungibility of military power? Should we accept Baldwin's view about it? I argue that we should not. To see why, let us look in greater detail at what else he has to say.

Baldwin adduces four examples that purport to demonstrate the limited versatility of military power.[3] The examples are hypothetical, but are nonetheless useful to analyze because they are equivalent to thought experiments. These are the examples:

> Possession of nuclear weapons is not just irrelevant to securing the election of a U.S. citizen as UN secretary-general; it is a hindrance.
>
> . . . The owner of a political power resource, such as the means to deter atomic attack, is likely to have difficulty converting this resource into another resource that would, for instance, allow his country to become the leader of the Third World.
>
> Planes loaded with nuclear weapons may strengthen a state's ability to deter nuclear attacks but may be irrelevant to rescuing the *Pueblo* [a U.S. destroyer seized by the North Koreans in early 1968] on short notice.
>
> The ability to get other countries to refrain from attacking one's homeland is not the same as the ability to "win the hearts and minds of the people" in a faraway land [the reference is to the Vietnam War].[4]

Seemingly persuasive at first glance, the examples are, in fact, highly misleading. A little reflection about each will show how Baldwin has committed the cardinal error of conflating the insufficiency of an instrument with its low fungibility, and, therefore, how he has made military power look more domain-specific in each example than it really is.

Consider first the United Nations case. Throughout the United Nations' history, the United States never sought, nor did it ever favor, the election of an American as secretary-general. If it had, money and bribes would have been of as little use as a nuclear threat. The Soviet Union would have vetoed it, just as the United States would have vetoed a Soviet national as secretary-general. Neither state would have countenanced the appointment of a citizen from the other, or from one of its client states. The reason is clear: The Cold War polarized the United Nations between East and West, and neither superpower was willing to allow the other to gain undue influence in the institution if they could prevent it. Therefore, because neither superpower would have ever agreed on a national from the other camp, both sought a secretary-general from the ranks of the unaligned, neutral nations. This explains why cold war secretaries-general came from the unaligned Scandinavian or Third World nations (Dag Hammarskjold from Sweden; U Thant from Burma, for example), particularly during the heyday of the Cold War. This arrangement, moreover, served both superpowers' interest. At those rare times when they both agreed that the United Nations could be helpful, UN mediation was made more effective because it had a secretary-general that was neutral, not aligned.

Finally, even if America's military power had nothing to do with electing secretaries-general, we should not conclude that it has nothing to do with America's standing within the institution. America's preeminence within the United Nations has been clear. So, too, is the fact that this stems from America's position as the world's strongest nation, a position deriving from both its economic and military strength. Thus, although nuclear weapons cannot buy secretary-general elections, great military power brings great influence in an international organization, one of whose main purposes, after all, is to achieve collective security through the threat or use of force.

The Third World example is equally misleading. To see why, let us perform a simple "thought experiment." Although a Third World leader that had armed his state with nuclear weapons might not rise automatically to the top of the Third World pack, he or she would become a mighty important actor nonetheless. Think of how less weighty China and India, which have nuclear weapons, would appear to other states if they did not possess them; and think of how Iraq, Iran, or Libya, which do not have them, would be viewed if they did. For the former set of states, nuclear weapons add to their global political standing; for the latter set, their mere attempts to acquire them have caused their prominence to rise considerably. By themselves, nuclear weapons cannot buy the top slot in the Third World or elsewhere. Neither economic wealth, nor military power, nor any other power asset alone, can buy top dog. That slot is reserved for the state that surpasses the others in all the key categories of power. Although they do not buy the top position, nuclear weapons nevertheless do significantly enhance the international influence of any state that possesses them, if influence is measured by how seriously a state is taken by others. In this particular case, then, Baldwin is correct to argue that nuclear weapons are not readily convertible into another instrument asset. Although true, the point is irrelevant: They add to the ultimate resource for which all the other assets of a state are mustered—political influence.

The *Pueblo* example is the most complex of the cases, and the one, when reexamined, that provides the strongest support for Baldwin's general argument.[5] Even when reexamined, this strong case falls far short of demonstrating that military power has little fungibility.

The facts of the *Pueblo* case are straightforward. On 23 January 1968, North Korea seized the USS *Pueblo*, an intelligence ship that was fitted with sophisticated electronic eavesdropping capabilities and that was listening in on North Korea, and did not release the ship's crew members until 22 December 1968, almost a year after they had been captured. North Korea claimed the ship was patrolling inside its twelve-mile territorial waters limit; the United States denied the claim because its radio "fix" on the *Pueblo* showed that it was patrolling fifteen and a half nautical miles from the nearest North Korean land point. Immediately after the seizure, the United States beefed up its conventional and nuclear forces in East Asia, sending 14,000 Navy and Air Force reservists and 350 additional aircraft to South Korea, as well as moving the aircraft carrier USS *Enterprise* and its task force within a few minutes' flying time of Wonsan, North Korea. Some of the aircraft sent to South Korean bases and those on the *Enterprise* were nuclear capable. According to President Johnson, several military options were considered but ultimately rejected:

> mining Wonsan harbor; mining other North Korean harbors; interdicting coastal shipping; seizing a North Korean ship; striking selected North Korean targets by air and naval gunfire. In each case we decided that the risk was too great and the possible accomplishment too small. "I do not want to win the argument and lose the sale," I consistently warned my advisers.[6]

The American government's denial, its military measures, and its subsequent diplomatic efforts, were to no avail. North Korea refused to release the crew. In fact, right from the outset of the crisis, the North Korean negotiators made clear that only an American confession that it had spied on North Korea and had intruded into its territorial waters would secure the crew's release. For eleven months the United States continued to insist that the *Pueblo* was not engaged in illegal activity, and that it had not violated North Korea's territorial waters. Only on 22 December, when General Gilbert Woodward, the U.S. representative to the negotiations, signed a statement in which the U.S. government apologized for the espionage and the intrusion, did North Korea release the crew. The American admission of guilt, however, was made under protest: Immediately before signing the statement, the government disavowed what it was about to sign; and immediately after the signing, the government disavowed what it had just admitted.

Although the facts of the *Pueblo* case are straightforward, the interpretation to be put on them is not. This much is clear: Neither nuclear weapons, nor any of America's other military assets, appear to have secured the crew's release. Equally clear, however, is that none of its other assets secured the crew's release either. Should we then conclude from this case that military power, diplomacy, and whatever other assets were employed to secure the crew's release have low fungibility? Clearly, that would be a foolish conclusion to draw. There was only one thing that secured the crew's release: the public humiliation of the United States. If nothing but humiliation worked, it is reasonable to conclude that humiliation either was, or more likely, quickly became North Korea's goal. When an adversary is firmly fixed on humiliation, military posturing, economic bribes, diplomatic pressure, economic threats, or any other tool used in moderation is not likely to succeed. Only extreme measures, such as waging war or economic blockade, are likely to be successful. At that point, the costs of such actions must be weighed against the benefits. One clear lesson we can draw from the *Pueblo* case is that sometimes there are tasks for which none of the traditional tools of statecraft are sufficient. These situations are rare, but they do on occasion occur. The *Pueblo* was one of them.

There is, however, a second and equally important point to be drawn from this example. Although it is true that America's military power did not secure the crew's release, nevertheless, there were other reasons to undertake the military buildup the United States subsequently engaged in. Neither the United States nor South Korea knew why the North had seized the *Pueblo*. President Johnson and his advisors, however, speculated that the seizure was related to the Tet offensive in Vietnam that began eight days after the *Pueblo*'s capture. They reasoned that the *Pueblo*'s seizure was deliberately timed to distract the United States and to frighten the South Koreans. Adding weight to this reasoning was the fact that the *Pueblo* was not an isolated incident. Two days earlier, thirty-one special North Korean agents infiltrated into Seoul and got within one-half mile of the presidential palace before they were overcome in battle. Their mission was to kill President Park. The United States feared that through these two incidents, and perhaps others to come, North Korea was trying to divert American military resources from Vietnam to Korea and to make the South Koreans sufficiently nervous that they would bring their two divisions fighting in Vietnam back home.[7]

The *Pueblo*'s seizure thus raised three problems for the United States: how to get its crew and ship back; how to deter the North from engaging in further provocative acts; and how to reassure the South Koreans sufficiently so that they would keep their troops in South Vietnam. A strong case could be made that the last two tasks, not the first, were the primary purposes for the subsequent American military buildup in East Asia. After all, the United States did not need additional forces there to pressure the North militarily to release the crew. There were already about 100,000 American troops in East Asia. A military buildup, however, would be a useful signal for deterrence of further provocations and reassurance of its ally. Until (or if) North Korea's archives are opened up, we cannot know whether deterrence of further provocation worked, because we do not know what additional plans the North had. What we do know is that the reassurance function of the buildup did work: South Korea kept its divisions in South Vietnam. Thus, America's military buildup had three purposes. Of those, one was achieved, another was not, and the third we cannot be certain about. In sum, it is wrong to draw the conclusion that the *Pueblo* case shows that force has little fungibility, even though military posturing appears not to have gotten the crew released.

Baldwin's final example is equally problematic if the point is to show that military power has little fungibility. Yes, it is true that preventing an attack on one's homeland is a different task than winning the hearts and minds of a people in a distant land. Presumably, however, the point of the example is to argue that the latter task is not merely different from the former, but also more difficult. If this is the assertion, it is unexceptionable: Compelling another government to change its behavior has always been an inherently more difficult task than deterring a given government from attacking one's homeland. Not only is interstate compellence more difficult than interstate deterrence, but intrastate compellence is more diffi-cult than interstate compellence. Forcing the adversaries in a civil war to lay down their arms and negotiate an end to their dispute is a notoriously difficult task, as the Chinese civil war in the 1940s, the Vietnamese civil war in the 1960s, and the Bosn-ian civil war in the 1990s all too tragically show. It is an especially difficult task in a situation like Vietnam, where the outside power's internal ally faces an adversary that has the force of nationalism on its side. (Ho Chi Minh was Vietnam's greatest nationalist figure of the twentieth century and was widely recognized as such within Vietnam.) It is hard to prevail in a civil war when the adversary monopolizes the appeal of nationalism. Equally important, however, it is hard to prevail in a civil war without resort to force. The United States could not have won in Vietnam by force alone, but it would have had no chance at all to win without it.

No thoughtful analyst of military power would therefore disagree with the fol-lowing propositions that can be teased out of the fourth example: (1) military power works better for defense than for conquest; (2) military power alone cannot guarantee pacification once conquest has taken place; (3) military power alone is not sufficient to compel a populace to accept the legitimacy of its government; and (4) compellence is more difficult than deterrence. These are reasonable state-ments. There is, however, also a fifth that should be drawn from this example: (5) when an outside power arrays itself in a civil war on the wrong side of nationalism, not only will force be insufficient to win, but so, too, will nearly all the other tools of statecraft—money, political skill, propaganda, and so on. In such cases military power suffers from the same insufficiency as the other instruments. That makes it no more, but no less, fungible than they are.

All four of Baldwin's examples demonstrate an important fact about military power: Used alone, it cannot achieve many things. Surely, this is an important point to remember, but is it one that is peculiar to military power alone or that proves that it has little fungibility? Surely not. Indeed, no single instrument of statecraft is ever sufficient to attain any significant foreign policy objective—a fact I shall term "task insufficiency."[8] There are two reasons for this. First, a statesman must antici-pate the counteractions that will be undertaken by the states he is trying to influ-ence. They will attempt to counter his stratagems with those of their own; they will use different types of instruments to offset the ones he is using; and they will attempt to compensate for their weakness in one area with their strength in another. A well-prepared influence attempt therefore requires a multi-instrumen-tal approach to deal with the likely counters to it. Second, any important policy itself has many facets. A multifaceted policy by necessity requires many instru-ments to implement it. For both reasons, all truly important matters require a statesman to muster several, if not all, the instruments at his disposal, even though he may rely more heavily on some than on others. In sum, in statecraft no tool can stand alone.

For military power, then, as for the other instruments of statecraft, fungibility should not be equated with sufficiency, and insufficiency should not be equated with low fungibility. A given instrument can carry a state part of the way to a given goal, even though it cannot carry the state all the way there. At one and the same time, an instrument of statecraft can usefully contribute to attaining many goals and yet by itself be insufficient to attain any one of them. Thus, careful consideration of Baldwin's examples demonstrates the following: (1) military power was not sufficient to achieve the defined task; (2) none of the other traditional policy instruments were sufficient either; and (3) military power was of some value, either for the defined task or for another task closely connected to it. What the examples did not demonstrate is that states are unable to transfer military power from one policy task to another. Indeed, to the contrary: Each showed that military power can be used for a variety of tasks, even though it may not be sufficient, by itself, to achieve any of them.

HOW FORCE ACHIEVES FUNGIBILITY

If military power is a versatile instrument of statecraft, then exactly how does it achieve its fungibility? What are the paths through which it can influence events in other domains?

There are two paths. The first is through the spill-over effects that military power has on other policy domains; the second, through the phenomenon of "linkage politics." In the first case, military power encounters military power, but from this military encounter ensues an outcome with significant consequences for non-military matters. In the second case, military power is deliberately linked to a non-military issue, with the purpose of strengthening a state's bargaining leverage on that issue. In the first case, force is used against force; in the second, force is linked with another issue. In both cases, military power becomes fungible because it produces effects outside the strictly military domain. I explain how each path works and illustrate both with examples.

Spill-Over Effects

A military encounter, whether peaceful or forceful, yields a result that can be consequential to the interactions and the outcomes that take place in other domains. This result, which I term the "spill-over effect," is too often forgotten.[9] Military-to-military encounters do not produce only military results—cities laid waste, armies defeated, enemies subdued, attacks prevented, allies protected. They also bring about political effects that significantly influence events in other domains. Military power achieves much of its fungibility through this effect: The political shock waves of a military encounter reverberate beyond the military domain and extend into the other policy domains as well. The exercise of successful deterrence, compellence, or defense affects the overall political framework of relations between two states. Because all policy domains are situated within this overarching framework, what happens in the latter affects what happens in these domains. Spill-over effects define with more precision why force acts akin to a gravitational field.

A spill-over effect can be understood either as a prerequisite or a by-product. As a prerequisite, the result produced by the act of force checking force creates something that is deliberate and viewed as essential in order to reach a given out-come in another domain. As a by-product, the encounter produces something in another domain that may be beneficial but is incidental or even unintended. Of course, what is by-product and what is prerequisite hangs on what outcomes are valued in that other domain. Two examples will illustrate how the spill-over effect works and how it manifests itself either as a prerequisite or a by-product.

Examples: Banking and Cold War Interdependence

The first example has to do with banks; the second with recent history. The banking example demonstrates the role force plays in solvency; the historical example, the role that U.S. military power played in creating today's economic interdependence.

First, the banking example. Begin with this question, Why do we deposit our money in a bank? The answer is we put our money in a bank because we think we can take it out whenever we want. We believe the money is there when we want it. In short, we believe the bank to be solvent.

Solvency is usually thought of solely in economic terms: A bank is solvent because it has enough assets to meet its financial liabilities if they are called.[10] Sol-vency, however, is a function, not simply of finances, but of physical safety. A bank's solvency depends on the fact both that its assets exceed its liabilities (its balance sheet is in the black) and that its assets are physically secure (not easily stolen). Physical security is therefore as important to a bank's solvency as its liquidity, even though we generally take the former for granted when we reside in a stable domes-tic order. If the banks within a state could be robbed at will, then its citizens would not put their money in them. A state makes banks physically secure by using its military power to deter and defend against would-be robbers and to compel them to give back the funds if a robbery takes place (assuming they are caught and the funds recovered). Through its use of its legitimate monopoly on the use of force, a state seeks to neutralize the threat of forcible seizure. If the state succeeds in establishing the physical security of its banks, it produces one of the two prerequi-sites required for a bank's solvency.

In sum, in a well-ordered state, public force suppresses private force. The effect of this suppression is to create a generalized stability that sets the context within which all societal interactions take place. This effect spills over into numer-ous other domains and produces many manifestations, one of which is confidence about the physical security of banks. This confidence can be viewed as a by-prod-uct of the public suppression of private force, as a prerequisite to banking solvency, or, more sensibly, as both.

A good historical example of the spill-over effect of military power is the eco-nomic interdependence produced among the free world's economies during the Cold War. In a fundamental sense, this is the banking analogy writ large. The bank is the free world economies, the potential robber is the Soviet Union, and the provider of physical safety is the United States.

During the Cold War era, the United States used its military power to deter a Soviet attack on its major allies, the Western Europeans and the Japanese. American military power checked Soviet military power. This military-to-military encounter yielded a high degree of military security for America's allies, but it also produced several by-products, one of the most important of which was the creation of an open and interdependent economic order among the United States, Western Europe, and Japan. Today's era of economic interdependence is in no small part due to the exercise of American military power during the Cold War. A brief discussion will show how American military power helped create the economic interdependence from which much of today's world benefits.

America's forty-year struggle with the Soviets facilitated economic integration within Western Europe and among Western Europe, North America, and Japan. Obviously, American military power was not the sole factor responsible for today's interdependence among the major industrialized nations. Also crucial were the conversion of governments to Keynesian economics; their overwhelming desire to avoid the catastrophic experience of the Great Depression and the global war it brought in its wake; the lesson they learned from the 1930s about how noncooperative, beggar-thy-neighbor policies ultimately redound to the disadvantage of all; the willingness of the United States to underwrite the economic costs of setting up the system and of sustaining it for a time; the acceptance by its allies of the legitimacy of American leadership; the hard work of the peoples involved; and so on. Important as all these factors were, however, we must remember where economic openness first began and where it subsequently flourished most: among the great powers that were allied with the United States against the Soviet Union.

How, then, did the Soviet threat and the measures taken to counter it help produce the modern miracle of economic interdependence among America's industrial allies? And how, exactly, did America's military power and its overseas military presence contribute to it? There were four ways.

First, the security provided by the United States created a political stability that was crucial to the orderly development of trading relations. As I discussed at the outset of this article, markets do not exist in political vacuums; rather, they work best when embedded in political frameworks that yield predictable expectations. American military power deployed in the Far East and on the European continent brought these stable expectations, first, by providing the psychological reassurance that the Europeans and the Japanese needed to rebuild themselves and, second, by continuing to provide them thereafter with a sense of safety that enabled their economic energies to work their will. Indeed, we should remember that the prime reason NATO was formed was psychological, not military: to make the Europeans feel secure enough against the Soviets so that they would have the political will to rebuild themselves economically. The initial purpose of NATO is the key to its (and to the U.S.-Japan defense treaty's) long-lasting function: the creation of a politically stable island amidst a turbulent international sea.

Second, America's provision of security to its allies in Europe and in the Far East dampened their respective concerns about German and Japanese military rearmament. The United States presence protected its allies not only from the Soviets, but also from the Germans and the Japanese. Because German and Japanese military power was contained in alliances that the United States dominated, and especially because American troops were visibly present and literally within each nation, Germany's and Japan's neighbors, while they did not forget the horrors they suffered at the hands of these two during the Second World War, nevertheless, were not paralyzed from cooperating with them. The success of the European Common Market owes as much to the presence of American military power on the continent of Europe as it does to the vision of men like Monnet. The same can be said for the Far East. America's military presence has helped "oil the waters" for Japan's economic dominance there.

Third, America's military presence helped to dampen concerns about disparities in relative economic growth and about vulnerabilities inherent in interdependence, both of which are heightened in an open economic order. Freer trade benefits all nations, but not equally. The most efficient benefit the most; and economic efficiencies can be turned to military effect. Interdependence brings dependencies, all the greater the more states specialize economically. Unequal gains from trade and trade dependencies all too often historically have had adverse political and military effects. Through its provision of military protection to its allies, the United States mitigated the security externalities of interdependence and enabled the Germans and the Japanese to bring their neighbors (America's allies) into their economic orbits without those neighbors fearing that German or Japanese military conquest or political domination would follow. With the security issue dealt with, the economic predominance of the Germans and Japanese was easier for their neighbors to swallow.

Finally, America's military presence fostered a solidarity that came by virtue of being partners against a common enemy. That sense of solidarity, in turn, helped develop the determination and the goodwill necessary to overcome the inevitable economic disputes that interdependencies bring. The "spill-over" effects of military cooperation against the Soviets on the political will to sustain economic openness should not be underestimated, though they are difficult to pinpoint and quantify. Surely, however, the sense of solidarity and good will that alliance in a common cause bred must have had these spill-over effects. Finally, the need to preserve a united front against the common enemy put limits on how far the allies, and the United States, would permit their economic disputes to go. The need to maintain a united political-military front bounded the inevitable economic disputes and prevented them from escalating into a downward-spiraling economic nationalism. Political stability, protection from potential German and Japanese military resurgence, the dampening of concerns about relative gains and dependencies, and the sense of solidarity—all of these were aided by the American military presence in Europe and the Far East.

Linkage Politics

The second way force exerts influence on other domains of policy is through the power of linkage politics. In politics, whether domestic or foreign, issues are usually linked to one another. The link can be either functional or artificial. If two issues are linked functionally, then there is a causal connection between them: A change in one produces a change in the other. The price of the dollar (its exchange rate value) and the price of oil imports, for example, are functionally linked, because the global oil market is priced in dollars. (Not only that, oil can only be bought with dollars.) A decline in the value of the dollar will increase the cost of a given amount of oil imported to the United States. Similarly, a rise in the value of the dollar will decrease the cost of a given amount of imported oil. As long as oil remains priced in dollars, the functional tie between exchange rates and energy cannot be delinked. Moreover, as the oil-dollar example illustrates, functional linkages generally have corresponding spill-over effects. That is, weakness on one issue (a weaker dollar) produces more weakness on the other (more money spent on energy imports); and strength on one (a stronger dollar) produces greater strength on the other (cheaper energy imports). Thus, functional linkages produce causal effects that either magnify a state's weakness or add to its strength.

When two issues are linked artificially, there is no causal connection between them. A change in one does not automatically produce a change in the other. Instead, the two issues become linked because a statesman has made a connection where none before existed. Usually, but not always, this will be done to gain bargaining leverage. By making a link between two heretofore unconnected issues, statesmen try to bring about politically what is not produced functionally. They make a link in order to compensate for weakness on a given issue. Their method is to tie an issue where they are weak to an issue where they are strong. Their goal is to produce a more desirable outcome in the weak area either by threatening to do something undesirable in the strong area, or by promising to do something beneficial there. If they can make the connection stick, then the result of an artificial linkage is a strengthening of a state's overall position. Unlike a functional linkage, where weakness begets weakness and strength begets strength, in an artificial linkage, strength offsets weakness. Thus, an artificial linkage is a bargaining connection that is made in the head of a statesman, but it is not any less real or any less effective as a result. I provide an example of a bargaining linkage below.

Whether functional or artificial, issue linkages have a crucial consequence for both the analysis and the exercise of state power. We can put the point more strongly: Because issues are connected, domains cannot be wholly delinked from one another. If they cannot be delinked, then we should not view them in isolation from one another. Therefore, any explanation of an outcome in a given domain that is based only on what goes on in that domain will always be incomplete, if not downright wrong. In sum, issue linkages limit the explanatory power of a domain-restricted analysis.

Bargaining linkages in particular make state assets more fungible than they might otherwise be. Linkage politics is a fact of international political life. We should not expect otherwise. Statesmen are out to make the best deals they can by compensating for weakness in one area with strength in others. Powerful states can better engage in these compensatory linkages than can weak ones. They are stronger in more areas than they are weak; consequently, they can more easily utilize their leverage in the strong areas to make up for their deficit in the weak ones. Great powers are also better able to shift assets among issue areas in order to build positions of bargaining strength when necessary. They can, for example, more easily generate military power when they need to in order to link it to nonmilitary tasks. Therefore, because powerful states can link issues more easily than can weaker ones, can compensate for deficiencies better, can generate more resources and do so more quickly when needed, and can shift assets around with greater ease, how powerful a state is overall remains an essential determinant to how successful it is internationally, irrespective of how weak it may be at any given moment on any specific issue in any particular domain. In sum, linkage politics enhances the advantages of being powerful and boosts the fungibility of force by enabling it to cross domains. . . .

Examples: Deficits, Petrodollars, and Oil Prices

Three . . . brief examples show the range of state goals that can be served by constructing such linkages.

The first involves the relation between America's large and continuing balance of payments deficits and its global alliance system. Throughout most of the Cold War era, the United States ran an annual large balance of payments deficits. Historically, no nation has been able to buy more abroad than it sells abroad (import more than it exports) in as huge a volume and for as long a period as has the United States. There were many reasons why it was able to, ranging from the liquidity that deficit dollars provided, which enabled world trade to grow, to general confidence in the American economy, which caused foreigners to invest their dollar holdings in the United States. Part of the reason that foreigners continued to take America's continuing flow of dollars, however, was an implicit, if not explicit, tradeoff: In return for their acceptance of American IOU's (deficit dollars), the United States provided the largest holders of them (the Germans, the Japanese, and the Saudis) military protection against their enemies. America's military strength compensated for its lack of fiscal discipline.[11]

A second example involves the recycling of petrodollars.[12] After the oil price hikes of the 1970s, the OPEC producers, especially the Persian Gulf members, were accumulating more dollars than they could profitably invest at home. Where to put those dollars was an important financial decision, especially for the Saudis, who were generating the largest dollar surpluses. There is strong circumstantial evidence that the Saudis agreed to park a sizable portion of their petrodollars in U.S. Treasury bills (T-bills) in part because of an explicit American proposal "to provide a security umbrella for the Gulf."[13] As David Spiro notes: "By the fourth quarter of 1977, Saudi Arabia accounted for twenty percent of all holdings of Treasury notes and bonds by foreign central banks."[14] The Saudis also continued to agree to price oil in dollars rather than peg it to a basket of currencies. Although there were clear financial incentives for both Saudi decisions, the incentives are not sufficient to explain Saudi actions. The Kuwaitis, for example, never put as many of their petrodollars in the United States, nor as many in T-bills, as did the Saudis. Moreover, an internal U.S. Treasury study concluded that the Saudis would have done better if oil had been pegged to a basket of currencies than to dollars. Indeed, OPEC had decided in 1975 to price oil in such a basket, but never followed through.[15] America's provision of security to the Saudis was an important, even if not sufficient, ingredient in persuading them both to price oil in dollars and then to park the dollars in the United States. Both decisions were of considerable economic benefit to the United States. Parking Saudi dollars in T-bills gave the American government "access to a huge pool of foreign capital"; pricing oils in dollars meant that the United States "could print money to buy oil."[16] Military power bought economic benefits.

A third example, again involving the Saudis, concerns the link between American military protection and the price of oil. The Saudis have a long-term economic interest that dictates moderation in oil prices. With a relatively small population and with the world's largest proven oil reserves, their strategy lies in maximizing revenue from oil over the long term. It is therefore to their advantage to keep the price of oil high enough to earn sizable profits, but not so high as to encourage investment in alternative energy sources. Periodically, Saudi Arabia has faced considerable pressure from the price hawks within OPEC to push prices higher than its interest dictates. American military protection has strengthened Saudi willingness to resist the hawks.

A specific instance of this interaction between U.S. protection and Saudi moderation, for example, occurred in the fall of 1980, with the onset of the Iran-Iraq war. Iraq attacked Iran in September, and the two countries proceeded to bomb one another's oil facilities. The initial stages of the war removed about four million barrels of oil per day from world markets and drove the price of oil to its highest level ever ($42 per barrel).[17] As part of their balancing strategy in the Gulf, this time the Saudis had allied themselves with Iraq and, fearing Iranian retaliation against their oil fields, asked for American military intervention to deter Iranian attacks on their oil fields and facilities. The United States responded by sending AWACS aircraft to Saudi Arabia and by setting up a joint Saudi-American naval task force to guard against Iranian attacks on oil tankers in the Gulf.[18] In return, the Saudis increased their oil production from 9.7 million barrels per day (mbd) to 10.3, which was the highest level it could sustain, and kept it there for the next ten months. Saudi actions had a considerable effect on oil prices, as Safran argues:

> Physically, the Saudi increase of 0.5 mbd was hardly enough to make up for the short-fall caused by the war . . . . Psychologically, however, the Saudi action was crucial in preventing the development of the kind of panic that had sent oil prices soaring after the fall of the shah and the Saudis' April 1979 decision to cut production by 1 mbd.[19]

As in the other cases, in this instance, American military power alone was not sufficient to cause Saudi actions to lower oil prices, but it was essential because during this turbulent period Saudi decisions on how much oil they would pump were not determined solely by economic factors. True, the Saudis, against the desires of the price hawks, which included the Iranians, had been pumping more oil since 1978 in order to lower oil prices. The Saudis had also violated their long-term strategy in March 1979, however, when they decided to cut oil production by 1 mbd, primarily to appease Iran, a move that triggered a rapid increase in oil prices. This pumping decision followed a political decision to move diplomatically away from the United States. Only a few months later, however, the conflict within the Saudi ruling family between an American- versus an Arab-oriented strategy was resolved in a compromise that led to a political reconciliation with the United States; and this political decision was followed by another to increase oil production by 1 mbd, starting 1 July 1979.[20] Before the Iran-Iraq war, then, Saudi pumping decisions were affected by political calculations about their security, in which the strategic connection with the Americans played a prominent role. If this was true in peacetime, surely it was so in wartime, too. The military protection announced by the Americans on 30 September 1980 was a necessary condition for the Saudi increase in oil production that followed in October. Again, military power had bought an economic benefit.

In sum, these . . . examples— . . . America's ability to run deficits, petrodollar recycling, and moderate oil prices—all illustrate just how pervasive bargaining linkages are in international politics and specifically how military power can be linked politically to produce them. In all cases, military power was not sufficient. Without it, however, the United States could not have produced the favorable economic outcomes it achieved.

NOTES

1. David Baldwin, *Paradoxes of Power* (New York: Blackwell, 1989), 151–52. Baldwin first developed his argument in his "Power Analysis and World Politics," *World Politics* 31, 1 (January 1979), 161–94, which is reprinted in *Paradoxes of Power.*
2. Quotes from Baldwin, *Paradoxes of Power,* 134–35, 135, and 136, respectively.
3. In fairness to Baldwin, these examples were not fully developed, but consist of only a sentence or two. Nevertheless, they are fair game because Baldwin used them as illustrations of his more general point about the limits to the utility of military power. The fact that he did not develop them further led him astray, in my view. He was trying to show with them that military power is less effective than commonly thought. I reinterpret these examples to show how versatile military power in fact is. Neither Baldwin nor I, however, can put a number on the fungibility of military power, and I certainly agree with him that "no political power resource begins to approach the degree of fungibility of money" (Baldwin, *Paradoxes of Power,* 135).
4. Baldwin, *Paradoxes of Power,* 134, 135, 133.
5. For the facts and interpretation of this case, I have relied on Lyndon Baines Johnson, *The Vantage Point: Perspectives of the Presidency, 1963–1969* (New York: Holt, Rinehart, Winston, 1971), 385, 387, and 532–37; Barry M. Blechman and Stephen S. Kaplan, *Force Without War: U.S. Armed Forces as a Political Instrument* (Washington, D.C.: Brookings, 1978), 48 and 71–72; Richard P. Stebbins and Elaine P. Adam, *Documents on American Foreign Relations, 1968–69* (New York: Simon & Schuster, 1972), 292–302; and the *New York Times Index,* 1968, 732–36.
6. Johnson, 536.
7. Johnson, 535; Blechman and Kaplan, 72.
8. Baldwin, of course, agrees with this point. He has written: "Actually, any technique of statecraft works poorly in isolation from the others." See David A. Baldwin, *Economic Statecraft* (Princeton: Princeton University Press, 1985), 143.
9. I have borrowed this term from Ernst Haas, even though I am using it differently than he does. He used the phrase to describe the effects that cooperation on economic

matters among the states of Western Europe could have on their political relations. He argued that cooperation on economic matters would spill over into their political relations, induce greater cooperation there, and lead ultimately to the political integration of Western Europe. See Ernst Haas, *Beyond the Nation State: Functionalism and International Organization* (Stanford: Stanford University Press, 1964), 48. For Haas's later assessment of how effective spill-over effects were, see Ernst Haas, *The Obsolescence of Regional Integration Theory* (Berkeley: Institute of International Studies, University of California, 1974).

10. Solvency is to be distinguished from liquidity. A bank can be solvent but not liquid. Liquidity refers to the ability of a bank to meet all its liabilities upon demand. Most banks are not able to do so if all the demands are called at the same time. The reason is that many assets of any given bank are tied up in investments that cannot be called back on short notice but take time to convert into cash. The function of a central bank is to solve the liquidity problem of a nation's banking system by providing the liquidity in the short term in order to prevent runs on a bank.

11. As Gilpin put it: "Partially for economic reasons, but more importantly for political and strategic ones, Western Europe (primarily West Germany) and Japan agreed to finance the American balance of payments deficit." See Robert Gilpin, *U.S. Power and the Multinational Corporation: The Political Economy of Direct Investment* (New York: Basic Books, 1975), 154.

12. For this example, I have relied exclusively on David Spiro's original and thorough research. See David E. Spiro, *Hegemony Unbound: Petrodollar Recycling and the De-Legitimation of American Power* (Ithaca: Cornell University Press, forthcoming), chap. 4.

13. The quote is from an interview conducted by Spiro in Boston in 1984 with a former American ambassador to the Middle East. See Spiro, 271. (All page references are for the manuscript version.)

14. Spiro, 261.

15. Spiro, 263–66, 281–83.

16. Spiro, 259, 287.

17. Daniel Yergin, *The Prize: The Epic Quest for Oil, Money and Power* (New York: Simon & Schuster, 1992), 711.

18. Nadar Safran, *Saudi Arabia: The Ceaseless Quest for Security* (Ithaca: Cornell University Press, 1988), 322, 410–11.

19. Safran, 411.

20. Safran, 237.

The Strategic Logic of Suicide Terrorism

ROBERT A. PAPE

Terrorist organizations are increasingly relying on suicide attacks to achieve major political objectives. For example, spectacular suicide terrorist attacks have recently been employed by Palestinian groups in attempts to force Israel to abandon the West Bank and Gaza, by the Liberation Tigers of Tamil Eelam to compel the Sri Lankan government to accept an independent Tamil homeland, and by Al Qaeda to pressure the United States to withdraw from the Saudi Arabian Peninsula. Moreover, such attacks are increasing both in tempo and location. Before the early 1980s, suicide terrorism was rare but not unknown. However, since the attack on the U.S. embassy in Beirut in April 1983, there have been at least 188 separate suicide terrorist attacks worldwide, in Lebanon, Israel, Sri Lanka, India, Pakistan, Afghanistan, Yemen, Turkey, Russia and the United States. The rate has increased from 31 in the 1980s, to 104 in the 1990s, to 53 in 2000–2001 alone. The rise of suicide terrorism is especially remarkable, given that the total number of terrorist incidents worldwide fell during the period, from a peak of 666 in 1987 to a low of 274 in 1998, with 348 in 2001.

What accounts for the rise in suicide terrorism, especially, the sharp escalation from the 1990s onward? Although terrorism has long been part of international politics, we do not have good explanations for the growing phenomenon of suicide terrorism. Traditional studies of terrorism tend to treat suicide attack as one of many tactics that terrorists use and so do not shed much light on the recent rise of this type of attack. The small number of studies addressed explicitly to suicide terrorism tend to focus on the irrationality of the act of suicide from the perspective of the individual attacker. As a result, they focus on individual motives—either religious indoctrination (especially Islamic Fundamentalism) or psychological predispositions that might drive individual suicide bombers.

The first-wave explanations of suicide terrorism were developed during the 1980s and were consistent with the data from that period. However, as suicide attacks mounted from the 1990s onward, it has become increasingly evident that these initial explanations are insufficient to account for which individuals become

From Robert A. Pape, "The Strategic Logic of Suicide Terrorism," *American Political Science Review,* Vol. 97, No. 3 (August 2003), pp. 343–361. Copyright © 2003 by The American Political Science Association. Reprinted with the permission of Cambridge University Press.

suicide terrorists and, more importantly, why terrorist organizations are increasingly relying on this form of attack. First, although religious motives may matter, modern suicide terrorism is not limited to Islamic Fundamentalism. Islamic groups receive the most attention in Western media, but the world's leader in suicide terrorism is actually the Liberation Tigers of Tamil Eelam (LTTE), a group who recruits from the predominantly Hindu Tamil population in northern and eastern Sri Lanka and whose ideology has Marxist/Leninist elements. The LTTE alone accounts for 75 of the 186 suicide terrorist attacks from 1980 to 2001. Even among Islamic suicide attacks, groups with secular orientations account for about a third of these attacks.

Second, although study of the personal characteristics of suicide attackers may someday help identify individuals terrorist organizations are likely to recruit for this purpose, the vast spread of suicide terrorism over the last two decades suggests that there may not be a single profile. Until recently, the leading experts in psychological profiles of suicide terrorists characterized them as uneducated, unemployed, socially isolated, single men in their late teens and early 20s. Now we know that suicide terrorists can be college educated or uneducated, married or single, men or women, socially isolated or integrated, from age 13 to age 47. In other words, although only a tiny number of people become suicide terrorists, they come from a broad cross section of lifestyles, and it may be impossible to pick them out in advance.

In contrast to the first-wave explanations, this article shows that suicide terrorism follows a strategic logic. Even if many suicide attackers are irrational or fanatical, the leadership groups that recruit and direct them are not. Viewed from the perspective of the terrorist organization, suicide attacks are designed to achieve specific political purposes: to coerce a target government to change policy, to mobilize additional recruits and financial support, or both. Crenshaw has shown that terrorism is best understood in terms of its strategic function; the same is true for suicide terrorism. In essence, suicide terrorism is an extreme form of what Thomas Schelling calls "the rationality of irrationality," in which an act that is irrational for individual attackers is meant to demonstrate credibility to a democratic audience that still more and greater attacks are sure to come. As such, modern suicide terrorism is analogous to instances of international coercion. For states, air power and economic sanctions are often the preferred coercive tools. For terrorist groups, suicide attacks are becoming the coercive instrument of choice.

To examine the strategic logic of suicide terrorism, this article collects the universe suicide terrorist attacks worldwide from 1980 to 2001, explains how terrorist organizations have assessed the effectiveness of these attacks, and evaluates the limits on their coercive utility.

Five principal findings follow. First, suicide terrorism is strategic. The vast majority of suicide terrorist attacks are not isolated or random acts by individual fanatics but, rather, occur in clusters as part of a larger campaign by an organized group to achieve a specific political goal. Groups using suicide terrorism consistently announce specific political goals and stop suicide attacks when those goals have been fully or partially achieved.

Second, the strategic logic of suicide terrorism is specifically designed to coerce modern democracies to make significant concessions to national self-determination. In general, suicide terrorist campaigns seek to achieve specific territorial goals, most often the withdrawal of the target state's military forces from what the terrorists see as national homeland. From Lebanon to Israel to Sri Lanka to Kashmir to Chechnya, every suicide terrorist campaign from 1980 to 2001 has been waged by terrorist groups whose main goal has been to establish or maintain self-determination for their community's homeland by compelling an enemy to withdraw. Further, every suicide terrorist campaign since 1980 has been targeted against a state that had a democratic form of government.

Third, during the past 20 years, suicide terrorism has been steadily rising because terrorists have learned that it pays. Suicide terrorists sought to compel American and French military forces to abandon Lebanon in 1983, Israeli forces to leave Lebanon in 1985, Israeli forces to quit the Gaza Strip and the West Bank in 1994 and 1995, the Sri Lankan government to create an independent Tamil state from 1990 on, and the Turkish government to grant autonomy to the Kurds in the late 1990s. Terrorist groups did not achieve their full objectives in all these cases. However, in all but the case of Turkey, the terrorist political cause made more gains after the resort to suicide operations than it had before. . . .

Fourth, although moderate suicide terrorism led to moderate concessions, these more ambitious suicide terrorist campaigns are not likely to achieve still greater gains and may well fail completely. In general, suicide terrorism relies on the threat to inflict low to medium levels of punishment on civilians. In other circumstances, this level of punishment has rarely caused modern nation states to surrender significant political goals, partly because modern nation states are often willing to countenance high costs for high interests and partly because modern nation states are often able to mitigate civilian costs by making economic and other adjustments. Suicide terrorism does not change a nation's willingness to trade high interests for high costs, but suicide attacks can overcome a country's efforts to mitigate civilian costs. Accordingly, suicide terrorism may marginally increase the punishment that is inflicted and so make target nations somewhat more likely to surrender modest goals, but it is unlikely to compel states to abandon important interests related to the physical security or national wealth of the state. National governments have in fact responded aggressively to ambitious suicide terrorist campaigns in recent years, events which confirm these expectations.

Finally, the most promising way to contain suicide terrorism is to reduce terrorists' confidence in their ability to carry out such attacks on the target society. States that face persistent suicide terrorism should recognize that neither offensive military action nor concessions alone are likely to do much good and should invest significant resources in border defenses and other means of homeland security.

THE LOGIC OF SUICIDE TERRORISM

Most suicide terrorism is undertaken as a strategic effort directed toward achieving particular political goals; it is not simply the product of irrational individuals or an expression of fanatical hatreds. The main purpose of suicide terrorism is to use the threat of punishment to coerce a target government to change policy, especially to cause democratic states to withdraw forces from territory terrorists view as their homeland. The record of suicide terrorism from 1980 to 2001 exhibits tendencies in the timing, goals, and targets of attack that are consistent with this strategic logic but not with irrational or fanatical behavior: (1) *timing*—nearly all suicide attacks occur in organized, coherent campaigns, not as isolated or randomly timed incidents; (2) *nationalist goals*—suicide terrorist campaigns are directed at gaining control of what the terrorists see as their national homeland territory, specifically at ejecting foreign forces from that territory; and (3) *target selection*—all suicide terrorist campaigns in the last two decades have been aimed at democracies, which make more suitable targets from the terrorists' point of view.

Defining Suicide Terrorism

Terrorism involves the use of violence by an organization other than a national government to cause intimidation or fear among a target audience. Although one could broaden the definition of terrorism so as to include the actions of a national government to cause terror among an opposing population, adopting such a broad definition would distract attention from what policy makers would most like to know: how to combat the threat posed by subnational groups to state security. Further, it could also create analytic confusion. Terrorist organizations and state governments have different levels of resources, face different kinds of incentives, and are susceptible to different types of pressures. Accordingly, the determinants of their behavior are not likely to be the same and, thus, require separate theoretical investigations.

In general, terrorism has two purposes—to gain supporters and to coerce opponents. Most terrorism seeks both goals to some extent, often aiming to affect enemy calculations while simultaneously mobilizing support for the terrorists cause and, in some cases, even gaining an edge over rival groups in the same social movement. However, there are trade-offs between these objectives and terrorists can strike various balances between them. These choices represent different forms of terrorism, the most important of which are demonstrative, destructive, and suicide terrorism.

Demonstrative terrorism is directed mainly at gaining publicity, for any or all of three reasons: to recruit more activists, to gain attention to grievances from softliners on the other side, and to gain attention from third parties who might exert pressure on the other side. Groups that emphasize ordinary, demonstrative terrorism include the Orange Volunteers (Northern Ireland), National Liberation Army (Columbia), and Red Brigades (Italy). Hostage taking, airline hijacking, and explosions announced in advance are generally intended to use the possibility of harm to bring issues to the attention of the target audience. In these cases, terrorists often avoid doing serious harm so as not to undermine sympathy for the political cause. Brian Jenkins captures the essence of demonstrative terrorism with his well-known remark, "Terrorists want a lot of people watching, not a lot of people dead."

Destructive terrorism is more aggressive, seeking to coerce opponents as well as mobilize support for the cause. Destructive terrorists seek to inflict real harm on members of the target audience at the risk of losing sympathy for their cause. Exactly how groups strike the balance between harm and sympathy depends on the nature of the political goal. For instance, the Baader-Meinhoff group selectively assassinated rich German industrialists, which alienated certain segments of German society but not others. Palestinian terrorists in the 1970s often sought to kill as many Israelis as possible, fully alienating Jewish society but still evoking sympathy from Muslim communities. Other groups that emphasize destructive terrorism include the Irish Republican Army, the Revolutionary Armed Forces of Colombia (FARC), and the nineteenth-century Anarchists.

Suicide terrorism is the most aggressive form of terrorism, pursuing coercion even at the expense of losing support among the terrorists' own community. What distinguishes a suicide terrorist is that the attacker does not expect to survive a mission and often employs a method of attack that requires the attacker's death in order to succeed (such as planting a car bomb, wearing a suicide vest, or ramming an airplane into a building). In essence, a suicide terrorist kills others at the same time that he kills himself. In principle, suicide terrorists could be used for demonstrative purposes or could be limited to targeted assassinations. In practice, however, suicide terrorists often seek simply to kill the largest number of people. Although this maximizes the coercive leverage that can be gained from terrorism, it does so at the greatest cost to the basis of support for the terrorist cause. Maximizing the number of enemy killed alienates those in the target audience who might be sympathetic to the terrorists cause, while the act of suicide creates a debate and often loss of support among moderate segments of the terrorists' community, even if also attracting support among radical elements. Thus, while coercion is an element in all terrorism, coercion is the paramount objective of suicide terrorism.

The Coercive Logic of Suicide Terrorism

At its core, suicide terrorism is a strategy of coercion, a means to compel a target government to change policy. The central logic of this strategy is simple: Suicide terrorism attempts to inflict enough pain on the opposing society to overwhelm their interest in resisting the terrorists demands and, so, to cause either the government to concede or the population to revolt against the government. The common feature of all suicide terrorist campaigns is that they inflict punishment on the opposing society, either directly by killing civilians or indirectly by killing military personnel in circumstances that cannot lead to meaningful battlefield victory. As we shall see, suicide terrorism is rarely a one-time event but often occurs in a series of suicide attacks. As such, suicide terrorism generates coercive leverage both from the immediate panic associated with each attack and from the risk of civilian punishment in the future.

Suicide terrorism does not occur in the same circumstances as military coercion used by states, and these structural differences help to explain the logic of the strategy. In virtually all instances of international military coercion, the coercer is the stronger state and the target is the weaker state; otherwise, the coercer would likely be deterred or simply unable to execute the threatened military operations.

In these circumstances, coercers have a choice between two main coercive strategies, punishment and denial. Punishment seeks to coerce by raising the costs or risks to the target society to a level that overwhelms the value of the interests in dispute. Denial seeks to coerce by demonstrating to the target state that it simply cannot win the dispute regardless of its level of effort, and therefore fighting to a finish is pointless—for example, because the coercer has the ability to conquer the disputed territory. Hence, although coercers may initially rely on punishment, they often have the resources to create a formidable threat to deny the opponent victory in battle and, if necessary, to achieve a brute force military victory if the target government refuses to change its behavior. The Allied bombing of Germany in World War II, American bombing of North Vietnam in 1972, and Coalition attacks against Iraq in 1991 all fit this pattern.

Suicide terrorism (and terrorism in general) occurs under the reverse structural conditions. In suicide terrorism, the coercer is the weaker actor and the target is the stronger. Although some elements of the situation remain the same, flipping the stronger and weaker sides in a coercive dispute has a dramatic change on the relative feasibility of punishment and denial. In these circumstances, denial is impossible, because military conquest is ruled out by relative weakness. Even though some groups using suicide terrorism have received important support from states and some have been strong enough to wage guerrilla military campaigns as well as terrorism, none have been strong enough to have serious prospects of achieving their political goals by conquest. The suicide terrorist group with the most significant military capacity has been the LTTE, but it has not had a real prospect of controlling the whole of the homeland that it claims, including Eastern and Northern Provinces of Sri Lanka.

As a result, the only coercive strategy available to suicide terrorists is punishment. Although the element of "suicide" is novel and the pain inflicted on civilians is often spectacular and gruesome, the heart of the strategy of suicide terrorism is the same as the coercive logic used by states when they employ air power or economic sanctions to punish an adversary: to cause mounting civilian costs to overwhelm the target state's interest in the issue in dispute and so to cause it to concede the terrorists' political demands. What creates the coercive leverage is not so much actual damage as the expectation of future damage. Targets may be economic or political, military or civilian, but in all cases the main task is less to destroy the specific targets than to convince the opposing society that they are vulnerable to more attacks in the future. These features also make suicide terrorism convenient for retaliation, a tit-for-tat interaction that generally occurs between terrorists and the defending government (Crenshaw 1981). . . .

Suicide terrorists' willingness to die magnifies the coercive effects of punishment in three ways. First, suicide attacks are generally more destructive than other terrorist attacks. An attacker who is willing to die is much more likely to accomplish the mission and to cause maximum damage to the target. Suicide attackers can conceal weapons on their own bodies and make last-minute adjustments more easily than ordinary terrorists. They are also better able to infiltrate heavily guarded targets because they do not need escape plans or rescue teams. Suicide attackers are also able to use certain especially destructive tactics such as wearing "suicide vests" and ramming vehicles into targets. The 188 suicide terrorist attacks from 1980 to 2001 killed an average of 13 people each, not counting the unusually large number of fatalities on September 11 and also not counting the attackers themselves. During the same period, there were about 4,155 total terrorist incidents worldwide, which killed 3,207 people (also excluding September 11), or less than one person per incident. Overall, from 1980 to 2001, suicide attacks amount to 3% of all terrorist attacks but account for 48% of total deaths due to terrorism, again excluding September 11.

Second, suicide attacks are an especially convincing way to signal the likelihood of more pain to come, because suicide itself is a costly signal, one that suggests that the attackers could not have been deterred by a threat of costly retaliation. Organizations that sponsor suicide attacks can also deliberately orchestrate the circumstances around the death of a suicide attacker to increase further expectations of future attacks. This can be called the "art of martyrdom." The more suicide terrorists justify their actions on the basis of religious or ideological motives that match the beliefs of a broader national community, the more the status of terrorist martyrs is elevated, and the more plausible it becomes that others will follow in their footsteps. Suicide terrorist organizations commonly cultivate "sacrificial myths" that include elaborate sets of symbols and rituals to mark an individual attacker's death as a contribution to the nation. Suicide attackers' families also often receive material rewards both from the terrorist organizations and from other supporters. As a result, the art of martyrdom elicits popular support from the terrorists' community, reducing the moral backlash that suicide attacks might otherwise produce, and so establishes the foundation for credible signals of more attacks to come.

Third, suicide terrorist organizations are better positioned than other terrorists to increase expectations about escalating future costs by deliberately violating norms in the use of violence. They can do this by crossing thresholds of damage, by breaching taboos concerning legitimate targets, and by broadening recruitment to confound expectations about limits on the number of possible terrorists. The element of suicide itself helps increase the credibility of future attacks, because it suggests that attackers cannot be deterred. Although the capture and conviction of Timothy McVeigh gave reason for some confidence that others with similar political views might be deterred, the deaths of the September 11 hijackers did not, because Americans would have to expect that future Al Qaeda attackers would be equally willing to die.

The Record of Suicide Terrorism, 1980 to 2001

To characterize the nature of suicide terrorism, this study identified every suicide terrorist attack from 1980 to 2001 that could be found in Lexis Nexis's on-line database of world news media. Examination of the universe shows that suicide terrorism has three properties that are consistent with the above strategic logic but not with irrational or fanatical behavior: (1) *timing*—nearly all suicide attacks occur in organized, coherent campaigns, not as isolated or randomly timed incidents; (2) *nationalist goals*—suicide terrorist campaigns are directed at gaining control of what the terrorists see as their national homeland territory, specifically at ejecting foreign forces from that territory; and (3) *target selection*—all suicide terrorist campaigns in the last two decades have been aimed at democracies, which make more suitable targets from the terrorists' point of view. Nationalist movements that face nondemocratic opponents have not resorted to suicide attack as a means of coercion.

Timing

As Table 1 indicates, there have been 188 separate suicide terrorist attacks between 1980 and 2001. Of these, 179, or 95%, were parts of organized, coherent campaigns, while only nine were isolated or random events. Seven separate disputes have led to suicide terrorist campaigns: the presence of American and French forces in Lebanon, Israeli occupation of West Bank and Gaza, the independence of the Tamil regions of Sri Lanka, the independence of the Kurdish region of Turkey, Russian occupation of Chechnya, Indian occupation of Kashmir, and the presence of American forces on the Saudi Arabian Peninsula. Overall, however, there have been 16 distinct campaigns, because in certain disputes the terrorists elected to suspend operations one or more times either in response to concessions or for other reasons. Eleven of the campaigns have ended and five were ongoing as of the end of 2001. The attacks comprising each campaign were organized by the same terrorist group (or, sometimes, a set of cooperating groups as in the ongoing "second *intifada*" in Israel/Palestine), clustered in time, publicly justified in terms of a specified political goal, and directed against targets related to that goal.

The most important indicator of the strategic orientation of suicide terrorists is the timing of the suspension of campaigns, which most often occurs based on a strategic decision by leaders of the terrorist organizations that further attacks would be counterproductive to their coercive purposes—for instance, in response to full or partial concessions by the target state to the terrorists' political goals. Such suspensions are often accompanied by public explanations that justify the decision to opt for a "cease-fire." Further, the terrorist organizations' discipline is usually fairly good; although there are exceptions, such announced cease-fires usually do stick for a period of months at least, normally until the terrorist leaders take a new strategic decision to resume in pursuit of goals not achieved in the earlier campaign. This pattern indicates that both terrorist leaders and their recruits are sensitive to the coercive value of the attacks.

As an example of a suicide campaign, consider Hamas's suicide attacks in 1995 to compel Israel to withdraw from towns in the West Bank. Hamas leaders deliberately withheld attacking during the spring and early summer in order to give PLO negotiations with Israel an opportunity to finalize a withdrawal. However, when in early July, Hamas leaders came to believe that Israel was backsliding and delaying withdrawal, Hamas launched a series of suicide attacks. Israel accelerated the pace of its withdrawal, after which Hamas ended the campaign. . . .

If suicide terrorism were mainly irrational or even disorganized, we would expect a much different pattern in which either political goals were not articulated

TABLE 1 ■ SUICIDE TERRORIST CAMPAIGNS, 1980–2001

Date	Terrorist Group	Terrorist's Goal	No. of Attacks	No. Killed	Target Behavior
		Completed Campaigns			
1. Apr–Dec 1983	Hezboliah	U.S./France out of Lebanon	6	384	Complete withdrawal
2. Nov 1983– Apr 1985	Hezbollah	Israel out of Lebanon	6	96	Partial withdrawal
3. June 1985– June 1986	Hezbollah	Israel out of Lebanon security zone	16	179	No change
4. July 1990– Nov 1994	LTTE	Sri Lanka accept Tamil state	14	164	Negotiations
5. Apr 1995– Oct 2000	LTTE	Sri Lanka accept Tamil state	54	629	No change
6. Apr 1994	Hamas	Israel out of Palestine	2	15	Partial withdrawal Gaza
7. Oct 1994– Aug 1995	Hamas	Israel out of Palestine	7	65	Partial withdrawal from West Bank
8. Feb–Mar 1996	Hamas	Retaliation for Israeli assassination	4	58	No change
9. Mar–Sept 1997	Hamas	Israel out of Palestine	3	24	Hamas leader released
10. June–Oct 1996	PKK	Turkey accept Kurd autonomy	3	17	No change
11. Mar–Aug 1999	PKK	Turkey release jailed leader	6	0	No change
		Ongoing Campaigns, as of December 2001			
12. 1996–	Al Qaeda	U.S. out of Saudi Peninsula	5	3,329	TBD*
13. 2000– Rebels	Chechnen	Russia out of Chechnya	4	53	TBD
14. 2000– Rebels	Kashmir	India out of Kashmir	3	45	TBD
15. 2001–	LTTE	Sri Lanka accept Tamil state	6	51	TBD
16. 2000–	Several	Israel out of Palestine	39	177	TBD
Total incidents	188				
No. of campaigns	179				
No. isolated	9				

Source: Robert Pape, "The Universe of Suicide Terrorist Attacks Worldwide, 1980–2001," University of Chicago, Typescript.

(e.g., references in news reports to "rogue" attacks) or the stated goals varied considerably even within the same conflict. We would also expect the timing to be either random or, perhaps, event-driven, in response to particularly provocative or infuriating actions by the other side, but little if at all related to the progress of negotiations over issues in dispute that the terrorists want to influence.

Nationalist Goals

Suicide terrorism is a high-cost strategy, one that would only make strategic sense for a group when high interests are at stake and, even then, as a last resort. The reason is that suicide terrorism maximizes coercive leverage at the expense of support among the terrorists' own community and so can be sustained over time only when there already exists a high degree of commitment among the potential pool of recruits. The most important goal that a community can have is the independence of its homeland (population, property, and way of life) from foreign influence or control. As a result, a strategy of suicide terrorism is most likely to be used to achieve nationalist goals, such as gaining control of what the terrorists see as their national homeland territory and expelling foreign military forces from that territory.

In fact, every suicide campaign from 1980 to 2001 has had as a major objective—or as its central objective—coercing a foreign government that has military forces in what they see as their homeland to take those forces out. Table 2 summarizes the disputes that have engendered suicide terrorist campaigns. Since 1980, there has not been a suicide terrorist campaign directed mainly against domestic opponents or against foreign opponents who did not have military forces in the terrorists homeland. Although attacks against civilians are often the most salient to Western observers, actually every suicide terrorist campaign in the past two decades has included attacks directly against the foreign military forces in the country, and most have been waged by guerrilla organizations that also use more conventional methods of attack against those forces.

TABLE 2 ■ MOTIVATION AND TARGETS OF SUICIDE TERRORIST CAMPAIGNS, 1980–2001

Region Dispute	Homeland Status	Terrorist Goal	Target a Democracy?
Lebanon, 1983–86	U.S./F/IDF military presence	U.S./F/IDF withdrawal	Yes
West Bank/ Gaza, 1994–	IDF military presence	IDF withdrawal	Yes
Tamils in Sri Lanka, 1990–	SL military presence	SL withdrawal	Yes (1950)
Kurds in Turkey, 1990s	Turkey military presence	Turkey withdrawal	Yes (1983)
Chechnya, 2000–	Russia military presence	Russian withdrawal	Yes (1993)
Kashmir, 2000–	Indian military presence	Indian withdrawal	Yes
Saudi Peninsula, 1996–	U.S. military presence	U.S. withdrawal	Yes

Even Al Qaeda fits this pattern. Although Saudi Arabia is not under American military occupation per se and the terrorists have political objectives against the Saudi regime and others, one major objective of Al Qaeda is the expulsion of U.S. troops from the Saudi Peninsula and there have been attacks by terrorists loyal to Osama Bin Laden against American troops in Saudi Arabia. To be sure, there is a major debate among Islamists over the morality of suicide attacks, but within Saudi Arabia there is little debate over Al Qaeda's objection to American forces in the region and over 95% of Saudi society reportedly agrees with Bin Laden on this matter.

Still, even if suicide terrorism follows a strategic logic, could some suicide terrorist campaigns be irrational in the sense that they are being waged for unrealistic goals? The answer is that some suicide terrorist groups have not been realistic in expecting the full concessions demanded of the target, but this is normal for disputes involving overlapping nationalist claims and even for coercive attempts in general. Rather, the ambitions of terrorist leaders are realistic in two other senses. First, suicide terrorists' political aims, if not their methods, are often more mainstream than observers realize; they generally reflect quite common, straightforward nationalist self-determination claims of their community. Second, these groups often have significant support for their policy goals versus the target state, goals that are typically much the same as those of other nationalists within their community. Differences between the terrorists and more "moderate" leaders usually concern the usefulness of a certain level of violence and—sometimes—the legitimacy of attacking additional targets besides foreign troops in the country, such as attacks in other countries or against third parties and civilians. Thus, it is not that the terrorists pursue radical goals and then seek others' support. Rather, the terrorists are simply the members of their societies who are the most optimistic about the usefulness of violence for achieving goals that many, and often most, support.

The behavior of Hamas illustrates the point. Hamas terrorism has provoked Israeli retaliation that has been costly for Palestinians, while pursuing the—apparently unrealistic—goal of abolishing the state of Israel. Although prospects of establishing an Arab state in all of "historic Palestine" may be poor, most Palestinians agree that it would be desirable if possible. Hamas's terrorist violence was in fact carefully calculated and controlled. In April 1994, as its first suicide campaign was beginning, Hamas leaders explained that "martyrdom operations" would be used to achieve intermediate objectives, such as Israeli withdrawal from the West Bank and Gaza, while the final objective of creating an Islamic state from the Jordan River to the Mediterranean may require other forms of armed resistance.

Democracies as the Targets

Suicide terrorism is more likely to be employed against states with democratic political systems than authoritarian governments for several reasons. First, democracies are often thought to be especially vulnerable to coercive punishment. Domestic critics and international rivals, as well as terrorists, often view democracies as "soft," usually on the grounds that their publics have low thresholds of cost tolerance and high ability to affect state policy. Even if there is little evidence that democracies are easier to coerce than other regime types, this image of democracy matters. Since terrorists can inflict only moderate damage in comparison to even small interstate wars, terrorism can be expected to coerce only if the target state is viewed as especially vulnerable to punishment. Second, suicide terrorism is a tool of the weak, which means that, regardless of how much punishment the terrorists inflict, the target state almost always has the capacity to retaliate with far more extreme punishment or even by exterminating the terrorists' community. Accordingly, suicide terrorists must not only have high interests at stake, they must also be confident that their opponent will be at least somewhat restrained. While there are infamous exceptions, democracies have generally been more restrained in their use of force against civilians, at least since World War II. Finally, suicide attacks may also be harder to organize or publicize in authoritarian police states, although these possibilities are weakened by the fact that weak authoritarian states are also not targets.

In fact, the target state of every modern suicide campaign has been a democracy. The United States, France, Israel, India, Sri Lanka, Turkey, and Russia were all democracies when they were attacked by suicide terrorist campaigns, even though the last three became democracies more recently than the others. . . .

The Kurds, which straddle Turkey and Iraq, illustrate the point that suicide terrorist campaigns are more likely to be targeted against democracies than authoritarian regimes. Although Iraq has been far more brutal toward its Kurdish population than has Turkey, violent Kurdish groups have used suicide attacks exclusively against democratic Turkey and not against the authoritarian regime in Iraq. There are plenty of national groups living under authoritarian regimes with grievances that could possibly inspire suicide terrorism, but none have. Thus, the fact that rebels have resorted to this strategy only when they face the more suitable type of target counts against arguments that suicide terrorism is a nonstrategic response, motivated mainly by fanaticism or irrational hatreds.

TERRORISTS' ASSESSMENTS OF SUICIDE TERRORISM

The main reason that suicide terrorism is growing is that terrorists have learned that it works. Even more troubling, the encouraging lessons that terrorists have learned from the experience of the 1980s and 1990s are not, for the most part, products of wild-eyed interpretations or wishful thinking. They are, rather, quite reasonable assessments of the outcomes of suicide terrorist campaigns during this period.

To understand how terrorists groups have assessed the effectiveness of suicide terrorism requires three tasks: (1) explanation of appropriate standards for evaluating the effectiveness of coercion from the standpoint of coercers; (2) analysis of the 11 suicide terrorist campaigns that have ended as of 2001 to determine how frequently target states made concessions that were, or at least could have been, interpreted as due to suicide attack; and (3) close analysis of terrorists' learning from particular campaigns. Because some analysts see suicide terrorism as fundamentally irrational, it is important to assess whether the lessons that the terrorists drew were reasonable conclusions from the record. The crucial cases are the Hamas and

Islamic Jihad campaigns against Israel during the 1990s, because they are most frequently cited as aimed at unrealistic goals and therefore as basically irrational.

Standards of Assessment

Terrorists, like other people, learn from experience. Since the main purpose of suicide terrorism is coercion, the learning that is likely to have the greatest impact on terrorists' future behavior is the lessons that they have drawn from past campaigns about the coercive effectiveness of suicide attack.

Most analyses of coercion focus on the decision making of target states, largely to determine their vulnerability to various coercive pressures. The analysis here, however, seeks to determine why terrorist coercers are increasingly attracted to a specific coercive strategy. For this purpose, we must develop a new set of standards, because assessing the value of coercive pressure for the coercer is not the same problem as assessing its impact on the target.

From the perspective of a target state, the key question is whether the value of the concession that the coercer is demanding is greater than the costs imposed by the coercive pressure, regardless of whether that pressure is in the form of lives at risk, economic hardship, or other types of costs. However, from the perspective of the coercer, the key question is whether a particular coercive strategy promises to be more effective than alternative methods of influence and, so, warrants continued (or increased) effort. This is especially true for terrorists who are highly committed to a particular goal and so willing to exhaust virtually any alternative rather than abandoning it. In this search for an effective strategy, coercers' assessments are likely to be largely a function of estimates of the success of past efforts; for suicide terrorists, this means assessments of whether past suicide campaigns produced significant concessions.

A glance at the behavior of suicide terrorists reveals that such trade-offs between alternative methods are important in their calculations. All of the organizations that have resorted to suicide terrorism began their coercive efforts with more conventional guerrilla operations, nonsuicide terrorism, or both. Hezbollah, Hamas, Islamic Jihad, the PKK, the LTTE, and Al Qaeda all used demonstrative and destructive means of violence long before resorting to suicide attack. Indeed, looking at the trajectory of terrorist groups over time, there is a distinct element of experimentation in the techniques and strategies used by these groups and distinct movement toward those techniques and strategies that produce the most effect. Al Qaeda actually prides itself for a commitment to even tactical learning over time—the infamous "terrorist manual" stresses at numerous points the importance of writing "lessons learned" memoranda that can be shared with other members to improve the effectiveness of future attacks. . . .

The Apparent Success of Suicide Terrorism

Perhaps the most striking aspect of recent suicide terrorist campaigns is that they are associated with gains for the terrorists' political cause about half the time.

As Table 1 shows, of the 11 suicide terrorist campaigns that were completed during 1980–2001, six closely correlate with significant policy changes by the target state toward the terrorists' major political goals. In one case, the terrorists' territorial goals were fully achieved (Hezbollah v. US/F, 1983); in three cases, the terrorists' territorial aims were partly achieved (Hezbollah v. Israel, 1983–85; Hamas v. Israel, 1994; and Hamas v. Israel, 1994–95); in one case, the target government entered into sovereignty negotiations with the terrorists (LTTE v. Sri Lanka, 1993–94); and in one case, the terrorist organization's top leader was released from prison (Hamas v. Israel, 1997). Five campaigns did not lead to noticeable concessions (Hezbollah's second effort against Israel in Lebanon, 1985–86; a Hamas campaign in 1996 retaliating for an Israeli assassination; the LTTE v. Sri Lanka, 1995–2002; and both PKK campaigns). Coercive success is so rare that even a 50% success rate is significant, because international military and economic coercion, using the same standards as above, generally works less than a third of the time.

There were limits to what suicide terrorism appeared to gain in the 1980s and 1990s. Most of the gains for the terrorists' cause were modest, not involving interests central to the target countries' security or wealth, and most were potentially revocable. For the United States and France, Lebanon was a relatively minor foreign policy interest. Israel's apparent concessions to the Palestinians from 1994 to 1997 were more modest than they might appear. Although Israel withdrew its forces from parts of Gaza and the West Bank and released Sheikh Yassin, during the same period Israeli settlement in the occupied territories almost doubled, and recent events have shown that Israel is not deterred from sending force back in when necessary. In two disputes, the terrorists achieved initial success but failed to reach greater goals. Although Israel withdrew from much of Lebanon in June 1985, it retained a six-mile security buffer zone along the southern edge of the country for another 15 years from which a second Hezbollah suicide terrorist campaign failed to dislodge it. The Sri Lankan government did conduct apparently serious negotiations with the LTTE from November 1994 to April 1995, but did not concede the Tamil's main demand for independence, and since 1995, the government has preferred to prosecute the war rather than consider permitting Tamil secession.

Still, these six concessions, or at least apparent concessions, help to explain why suicide terrorism is on the rise. In three of the cases, the target government policy changes are clearly due to coercive pressure from the terrorist group. The American and French withdrawal was perhaps the most clear-cut coercive success for suicide terrorism. In his memoirs, President Ronald Reagan explained the U.S. decision to withdraw from Lebanon:

> The price we had to pay in Beirut was so great, the tragedy at the barracks was so enormous. . . . We had to pull out. . . . We couldn't stay there and run the risk of another suicide attack on the Marines.

The IDF withdrawal from most of southern Lebanon in 1985 and the Sri Lankan government decision to hold negotiations with the LTTE were also widely understood to be a direct result of the coercive punishment imposed by Hezbollah and LTTE respectively. In both cases, the concessions followed periods in which the terrorists had turned more and more to suicide attacks, but since Hezbollah and the LTTE employed a combination of suicide attack and conventional attack on their opponents, one can question the relative weight of suicide attack in coercing these target states. However, there is little question in either case that punishment pressures inflicted by these terrorist organizations were decisive in the outcomes. For instance, as a candidate in the November 9, 1994, presidential election of Sri Lanka, Mrs. Chandrika Kumaratunga explicitly asked for a mandate to redraw boundaries so as to appease the Tamils in their demand for a separate homeland in the island's northeast provinces, often saying, "We definitely hope to begin discussions with the Tamil people, with their representatives—including the Tigers—and offer them political solutions to end the war . . . [involving] extensive devolution." This would, Kumaratunga said, "create an environment in which people could live without fear."

The other three concessions, or arguable concessions, are less clear-cut. All three involve Hamas campaigns against Israel. Not counting the ongoing second intifada, Hamas waged four separate suicide attack campaigns against Israel, in 1994, 1995, 1996, and 1997. One, in 1996, did not correspond with Israeli concessions. This campaign was announced as retaliation for Israel's assassination of a Hamas leader; no particular coercive goal was announced, and it was suspended by Hamas after four attacks in two weeks. The other three all do correspond with Israeli concessions. In April 1994, Hamas began a series of suicide bombings in relation to the Hebron Massacre. After two attacks, Israel decided to accelerate its withdrawal from Gaza, which was required under the Oslo Agreement but which had been delayed. Hamas then suspended attacks for five months. From October 1994 to August 1995, Hamas (and Islamic Jihad) carried out a total of seven suicide attacks against Israel. In September 1995, Israel agreed to withdraw from certain West Bank towns that December, which it earlier had claimed could not be done before April 1996 at the soonest. Hamas then suspended attacks until its retaliation campaign during the last week of February and first week of March 1996. Finally, in March 1997, Hamas began a suicide attack campaign that included an attack about every two months until September 1997. In response Israeli Prime Minister Netanyahu authorized the assassination of a Hamas leader. The attempt, in Amman, Jordan, failed and the Israeli agents were captured. To get them back Israel agreed to release Sheikh Ahmed Yassin, spiritual leader of Hamas. While this was not a concession to the terrorists' territorial goals, there is no evidence that Hamas interpreted this in any way different from the standard view that this release was the product of American and Jordanian pressure. . . .

THE LIMITS OF SUICIDE TERRORISM

Despite suicide terrorists' reasons for confidence in the coercive effectiveness of this strategy, there are sharp limits to what suicide terrorism is likely to accomplish in the future. During the 1980s and 1990s, terrorist leaders learned that moderate punishment often leads to moderate concessions and so concluded that more ambitious suicide campaigns would lead to greater political gains. However, today's more ambitious suicide terrorist campaigns are likely to fail. Although suicide terrorism is somewhat more effective than ordinary coercive punishment using air power or economic sanctions, it is not drastically so.

Suicide Terrorism is Unlikely to Achieve Ambitious Goals

In international military coercion, threats to inflict military defeat often generate more coercive leverage than punishment. Punishment, using anything short of nuclear weapons, is a relatively weak coercive strategy because modern nation states generally will accept high costs rather than abandon important national goals, while modern administrative techniques and economic adjustments over time often allow states to minimize civilian costs. The most punishing air attacks with conventional munitions in history were the American B-29 raids against Japan's 62 largest cities from March to August 1945. Although these raids killed nearly 800,000 Japanese civilians—almost 10% died on the first day, the March 9, 1945, fire-bombing of Tokyo, which killed over 85,000—the conventional bombing did not compel the Japanese to surrender.

Suicide terrorism makes adjustment to reduce damage more difficult than for states faced with military coercion or economic sanctions. However, it does not affect the target state's interests in the issues at stake. As a result, suicide terrorism can coerce states to abandon limited or modest goals, such as withdrawal from territory of low strategic importance or, as in Israel's case in 1994 and 1995, a temporary and partial withdrawal from a more important area. However, suicide terrorism is unlikely to cause targets to abandon goals central to their wealth or security, such as a loss of territory that would weaken the economic prospects of the state or strengthen the rivals of the state.

Suicide terrorism makes punishment more effective than in international military coercion. Targets remain willing to countenance high costs for important goals, but administrative, economic, or military adjustments to prevent suicide attack are harder, while suicide attackers themselves are unlikely to be deterred by the threat of retaliation. Accordingly, suicide attack is likely to present a threat of continuing limited civilian punishment that the target government cannot completely eliminate, and the upper bound on what punishment can gain for coercers is recognizably higher in suicidal terrorism than in international military coercion.

The data on suicide terrorism from 1980 to 2001 support this conclusion. While suicide terrorism has achieved modest or very limited goals, it has so far failed to compel target democracies to abandon goals central to national wealth or security. When the United States withdrew from Lebanon in 1984, it had no important security, economic, or even ideological interests at stake. Lebanon was largely a humanitarian mission and not viewed as central to the national welfare of the United States. Israel withdrew from most of Lebanon in June 1985 but remained in a security buffer on the edge of southern Lebanon for more than a decade afterward, despite the fact that 17 of 22 suicide attacks occurred in 1985 and 1986. Israel's withdrawals from Gaza and the West Bank in 1994 and 1995 occurred at the same time that settlements increased and did little to hinder the IDF's return, and so these concessions were more modest than they may appear. Sri Lanka has suffered more casualties from suicide attack than Israel but has not acceded to demands that it surrender part of its national territory. Thus, the logic of punishment and the record of suicide terrorism suggests that, unless suicide terrorists acquire far more destructive technologies, suicide attacks for more ambitious goals are likely to fail and will continue to provoke more aggressive military responses.

POLICY IMPLICATIONS FOR CONTAINING SUICIDE TERRORISM

While the rise in suicide terrorism and the reasons behind it seem daunting, there are important policy lessons to learn. The current policy debate is misguided. Offensive military action or concessions alone rarely work for long. For over 20 years, the governments of Israel and other states targeted by suicide terrorism have engaged in extensive military efforts to kill, isolate, and jail suicide terrorist leaders and operatives, sometimes with the help of quite good surveillance of the terrorists' communities. Thus far, they have met with meager success. Although decapitation of suicide terrorist organizations can disrupt their operations temporarily, it rarely yields long-term gains. Of the 11 major suicide terrorist campaigns that had ended as of 2001, only one—the PKK versus Turkey—did so as a result of leadership decapitation, when the leader, in Turkish custody, asked his followers to stop. So far, leadership decapitation has also not ended Al Qaeda's campaign. Although the United States successfully toppled the Taliban in Afghanistan in December 2001, Al Qaeda launched seven successful suicide terrorist attacks from April to December 2002, killing some 250 Western civilians, more than in the three years before September 11, 2001, combined.

Concessions are also not a simple answer. Concessions to nationalist grievances that are widely held in the terrorists' community can reduce popular support for further terrorism, making it more difficult to recruit new suicide attackers and improving the standing of more moderate nationalist elites who are in competition with the terrorists. Such benefits can be realized, however, only if the concessions really do substantially satisfy the nationalist or self-determination aspirations of a large fraction of the community.

Partial, incremental, or deliberately staggered concessions that are dragged out over a substantial period of time are likely to become the worst of both worlds. Incremental compromise may appear—or easily be portrayed—to the terrorists' community as simply delaying tactics and, thus, may fail to reduce, or actually increase, their distrust that their main concerns will ever be met. Further, incrementalism provides time and opportunity for the terrorists to intentionally provoke the target state in hopes of derailing the smooth progress of negotiated compromise in the short term, so that they can reradicalize their own community and actually escalate their efforts toward even greater gains in the long term. Thus, states that are willing to make concessions should do so in a single step if at all possible.

Advocates of concessions should also recognize that, even if they are successful in undermining the terrorist leaders' base of support, almost any concession at all will tend to encourage the terrorist leaders further about their own coercive effectiveness. Thus, even in the aftermath of a real settlement with the opposing community, some terrorists will remain motivated to continue attacks and, for the medium term, may be able to do so, which in term would put a premium on combining concessions with other solutions.

Given the limits of offense and of concessions, homeland security and defensive efforts generally must be a core part of any solution. Undermining the feasibility of suicide terrorism is a difficult task. After all, a major advantage of suicide attack is that it is more difficult to prevent than other types of attack. However, the difficulty of achieving perfect security should not keep us from taking serious measures to prevent would-be terrorists from easily entering their target society. As Chaim Kaufmann has shown, even intense ethnic civil wars can often be stopped by demographic separation because it greatly reduces both means and incentives for the sides to attack each other. This logic may apply with even more force to the related problem of suicide terrorism, since, for suicide attackers, gaining physical access to the general area of the target is the only genuinely demanding part of an operation, and as we have seen, resentment of foreign occupation of their national homeland is a key part of the motive for suicide terrorism.

The requirements for demographic separation depend on geographic and other circumstances that may not be attainable in all cases. For example, much of Israel's difficulty in containing suicide terrorism derives from the deeply intermixed settlement patterns of the West Bank and Gaza, which make the effective length of the border between Palestinian and Jewish settled areas practically infinite and have rendered even very intensive Israeli border control efforts ineffective. As a result, territorial concessions could well encourage terrorist leaders to strive for still greater gains while greater repression may only exacerbate the conditions of occupation that cultivate more recruits for terrorist organizations. Instead, the best course to improve Israel's security may well be a combined strategy: abandoning territory on the West Bank along with an actual wall that physically separates the populations.

Similarly, if Al Qaeda proves able to continue suicide attacks against the American homeland, the United States should emphasize improving its domestic security. In the short term, the United States should adopt stronger border controls to make it more difficult for suicide attackers to enter the United States. In the long term, the United States should work toward energy independence and, thus, reduce the need for American troops in the Persian Gulf countries where their presence has helped recruit suicide terrorists to attack America. These measures will not provide a perfect solution, but they may make it far more difficult for Al Qaeda to continue attacks in the United States, especially spectacular attacks that require elaborate coordination.

Perhaps most important, the close association between foreign military occupations and the growth of suicide terrorist movements in the occupied regions should give pause to those who favor solutions that involve conquering countries in order to transform their political systems. Conquering countries may disrupt terrorist operations in the short term, but it is important to recognize that occupation of more countries may well increase the number of terrorists coming at us.

New and Old Wars

MARY KALDOR

My central argument is that, during the last decades of the twentieth century, a new type of organized violence developed, especially in Africa and Eastern Europe, which is one aspect of the current globalized era. I describe this type of violence as "new war." I use the term "new" to distinguish such wars from prevailing perceptions of war drawn from an earlier era. . . . I use the term "war" to emphasize the political nature of this new type of violence, even though, as will become clear in the following pages, the new wars involve a blurring of the distinctions between war (usually defined as violence between states or organized political groups for political motives), organized crime (violence undertaken by privately organized groups for private purposes, usually financial gain) and large-scale violations of human rights (violence undertaken by states or politically organized groups against individuals). . . .

The new wars have to be understood in the context of the process known as globalization. By globalization, I mean the intensification of global interconnectedness—political, economic, military and cultural—and the changing character of political authority. Even though I accept the argument that globalization has its roots in modernity or even earlier, I consider that the globalization of the 1980s and 1990s was a qualitatively new phenomenon which can, at least in part, be explained as a consequence of the revolution in information technologies and dramatic improvements in communication and data-processing. This process of intensifying interconnectedness is a contradictory process involving both integration and fragmentation, homogenization and diversification, globalization and localization. It is often argued that the new wars are a consequence of the end of the Cold War; they reflect a power vacuum which is typical of transition periods in world affairs. It is undoubtedly true that the consequences of the end of the Cold War—the availability of surplus arms, the discrediting of socialist ideologies, the disintegration of totalitarian empires, the withdrawal of superpower support to client regimes—contributed in important ways to the new wars. But equally, the end of the Cold War could be viewed as the way in which the Eastern bloc succumbed to the inevitable encroachment of globalization—the crumbling of the last bastions of territorial autarchy, the moment when Eastern Europe was "opened up" to the rest of the world.

The impact of globalization is visible in many of the new wars. The global presence in these wars can include international reporters, mercenary troops and military advisers, and diaspora volunteers as well as a veritable "army" of international agencies ranging from nongovernmental organizations (NGOs) such as Oxfam, Save the Children, Médecins Sans Frontières, Human Rights Watch and the International Red Cross to international institutions such as the United Nations High Commissioner for Refugees (UNHCR), the European Union (EU), the United Nations Children's Fund (UNICEF), the Organization for Security and Cooperation in Europe (OSCE), the African Union (AU) and the United Nations (UN) itself, including peacekeeping troops. Indeed, the wars epitomize a new kind of global/local divide between those members of a global class who can speak English, have access to faxes, the Internet and satellite television, who use dollars or euros or credit cards, and who can travel freely, and those who are excluded from global processes, who live off what they can sell or barter or what they receive in humanitarian aid, whose movement is restricted by roadblocks, visas and the cost of travel, and who are prey to sieges, forced famines, landmines, etc. . . .

The new wars arise in the context of the erosion of the autonomy of the state and in some extreme cases the disintegration of the state. In particular, they occur in the context of the erosion of the monopoly of legitimate organized violence. This monopoly is eroded from above and from below. It has been eroded from above by the transnationalization of military forces which began during the two world wars and was institutionalized by the bloc system during the Cold War and by innumerable transnational connections between armed forces that developed in the post-war period. The capacity of states to use force unilaterally against other states has been greatly weakened. This is partly for practical reasons—the growing destructiveness of military technology and the increasing interconnectedness of states, especially in the military field. It is difficult to imagine nowadays a state or group of states risking a large-scale war which could be even more destructive than what was experienced during the two world wars. Moreover, military alliances, international arms production and trade, various forms of military cooperation and exchanges, arms control agreements, etc., have created a form of global military integration. The weakening of states' capacity to use unilateral force is also due to the evolution of international norms. The principle that unilateral aggression is illegitimate was first codified in the Kellogg–Briand pact of 1928, and reinforced after World War II in the UN Charter and through the reasoning used in the war crimes trials in Nuremberg and Tokyo.

At the same time, the monopoly of organized violence is eroded from below by privatization. Indeed, it could be argued that the new wars are part of a process which is more or less a reversal of the processes through which modern states evolved. . . . The rise of the modern state was intimately connected to war. In order to fight wars, rulers needed to increase taxation and borrowing, to eliminate "wastage" as a result of crime, corruption and inefficiency, to regularize armed forces and police and to eliminate private armies, and to mobilize popular support in order to raise money and men. As war became the exclusive province of the state, so the growing destructiveness of war against other states was paralleled by a process of growing security at home; hence the way in which the term "civil" came to mean internal. The new wars occur in situations in which state revenues decline because of the decline of the economy as well as the spread of criminality, corruption and inefficiency, violence is increasingly privatized both as a result of growing organized crime and the emergence of paramilitary groups, and political legitimacy is disappearing. Thus the distinctions are breaking down between external barbarity and domestic civility, between the combatant as the legitimate bearer of arms and the noncombatant, or between the soldier or policeman and the criminal. The barbarity of war between states may have become a thing of the past. In its place is a new type of organized violence that is more pervasive, but also perhaps less extreme. . . .

The new wars can be contrasted with earlier wars in terms of their goals, the methods of warfare and how they are financed. The goals of the new wars are about identity politics in contrast to the geopolitical or ideological goals of earlier wars. In . . . the context of globalization, ideological and/or territorial cleavages of an earlier era have increasingly been supplanted by an emerging political cleavage between what I call cosmopolitanism, based on inclusive, universalist, multicultural values, and the politics of particularist identities. This cleavage can be explained in terms of the growing divide between those who are part of global processes and those who are excluded, but it should not be equated with this division. Among the global class are members of transnational networks based on exclusivist identity, while at the local level there are many courageous individuals who refuse the politics of particularism.

By identity politics, I mean the claim to power on the basis of a particular identity—be it national, clan, religious or linguistic. In one sense, all wars involve a clash of identities—British against French, communists against democrats. But my point is that these earlier identities were linked either to a notion of state interest or to some forward-looking project—ideas about how society should be organized. Nineteenth-century European nationalisms or postcolonial nationalisms, for example, presented themselves as emancipatory nation-building projects. The new identity politics is about the claim to power on the basis of labels—in so far as there are ideas about political or social change, they tend to relate to an idealized nostalgic representation of the past. It is often claimed that the new wave of identity politics is merely a throwback to the past, a resurgence of ancient hatreds kept under control by colonialism and/or the Cold War. While it is true that the narratives of identity politics depend on memory and tradition, it is also the case that these are "reinvented" in the context of the failure or the corrosion of other sources of political legitimacy—the discrediting of socialism or the nation-building rhetoric of the first generation of postcolonial leaders. These backward-looking political projects arise in the vacuum created by the absence of forward-looking projects. Unlike the politics of ideas which are open to all and therefore tend to be integrative, this type of identity politics is inherently exclusive and therefore tends towards fragmentation.

There are two aspects of the new wave of identity politics which specifically relate to the process of globalization. First, the new wave of identity politics is both local and global, national as well as transnational. In many cases, there are significant diaspora communities whose influence is greatly enhanced by the ease of travel and improved communication. Alienated diaspora groups in advanced industrial or oil-rich countries provide ideas, funds and techniques, thereby imposing their own frustrations and fantasies on what is often a very different situation. Second, this politics makes use of the new technology. The speed of political mobilization is greatly increased by the use of the electronic media. The effect of television, radio or videos on what is often a nonreading public cannot be overestimated. The protagonists of the new politics often display the symbols of a global mass culture—Mercedes cars, Rolex watches, Ray-Ban sunglasses—combined with the labels that signify their own brand of particularistic cultural identity.

The second characteristic of the new wars is the changed mode of warfare—the means through which the new wars are fought. The strategies of the new warfare draw on the experience of both guerrilla warfare and counterinsurgency, yet they are quite distinctive. In conventional or regular war, the goal is the capture of territory by military means; battles are the decisive encounters of the war. Guerrilla warfare developed as a way of getting round the massive concentrations of military force which are characteristic of conventional war. In guerrilla warfare, territory is captured through political control of the population rather than through military advance, and battles are avoided as far as possible. The new warfare also tends to avoid battle and to control territory through political control of the population, but whereas guerrilla warfare, at least in theory as articulated by Mao Tse-tung or Che Guevara, aimed to capture "hearts and minds," the new warfare borrows from counterinsurgency techniques of destabilization aimed at sowing "fear and hatred." The aim is to control the population by getting rid of everyone of a different identity (and indeed of a different opinion) and by instilling terror. Hence the strategic goal of these wars is to mobilize extremist politics based on fear and hatred. This often involves population expulsion through various means such as mass killing and forcible resettlement, as well as a range of political, psychological and economic techniques of intimidation. This is why, in all these wars, there has been a dramatic increase in the number of refugees and displaced persons, and why most violence is directed against civilians. At the turn of the twentieth century, the ratio of military to civilian casualties in wars was 8:1. Today, this has been almost exactly reversed; in the wars of the 1990s, the ratio of military to civilian casualties is approximately 1:8. Behaviour that was proscribed according to the classical rules of warfare and codified in the laws of war in the late nineteenth century and early twentieth century, such as atrocities against noncombatants, sieges, destruction of historic monuments, etc., constitutes an essential component of the strategies of the new mode of warfare. The terrorism experienced in places such as New York, Madrid or London, as well as in Israel or Iraq, can be understood as a variant of new strategy—the use of spectacular, often gruesome, violence to create fear and conflict.

In contrast to the vertically organized hierarchical units that were typical of "old wars," among the units that fight these wars are a disparate range of different types of groups, such as paramilitary units, local warlords, criminal, gangs, police forces, mercenary groups and also regular armies, including breakaway units from regular armies. In organizational terms, they are highly decentralized and they operate through a mixture of confrontation and cooperation even when on opposing sides. They make use of advanced technology even if it is not what we tend to call "high technology" (stealth bombers or cruise missiles, for example). In the last fifty years, there have been significant advances in lighter weapons—undetectable landmines, for example, or small arms which are light, accurate and easy to use so that they can even be operated by children. Modern communications—cellular phones or computer links—are also used in order to coordinate, mediate and negotiate among the disparate fighting units.

The third way in which the new wars can be contrasted with earlier wars is what I call the new ["globalized" war economy,] which . . . is almost exactly the opposite of the war economies of the two world wars. The latter were centralized, totalizing and autarchic. The new war economies are decentralized. Participation in the war is low and unemployment is extremely high. Moreover, these economies are heavily dependent on external resources. In these wars, domestic production declines dramatically because of global competition, physical destruction or inter-ruptions to normal trade, as does tax revenue. In these circumstances, the fighting units finance themselves through plunder, hostage-taking and the black market or through external assistance. The latter can take the following forms: remittances from the diaspora, "taxation" of humanitarian assistance, support from neighbour-ing governments, or illegal trade in arms, drugs or valuable commodities such as oil or diamonds or human trafficking. All of these sources can only be sustained through continued violence so that a war logic is built into the functioning of the economy. This retrograde set of social relationships, which is entrenched by war, has a tendency to spread across borders through refugees or organized crime or ethnic minorities. It is possible to identify clusters of war economies or near war economies in places such as the Balkans, the Caucasus, Central Asia, the Horn of Africa, Central Africa or West Africa.

Because the various warring parties share the aim of sowing "fear and hatred," they operate in a way that is mutually reinforcing, helping each other to create a climate of insecurity and suspicion. . . . Often, among the first civilians to be tar-geted are those who espouse a different politics, those who try to maintain inclu-sive social relations and some sense of public morality. Thus though the new wars appear to be between different linguistic, religious or tribal groups, they can also be presented as wars in which those who represent particularistic identity politics cooperate in suppressing the values of civility and multiculturalism. In other words, they can be understood as wars between exclusivism and cosmopolitanism.

This analysis of new wars has implications for the management of conflicts. . . . There is no possible long-term solution within the framework of identity politics. And because these are conflicts with extensive social and economic ramifications, top-down approaches are likely to fail. In the early 1990s there was great optimism about the prospects for humanitarian intervention to protect civilians. However, the practice of humanitarian intervention has, I would argue, been shackled by a kind of myopia about the character of the new warfare. On the one hand, the persistence of inherited mandates, the tendency to interpret these wars in traditional terms, has been the main reason why humanitarian intervention has often failed to prevent the wars and may actually have helped to sustain them in various ways—for example, through the provision of humanitarian aid, which is an important source of income for the warring parties, or through the legitimation of war criminals by inviting them to the negotiating table, or through the effort to find political compromises based on exclusivist assumptions. On the other hand, humanitarian intervention has been used to legitimize updated "old wars" such as in Kosovo or Iraq.

The key to any long-term solution is the restoration of legitimacy, the reconstitution of the control of organized violence by public authorities, whether local, national or global. This is both a political process—the rebuilding of trust in and support for public authorities—and a legal process—the re-establishment of a rule of law within which public authorities operate. This cannot be done on the basis of particularistic politics. An alternative forward-looking cosmopolitan political project which would cross the global/local divide and reconstruct legitimacy around an inclusive, democratic set of values has to be counterposed against the politics of exclusivism. In all the new wars there are local people and places who struggle against the politics of exclusivism—the Hutus and Tutsis who called themselves Hutsis and tried to defend their localities against genocide, the non-nationalists in the cities of Bosnia–Herzegovina, particularly Sarajevo and Tuzla, who kept alive civic multicultural values, the elders in Northwest Somaliland who negotiated peace. What is needed is an alliance between local defenders of civility and transnational institutions which would guide a strategy aimed at controlling violence. Such a strategy would include political, military and economic components. It would operate within a framework of international law, based on that body of international law that comprises both the "laws of war" and human rights law, which could perhaps be termed cosmopolitan law. In this context, peace-keeping could be reconceptualized as cosmopolitan law-enforcement. Since the new wars are, in a sense, a mixture of war, crime and human rights violations, so the agents of cosmopolitan law-enforcement have to be a mixture of soldiers and police. I also argue that a new strategy of reconstruction, which includes the reconstruction of social, civic and institutional relationships, should supplant the current dominant approaches of structural adjustment or humanitarianism. . . .

In the final chapter of the book, I discuss the implications. Although the new wars are concentrated in Africa, Eastern Europe and Asia, they are a global phenomenon not just because of the presence of global networks, or because they are reported globally. The characteristics of the new wars I have described are to be found in North America and Western Europe as well. The right-wing militia groups in the United States are not so very different from the paramilitary groups in Eastern Europe or Africa. Indeed, in the United States it is reported that private security officers outnumber police officers by two to one. Nor is the salience of identity politics and the growing disillusionment with formal politics just a Southern and Eastern phenomenon. The violence in the inner cities of Western Europe and North America can, in some senses, be described as new wars. The suicide bombers responsible for the attacks of 7 July [2005] on London were, after all, homegrown. It is sometimes said that the advanced industrial world is integrating and the poorer parts of the world are fragmenting. I would argue that all parts of the world are characterized by a combination of integration and fragmentation even though the tendencies to integration are greater in the North and the tendencies to fragmentation may be greater in the South and East.

Since 9/11 it has become clear that it is no longer possible to insulate some parts of the world from others. Neither the idea that we can re-create some kind of bipolar or multipolar world order on the basis of identity—Christianity versus Islam, for example—nor the idea that the "anarchy" in places such as Africa and Eastern Europe can be contained is feasible if my analysis of the changing character of organized violence has some basis in reality. This is why the cosmopolitan project has to be a global project even if it is, as it must be, local or regional in application.

 Exercises for the Political Utility of Force Today

Apply what you learned in this chapter by using the online resources on MyPoliSciKit (www.mypoliscikit.com).

 Practice Tests

Videos:
- "Iraq and Vietnam: An Unfair Comparison"
- "Toppling Hussein"

Reading Guides:
- Robert J. Art, "The Fungibility of Force"
- Robert A. Pape, "The Strategic Logic of Suicide Terrorism"
- Mary Kaldor, "New and Old Wars"

NUCLEAR DETERRENCE AND NUCLEAR SPREAD

Getting Ready for a Nuclear-Ready Iran

HENRY SOKOLSKI

[This chapter] reflects analysis done at a series of competitive strategies workshops that focused on the next two decades of likely competition between America and Iran and what comparative strengths the United States and its allies might use to leverage Iranian behavior.

These workshops identified three threats that are likely to increase following Iran's acquisition of a nuclear weapons option.

1. **Even More Nuclear Proliferation.** Iran's continued insistence that it acquired its nuclear capabilities legally under the Nuclear Nonproliferation Treaty (NPT) would, if unchallenged, encourage its neighbors (including Iraq, Saudi Arabia, Egypt, Syria, Turkey, and Algeria) to develop nuclear options of their own by emulating Iran's example, by overtly declaring possession (in Israel's case) or by importing nuclear weapons (in Saudi Arabia's case). Such announcements and efforts, in turn, would likely undermine nuclear nonproliferation restraints internationally and strain American relations with most of its key friends in the Middle East.

2. **Dramatically Higher Oil Prices.** A nuclear-ready Iran could be emboldened to manipulate oil prices upward. It might attempt this either by threatening the freedom of the seas (by mining oil transit points as it did in the 1980s, or by threatening to close the Straits of Hormuz), or by using

Henry Sokolski, "Getting Ready for a Nuclear-Ready Iran: Report of the NPEC Working Group," in *Getting Ready for a Nuclear-Ready Iran,* ed. Henry Sokolski and Patrick Clawson. Carlisle, PA: Strategic Studies Institute, U.S. Army War College, October 2005, pp. 1–10. Portions of the text and the footnotes have been omitted.

terrorist proxies to threaten the destruction of Saudi and other Gulf state oil facilities and pipelines.

3. **Increased Terrorism Designed to Diminish U.S. Influence.** With a nuclear weapons option acting as a deterrent to the United States and allied action against it, Iran would likely lend greater support to terrorists operating against Israel, Iraq, Libya, Saudi Arabia, Europe, and the United States. The aim of such support would be to reduce American support for U.S. involvement in the Middle East, for Israel, and for actions against Iran generally, and to elevate Iran as an equal to the United States and its allies on all matters relating to the Persian Gulf and related regions. An additional aim of the terrorism that Iran would support would be to keep other nations from supporting U.S. policies and the continued U.S. military presence in the Middle East.

All of these threats are serious. If realized, they would undermine U.S. and allied efforts to foster moderate rule in much of the Middle East and set into play a series of international competitions that could ultimately result in major wars. . . .

The United States and its allies should continue to do all they can to head Iran off, including efforts to throttle Iran's "civilian" program. Indeed, if all Washington and its allies do is pressure Iran not to acquire nuclear arms openly, without pressuring Iran to give up its "civilian" nuclear efforts, Iran will best them easily by using these civilian facilities to develop a quick nuclear breakout capability, claiming its entire nuclear program is legal under the NPT, and wielding it diplomatically much as it would if it actually had nuclear weapons.

What should we expect when . . . Iran secures such a breakout option? If the United States and its allies do no more than they have already done, two things. First, many of Iran's neighbors will do their best to follow its "peaceful" example. Egypt, Algeria, Syria, and Saudi Arabia will all claim that they too need to pursue nuclear research and development to the point of having nuclear weapons options and, as a further slap in Washington's face (and Tel Aviv's), will point to Iran's "peaceful" nuclear program and Israel's undeclared nuclear weapons arsenal to help justify their own "civil" nuclear activities. Second, an ever more nuclear-ready Iran will try to lead the revolutionary Islamic vanguard throughout the Islamic world by becoming the main support for terrorist organizations aimed against Washington's key regional ally, Israel; America's key energy source, Saudi Arabia; and Washington's prospective democratic ally, Iraq.

Early in 2004, senior Saudi officials announced they were studying the possibility of acquiring or "leasing" nuclear weapons from China or Pakistan (this would be legal under the NPT so long as the weapons were kept under Chinese or Pakistani "control"). Egypt earlier announced its plans to develop a large nuclear desalinization plant and is reported recently to have received sensitive nuclear technology from Libya. Syria, meanwhile, is now interested in uranium enrichment. . . . And Algeria is in the midst of upgrading its second large research reactor facility, which is still ringed with air defense units.

If these states continue to pursue their nuclear dreams (spurred on by Iran's example), could Iraq, which still has a considerable number of nuclear scientists and engineers, be expected to stand idly by? And what of Turkey, whose private sector was recently revealed to have been part of the A. Q. Khan network? Will nuclear agitation to its south and its repeated rejection from the EU cause Turkey to reconsider its non-nuclear status? Most of these nations are now friends of the United States. Efforts on their part to acquire a bomb under the guise of developing "peaceful" nuclear energy (with Latin American, Asian, European, Russian, or Chinese help), will only serve to strain their relations with Washington.

With such regional nuclear enthusiasms will come increased diplomatic pressure on Israel, an undeclared nuclear weapons state and America's closest Middle East ally. In July 2004, the IAEA's Director General and the major states within the Middle East urged Israel to give up its nuclear arms in proposed regional arms control negotiations. Israel's understandable reluctance to be dragged into such talks or to admit to having nuclear arms now will not end these pressures. If Israel has a secret nuclear arsenal, Arabs argue, why not balance it with Iranian, Saudi, Egyptian, or other covert nuclear weapons programs? How fair is it for the United States and Europe to demand that Middle Eastern Muslim states restrain their own "peaceful" nuclear ambitions if Israel itself already has the bomb and is publicly arguing that it will not be "second" to introduce nuclear weapons into the region? Wouldn't it make more sense to force Israel to admit it has nuclear weapons and then to demand that it give them up in a regional arms control negotiations effort (even though once Israel admits it has weapons, many of its Muslim neighbors, who still do not recognize Israel, are likely to then use Israel's admission to justify getting nuclear weapons themselves)?

This then brings us to the second likely result of Iran becoming ever more nuclear-ready: A more confident Iran more willing to sponsor terrorist organizations, especially those opposed to Israel and the current government in Iraq . . . Iran already has been seen to be increasing its support to groups like Hezbollah . . . groups which want to liberate their lands from American and Israeli "occupation." Increasing its aid to these groups certainly would help Iran take the lead in the Islamic crusade to rid the region of Zionist—American forces and thereby become worthy of tribute and consideration by other Islamic states. Also, bolstering such terrorist activity would help Tehran deter Israel and the United States from striking it militarily.

Beyond this, Iran is likely to increase its assistance to groups willing to risk striking the United States. News reports in August 2004 claimed that Iranian diplomats assigned to UN headquarters in New York were to survey 29 American targets to help terrorist organizations interested in hitting the United States. The aim here appears to be, again, to deter the United States from hitting Iran and to divide U.S. opinion about the merits of backing Israel, or supporting any other anti-Iranian measure or group.

A nuclear-ready Iran is also likely step up its terrorist activities against Iraq, Libya, and Saudi Arabia. . . .

Iran . . . has a history of supporting terrorist activity in Saudi Arabia. Although only roughly 10 percent of Saudi Arabia's population is Shia, this sect constitutes an overwhelming majority of the population living in Saudi Arabia's key northern oil-producing region. Any terrorist action anywhere in Saudi Arabia, though, tends to raise questions about the general viability of the Saudi regime and the security of the world's largest oil reserves. Historically, after a major terrorist attack in Saudi Arabia, markets worry, the price of oil increases, and Iran's own oil revenues, in turn, surge upward. The reason is simple: Saudi Arabia has the world's largest reserve oil production capacity. . . . Damage Saudi Arabia's ability to ramp up production or to export what it can produce (or merely raise doubts about the current Saudi government's continued ability to protect these capabilities), and you effectively cripple the world's capacity to meet increased demand for oil internationally. Terrorism in Saudi Arabia, in short, provides Iran with a quick, effective way to manipulate international oil prices. This cannot help but garner Iran greater leverage in getting the Organization of Petroleum Exporting Countries (OPEC) to support its long-ignored calls to increase oil prices. It also will help Iran garner increased European and Asian regard for its calls for more financial support, investment, and advanced technology. Iranian progress on these fronts is likely to be fortified by Tehran's offers of oil rights to European states, Russia, and China. This, in turn, will help keep the current regime in power longer, will further reduce U.S. influence in the region, and will make action in the UN Security Council (UNSC) against Tehran far less likely.

Yet, another way Iran could drive up oil prices is by threatening free passage of oil through the Straits of Hormuz or by engaging in naval mining in the Gulf and other key locations, using its surface fleet of fast boats or its smaller submarines as it did in the late 1980s. Iran already has deployed anti-shipping missiles at Qeshm, Abu Musa Island, and on Sirri Island, all of which are in range of shipping through the Strait. It has also occupied and fortified three islands inside the shipping lanes of the Strait of Hormuz—Abu Musa, The Greater Tunbs and the Lesser Tunbs. Given that one-fifth of the world's entire oil demand flows through the Straits (as well as roughly a quarter of America's supply of oil) and no other nation has fortified its shores near Hormuz, an Iranian threat to disrupt commerce there would have to be taken seriously by commercial concerns (e.g., insurers and commodity markets) and other nations.

A Nuclear-Armed Iran: A Difficult but Not Impossible Policy Problem

BARRY R. POSEN

Iran's nuclear energy research and development efforts seem on course to achieve an ability to produce highly enriched uranium, the key element of a nuclear weapon. . . . France, Germany, and the United Kingdom, acting under the auspices of the European Union, and with the support of the United States, have negotiated intensively with Iran since 2003 to discourage further Iranian nuclear enrichment progress; the United Nations Security Council demanded that Iran suspend enrichment and implement other important arms control measures with Resolution 1696 in July 2006. Nevertheless diplomacy has thus far been unsuccessful, and there is no guarantee of future success.

If negotiations fail, interested powers such as the United States, the European Union, and Iran's neighbors will face three alternatives: (1) they could move from diplomacy to economic and political coercion; (2) one or more states (most probably the United States or Israel) could launch a preventive attack to erode or destroy the Iranian nuclear program; or (3) these powers could develop strategies of containment and deterrence to coexist with a nuclear-armed Iran—if Iran achieves weapons capability.

The primary purpose of this paper is to address the third option—to spell out a strategy of containment and deterrence and show how it could work. I systematically review the standard objections to this strategy, and explain why they are misplaced. Summarizing the other options, I then argue that a containment and deterrence strategy is more likely to achieve U.S. strategic goals, and do so at lower risks and costs. Finally, I briefly review the proliferation risks that would arise from an Iranian nuclear program, and argue that these risks can be reduced by a deterrence and containment strategy. That said, containment of a nuclear-armed Iran is not the preferred outcome. It would be better if diplomacy were to succeed. Thus, one implication of this analysis is that the United States and its allies should review their current diplomatic approach to Iran and try to devise a more promising political strategy. . . .

From Barry R. Posen, "A Nuclear-Armed Iran: A Difficult but Not Impossible Problem," *A Century Foundation Report*, December 6, 2006. Reprinted by permission of The Century Foundation. Portions of the text have been omitted.

ECONOMIC COERCION

Though economic coercion should be attempted if the current round of diplomacy fails, this seems unlikely to work unless it is combined with a new set of incentives. First, it is improbable that a particularly strong international sanctions regime can be organized against Iran. Russia, China, and even many European states fear that the initiation of a strong sanctions policy, blessed by the UN, is the first step on the road to war. Sanctions may not change Iranian behavior, but they will have further committed the international community to do something about Iran's program. Some states also will oppose a strong sanctions policy because they profit from their relationships with Iran, due to its energy resources, or expect to profit even more if they help shield Iran from stern measures. Finally, given tight oil markets and high prices, most states would not support a sanctions regime that embargoed the export of Iranian oil.[1]

Second, though Iran is not a wealthy country, it has a relatively well-rounded economy. Aside from its obvious strengths in oil and gas production, Iran is endowed with abundant raw materials and agricultural land, and has a moderately well developed industrial sector. If a sanctions regime did not close off Iran's oil exports, it seems very likely that, with its own endowments and the cash it raises from energy exports, it could weather any plausible sanctions regime.[2]

If the threat of international economic sanctions were accompanied by more focused diplomacy, it might find more support and be more credible. In particular, the United States would need to assure Iran that it has abandoned any hopes to overthrow the current regime. Some have suggested a "grand bargain" in which the United States would offer Iran a security guarantee, an end to sanctions, and the normalization of diplomatic relations, in exchange for major concessions on Iran's nuclear program and an end to support for terrorism.[3] Such a negotiating offer might reduce the concerns of fence sitters such as Russia and China, who fear that the ultimate U.S. objective is regime change, and that the United States intends to leverage ineffective sanctions into an argument for war. The offer of a grand bargain also would put Iran in a difficult position, insofar as declining the offer would be tantamount to admitting its ambitions to produce a nuclear weapon. Moreover, if such a negotiating gambit fails, and the United States turns to a strategy of containment, states in the region will be even more likely to want U.S. assistance, and will more easily be able to portray a strengthened relationship with the United States as an essential counter to Iranian ambitions.

PREVENTIVE MILITARY ACTION

A military attack on Iran's nuclear infrastructure could set back the program, but probably not prevent its recovery, unless the attack were somehow to topple the Iranian government and bring a very different ruling group to power. A military strike carries significant political and military risks. If time bought by setting back the Iranian program through military strikes would be used to good effect—that is, if in the interim other disputes in which Iran is directly or indirectly involved were solved, or if Iran became a liberal-democratic mirror-image of a Western democracy—a preventive attack might look attractive. But there is no reason to believe that this will be the case, and the reverse is more probable. Small or large attacks on Iran will inject energy into Persian nationalism, strengthen the regime's argument that the West is a threat, and leave Iran with a grudge that it may express by deepening or initiating relationships with other states and groups hostile to U.S. purposes. Even regional states with something to fear from a nuclear-armed Iran probably would not welcome a preventive attack, simply because the region is already so roiled with violence, much of it attributed to mistaken U.S. policies.

Published assessments of possible attacks on Iran's nuclear infrastructure necessarily involve some speculation. There are nuclear facilities that we have good public information about, but there is likely a great deal of information that is known by western intelligence agencies that has not leaked into the public domain, and more information in Iran that has not leaked to anyone. Poor intelligence alone is one factor that might hinder the success of these operations. That said, three types of attack, of increasing strength, have been suggested.

First, some have considered very limited attacks on what seem to be critical nodes in a nuclear weapons production chain—especially Iran's plants at Isfahan to produce uranium hexafluoride gas and its facilities at Natanz to process this gas through centrifuges in order to enrich its fissionable material content. One careful analysis suggests that even Israeli fighter-bombers, armed with precision guided weapons Israel is known to possess, could destroy these facilities, presuming that they could refuel from aerial tankers en route, and fly over Jordan and Iraq, or Saudi Arabia, or Turkey.[4] For the United States, destroying these facilities would be a trivial matter. That said, the rest of the Iranian nuclear research and development effort would survive, and it seems likely that failing a change of government, Iran would persevere, and do so in a way that leaves the program less vulnerable. One might believe that a limited attack, however, would produce a relatively modest Iranian military response.

Second, some have suggested that one should try for maximum damage to the entire Iranian nuclear program. A recent analysis suggests that an attack on the Iranian nuclear infrastructure would involve four hundred aim points. The Pentagon's own intelligence would produce an even bigger target set. The United States easily could strike four hundred aim points with precision guided munitions in a single night.[5] Though no one could guarantee that this would be the end of Iran's program, it seems likely that the setback would be far greater than the limited attack on two critical nodes. An Iranian regime might determine that an attack of this size needed to be answered with a forceful response. The regime would look weak regionally, and domestically, if it simply accepted such an attack without a response. The regime reasonably could fear that failure to respond simply would invite further attacks, because the United States would doubt Iran's capability and will. Insofar as the United States has made plain that it wants to overthrow the Iranian regime, it is unlikely that Iran would view such a large attack as the final move.

Finally, . . . rumors have surfaced of even larger attack plans. To the target list associated with Iran's nuclear infrastructure, would be added an array of conventional targets—including naval bases, airfields, surface-to-air missile sites, surface-to-surface missile sites, and so on. During the first three nights of the 1991 Gulf War, coalition aircraft struck nearly three thousand targets of this kind.[6] Such attacks would have the purpose of forestalling an Iranian military retaliation against countries as close as Kuwait and as distant as Israel, U.S. forces in the region including those in Iraq, and oil tanker routes. Attacks of this size may also have the purpose of weakening the Iranian regime, though the precise mechanism is unclear, insofar as attacks of this kind have typically strengthened rather than weakened national cohesion and public support of governments, at least in the first instance. Though such an attack may succeed in reducing Iran's retaliatory options, it is implausible that it can reduce them to zero. U.S. forces in Iraq, and their line of communication, which runs through Shia populated areas where Iran has considerable influence, are quite vulnerable to tactical rocket and commando attacks that U.S. air strikes probably cannot prevent.[7] Beyond these significant immediate local costs, the United States attack will become a significant factor in future Iranian politics, discrediting any political faction that seems remotely associated with the United States or its purposes, and providing a potent political/ideological rationale for violence against the United States and its friends for many years to come.

Given that the odds of nonmilitary coercion achieving a success seem low, and the possible costs of a significant, if partly successful, large military operation seem high, it is reasonable to consider the remaining alternative systematically—containment and deterrence of a nuclear-armed Iran.

"GRAND STRATEGY"–IRAN AND THE UNITED STATES

Before considering the consequences of a nuclear-armed Iran for both the stability of the Middle East and Persian Gulf region and the security interests of the United States, one ought to consider the objectives that an Iranian nuclear force might be meant to serve. This requires some speculation about Iran's own "grand strategy."

Given that Iran is the most populous and economically developed state in the Persian Gulf area, a realist expects it to have ambitions to expand its power and influence in the region. Indeed, it is reasonable to expect that revolutionary Iran, like Iran under the Shah, has pretensions to regional hegemony. This is a general prediction, however, and much depends on what this means to Iran. For example, though many analysts do believe Iran has hegemonic ambitions, they usually couch this in cultural and political terms, not military terms.[8] Iran is active in expanding its influence, especially among Shia Arab populations in Iraq, in the Gulf region, and in Lebanon. Though Iran does have some disputes about islands, water rights, waterways, and coastal zones, according to the Central Intelligence Agency it has no major territorial claims beyond its borders.[9] The United States is no doubt perceived as an obstacle to Iran's regional ambitions. Iran surely would like to reduce the United States presence in the Gulf region, especially since the Bush administration adopted regime change in Iran as an objective.

Iran uses military force with some calculation, to increase the costs to others who might obstruct its goals, rather than to remove obstacles directly. Iran is not shy about using military assistance to nonstate actors as a way to discomfit those it defines as enemies, such as the United States and Israel. Iran sees some interest in maintaining a plausible capability to disrupt the flow of oil from the Persian Gulf, by leveraging its own limited naval capacity and its geographic control of one side of the narrow Strait of Hormuz to create a threat to Western economies. This threat is probably dissuasive—a retaliatory capability, as Iran cannot disrupt the flow of oil out of the Gulf without losing its own ability to export, which is vital to its economy. On the whole, Iran seems deliberate, unafraid to use violence in limited ways, but cautious as it tries to increase its influence and reduce that of others. The main exception to this description is its inflammatory rhetoric about Israel. I hypothesize, however, that much of this rhetoric is instrumental. Iran faces a major obstacle in expanding its influence—it is a Persian state amidst Arabs, and a Shia state amidst Sunnis. These differences are important and cause most Arab regimes to mistrust Iran. Iran may be using the struggle with Israel to submerge these differences in the face of a common enemy, and so legitimate itself among those not affectively inclined to follow its leadership, and weak enough to fear its power.

The United States pursues an ambitious inter-related complex of economic, security, and political objectives in the Persian Gulf. At this moment, political and security goals loom largest. . . .

The United States . . . has . . . traditional economic interests in the Gulf, which also are connected to security interests. Much of the world's internationally traded oil comes from the Gulf, so the United States is interested in the free flow of oil from the region. It also wishes to ensure that the oil resources not come under the control of hostile powers that might use it as a coercive lever. And finally, the United States wants to assure that the earnings from oil exports not end up in mischievous hands. These concerns generate a broad security agenda—including the defense of oil routes, the prevention of the conquest of any oil state by another, and watchful oversight of the internal politics of certain countries to ensure that dangerous elements not come to power. U.S. strategists may also believe that U.S. hegemony in the Gulf region gives them some leverage over oil exports, and thus increases U.S. power in other parts of the world. For all these reasons, the United States must maintain a very large military presence, and remain the predominant military power in the Gulf region.

This brief assessment of Iranian and U.S. goals suggests that these two powers are destined to be in an intensely competitive relationship. Each has cards to play in this competition. Iran knows the region well, has an excellent geographic position, and may be able to find support in Shiite Arab populations in neighboring countries. Though economically and militarily weak compared to the United States, it is the strongest power in the Gulf, and has proven itself capable of mobilizing very large ground forces. The United States has a giant economy and the world's most advanced military. The United States also has two potential political advantages. Historically, most states consider large proximate land powers such as Iran to be more dangerous to them than distant sea powers such as the United States. And, Iran—an Islamic country, with potential Shia domestic allies in many gulf states—poses a more credible threat of domestic destabilization than does the U.S. rhetoric of democratization. However powerful and assertive the United States may be, neighboring Iran poses at least as great a threat—and perhaps a greater threat. Hence, despite the present diplomatic ill effects of its mistakes in Iraq, over time the United States is likely to prove the more attractive ally to most states in the region.

Nuclear weapons would make Iran a somewhat more powerful state, which could allow it to pursue certain interests with greater vigor. Fear of Iranian nuclear weapons may cause other states in the region to want their own nuclear weapons, which may in turn cause still others to want nuclear weapons. This would not only be a problem in its own terms, it could further damage the Nuclear Non-Proliferation Treaty and the institutions that sustain it. The ability of the United States and its allies and friends outside and inside the region to contain and deter Iran will affect whether or not significant nuclear proliferation occurs in the region, so I turn first to the likely U.S. and regional responses to a nuclear Iran.

NUCLEAR-ARMED IRAN'S FOUR THREATS

Reviewing the debate over Iranian nuclear weapons, one can find four different strategic fears of a nuclear-armed Iran: (1) Iran could be emboldened by the possession of a deterrent force and its foreign policy thus would become more adventurous and more violent; (2) Iran could directly threaten others with nuclear attack unless certain demands were met; (3) Iran could give nuclear weapons to nonstate actors; and (4) Iran simply could attack Israel with nuclear weapons—heedless of the inevitable Israeli nuclear retaliation.

A More Adventurous Iran

During the recent fighting between Israel and Hezbollah, President Bush averred that the event would have been much more dangerous had Iran possessed nuclear weapons, but he did not explain why. His implication was that Iran would have been more inclined to involve itself directly in the crisis. The argument would be that Iran's leadership would shelter behind its nuclear deterrent. Great powers would be afraid to attack Iran directly, especially to invade Iran, if they faced the risk of nuclear escalation. So Iran would be free to do anything from meddling in the internal affairs of other countries to invading them with conventional forces, because it could control its costs. This concern is quite reasonable; Iran's leaders might have this idea, but how much different would the situation be than it is today?

Iran already dabbles in subversion and terror. Its leaders do not seem too concerned about invasion, and overthrow, and with good reason. Iran's population is some 70 million, and its land area is roughly three times the size of France.

The United States, with the most capable army in the world, is having a difficult time controlling five of Iraq's eighteen provinces, and perhaps 12 million of its 26.8 million people. Iran is surely concerned about other retaliatory responses, including air attacks and even embargos. This is why Iran is somewhat careful to limit its activities and cover its tracks. It might perceive itself to be more secure from retaliatory air attack with a nuclear deterrent, but Israel's nuclear deterrent did not save it from rocket attack in the recent fighting in Lebanon. And from what is known about U.S. Cold War military planning for war against the Soviet Union, and for that matter possible conflict with China today, large nuclear retaliatory forces do not deter the United States from planning large scale conventional air operations against nuclear-armed countries.

Iran's leaders might also perceive that actual conventional attacks on its neighbors would carry less risk than in the past, due to possession of a nuclear deterrent. But counterattacks on its homeland are only one cost of such a gambit. Iran's conventional military offensive capability is not very great, and it would take enormous investments to improve them much. U.S. military spending is currently nearly three times Iran's total GDP, and ninety times Iran's defense effort.[10] Saudi Arabia might be able to defend itself without U.S. help, but we know from the 1991 Iraqi invasion of Kuwait that the kingdom and the United States have cooperated to assure that U.S. reinforcements can reach Saudi Arabia very quickly. Though tiny countries such as Kuwait and the Gulf sheikdoms cannot hope to defend themselves against Iran on their own, reinforcement with high-technology U.S. military forces would assure that Iran's offensive forces could not conquer these countries, and there again preparations have already been made to enable rapid U.S. reinforcement. And, for the foreseeable future, it seems very likely that considerable U.S. forces will be based in the Gulf states and the adjacent waters. Even if Iran's leaders somehow feel safe at home, the forces they dispatch abroad would surely be destroyed, and they likely understand this very well as they have had a box seat at two U.S. conventional wars in the region, and seen much of their own surface fleet sunk by the United States.

Direct Threats from Iran

A second possible use of Iran's nuclear weapons is bald nuclear coercion—especially against nonnuclear neighbors. Nuclear coercion, even against the weak, has certain risks, so it is hard to guess what Iranian interest would be worth such a gambit. In a drive for Gulf hegemony, Iran might demand that those of its neighbors who are close to the United States should weaken these ties—throw out U.S. forces, deny them ports of call and landing rights, destroy prepositioned equipment sites, and cease importing U.S. weapons. Less plausibly, Iran might demand that other oil producing states agree with its own views at any given time about how much oil to pump, or what to charge for it, though this does not seem worth a nuclear crisis. It is worth noting that, since the end of World War II, no nuclear power has found a way to use nuclear threats to achieve offensive strategic objectives.

These gambits are unlikely to work, and the United States and its allies can act to forestall them. During the Cold War, the United States offered the protection of its nuclear deterrent forces to many allies who did not possess nuclear weapons—every NATO member state except Britain and France. The United States promised that if NATO were to be attacked by the Soviet Union with nuclear weapons, it would respond. Indeed, NATO strategy called for the employment of nuclear weapons in the event of a successful Soviet conventional invasion of NATO states. The United States made this commitment in spite of virtual nuclear parity with the Soviet Union. The United States risked annihilation to secure its interests in Europe.

The United States has, at least since the late 1970s, perceived itself through Democratic and Republican administrations to have a very strong interest in the security of Persian Gulf countries. It is likely that the United States would offer the Gulf Arab countries a nuclear "guarantee." Given that U.S. strategic nuclear forces today are vastly more powerful than anything Iran is likely to be able to deploy, the United States runs less risk in offering such an assurance than it did during the Cold War, and Iran would face very grave risks if it challenged them. Indeed, given U.S. nuclear advantages, Iran would be running the risk of a preemptive U.S. nuclear strike against Iranian forces, in the event that it began to alert these forces to add credibility to its threat. Put bluntly, to be a nuclear-armed state is to be a nuclear target.

Would a state such as Saudi Arabia be willing to count on the U.S. nuclear guarantee? Would it be willing to stand up to an Iranian threat, and risk the possibility that Iran might not be deterred? This is impossible to know. But, Saudi Arabia would know one thing: if it succumbed to Iran's blandishments once, and severed its connections to the United States, it essentially would become a satellite of Iran, and there would be no end to Iran's demands.

Iran and Nonstate Actors

Since the September 11, 2001, attacks on the United States, many have been concerned that nuclear weapons could fall into the hands of terrorists. One way this could occur, it is feared, would be for a state with a weapons program to give or sell one to a terrorist group. Such action seems unlikely in the case of Iran, or any state, because it serves no strategic purpose, invites retaliation, and cannot be controlled. It is perhaps the most self-destructive thing that any nation state can do.

What strategic purpose, other than pure destruction, could such an action serve? A single nuclear weapon exploded in the United States, or any other state, would be a truly horrible event. But it would not destroy the existence of that state, or destroy its political power. And it would enrage that state, and no doubt cause extraordinary efforts to discover, and punish, the source of the attack.

If the weapon is tracked back to the source, the source country will be blamed. It will be blamed not only by the victim, but by other states, terrified by the implications of the action. The victim surely will try to punish the supplier, and it is likely that this punishment would involve nuclear strikes. Iran or any other nuclear weapons provider might hope to avoid detection, but they could only hope—they could not count on it. The characteristics of the explosion may provide some indications of the origin of the weapon.[11] Moreover, once the explosion occurs, intelligence collected and either ignored or misunderstood prior to the event will be reviewed in light of the event, and may have new meaning. Additionally, there are not all that many potential sources of a nuclear weapon—wherever an explosion occurs one can be sure that intelligence would quickly focus on nuclear problem states such as North Korea, Iran, and Pakistan. Indeed, these states are so likely to end up in the spotlight for a terrorist use of a nuclear weapon, they probably have an interest in stopping *any* conspiracies of this kind that they discover.

Once a weapon is supplied to the nonstate actor, the supplying state has no guarantee that it will be used for the original agreed purpose. The nonstate actor may have promised to attack Israel, but instead may attack France, or the United States. Alternatively, that actor may simply be a middleman, and sell or trade the device to someone else. The risks cannot be controlled by the supplying state.

Iran and Israel

It is occasionally suggested that Iran in particular, because of its leaders' undisguised hatred for the state of Israel, and quite open assertions that the Middle East would be better off if Israel disappeared, might act to make their fantasies a reality. Iran could use its future nuclear weapons to annihilate the state of Israel, unconcerned about Israeli nuclear retaliation because Iran is a large country that would somehow survive a nuclear exchange with Israel, while Israel is a small country that would be entirely destroyed.

A few fission weapons would horribly damage the state of Israel, and a few fusion weapons would surely destroy it. But neither kind of attack could reliably shield Iran from a devastating response. Israel has had years to work on developing and shielding its nuclear deterrent. It is generally attributed with as many as 200 fission warheads, deliverable by several different methods, including Intermediate Range Ballistic Missile.[12] Were Iran to proceed with a weapons program, Israel would surely improve its own capabilities. Though Iran's population is large, and much of it is dispersed, about a quarter of Iranians (over fifteen million people) live in eight cities conservatively within range of Israel's Jericho II missile.[13] Much of Iran's economic capacity is also concentrated in these cities.[14] Nuclear attacks on these cities, plus some oil industry targets, would destroy Iran as a functioning society and prevent its recovery. There is little in the behavior of the leaders of revolutionary Iran that suggests they would see this as a good trade.

A premise of the foregoing fears is that Iran is led by religious fanatics, who might be more interested in the next world than this one. The current president of Iran, Mahmoud Ahmadinejad, has made statements that have caused observers to doubt his risk aversion and his grasp on reality. It is important to note, however, that in Iran's governing structure, the president does not have much influence over security policy. This belongs to the Supreme Leader Ayatollah Khamenei. Though its implications are much disputed, he has issued a *fatwa* against the development, production, stockpiling, and use of nuclear weapons.[15] This suggests awareness that nuclear weapons are particularly destructive and terrible. Iran's religious leaders have in the past shown themselves sensitive to costs. The founder of Iran's revolution, Ayatollah Khomeini, ceased the war with Iraq in the 1980s when he determined that the costs were too great.[16] By modern standards these costs were high, perhaps half a million dead. But those casualties pale against the casualties of a nuclear exchange with Israel. And Iran's suffering in a nuclear exchange with Israel would pale against its likely suffering in an exchange with the United States.

Mahmoud Ahmadinejad is nevertheless a worrying figure. He has denied that the Jewish Holocaust is a proven fact. He has said, or implied, that Israel should disappear from the map of the Middle East. In the first instance he denies a horror for world Jewry. In the second, he promises a new horror for the Jews, and given Israel's nuclear capabilities, a horror for Iranians as well if his own country were involved. What we cannot know is whether these observations are offered to produce a certain emotional effect, or whether he understands the implications of his utterances and believes and accepts them. Fortunately, few predict that Iran can acquire nuclear weapons soon, which gives time to assess and monitor Ahmadinejad's actual strategic influence in Iran, and to discredit him in Iran and in the wider world by regularly pointing out the very grave risks that his ideas hold for his country. Iranians will have a chance to reconsider this man's leadership abilities. He came in with a vote; he can go out the same way. The time in office of Iranian presidents is fixed in any case—limited to two four-year terms.

OTHER ISSUES RESULTING FROM A NUCLEAR-ARMED IRAN

A final set of concerns about a nuclear-armed Iran arise not from what Iran would or would not do from the point of view of considered strategy, but from a mixed bag of concerns about inadequate Iranian resources, organizational incompetence, and political decentralization. These concerns are not trivial, but even those who raise them do not advocate preventive war to avoid them, which helps put the risks in context.[17]

The first problem is the risk that, due to their relative poverty and inexperience, new nuclear states, such as Iran, will be unable or unwilling to develop the secure retaliatory forces necessary for a stable deterrent relationship. Iran's nuclear force could be small, vulnerable to attack, and lacking secure command and control. Such a force could attract preemption by a neighbor. Or, fearing preemption by a neighbor, Iran could adopt "hair-trigger" alert postures, or due to poor command and control, a fearful Iran might in a crisis inadvertently launch a nuclear weapon. These are all valid concerns, but many of these problems would be in Iran's hands to solve.

Precisely because even a single nuclear explosion is so destructive, Iran does not need a particularly large nuclear force to deter nuclear attacks by other nuclear states. If Iran's secondary purpose is to discourage further any effort to conquer Iran and change the government, then the state attempting to do that will inevitably present lucrative proximate targets for Iranian nuclear weapons. To deter its neighbors, or invaders, Iran does not need particularly long-ranged survivable systems—short-range mobile missiles should be sufficient and these are the easiest to hide.

Iran's most reasonable strategy is to disperse and hide its small force as best it can, and keep it quiet so that foreign intelligence means cannot attack it. This means eschewing dangerous alert postures, firststrike doctrines, and the like. Dispersal, secrecy, stealth, and communications security are the means to survival, though they may present some command and control issues, and some nuclear security issues. There is no reason in principle, however, why a state such as Iran cannot use multiple-key arrangements to ensure against the unauthorized launch of its weapons.

Analysts of nuclear weapons organizations, however, fairly point to the fact that states do not always base their nuclear weapons in reasonable ways. And they do not necessarily confine their objectives to basic deterrence. Iran may decide that it wants a first-strike capability versus its neighbors, such as Israel. Such a dream is probably unachievable, but Iran might attempt to develop such a capability. This would set up an unstable strategic relationship between the two countries, and any crises would include an element of great risk, as one or the other became tempted to preempt. In the U.S.-Soviet case, these problems ultimately lead the two sides to ensure that some piece of their nuclear forces would likely survive an exchange to visit a horrible retaliation, and thus deter the other's first-strike temptations. These risks also led them to become quite cautious in their political competition, but there were hair-raising episodes along the way, and there is no reason to rule out similar events in the case of Iran.

On the other hand, it is virtually impossible for Iran to achieve a first-strike capability versus the United States. Any risks that Iran took in its basing mode and alert posture to get ready for a first strike against Israel could easily make it more vulnerable to a first strike from the United States. Spending its nuclear forces on Israel would leave Iran politically and militarily vulnerable to a huge U.S. retaliation. By striking first, it would have legitimated a U.S. nuclear attack, while simultaneously weakening its own deterrent with the weapons it had expended. The United States is the greater threat to Iran because it is much more powerful than Israel, and has actual strategic objectives in the Gulf. It is strategically reasonable for Iran to focus its deterrent energies on the United States, which it can only influence with a secure retaliatory force, capable of threatening U.S. forces and interests in the region.

A final potential problem in Iran is the apparent decentralization of power in the country. Iran essentially has two military organizations: the "professional" military, and the Revolutionary Guard Corps. The latter is ideologically motivated, secretive, and involved in assisting armed groups abroad in Iraq and Lebanon. Many fear that the latter would end up in control of the weapons, or at least with considerable access to them. Given the nature of this organization, some of its members might be willing to do things that the higher political authorities in the state would not choose to do. They might give the weapons away, or use them without authorization. It is impossible to know whether this would occur in Iran. The Revolutionary Guards are generally considered to be very loyal to the Supreme Leader, the ultimate political authority.[18] This should work against renegade behavior. Iran is dedicating considerable national resources to nuclear energy, and if it pursued its current path through to a complete weapons program, it will have devoted many more resources. It is likely, though not guaranteed, that Iran's leaders will take care to put the weapons under the control of people they trust to obey their orders. All states having relations with Iran have an interest in this matter. Nuclear powers must make clear to Iran that its nuclear weapons would be a state responsibility. It will not matter to others whether an Iranian nuclear weapon was employed or exported by "rogue" elements within the state. Even nonnuclear powers can convey this message to Iran, letting Iran know that such an excuse would not win Iran any diplomatic cover. Iran must also be carefully watched for signs of sloppy control practices, and if they appear, other states must make these practices a primary issue in their relations with Iran.

REGIONAL NUCLEAR PROLIFERATION AND RISKS TO THE NON-PROLIFERATION TREATY

States in range of Iran's nuclear weapons will reasonably wish to take measures to protect themselves against nuclear coercion and nuclear attack. Iran's neighbors have three policy options to ensure themselves against a nuclear-armed Iran. They can choose to appease Iran comprehensively; they can find a nuclear guarantor; they can build their own nuclear weapons. Though elements of these three policies could be combined, one will tend to dominate.

Most countries will decline to appease Iran, if they have another plausible option, because most nation-states enjoy their autonomy and do not wish to give it up. Comprehensive appeasement is the road to ruin; one set of concessions to a demanding Iran could easily lead to another, until the state in question loses the ability to recover any shred of sovereignty. Comprehensive appeasement will likely only prove preferable to states facing a disastrous war, or disastrous defeat, with no hope of survival. Historically, this sort of behavior is generally only found among the very weak, and typically when they lack any other option.

The most important choice is whether states will seek their own nuclear weapons, or seek the protection of another nuclear power, if that protection is offered. That said, only a few states in the Middle East and Persian Gulf have the resources to attempt their own autonomous nuclear weapons programs. I have argued above that the United States likely would offer protection to regional states in order to protect its interests in the Persian Gulf from Iran. It also may offer such protection in order to forestall a spasm of nuclear proliferation in the region. The policies of the United States, and to a lesser extent the principal European states and the European Union, will be the most decisive determinant of whether or not Iran's nuclear programs are emulated.

At this time, and for the foreseeable future, four regional powers can be considered candidate nuclear competitors with Iran: Israel (already a nuclear-armed state), Egypt, Saudi Arabia, and Turkey.

Israel depends on the United States for its advanced conventional weaponry, but it is unwilling to count on any state for its immediate defense. Israel has had a nuclear weapons program for a very long time, though it declines to discuss the matter publicly. Open sources estimate a stockpile of two hundred weapons. Israel is believed to be able to deliver weapons by ballistic missile and by aircraft, and perhaps by submarine-launched cruise missile. It seems to have taken care to produce a secure second-strike capability. In the face of an open Iranian program, Israel may be tempted to go public with its own program.

Though Iran is quite vulnerable to nuclear attack today, Israel might intensify its preparations to ensure that Iran understands just how dangerous nuclear threats toward Israel would be. Not many Israeli nuclear weapons would need to survive an attempted Iranian first strike to ruin Iran forever. Open improvements in Israeli nuclear capabilities, especially if accompanied by extensive public rhetoric, would likely raise security and prestige concerns among its neighbors. The United States would be wise to urge Israel to refrain from strong nuclear declarations, unless Iran's own public declarations about its nuclear capability demand a response.

Egypt would be concerned for reasons of both prestige and security if Iran was to become a nuclear weapons state, and Israel was to become an open nuclear power. Egypt at one time had an active nuclear energy research program, and there was concern that it could become a nuclear weapons program. It has the technological and scientific expertise and has recently announced a new civilian nuclear energy program.[19] Absent active U.S. diplomacy, and strategic guarantees, Egypt probably would follow suit in developing nuclear weapons. Egypt faces a number of barriers, however. First, it is highly dependent on the United States for conventional weaponry. The United States surely would suspend this relationship if Egypt decided to pursue nuclear weapons. This would be quite unsettling to Egypt's internal politics. Second, Egypt is a poor country; foreign economic assistance would also dry up if Egypt decided to go nuclear. Third, given that Israel is already a nuclear weapons state, and Iran is well ahead of Egypt, Egypt would go through a period of both conventional and nuclear vulnerability as it attempted to produce nuclear weapons. Egypt could choose to accept all these risks and costs, but it seems more plausible that the United States and the European Union could find a package of assurances and incentives that would be acceptable to Egypt.

Saudi Arabia would face similar, though stronger temptations, than Egypt. Saudi Arabia is arguably the other "great power" of the Persian Gulf region, and thus a natural competitor with Iran. With the demise of Iraq, it is the undisputed leader of the Arab states in the Gulf, and thus a rival to an Iran trying to expand its sphere of influence. Due to their proximity, Iran and Saudi Arabia are vulnerable to one another's conventional military power. Saudi Arabia likely views itself as the protector of Sunni Arabs from Shia Arabs, and from Shia Iran.

Saudi Arabia does not, however, have a developed nuclear science and technology effort. And it does not have the other industrial capabilities needed to support a nuclear weapons program and associated delivery systems. Saudi Arabia would thus take quite a long time to develop its own nuclear forces, and like Egypt, would be vulnerable in the interval. They would have to rely on an external guarantee, and the guarantor probably would not want to be a party to any nuclear program. With its wealth, however, it cannot be ruled out that the Saudis would simply try to buy nuclear weapons. They would need more than a few to compete with an Iranian program, and they would need delivery systems. Pakistan seems the only possible source, but it is under a great deal of scrutiny. Pakistan would face enormous pressure not to transfer complete weapons to another party. Finally, Saudi Arabia does have good reason to believe that outsiders are committed to its security. The United States and other great powers have extensive economic and military interests in maintaining Saudi security. The United States has demonstrated its commitment in many ways, including war. The Saudis are accustomed to security cooperation with the United States. A U.S. guarantee likely would prove the most attractive option for Saudi Arabia.

Turkey also will be concerned, for security and prestige reasons, about a nuclear weapons capability in neighboring Iran. Turkey's economic, scientific, and engineering capabilities probably make it more capable of going nuclear than either Egypt or Saudi Arabia. Turkey's calculation will be affected by other political interests, however. Turkey is a member of NATO, a nuclear alliance, and thus already enjoys a nuclear guarantee by the United States. Dozens of tactical nuclear weapons are based in Turkey, and some of Turkey's aircraft are wired to deliver these weapons, which could be turned over to them under circumstances determined by the United States, and based on long-standing procedures agreed within NATO. This relationship would be jeopardized were Turkey to embark on its own independent nuclear weapons program. Turkey also aspires to membership in the European Union. Though the Europeans have been only moderately encouraging, it seems likely that the EU would discourage an independent Turkish nuclear effort. Conversely, it seems possible that the EU might become more accommodating of Turkey's effort to join the EU if that helped discourage a Turkish nuclear program. . . .

CONCLUSION

A nuclear-armed Iran is not a trivial problem—for its neighbors or the United States. Indeed, Iran itself would be entering a difficult new period in its history. It would be better by far for Iran to forgo those technology development initiatives that would allow it to make a decision to become a nuclear weapons state. But current diplomatic efforts may fail, and the question arises as to whether preventive war dominates a strategy of containment and deterrence. This choice can only be considered if a strategy of containment is elucidated, and its odds of success assessed. Should Iran become a nuclear power, both the immediate strategic risks and the proliferation risks can be addressed with a reinvigorated commitment of U.S. power to stability and security in the Persian Gulf and the Middle East. Such a commitment is reasonable given U.S. strategic interests in the region. The United States should seek the help of outside partners in Europe and elsewhere in making this commitment. The United States can and should make it clear to Iran that the overt or covert use of its nuclear weapons, for blackmail or for war, would put Iran in the gravest danger of nuclear retaliation. The United States should similarly explain to regional actors why it is willing to make this commitment. Both the United States and regional actors may wish to reinforce this commitment with security agreements and some visible military preparations. At the same time, it will be necessary for the United States to forgo any future efforts to replace the Iranian regime. This would run nuclear risks that neither the United States, nor other great powers, nor regional powers will wish to run.

The strategy of deterrence and containment has worked for the United States before; there is no reason why it cannot work again. Relative to Iran, the United States and its likely allies have vastly superior material capabilities, a far more favorable situation than in the Cold War. In a confrontation with the United States, Iran would run risks of complete destruction, and it cannot threaten the United States with comparable damage.

Bismarck said of preventive war that it was like committing suicide out of fear of death. A preventive war versus Iran might not be suicidal, but it will definitely hurt. The United States and its allies have many military and diplomatic cards to play to manage the dangers posed by a nuclear-armed Iran. That said, a replay of the Cold War competition in the Persian Gulf is not a happy outcome. Though I think it is preferable to preventive war, far better would be a diplomatic solution. Since it is unlikely that economic pressure alone will bring diplomatic success, it would be wise to offer Iran a package of incentives more consistent with its apparent concerns than has been offered thus far. If Iran were to decline such an offer, this clarification of its purposes would assist the ultimate diplomacy of containment and deterrence.

NOTES

1. Jeffrey J. Schott, Institute for International Economics, "Economic Sanctions, Oil, and Iran," Testimony before the Joint Economic Committee, U.S. Congress, Hearing on "Energy and the Iranian Economy," July 25, 2006, available online at http://www.iie.com/publications/papers/paper.cfm?ResearchID=649.
2. Lionel Beehner, "What Sanctions Mean for Iran's Economy," Council on Foreign Relations Background Paper, May 2006, available online at http://www.cfr.org/publication/10590/what_sanctions_mean_for_irans_economy.html?
3. Flynt Leverett, "The Race for Iran," *New York Times*, June 20, 2006.
4. Austin Long and Whitney Raas, "Osirak Redux? Assessing Israeli Capabilities to Destroy Iranian Nuclear Facilities," April 2006, SSP Working Paper, available online at http://web.mit.edu/ssp/Publications/working_papers/wp_06–1.pdf.
5. For example, two hundred fighter bombers could easily deliver four hundred precision-guided weapons against four hundred aim points. Given the U.S. naval and air presence in the Persian Gulf, this rather limited attack could probably be launched with little reinforcement.

6. Thomas A. Keaney and Eliot A. Cohen, *Gulf War Air Power Survey Summary Report* (Washington, D.C.: Government Printing Office, 1993), Figure 5, "Coalition Air Strikes by Day Against Iraqi Target Sets," p. 13 (numbers estimated from graph).

7. The recent Israeli experience in Lebanon is relevant. Neither the Israeli Air Force nor the powerful counterbattery attacks of the Israeli Army's artillery could prevent Hezbollah from launching a hundred or more artillery rockets into northern Israel almost every night. Given the length of the Iran/Iraq border, it seems likely that Iran could infiltrate small units into Iraq to raid bases and truck convoys. At this moment, Iran likely has agents in Southern Iraq, and has sufficiently strong relationships with Shiite militias that some of these militias might assist Iran. Finally, Iran's intelligence on the location and strength of coalition forces is likely very good. It would not be surprising if Iran had precise coordinates for many of these potential targets, and spotters close to these targets, both of which would improve the performance of its otherwise inaccurate long range artillery rockets.

8. Robert Lowe and Claire Spencer, eds., *Iran, its Neighbors and the Regional Crises, A Middle East Programme Report* (London: Royal Institute of International Affairs, 2006), pp. 6, 8–12; See also Vali Nasr, "When the Shiites Rise," *Foreign Affairs* 85 (July/August 2006): 58–74, esp. 66–68. Ray Takeyh, "A Profile in Defiance, Being Mahmoud Admadinejad," *National Interest*, no. 83 (Spring 2006): pp. 16–21 makes the point that the new Iranian president and his coterie of Iraq war veterans seem more religious, more nationalistic, and more confrontational than others in the Iranian political elite, but that they are only one faction.

9. *The World Factbook,* U.S. Central Intelligence Agency, available online at https://www.cia.gov/cia/publications/factbook/geos/ir.html, accessed Sept. 25, 2006.

10. *The Military Balance 2006* (London: International Institute for Strategic Studies, and Routledge, 2006), pp. 18, 187.

11. William Dunlop and Harold Smith, "Who Did It? Using International Forensics to Detect and Deter Nuclear Terrorism," *Arms Control Today,* October 2006, available online at http://www.armscontrol.org/act/2006_10/CVRForensics.asp, accessed October 29, 2006.

12. *The Military Balance 2006*, p. 191.

13. For population concentrations see, "World Urbanization Prospects: The 2005 Revision Population Database," "Iran," U.N. Population Division, available online at http://esa.un.org/unup, accessed 23 September 2006. Jericho II range estimates by Austin Long.

14. Perhaps a third of Iranian manufacturing industry is concentrated in or near Tehran, Karaj, and Isfahan alone. See "Table 7.9, Manufacturing Establishments by Legal Status and Ostan: 1381," Statistical Centre of Iran, available online at http://www.sci.org.ir/portal/faces/public/sci_en/sci_en.selecteddata/sci_en.yearbookdata, accessed September 29, 2006.

15. Mark Fitzpatrick, "Assessing Iran's Nuclear Program," *Survival* 48, no. 3 (Autumn 2006): 13.

16. Graham E. Fuller, "War and Revolution in Iran," *Current History* (February 1989): 81–100. "In basic terms, Khomeini faced a stark choice between pursuing an increasingly unattainable revolutionary victory over Iraq and the survival of the Islamic Revolution itself" (p. 81).

17. Scott D. Sagan, "How to Keep the Bomb From Iran," *Foreign Affairs* 85 (September/October 2006): 45–59. Sagan raises many of the concerns outlined here. These concerns lead him to advise a focused diplomatic effort to discourage Iran from proceeding with its enrichment program. He explicitly concludes, however, that preventive war is not an

appropriate answer to the Iranian program. Implicitly, therefore, he accepts that however problematical a nuclear Iran might be, these risks do not exceed those associated with a preventive war.

18. Jim Walsh, "Iran and the Nuclear Issue: Negotiated Settlement or Escalation?" Testimony before the Subcommittee on Federal Financial Management, Government Information and International Security, Committee on Homeland Security and Governmental Affairs, United States Senate, July 20, 2006, Washington, D.C.

19. For an excellent review of the nuclear potential of Egypt, Turkey, and Saudi Arabia, see Wyn Q. Bowen and Joanna Kidd, "The Nuclear Capabilities and Ambitions of Iran's Neighbors," in *Getting Ready for a Nuclear-Ready Iran,* Henry Sokolski and Patrick Clawson, eds. (Carlyle Barracks, Penn.: U.S. Army War College, Strategic Studies Institute, 2005), pp. 51–88, available online at www.strategicstudiesinstitute.army.mil/. See also William Wallis and Roula Khalaf, "Speculation after Egypt Revives Nuclear Plans," *Financial Times,* September 25, 2006, available online at http://www.ft.com/cms/s/6e01b312–4cba-11db-b03c-0000779e2340.html, accessed October 29, 2006.

 Exercises for Nuclear Deterrence and Nuclear Spread

Apply what you learned in this chapter by using the online resources on MyPoliSciKit (www.mypoliscikit.com).

 Practice Tests

Videos:
- "Nuclear Disarmament under the INF Treaty"
- "Hiroshima, 1945"

 Reading Guides:
- Henry Sokolski, "Getting Ready for a Nuclear-Ready Iran"
- Barry R. Posen, "A Nuclear-Armed Iran: A Difficult but Not Impossible Policy Problem"

International Political Economy and Globalization

In Part 1, we examined the meaning of anarchy and saw the consequences for state behavior that flowed from it. In Part 2, we analyzed in more detail one of the primary instruments that states can and must use, namely, military power. In Part 3, we are concerned with the other primary instrument of state action—economic power—and with the economically globalized world in which we now live.

Disparities in power, as we saw earlier, have important effects on state behavior. Such disparities occur not simply because of the differences in military power that states wield, but also because of the differences in economic resources that they generate. In the first instance, the force that a nation can deploy is dependent in part on the economic wealth that it can muster to support and sustain its military forces. Wealth is therefore a component of state power. But the generation of wealth, unlike the generation of military power, is also an end of state action. Except in the rarest of circumstances, military power is never sought as an end in itself, but rather is acquired as a means to attain security or the other ends that a state pursues. By contrast, wealth is both a component of state power and a good that can be consumed by its citizenry. Force is mustered primarily for the external arena. Wealth is sought for both the external and the domestic arena. Moreover, wealth and power differ in the degree to which states can pursue each without detriment to the positions and interests of other nations. No situation in international politics is ever totally cooperative or conflictual, but the potential for cooperative behavior is greater in the realm of wealth than in the realm of power.

It is the duality of economic power (as a component and end of state action) and its greater potential for common gains that make the analysis of the role it plays in state behavior and international interactions complex and elusive. The study of international political economy, as it has been traditionally understood, encompasses both these aspects of economic power. More recently, scholars and citizens have become concerned about the costs and benefits of the globalized world that we now inhabit.

PERSPECTIVES ON POLITICAL ECONOMY

"The science of economics presupposes a given political order, and cannot be profitably studied in isolation from politics." So wrote E. H. Carr in his seminal work, *The Twenty Years' Crisis*, in 1939. Fifty years earlier, in an essay titled "Socialism: Utopian or Scientific," Karl Marx's coauthor, Friedrich Engels, asserted: "The materialist conception of history starts from the proposition that the production of the means to support human life . . . is the basis of all social structure. . . ." These two views—that economic processes are not autonomous but require political structures to support them, and that economic factors determine the social and political structures of states—represent the polar extremes on the relationship of politics and economics.

Which view is correct? To this question there is no simple or single answer. Any reply is as much philosophical as it is empirical. The economic interests of individuals in a state and of states within the international arena do powerfully affect the goals that are sought and the degree of success with which they are attained. But the fundamental political structure of international action is also a constraint. Anarchy makes cooperative actions more difficult to attain than would otherwise be the case and requires that statesmen consider both relative and absolute positions when framing actions in the international economic realm. And often in international politics the imperatives of security and survival override the dictates of economic interests. War, after all, almost never pays in a strict balance-sheet sense, particularly when waged between states of roughly equal power. The economic wealth lost in fighting is usually not recouped in the peace that follows.

The best discussions of the relations between politics and economics in international affairs have been by the classical theorists of international politics. Robert Gilpin examines three schools of thought—liberalism, Marxism, and mercantilism. Unlike the other two, liberal political economists have stressed the cooperative, not the conflictual, nature of international economic relations. They have extended Adam Smith's arguments about the domestic economy to the international economy. Smith argued that the specialization of function by individuals within a state, together with their unfettered pursuit of their own self-interests, would increase the wealth of a nation and thereby benefit all. Collective harmony and national wealth could thus be the product of self-interested behavior, if only the government would provide order with as little restraint on individual action as was necessary. The eighteenth-century philosophers and the nineteenth- and twentieth-century free traders argued that what was good for individuals within a state would also be good for states in the international arena. By trading freely with one another, states could specialize according to their respective comparative advantages and the wealth of all nations would, as a consequence, increase. "Make trade, not war" has been the slogan of the liberal free traders.

By contrast, both mercantilists and Marxists have seen state relations as inherently conflictual. For Marxists, this is so because capitalists within and among states compete fiercely with one another to maximize their profits. Driven by their greed, they are incapable of cooperating with one another. Because a state's policy is determined by the capitalist ruling class, states will wage wars for profit and, under

Lenin's dictum, will wage wars to redivide the world's wealth. Imperialism as the highest stage of capitalism is a classic zero-sum situation. Mercantilists also argue that economic factors make relations among states conflictual. Their analysis, however, rests not on the externalization of class conflict, but on the nature of political and economic power. For eighteenth-century mercantilists, the world's wealth was fixed and could only be redivided. For nineteenth- and twentieth-century mercantilists, wealth could be increased for all, but because wealth contributes to national power and power is relative, not absolute, conflict would continue.

All three schools of thought are motivated by their views on the relation of politics to economics. Mercantilists stress the primacy of politics and the consequent pursuit of national power and relative position in the international arena. Both liberals and Marxists stress the primacy of economics. For the former, the potential for economic harmony can override the forces of nationalism if free trade is pursued. For the latter, economic interests determine political behavior and, because the first is conflictual, the second must be also. Both liberals and Marxists want to banish politics from international relations, the former through free trade, the latter through the universal spread of communism. Mercantilists, like realists, view these prescriptions as naive and believe that the national interests of every state are only partly determined by their economic interests.

Scholars continue to wrestle with the relation between politics and economics in international affairs. Michael J. Hiscox presents a view that combines liberalism and Marxism. Unlike the realist perspective discussed in earlier sections and mercantilism presented by Gilpin, Hiscox stresses the role played by domestic economic interests in formulating a state's foreign economic policy. This perspective is similar to Marxism in stressing the importance of economic motives and groups, but unlike it in focusing on economic interests rather than economic classes and on the role of institutions in aggregating preferences. Indeed, on many issues such as tariff levels and exchange rates, workers and owners in one economic sector may work together against workers and owners in other sectors.

Bruce R. Scott looks at the political-economic relations between rich and poor states, and asks why the gap between these two has increased during the globalization era of the last 20 years, when, in fact, neoclassical economic theory predicts that the gap should have decreased. According to this theory, in a free global market poor states lessen the gap because they are supposed to grow faster than rich states. That this has not happened is due, according to Scott, to the barriers imposed by the rich states on immigration and agriculture from the poorer states, and to the inadequate government structures in the poor states that make them less than ideal outlets for capital investments from the rich states. Thus, the reasons are political-economic in nature, and the fault lies with both the rich and the poor states.

THE NATURE OF GLOBALIZATION

At the beginning of the twenty-first century, which way will the international political economy go? Where should it go? Has globalization fundamentally changed the world economy, and, if so, will national borders lose even more of their economic significance in the future? Will there be a protectionist backlash? Are new forms of protectionism now more important than tariffs as technology, innovation, and services become more important? Have the poor, in both the United States and abroad, suffered because of globalization?

These are difficult questions to answer. How they are answered depends heavily on how economically interdependent one sees the nations of the world today. "Interdependence" is one of those terms that has developed a myriad of meanings. The most fruitful way to use the term, when considering the relationship between this concept and peaceful cooperation among states, is as follows: Interdependence is the size of the stake that a state believes it has in seeing other states' economies prosper so as to help its own economy prosper too. Interdependence can be high or low. The more highly perceived interdependence is, the larger a state's stake in the economic well-being of the countries with which it heavily interacts; the less interdependence, the smaller is its stake. Many analysts believe that high levels of interdependence should facilitate cooperation among states for their mutual gain. Others argue that interdependence increases conflict by reducing autonomy, and even if this is not correct, myriad disputes are possible about how to divide the gains from high levels of economic intercourse.

Interdependence can exist between pairs of countries and can be generated by important but narrow flows of goods. Globalization, as the term indicates, involves most if not all countries and a wide range of economic transactions. The potential loss of autonomy is broader because the nature of national economies, the abilities of states to direct their individual economic and even social policies, and the stability of governments are affected by the movement toward a truly worldwide (or global) economy.

After World War II, the United States used its considerable economic and military power to create an open international economic order by working to lower the barriers among nations to the flow of manufactured goods, raw materials other than agriculture, and capital. The result of this international economic openness was a rise in the level of globalization, particularly among the industrialized nations of the world, but also, to a considerable degree, among the industrializing nations in East Asia and Latin America. But globalization has its costs as well as its benefits. High levels of participation in the international economy can bring the benefits of efficiency that flow from specialization, but also the destruction of national industries that can no longer compete internationally. States today must reconcile the imperatives of what Gilpin has called "Keynes at home" with "Smith abroad": maintenance of full employment domestically and competitive participation in the international economy. Through exports and capital inflows, globalization can help a state increase its wealth, but it also brings vulnerabilities that derive from the need to rely partially on others for one's own prosperity. Balancing the two imperatives is a difficult political act.

The readings in this section pick up on some of these themes and deal with the nature of globalization today. Jeffrey Frankel provides several benchmarks by which to measure the globalization and integration of the current world economy and then presents a tentative balance sheet on the economic and social effects of globalization. Pankaj Ghemawat argues that the summary phrase of the *New York Times'* columnist Thomas Friedman—"the world is flat"—is inaccurate: the bulk of economic activity remains within national borders even more than would be the case if only economic factors were at work. Alan S. Blinder suggests that we are now entering the third industrial revolution of the last 150 years: having moved from agriculture to manufacturing, then from manufacturing to services, we are now into the information age in which information technology vastly expands the scope of services that can be traded. One concrete manifestation of this change is offshoring: the migration abroad of those jobs that can be digitalized, with all the attendant political effects this will have.

CRITICS OF GLOBALIZATION

Globalization should not only be described, measured and compared, however; it must also be assessed. Does it benefit all states that become entangled in it, or do a few benefit at the expense of the many? Is heavy participation in the global economy a prerequisite to economic development, or can such participation actually harm development? Does globalization hasten the degradation of the environment, weaken protection of worker rights in both the rich and poor countries, and give too much power to multinational corporations? Is a world in which capital moves freely and finance is largely unregulated one that contains the seeds of its own destruction? Globalization may be a fact of today's world, but it is no longer seen as an unalloyed good.

The readings in this section take differing stands on these questions. Dani Rodrik asserts that globalization can be a false promise to developing states. He challenges free-trade orthodoxy by showing that high tariff and nontariff barriers do not necessarily bring with them low growth, and argues that the preparations that poorer states must take to open themselves up to international trade and investment divert precious and scarce resources from the task of economic development. John Micklethwait and Adrian Wooldridge disagree. Global economic growth, they argue, has been aided significantly by the growth in world trade. Globalization can also be a force for protecting the environment because the wealthier states become, the more they tend to clean up their environment. Finally, in their view globalization aids workers because multinational companies generally pay better wages and provide better working conditions than their local competitors. Robert Wade tackles the question of global finance, arguing that significant changes to the current global financial order are imperative and that the current financial conglomerates are too powerful and need to be regulated more closely by states, both domestically and internationally.

Politics created today's globalized world. What politics has created politics can rend asunder. Globalization should neither be taken for granted nor viewed as an irresistible force.

PERSPECTIVES ON POLITICAL ECONOMY

The Nature of Political Economy

ROBERT GILPIN

> *The international corporations have evidently declared ideological war on the "antiquated" nation state. . . . The charge that materialism, modernization and internationalism is the new liberal creed of corporate capitalism is a valid one. The implication is clear: The nation state as a political unit of democratic decision-making must, in the interest of "progress," yield control to the new mercantile mini-powers.*[1]

> *While the structure of the multinational corporation is a modern concept, designed to meet the requirements of a modern age, the nation state is a very old-fashioned idea and badly adapted to serve the needs of our present complex world.*[2]

These two statements—the first by Kari Levitt, a Canadian nationalist, the second by George Ball, a former United States undersecretary of state—express a dominant theme of contemporary writings on international relations. International society, we are told, is increasingly rent between its economic and its political organization. On the one hand, powerful economic and technological forces are creating a highly interdependent world economy, thus diminishing the traditional significance of national boundaries. On the other hand, the nation-state continues to command men's loyalties and to be the basic unit of political decision making. As one writer has put the issue, "The conflict of our era is between ethnocentric nationalism and geocentric technology."[3]

Ball and Levitt represent two contending positions with respect to this conflict. Whereas Ball advocates the diminution of the power of the nation-state in

From *U.S. Power and the Multinational Corporation* by Robert Gilpin, pp. 20–44. Copyright © 1975 by Basic Books, Inc. Reprinted by permission of Basic Books, a member of Perseus Books Group.

order to give full rein to the productive potentialities of the multinational corporation, Levitt argues for a powerful nationalism which could counterbalance American corporate domination. What appears to one as the logical and desirable consequence of economic rationality seems to the other to be an effort on the part of American imperialism to eliminate all contending centers of power.

Although the advent of the multinational corporation has put the question of the relationship between economics and politics in a new guise, it is an old issue. In the nineteenth century, for example, it was this issue that divided classical liberals like John Stuart Mill from economic nationalists, represented by Georg Friedrich List. Whereas the former gave primacy in the organization of society to economics and the production of wealth, the latter emphasized the political determination of economic relations. As this issue is central both to the contemporary debate on the multinational corporation and to the argument of this study, this chapter analyzes the three major treatments of the relationship between economics and politics—that is, the three major ideologies of political economy.

THE MEANING OF POLITICAL ECONOMY

The argument of this study is that the relationship between economics and politics, at least in the modern world, is a reciprocal one. On the one hand, politics largely determines the framework of economic activity and channels it in directions intended to serve the interests of dominant groups; the exercise of power in all its forms is a major determinant of the nature of an economic system. On the other hand, the economic process itself tends to redistribute power and wealth; it transforms the power relationships among groups. This in turn leads to a transformation of the political system, thereby giving rise to a new structure of economic relationships. Thus, the dynamics of international relations in the modern world is largely a function of the reciprocal interaction between economics and politics.

First of all, what do I mean by "politics" or "economics"? Charles Kindleberger speaks of economics and politics as two different methods of allocating scarce resources: the first through a market mechanism, the latter through a budget.[4] Robert O. Keohane and Joseph Nye, in an excellent analysis of international political economy, define economics and politics in terms of two levels of analysis: those of structure and of process.[5] Politics is the domain "having to do with the establishment of an order of relations, a structure. . . ."[6] Economics deals with "short-term allocative behavior (i.e., holding institutions, fundamental assumptions, and expectations constant). . . ."[7] Like Kindleberger's definition, however, this definition tends to isolate economic and political phenomena except under certain conditions, which Keohane and Nye define as the "politicization" of the economic system. Neither formulation comes to terms adequately with the dynamic and intimate nature of the relationship between the two.

In this study, the issue of the relationship between economics and politics translates into that between wealth and power. According to this statement of the problem, economics takes as its province the creation and distribution of wealth;

politics is the realm of power. I shall examine their relationship from several ideological perspectives, including my own. But what is wealth? What is power?

In response to the question, What is wealth?, an economist-colleague responded, "What do you want, my thirty-second or thirty-volume answer?" Basic concepts are elusive in economics, as in any field of inquiry. No unchallengeable definitions are possible. Ask a physicist for his definition of the nature of space, time, and matter, and you will not get a very satisfying response. What you will get is an *operational* definition, one which is usable: It permits the physicist to build an intellectual edifice whose foundations would crumble under the scrutiny of the philosopher.

Similarly, the concept of wealth, upon which the science of economics ultimately rests, cannot be clarified in a definitive way. Paul Samuelson, in his textbook, doesn't even try, though he provides a clue in his definition of economics as "the study of how men and society *choose* . . . to employ *scarce* productive resources . . . to produce various commodities . . . and distribute them for consumption."[8] Following this lead, we can say that wealth is anything (capital, land, or labor) that can generate future income; it is composed of physical assets and human capital (including embodied knowledge).

The basic concept of political science is power. Most political scientists would not stop here; they would include in the definition of political science the purpose for which power is used, whether this be the advancement of the public welfare or the domination of one group over another. In any case, few would dissent from the following statement of Harold Lasswell and Abraham Kaplan:

> The concept of power is perhaps the most fundamental in the whole of political science: The political process is the shaping, distribution, and exercise of power (in a wider sense, of all the deference values, or of influence in general).[9]

Power as such is not the sole or even the principal goal of state behavior. Other goals or values constitute the objectives pursued by nation-states: welfare, security, prestige. But power in its several forms (military, economic, psychological) is ultimately the necessary means to achieve these goals. For this reason, nation-states are intensely jealous of and sensitive to their relative power position. The distribution of power is important because it profoundly affects the ability of states to achieve what they perceive to be their interests.

The nature of power, however, is even more elusive than that of wealth. The number and variety of definitions should be an embarrassment to political scientists. Unfortunately, this study cannot bring the intradisciplinary squabble to an end. Rather, it adopts the definition used by Hans J. Morgenthau in his influential *Politics Among Nations:* "man's control over the minds and actions of other men."[10] Thus, power, like wealth, is the capacity to produce certain results.

Unlike wealth, however, power cannot be quantified; indeed, it cannot be overemphasized that power has an important psychological dimension. Perceptions of power relations are of critical importance; as a consequence, a fundamental task of statesmen is to manipulate the perceptions of other statesmen regarding the distribution of power. Moreover, power is relative to a specific situation or set of circumstances; there is no single hierarchy of power in international relations. Power may take many forms—military, economic, or psychological—though, in the final analysis, force is the ultimate form of power. Finally, the inability to predict the behavior of others or the outcome of events is of great significance. Uncertainty regarding the distribution of power and the ability of the statesmen to control events plays an important role in international relations. Ultimately, the determination of the distribution of power can be made only in retrospect as a consequence of war. It is precisely for this reason that war has had, unfortunately, such a central place in the history of international relations. In short, power is an elusive concept indeed upon which to erect a science of politics.

Such mutually exclusive definitions of economics and politics as these run counter to much contemporary scholarship by both economists and political scientists, for both disciplines are invading the formerly exclusive jurisdictions of the other. Economists, in particular, have become intellectual imperialists; they are applying their analytical techniques to traditional issues of political science with great success. These developments, however, really reinforce the basic premise of this study, namely, the inseparability of economics and politics.

The distinction drawn above between economics as the science of wealth and politics as the science of power is essentially an analytical one. In the real world, wealth and power are ultimately joined. This, in fact, is the basic rationale for a political economy of international relations. But in order to develop the argument of this study, wealth and power will be treated, at least for the moment, as analytically distinct.

To provide a perspective on the nature of political economy, the next section will discuss the three prevailing conceptions of political economy: liberalism, Marxism, and mercantilism. Liberalism regards politics and economics as relatively separable and autonomous spheres of activities; I associate most professional economists as well as many other academics, businessmen, and American officials with this outlook. Marxism refers to the radical critique of capitalism identified with Karl Marx and his contemporary disciples; according to this conception, economics determines politics and political structure. Mercantilism is a more questionable term because of its historical association with the desire of nation-states for a trade surplus and for treasure (money). One must distinguish, however, between the specific form mercantilism took in the seventeenth and eighteenth centuries and the general outlook of mercantilistic thought. The essence of the mercantilistic perspective, whether it is labeled economic nationalism, protectionism, or the doctrine of the German Historical School, is the subservience of economy to the state and its interests—interests that range from matters of domestic welfare to those of international security. It is this more general meaning of mercantilism that is implied by the use of the term in this study.

Following the discussion of these three schools of thought, I shall elaborate my own, more eclectic, view of political economy and demonstrate its relevance for understanding the phenomenon of the multinational corporation.

THREE CONCEPTIONS OF POLITICAL ECONOMY

The three prevailing conceptions of political economy differ on many points. Several critical differences will be examined in this brief comparison. (See Table 1.)

The Nature of Economic Relations

The basic assumption of liberalism is that the nature of international economic relations is essentially harmonious. Herein lay the great intellectual innovation of Adam Smith. Disputing his mercantilist predecessors, Smith argued that international economic relations could be made a positive-sum game; that is to say, everyone could gain, and no one need lose, from a proper ordering of economic relations, albeit the distribution of these gains may not be equal. Following Smith, liberalism assumes that there is a basic harmony between true national interest and cosmopolitan economic interest. Thus, a prominent member of this school of thought has written, in response to a radical critique, that the economic efficiency of the sterling standard in the nineteenth century and that of the dollar standard in the twentieth century serve "the cosmopolitan interest in a national form."[11] Although Great Britain and the United States gained the most from the international role of their respective currencies, everyone else gained as well.

Liberals argue that, given this underlying identity of national and cosmopolitan interests in a free market, the state should not interfere with economic transactions across national boundaries. Through free exchange of commodities, removal of restrictions on the flow of investment, and an international division of labor, everyone will benefit in the long run as a result of a more efficient utilization of the world's scarce resources. The national interest is therefore best served, liberals maintain, by a generous and cooperative attitude regarding economic relations with other countries. In essence, the pursuit of self-interest in a free, competitive economy achieves the greatest good for the greatest number in international no less than in the national society.

TABLE 1 ■ COMPARISON OF THE THREE CONCEPTIONS OF POLITICAL ECONOMY

	Liberalism	Marxism	Mercantilism
Nature of economic relations	Harmonious	Conflictual	Conflictual
Nature of the actors	Households and firms	Economic classes	Nation-states
Goal of economic activity	Maximization of global welfare	Maximization of class interests	Maximization of national interest
Relationship between economics and politics	Economics *should* determine politics	Economics *does* determine politics	Politics determines economics
Theory of change	Dynamic equilibrium	Tendency toward disequilibrium	Shifts in the distribution of power

Both mercantilists and Marxists, on the other hand, begin with the premise that the essence of economic relations is conflictual. There is no underlying harmony; indeed, one group's gain is another's loss. Thus, in the language of game theory, whereas liberals regard economic relations as a non-zero-sum game, Marxists and mercantilists view economic relations as essentially a zero-sum game.

The Goal of Economic Activity

For the liberal, the goal of economic activity is the optimum or efficient use of the world's scarce resources and the maximization of world welfare. While most liberals refuse to make value judgments regarding income distribution, Marxists and mercantilists stress the distributive effects of economic relations. For the Marxist the distribution of wealth among social classes is central; for the mercantilist it is the distribution of employment, industry, and military power among nation-states that is most significant. Thus, the goal of economic (and political) activity for both Marxists and mercantilists is the redistribution of wealth and power.

The State and Public Policy

These three perspectives differ decisively in their view regarding the nature of the economic actors. In Marxist analysis, the basic actors in both domestic and international relations are economic classes; the interests of the dominant class determine the foreign policy of the state. For mercantilists, the real actors in international economic relations are nation-states; national interest determines foreign policy. National interest may at times be influenced by the peculiar economic interests of classes, elites, or other subgroups of the society; but factors of geography, external configurations of power, and the exigencies of national survival are primary in determining foreign policy. Thus, whereas liberals speak of world welfare and Marxists of class interests, mercantilists recognize only the interests of particular nation-states.

Although liberal economists such as David Ricardo and Joseph Schumpeter recognized the importance of class conflict and neoclassical liberals analyze economic growth and policy in terms of national economies, the liberal emphasis is on the individual consumer, firm, or entrepreneur. The liberal ideal is summarized in the view of Harry Johnson that the nation-state has no meaning as an economic entity.[12]

Underlying these contrasting views are differing conceptions of the nature of the state and public policy. For liberals, the state represents an aggregation of private interests: public policy is but the outcome of a pluralistic struggle among interest groups. Marxists, on the other hand, regard the state as simply the "executive committee of the ruling class," and public policy reflects its interests. Mercantilists, however, regard the state as an organic unit in its own right: the whole is greater than the sum of its parts. Public policy, therefore, embodies the national interest or Rousseau's "general will" as conceived by the political elite.

The Relationship between Economics and Politics: Theories of Change

Liberalism, Marxism, and mercantilism also have differing views on the relationship between economics and politics. And their differences on this issue are directly relevant to their contrasting theories of international political change.

Although the liberal ideal is the separation of economics from politics in the interest of maximizing world welfare, the fulfillment of this ideal would have important political implications. The classical statement of these implications was that of Adam Smith in *The Wealth of Nations*.[13] Economic growth, Smith argued, is primarily a function of the extent of the division of labor, which in turn is dependent upon the scale of the market. Thus he attacked the barriers erected by feudal principalities and mercantilistic states against the exchange of goods and the enlargement of markets. If men were to multiply their wealth, Smith argued, the contradiction between political organization and economic rationality had to be resolved in favor of the latter. That is, the pursuit of wealth should determine the nature of the political order.

Subsequently, from nineteenth-century economic liberals to twentieth-century writers on economic integration, there has existed "the dream . . . of a great republic of world commerce, in which national boundaries would cease to have any great economic importance and the web of trade would bind all the people of the world in the prosperity of peace."[14] For liberals the long-term trend is toward world integration, wherein functions, authority, and loyalties will be transferred from "smaller units to larger ones; from states to federalism; from federalism to supranational unions and from these to superstates."[15] The logic of economic and technological development, it is argued, has set mankind on an inexorable course toward global political unification and world peace.

In Marxism, the concept of the contradiction between economic and political relations was enacted into historical law. Whereas classical liberals—although Smith less than others—held that the requirements of economic rationality *ought* to determine political relations, the Marxist position was that the mode of production does in fact determine the superstructure of political relations. Therefore, it is argued, history can be understood as the product of the dialectical process—the contradiction between the evolving techniques of production and the resistant sociopolitical system.

Although Marx and Engels wrote remarkably little on international economics, Engels, in his famous polemic, *Anti-Duhring*, explicitly considers whether economics or politics is primary in determining the structure of international relations.[16] E. K. Duhring, a minor figure in the German Historical School, had argued, in contradiction to Marxism, that property and market relations resulted less from the economic logic of capitalism than from extraeconomic political factors: "The basis of the exploitation of many by man was an historical act of force which created an exploitative economic system for the benefit of the stronger man or class."[17] Since Engels, in his attack on Duhring, used the example of the unification of Germany through the Zollverein or customs union of 1833, his analysis is directly relevant to this discussion of the relationship between economics and political organization.

Engels argued that when contradictions arise between economic and political structures, political power adapts itself to the changes in the balance of economic forces; politics yields to the dictates of economic development. Thus, in the case of nineteenth-century Germany, the requirements of industrial production had become incompatible with its feudal, politically fragmented structure. "Though political reaction was victorious in 1815 and again in 1848," he argued, "it was unable to prevent the growth of large-scale industry in Germany and the growing participation of German commerce in the world market."[18] In summary, Engels wrote, "German unity had become an economic necessity."[19]

In the view of both Smith and Engels, the nation-state represented a progressive stage in human development, because it enlarged the political realm of economic activity. In each successive economic epoch, advances in technology and an increasing scale of production necessitate an enlargement of political organization. Because the city-state and feudalism restricted the scale of production and the division of labor made possible by the Industrial Revolution, they prevented the efficient utilization of resources and were, therefore, superseded by larger political units. Smith considered this to be a desirable objective; for Engels it was an historical necessity. Thus, in the opinion of liberals, the establishment of the Zollverein was a movement toward maximizing world economic welfare;[20] for Marxists it was the unavoidable triumph of the German industrialists over the feudal aristocracy.

Mercantilist writers from Alexander Hamilton to Frederich List to Charles de Gaulle, on the other hand, have emphasized the primacy of politics; politics, in this view, determines economic organization. Whereas Marxists and liberals have pointed to the production of wealth as the basic determinant of social and political organization, the mercantilists of the German Historical School, for example, stressed the primacy of national security, industrial development, and national sentiment in international political and economic dynamics.

In response to Engels's interpretation of the unification of Germany, mercantilists would no doubt agree with Jacob Viner that "Prussia engineered the customs union primarily for political reasons, in order to gain hegemony or at least influence over the lesser German states. It was largely in order to make certain that the hegemony should be Prussian and not Austrian that Prussia continually opposed Austrian entry into the Union, either openly or by pressing for a customs union tariff lower than highly protectionist Austria could stomach."[21] In pursuit of this strategic interest, it was "Prussian might, rather than a common zeal for political unification arising out of economic partnership, [that] . . . played the major role."[22]

In contrast to Marxism, neither liberalism nor mercantilism has a developed theory of dynamics. The basic assumption of orthodox economic analysis (liberalism) is the tendency toward equilibrium; liberalism takes for granted the existing social order and given institutions. Change is assumed to be gradual and adaptive—a continuous process of dynamic equilibrium. There is no necessary connection between such political phenomena as war and revolution and the evolution of the economic system, although they would not deny that misguided statesmen can blunder into war over economic issues or that revolutions are conflicts over the distribution of wealth; but neither is inevitably linked to the evolution of the productive system. As for mercantilism, it sees change as taking place owing to shifts in the balance of power; yet, mercantilist writers such as members of the German Historical School and contemporary political realists have not developed a systematic theory of how this shift occurs.

On the other hand, dynamics is central to Marxism; indeed Marxism is essentially a theory of social *change*. It emphasizes the tendency toward *dis*equilibrium owing to changes in the means of production and the consequent effects on the ever-present class conflict. When these tendencies can no longer be contained, the sociopolitical system breaks down through violent upheaval. Thus war and revolution are seen as an integral part of the economic process. Politics and economics are intimately joined.

Why an International Economy?

From these differences among the three ideologies, one can get a sense of their respective explanations for the existence and functioning of the international economy.

An interdependent world economy constitutes the normal state of affairs for most liberal economists. Responding to technological advances in transportation and communications, the scope of the market mechanism, according to this analysis, continuously expands. Thus, despite temporary setbacks, the long-term trend is toward global economic integration. The functioning of the international economy is determined primarily by considerations of efficiency. The role of the dollar as the basis of the international monetary system, for example, is explained by the preference for it among traders and nations as the vehicle of international commerce.[23] The system is maintained by the mutuality of the benefits provided by trade, monetary arrangements, and investment.

A second view—one shared by Marxists and mercantilists alike—is that every interdependent international economy is essentially an imperial or hierarchical system. The imperial or hegemonic power organizes trade, monetary, and investment relations in order to advance its own economic and political interests. In the absence of the economic and especially the political influence of the hegemonic power, the system would fragment into autarkic economies or regional blocs. Whereas for liberalism maintenance of harmonious international market relations is the norm, for Marxism and mercantilism conflicts of class or national interests are the norm.

PERSPECTIVE OF THE AUTHOR

My own perspective on political economy rests on what I regard as a fundamental difference in emphasis between economics and politics; namely, the distinction between absolute and relative gains. The emphasis of economic science—or, at least, of liberal economics—is on *absolute* gains; the ultimate defense of liberalism is that over the long run everyone gains, albeit in varying degrees, from a liberal economic regime. Economics, according to this formulation, need not be a zero-sum game. Everyone can gain in wealth through a more efficient division of labor; moreover, everyone can lose, in absolute terms, from economic inefficiency. Herein lies the strength of liberalism.

This economic emphasis on absolute gains is in fact embodied in what one can characterize as the ultimate ideal of liberal economics: the achievement of a "Pareto optimum" world. Such a properly ordered world would be one wherein "by improving the position of one individual (by adding to his possessions) no one else's position is deteriorated." As Oskar Morgenstern has observed, "[e]conomic literature is replete with the use of the Pareto optimum thus formulated or in equivalent language."[24] It is a world freed from "interpersonal comparisons of utility," and thus a world freed from what is central to politics, i.e., ethical judgment and conflict regarding the just and relative distribution of utility. That the notion of a Pareto optimum is rife with conceptual problems and is utopian does not detract from its centrality as the implicit objective of liberal economics. And this emphasis of economics on absolute gains for all differs fundamentally from the nature of political phenomena as studied by political scientists: viz., struggles for power as a goal itself or as a means to the achievement of other goals.

The essential fact of politics is that power is always relative; one state's gain in power is by necessity another's loss. Thus, even though two states may be gaining absolutely in wealth, in political terms it is the effect of these gains on relative power positions which is of primary importance. From this *political* perspective, therefore, the mercantilists are correct in emphasizing that in power terms, international relations is a zero-sum game.

In a brilliant analysis of international politics, the relativity of power and its profound implications were set forth by Jean-Jacques Rousseau:

> The state, being an artificial body is not limited in any way. . . . It can always increase; it always feels itself weak if there is another that is stronger. Its security and preservation demand that it make itself more powerful than its neighbors. It can increase, nourish and exercise its power only at their expense . . . while the inequality of man has natural limits that between societies can grow without cease, until one absorbs all the others. . . . Because the grandeur of the state is purely relative it is forced to compare itself with that of the others. . . . It is in vain that it wishes to keep itself to itself; it becomes small or great, weak or strong, according to whether its neighbor expands or contracts, becomes stronger or declines. . . .
>
> The chief thing I notice is a patent contradiction in the condition of the human race. . . . Between man and man we live in the condition of the civil state, subjected to laws; between people and people we enjoy natural liberty, which makes the situation worse. Living at the same time in the social order and in the state of nature, we suffer from the inconveniences of both without finding . . . security in either. . . . We see men united by artificial bonds, but united to destroy each other; and all the horrors of war take birth from the precautions they have taken in order to prevent them. . . . War is born of peace, or at least of the precautions which men have taken for the purpose of achieving durable peace.[25]

Because of the relativity of power, therefore, nation-states are engaged in a never-ending struggle to improve or preserve their relative power positions.

This rather stark formulation obviously draws too sharp a distinction between economics and politics. Certainly, for example, liberal economists may be interested in questions of distribution; the distributive issue was, in fact, of central concern to Ricardo and other classical writers. However, when economists stop taking the system for granted and start asking questions about distribution, they have really ventured into what I regard as the essence of politics, for distribution is really a political issue. In a world in which power rests on wealth, changes in the relative distribution of wealth imply changes in the distribution of power and in the political system itself. This, in fact, is what is meant by saying that politics is about relative gains. Politics concerns the efforts of groups to redistribute gains to their own advantage.

Similarly, to argue that politics is about relative gains is not to argue that it is a constant-sum game. On the contrary, man's power over nature and his fellow man has grown immensely in absolute terms over the past several centuries. It is certainly the case that everyone's absolute capabilities can increase due to the development of new weaponry, the expansion of productive capabilities, or changes in the political system itself. Obviously such absolute increases in power are important politically. Who can deny, for example, that the advent of nuclear weapons has profoundly altered international politics? Obviously, too, states can negotiate disarmament and other levels of military capability.

Yet recognition of these facts does not alter the prime consideration that changes in the relative distribution of power are of fundamental significance politically. Though all may be gaining or declining in absolute capability, what will concern states principally are the effects of these absolute gains or losses on relative positions. How, for example, do changes in productive capacity or military weaponry affect the ability of one state to impose its will on another? It may very well be that in a particular situation absolute gains will not affect relative positions. But the efforts of groups to cause or prevent such shifts in the relative distribution of power constitute the critical issue of politics.

This formulation of the nature of politics obviously does not deny that nations may cooperate in order to advance their mutual interest. But even cooperative actions may have important consequences for the distribution of power in the system. For example, the Strategic Arms Limitation Talks (SALT) between the United States and the Soviet Union are obviously motivated by a common interest in preventing thermonuclear war. Other states will also benefit if the risk of war between the superpowers is reduced. Yet, SALT may also be seen as an attempt to stabilize the international distribution of power to the disadvantage of China and other third powers. In short, in terms of the system as a whole, political cooperation can have a profound effect on the relative distribution of power among nation-states.

The point may perhaps be clarified by distinguishing between two aspects of power. When one speaks of absolute gains in power, such as advances in economic capabilities or weapons development, one is referring principally to increases in physical or material capabilities. But while such capabilities are an important component of power, power, as we have seen, is more than physical capability. Power is also a psychological relationship: Who can influence whom to do what? From this perspective, what may be of most importance is how changes in capability affect this psychological relationship. Insofar as they do, they alter the relative distribution of power in the system.

In a world in which power rests increasingly on economic and industrial capabilities, one cannot really distinguish between wealth (resources, treasure, and industry) and power as national goals. In the short run there may be conflicts between the pursuit of power and the pursuit of wealth; in the long run the two pursuits are identical. Therefore, the position taken in this study is similar to Viner's interpretation of classical mercantilism:

> What then is the correct interpretation of mercantilist doctrine and practice with respect to the roles of power and plenty as ends of national policy? I believe that practically all mercantilists, whatever the period, country, or status of the particular individual, would have subscribed to all of the following propositions: (1) wealth is an absolutely essential means to power, whether for security or for aggression; (2) power is essential or valuable as a means to the acquisition or retention of wealth; (3) wealth and power are each proper ultimate ends of national policy; (4) there is long-run harmony between these ends, although in particular circumstances it may be necessary for a time to make economic sacrifices in the interest of military security and therefore also of long-run prosperity.[26]

This interpretation of the role of the economic motive in international relations is substantially different from that of Marxism. In the Marxist framework of analysis, the economic factor is reduced to the profit motive, as it affects the behavior of individuals or firms. Accordingly, the foreign policies of capitalist states are determined by the desire of capitalists for profits. This is, in our view, far too narrow a conception of the economic aspect of international relations. Instead, in this study we label "economic" those sources of wealth upon which national power and domestic welfare are dependent.

Understood in these broader terms, the economic motive and economic activities are fundamental to the struggle for power among nation-states. The objects of contention in the struggles of the balance of power include the centers of economic power. As R. G. Hawtrey has expressed it, "the political motives at work can only be expressed in terms of the economic. Every conflict is one of power and power depends on resources."[27] In pursuit of wealth *and* power, therefore, nations (capitalist, socialist, or fascist) contend over the territorial division and exploitation of the globe.

Even at the level of peaceful economic intercourse, one cannot separate out the political element. Contrary to the attitude of liberalism, international economic relations are in reality political relations. The interdependence of national economies creates economic power, defined as the capacity of one state to damage another through the interruption of commercial and financial relations.[28] The attempts to create and to escape from such dependency relationships constitute an important aspect of international relations in the modern era.

The primary actors in the international system are nation-states in pursuit of what they define as their national interest. This is not to argue, however, that nation-states are the only actors, nor do I believe that the "national interest" is something akin to Rousseau's "general will"—the expression of an organic entity separable from its component parts. Except in the abstract models of political scientists, it has never been the case that the international system was composed solely of nation-states. In an exaggerated acknowledgment of the importance of nonstate or transnational actors at an earlier time, John A. Hobson asked rhetorically whether "a great war could be undertaken by any European state, or a great state loan subscribed, if the House of Rothschild and its connexions set their face against it."[29] What has to be explained, however, are the economic and political circumstances that enable such transnational actors to play their semi-independent role in international affairs. The argument of this study is that the primary determinants of the role played by these non-state actors are the larger configurations of power among nation-states. What is determinant is the interplay of national interests.

As for the concept of "national interest," the national interest of a given nation-state is, of course, what its political and economic elite determines it to be. In part, as Marxists argue, this elite will define it in terms of its own group or class interests. But the national interest comprehends more than this. More general influences, such as cultural values and considerations relevant to the security of the state itself—geographical position, the evolution of military technology, and the international distribution of power—are of greater importance. There is a sense, then, in which the factors that determine the national interest are objective. A ruling elite that fails to take these factors into account does so at its peril. In short, then, there is a basis for considering the nation-state itself as an actor pursuing its own set of security, welfare, and status concerns in competition or cooperation with other nation-states.

Lastly, in a world of conflicting nation-states, how does one explain the existence of an interdependent international economy? Why does a liberal international economy—that is, an economy characterized by relatively free trade, currency convertibility, and freedom of capital movement—remain intact rather than fragment into autarkic national economies and regional or imperial groupings? In part, the answer is provided by liberalism: economic cooperation, interdependence, and an international division of labor enhance efficiency and the maximization of aggregate wealth. Nation-states are induced to enter the international system because of the promise of more rapid growth; greater benefits can be had than could be obtained by autarky or a fragmentation of the world economy. The historical record suggests, however, that the existence of mutual economic benefits is not always enough to induce nations to pay the costs of a market system or to forgo opportunities of advancing their own interests at the expense of others. There is always the danger that a nation may pursue certain short-range policies, such as the imposition of an optimum tariff, in order to maximize its own gains at the expense of the system as a whole.

For this reason, a liberal international economy requires a power to manage and stabilize the system. As Charles Kindleberger has convincingly shown, this governance role was performed by Great Britain throughout the nineteenth century and up to 1931, and by the United States after 1945.[30] The inability of Great Britain in 1929 to continue running the system and the unwillingness of the United States to assume this responsibility led to the collapse of the system in the "Great Depression." The result was the fragmentation of the world economy into rival economic blocs. Both dominant economic powers had failed to overcome the divisive forces of nationalism and regionalism.

The argument of this study is that the modern world economy has evolved through the emergence of great national economies that have successively become dominant. In the words of the distinguished French economist François Perroux, "the economic evolution of the world has resulted from a succession of dominant economies, each in turn taking the lead in international activity and influence. . . . Throughout the nineteenth century the British economy was the dominant economy in the world. From the [eighteen] seventies on, Germany was dominant in respect to certain other Continental countries and in certain specified fields. In the twentieth century, the United States economy has clearly been and still is the internationally dominant economy."[31]

An economic system, then, does not arise spontaneously owing to the operation of an invisible hand and in the absence of the exercise of power. Rather, every economic system rests on a particular political order; its nature cannot be understood aside from politics. This basic point was made some years ago by E. H. Carr when he wrote that "the science of economics presupposes a given political order, and cannot be profitably studied in isolation from politics."[32] Carr sought to convince his fellow Englishmen that an international economy based on free trade was not a natural and inevitable state of affairs but rather one that reflected the economic and political interests of Great Britain. The system based on free trade had come into existence through, and was maintained by, the exercise of British economic and military power. With the rise after 1880 of new industrial and military powers with contrasting economic interests—namely, Germany, Japan, and the United States—an international economy based on free trade and British power became less and less viable. Eventually this shift in the locus of industrial and military power led to the collapse of the system in World War I. Following the interwar period, a liberal international economy was revived through the exercise of power by the world's newly emergent dominant economy—the United States.

Accordingly, the regime of free investment and the preeminence of the multinational corporation in the contemporary world have reflected the economic and political interests of the United States. The multinational corporation has prospered because it has been dependent on the power of, and consistent with the political interests of, the United States. This is not to deny the analyses of economists who argue that the multinational corporation is a response to contemporary technological and economic developments. The argument is rather that these economic and technological factors have been able to exercise their profound effects because the United States—sometimes with the cooperation of other states and sometimes over their opposition—has created the necessary political framework. As former Secretary of the Treasury Henry Fowler stated several years ago, "it is . . . impossible to overestimate the extent to which the efforts and opportunities for American firms abroad depend upon the vast presence and influence and prestige that America holds in the world."[33]

By the mid-1970s, however, the international distribution of power and the world economy resting on it were far different from what they had been when Fowler's words were spoken. The rise of foreign economic competitors, America's growing dependence upon foreign sources of energy and other resources, and the expansion of Soviet military capabilities have greatly diminished America's presence and influence in the world. One must ask if, as a consequence, the reign of the American multinationals over international economic affairs will continue into the future.

In summary, although nation-states, as mercantilists suggest, do seek to control economic and technological forces and channel them to their own advantage, this is impossible over the long run. The spread of economic growth and industrialization cannot be prevented. In time the diffusion of industry and technology undermines the position of the dominant power. As both liberals and Marxists have emphasized, the evolution of economic relations profoundly influences the nature of the international political system. The relationship between economics and politics is a reciprocal one.

Although economic and accompanying political change may well be inevitable, it is not inevitable that the process of economic development and technological advance will produce an increasingly integrated world society. In the 1930s, Eugene Staley posed the issue:

> A conflict rages between technology and politics. Economics, so closely linked to both, has become the major battlefield. Stability and peace will reign in the world economy only when, somehow, the forces on the side of technology and the forces on the side of politics have once more become accommodated to each other.[34]

Staley believed, as do many present-day writers, that politics and technology must ultimately adjust to one another. But he differed with contemporary writers with regard to the inevitability with which politics would adjust to technology. Reflecting the intense economic nationalism of the period in which he wrote, Staley pointed out that the adjustment may very well be the other way around. As he reminds us, in his own time and in earlier periods economics has had to adjust to political realities: "In the 'Dark Ages' following the collapse of the Roman Empire, technology adjusted itself to politics. The magnificent Roman roads fell into disrepair, the baths and aqueducts and amphitheatres and villas into ruins. Society lapsed back to localism in production and distribution, forgot much of the learning and the technology and the governmental systems of earlier days."[35]

CONCLUSION

The purpose of this chapter has been to set forth the analytical framework that will be employed in this study. This framework is a statement of what I mean by "political economy." In its eclecticism it has drawn upon, while differing from, the three prevailing perspectives of political economy. It has incorporated their respective strengths and has attempted to overcome their weaknesses. In brief, political economy in this study means the reciprocal and dynamic interaction in international relations of the pursuit of wealth and the pursuit of power. In the short run, the distribution of power and the nature of the political system are major determinants of the framework within which wealth is produced and distributed. In the long run, however, shifts in economic efficiency and in the location of economic activity tend to undermine and transform the existing political system. This political transformation in turn gives rise to changes in economic relations that reflect the interests of the politically ascendant state in the system.

NOTES

1. Kari Levitt, "The Hinterland Economy," *Canadian Forum* 50 (July–August 1970): p. 163.
2. George W. Ball, "The Promise of the Multinational Corporation," *Fortune,* June 1, 1967, p. 80.
3. Sidney Rolfe, "Updating Adam Smith," *Interplay* (November 1968): p. 15.
4. Charles Kindleberger, *Power and Money: The Economics of International Politics and the Politics of International Economics* (New York: Basic Books, 1970), p. 5.
5. Robert Keohane and Joseph Nye, "World Politics and the International Economic System," in C. Fred Bergsten, ed., *The Future of the International Economic Order: An Agenda for Research* (Lexington, Mass.: D.C. Heath, 1973), p. 116.
6. Ibid.
7. Ibid., p. 117.
8. Paul Samuelson, *Economics: An Introductory Analysis* (New York: McGraw-Hill, 1967), p. 5.
9. Harold Lasswell and Abraham Kaplan, *Power and Society: A Framework for Political Inquiry* (New Haven, Conn.: Yale University Press, 1950), p. 75.
10. Hans Morgenthau, *Politics Among Nations* (New York: Alfred A. Knopf), p. 26. For a more complex but essentially identical view, see Robert Dahl, *Modern Political Analysis* (Englewood Cliffs, N.J.: Prentice-Hall, 1963).
11. Kindleberger, *Power and Money*, p. 227.
12. For Johnson's critique of economic nationalism, see Harry Johnson, ed., *Economic Nationalism in Old and New States* (Chicago: University of Chicago Press, 1967).
13. Adam Smith, *The Wealth of Nations* (New York: Modern Library, 1937).
14. J. B. Condliffe, *The Commerce of Nations* (New York: W. W. Norton, 1950), p. 136.
15. Amitai Etzioni, "The Dialectics of Supernational Unification" in *International Political Communities* (New York: Doubleday, 1966), p. 147.
16. The relevant sections appear in Ernst Wangerman, ed., *The Role of Force in History: A Study of Bismarck's Policy of Blood and Iron,* trans. Jack Cohen (New York: International Publishers, 1968).
17. Ibid., p. 12.
18. Ibid., p. 13.
19. Ibid., p. 14.
20. Gustav Stopler, *The German Economy* (New York: Harcourt, Brace and World, 1967), p. 11.

21. Jacob Viner, *The Customs Union Issue*, Studies in the Administration of International Law and Organization, No. 10 (New York: Carnegie Endowment for International Peace, 1950), pp. 98–99.

22. Ibid., p. 101.

23. Richard Cooper, "Eurodollars, Reserve Dollars, and Asymmetrics in the International Monetary System," *Journal of International Economics* 2 (September 1972): pp. 325–44.

24. Oskar Morgenstern, "Thirteen Critical Points in Contemporary Economic Theory: An Interpretation," *Journal of Economic Literature* 10 (December 1972): p. 1169.

25. Quoted in F. H. Hinsley, *Power and the Pursuit of Peace* (Cambridge: Cambridge University Press, 1963), pp. 50–51.

26. Jacob Viner, "Power versus Plenty as Objectives of Foreign Policy in the Seventeenth and Eighteenth Centuries," in *The Long View and the Short: Studies in Economic Theory and Practice* (Glencoe, Ill.: The Free Press, 1958), p. 286.

27. R. G. Hawtrey, *Economic Aspects of Sovereignty* (London: Longmans, Green, 1952), p. 120.

28. Albert Hirshman, *National Power and the Structure of Foreign Trade* (Berkeley: University of California Press, 1969), p. 16.

29. John A. Hobson, *Imperialism: A Study* (1902; 3rd ed., rev., London: G. Allen and Unwin, 1938), p. 57.

30. Charles Kindleberger, *The World in Depression 1929–1939* (Berkeley: University of California Press, 1973), p. 293.

31. François Perroux, "The Domination Effect and Modern Economic Theory," in *Power in Economics*, ed. K. W. Rothschild (London: Penguin, 1971), p. 67.

32. E. H. Carr, *The Twenty Years' Crisis, 1919–1939* (New York: Macmillan, 1951), p. 117.

33. Quoted in Kari Levitt, *Silent Surrender: The American Economic Empire in Canada* (New York: Liveright Press, 1970), p. 100.

34. Eugene Staley, *World Economy in Transition: Technology vs. Politics, Laissez Faire vs. Planning, Power vs. Welfare* (New York: Council on Foreign Relations [under the auspices of the American Coordinating Committee for International Studies], 1939), pp. 51–52.

35. Ibid., p. 52.

The Domestic Sources
of Foreign Economic Policies

MICHAEL J. HISCOX

Each government must make choices about how best to manage the way its own economy is linked to the global economy. It must choose whether to open the national market to international trade, whether to liberalize trade with some nations more than with others, and whether to allow more trade in some sectors of the economy than in other sectors. Each government must also decide whether to restrict international flows of investment in different sectors and whether to regulate immigration and emigration by different types of workers. And it must either fix the exchange rate for the national currency or allow the rate to fluctuate to some degree in response to supply and demand in international financial markets.

Of course, if every government always made the same choices in all these areas of policy, things would be very simple for us as scholars (and much more predictable for us as citizens of the world). But governments in different countries, and at different moments in history, have often chosen radically different foreign economic policies. . . .

Politics, we know, is all about who gets what, when, and how. Different individuals and groups in every society typically have very different views about what their government should do when it comes to setting the policies that regulate international trade, immigration, investment, and exchange rates. These competing demands must be reconciled in some way by the political institutions that govern policy making. To really understand the domestic origins of foreign economic policies we thus need to perform two critical tasks:

1. Identify or map the policy preferences of different groups in the domestic economy.
2. Specify how political institutions determine the way these preferences are aggregated or converted into actual government decisions.

The first step will require some economic analysis. How people are affected by their nation's ties with the global economy, and thus what types of policies they prefer to manage those ties, depends primarily on how they make their living.

From Michael J. Hiscox, "The Domestic Sources of Foreign Economic Policies," in *Global Political Economy*, ed. John Ravenhill. Oxford: Oxford University Press, 2005, pp. 51–54, 57–62, 65–68. By permission of Oxford University Press. Portions of the text have been omitted.

Steelworkers typically have very different views about most foreign economic policies from wheat farmers, for instance, because such policies rarely affect the steel and wheat industries in similar fashion. Of critical importance here are the types of assets that individuals own and how the income earned from those assets is affected by different policy choices. The second step calls for political analysis. How political representatives are elected, how groups organize to lobby or otherwise influence politicians, and how policies are proposed, debated, amended, and passed in legislatures, and then implemented by government agencies, all depend on the structure of political institutions. Democratically elected leaders face very different institutional constraints from military dictators, of course, and even among our democracies there is quite a wide range of institutional variation that can have a large impact on the behaviour of policy makers. . . .

POLICY PREFERENCES

The guiding assumption here is that, when it comes to taking positions on how to regulate ties with the global economy, individuals and groups are fundamentally concerned with how different policy choices affect their incomes. Of course people may also have important non-material concerns that affect their attitudes toward foreign economic policies. Many people are concerned about the cultural implications of globalization, for instance, and its impact on the world's environment and on human rights, and these concerns may have an impact on their views about the regulation of international trade, immigration, and investment. We will discuss some of these important considerations in more detail later in the chapter. But we begin here with the simplest possible framework in which economic policies are evaluated only in terms of their economic effects. . . .

Trade

The dramatic growth in international trade over the last few decades has intensified political debate over the costs and benefits of trade openness. In the United States, the controversy surrounding the creation of the North American Free Trade Agreement (NAFTA) in 1993 was especially intense, and similar arguments have arisen in Europe over the issue of enlargement of the European Union and over attempts to reform the Common Agricultural Policy. Rapid trade policy reforms have also generated a significant political backlash in many developing nations. And recent years have witnessed violent protests and demonstrations by groups from a variety of countries that hope to disrupt meetings of the World Trade Organization (WTO). Political leaders around the world frequently voice concerns about the negative effects of trade and the need to protect their firms and workers from foreign competition.

What is behind all of this political fuss and bother? At first glance it may seem puzzling that there is so much conflict over trade. After all, the most famous insight from all of international economics is the proof that trade provides mutual gains:

that is, when countries exchange goods and services they are all generally better off. Trade allows each country to specialize in producing those goods and services in which it has a comparative advantage, and in doing so world welfare is improved.

While there are gains from trade for all countries in the aggregate, what makes trade so controversial is that, among individuals within each country, trade creates winners and losers. How trade affects different individuals depends upon how they earn their living. To flesh out this story, economists have traditionally relied upon a very simple theory of trade devised by two Swedish economists, Eli Heckscher and Bertil Ohlin. In the Heckscher-Ohlin model of trade, each nation's comparative advantage is traced to its particular endowments of different factors of production: that is, basic inputs such as land, labour, and capital that are used in different pro-portions in the production of different goods and services. Since the costs of these inputs in each country will depend on their availability, differences in factor endowments across countries will create differences in comparative advantage. Each country will tend to export items whose production requires intensive use of the factors with which it is abundantly endowed relative to other nations; con-versely, each country will import goods whose production requires intensive use of factors that are relatively scarce. Countries well endowed with land, like Australia and Canada, are expected to export agricultural products (for example, wheat and wool), while importing products that require the intensive use of labour (for example, textiles and footwear) from more labour-abundant economies like China and India. The advanced economies of Europe, Japan, and the United States, well endowed with capital relative to the rest of the world, should export capital-inten-sive products (for example, automobiles and pharmaceuticals), while importing labour-intensive goods from less developed trading partners where supplies of cap-ital are scarce compared to supplies of labour.

Building on this simple model of trade, Wolfgang Stolper and Paul Samuelson derived a famous theorem in 1941 that outlined the likely effects of trade on the real incomes of different sets of individuals within any economy. According to the Stolper-Samuelson theorem, trade benefits those who own the factors of produc-tion with which the economy is relatively well endowed and trade hurts owners of scarce factors. The reasoning is straightforward: by encouraging specialization in each economy in export-oriented types of production, trade increases the demand for locally abundant factors (and bids up the earnings of those who own those fac-tors), while reducing demand for locally scarce factors (and lowering the earnings of owners of such factors). In Australia and Canada, the theorem tells us that landowners should benefit most from trade, while workers can expect lower real wages as a consequence of increased imports of labour-intensive goods. In Europe, Japan, and the United States, the theorem predicts a fairly simple class division over trade: the trade issue should benefit owners of capital at the expense of work-ers. The converse should hold in relatively labour-abundant (and capital-scarce) developing economies like China and India, where trade will raise the wages of workers relative to the profits earned by local owners of capital.

By revealing how trade benefits some people while making others worse off, the Stolper-Samuelson theorem thus accounts for why trade is such a divisive political issue. The theorem also provides a neat way to map the policy preferences of individuals in each economy. In each nation, owners of locally abundant factors should support greater trade openness, while owners of locally scarce factors should be protectionist. There is a good deal of evidence in the histories of political conflict over trade in a variety of nations that fits with this simple prediction (see Rogowski 1989). In Australia, for instance, the first national elections in 1901 were actually fought between a Free Trade party, representing predominantly rural voters, and a Protectionist party that was supported overwhelmingly by urban owners of capital and labour. A very similar kind of political division characterized most debates over trade policy in Canada in the late nineteenth century, with support for trade openness emanating mostly from farmers in the vast western provinces. In Europe and Japan, in contrast, much of the opposition to trade over the last century or so has come from agricultural interests, anxious to block cheap imports of farm products from abroad. In the United States and Europe, at least since the 1960s, labour unions have voiced some of the loudest opposition to trade openness and have called for import restrictions aimed at protecting jobs in labour-intensive industries threatened by foreign competition.

On the other hand, political divisions and coalitions in trade politics often appear to contradict this simple model of preferences. It is quite common to see workers and owners in the same industry banding together to lobby for protective import barriers, for instance, in contemporary debates about policy in Europe and the United States, even though the Stolper-Samuelson theorem tells us that capital and labour are supposed to have directly opposing views. So what is going on here? The critical problem seems to be that the theorem is derived by assuming that factors of production are highly mobile between different industries in each economy. An alternative approach to mapping the effects of trade on incomes, often referred to as the 'specific factors' model, allows instead that it can be quite costly to move some factors of production between different sectors in the economy. That is, different types of land, labour skills, and capital equipment often have a very limited or specific use (or range of uses) to which they can be put when it comes to making products. The plant and machinery used in modern manufacturing industries is very specialized: the presses used to stamp out automobile bodies are only designed for that purpose, for instance, and cannot be adapted easily or quickly to perform other tasks. Steel factories cannot easily be converted into pharmaceutical factories or software design houses. Nor can steelworkers quickly adapt their skills and become chemical engineers or computer programmers.

In the specific factors model, the real incomes of different individuals are tied very closely to the fortunes of the particular industries in which they make their living. Individuals employed or invested in export industries benefit from trade according to this model, while those who are attached to import-competing industries are harmed. In the advanced economies of Europe and the United States, the implication is that owners and employees in export-oriented industries like aerospace, pharmaceuticals, computer software, construction equipment, and financial services, should be much more supportive of trade than their counterparts in, say, the steel, textiles, and footwear industries, which face intense pressure from import competition. There is much evidence supporting these predictions in the real world of trade politics especially in the debates over trade in the most advanced economies where technologies (and the skills that complement them) have become increasingly specialized in many different manufacturing and service industries, and even in various areas of agriculture and mining production. In the recent debates over regional and multilateral trade agreements in the United States, for instance, some of the most vociferous opposition to removing barriers to trade has come from owners and workers aligned together in the steel and textile industries. . . .

Foreign Investment

Capital can also move from one country to another. These movements usually do not take the form of a physical relocation of some existing buildings and machinery from a site in one nation to another site abroad (the equivalent to worker migration). Instead, they take the form of financial transactions between citizens of different nations that transfer ownership rights over assets: a firm in one country buys facilities abroad that it can operate as a subsidiary, for instance, or individuals in one country buy shares of foreign companies, or a bank in one country lends money to foreign firms. All such transactions increase the stock of capital available for productive use in one country, and decrease the stock of capital in another country.

The dramatic increase in the volume of international capital flows over the past forty years, out-stripping the increase in trade, has had a profound impact on the international economy. Short-term flows of capital in the form of 'portfolio' investment (purchases of company shares and other forms of securities including government bonds), which can change direction quite rapidly in response to news and speculation about changing macro-economic conditions and possible adjustments in exchange rates, have had a major impact on the choices governments can make when it comes to monetary and exchange-rate policies. Longer-term capital flows in the form of 'direct foreign investment' (where the purchase of foreign assets by a firm based in one country gives it ownership control of a firm located on foreign soil), have perhaps been even more politically controversial since the activities of these multinational firms can have a major impact on economic conditions in the host nations in which they manage affiliates. Many critics of multinational corporations fear that the economic leverage enjoyed by these firms, especially in small developing nations, can undermine national policies aimed at improving environment standards and human rights. The political debate over direct foreign investment is thus highly charged.

Tight restrictions on both short- and long-term investment by foreigners have been quite common historically, although the controls have been much less strict than those typically imposed on immigration. Clearly these controls cannot be motivated by a desire for economic efficiency. If such controls are removed and capital is allowed to move freely to those locations in which it is used most productively (and where it will be rewarded, as a result, with higher earnings), it is easy to show that the total output of goods and services will be increased in both the country to which the capital is flowing and in the world economy as a whole. Again, this expansion in aggregate production makes it possible, in principle, to raise the standard of living for people everywhere. International investment, just like the migration of workers examined above, can serve the same economic purpose that is otherwise served by trade. International flows of capital substitute for the exports of capital-intensive goods and services in the benchmark Heckscher-Ohlin model. In general, then, we can expect that the advanced industrial economies of Europe and the United States, which have abundant local supplies of capital for investment and in which rates of return on capital are thus quite low compared with earnings elsewhere, are the natural suppliers of capital (as well as capital-intensive goods) to poorer nations in which capital is in relatively scarce supply. . . .

Now, putting aside the aggregate welfare gains that international movements of capital make possible, which individuals are likely to benefit from such capital flows and which individuals will lose out? Here we can simply apply the logic of the same 'factor proportions' approach we used above to outline the effects of immigration. We might distinguish between different types of capital, in the same way we distinguished between low- and high-skilled labour above, and set apart lending and short-term or portfolio investment flows from direct foreign investment. But to keep things simple here we will just consider them all as a single form of capital. What is critical here, of course, is the impact that inflows of any foreign capital have on relative supplies of factors of production in the local economy. Allowing more inflows of capital from abroad will increase the local supply of capital relative to other factors and thus lower real returns for local owners of capital. At the same time, inflows of investment will raise the real earnings of local owners of land and labour by increasing demand for these other factors of production. . . . We can thus expect that policies allowing greater inflows of foreign capital will be strongly opposed by individuals who own capital in the local economy, but such policies will be supported by local landowners and workers. . . .

Foreign investment tends to be even more politically controversial in developing nations, where the behaviour of large foreign corporations can have profound effects on the local economy and on local politics. One particular concern among critics of multinational firms has been the role that several large corporations have apparently played in supporting authoritarian governments that have restricted political organization among labour groups, limited growth in wage rates, and permitted firms to mistreat workers and pollute the environment. While the evidence is not very clear, local owners of capital may well have muted their opposition to investments by foreign firms in order to support authoritarian policies adopted by military regimes in some cases: in *Nigeria*, for instance, where Shell (the European oil company) has long been the major foreign investor, or more recently in Myanmar, where Unocal (an American oil and gas firm) is the key foreign player. But the basic competitive tension between local capitalists and foreign firms (whose entry into the economy bids down local profits) is typically very obvious even in these unstable and non-democratic environments, as local firms have often encouraged their governments to impose severe restrictions on foreign investments, including onerous regulations stipulating that foreign firms use local rather than imported inputs, exclusion from key sectors of the economy, and even nationalization (seizure) of firms' assets. Newer evidence suggests that, as we might expect given the preferences of labour in capital-poor developing nations, left-wing governments backed by organized labour have made the strongest efforts to lure foreign firms to make investments. . . .

Exchange Rates

Of course a critical difference between transactions that take place between individuals living in the same country and transactions between people in different countries is that the latter require that people can convert one national currency into another. If a firm in Australia wants to import DVDs from a film studio in the United States, for example, it will need to exchange its Australian dollars for US dollars to pay the American company. The rate at which this conversion takes place will obviously affect the transaction: the more Australian dollars it takes to buy the number of US dollars required (the price of the DVDs), the more costly are the imports for movie loving Australian buyers. All the trade and investment transactions taking place every day in the world economy are affected by the rates at which currencies are exchanged.

Prior to the First World War, almost all governments fixed the value of their currency in terms of gold, thereby creating an international monetary system in which all rates of conversion between individual currencies were held constant. . . . Between the Second World War and 1973, most currencies were fixed in value to the US dollar, the most important currency in the post-war world economy. In this system, often referred to as the 'Bretton Woods' system, the United States agreed to guarantee the value of the dollar by committing to exchange dollars for gold at a set price of $35 per ounce. Since 1973, when the Nixon administration officially abandoned the fixed rate between the dollar and gold, all the major currencies have essentially been allowed to fluctuate freely in value in world financial markets. Among developing nations, however, many governments continue to fix the value of their currency in terms of dollars or another of the major currencies (see Frieden, Ghezzi, and Stein 2001). And groups of nations in different regions of the world, including the members of the European Union, have made separate efforts to stabilize exchange rates at the regional level, even progressing to the adoption of a common regional currency.

The fundamental choice each government must make involves whether to allow the value of the national currency to fluctuate freely in response to market demand and supply, or instead fix the value of the currency in terms of some other currency or external standard—typically, the currency of a major trading partner or, as was common in the past, gold (a precious metal valued highly in most societies throughout history). When a government chooses to fix the value of the national currency, it sets the official rate of exchange and commits itself to buy the currency at that fixed rate when requested to by private actors or foreign governments. Between a 'pure float' and a fixed exchange rate there are intermediate options: a government can choose a target value for the exchange rate and only allow the currency to fluctuate in value within some range around the target rate. The wider this range, of course, the more policy approximates floating the currency. . . .

The crux of the choice between fixed and floating exchange rates is the choice between stability and policy control: a stable exchange rate will increase the economic benefits attainable from international trade and investment, but this requires giving up the ability to adjust monetary policy to suit domestic economic conditions. Governments in the most advanced economies have generally decided that policy control is more important to them than exchange-rate stability, at least since the early 1970s. Governments in smaller, developing nations have mostly chosen exchange-rate stability over policy control. In part this is because these countries tend to rely more heavily upon trade and foreign investment as sources of economic growth. This choice is also more attractive for governments in smaller countries trying to defeat chronic inflation. . . .

INSTITUTIONS

Once we have specified the preferences of different individuals and groups on any particular issue we need to think about how much influence they will have over policy outcomes. This is where political institutions come in. Political institutions establish the rules by which policy is made, and thus how the policy preferences of different groups are weighed in the process that determines the policy outcome. It is appropriate here to start with the broadest types of rules first, and consider the formal mechanisms by which governments and representatives in legislative bodies are elected (or otherwise come to power). These broad features of the institutional environment have large effects on all types of policies. But then we can move on to discuss more specific aspects of the legislative process and administrative agencies that have implications for the formulation and implementation of trade, immigration, investment, and exchange-rate policies.

Elections and Representation

Perhaps it is best to start with the observation that the general relationship between democratization and foreign economic policy making is a matter that is still open to considerable theoretical and empirical doubt. Part of the puzzle is that there is a great deal of variation in the levels of economic openness we have observed among autocratic nations. In autocratic regimes, the orientation of policy will depend upon the particular desires and motivations of the (non-elected) leadership, and there are different theoretical approaches to this issue. Non-elected governments could pursue trade and investment liberalization in an effort to maximize tax returns over the long term by increasing aggregate economic output. Such policies may be easier to adopt because autocratic leaders are more insulated than democratic counterparts from the political demands made by any organized domestic groups that favour trade protection and limits on foreign investment. Perhaps this is an apt description of the state of affairs in China as it has been gradually opening its economy to trade and investment over the past two decades, and non-democratic governments in Taiwan and South Korea pursued trade liberalization even more rapidly in the 1960s. On the other hand, autocratic governments may draw political support from small, powerful groups in the system that favour protection. Many such governments appear to have used trade and investment barriers in ways aimed at consolidating their rule. The experience in Sub-Saharan African nations since the 1960s, and in Pakistan and Myanmar, seems to fit this mould. Without a detailed assessment of the particular groups upon which a particular authoritarian regime depends for political backing, it is quite difficult to make predictions about likely policy outcomes under non-democratic rule.

In formal democracies that hold real elections, the most fundamental set of political rules is the set that defines which individuals get to vote. If the franchise law gives more weight to one side in a policy contest compared to others, it can obviously have a large impact on policy outcomes. Where only those who own land can vote, for instance, agricultural interests will be privileged in the policy-making process. If this landowning elite favours trade protection, as it did in Britain in the years before the Great Reform Act of 1832, then such a policy is almost sure to be held firmly in place. By shifting political power away from landowners and towards urban owners of capital and labour, extensions of the franchise had a major impact on all forms of economic policy during the late nineteenth and early twentieth centuries in Europe, America, and elsewhere. In England, the extension of voting power to the middle and working classes, achieved in the reforms of 1832 and 1867, had the effect of making free trade politically invincible—with a huge block of workers along with the urban business class supporting trade openness, and only a tiny fraction of the electorate (the traditional rural elites) against it, a government that endorsed tariffs or restrictions on investment would have been committing electoral suicide. In the United States and Australia, on the other hand, where labour and capital were in relatively scarce supply, the elimination of property qualifications for voting and the extension of suffrage had exactly the opposite effect, empowering a larger block of urban voters who favoured high tariffs. In general, extensions of the franchise to urban classes tend to produce more open policies toward trade, immigration, and investment in labour and capital-abundant countries, and more closed or protectionist policies in labour and capital-scarce economies.

The precise rules by which representatives are elected to national legislatures are the next critical feature of the institutional environment. Scholars have suggested that in parliamentary systems in which legislative seats are apportioned among parties according to the proportion of votes they receive ('proportional representation'), narrowly organized groups have far less impact on policy making in general than they do in electoral systems in which individual seats are decided by plurality rule. Parliamentary systems with proportional representation tend to encourage the formation of strong, cohesive political parties, which appeal to a national constituency and have less to gain in electoral terms by responding to localized and particularistic demands. Other types of systems, in contrast, tend to encourage intra-party competition among individual politicians and the development of a 'personal vote' in particular electoral districts and thus are more conducive to interest group lobbying. The implications for foreign economic policies are usually spelled out in very clear terms: we expect that proportional representation systems with strong political parties (e.g. Sweden) will typically produce lower levels of trade protection and other restrictions than alternative types of electoral systems (e.g. Britain, the United States) in which particular local and regional interests have a greater influence.

These conclusions about the impact of particularistic groups in different types of electoral systems rest upon a critical insight derived from theoretical work on collective action in trade politics: that there is a fundamental asymmetry between the lobbying pressure generated from groups seeking protectionist policies and the lobbying pressure that comes from groups who oppose such restrictions. The main reason for this is that restrictions on imports and other types of exchange, when imposed one at a time, tend to have very lopsided effects. . . . Thus it is unlikely that those hurt by the new tariff will be prepared to devote resources to lobbying against the policy proposal. Collective political action will always be much easier to organize in the relatively small groups that benefit from a particular trade restriction than in the much larger groups (the rest of the economy) that are hurt by the restriction. Perhaps the best example of this logic is the extraordinary political power that has been demonstrated by the small, highly organized agricultural groups in Europe, the United States, and Japan over the past fifty years. These groups, which together represent a tiny fraction of the population in each political system, have been able to win extremely high (if not prohibitive) rates of protection from imports and lavish subsidies.

Other aspects of electoral institutions may also play a role in shaping policy outcomes. In general, smaller electoral districts in plurality systems may be expected to increase the influence of sectoral or particularistic groups over elected representatives and thus lead to higher levels of protection. In larger districts, political representatives will be forced to balance the interests of a greater variety of industry groups when making decisions about policies and will be less affected by the demands of any one industry lobby, and a larger share of the costs of any tariff or restriction will be 'internalized' among voters within the district. From this perspective, upper chambers of parliaments, which typically allocate seats among representatives of much larger electoral districts than those in lower chambers, tend to be less inclined toward trade protection and other types of restrictive foreign economic policies. Meanwhile, in legislative chambers in which seats are defined along political-geographic lines without regard for population (for example, in the United States Senate, where each state receives two seats), agricultural, forestry, and mining interests in underpopulated areas typically gain a great deal more influence over policy making than they can wield in chambers (e.g. the United States House of Representatives) where legislative seats are defined based upon the number of voters in each district.

The Great Divide in the Global Village

BRUCE R. SCOTT

INCOMES ARE DIVERGING

Mainstream economic thought promises that globalization will lead to a widespread improvement in average incomes. Firms will reap increased economies of scale in a larger market, and incomes will converge as poor countries grow more rapidly than rich ones. In this "win-win" perspective, the importance of nation-states fades as the "global village" grows and market integration and prosperity take hold.

But the evidence paints a different picture. Average incomes have indeed been growing, but so has the income gap between rich and poor countries. Both trends have been evident for more than 200 years, but improved global communications have led to an increased awareness among the poor of income inequalities and heightened the pressure to emigrate to richer countries. In response, the industrialized nations have erected higher barriers against immigration, making the world economy seem more like a gated community than a global village. And although international markets for goods and capital have opened up since World War II and multilateral organizations now articulate rules and monitor the world economy, economic inequality among countries continues to increase. Some two billion people earn less than $2 per day.

At first glance, there are two causes of this divergence between economic theory and reality. First, the rich countries insist on barriers to immigration and agricultural imports. Second, most poor nations have been unable to attract much foreign capital due to their own government failings. These two issues are fundamentally linked: by forcing poor people to remain in badly governed states, immigration barriers deny those most in need the opportunity to "move up" by "moving out." In turn, that immobility eliminates a potential source of pressure on ineffective governments, thus facilitating their survival.

Since the rich countries are unlikely to lower their agricultural and immigration barriers significantly, they must recognize that politics is a key cause of economic inequality. And since most developing countries receive little foreign investment, the wealthy nations must also acknowledge that the "Washington consensus," which assumes that free markets will bring about economic convergence, is mistaken. If

Bruce R. Scott, "The Great Divide in the Global Village." Reprinted by permission of *Foreign Affairs*, Vol. 80, No. 1 (January/February 2001), pp. 160–177. Copyright 2001 by the Council on Foreign Relations, Inc. www.ForeignAffairs.org.

they at least admit these realities, they will abandon the notion that their own particular strategies are the best for all countries. In turn, they should allow poorer countries considerable freedom to tailor development strategies to their own circumstances. In this more pragmatic view, the role of the state becomes pivotal.

Why have economists and policymakers not come to these conclusions sooner? Since the barriers erected by rich countries are seen as vital to political stability, leaders of those countries find it convenient to overlook them and focus instead on the part of the global economy that has been liberalized. The rich countries' political power in multilateral organizations makes it difficult for developing nations to challenge this self-serving world-view. And standard academic solutions may do as much harm as good, given their focus on economic stability and growth rather than on the institutions that underpin markets. Economic theory has ignored the political issues at stake in modernizing institutions, incorrectly assuming that market-based prices can allocate resources appropriately.

The fiasco of reform in Russia has forced a belated reappraisal of this blind trust in markets. Many observers now admit that the transition economies needed appropriate property rights and an effective state to enforce those rights as much as they needed the liberalization of prices. Indeed, liberalization without property rights turned out to be the path to gangsterism, not capitalism. China, with a more effective state, achieved much greater success in its transition than did Russia, even though Beijing proceeded much more slowly with liberalization and privatization.

Economic development requires the transformation of institutions as well as the freeing of prices, which in turn requires political and social modernization as well as economic reform. The state plays a key role in this process; without it, developmental strategies have little hope of succeeding. The creation of effective states in the developing world will not be driven by familiar market forces, even if pressures from capital markets can force fiscal and monetary discipline. And in a world still governed by "states rights," real progress in achieving accountable governments will require reforms beyond the mandates of multilateral institutions.

GO WITH THE FLOW

In theory, globalization provides an opportunity to raise incomes through increased specialization and trade. This opportunity is conditioned by the size of the markets in question, which in turn depends on geography, transportation costs, communication networks, and the institutions that underpin markets. Free trade increases both the size of the market and the pressure to improve economic performance. Those who are most competitive take advantage of the enhanced market opportunities to survive and prosper.

Neoclassical economic theory predicts that poor countries should grow faster than rich ones in a free global market. Capital from rich nations in search of cheaper labor should flow to poorer economies, and labor should migrate from low-income areas toward those with higher wages. As a result, labor and capital costs—and eventually income—in rich and poor areas should eventually converge.

The U.S. economy demonstrates how this theory can work in a free market with the appropriate institutions. Since the 1880s, a remarkable convergence of incomes among the country's regions has occurred. The European Union has witnessed a similar phenomenon, with the exceptions of Greece and Italy's southern half, the *Mezzogiorno*. What is important, however, is that both America and the EU enjoy labor and capital mobility as well as free internal trade.

But the rest of the world does not fit this pattern. The most recent *World Development Report* shows that real per capita incomes for the richest one-third of countries rose by an annual 1.9 percent between 1970 and 1995, whereas the middle third went up by only 0.7 percent and the bottom third showed no increase at all. In the Western industrial nations and Japan alone, average real incomes have been rising about 2.5 percent annually since 1950—a fact that further accentuates the divergence of global income. These rich countries account for about 60 percent of world GDP but only 15 percent of world population.

Why is it that the poor countries continue to fall further behind? One key reason is that most rich countries have largely excluded the international flow of labor into their markets since the interwar period. As a result, low-skilled labor is not free to flow across international boundaries in search of more lucrative jobs. From an American or European perspective, immigration appears to have risen in recent years, even approaching its previous peak of a century ago in the United States. Although true, this comparison misses the central point. Billions of poor people could improve their standard of living by migrating to rich countries. But in 1997, the United States allowed in only 737,000 immigrants from developing nations, while Europe admitted about 665,000. Taken together, these flows are only 0.04 percent of all potential immigrants.

The point is not that the rich countries should permit unfettered immigration. A huge influx of cheap labor would no doubt be politically explosive; many European countries have already curtailed immigration from poor countries for fear of a severe backlash. But the more salient issue is that rich nations who laud liberalism and free markets are rejecting those very principles when they restrict freedom of movement. The same goes for agricultural imports. Both Europe and Japan have high trade barriers in agriculture, while the United States remains modestly protectionist.

Mainstream economic theory does provide a partial rationalization for rich-country protectionism: Immigration barriers need not be a major handicap to poor nations because they can be offset by capital flows from industrialized economies to developing ones. In other words, poor people need not demand space in rich countries because the rich will send their capital to help develop the poor countries. This was indeed the case before World War I, but it has not been so since World War II.

But the question of direct investment, which typically brings technologies and know-how as well as financial capital, is more complicated than theories would predict. The total stock of foreign direct investment did rise almost sevenfold from 1980 to 1997, increasing from 4 percent to 12 percent of world GDP during that period. But very little has gone to the poorest countries. In 1997, about 70 percent went from one rich country to another, 8 developing countries received about 20 percent, and the remainder was divided among more than 100 poor nations. According to the World Bank, the truly poor countries received less than 7 percent of the foreign direct investment to all developing countries in 1992–98. At the same time, the unrestricted opening of capital markets in developing countries gives larger firms from rich countries the opportunity for takeovers that are reminiscent of colonialism. It is not accidental that rich countries insist on open markets where they have an advantage and barriers in agriculture and immigration, where they would be at a disadvantage.

As for the Asian "tigers," their strong growth is due largely to their high savings rate, not foreign capital. Singapore stands out because it has enjoyed a great deal of foreign investment, but it has also achieved one of the highest domestic-savings rates in the world, and its government has been a leading influence on the use of these funds. China is now repeating this pattern, with a savings rate of almost 40 percent of GDP. This factor, along with domestic credit creation, has been its key motor of economic growth. China now holds more than $100 billion in low-yielding foreign-exchange reserves, the second largest reserves in the world.

In short, global markets offer opportunities for all, but opportunities do not guarantee results. Most poor countries have been unable to avail themselves of much foreign capital or to take advantage of increased market access. True, these countries have raised their trade ratios (exports plus imports) from about 35 percent of their GDP in 1981 to almost 50 percent in 1997. But without the Asian tigers, developing-country exports remain less than 25 percent of world exports.

Part of the problem is that the traditional advantages of poor countries have been in primary commodities (agriculture and minerals), and these categories have shrunk from about 70 percent of world trade in 1900 to about 20 percent at the end of the century. Opportunities for growth in the world market have shifted from raw or semiprocessed commodities toward manufactured goods and services—and, within these categories, toward more knowledge-intensive segments. This trend obviously favors rich countries over poor ones, since most of the latter are still peripheral players in the knowledge economy. (Again, the Asian tigers are the exception. In 1995, they exported as much in high-technology goods as did France, Germany, Italy, and Britain combined—which together have three times the population of the tigers.)

ONE COUNTRY, TWO SYSTEMS

Why is the performance of poor countries so uneven and out of sync with theoretical forecasts? Systemic barriers at home and abroad inhibit the economic potential of poorer nations, the most formidable of these obstacles being their own domestic political and administrative problems. These factors, of course, lie outside the framework of mainstream economic analysis. A useful analogy is the antebellum economy of the United States, which experienced a similar set of impediments.

Like today's "global village," the U.S. economy before the Civil War saw incomes diverge as the South fell behind the North. One reason for the Confederacy's secession and the resulting civil war was Southern recognition that it was falling behind in both economic and political power, while the richer and more populous North was attracting more immigrants. Half of the U.S. population lived in the North in 1780; by 1860, this share had climbed to two-thirds. In 1775, incomes in the five original Southern states equaled those in New England, even though wealth (including slaves) was disproportionately concentrated in the South. By 1840, incomes in the northeast were about 50 percent higher than those in the original Southern states; the North's railroad mileage was about 40 percent greater (and manufacturing investment four times higher) than the South's. As the economist Robert Fogel has pointed out, the South was not poor—in 1860 it was richer than all European states except England—but Northern incomes were still much higher and increasing.

Why had Southern incomes diverged from those in the North under the same government, laws, and economy? Almost from their inception, the Southern colonies followed a different path from the North—specializing in plantation agriculture rather than small farms with diversified crops—due to geography and slavery. Thanks to slave labor, Southerners were gaining economies of scale and building comparative advantage in agriculture, exporting their goods to world markets and the North. Gang labor outproduced "free" (paid) labor. But the North was building even greater advantages by developing a middle class, a manufacturing sector, and a more modern social and political culture. With plans to complete transcontinental railroads pending, the North was on the verge of achieving economic and political dominance and the capacity to shut off further expansion of slavery in the West. The South chose war over Northern domination—and modernization.

Although the Constitution guaranteed free trade and free movement of capital and labor, the institution of slavery meant that the South had much less factor mobility than the North. It also ensured less development of its human resources, a less equal distribution of income, a smaller market for manufactures, and a less dynamic economy. It was less attractive to both European immigrants and external capital. With stagnant incomes in the older states, it was falling behind. In these respects, it was a forerunner of many of today's poor countries, especially those in Latin America.

What finally put the South on the path to economic convergence? Four years of civil war with a total of 600,000 deaths and vast destruction of property were only a start. Three constitutional amendments and twelve years of military "reconstruction" were designed to bring equal rights and due process to the South. But the reestablishment of racial segregation following Reconstruction led to sharecropping as former slaves refused to return to the work gangs. Labor productivity dropped so much that Southern incomes fell to about half of the North's in 1880. In fact, income convergence did not take off until the 1940s, when a wartime boom in the North's industrial cities attracted Southern migrants in search of better jobs. At the same time, the South began drawing capital as firms sought lower wages, an anti-union environment, and military contracts in important congressional districts. But this process did not fully succeed until the 1960s, as new federal laws and federal troops brought full civil rights to the South and ensured that the region could finally modernize.

THE GREAT DIVIDE

Although slavery is a rarity today, the traditional U.S. divide between North and South provides a good model for understanding contemporary circumstances in many developing countries. In the American South, voter intimidation, segregated housing, and very unequal schooling were the rule, not the exception—and such tactics are repeated today by the elites in today's poor countries. Brazil, Mexico, and Peru had abundant land relative to population when the Europeans arrived, and their incomes roughly approximated those in North America, at least until 1700. The economists Stanley Engerman and Kenneth Sokoloff have pointed out that these states, like the Confederacy, developed agricultural systems based on vast landholdings for the production of export crops such as sugar and coffee. Brazil and many Caribbean islands also adopted slavery, while Peru and Mexico relied on forced indigenous labor rather than African slaves.

History shows that the political development of North America and developing nations—most of which were colonized by Europeans at some point—was heavily influenced by mortality. In colonies with tolerable death rates (Australia, Canada, New Zealand, and the United States), the colonists soon exerted pressure for British-style protections of persons and property. But elsewhere (most of Africa, Latin America, Indonesia, and to a lesser degree, India), disease caused such high mortality rates that the few resident Europeans were permitted to exploit a disenfranchised laboring class, whether slave or free. When the colonial era ended in these regions, it was followed by "liberationist" regimes (often authoritarian and incompetent) that maintained the previous system of exploitation for the advantage of a small domestic elite. Existing inequalities within poor countries continued; policies and institutions rarely protected individual rights or private initiative for the bulk of the population and allowed elites to skim off rents from any sectors that could bear it. The economist Hernando de Soto has shown how governments in the developing world fail to recognize poor citizens' legal titles to their homes and businesses, thereby depriving them of the use of their assets for collateral. The losses in potential capital to these countries have dwarfed the cumulative capital inflows going to these economies in the last century.

The legacy of these colonial systems also tends to perpetuate the unequal distribution of income, wealth, and political power while limiting capital mobility. Thus major developing nations such as Brazil, China, India, Indonesia, and Mexico are experiencing a divergence of incomes by province within their economies, as labor and capital fail to find better opportunities. Even in recent times, local elites have fought to maintain oppressive conditions in Brazil, El Salvador, Guatemala, Mexico, Nicaragua, and Peru. Faced with violent intimidation, poor people in these countries have suffered from unjust law enforcement similar to what was once experienced by black sharecroppers in the American South.

Modernization and economic development inevitably threaten the existing distribution of power and income, and powerful elites continue to protect the status quo—even if it means that their society as a whole falls further behind. It takes more than a constitution, universal suffrage, and regular elections to achieve governmental accountability and the rule of law. It may well be that only the right of exit—emigration—can peacefully bring accountability to corrupt and repressive regimes. Unlike the U.S. federal government, multilateral institutions lack the legitimacy to intervene in the internal affairs of most countries. Europe's economic takeoff in the second half of the nineteenth century was aided by the emigration of 60 million people to North America, Argentina, Brazil, and Australia. This emigration—about 10 percent of the labor force—helped raise European wages while depressing inflated wages in labor-scarce areas such as Australia and the United States. A comparable out-migration of labor from today's poor countries would involve hundreds of millions of people.

Of course, Latin America has seen some success. Chile has received the most attention for its free market initiatives, but its reforms were implemented by a brutally repressive military regime—hardly a model for achieving economic reform through democratic processes. Costa Rica would seem to be a much better model for establishing accountability, but its economic performance has not been as striking as Chile's.

Italy, like the United States in an earlier era, is another good example of "one country, two systems." Italy's per capita income has largely caught up with that of its European neighbors over the past 20 years, even exceeding Britain's and equaling France's in 1990, but its *Mezzogiorno* has failed to keep up. Whereas overall Italian incomes have been converging toward those of the EU, *Mezzogiorno* incomes have been diverging from those in the north. Southern incomes fell from 65 percent of the northern average in 1975 to 56 percent 20 years later; in Calabria, they fell to 47 percent of the northern average. Southern unemployment rose from 8 percent in 1975 to 19 percent in 1995—almost three times the northern average. In short, 50 years of subsidies from Rome and the EU have failed to stop the *Mezzogiorno* from falling further behind. Instead, they have yielded local regimes characterized by greatly increased public-sector employment, patronage, dependency, and corruption—not unlike the results of foreign aid for developing countries. And the continuing existence of the Mafia further challenges modernization.

Democracy, then, is not enough to ensure that the governed are allowed to reap the gains of their own efforts. An effective state requires good laws as well as law enforcement that is timely, evenhanded, and accessible to the poor. In many countries, achieving objective law enforcement means reducing the extralegal powers of vested interests. When this is not possible, the only recourse usually available is emigration. But if the educated elite manages to emigrate while the masses remain trapped in a society that is short of leaders, the latter will face even more formidable odds as they try to create effective institutions and policies. Although Italians still emigrate from south to north, the size of this flow is declining, thanks in part to generous transfer payments that allow them to consume almost as much as northerners. In addition, policymaking for the *Mezzogiorno* is still concentrated in Rome.

The immigration barriers in rich countries not only foreclose opportunities in the global village to billions of poor people, they help support repressive, pseudo-democratic governments by denying the citizens of these countries the right to vote against the regime with their feet. In effect, the strict dictates of sovereignty allow wealthy nations to continue to set the rules in their own favor while allowing badly governed poor nations to continue to abuse their own citizens and retard economic development. Hence the remedy for income divergence must be political as well as economic.

GETTING INSTITUTIONS RIGHT

According to economic theory, developing nations will create and modernize the institutions needed to underpin their markets so that their markets and firms can gradually match the performance of rich countries. But reality is much more complex than theory. For example, de Soto's analysis makes clear that effectively mobilizing domestic resources offers a much more potent source of capital for most developing nations than foreign inflows do. Yet mainstream economists and their formal models largely ignore these resources. Western economic advisers in Russia were similarly blindsided by their reliance on an economic model that had no institutional context and no historical perspective. Economists have scrambled in recent years to correct some of these shortcomings, and the Washington consensus now requires the "right" institutions as well as the "right" prices. But little useful theory exists to guide policy when it comes to institutional analysis, and gaps in the institutional foundations in most developing countries leave economic models pursuing unrealistic solutions or worse.

The adjustment of institutions inevitably favors certain actors and disadvantages others. As a result, modernization causes conflict that must be resolved through politics as well as economics. At a minimum, successful development signifies that the forces for institutional change have won out over the status quo. Achieving a "level playing field" signifies that regulatory and political competition is well governed.

Economists who suggest that all countries must adopt Western institutions to achieve Western levels of income often fail to consider the changes and political risks involved. The experts who recommended that formerly communist countries apply "shock therapy" to markets and democracy disregarded the political and regulatory issues involved. Each change requires a victory in the "legislative market" and successful persuasion within the state bureaucracy for political approval. Countries with lower incomes and fewer educated people than Russia face even more significant developmental challenges just to achieve economic stability, let alone attract foreign investment or make effective use of it. Institutional deficiencies, not capital shortages, are the major impediment to development, and as such they must be addressed before foreign investors will be willing to send in capital.

Although price liberalization can be undertaken rapidly, no rapid process (aside from revolution) exists for an economy modernizing its institutions. Boris Yeltsin may be credited with a remarkable turnover, if not a coup d'état, but his erratic management style and the lack of parliamentary support ensured that his government would never be strong. In these circumstances, helping the new Russian regime improve law enforcement should have come ahead of mass privatization. Launching capitalism in a country where no one other than apparatchiks had access to significant amounts of capital was an open invitation to gangsterism and a discredited system. Naive economic models made for naive policy recommendations.

HOW THE WEST WON

The state's crucial role is evident in the West's economic development. European economic supremacy was forged not by actors who followed a "Washington consensus" model but by strong states. In the fifteenth century, European incomes were not much higher than those in China, India, or Japan. The nation-state was a European innovation that replaced feudalism and established the rule of law; in turn, a legal framework was formed for effective markets. Once these countries were in the lead, they were able to continuously increase their edge through technological advances. In addition, European settlers took their civilization with them to North America and the South Pacific, rapidly raising these areas to rich-country status as well. Thus Europe's early lead became the basis for accumulating further advantages with far-reaching implications.

Europe's rise to economic leadership was not rapid at first. According to the economist Angus Maddison, Europe's economy grew around 0.07 percent a year until 1700; only after 1820 did it reach one percent. But the pace of technological and institutional innovation accelerated thereafter. Meanwhile, discovery of new markets in Africa, Asia, and the Americas created new economic opportunities. Secular political forces overthrew the hegemony of the Catholic Church. Feudalism was eroded by rising incomes and replaced by a system that financed government through taxes, freeing up land and labor to be traded in markets. Markets permitted a more efficient reallocation of land and labor, allowing further rises in incomes. Effective property rights allowed individuals to keep the fruits of their own labor, thereby encouraging additional work. And privatization of common land facilitated the clearing of additional acreage.

The nation-state helped forge all these improvements. It opened up markets by expanding territory; reduced transaction costs; standardized weights, measures, and monetary units; and cut transport costs by improving roads, harbors, and canals. In addition, it was the state that established effective property rights. The European state system thrived on flexible alliances, which constantly changed to maintain a balance of power. Military and economic rivalries prompted states to promote development in agriculture and commerce as well as technological innovation in areas such as shipping and weaponry. Absent the hegemony of a single church or state, technology was diffused and secularized. Clocks, for instance, transferred timekeeping from the monastery to the village clock tower; the printing press did much the same for the production and distribution of books.

Europe's development contrasts sharply with Asia's. In the early modern era, China saw itself as the center of the world, without real rivals. It had a much larger population than Europe and a far bigger market as well. But though the Chinese pioneered the development of clocks, the printing press, gunpowder, and iron, they did not have the external competitive stimulus to promote economic development. Meanwhile, Japan sealed itself off from external influences for more than 200 years, while India, which had continuous competition within the subcontinent, never developed an effective national state prior to the colonial era.

The Europeans also led in establishing accountable government, even though it was achieved neither easily nor peacefully. Most European states developed the notion that the sovereign (whether a monarch or a parliament) had a duty to protect subjects and property in return for taxes and service in the army. Rulers in the Qing, Mughal, and Ottoman Empires, in contrast, never recognized a comparable responsibility to their subjects. During the Middle Ages, Italy produced a number of quasi-democratic city-states, and in the seventeenth century Holland created the first modern republic after a century of rebellion and warfare with Spain. Britain achieved constitutional monarchy in 1689, following two revolutions. After a bloody revolution and then dictatorship, France achieved accountable government in the nineteenth century.

Europe led the way in separating church and state—an essential precursor to free inquiry and adoption of the scientific method—after the Thirty Years' War. The secular state in turn paved the way for capitalism and its "creative destruction." Creative destruction could hardly become the norm until organized religion lost its power to execute as heretics those entrepreneurs who would upset the status quo. After the Reformation, Europeans soon recognized another fundamental tenet of capitalism: the role of interest as a return for the use of capital. Capitalism required that political leaders allow private hands to hold power as well as wealth; in turn, power flowed from the rural nobility to merchants in cities. European states also permitted banks, insurance firms, and stock markets to develop. The "yeast" in this recipe lay in the notion that private as well as state organizations could mobilize and reallocate society's resources—an idea with profound social, political, and economic implications today.

Most of Europe's leading powers did not rely on private initiative alone but adopted mercantilism to promote their development. This strategy used state power to create a trading system that would raise national income, permitting the government to enhance its own power through additional taxes. Even though corruption was sometimes a side effect, the system generally worked well. Venice was the early leader, from about 1000 to 1500; the Dutch followed in the sixteenth and seventeenth centuries; Britain became dominant in the eighteenth century. In Britain, as in the other cases, mercantilist export promotion was associated with a dramatic rise in state spending and employment (especially in the navy), as well as "crony capitalism." After World War II, export-promotion regimes were adopted by Japan, South Korea, Singapore, and Taiwan with similar success. Today, of course, such strategies are condemned as violations of global trade rules, even for poor countries.

Finally, geography played a pivotal role in Europe's rise, providing a temperate climate, navigable rivers, accessible coastline, and defensible boundaries for future states. In addition, Europe lacked the conditions for the production of labor-intensive commodities such as coffee, cotton, sugar, or tobacco—production that might have induced the establishment of slavery. Like in the American North, European agriculture was largely rain-fed, diversified, and small-scale.

Europe's rise, then, was partly due to the creation and diffusion of technological innovations and the gradual accumulation of capital. But the underlying causes were political and social. The creation of the nation-state and institutionalized state rivalry fostered government accountability. Scientific enlightenment and upward social mobility, spurred by healthy competition, also helped Europe achieve such transformations. But many of today's developing countries still lack these factors crucial for economic transformation.

PLAYING CATCH-UP

Globalization offers opportunities for all nations, but most developing countries are very poorly positioned to capitalize on them. Malarial climates, limited access to navigable water, long distances to major markets, and unchecked population growth are only part of the problem. Such countries also have very unequal income structures inherited from colonial regimes, and these patterns of income distribution are hard to change unless prompted by a major upheaval such as a war or a revolution. But as serious as these disadvantages are, the greatest disadvantage has been the poor quality of government.

If today's global opportunities are far greater and potentially more accessible than at any other time in world history, developing countries are also further behind than ever before. Realistic political logic suggests that weak governments need to show that they can manage their affairs much better before they pretend to have strategic ambitions. So what kind of catch-up models could they adopt?

Substituting domestic goods for imports was the most popular route to economic development prior to the 1980s. But its inward orientation made those who adopted it unable to take advantage of the new global opportunities and ultimately it led to a dead end. Although the United States enjoyed success with such a strategy from 1790 until 1940, no developing country has a home market large enough to support a modern economy today. The other successful early growth model was European mercantilism, namely export promotion, as pioneered by Venice, the Dutch republic, Britain, and Germany. Almost all of the East Asian success stories, China included, are modern versions of the export-oriented form of mercantilism.

For its part, free trade remains the right model for rich countries because it provides decentralized initiatives to search for tomorrow's market opportunities. But it does not necessarily promote development. Britain did not adopt free trade until the 1840s, long after it had become the world's leading industrial power. The prescription of lower trade barriers may help avoid even worse strategies at the hands of bad governments, but the Washington-consensus model remains best suited for those who are ahead rather than behind.

Today's shareholder capitalism brings additional threats to poor countries, first by elevating compensation for successful executives, and second by subordinating all activities to those that maximize shareholder value. Since 1970, the estimated earnings of an American chief executive have gone from 30 times to 450 times that of the average worker. In the leading developing countries, this ratio is still less than 50. Applying a similar "market-friendly" rise in executive compensation within the developing world would therefore only aggravate the income gap, providing new ammunition for populist politicians. In addition, shareholder capitalism calls for narrowing the managerial focus to the interests of shareholders, even if this means dropping activities that offset local market imperfections. A leading South African bank has shed almost a million small accounts—mostly held by blacks—to raise its earnings per share. Should this bank, like its American counterparts, have an obligation to serve its community, including its black members, in return for its banking license?

Poor nations must improve the effectiveness of their institutions and bureaucracies in spite of entrenched opposition and poorly paid civil servants. As the journalist Thomas Friedman has pointed out, it is true that foreign-exchange traders can dump the currencies of poorly managed countries, thereby helping discipline governments to restrain their fiscal deficits and lax monetary policies. But currency pressures will not influence the feudal systems in Pakistan and Saudi Arabia, the theocracies in Afghanistan and Iran, or the kleptocracies in Kenya or southern Mexico. The forces of capital markets will not restrain Brazilian squatters as they take possession of "public lands" or the slums of Rio de Janeiro or São Paulo, nor will they help discipline landlords and vigilantes in India's Bihar as they fight for control of their state. Only strong, accountable government can do that.

LOOKING AHEAD

Increased trade and investment have indeed brought great improvements in some countries, but the global economy is hardly a win-win situation. Roughly one billion people earn less than $1 per day, and their numbers are growing. Economic resources to ameliorate such problems exist, but the political and administrative will to realize the potential of these resources in poor areas is lacking. Developing-nation governments need both the pressure to reform their administrations and institutions, and the access to help in doing so. But sovereignty removes much of the external pressure, while immigration barriers reduce key internal motivation. And the Washington consensus on the universality of the rich-country model is both simplistic and self-serving.

The world needs a more pragmatic, country-by-country approach, with room for neomercantilist regimes until such countries are firmly on the convergence track. Poor nations should be allowed to do what today's rich countries did to get ahead, not be forced to adopt the laissez-faire approach. Insisting on the merits of comparative advantage in low-wage, low-growth industries is a sure way to stay poor. And continued poverty will lead to rising levels of illegal immigration and low-level violence, such as kidnappings and vigilante justice, as the poor take the only options that remain. Over time, the rich countries will be forced to pay more attention to the fortunes of the poor—if only to enjoy their own prosperity and safety.

Still, the key initiatives must come from the poor countries, not the rich. In the last 50 years, China, India, and Indonesia have led the world in reducing poverty. In China, it took civil war and revolution, with tens of millions of deaths, to create a strong state and economic stability; a de facto coup d'état in 1978 brought about a very fortunate change of management. The basic forces behind Chinese reform were political and domestic, and their success depended as much on better using resources as opening up markets. Meanwhile, the former Soviet Union and Africa lie at the other extreme. Their economic decline stems from their failure to maintain effective states and ensure the rule of law.

It will not be surprising if some of today's states experience failure and economic decline in the new century. Argentina, Colombia, Indonesia, and Pakistan will be obvious cases to watch, but other nations could also suffer from internal regional failures—for example, the Indian state of Bihar. Income growth depends heavily on the legal, administrative, and political capabilities of public actors in sovereign states. That is why, in the end, external economic advice and aid must go beyond formal models and conform to each country's unique political and social context.

mypoliscikit Exercises for Perspectives on Political Economy

Apply what you learned in this chapter by using the online resources on MyPoliSciKit (www.mypoliscikit.com).

 Practice Tests

 Videos:
- "Liberalizing Chinese-British Trade"
- "Global Migration and Unemployment"

 Simulation: "Business: You Are a Foreign Market Analyst"

 Reading Guides:
- Robert Gilpin, "The Nature of Political Economy"
- Michael J. Hiscox, "The Domestic Sources of Foreign Economic Policies"
- Bruce R. Scott, "The Great Divide in the Global Village"

THE NATURE
OF GLOBALIZATION

Globalization of the Economy

JEFFREY FRANKEL

Economic globalization is one of the most powerful forces to have shaped the postwar world. In particular, international trade in goods and services has become increasingly important over the past fifty years, and international financial flows over the past thirty years. This chapter documents quantitatively the process of globalization for trade and finance. It then briefly goes beyond the causes of international economic integration to consider its effects, concluding that globalization is overall a good thing, not just for economic growth but also when noneconomic goals are taken into account.

The two major drivers of economic globalization are reduced costs to transportation and communication in the private sector and reduced policy barriers to trade and investment on the part of the public sector. Technological progress and innovation have long been driving the costs of transportation and communication steadily lower. In the postwar period we have seen major further cost-saving advances, even within ocean shipping: supertankers, roll-on-roll-off ships, and containerized cargo. Between 1920 and 1990 the average ocean freight and port charges per short ton of U.S. import and export cargo fell from $95.00 to $29.00 (in 1990 dollars). An increasing share of cargo goes by air. Between 1930 and 1990, average air transport revenue per passenger mile fell from $0.68 to $0.11. Jet air shipping and refrigeration have changed the status of goods that had previously been classified altogether as not tradable internationally. Now fresh-cut flowers, perishable broccoli and strawberries, live lobsters, and even ice cream are sent between continents. Communications costs have fallen even more rapidly. Over this period the cost of a

Jeffrey Frankel, "Globalization of the Economy," in Joseph S. Nye and John D. Donahue, eds. *Governance in a Globalizing World*. Washington, DC: Brookings Institution, 2000, pp. 45–69. Portions of the text and footnotes have been omitted.

305

three-minute telephone call from New York to London fell from $244.65 to $3.32. Recent inventions such as faxes and the Internet require no touting.

It is easy to exaggerate the extent of globalization. Much excited discussion of the topic makes it sound as though the rapid increase in economic integration across national borders is unprecedented. Some commentators imply that it has now gone so far that it is complete; one hears that distance and national borders no longer matter, that the nation-state and geography are themselves no longer relevant for economic purposes, and that it is now as easy to do business with a customer across the globe as across town. After all, has not the World Wide Web reduced cross-border barriers to zero?

It would be a mistake for policymakers or private citizens to base decisions on the notion that globalization is so new that the experience of the past is not relevant, or that the phenomenon is now irreversible, or that national monetary authorities are now powerless in the face of the global marketplace, or that the quality of life of Americans—either economic or noneconomic aspects—is determined more by developments abroad than by American actions at home.

It is best to recognize that at any point in history many powerful forces are working to drive countries apart, at the same time as other powerful forces are working to shrink the world. In the 1990s, for example, at the same time that forces such as the Internet and dollarization have led some to proclaim the decline of the nation-state, more new nations have been created (out of the ruins of the former Soviet bloc) than in any decade other than the decolonizing 1960s, each with its own currencies and trade policies. The forces of shrinkage have dominated in recent decades, but the centrifugal forces are important as well.

TWO BENCHMARKS FOR MEASURING ECONOMIC INTEGRATION

The overall post–World War II record of economic integration across national borders, powerful as it has been, is, in two respects, not as striking as widely believed. The first perspective is to judge by the standard of 100 years ago. The second is to judge by the standard of what it would mean to have truly perfect global integration.

Judging Globalization 2000 by the Standard of 1900

The globalization that took place in the nineteenth century was at least as impressive as the current episode. The most revolutionary breakthroughs in transportation and communication had already happened by 1900—for example, the railroad, steamship, telegraph, and refrigeration. Freight rates had fallen sharply throughout the century. An environment of political stability was provided by the Pax Britannica, and an environment of monetary stability was provided by the gold standard. Kevin O'Rourke and Jeffrey Williamson show that, as a result of rapidly growing trade, international differences in commodity prices narrowed dramatically.

It is inescapable to invoke a particularly famous quote from John Maynard Keynes: "What an extraordinary episode in the progress of man that age was which came to an end in August 1914! . . . The inhabitant of London could order by telephone, sipping his morning tea in bed, the various products of the whole earth . . .he could at the same time and by the same means adventure his wealth in the natural resources and new enterprise of any quarter of the world."[1]

The world took a giant step back from economic globalization during the period 1914–1944. Some of the causes of this retrogression were isolationist sentiments in the West that followed World War I, the monetary instability and economic depression that plagued the interwar period, increases in tariffs and other trade barriers including most saliently the adoption by the U.S. Congress of the Smoot-Hawley tariff of 1930, the rise of the fascist bloc in the 1930s, and the rise of the communist bloc in the 1940s. All of these factors pertain to barriers that were created by governments, in contrast to the forces of technology and the private marketplace, which tend to reduce barriers. As a result, the world that emerged in 1945 was far more fragmented economically than the world that had turned to war in 1914.

The victors, however, were determined not to repeat the mistakes they had made at the time of the first world war. This time, they would work to promote economic integration in large part to advance long-term political goals. To govern international money, investment, and trade, they established multilateral institutions—the International Monetary Fund, World Bank, and General Agreement on Tariffs and Trade. The United States initially led the way by reducing trade barriers and making available gold-convertible dollars.

By one basic measure of trade, exports or imports of merchandise as a fraction of total output, it took more than twenty-five years after the end of World War II before the United States around 1970 reached the same level of globalization that it had experienced on the eve of World War I. This fraction continued to increase rapidly between 1971 and 1997—reaching about 9 percent today, still far lower than that in Britain throughout the late and early twentieth centuries. By other measures, some pertaining to the freedom of factor movements, the world even by the turn of the millennium was no more integrated than that of the preceding turn of the century.

Most people find it surprising that trade did not reattain its pre–World War I importance until the early 1970s. The significance of the comparison with 100 years ago goes well beyond factoids that economic historians enjoy springing on the uninitiated. Because technological know-how is irreversible—or was irreversible over the second millennium, if not entirely over the first—there is a tendency to see globalization as irreversible. But the political forces that fragmented the world for thirty years (1914–44) were evidently far more powerful than the accretion of technological progress in transport that went on during that period. The lesson is that nothing is inevitable about the process of globalization. For it to continue, world leaders must make choices of the sort made in the aftermath of World War II, instead of those made in the aftermath of World War I.

Judging by the Globalization 2000 Standard
of Perfect International Integration

Perhaps perfect economic integration across national borders is a straw man. . . . But straw men have their purposes, and in this case ample rhetoric exists to justify the interest. A good straw man needs to be substantial enough to impress the crows and yet not so substantial that he can't be knocked flat. On both scores the proposition of complete international integration qualifies admirably.

Consider again the basic statistics of trade integration—a country's total exports of goods and services, or total imports, as a fraction of GDP. With the rapid increase in services included, these ratios now average 12 percent for the United States. The current level of trade likely represents a doubling from 100 years ago. As remarkable as is this evidence of declining transportation costs, tariffs, and other barriers to trade, it is still very far from the condition that would prevail if these costs and barriers were zero. More sophisticated statistics below will document this claim. But a very simple calculation is sufficient to make the point. U.S. output is about one-fourth of gross world product. The output of producers in other countries is thus about three-fourths of gross world product. If Americans were prone to buy goods and services from foreign producers as easily as from domestic producers, then foreign products would constitute a share of U.S. spending equal to that of the spending of the average resident of the planet. The U.S. import-GDP ratio would equal .75. The same would be true of the U.S. export-GDP ratio. And yet these ratios are only about one-sixth of this hypothetical level (12 percent/75 percent = one-sixth). In other words, globalization would have to increase another sixfold, as measured by the trade ratio, before it would literally be true that Americans did business as easily across the globe as across the country.

Other countries are also a long way from perfect openness in this sense. The overall ratio of merchandise trade to output worldwide is about twice the U.S. ratio. This is to be expected, as other countries are smaller. For the other two large economies—Japan and the European Union considered as a whole—the ratio is closer to the U.S. level. In almost all cases, the ratio falls far short of the level that would prevail in a perfectly integrated world. In Figure 1, the vertical dimension represents the share of a country's output that is sold to its fellow citizens, rather than exported. The downward movement for most countries illustrates that they have become more open over the past 130 years. (One can also see that the integration trend was interrupted during the interwar period.) The United States is still far from perfect openness: the share of output sold at home is disproportionate to the share of world output. Other countries have a higher ratio of trade to GDP than the United States as a result of being smaller and less self-sufficient. Nonetheless, they are similarly far from perfect openness.

Why is globalization still so far from complete? To get an idea of the combination of transportation costs, trade barriers, and other frictions that remains yet to be dismantled, we must delve more deeply into the statistics.

Share of output sold at home

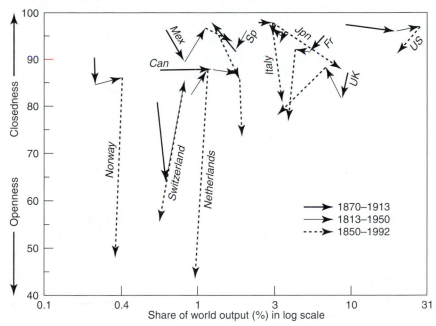

FIGURE 1 ■ Country Size (Share of World Output) versus Closedness (Sales at Home/Total Output)

Source: Author's calculations and data from Angus Maddison, Monitoring the World Economy (Paris: Development Center of the Organization for Economic Cooperation and Development, 1995).
Note: Closedness = (1 - (x/GDP))*100.

STATISTICAL MEASURES OF ECONOMIC INTEGRATION

It can be instructive to look at direct measures of how some of the barriers to transborder integration have changed during the twentieth century—the level of tariffs on manufactures as an illustration of trade policy, or the price of a trans-Atlantic telephone call as an illustration of technological change in communications and transportation. Nevertheless, the political and physical determinants are too numerous and varied to be aggregated into a few key statistics that are capable of measuring the overall extent of integration in trade or finance. Tariff rates, for example, differ tremendously across commodities, and there is no single sensible way to aggregate them. The situation is even worse for nontariff barriers. Alternative possible measures of the importance of tariffs and other trade barriers have very low correlation with each other. . . .

It is more rewarding to look at summary measures of the *effects* of cross-border barriers on the patterns of trade and investment than to look at measures of the barriers themselves. Two sorts of measures are in use: those pertaining to quantities and those pertaining to prices.

Measures of quantities might appear more direct: "just how big are international flows?" But economists often prefer to look at price measures. In the first place, the quality of the data is often higher for prices than quantities. (This is particularly true of data on international financial markets—the data on the prices of foreign securities are extremely good, the data on aggregate international trade in securities are extremely bad.) In the second place, even at a conceptual level, international differentials in the prices of specific goods or specific assets, which measure the ability of international arbitrage to hold these prices in line, are more useful indicators of the extent of integration in a causal sense. Consider the example of U.S. trade in petroleum products. It is not especially large as a percentage of total U.S. output or consumption of petroleum products. And yet arbitrage ties the price of oil within the United States closely to the price in the world market. Even a pair of countries that records no bilateral oil trade whatsoever will find that their prices move closely together. It is the absence of barriers and the *potential* for large-scale trade that keeps prices in line and makes the markets integrated in the most meaningful sense, not the magnitude of trade that takes place.

The Ability of Arbitrage to Eliminate International Differentials in Goods Prices

According to basic economic theory, arbitrage, defined as the activity of buying an item in a place where it is cheap and simultaneously selling the same item where it is expensive, should drive prices into equality. Its failure to do so perfectly is a source of repeated surprise to economists (though perhaps to nobody else). Often the explanation is that the commodities in question are not in fact identical. Brand names matter, if for no other reason than matters of retailing, warranty, and customer service. A BMW is certainly not the same automobile as a Lexus, and even a BMW sold in Germany is not the same as a BMW sold in the United States (different air pollution control equipment, for example). When the comparison across countries uses aggregate price indexes, as in standard tests of "purchasing power parity," it is no surprise to find only weak evidence of arbitrage. The finding of international price differentials is more surprising in the case of nondifferentiated non-brand-name commodities such as standardized ball bearings. Tests find that price differentials for specific goods are far larger across national borders than they are within countries. Exchange rate variability is a likely culprit.

Even more surprising is the paucity of evidence of a tendency for price differentials to diminish over the long sweep of history. Kenneth Froot, Michael Kim, and Kenneth Rogoff have obtained data on prices in England and Holland since the year 1273 for eight commodities (barley, butter, cheese, eggs, oats, peas, silver, and wheat).[2] Deviations from the so-called Law of One Price across the English Channel are no smaller or less persistent now than they were in the past, even though technological progress has certainly reduced the cost of shipping these products dramatically. Evidently other forces have counteracted the fall in transport costs; candidates are trade barriers under Europe's Common Agricultural Policy and volatility in the exchange rate between the guilder and the pound.

Factors Contributing to Home-Country Bias in Trade

Geography in general—and distance in particular—remain far more important inhibitions to trade than widely believed.

Distance

Distance is still an important barrier to trade and not solely because of physical shipping costs. The effects of informational barriers are observed to decrease with proximity and with linguistic, cultural, historical, and political links. We might call it social distance. Hans Linnemann called it "psychic distance," and Peter Drysdale and Ross Garnaut named it "subjective resistance."[3]

Among many possible proofs that distance is still important, one of the simplest is the observed tendency toward geographical agglomeration of industries. The tendency for industry to concentrate regionally is evidence both of costs to transportation and communication and of increasing returns to scale in production.

The agglomeration occurs even in sectors where physical transport costs are negligible, as in financial services or computer software. Financial firms concentrate in Manhattan and information technology firms concentrate in Silicon Valley. The reason they choose to locate near each other is not because they are trading physical commodities with each other and wish to save on shipping costs. Rather, face-to-face contact is important for exchanging information and negotiating deals.

The importance of distance is also revealed by analysis of data on prices of goods in different locations. If transport costs and other costs of doing business at a distance are important, then arbitrage should do a better job of keeping prices of similar goods in line when they are sold at locations close together rather than far apart. Charles Engel and John Rogers study prices in fourteen consumption categories for twenty-three Canadian and U.S. cities. They find that the distance between two North American cities significantly affects the variability of their relative prices. . . .

Statistical estimates find highly significant effects of distance on bilateral trade. When the distance between two countries is increased by 1 percent, trade between them falls by 0.7 to 1.0 percent. This statistic, like the others that follow, pertains to the effect in isolation, holding constant other effects on trade, such as the size of the trading partners. . . .

Other Geographical Variables

Other physical attributes of location also have statistically significant effects. Landlocked countries engage in less trade by a factor of about one-third, holding other factors equal. Two countries that are adjacent to each other trade about 80 percent more than two otherwise similar countries.

Linguistic and Colonial Factors

Linguistic barriers remain an impediment to trade. Two countries that speak the same language trade about 50 percent more than two otherwise similar countries. The multitude of languages is one of the reasons why economic integration remains far from complete in the European Union.

Colonial links have also been important historically. In 1960, the year when the break-up of the largest colonial empires began in earnest, trade between colonies and the colonial power was on average two to four times greater than for otherwise similar pairs of countries. This effect, already reduced from an earlier peak in the colonial era, has continued to decline in the 1970s and 1980s. But it has not disappeared. Indeed, if small dependencies are included in the sample, then two units that share the same colonizer still trade on average an estimated 80 percent more with each other than two otherwise similar countries (as recently as 1990). In addition, if one of the pair is the colonial mother country, trade is five to nine times greater than it would otherwise be.

Military Factors

The effects on bilateral trade of politico-military alliances, wars, have also been examined. Theoretically and empirically (in the gravity framework) trade is generally higher among countries that are allies and lower among countries that are actual or potential adversaries. Understandably, if two countries are currently at war, there is usually a negative effect on trade. It runs as high as a 99 percent reduction in 1965. More typical is an 82 percent reduction in 1990.[4]

Free Trade Areas

Regional trading arrangements reduce tariffs and other trade barriers within a group of countries, though there is a range from mild preferential trading arrangements to full-fledged economic unions. Often the members of such groups are already tightly linked through proximity, common language, or other ties. But even holding constant for such factors, in the gravity model, the formation of a free trade area is estimated on average to raise trade by 70 to 170 percent. A serious common market, such as the European Union, can have a bigger effect. Nevertheless, in each of the EU member countries, a large bias toward trade within that country remains.

Political Links

A naive economist's view would be that once tariffs and other explicit trade barriers between countries are removed, and geographic determinants of transportation costs are held constant, trade should move as easily across national boundaries as within them. But this is far from the case in reality. If two geographic units belong to the same sovereign nation, such as France and its overseas departments, trade is roughly tripled. Thus political relationships among geographic units have larger effects on trade than such factors as explicit trade policies or linguistic barriers.

Common Country

Even after adjusting for distance (including noncontiguity) and linguistic barriers, all countries still exhibit a substantial bias toward buying domestic goods rather than foreign. . . .

There would be some great advantages of having data at the level of states or provinces within countries. We would be able to ascertain how trade between two geographical entities is affected by their common membership in a political union. We have learned that when two geographical units share such links as speaking a common language, their bilateral trade is clearly boosted. It stands to reason that when two units share a common cultural heritage or legal system, their trade will be enhanced by even more. Data are not generally available on trade among U.S. states, Japanese prefectures, German länder, British counties, or French departments. But there do exist data on trade undertaken by Canadian provinces, among one another and with major American states. They show a strong intranational bias to trade. Ontario exports three times as much to British Columbia as to California, even though the latter has ten times as many people. (The figures are for 1988.) . . .

Currencies

There has long been reason to suspect that the existence of different currencies, and especially the large fluctuation in the exchange rates between currencies since the break-up of the Bretton Woods monetary system in 1971, has been a barrier to international trade and investment. Exchange rate fluctuations are clearly related to the failures of the law of one price observed in goods markets. When it is observed that, for example, Canadians and Americans trade far more with their countrymen than with each other, in a context where trade barriers, geography, and linguistic barriers have been eliminated, the currency difference is one of the prime suspects. . . .

Promoting trade and finance is one of several motivations for the recent adoption of common currencies or currency boards by roughly twenty countries over the past decade (including the eleven members of the European Economic and Monetary Union in 1999). At the same time, however, approximately the same number of new currencies have come into existence, as a result of the breakup of the former Soviet bloc.

Measures of Financial Market Integration

The delegates who met at Bretton Woods in 1944 had a design for the world monetary system that explicitly did not accord financial markets the presumption that was accorded trade in goods, the presumption that international integration was unambiguously good and that barriers should be liberalized as rapidly as possible. Although economic theory can make as elegant a case in favor of free trade in assets as for free trade in goods and services, the delegates had been persuaded by the experience of the 1930s that some degree of controls on international capital movements was desirable. It was not until the final 1973 breakdown of the system of fixed exchange rates that Germany and the United States removed their capital controls. Japan and the United Kingdom kept theirs until the end of the 1970s, and most other European countries did not liberalize until the end of the 1980s. Many emerging-market countries also opened up to large-scale international capital movements in the 1990s (though the subsequent crises have convinced some observers that those delegates at Bretton Woods might have had it right in the first place).

Tests regarding financial markets show international integration that has increased tremendously over the past thirty years but that is less complete than often supposed. This generalization applies to quantity-based tests as well as to price-based tests.

It is true that the gross volume of cross-border capital flows has grown very large. Perhaps the most impressive and widely cited statistic is the gross volume of turnover in foreign exchange markets: $1.5 trillion per day worldwide, by April 1998, which is on the order of a hundred times greater than the volume of trade in goods and services. *Net* capital flows are for most purposes more interesting than gross flows, however. Net capital flows today are far smaller as a share of GDP than were pre-World War I net flows out of Great Britain and into such land-abundant countries as Argentina, Australia, and Canada. Furthermore, Martin Feldstein and Charles Horioka argued in a very influential paper that net capital flows are far smaller than one would expect them to be in a world of perfect international capital mobility: a country that suffers a shortfall in national saving tends to experience an almost commensurate fall in investment, rather than making up the difference by borrowing from abroad. Similarly, investors in every country hold far lower proportions of their portfolios in the form of other countries' securities than they would in a well-diversified portfolio, a puzzle known as home country bias. Evidently, imperfect information and transactions costs are still important barriers to cross-country investment.

The ability of arbitrage to equate asset prices or rates of return across countries has been widely tested. One would expect that in the absence of barriers to cross-border financial flows, arbitrage would bring interest rates into equality. But the answer depends on the precise condition tested. Interest rates that have had the element of exchange risk removed by forward market cover are indeed virtually equated across national borders among industrialized countries, showing that they have few controls on international capital movements. But interest rates seem not to be equalized across countries when they are adjusted for expectations of exchange rate changes rather than for forward exchange rates, and interest rates are definitely not equalized when adjusted for expected inflation rates. Evidently, currency differences are important enough to drive a wedge between expected rates of return. Furthermore, residual transactions costs or imperfect information apparently affects cross-border investment in equities. They discourage investors altogether from investing in some information-intensive assets, such as mortgages, across national borders. Furthermore, country risk still adds a substantial penalty wedge to all investments in developing countries.

In short, though international financial markets, much like goods markets, have become far more integrated in recent decades, they have traversed less of the distance to perfect integration than is widely believed. Globalization is neither new, nor complete, nor irreversible.

The Impact of Economic Globalization

What are the effects of globalization and its merits? We must acknowledge a lower degree of certainty in our answers. It becomes harder to isolate cause and effect.

Moreover, once we extend the list of objectives beyond maximizing national incomes, value judgments come into play. Nevertheless, economic theory and empirical research still have much to contribute.

The Effect of Trade on the Level and Growth of Real Income

Why do economists consider economic integration so important? What are the benefits of free trade for the economy?

The Theoretical Case for Trade

Classical economic theory tells us that there are national gains from trade, associated with the phrase "comparative advantage." Over the past two decades, scholars have developed a "new trade theory." It suggests the existence of additional benefits from trade, which are termed dynamic. We consider each theory in turn.

The classical theory goes back to Adam Smith and David Ricardo. Adam Smith argued that specialization—the division of labor—enhances productivity. David Ricardo extended this concept to trade between countries. The notion is that trade allows each country to specialize in what it does best, thus maximizing the value of its output. If a government restricts trade, resources are wasted in the production of goods that could be imported more cheaply than they can be produced domestically.

What if one country is better than anyone else at producing *every* good? The argument in favor of free trade still carries the day. All that is required is for a country to be *relatively* less skilled than another in the production of some good in order for it to benefit from trade. This is the doctrine of comparative advantage—the fundamental (if perhaps counterintuitive) principle that underlies the theory of international trade. It makes sense for Michael Jordan to pay someone else to mow his lawn, even if Jordan could do it better himself, because he has a comparative advantage at basketball over lawn mowing. Similarly, it makes sense for the United States to pay to import certain goods that can be produced more efficiently abroad (apparel, shoes, tropical agriculture, consumer electronics), because the United States has a comparative advantage in other goods (aircraft, financial services, wheat, and computer software).

This is the classical view of the benefits of free trade in a nutshell. Two key attributes of the classical theory are worth flagging. First, it assumes perfect competition, constant returns to scale, and fixed technology, assumptions that are not very realistic. Second, the gains from trade are primarily static in nature—that is, they affect the *level* of real income. The elimination of trade barriers raises income, but this is more along the lines of a one-time increase.

What of the "new trade theory"? It is more realistic than the classical theory, in that it takes into account imperfect competition, increasing returns to scale, and changing technology. It can be viewed as providing equally strong, or stronger, support for the sort of free trade policies that the United States has followed throughout the postwar period, that is, multilateral and bilateral negotiations to reduce trade barriers, than did the classical theory.

To be sure, these theories say that, under certain very special conditions, one country can get ahead by interventions (for example, subsidies to strategic sectors), provided the government gets it exactly right and provided the actions of other countries are taken as given. But these theories also tend to have the property that a world in which everyone is subsidizing at once is a world in which everyone is worse off, and that we are all better off if we can agree to limit subsidies or other interventions.

Bilateral or multilateral agreements where other sides make concessions to U.S. products, in return for whatever concessions the United States makes, are virtually the only sorts of trade agreements the United States has made. Indeed, most recent trade agreements (like the North American Free Trade Agreement and China's accession to the WTO) have required much larger reductions in import barriers by U.S. trading partners than by the United States. The reason is that their barriers were higher than those of the United States to start with. But the natural implication is that such agreements raise foreign demand for U.S. products by more than they raise U.S. demand for imports. Hence the United States is likely to benefit from a positive "terms of trade effect." This just adds to the usual benefits of increased efficiency of production and gains to consumers from international trade.

Furthermore, even when a government does not fear retaliation from abroad for trade barriers, intervention in practice is usually based on inadequate knowledge and is corrupted by interest groups. Seeking to rule out all sector-specific intervention is the most effective way of discouraging rent-seeking behavior. Globalization increases the number of competitors operating in the economy. Not only does this work to reduce distortionary monopoly power in the marketplace (which is otherwise exercised by raising prices), it can also reduce distortionary corporate power in the political arena (which is exercised by lobbying).

Most important, new trade theory offers reason to believe that openness can have a permanent effect on a country's rate of growth, not just the level of real GDP. A high rate of economic interaction with the rest of the world speeds the absorption of frontier technologies and global management best practices, spurs innovation and cost-cutting, and competes away monopoly.

These dynamic gains come from a number of sources. They include the benefits of greater market size and enhanced competition. Other sources include technological improvements through increased contact with foreigners and their alternative production styles. Such contact can come, for example, from direct investment by foreign firms with proprietary knowledge or by the exposure to imported goods that embody technologies developed abroad. Each of these elements of international trade and interactions has the effect of promoting growth in the domestic economy. When combined with the static effects, there is no question that the efforts to open markets, when successful, can yield significant dividends.

The Empirical Case for Trade

Citing theory is not a complete answer to the question, "how do we know that trade is good?" We need empirical evidence. Economists have undertaken statistical tests of the determinants of countries' growth rates. Investment in physical capital and investment in human capital are the two factors that emerge the most strongly. But other factors matter. Estimates of growth equations have found a role for openness, measured, for example, as the sum of exports and imports as a share of GDP. David Romer and I look at a cross-section of 100 countries during the period since 1960. The study sought to address a major concern about simultaneous causality between growth and trade: does openness lead to growth, or does growth lead to openness? We found that the effect of openness on growth is even stronger when we correct for the simultaneity compared with standard estimates.

The estimate of the effect of openness on income per capita ranges from 0.3 to 3.0. Consider a round middle number such as 1.0. The increase in U.S. openness since the 1950s is 0.12. Multiplying the two numbers together implies that the increased integration has had an effect of 12 percent on U.S. income. More dramatically, compare a stylized Burma, with a ratio close to zero, versus a stylized Singapore, with a ratio close to 100 percent. Our ballpark estimate, the coefficient of 1.0, implies that Singapore's income is 100 percent higher than Burma's as a result of its openness. The fact that trade can affect a country's growth rate—as opposed to affecting the level of its GDP in a "one-shot" fashion—makes the case for trade liberalization even more compelling. . . .

Macroeconomic Interdependence

Trade and financial integration generally increase the transmission of business cycle fluctuations among countries. Floating exchange rates give countries some insulation against one another's fluctuations. When capital markets are highly integrated, floating rates do not give complete insulation, as the post-1973 correlation among major industrialized economies shows. But international transmission can be good for a country as easily as bad, as happens when adverse domestic developments are in part passed off to the rest of the world. The trade balance can act as an important automatic stabilizer for output and employment, improving in recessions and worsening in booms.

Contagion of financial crises is more worrying. The decade of the 1990s alone abounds with examples: the 1992–93 crises in the European exchange rate mechanism, the "tequila crisis" that began with the December 1994 devaluation of the Mexican peso, and the crises in East Asia and emerging markets worldwide from July 1997 to January 1999. Evidently when one country has a crisis it affects others. There is now a greater consensus among economists than before that not all of the observed volatility, or its cross-country correlation, can be attributed to efficient capital markets punishing or rewarding countries based on a rational evaluation of the economic fundamentals. It is difficult to do justice in one paragraph to a discussion that is as voluminous and vigorous as the debate over the welfare implications of the swelling international capital flows. Still, the majority view remains that countries are overall better off with modern globalized financial markets than without them.

The Effect of Trade on Other Social Goals

Many who fear globalization concede that trade has a positive effect on aggregate national income but suspect that it has adverse effects on other highly valued goals such as labor rights, food safety, culture, and so forth. Here we consider only two major values—equality and the environment—and briefly at that.

Income Distribution

International trade and investment can be a powerful source of growth in poor countries, helping them catch up with those who are ahead in endowments of capital and technology. This was an important component of the spectacular growth of East Asian countries between the 1960s and the 1990s, which remains a miracle even in the aftermath of the 1997–98 currency crises. By promoting convergence, trade can help reduce the enormous worldwide inequality in income. Most of those who are concerned about income distribution, however, seem more motivated by within-country equality than global equality.

A standard textbook theory of international trade, the Heckscher-Ohlin-Samuelson model, has a striking prediction to make regarding within-country income distribution. It is that the scarce factors of production will lose from trade, and the abundant factors will benefit. This means that in rich countries, those who have capital and skills will benefit at the expense of unskilled labor, whereas in poor countries it will be the other way around. The same prediction holds for international capital mobility (or, for that matter, for international labor mobility). It has been very difficult, however, to find substantial direct evidence of the predictions of the model during the postwar period, including distribution effects within either rich or poor countries. Most likely the phenomena of changing technology, intraindustry trade, and worker ties to specific industries are more important today than the factor endowments at the heart of the Heckscher-Ohlin-Samuelson model.

In the United States, the gap between wages paid to skilled workers and wages paid to unskilled workers rose by 18 percentage points between 1973 and 1995 and then leveled off. The fear is that trade is responsible for some of the gap, by benefiting skilled workers more than unskilled workers. Common statistical estimates—which typically impose the theoretical framework rather than testing it—are that between 5 and 30 percent of the increase is attributable to trade. Technology, raising the demand for skilled workers faster than the supply, is the major factor responsible for the rest. One of the higher estimates is that trade contributes one-third of the net increase in the wage gap.

On a sample of seventy-three countries, Chakrabarti finds that trade actually reduces inequality, as measured by the Gini coefficient. This relationship also holds for each income class.

Clearly, income distribution is determined by many factors beyond trade. One is redistribution policies undertaken by the government. In some cases such policies are initiated in an effort to compensate or "buy off" groups thought to be adversely affected by trade. But a far more important phenomenon is the tendency for countries to implement greater redistribution as they grow richer.

A long-established empirical regularity is the tendency for income inequality to worsen at early stages of growth and then to improve at later stages. The original explanation for this phenomenon, known as the Kuznets curve, had to do with rural-urban migration. But a common modern interpretation is that income redistribution is a "superior good"—something that societies choose to purchase more of, even though at some cost to aggregate income, as they grow rich enough to be able to afford to do so. If this is right, then trade can be expected eventually to raise equality, by raising aggregate income.

Environment

Similar logic holds that trade and growth can also be good for the environment, once the country gets past a certain level of per capita income. Gene Grossman and Alan Krueger found what is called the environmental Kuznets curve: growth is bad for air and water pollution at the initial stages of industrialization but later on reduces pollution as countries become rich enough to pay to clean up their environments. . . . A key point is that popular desires need not translate automatically into environmental quality; rather government intervention is usually required to address externalities.

The idea that trade can be good for the environment is surprising to many. The pollution-haven hypothesis instead holds that trade encourages firms to locate production of highly polluting sectors in low-regulation countries in order to stay competitive. But economists' research suggests that environmental regulation is not a major determinant of firms' ability to compete internationally. Furthermore, running counter to fears of a "race to the bottom," is the Pareto-improvement point: trade allows countries to attain more of whatever their goals are, including higher market-measured income for a given level of environmental quality or a better environment for a given level of income. . . .

The econometric studies of the effects of trade and growth on the environment get different results depending on what specific measures of pollution they use. There is a need to look at other environmental criteria as well. It is difficult to imagine, for example, that trade is anything but bad for the survival of tropical hardwood forests or endangered species, without substantial efforts by governments to protect them.

The argument that richer countries will take steps to clean up their environments holds only for issues when the effects are felt domestically—where the primary "bads," such as smog or water pollution, are external to the firm or household but internal to the country. Some environmental externalities that have received increased attention in recent decades, however, are global. Biodiversity, overfishing, ozone depletion, and greenhouse gas emissions are four good examples. A ton of carbon dioxide has the same global warming effect regardless of where in the world it is emitted. In these cases, individual nations can do little to improve the environment on their own, no matter how concerned their populations or how effective their governments. For each of the four examples, governments have negotiated international treaties in an attempt to deal with the problem. But only the attempt to address ozone depletion, the Montreal Protocol, can be said as yet to have met with much success.

Is the popular impression then correct, that international trade and finance exacerbates these global environmental externalities? Yes, but only in the sense that trade and finance promote economic growth. Clearly if mankind were still a population of a few million people living in preindustrial poverty, greenhouse gas emissions would not be a big issue. Industrialization leads to environmental degradation, and trade is part of industrialization. But virtually everyone wants industrialization, at least for themselves. Deliberate self-impoverishment is not a promising option. Once this point is recognized, there is nothing special about trade compared with the other sources of economic growth: capital accumulation, rural-urban migration, and technological progress. . . .

SUMMARY OF CONCLUSIONS

This chapter gives confident answers to questions about the extent and sources of economic globalization and moderately confident answers to some questions about its effects.

The world has become increasingly integrated with respect to trade and finance since the end of World War II, owing to declining costs to transportation and communication and declining government barriers. The phenomenon is neither new nor complete, however. Globalization was more dramatic in the half-century preceding World War I, and much of the progress during the last half-century has merely reversed the closing off that came in between. In the second regard, globalization is far from complete. Contrary to popular impressions, national borders and geography still impede trade and investment substantially. A simple calculation suggests that the ratio of trade to output would have to increase at least another sixfold before it would be true that Americans trade across the globe as readily as across the country. Such barriers as differences in currencies, languages, and political systems each have their own statistically estimated trade-impeding influences, besides the remaining significant effects of distance, borders, and other geographical and trade policy variables.

The chapter's discussion of the impacts of economic globalization has necessarily been exceedingly brief. Both theory and evidence are read as clearly supportive of the proposition that trade has a positive effect on real incomes. This is why economists believe it is important that the process of international integration be allowed to continue, especially for the sake of those countries that are still poor.

Effects on social values other than aggregate incomes can be positive or negative, depending on the details, and the statistical evidence does not always give clear-cut answers about the bottom line. In the two most studied cases, income distribution and environmental pollution, there seems to be a pattern whereby things get worse in the early stages of industrialization but then start to get better at higher levels of income. Societies that become rich in terms of market-measured output choose to improve their quality of life in other ways as well. It is possible that the same principle extends to noneconomic values such as safety, human rights, and democracy. In short, there is reason to hope that, aside from the various more direct effects of trade on noneconomic values, there is a general indirect beneficial effect that comes through the positive effect of trade on income. . . .

NOTES

1. John Maynard Keynes, *The Economic Consequences of the Peace* (Harcourt Brace, and Howe, 1920).
2. Kenneth Froot, Michael Kim, and Kenneth Rogoff, "The Law of One Price over 700 Years," Working Paper 5132 (Cambridge, Mass.: National Bureau of Economic Research, May 1995).
3. Hans Linnemann, *An Econometric Study of International Trade Flows* (Amsterdam: North-Holland, 1960); and Peter Drysdale and Ross Garnaut, "Trade Intensities and the Analysis of Bilateral Trade Flows in a Many-Country World," *Hitotsubashi Journal of Economics*, Vol. 22 (1982), pp. 62–84.
4. Edward Mansfield, "Effects of International Politics on Regionalism in International Trade," in Kym Anderson and Richard Blackhurst, eds., *Regional Integration and the Global Trading System* (Harvester Wheatsheaf, 1993); Edward Mansfield and Rachel Bronson, "The Political Economy of Major-Power Trade Flows," in Edward Mansfield and Helen Milner, eds., *The Political Economy of Regionalism* (Columbia University Press 1997); and Joanne Gowa and Edward Mansfield, "Power Politics and International Trade," *American Political Science Review*, Vol. 87 (June 1993), pp. 408–20.

Why the World Isn't Flat

PANKAJ GHEMAWAT

Ideas will spread faster, leaping borders. Poor countries will have immediate access to information that was once restricted to the industrial world and traveled only slowly, if at all, beyond it. Entire electorates will learn things that once only a few bureaucrats knew. Small companies will offer services that previously only giants could provide. In all these ways, the communications revolution is profoundly democratic and liberating, leveling the imbalance between large and small, "rich and poor." . . . We seem to live in a world that is no longer a collection of isolated, "local" nations, effectively separated by high tariff walls, poor communications networks and mutual suspicion. It's a world that, if you believe the most prominent proponents of globalization, is increasingly wired, informed, and, well, "flat." . . .

Amid all this clutter, several books on the subject have managed to attract significant attention. During a recent TV interview, the first question I was asked—quite earnestly—was why I still thought the world was round. The interviewer was referring of course to the thesis of *New York Times* columnist Thomas L. Friedman's bestselling book *The World Is Flat*. Friedman asserts that 10 forces—most of which enable connectivity and collaboration at a distance—are "flattening" the Earth and leveling a playing field of global competitiveness, the likes of which the world has never before seen.

It sounds compelling enough. But Friedman's assertions are simply the latest in a series of exaggerated visions that also include the "end of history" and the "convergence of tastes." Some writers in this vein view globalization as a good thing—an escape from the ancient tribal rifts that have divided humans, or an opportunity to sell the same thing to everyone on Earth. Others lament its cancerous spread, a process at the end of which everyone will be eating the same fast food. Their arguments are mostly characterized by emotional rather than cerebral appeals, a reliance on prophecy, semiotic arousal (that is, treating everything as a sign), a focus on technology as the driver of change, an emphasis on education that creates "new" people, and perhaps above all, a clamor for attention. But they all have one thing in common: They're wrong.

In truth, the world is not nearly as connected as these writers would have us believe. Despite talk of a new, wired world where information, ideas, money, and people can move around the planet faster than ever before, just a fraction of what we consider globalization actually exists. The portrait that emerges from a hard look at the way companies, people, and states interact is a world that's only beginning to realize the potential of true global integration. And what these trend's backers won't tell you is that globalization's future is more fragile than you know.

THE 10 PERCENT PRESUMPTION

The few cities that dominate international financial activity—Frankfurt, Hong Kong, London, New York—are at the height of modern global integration; which is to say, they are all relatively well connected with one another. But when you examine the numbers, the picture is one of extreme connectivity at the local level, not a flat world. What do such statistics reveal? Most types of economic activity that could be conducted either within or across borders turn out to still be quite domestically concentrated.

One favorite mantra from globalization champions is how "investment knows no boundaries." But how much of all the capital being invested around the world is conducted by companies outside of their home countries? The fact is, the total amount of the world's capital formation that is generated from foreign direct

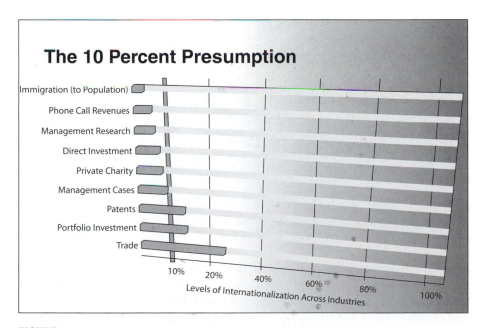

FIGURE 1 ■

investment (FDI) has been less than 10 percent for the last three years for which data are available (2003–05). In other words, more than 90 percent of the fixed investment around the world is still domestic. And though merger waves can push the ratio higher, it has never reached 20 percent. In a thoroughly globalized environment, one would expect this number to be much higher—about 90 percent, by my calculation. And FDI isn't an odd or unrepresentative example.

As the chart above demonstrates, the levels of internationalization associated with cross-border migration, telephone calls, management research and education, private charitable giving, patenting, stock investment, and trade, as a fraction of gross domestic product (GDP), all stand much closer to 10 percent than 100 percent. The biggest exception in absolute terms—the trade-to-GDP ratio shown at the bottom of the chart—recedes most of the way back down toward 20 percent if you adjust for certain kinds of double-counting. So if someone asked me to guess the internationalization level of some activity about which I had no particular information, I would guess it to be much closer to 10 percent—the average for the nine categories of data in the chart—than to 100 percent. I call this the "10 Percent Presumption."

More broadly, these and other data on cross-border integration suggest a semi-globalized world, in which neither the bridges nor the barriers between countries can be ignored. From this perspective, the most astonishing aspect of various writings on globalization is the extent of exaggeration involved. In short, the levels of internationalization in the world today are roughly an order of magnitude lower than those implied by globalization proponents.

A STRONG NATIONAL DEFENSE

If you buy into the more extreme views of the globalization triumphalists, you would expect to see a world where national borders are irrelevant, and where citizens increasingly view themselves as members of ever broader political entities. True, communications technologies have improved dramatically during the past 100 years. The cost of a three-minute telephone call from New York to London fell from $350 in 1930 to about 40 cents in 1999, and it is now approaching zero for voice-over-Internet telephony. And the Internet itself is just one of many newer forms of connectivity that have progressed several times faster than plain old telephone service. This pace of improvement has inspired excited proclamations about the pace of global integration. But it's a huge leap to go from predicting such changes to asserting that declining communication costs will obliterate the effects of distance. Although the barriers at borders have declined significantly, they haven't disappeared.

To see why, consider the Indian software industry—favorite of Friedman and others. Friedman cites Nandan Nilekani, the CEO of the second-largest such firm, Infosys, as his muse for the notion of a flat world. But what Nilekani has pointed out privately is that while Indian software programmers can now serve the United

States from India, access is assured, in part, by U.S. capital being invested—quite literally—in that outcome. In other words, the success of the Indian IT industry is not exempt from political and geographic constraints. The country of origin matters—even for capital, which is often considered stateless.

Or consider the largest Indian software firm, Tata Consultancy Services (TCS). Friedman has written at least two columns in the *New York Times* on TCS's Latin American operations: "[I]n today's world, having an Indian company led by a Hungarian-Uruguayan servicing American banks with Montevidean engineers managed by Indian technologists who have learned to eat Uruguayan veggie is just the new normal," Friedman writes. Perhaps. But the real question is why the company established those operations in the first place. Having worked as a strategy advisor to TCS since 2000, I can testify that reasons related to the tyranny of time zones, languages, and the need for proximity to clients' local operations loomed large in that decision. This is a far cry from globalization proponents' oft-cited world in which geography, language, and distance don't matter.

Trade flows certainly bear that theory out. Consider Canadian-U.S. trade, the largest bilateral relationship of its kind in the world. In 1988, before the North American Free Trade Agreement (NAFTA) took effect, merchandise trade levels between Canadian provinces—that is, within the country—were estimated to be 20 times as large as their trade with similarly sized and similarly distant U.S. states. In other words, there was a built-in "home bias." Although NAFTA helped reduce this ratio of domestic to international trade—the home bias—to 10 to 1 by the mid-1990s, it still exceeds 5 to 1 today. And these ratios are just for merchandise; for services, the ratio is still several times larger. Clearly, the borders in our seemingly "borderless world" still matter to most people.

Geographical boundaries are so pervasive, they even extend to cyberspace. If there were one realm in which borders should be rendered meaningless and the globalization proponents should be correct in their overly optimistic models, it should be the Internet. Yet Web traffic within countries and regions has increased far faster than traffic between them. Just as in the real world, Internet links decay with distance. People across the world may be getting more connected, but they aren't connecting with each other. The average South Korean Web user may be spending several hours a day online—connected to the rest of the world in theory—but he is probably chatting with friends across town and e-mailing family across the country rather than meeting a fellow surfer in Los Angeles. We're more wired, but no more "global."

Just look at Google, which boasts of supporting more than 100 languages and, partly as a result, has recently been rated the most globalized Web site. But Google's operation in Russia (cofounder Sergey Brin's native country) reaches only 28 percent of the market there, versus 64 percent for the Russian market leader in search services, Yandex, and 53 percent for Rambler.

Indeed, these two local competitors account for 91 percent of the Russian market for online ads linked to Web searches. What has stymied Google's expansion into the Russian market? The biggest reason is the difficulty of designing a search engine to handle the linguistic complexities of the Russian language. In addition, these local competitors are more in tune with the Russian market, for example, developing payment methods through traditional banks to compensate for the dearth of credit cards. And, though Google has doubled its reach since 2003, it had to set up a Moscow office in Russia and hire Russian software engineers, underlining the continued importance of physical location. Even now, borders between countries define—and constrain—our movements more than globalization breaks them down.

TURNING BACK THE CLOCK

If globalization is an inadequate term for the current state of integration, there's an obvious rejoinder: Even if the world isn't quite flat today, it will be tomorrow. To respond, we have to look at trends, rather than levels of integration at one point in time. The results are telling. Along a few dimensions, integration reached its all-time high many years ago. For example, rough calculations suggest that the number of long-term international migrants amounted to 3 percent of the world's population in 1900—the high-water mark of an earlier era of migration—versus 2.9 percent in 2005.

Along other dimensions, it's true that new records are being set. But this growth has happened only relatively recently, and only after long periods of stagnation and reversal. For example, FDI stocks divided by GDP peaked before World War I and didn't return to that level until the 1990s. Several economists have argued that the most remarkable development over the long term was the declining level of internationalization between the two World Wars. And despite the records being set, the current level of trade intensity falls far short of completeness, as the Canadian-U.S. trade data suggest. In fact, when trade economists look at these figures, they are amazed not at how much trade there is, but how little.

It's also useful to examine the considerable momentum that globalization proponents attribute to the constellation of policy changes that led many countries—particularly China, India, and the former Soviet Union—to engage more extensively with the international economy. One of the better-researched descriptions of these policy changes and their implications is provided by economists Jeffrey Sachs and Andrew Warner:

"The years between 1970 and 1995, and especially the last decade, have witnessed the most remarkable institutional harmonization and economic integration among nations in world history. While economic integration was increasing throughout the 1970s and 1980s, the extent of integration has come sharply into focus only since the collapse of communism in 1989. In 1995, one dominant global economic system is emerging."

Yes, such policy openings are important. But to paint them as a sea change is inaccurate at best. Remember the 10 Percent Presumption, and that integration is only beginning. The policies that we fickle humans enact are surprisingly reversible. Thus, Francis Fukuyama's *The End of History,* in which liberal democracy and technologically driven capitalism were supposed to have triumphed over other ideologies, seems quite quaint today. In the wake of Sept. 11, 2001, Samuel Huntington's *Clash of Civilizations* looks at least a bit more prescient. But even if you stay on the economic plane, as Sachs and Warner mostly do, you quickly see counterevidence to the supposed decisiveness of policy openings. The so-called Washington Consensus around market-friendly policies ran up against the 1997 Asian currency crisis and has since frayed substantially—for example, in the swing toward neopopulism across much of Latin America. In terms of economic outcomes, the number of countries—in Latin America, coastal Africa, and the former Soviet Union—that have dropped out of the "convergence club" (defined in terms of narrowing productivity and structural gaps vis-à-vis the advanced industrialized countries) is at least as impressive as the number of countries that have joined the club. At a multilateral level, the suspension of the Doha round of trade talks in the summer of 2006—prompting *The Economist* to run a cover titled "The Future of Globalization" and depicting a beached wreck—is no promising omen. In addition, the recent wave of cross-border mergers and acquisitions seems to be encountering more protectionism, in a broader range of countries, than did the previous wave in the late 1990s.

Of course, given that sentiments in these respects have shifted in the past 10 years or so, there is a fair chance that they may shift yet again in the next decade. The point is, it's not only possible to turn back the clock on globalization-friendly policies, it's relatively easy to imagine it happening. Specifically, we have to entertain the possibility that deep international economic integration may be inherently incompatible with national sovereignty—especially given the tendency of voters in many countries, including advanced ones, to support more protectionism, rather than less. As Jeff Immelt, CEO of GE, put it in late 2006, "If you put globalization to a popular vote in the U.S., it would lose." And even if cross-border integration continues on its upward path, the road from here to there is unlikely to be either smooth or straight. There will be shocks and cycles, in all likelihood, and maybe even another period of stagnation or reversal that will endure for decades. It wouldn't be unprecedented.

The champions of globalization are describing a world that doesn't exist. It's a fine strategy to sell books and even describe a potential environment that may someday exist. Because such episodes of mass delusion tend to be relatively short-lived even when they do achieve broad currency, one might simply be tempted to wait this one out as well. But the stakes are far too high for that. Governments that buy into the flat world are likely to pay too much attention to the "golden straitjacket" that Friedman emphasized in his earlier book, *The Lexus and the Olive Tree,* which is supposed to ensure that economics matters more and more and politics less and less. Buying into this version of an integrated world—or worse, using it as a basis for policymaking—is not only unproductive. It is dangerous.

Offshoring: The Next Industrial Revolution?

ALAN S. BLINDER

A CONTROVERSY RECONSIDERED

In February 2004, when N. Gregory Mankiw, a Harvard professor then serving as chairman of the White House Council of Economic Advisers, caused a national uproar with a "textbook" statement about trade, economists rushed to his defense. Mankiw was commenting on the phenomenon that has been clumsily dubbed "offshoring" (or "offshore outsourcing")—the migration of jobs, but not the people who perform them, from rich countries to poor ones. Offshoring, Mankiw said, is only "the latest manifestation of the gains from trade that economists have talked about at least since Adam Smith. . . . More things are tradable than were tradable in the past, and that's a good thing." Although Democratic and Republican politicians alike excoriated Mankiw for his callous attitude toward American jobs, economists lined up to support his claim that offshoring is simply international business as usual.

Their economics were basically sound: the well-known principle of comparative advantage implies that trade in new kinds of products will bring overall improvements in productivity and well-being. But Mankiw and his defenders underestimated both the importance of offshoring and its disruptive effect on wealthy countries. Sometimes a quantitative change is so large that it brings about qualitative changes, as offshoring likely will. We have so far barely seen the tip of the offshoring iceberg, the eventual dimensions of which may be staggering.

To be sure, the furor over Mankiw's remark was grotesquely out of proportion to the current importance of offshoring, which is still largely a prospective phenomenon. Although there are no reliable national data, fragmentary studies indicate that well under a million service-sector jobs in the United States have been lost to offshoring to date. (A million seems impressive, but in the gigantic and rapidly churning U.S. labor market, a million jobs is less than two weeks' worth of normal gross job losses.) However, constant improvements in technology and global communications virtually guarantee that the future will bring much more offshoring of "impersonal services" —that is, services that can be delivered electronically over long distances with little or no degradation in quality.

Alan S. Blinder, "Offshoring: The Next Industrial Revolution?" Reprinted by permission of *Foreign Affairs*, Vol. 85, No. 2 (March/April 2006), pp. 113–129. Copyright 2006 by the Council on Foreign Relations, Inc. www.ForeignAffairs.org.

That said, we should not view the coming wave of offshoring as an impending catastrophe. Nor should we try to stop it. The normal gains from trade mean that the world as a whole cannot lose from increases in productivity, and the United States and other industrial countries have not only weathered but also benefited from comparable changes in the past. But in order to do so again, the governments and societies of the developed world must face up to the massive, complex, and multifaceted challenges that offshoring will bring. National data systems, trade policies, educational systems, social welfare programs, and politics all must adapt to new realities. Unfortunately, none of this is happening now.

MODERNIZING COMPARATIVE ADVANTAGE

Countries trade with one another for the same reasons that individuals, businesses, and regions do: to exploit their comparative advantages. Some advantages are "natural": Texas and Saudi Arabia sit atop massive deposits of oil that are entirely lacking in New York and Japan, and nature has conspired to make Hawaii a more attractive tourist destination than Greenland. There is not much anyone can do about such natural advantages.

But in modern economies, nature's whimsy is far less important than it was in the past. Today, much comparative advantage derives from human effort rather than natural conditions. The concentration of computer companies around Silicon Valley, for example, has nothing to do with bountiful natural deposits of silicon; it has to do with Xerox's fabled Palo Alto Research Center, the proximity of Stanford University, and the arrival of two young men named Hewlett and Packard. Silicon Valley could have sprouted up elsewhere.

One important aspect of this modern reality is that patterns of man-made comparative advantage can and do change over time. The economist Jagdish Bhagwati has labeled this phenomenon "kaleidoscopic comparative advantage," and it is critical to understanding offshoring. Once upon a time, the United Kingdom had a comparative advantage in textile manufacturing. Then that advantage shifted to New England, and so jobs were moved from the United Kingdom to the United States. Then the comparative advantage shifted once again—this time to the Carolinas—and jobs migrated south within the United States. Now the comparative advantage in textile manufacturing resides in China and other low-wage countries, and what many are wont to call "American jobs" have been moved there as a result.

Of course, not everything can be traded across long distances. At any point in time, the available technology—especially in transportation and communications—largely determines what can be traded internationally and what cannot. Economic theorists accordingly divide the world's goods and services into two bins: tradable and nontradable. Traditionally, any item that could be put in a box and shipped (roughly, manufactured goods) was considered tradable, and anything that could not be put in a box (such as services) or was too heavy to ship (such as houses) was thought of as nontradable. But because technology is always improving and transportation is becoming cheaper and easier, the boundary between what is tradable and what is not is constantly shifting. And unlike comparative advantage, this change is not kaleido-scopic; it moves in only one direction, with more and more items becoming tradable.

The old assumption that if you cannot put it in a box, you cannot trade it is thus hopelessly obsolete. Because packets of digitized information play the role that boxes used to play, many more services are now tradable and many more will surely become so. In the future, and to a great extent already, the key distinction will no longer be between things that can be put in a box and things that cannot. Rather, it will be between services that can be delivered electronically and those that cannot.

THE THREE INDUSTRIAL REVOLUTIONS

Adam Smith wrote *The Wealth of Nations* in 1776, at the beginning of the first Industrial Revolution. Although Smith's vision was extraordinary, even he did not imagine what was to come. As workers in the industrializing countries migrated from farm to factory, societies were transformed beyond recognition. The shift was massive. It has been estimated that in 1810, 84 percent of the U.S. work force was engaged in agriculture, compared to a paltry 3 percent in manufacturing. By 1960, manufacturing's share had risen to almost 25 percent and agriculture's had dwindled to just 8 percent. (Today, agriculture's share is under 2 percent.) How and where people lived, how they educated their children, the organization of businesses, the forms and practices of government—all changed dramatically in order to accommodate this new reality.

Then came the second Industrial Revolution, and jobs shifted once again—this time away from manufacturing and toward services. The shift to services is still viewed with alarm in the United States and many other rich countries, where people bemoan rather than welcome the resulting loss of manufacturing jobs. But in reality, new service-sector jobs have been created far more rapidly than old manufacturing jobs have disappeared. In 1960, about 35 percent of nonagricultural workers in the United States produced goods and 65 percent produced services. By 2004, only about one-sixth of the United States' nonagricultural jobs were in goods-producing industries, while five-sixths produced services. This trend is worldwide and continuing. Between 1967 and 2003, according to the Organization for Economic Cooperation and Development, the service sector's share of total jobs increased by about 19 percentage points in the United States, 21 points in Japan, and roughly 25 points in France, Italy, and the United Kingdom.

We are now in the early stages of a third Industrial Revolution—the information age. The cheap and easy flow of information around the globe has vastly expanded the scope of tradable services, and there is much more to come. Industrial revolutions are big deals. And just like the previous two, the third Industrial Revolution will require vast and unsettling adjustments in the way Americans and residents of other developed countries work, live, and educate their children.

But a bit of historical perspective should help temper fears of offshoring. The first Industrial Revolution did not spell the end of agriculture, or even the end of food production, in the United States. It just meant that a much smaller percentage of Americans had to work on farms to feed the population. (By charming historical coincidence, the actual number of Americans working on farms today—around 2 million—is about what it was in 1810.) The main reason for this shift was not foreign trade, but soaring farm productivity. And most important, the massive movement of labor off the farms did not result in mass unemployment. Rather, it led to a large-scale reallocation of labor to factories.

Similarly, the second Industrial Revolution has not meant the end of manufacturing, even in the United States, which is running ahead of the rest of the world in the shift toward services. The share of the U.S. work force engaged in manufacturing has fallen dramatically since 1960, but the number of manufacturing workers has declined only modestly. Three main forces have driven this change. First, rising productivity in the manufacturing sector has enabled the production of more and more goods with less and less labor. Second, as people around the world have gotten richer, consumer tastes have changed, with consumers choosing to spend a greater share of their incomes on services (such as restaurant meals and vacations) and a smaller share on goods (such as clothing and refrigerators). Third, the United States now imports a much larger share of the manufactured goods it consumes than it did 50 years ago. All told, the share of manufacturing in U.S. GDP declined from a peak near 30 percent in 1953 to under 13 percent in 2004. That may be the simplest quantitative indicator of the massive extent of the second Industrial Revolution to date. But as with the first Industrial Revolution, the shift has not caused widespread unemployment.

The third Industrial Revolution will play out similarly over the next several decades. The kinds of jobs that can be moved offshore will not disappear entirely from the United States or other rich countries, but their shares of the work force will shrink dramatically. And this reduction will transform societies in many ways, most of them hard to foresee, as workers in rich countries find other things to do. But just as with the first two industrial revolutions, massive offshoring will not lead to massive unemployment. In fact, the world gained enormously from the first two industrial revolutions, and it is likely to do so from the third—so long as it makes the necessary economic and social adjustments.

THIS TIME IT'S PERSONAL

What sorts of jobs are at risk of being offshored? In the old days, when tradable goods were things that could be put in a box, the key distinction was between manufacturing and nonmanufacturing jobs. Consistent with that, manufacturing workers in the rich countries have grown accustomed to the idea that they compete with foreign labor. But as the domain of tradable services expands, many service workers will also have to accept the new, and not very pleasant, reality that they too must compete with workers in other countries. And there are many more service than manufacturing workers.

Many people blithely assume that the critical labor-market distinction is, and will remain, between highly educated (or highly skilled) people and less-educated (or less-skilled) people—doctors versus call-center operators, for example. The supposed remedy for the rich countries, accordingly, is more education and a general "upskilling" of the work force. But this view may be mistaken. Other things being equal, education and skills are, of course, good things; education yields higher returns in advanced societies, and more schooling probably makes workers more flexible and more adaptable to change. But the problem with relying on education as the remedy for potential job losses is that "other things" are not remotely close to equal. The critical divide in the future may instead be between those types of work that are easily deliverable through a wire (or via wireless connections) with little or no diminution in quality and those that are not. And this unconventional divide does not correspond well to traditional distinctions between jobs that require high levels of education and jobs that do not.

A few disparate examples will illustrate just how complex—or, rather, how untraditional—the new divide is. It is unlikely that the services of either taxi drivers or airline pilots will ever be delivered electronically over long distances. The first is a "bad job" with negligible educational requirements; the second is quite the reverse. On the other hand, typing services (a low-skill job) and security analysis (a high-skill job) are already being delivered electronically from India—albeit on a small scale so far. Most physicians need not fear that their jobs will be moved offshore, but radiologists are beginning to see this happening already. Police officers will not be replaced by electronic monitoring, but some security guards will be. Janitors and crane operators are probably immune to foreign competition; accountants and computer programmers are not. In short, the dividing line between the jobs that produce services that are suitable for electronic delivery (and are thus threatened by offshoring) and those that do not does not correspond to traditional distinctions between high-end and low-end work.

The fraction of service jobs in the United States and other rich countries that can potentially be moved offshore is certain to rise as technology improves and as countries such as China and India continue to modernize, prosper, and educate their work forces. Eventually, the number of service-sector jobs that will be vulnerable to competition from abroad will likely exceed the total number of manufacturing jobs. Thus, coping with foreign competition, currently a concern for only a minority of workers in rich countries, will become a major concern for many more.

There is currently not even a vocabulary, much less any systematic data, to help society come to grips with the coming labor-market reality. So here is some suggested nomenclature. Services that cannot be delivered electronically, or that are notably inferior when so delivered, have one essential characteristic: personal, face-to-face contact is either imperative or highly desirable. Think of the waiter who serves you dinner, the doctor who gives you your annual physical, or the cop on the beat. Now think of any of those tasks being performed by robots controlled from India—not quite the same. But such face-to-face human contact is not necessary in the relationship you have with the telephone operator who arranges your conference call or the clerk who takes your airline reservation over the phone. He or she may be in India already.

The first group of tasks can be called personally delivered services, or simply personal services, and the second group impersonally delivered services, or impersonal services. In the brave new world of globalized electronic commerce, impersonal services have more in common with manufactured goods that can be put in boxes than they do with personal services. Thus, many impersonal services are destined to become tradable and therefore vulnerable to offshoring. By contrast, most personal services have attributes that cannot be transmitted through a wire. Some require face-to-face contact (child care), some are inherently "high-touch" (nursing), some involve high levels of personal trust (psychotherapy), and some depend on location specific attributes (lobbying).

However, the dividing line between personal and impersonal services will move over time. As information technology improves, more and more personal services will become impersonal services. No one knows how far this process will go. . . .

To obtain a ballpark figure of the number of U.S. jobs threatened by offshoring, consider the composition of the U.S. labor market at the end of 2004. There were 14.3 million manufacturing jobs. The vast majority of those workers produced items that could be put in a box, and so virtually all of their jobs were potentially movable offshore. About 7.6 million Americans worked in construction and mining. Even though these people produced goods, not services, their jobs were not in danger of moving offshore. (You can't hammer a nail over the Internet.) Next, there were 22 million local, state, and federal government jobs. Even though many of these jobs provide impersonal services that need not be delivered face to face, hardly any are candidates for offshoring—for obvious political reasons. Retail trade employed 15.6 million Americans. Most of these jobs require physical presence, although online retailing is increasing its share of the market, making a growing share of retail jobs vulnerable to offshoring as well.

Those are the easy cases. But the classification so far leaves out the majority of private-service jobs—some 73.6 million at the end of 2004. This extremely heterogeneous group breaks down into educational and health services (17.3 million), professional and business services (16.7 million), leisure and hospitality services (12.3 million), financial services (8.1 million), wholesale trade (5.7 million), transportation (4.3 million), information services (3.2 million), utilities (0.6 million), and "other services" (5.4 million). It is hard to divide such broad job categories into personal and impersonal services, and it is even more difficult to know what possibilities for long-distance electronic delivery the future will bring. Still, it is possible to get a rough sense of which of these jobs may be vulnerable to offshoring.

The health sector is currently about five times as large as the educational sector, and the vast majority of services in the health sector seem destined to be delivered in person for a very long time (if not forever). But there are exceptions, such as radiology. More generally, laboratory tests are already outsourced by most physicians. Why not out of the country rather than just out of town? And with a little imagination, one can envision other medical procedures being performed by doctors who are thousands of miles away. Indeed, some surgery has already been performed by robots controlled by doctors via fiber-optic links.

Educational services are also best delivered face to face, but they are becoming increasingly expensive. Electronic delivery will probably never replace personal contact in K–12 education, which is where the vast majority of the educational jobs are. But college teaching is more vulnerable. As college tuition grows evermore expensive, cheap electronic delivery will start looking more and more sensible, if not imperative.

The range of professional- and business-service jobs includes everything from CEOs and architects to typists and janitors—a heterogeneous lot. That said, in scanning the list of detailed subcategories, it appears that many of these jobs are at least potentially offshorable. For example, future technological developments may dictate how much accounting stays onshore and how much comes to be delivered electronically from countries with much lower wages.

The leisure and hospitality industries seem much safer. If you vacation in Florida, you do not want the beachboy or the maid to be in China. Reservation clerks can be (and are) located anywhere. But on balance, only a few of these jobs can be moved offshore.

Financial services, a sector that includes many highly paid jobs, is another area where the future may look very different from the present. Today, the United States "onshores" more financial jobs (by selling financial services to foreigners) than it offshores. Perhaps that will remain true for years. But improvements in telecommunications and rising educational levels in countries such as China and, especially, India (where many people speak English) may change the status quo dramatically.

Wholesale trade is much like retail trade, but with a bit less personal contact and thus somewhat greater potential for offshoring. The same holds true for transportation and utilities. Information service jobs, however, are the quintessential types of jobs that can be delivered electronically with ease. The majority of these jobs are at risk. Finally, the phrase "other services" is not very informative, but detailed scrutiny of the list (repair and laundry workers appear, for example) reveals that most of these services require personal delivery.

The overall picture defies generalization, but a rough estimate, based on the preceding numbers, is that the total number of current U.S. service-sector jobs that will be susceptible to offshoring in the electronic future is two to three times the total number of current manufacturing jobs (which is about 14 million). That said, large swaths of the U.S. labor market look to be immune. But, of course, no one knows exactly what technological changes the future will bring.

A DISEASE WITHOUT A CURE

One additional piece of economic analysis will complete the story, and in a somewhat worrisome way. Economists refer to the "cost disease" of the personal services as Baumol's disease, after the economist who discovered it, William Baumol. The problem stems from the fact that in many personal services, productivity improvements are either impossible or highly undesirable. In the "impossible" category think of how many musician hours it took to play one of Mozart's string quartets in 1790 versus in 1990, or how many bus drivers it takes to get children to school today versus a generation ago. In the "undesirable" category, think of school teachers. Their productivity can be increased rather easily: by raising class size, which squeezes more student output from the same teacher input. But most people view such "productivity improvements" as deteriorations in educational quality, a view that is well supported by research findings. With little room for genuine productivity improvements, and with the general level of real wages rising all the time, personal services are condemned to grow ever more expensive (relative to other items) over time. That is the essence of Baumol's disease.

No such problem besets manufacturing. Over the years, automakers, to take one example, have drastically reduced the number of labor hours it takes to build a car—a gain in productivity that has not come at the expense of quality. Here once again, impersonal services are more like manufactured goods than personal services. Thanks to stunning advances in telecommunications technology, for example, your telephone company now handles vastly more calls with many fewer human operators than it needed a generation ago. And the quality of telephony has improved, not declined, as its relative price has plummeted.

The prediction of Baumol's disease—that the prices of personal services (such as education and entertainment) will rise relative to the prices of manufactured goods and impersonal services (such as cars and telephone calls)—is borne out by history. For example, the theory goes a long way toward explaining why the prices of health care and college tuition have risen faster than the consumer price index for decades.

Constantly rising relative prices have predictable consequences. Demand curves slope downward—meaning that the demand for an item declines as its relative price rises. Applied in this context, this should mean decreasing relative demand for many personal services and increasing relative demand for many goods and impersonal services over time. The main exceptions are personal services that are strong "luxury goods" (as people get richer, they want relatively more of them) and those few goods and impersonal services that economists call "inferior" (as people get richer, they want fewer of them).

Baumol's disease connects to the offshoring problem in a rather disconcerting way. Changing trade patterns will keep most personal service jobs at home while many jobs producing goods and impersonal services migrate to the developing world. When you add to that the likelihood that the demand for many of the increasingly costly personal services is destined to shrink relative to the demand for ever-cheaper impersonal services and manufactured goods, rich countries are likely to have some major readjustments to make. One of the adjustments will involve reallocating labor from one industry to another. But another will show up in real wages. As more and more rich-country workers seek employment in personal services, real wages for those jobs are likely to decline, unless the offset from rising demand is strong enough. Thus, the wage prognosis is brighter for luxury personal-service jobs (such as plastic surgery and chauffeuring) than for ordinary personal service jobs (such as cutting hair and teaching elementary school).

IS FOREWARNED FOREARMED?

What is to be done about all of this? It is easier to describe the broad contours of a solution than to prescribe specific remedies. Indeed, this essay is intended to get as many smart people as possible thinking creatively about the problem.

Most obvious is what to avoid: protectionist barriers against offshoring. Building walls against conventional trade in physical goods is hard enough. Humankind's natural propensity to truck and barter, plus the power of comparative advantage, tends to undermine such efforts—which not only end in failure but also cause wide-ranging collateral damage. But it is vastly harder (read "impossible") to stop electronic trade. There are just too many "ports" to monitor. The Coast Guard cannot interdict "shipments" of electronic services delivered via the Internet. Governments could probably do a great deal of harm by trying to block such trade, but in the end they would not succeed in repealing the laws of economics, nor in holding back the forces of history. What, then, are some more constructive—and promising—approaches to limiting the disruption?

In the first place, rich countries such as the United States will have to reorganize the nature of work to exploit their big advantage in nontradable services: that they are close to where the money is. That will mean, in part, specializing more in the delivery of services where personal presence is either imperative or highly beneficial. Thus, the U.S. work force of the future will likely have more divorce lawyers and fewer attorneys who write routine contracts, more internists and fewer radiologists, more salespeople and fewer typists. The market system is very good at making adjustments like these, even massive ones. It has done so before and will do so again. But it takes time and can move in unpredictable ways. Furthermore, massive transformations in the nature of work tend to bring wrenching social changes in their wake.

In the second place, the United States and other rich nations will have to transform their educational systems so as to prepare workers for the jobs that will actually exist in their societies. Basically, that requires training more workers for personal services and fewer for many impersonal services and manufacturing. But what does that mean, concretely, for how children should be educated? Simply providing more education is probably a good thing on balance, especially if a more educated labor force is a more flexible labor force, one that can cope more readily with nonroutine tasks and occupational change. However, education is far from a panacea, and the examples given earlier show that the rich countries will retain many jobs that require little education. In the future, how children are educated may prove to be more important than how much. But educational specialists have not even begun to think about this problem. They should start right now.

Contrary to what many have come to believe in recent years, people skills may become more valuable than computer skills. The geeks may not inherit the earth after all—at least not the highly paid geeks in the rich countries. Creativity will be prized. Thomas Friedman has rightly emphasized that it is necessary to steer youth away from tasks that are routine or prone to routinization into work that requires real imagination. Unfortunately, creativity and imagination are notoriously difficult to teach in schools—although, in this respect, the United States does seem to have a leg up on countries such as Germany and Japan. Moreover, it is hard to imagine that truly creative positions will ever constitute anything close to the majority of jobs. What will everyone else do?

One other important step for rich countries is to rethink the currently inadequate programs for trade adjustment assistance. Up to now, the performance of trade adjustment assistance has been disappointing. As more and more Americans—and Britons, and Germans, and Japanese—are faced with the necessity of adjusting to the dislocations caused by offshoring, these programs must become both bigger and better.

Thinking about adjustment assistance more broadly, the United States may have to repair and thicken the tattered safety net that supports workers who fall off the labor-market trapeze—improving programs ranging from unemployment insurance to job retraining, health insurance, pensions, and right down to public assistance. At present, the United States has one of the thinnest social safety nets in the industrialized world, and there seems to be little if any political force seeking to improve it. But this may change if a larger fraction of the population starts falling into the safety net more often. The corresponding problem for western Europe is different. By U.S. standards, the social safety nets there are broad and deep. The question is, are they affordable, even now? And if so, will they remain affordable if they come to be utilized more heavily?

To repeat, none of this is to suggest that there will be massive unemployment; rather, there will be a massive transition. An effective safety net would ease the pain and, by so doing, speed up the adjustment.

IMPERFECT VISION

Despite all the political sound and fury, little service-sector offshoring has happened to date. But it may eventually amount to a third Industrial Revolution, and industrial revolutions have a way of transforming societies.

That said, the "threat" from offshoring should not be exaggerated. Just as the first Industrial Revolution did not banish agriculture from the rich countries, and the second Industrial Revolution has not banished manufacturing, so the third Industrial Revolution will not drive all impersonal services offshore. Nor will it lead to mass unemployment. But the necessary adjustments will put strains on the societies of the rich countries, which seem completely unprepared for the coming industrial transformation.

Perhaps the most acute need, given the long lead-times, is to figure out how to educate children now for the jobs that will actually be available to them 10 and 20 years from now. Unfortunately, since the distinction between personal services (likely to remain in rich countries) and impersonal services (likely to go) does not correspond to the traditional distinction between high-skilled and low-skilled work, simply providing more education cannot be the whole answer.

As the transition unfolds, the number of people in the rich countries who will feel threatened by foreign job competition will grow enormously. It is predictable that they will become a potent political force in each of their countries. In the United States, job-market stress up to now has been particularly acute for the uneducated and the unskilled, who are less inclined to exercise their political voice and less adept at doing so. But the new cadres of displaced workers, especially those who are drawn from the upper educational reaches, will be neither as passive nor as quiet. They will also be numerous. Open trade may therefore be under great strain.

Large-scale offshoring of impersonal-service jobs from rich countries to poor countries may also bear on the relative economic positions of the United States and Europe. The more flexible, fluid American labor market will probably adapt more quickly and more successfully to dramatic workplace and educational changes than the more rigid European labor markets will.

Contrary to current thinking, Americans, and residents of other English-speaking countries, should be less concerned about the challenge from China, which comes largely in manufacturing, and more concerned about the challenge from India, which comes in services. India is learning to exploit its already strong comparative advantage in English, and that process will continue. The economists Jagdish Bhagwati, Arvind Panagariya, and T. N. Srinivasan meant to reassure Americans when they wrote, "Adding 300 million to the pool of skilled workers in India and China will take some decades." They were probably right. But decades is precisely the free frame that people should be thinking about—and 300 million people is roughly twice the size of the U.S. work force.

Many other effects of the coming industrial transformation are difficult to predict, or even to imagine. Take one possibility: for decades, it has seemed that modern economic life is characterized by the ever more dehumanized workplace parodied by Charlie Chaplin in *Modern Times*. The shift to personal services could well reverse that trend for rich countries—bringing less alienation and greater overall job satisfaction. Alas, the future retains its mystery. But in any case, offshoring will likely prove to be much more than just business as usual.

mypoliscikit Exercises for The Nature of Globalization

Apply what you learned in this chapter by using the online resources on MyPoliSciKit (www.mypoliscikit.com).

 Practice Tests

 Videos:
- "Brazil's Biofuel Boom"
- "China's New Middle Class"

 Simulation:
- "International Development: You Are the Minister of Trade and Finance"
- "International Trade: You Are a Trade Expert"

 Reading Guides:
- Jeffrey Frankel, "Globalization of the Economy"
- Pankaj Ghemawat, "Why the World Isn't Flat"
- Alan S. Blinder, "Offshoring: The Next Industrial Revolution?"

CRITICS
OF GLOBALIZATION

Trading in Illusions

DANI RODRIK

A senior U.S. Treasury official recently urged Mexico's government to work harder to reduce violent crime because "such high levels of crime and violence may drive away foreign investors." This admonition nicely illustrates how foreign trade and investment have become the ultimate yardstick for evaluating the social and economic policies of governments in developing countries. Forget the slum dwellers or *campesinos* who live amidst crime and poverty throughout the developing world. Just mention "investor sentiment" or "competitiveness in world markets" and policymakers will come to attention in a hurry.

Underlying this perversion of priorities is a remarkable consensus on the imperative of global economic integration. Openness to trade and investment flows is no longer viewed simply as a component of a country's development strategy; it has mutated into the most potent catalyst for economic growth known to humanity. Predictably, senior officials of the World Trade Organization (WTO), International Monetary Fund (IMF), and other international financial agencies incessantly repeat the openness mantra. In recent years, however, faith in integration has spread quickly to political leaders and policymakers around the world.

Joining the world economy is no longer a matter simply of dismantling barriers to trade and investment. Countries now must also comply with a long list of admission requirements, from new patent rules to more rigorous banking standards. The apostles of economic integration prescribe comprehensive institutional reforms that took today's advanced countries generations to accomplish, so that developing countries can, as the cliché goes, maximize the gains and minimize the risks of

From Dani Rodrik, "Trading in Illusions," *Foreign Policy,* issue #123 (March/April 2001), pp. 54–62. © 2001 by the Carnegie Endowment for International Peace. Reprinted with permission. www .foreignpolicy.com.

participation in the world economy. Global integration has become, for all practical purposes, a substitute for a development strategy.

This trend is bad news for the world's poor. The new agenda of global integration rests on shaky empirical ground and seriously distorts policymakers' priorities. By focusing on international integration, governments in poor nations divert human resources, administrative capabilities, and political capital away from more urgent development priorities such as education, public health, industrial capacity, and social cohesion. This emphasis also undermines nascent democratic institutions by removing the choice of development strategy from public debate.

World markets are a source of technology and capital; it would be silly for the developing world not to exploit these opportunities. But globalization is not a shortcut to development. Successful economic growth strategies have always required a judicious blend of imported practices with domestic institutional innovations. Policymakers need to forge a domestic growth strategy by relying on domestic investors and domestic institutions. The costliest downside of the integrationist faith is that it crowds out serious thinking and efforts along such lines.

EXCUSES, EXCUSES

Countries that have bought wholeheartedly into the integration orthodoxy are discovering that openness does not deliver on its promise. Despite sharply lowering their barriers to trade and investment since the 1980s, scores of countries in Latin America and Africa are stagnating or growing less rapidly than in the heyday of import substitution during the 1960s and 1970s. By contrast, the fastest growing countries are China, India, and others in East and Southeast Asia. Policymakers in these countries have also espoused trade and investment liberalization, but they have done so in an unorthodox manner—gradually, sequentially, and only after an initial period of high growth—and as part of a broader policy package with many unconventional features.

The disappointing outcomes with deep liberalization have been absorbed into the faith with remarkable aplomb. Those who view global integration as the prerequisite for economic development now simply add the caveat that opening borders is insufficient. Reaping the gains from openness, they argue, also requires a full complement of institutional reforms.

Consider trade liberalization. Asking any World Bank economist what a successful trade-liberalization program requires will likely elicit a laundry list of measures beyond the simple reduction of tariff and nontariff barriers: tax reform to make up for lost tariff revenues; social safety nets to compensate displaced workers; administrative reform to bring trade practices into compliance with WTO rules; labor market reform to enhance worker mobility across industries; technological assistance to upgrade firms hurt by import competition; and training programs to ensure that export-oriented firms and investors have access to skilled workers. As the promise of trade liberalization fails to materialize, the prerequisites keep expanding. For example, Clare Short, Great Britain's secretary of state for international development, recently added universal provision of health and education to the list.

In the financial arena, integrationists have pushed complementary reforms with even greater fanfare and urgency. The prevailing view in Washington and other Group of Seven (G-7) capitals is that weaknesses in banking systems, prudential regulation, and corporate governance were at the heart of the Asian financial crisis of the late 1990s. Hence the ambitious efforts by the G-7 to establish international codes and standards covering fiscal transparency, monetary and financial policy, banking supervision, data dissemination, corporate governance, and accounting standards. The Financial Stability Forum (FSF)—a G-7 organization with minimal representation from developing nations—has designated 12 of these standards as essential for creating sound financial systems in developing countries. The full FSF compendium includes an additional 59 standards the agency considers "relevant for sound financial systems," bringing the total number of codes to 71. To fend off speculative capital movements, the IMF and G-7 also typically urge developing countries to accumulate foreign reserves and avoid exchange-rate regimes that differ from a "hard peg" (tying the value of one's currency to that of a more stable currency, such as the U.S. dollar) or a "pure float" (letting the market determine the appropriate exchange rate).

A cynic might wonder whether the point of all these prerequisites is merely to provide easy cover for eventual failure. Integrationists can conveniently blame disappointing growth performance or a financial crisis on "slippage" in the implementation of complementary reforms rather than on a poorly designed liberalization. So if Bangladesh's freer trade policy does not produce a large enough spurt in growth, the World Bank concludes that the problem must involve lagging reforms in public administration or continued "political uncertainty" (always a favorite). And if Argentina gets caught up in a confidence crisis despite significant trade and financial liberalization, the IMF reasons that structural reforms have been inadequate and must be deepened.

FREE TRADE-OFFS

Most (but certainly not all) of the institutional reforms on the integrationist agenda are perfectly sensible, and in a world without financial, administrative, or political constraints, there would be little argument about the need to adopt them. But in the real world, governments face difficult choices over how to deploy their fiscal resources, administrative capabilities, and political capital. Setting institutional priorities to maximize integration into the global economy has real opportunity costs.

Consider some illustrative trade-offs. World Bank trade economist Michael Finger has estimated that a typical developing country must spend $150 million to implement requirements under just three WTO agreements (those on customs valuation, sanitary and phytosanitary measures, and trade-related intellectual property rights). As Finger notes, this sum equals a year's development budget for many least-developed countries. And while the budgetary burden of implementing financial codes and standards has never been fully estimated, it undoubtedly entails a substantial diversion of fiscal and human resources as well. Should governments in developing countries train more bank auditors and accountants, even if those investments mean fewer secondary-school teachers or reduced spending on primary education for girls?

In the area of legal reform, should governments focus their energies on "importing" legal codes and standards or on improving existing domestic legal institutions? In Turkey, a weak coalition government spent several months during 1999 gathering political support for a bill providing foreign investors the protection of international arbitration. But wouldn't a better long-run strategy have involved reforming the existing legal regime for the benefit of foreign and domestic investors alike?

In public health, should governments promote the reverse engineering of patented basic medicines and the importation of low-cost generic drugs from "unauthorized" suppliers, even if doing so means violating WTO rules against such practices? When South Africa passed legislation in 1997 allowing imports of patented AIDS drugs from cheaper sources, the country came under severe pressure from Western governments, which argued that the South African policy conflicted with WTO rules on intellectual property.

How much should politicians spend on social protection policies in view of the fiscal constraints imposed by market "discipline"? Peru's central bank holds foreign reserves equal to 15 months of imports as an insurance policy against the sudden capital outflows that financially open economies often experience. The opportunity cost of this policy amounts to almost 1 percent of gross domestic product annually—more than enough to fund a generous antipoverty program.

How should governments choose their exchange-rate regimes? During the last four decades, virtually every growth boom in the developing world has been accompanied by a controlled depreciation of the domestic currency. Yet financial openness makes it all but impossible to manage the exchange rate.

How should policymakers focus their anticorruption strategies? Should they target the high-level corruption that foreign investors often decry or the petty corruption that affects the poor the most? Perhaps, as the proponents of permanent normal trade relations with China argued in the recent U.S. debate, a government that is forced to protect the rights of foreign investors will become more inclined to protect the rights of its own citizens as well. But this is, at best, a trickledown strategy of institutional reform. Shouldn't reforms target the desired ends directly—whether those ends are the rule of law, improved observance of human rights, or reduced corruption?

The rules for admission into the world economy not only reflect little awareness of development priorities, they are often completely unrelated to sensible economic principles. For instance, WTO agreements on anti-dumping, subsidies and countervailing measures, agriculture, textiles, and trade-related intellectual property rights lack any economic rationale beyond the mercantilist interests of a narrow set of powerful groups in advanced industrial countries. Bilateral and regional trade agreements are typically far worse, as they impose even tighter prerequisites on developing countries in return for crumbs of enhanced "market access." For example, the African Growth and Opportunity Act signed by U.S. President Clinton in May 2000 provides increased access to the U.S. market only if African apparel manufacturers use U.S.-produced fabric and yarns. This restriction severely limits the potential economic spillovers in African countries.

There are similar questions about the appropriateness of financial codes and standards. These codes rely heavily on an Anglo-American style of corporate governance and an arm's-length model of financial development. They close off alternative paths to financial development of the sort that have been followed by many of today's rich countries (for example, Germany, Japan, or South Korea).

In each of these areas, a strategy of "globalization above all" crowds out alternatives that are potentially more development-friendly. Many of the institutional reforms needed for insertion into the world economy can be independently desirable or produce broader economic benefits. But these priorities do not necessarily coincide with the priorities of a comprehensive development agenda.

ASIAN MYTHS

Even if the institutional reforms needed to join the international economic community are expensive and preclude investments in other crucial areas, pro-globalization advocates argue that the vast increases in economic growth that invariably result from insertion into the global marketplace will more than compensate for those costs. Take the East Asian tigers or China, the advocates say. Where would they be without international trade and foreign capital flows?

That these countries reaped enormous benefits from their progressive integration into the world economy is undeniable. But look closely at what policies produced those results, and you will find little that resembles today's rule book.

Countries like South Korea and Taiwan had to abide by few international constraints and pay few of the modern costs of integration during their formative growth experience in the 1960s and 1970s. At that time, global trade rules were sparse and economies faced almost none of today's common pressures to open their borders to capital flows. So these countries combined their outward orientation with unorthodox policies: high levels of tariff and non-tariff barriers, public ownership of large segments of banking and industry, export subsidies, domestic-content requirements, patent and copyright infringements, and restrictions on capital flows (including on foreign direct investment). Such policies are either precluded by today's trade rules or are highly frowned upon by organizations like the IMF and the World Bank.

China also followed a highly unorthodox two-track strategy, violating practically every rule in the guidebook (including, most notably, the requirement of private property rights). India, which significantly raised its economic growth rate in the early 1980s, remains one of the world's most highly protected economies.

All of these countries liberalized trade gradually, over a period of decades, not years. Significant import liberalization did not occur until after a transition to high economic growth had taken place. And far from wiping the institutional slate clean, all of these nations managed to eke growth out of their existing institutions, imperfect as they may have been. Indeed, when some of the more successful Asian economies gave in to Western pressure to liberalize capital flows rapidly, they were rewarded with the Asian financial crisis.

That is why these countries can hardly be considered poster children for today's global rules. South Korea, China, India, and the other Asian success cases had the freedom to do their own thing, and they used that freedom abundantly. Today's globalizers would be unable to replicate these experiences without running afoul of the IMF or the WTO.

The Asian experience highlights a deeper point: A sound overall development strategy that produces high economic growth is far more effective in achieving integration with the world economy than a purely integrationist strategy that relies on openness to work its magic. In other words, the globalizers have it exactly backwards. Integration is the result, not the cause, of economic and social development. A relatively protected economy like Vietnam is integrating with the world economy much more rapidly than an open economy like Haiti because Vietnam, unlike Haiti, has a reasonably functional economy and polity.

Integration into the global economy, unlike tariff rates or capital-account regulations, is not something that policymakers control directly. Telling finance ministers in developing nations that they should increase their "participation in world trade" is as meaningful as telling them that they need to improve technological capabilities—and just as helpful. Policymakers need to know which strategies will produce these results, and whether the specific prescriptions that the current orthodoxy offers are up to the task.

TOO GOOD TO BE TRUE

Do lower trade barriers spur greater economic progress? The available studies reveal no systematic relationship between a country's average level of tariff and nontariff barriers and its subsequent economic growth rate. If anything, the evidence for the 1990s indicates a positive relationship between import tariffs and economic growth [see chart]. The only clear pattern is that countries dismantle their trade restrictions as they grow richer. This finding explains why today's rich countries, with few exceptions, embarked on modern economic growth behind protective barriers but now display low trade barriers.

The absence of a strong negative relationship between trade restrictions and economic growth may seem surprising in view of the ubiquitous claim that trade liberalization promotes higher growth. Indeed, the economics literature is replete with cross-national studies concluding that growth and economic dynamism are strongly linked to more open trade policies. A particularly influential study finds that economies that are "open," by the study's own definition, grew 2.45 percentage points faster annually than closed ones—an enormous difference.

Upon closer look, however, such studies turn out to be unreliable. In a detailed review of the empirical literature, University of Maryland economist Francisco Rodríguez and I found a major gap between the results that economists have actually obtained and the policy conclusions they have typically drawn. For example, in many cases economists blame poor growth on the government's failure to liberalize trade policies, when the true culprits are ineffective institutions, geographic determinants (such as location in a tropical region), or inappropriate macroeconomic policies (such as an overvalued exchange rate). Once these misdiagnoses are corrected, any meaningful relationship across countries between the level of trade barriers and economic growth evaporates.

The evidence on the benefits of liberalizing capital flows is even weaker. In theory, the appeal of capital mobility seems obvious: If capital is free to enter (and leave) markets based on the potential return on investment, the result will be an efficient allocation of global resources. But in reality, financial markets are inherently unstable, subject to bubbles (rational or otherwise), panics, shortsightedness, and self-fulfilling prophecies. There is plenty of evidence that financial liberalization is often followed by financial crash—just ask Mexico, Thailand, or Turkey—while there is little convincing evidence to suggest that higher rates of economic growth follow capital-account liberalization.

Perhaps the most disingenuous argument in favor of liberalizing international financial flows is that the threat of massive and sudden capital movements serves to discipline policymakers in developing nations who might otherwise manage their economies irresponsibly. In other words, governments might be less inclined to squander their societies' resources if such actions would spook foreign lenders. In practice, however, the discipline argument falls apart. Behavior in international capital markets is dominated by mood swings unrelated to fundamentals. In good times, a government with a chronic fiscal deficit has an easier time financing its spending when it can borrow funds from investors abroad; witness Russia prior to 1998 or Argentina in the 1990s. And in bad times, governments may be forced to adopt inappropriate policies in order to conform to the biases of foreign investors; witness the excessively restrictive monetary and fiscal policies in much of East Asia in the immediate aftermath of the Asian financial crisis. A key reason why Malaysia was able to recover so quickly after the imposition of capital controls in September 1998 was that Prime Minister Mahathir Mohamad resisted the high interest rates and tight fiscal policies that South Korea, Thailand, and Indonesia adopted at the behest of the International Monetary Fund.

GROWTH BEGINS AT HOME

Well-trained economists are justifiably proud of the textbook case in favor of free trade. For all the theory's simplicity, it is one of our profession's most significant achievements. However, in their zeal to promote the virtues of trade, the most ardent proponents are peddling a cartoon version of the argument, vastly overstating the effectiveness of economic openness as a tool for fostering development.

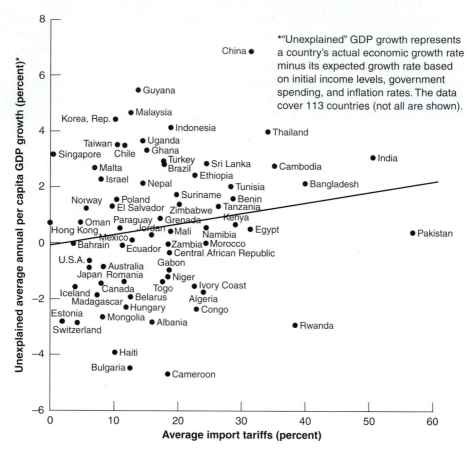

FIGURE 1 ■ High Tariffs Don't Mean Low Growth Gross Domestic Product (GDP) Growth and Tariff Rates, 1990s
Source: Author's calculations based on World Bank data.

Such claims only endanger broad public acceptance of the real article because they unleash unrealistic expectations about the benefits of free trade. Neither economic theory nor empirical evidence guarantees that deep trade liberalization will deliver higher economic growth. Economic openness and all its accouterments do not deserve the priority they typically receive in the development strategies pushed by leading multilateral organizations.

Countries that have achieved long-term economic growth have usually combined the opportunities offered by world markets with a growth strategy that mobilizes the capabilities of domestic institutions and investors. Designing such a growth strategy is both harder and easier than implementing typical integration policies. It is harder because the binding constraints on growth are usually country specific and do not respond well to standardized recipes. But it is easier because once those constraints are targeted, relatively simple policy changes can yield enormous economic payoffs and start a virtuous cycle of growth and additional reform.

Unorthodox innovations that depart from the integration rule book are typically part and parcel of such strategies. Public enterprises during the Meiji restoration in Japan; township and village enterprises in China; an export processing zone in Mauritius; generous tax incentives for priority investments in Taiwan; extensive credit subsidies in South Korea; infant-industry protection in Brazil during the 1960s and 1970s—these are some of the innovations that have been instrumental in kick-starting investment and growth in the past. None came out of a Washington economist's tool kit.

Few of these experiments have worked as well when transplanted to other settings, only underscoring the decisive importance of local conditions. To be effective, development strategies need to be tailored to prevailing domestic institutional strengths. There is simply no alternative to a homegrown business plan. Policymakers who look to Washington and financial markets for the answers are condemning themselves to mimicking the conventional wisdom du jour, and to eventual disillusionment.

Why the Globalization Backlash Is Stupid

JOHN MICKLETHWAIT
AND ADRIAN WOOLDRIDGE

"GLOBALIZATION MEANS THE TRIUMPH OF GIANT COMPANIES"

Nonsense. If you listen to antiglobalists, we live in a world of "Disneyfication" and "Coca-Colonization" in which giant companies simultaneously trample over their smaller commercial rivals and turn national governments into helpless lackeys. They are wrong on both counts.

The proportion of output from big companies has declined, not increased. Globalization radically shifts the balance of advantage from incumbents to challengers. Incumbents could once protect themselves behind lofty barriers such as the high cost of capital, the difficulty of acquiring new technology, or the importance of close relationships with national governments. Globalization reduces the importance of all these things. Lower barriers make capital easier to raise, technology easier to buy, markets easier to reach, and ties with national governments ever less important. You no longer have to be a multinational to have the reach of one.

By all rights, Motorola Inc. ought to be the undisputed ruler of the wireless world. The company was the first to mass-produce car phones. It also sits in the heart of the world's biggest market for them. But it has been humbled by Nokia Corp., a relatively small company from Finland that only a decade ago was more interested in bathroom tissue than mobile phones. Nokia's only weapons were better phones and better management. Against these, mere size proved a puny defense—which helps explain why giants such as AT&T Corp. and General Motors Corp. (GM) now look so vulnerable.

The idea that companies are now more important than governments is equally misleading. Far from getting smaller, governments in most Western countries remain colossal, consuming more than 40 percent of Western Europe's gross domestic product (GDP), for example. They continue to expand their influence over corporate behavior through regulatory policy. Bill Gates rapidly discovered that a rather obscure Justice Department antitrust lawyer, Joel Klein, was a much

From John Micklethwait and Adrian Wooldridge, "The Globalization Backlash," *Foreign Policy,* issue #126 (September/October 2001), pp. 16–28. © 2001 by the Carnegie Endowment for International Peace. Reprinted with permission. www.foreignpolicy.com.

more fearsome opponent than any mere company. Jack Welch, the face of American Big Business, met his Waterloo in Belgium when the similarly anonymous bureaucrats of the European Commission blocked what would have been the biggest merger in history, that between General Electric and Honeywell.

As for the oft-quoted "statistics" about so many companies being bigger than countries—the idea that GM is as big as Denmark—these compare sales figures with GDP. Since GDP measures value added, the correct corporate comparison is profits. As Martin Wolf of the *Financial Times* has pointed out, GM then slides from being as large as the 23rd biggest country to the 55th, about the same size as a basket case like Ukraine.

"GLOBALIZATION IS DESTROYING THE ENVIRONMENT"

Not really. Myth provides a prime example of a conceit that underlies a great deal of antiglobal thinking. Take one self-evident truth that all sensible people can agree upon—business of all sorts tends to despoil the environment. Then repeat that observation in highly emotive language, ignoring all other mitigating factors. Then heap all the blame on global companies, global regulators, and indeed globalization itself, when the bulk of the damage is done by local governments, local companies, and even local voters. And, whatever happens, keep running away from the really hard question: How much is greenery worth?

A good starting point is that almost all business that produces a physical product tends to be dirty. Until relatively recently, businesspeople were reluctant to admit this reality. That not only made them look shifty, it also meant that they never made arguments about the choices involved. For instance, during the furor in 1995 over the offshore disposal of its Brent Spar oil rig, Shell failed to argue with any force that Greenpeace's demand that the rig be disposed of on land was by no means the greener solution.

Nowadays, business, particularly multinational business, is better behaved. Businesspeople have not become softer. They have simply wised up to two things. The first is that dirty factories lose them consumers. The second is that environmental regulations are not prohibitively expensive, particularly for multinationals. A 1990 study by the U.S. Environmental Protection Agency, for instance, found that even the most polluting industries don't have to spend more than 2 percent of their revenues on being good environmental citizens. Go to a ghastly eyesore in the Third World, such as Cubatão, the capital of Brazil's chemical business (once dubbed the most polluted city on earth), and you find that multinational companies tend to be cleaner than their Brazilian counterparts—and keener to abide by international standards.

What about the idea that trade, by increasing business activity generally, harms the environment? This is certainly true in the short term. If open borders increase the market for a chemical factory in Lagos, the factory will create more chemicals. But as countries grow richer, they also tend to clean up their act: An elaborate index of environmental sustainability in 122 countries prepared for the World Economic Forum this year showed a strong correlation between a country's greenness and wealth (though, to be fair, an even stronger one with its lack of corruption). More generally, although environmentalism is a good thing, it must be balanced against other virtues, including, from a developing country's point of view, economic growth. It is patronizing for rich-world greens to decide that Africans should not tolerate dirtier air and water in exchange for more wealth.

Alas, the cost of the environment is nearly always tabulated incorrectly. In China, according to the World Bank, air and water pollution cost $54 billion a year—8 percent of the country's GDP. But it is not the polluting companies that bear this price. For that matter, what incentive do Indian polluters have to stop throwing rubbish into the Ganges that then wrecks Bangladesh's rice paddies? One reason why fish stocks are alarmingly low globally is because the seas of the world provide a textbook example of the "tragedy of the commons." Because nobody owns them, nobody feels responsible for them. If a Norwegian fisherman does not pillage them, then his British rival will. This dynamic is also dramatically evident in the current impasse over global warming.

But blaming these things on globalization seems a spurious way to let local politicians off the hook. The right way to protest, say, George W. Bush's decision to junk the Kyoto Protocol is not to blame "the market," but Bush himself. And how exactly would a less interlinked world help? Global warming would not go away if trade barriers went up. Far from being caused by unfettered capitalism, environmental damage is often caused by exactly the opposite. One reason fishing fleets can continue to ravage the oceans is because governments spend $21 billion a year supporting them. Brazil's government initially spurred on the despoliation of the rain forest. The World-watch Institute reckons that there are $650 billion worth of subsidies going to environmentally destructive activities. On the other hand, globalization sometimes directly benefits the environment by promoting things such as trade in pollution-control technology and the privatization of state-owned companies, which become less polluting as they are restructured.

"GLOBALIZATION MAKES GEOGRAPHY IRRELEVANT"

Wrong again. You might think that the death of distance also means the death of geography. The truth is probably the opposite. If most tangible resources are within anyone's reach, then what matters are the intangible things, which in turn means proximity to people.

The world economy is visibly organizing itself around various clusters of excellence, most obviously Hollywood, Silicon Valley, and Wall Street. The main challenge for companies in a global economy is to situate themselves in various centers of excellence and weave together different centers of excellence into a global production network. The main challenge for communities is to invest in their comparative advantage. Look at the way that Miami has exploited its connections with Latin America. Or the way that the energy cluster in Houston has used its expertise in oil to move into gas, electricity, and energy trading.

The idea that businesses can simply up-sticks and move is also rubbish. Considerable publicity has been given to the few Swedish and German companies that have eventually moved some operations out of their highly taxed homelands; the real story is how long those firms stuck it out. Wander around Los Angeles, America's main manufacturing center, and you will find squadrons of low-tech factories churning out toys, furniture, and clothes, all of which could probably be made cheaper elsewhere. They stay partly for personal reasons (many are family-owned), partly because they can compensate for high labor costs by using more machines, but mostly because Los Angeles is a hub for all three industries—a place where designers, suppliers, and distributors are just around the corner.

Finally, borders remain much more important than many people imagine. Canada and the United States are both English-speaking countries and members of the North American Free Trade Agreement. But the average Canadian province does 12 times as much trade in goods and 40 times as much trade in services with another Canadian province as it does with an American state of the same size and proximity. Similar figures exist for the European Union (EU) countries.

"GLOBALIZATION MEANS AMERICANIZATION"

Not necessarily. True, globalization certainly tilts the playing field in favor of liberal virtues such as accountability, transparency, and individual rights that are often deemed to be American.

Yet does this mean Americanization? Foreign dictators who want to use xenophobia to prop up their positions would no doubt argue that it does. But the United States has no monopoly on liberal virtues. Classical liberalism was first developed by a group of British thinkers—John Locke, David Hume, and Adam Smith. We still use a French phrase, laissez-faire, when we invoke the ideal of a free market economy. The first joint stock company was developed in Britain rather than the United States. Indeed, American democracy was arguably the product of British corporations such as the Virginia Company. For all its bureaucracy, the EU now enshrines liberal values such as democratic representation and individual rights every bit as firmly as the U.S. Constitution.

Certainly, Europe is now moving closer to the Anglo-American shareholder model of capitalism than it had in the immediate postwar years. A popular share-owning culture is slowly putting down roots in Europe. The euro, like the single market before it, is forcing European companies to slim. But these developments do not mean that European companies or European society will become mere facsimiles of America. Europeans will probably continue to put much more emphasis on social solidarity than the United States. France's tight labor laws (including a relatively new 35-hour week) have not stopped its global companies from being competitive, though they have arguably kept its unemployment rate unnecessarily high. The Nordic countries, whose economic performance has matched America's, argue that their well-developed welfare states make their economies more flexible because people are not afraid to change jobs. There are growing signs that Europe (with a potential internal market of 500 million people) is beginning to flex its muscles against the United States, whether it be through vetoing mergers, building its own army, or generally disagreeing with American foreign policy in areas such as the Middle East.

Nor does globalization necessarily mean the Americanization of popular culture. True, American films can be seen almost all over the world, the Big Mac™ is the closest thing we have to a universal food, and Britney Spears is hard to avoid, even if you are in Tibet. But cultural trade is a two-way process. If you look at popular musicals (Andrew Lloyd Webber's) or the bestseller lists (the *Harry Potter* series), Britain continues to exercise a powerful influence on the United States. The most successful programs on American television at the moment are "reality" programs imported from Europe. Foreigners own half of America's top 20 book-publishing houses and half of its film studios. On the whole, consumers have a marked taste for local products, something that is becoming easier to satisfy as technology makes economies of scale less important. The most popular television program in European countries is nearly always a local production. A few years ago hardly any self-respecting European teenager would have been caught listening to local groups. Now France has Air and Sweden has The Cardigans.

But there is a more important reason why globalization does not mean the triumph of a particular nationality. The essence of globalization is that it increases choice. And this includes the choice to live life according to your own lights. A nice example of this is the Bruderhof, a religious group that is rather like the Amish. The Bruderhof reject many features of the modern world. They don't have radios or televisions; they don't approve of feminism and homosexuality. But they have established a highly successful global toy business using a mixture of Japanese management techniques and American technology. The result: They have all the money that they need to keep their community flourishing, but they have not had to abandon their way of life.

"GLOBALIZATION MEANS A RACE TO THE BOTTOM IN LABOR STANDARDS"

No. This argument rests on four misconceptions.

The first is that employers are concerned, above all, with the price of labor. In fact, what really interests them is the value of labor. Some companies will undoubtedly move routine tasks to parts of the world where hourly wages are lower. But in general what employers want is not cheap workers but productive ones. And the most productive workers are usually those with the best education, access to the best machinery, and a support system that includes things like good infrastructure.

If the "race to the bottom" argument were correct, you would expect foreign direct investment (FDI) to be pouring into countries with the lowest wages and the weakest labor standards. Nothing could be further from the truth. The United States is the world's largest recipient of FDI. Year after year the United States has run a net surplus in its capital account (and the inflow of foreign capital has helped to keep interest rates low, build new factories, and bring new production methods to bear on the economy). About 80 percent of U.S. FDI goes to other rich countries. American investment in countries like Mexico and China is a mere fragment of U.S. investment at home.

The second is that globalization is weakening the ties of companies to their home regions. But companies depend on the environment that first created them in all sorts of ways, some obvious, some more subtle. During the Justice Department's investigation of Microsoft, Bill Gates could not have threatened to move his operation to the Bahamas, even though Microsoft has relatively few fixed assets. Microsoft depends not just on a supply of educated workers (who would have refused to move) but also on its close relationship with American universities.

The third idea—that global companies are hostile to "worker protection" such as trade-union rights and labor standards—contains a half-truth. Companies rarely react favorably to unions (or indeed to governments) that want to shackle their freedom of maneuver with inflexible rules about, say, hiring and firing. But, by and large, multinationals are much less hostile to things such as safe working environments, on-the-job training, and opportunities for promotion. Once again, the key factor for companies is boosting productivity rather than lowering the price they pay for labor, so a well-trained and healthy workforce is important. Survey after survey shows multinationals providing higher wages and better working conditions for their employees than their local competitors.

The fourth and largest misconception is that globalization is a zero-sum game: that if the rich are getting richer as a result of globalization, then the poor must be getting poorer. But the argument in favor of globalization is that it can improve the lot of everybody by leading to a more efficient use of resources.

Of course, globalization does not always achieve this goal, and of course it cannot impose efficiency without a certain amount of pain, but in general, globalization improves the living standards of the vast majority of people. In the half century since the foundation of the General Agreement on Tariffs and Trade (GATT), the world economy has grown sixfold, in part because trade has expanded 16-fold. The Organisation for Economic Co-operation and Development calculates that nations that are relatively open to trade grow about twice as fast as those that are relatively closed. Despite the Asian crisis, the World Bank calculates that some 800 million people moved out of absolute poverty in the past decade. And the people left behind still tend to suffer from too little globalization (be it trade barriers to the goods that they produce or restraints on the information they can get at home) rather than too much.

"GLOBALIZATION CONCENTRATES POWER IN UNDEMOCRATIC INSTITUTIONS LIKE THE WTO"

No. Organizations like the World Trade Organization (WTO) and the International Monetary Fund (IMF) are not quite paper tigers. But they are much less powerful than their detractors (and a few of their inmates) imagine. The WTO is essentially an arbitration mechanism: It deals with issues that clashing governments refer to it. The IMF is a crisis management agency. True, it can impose stringent require- ments for structural reforms on its clients, and it has often done so with breathtak- ing arrogance and insensitivity. But governments only resort to the IMF if they are already in serious trouble.

By any conceivable measure, national governments are far more important players in the international order than global institutions. During the Asian crisis, it was the U.S. Treasury Department that decided whether to bail out countries, not the IMF. (And why not? It was writing the checks.) For all the fears in the Ameri- can heartland about the U.N.'s black helicopters, national governments decide whether to send peacekeeping troops. And now the international institutions face a new constraint. The number of international nongovernmental organizations (NGOs) increased from 6,000 in 1990 to 26,000 by the end of the decade. Visit any old-fashioned multilateral institution and you will find it surrounded by NGOs monitoring it. There are 1,700 clustered around the United Nations' offices in Geneva, for example.

Membership of the WTO suggests that globalization is a bottom-up process. When GATT was founded in 1948, it only had 23 contracting parties, most of them industrialized nations; today the WTO has 142 members, more than three quarters of them developing nations, and 20 more countries are eagerly waiting to join. It may be true that the global civil servants who run most international institutions are not directly elected (just as the heads of civil service departments are not directly elected). But they are accountable to national governments, the majority of which are now democracies.

Indeed, you could argue that the real democratic deficit in global institutions is to be found not in the IMF and the WTO but in the NGOs that protest against them. NGOs claim to represent global civil society (whatever that is). But nobody elects them. They are not accountable to democratic governments. They represent nobody but their members and their activist cadres, which in some of the noisiest cases means a few hundred people.

Financial Regime Chang

ROBERT WADE

Since the 1930s the noncommunist world has experienced two shi~
national economic norms and rules substantial enough to be called `i~
changes." They were separated by an interval of roughly thirty years: the firs~
regime, characterized by Keynesianism and governed by the international Bretton
Woods arrangements, lasted from about 1945 to 1975; the second began after the
breakdown of Bretton Woods, and prevailed until the First World debt crisis of
2007–08. This latter regime, known variously as neoliberalism, the Washington
Consensus[1] or the globalization consensus, centred on the notion that all governments should liberalize, privatize, deregulate—prescriptions that have been so
dominant at the level of global economic policy as to constitute, in John Stuart
Mill's phrase, "the deep slumber of a decided opinion."

The two regimes differed in the role allotted to the state, in both developed
and developing countries. The Bretton Woods regime favoured "embedded liberalism," as it was later called, which sanctioned market allocation in much of the
economy but constrained it within limits set through a political process. The successor neoliberal regime, particularly associated with Reagan and Thatcher, moved
back towards the norms of *laissez-faire* embraced by classical liberalism, and hence
prescribed a roll-back of state "intervention" and an expansion of market allocation
in economic life. But it gave more emphasis than classical liberalism to the idea
that competition is not the "natural" state of affairs, and that the market can produce suboptimal results wherever producers have monopoly power (as in Adam
Smith's observation that "people of the same trade seldom meet together [without
concocting] a conspiracy against the public").

Neoliberalism accordingly sanctioned state intervention not only to supply a
range of public goods that could not be provided through competitive profit-
seeking (as did classical liberalism), but also to frame and enforce rules of competition, overriding private interests in order to do so; hence the "neo." Its principal
yardstick for judging business success was shareholder value, and its central notion
of the national economic interest was efficiency as determined by competition in
an economy fully open to world markets; there should be no "artificial" barriers
between national and world market prices, such as tariffs or subsidies to particular
industries. Of course, at the level of policy, many tactical, pragmatic modifications
were made to these principles, in order to subsidize corporations, channel more
wealth to the rich, and stabilize the economy and society with covertly Keynesian
policies.[2] But at the level of norms, the difference was clear.

From Robert Wade, "Financial Regime Change?" *New Left Review*, Vol. 53 (September/October
2008), pp. 5–21. Reprinted by permission of New Left Review, London, U.K. Figure 2 is reprinted by
permission of Alan Freeman. Portions of the text and some footnotes have been omitted.

realm of finance, neoliberal prescriptions were justified by the "efficient
hypothesis," which claimed that market prices convey all relevant infor-
and that markets clear continuously—rendering sustained disequilibria,
as bubbles, unlikely; and making policy action to stop them inadvisable, since
would constitute "financial repression." Milton Friedman and the Chicago
school gave their name to this theory; but as Paul Samuelson said, "Chicago is not
a place, it is a state of mind," and it came to prevail in finance ministries, central
banks and university economics departments around the noncommunist world.

The shocks of the past year—another thirty years on from the last major shift—
support the conjecture that we are witnessing a third regime change, propelled by a
wholesale loss of confidence in the Anglo-American model of transactions-oriented
capitalism and the neoliberal economics that legitimized it (and by the U.S.'s loss of
moral authority, now at rock bottom in much of the world). Governmental
responses to the crisis further suggest that we have entered the second leg of
Polanyi's "double movement," the recurrent pattern in capitalism whereby (to
oversimplify) a regime of free markets and increasing commodification generates
such suffering and displacement as to prompt attempts to impose closer regulation
of markets and de-commodification (hence "*embedded* liberalism").[3] The first leg
of the current double movement was the long reign of neoliberalism and its globalization consensus. The second as yet has no name, and may turn out to be a period
marked more by a lack of agreement than any new consensus. . . .

SYSTEMIC TREMORS

The events of September 2008 . . . make it hard to avoid the conclusion that we
have entered a new phase. Financial market conditions in much of the OECD have
sunk to their lowest levels since the banking shutdown of 1932, which was the
single most powerful factor in making the 1929 downturn and stock market crash
become the Great Depression. (Some 11,000 national and state banks failed in the
US between 1929 and 1933.) One bond trader described the current situation as
"the financial equivalent of the Reign of Terror during the French Revolution." In
these circumstances, the efficient markets hypothesis and the prescriptions
derived from it have been thoroughly discredited.

In particular, the second fortnight of September of this year saw not one but
three "game-changing" convulsions in the world's most sophisticated financial system. These do not include the nationalization of Freddie Mac and Fannie Mae:
giant though they are, these "quasi-government institutions" had an established
claim to a public safety net. Rather, the first upheaval was the run on two more of
the big five Wall Street-based broker-dealers or investment banks, following the
earlier run on Bear Stearns—in each case followed by the banks' demise. Only
Morgan Stanley and Goldman Sachs remain standing—for the time being—and
they have switched their legal status to that of bank holding companies, which
means they will be subject to closer regulation than before. The bankruptcy of
Lehman Brothers in mid-September trapped the funds of mega-investors, ratchet-
ing up the panic throughout financial markets and shutting down credit flows even

for normal business. It could have especially far-reaching consequences, since Lehman had a huge volume of derivative business, and there has never been a default of a counter-party to derivative contracts on anything like this scale.

The loss of three of the five giants fundamentally changes the politics of international finance, because these investment banks were immensely powerful actors in the political process—not only in the US but also in the EU. From their London bases, the US investment banks had a shaping influence on the content of EU financial legislation in Brussels. The upside of their disappearance, then, is that it weakens one major obstacle to financial re-regulation.

The second September game-changer was the U.S. Treasury's bail-out of AIG for a promised $85 bn. AIG was not just America's but the world's biggest insurer. Since it stood outside the banking system, its bail-out broke through the firewall separating financial intermediaries from the "real" economy. . . . The third great convulsion outdid even the second: in the most dramatic government rescue operation in history, the U.S. Treasury announced a plan to buy up to $700 bn of toxic securities from troubled banks, at a price well above current market value. Remarkably, it was improvised almost on the spot—Secretary Paulson's original proposal ran to only three typed pages—indicating that the Treasury had been convinced that it could muddle through without a contingency plan. . . .

CAUSES OF THE CRUNCH

If the wars in Iraq, Kosovo and Afghanistan were one expression of American post-Cold War triumphalism, globalized finance, launched during the Clinton Administration, was another. The mainstream press boasted that the U.S. financial system had broken through the sound barrier and was now operating in a new dimension, as it undertook more and more dazzling gambles. They were right to emphasize the novelty of the way in which U.S. finance operated in the 2000s, and the sense that it had no limits. The deeper causes, however, lay in economic developments. In much of the Western world the rate of profit of nonfinancial corporations fell steeply between 1950–73 and 2000–06—in the U.S. by roughly a quarter. In response, firms 'invested' increasingly in financial speculation, and the U.S. government helped offset the resulting shortfall of non-residential private investment by boosting military spending (the Pentagon's annual budget happens to be around the same as the figure put on the Treasury's recent rescue plan).

In addition, foreign currency markets have since 2000 persistently driven exchange rates in the wrong direction, causing many economies running large external deficits to experience currency appreciation, and others running surpluses to experience depreciation or no change. External deficits and surpluses have grown, increasing the fragility of the global economy. However, commentators who insist that the present turmoil is simply the latest in a long line of crises driven by bubble dynamics miss the point that this time, the asset bubble was propagated across the world through securitization technology and the "originate and distribute" model of banking, which only came to fruition in the 2000s. The model

TABLE 1 ■ U.S. DEBT AS A PERCENTAGE OF GDP

	1980	2007
Overall	163	346
Households	50	100
Finance	21	116

Source: *Financial Times*, September 24, 2008.

encouraged high leverage, complex financial instruments and opaque markets, all of which put this crisis in a league of its own.

Too much stress has been laid specifically on the housing bubble, as though it was a necessary and sufficient condition of the crisis. It was only one part of a much wider run-up of debt. Table 1, overleaf, shows the ratio of debt to GDP for the US economy as a whole, and for the two most indebted sectors—households and finance—for 1980 and 2007. The overall ratio more than doubled, and that for the financial sector increased more than fivefold.

The toxic combination of debt, asset bubble and securitization technology was itself enabled by lax regulation. The locus of the blow-up was not unregulated hedge funds, but supposedly regulated banks. Until recently it was acceptable in the eyes of the authorities for investment banks to operate with a debt to equity ratio of 30–35:1. It is no exaggeration to say that the crisis stems from the biggest regulatory failure in modern history. Many politicians and commentators are stressing that "we are all to blame"—the international economy, bankers, investors, ratings agencies, consumers. But this simply diverts attention from those whose job it was to regulate: the regulators and the political authorities who sanctioned them.

The UK's role in the crisis deserves emphasis, because contrary to conventional wisdom, the dynamics at its heart started there. The Thatcher government set out to attract financial business from New York by advertising London as a place where US firms could escape onerous domestic regulation. The government of Tony Blair and Chancellor Gordon Brown continued the strategy, leading Brown to boast that the UK had "not only light but limited regulation." In response, political momentum grew in the US over the course of the 1990s to repeal the Depression-era Glass–Steagall act, which separated commercial from investment banking. Its repeal in 1999 produced a de facto financial liberalization, by facilitating an unrestrained growth of the unregulated shadow-banking system of hedge funds, private equity funds, mortgage brokers and the like. This shadow system then undertook financial operations which tied in the banks, and it was these that eventually brought the banks' downfall.

The striking thing about the UK Financial Services Authority, set up with great fanfare by Brown in 1997, at the same time as he granted the Bank of England semi-autonomy in monetary policy, is that it has sweeping jurisdiction over the

British financial sector—in contrast to the U.S. system of multiple and fragmented regulators. Yet it regulates diffidently, and was evidently intended as little more than window-dressing. . . . Hence the FSA, in its covert and successful bid to attract US companies to London, allowed banks and insurance companies operating from the City to do so with much less capital than similar organizations in New York. Its commitment to light and limited regulation meant that to deal with British financial markets one-third the size of those in the US, it had eleven times fewer enforcement agents than the Securities and Exchange Commission (SEC)— 98 as compared to 1,111. . . . For a decade, the combined tails of the housing market and financial sector have wagged the dog of the British economy. As in the US, consumption grew much faster than GDP, financed by rising debt, thanks to booming house prices. A grateful electorate returned the Labour government to office twice in a row.

GOVERNMENTAL RESPONSES

The downward spiral of credit contraction . . . was being driven by a pervasive collapse of trust in the entire structure of financial intermediation that underpins capitalist economies. . . . Governments. . . therefore moved to stabilize credit markets by taking steps to encourage buyers to re-enter the market for securities—most notably the US Treasury, with its $700 bn bail-out scheme. Several European states . . . moved to steady the banking sector, with Ireland, Greece, Germany, Austria and Denmark guaranteeing all savings deposits in early October 2008. Competition rules have been set aside, as governments foster mega-mergers. In the UK, the recent merger of HBOS and Lloyds TSB creates a bank with a 30 per cent share of the retail market.

The sheer monopoly power of such new financial conglomerates is likely to prompt a stronger regulatory response. Another key area to watch in terms of gauging the robustness of governmental responses is the market for Over the Counter (OTC) derivative contracts—which Warren Buffet famously described in 2003 as "financial weapons of mass destruction." Buffet went on to say that, while the Federal Reserve system was created in part to prevent financial contagion, "there is no central bank assigned to the job of preventing the dominoes toppling in insurance or derivatives." In the event that more regulation of the OTC market is implemented—even in the minimal form of requiring the use of a standard contract format and registration of the details of each contract with a regulatory body—Brooksley Born will have some satisfaction. She was head of the Chicago Futures Trading Commission in the late 1990s, and proposed in a discussion paper that the OTC market should come under some form of regulation. Alan Greenspan, SEC Chairman Arthur Levitt and Treasury Secretary Robert Rubin were so angry at her for even raising such an idea that they sought Clinton's permission to have her fired; in January 1999 she duly resigned for "family reasons."

Beyond such immediate, firefighting responses, the crisis has also drawn attention to the matter of the system's overall stability—and specifically to the impact of international financial standards on national systems. A furious debate has been under way in recent years about international accounting standards. Both the leading sets used by listed companies around the world—the U.S. Generally Accepted Accounting Principles and the International Financial Reporting Standards (also known as IAS)—require listed companies to "mark to market"; that is, frequently to revalue their assets at current market prices or, if the assets are illiquid and have no market price, to revalue them according to the cost of guaranteeing them. Defenders of this method—principally investors—tendentiously call it the "fair value" standard (who could oppose "fair value"?), arguing that its adoption is crucial to maintaining investors' confidence in firms' published accounts.[4]

Critics, including the International Institute of Finance—the main lobbying group for bankers—counter that it amplifies booms and busts. During downswings "fair value" accounting obliges banks to record a drop in asset value which may be unjustified by economic "fundamentals." To maintain their solvency ratios they are then obliged to raise new capital at high cost or reduce lending. Upswings, meanwhile, permit banks to boost their balance sheets beyond levels justified by "fundamentals." But the alternative methods of "mark to historical prices" or "mark to model," in which each firm uses its own model to estimate shadow prices, are in turn open to attack. Warren Buffet observed that "mark to model" tends to degenerate into "mark to myth," while Goldman Sachs in June 2008 resigned its membership of the IIF in protest at the prospect of a move to what it called Alice in Wonderland accounting.

Critics of "mark to market" tend to conflate the important distinction between accounting standards and prudential standards. The former are concerned with the information provided to shareholders and others about the "integrity" of the market; their function is to ensure continuous and accurate information on the situation of companies as the basis for investment decisions. Prudential standards, on the other hand, focus on financial stability, and on preventing financial actors from behaving in ways that put stability at risk. Maintaining this distinction, and overhauling some prudential standards, is important in the current context.

CREDIT AND CREDIBILITY

One type of prudential standard ripe for revision concerns banks' capital adequacy. The Basel II standard of capital adequacy, which came into force at the start of 2007 after some nine years of negotiation, marked a shift from the external regulation of Basel I to self-regulation—making it an invitation to careless behaviour and "moral hazard" at a time when big banks are more confident than ever that they will be bailed out by the state. Basel II requires banks to use agencies' ratings and their own internal risk-assessment models—both of which have been shown to be pro-cyclical and to have failed spectacularly in the run-up to the present crisis—while raising capital standards during periods of illiquidity, precisely when banks are less able to meet them. Moreover, experience of Basel I and simulation of the effects of Basel II suggest that both sets of rules tip capital flows from developed-country banks to the developing world in favour of short-term bank credit, the most dangerous kind.[5] Basel II also raises the cost of finance for banks in the global South relative to those in the developed world, cementing the competitive advantage of the latter. Incremental revision of Basel II will not address any of these issues; for that, wholesale renegotiation will be required.

Among the many victims of the crisis, then, is the dominant "global" model of financial architecture of the last two decades, the credibility of which has been seriously damaged. All three of its main pillars malfunctioned in the run-up to the current crisis. Firstly, a financial services regulator is supposed to protect bank depositors and consumers from unsound behaviour by individual firms, such as holding inadequate reserves; as we have seen, however, regulation was lax in the extreme. Second, financial markets are meant independently to allocate investment capital and consumer credit between individuals, firms and states, with little influence from government; but the opacity created by leveraging and complex financial engineering resulted in market meltdown and eventual state rescue.

The third pillar is the maintenance of monetary stability—defined as keeping a tight lid on inflation—by the central bank. Focusing on the retail price index, central banks opted to keep interest rates very low and permit fast credit growth, lulled by low price inflation due to cheap imports from China. The rapid growth of credit blew out asset bubbles, especially in housing—which many central banks ignored, since their mandate was confined to consumer prices. Indeed, they and the politicians behind them applauded the housing boom because it propelled sharp increases in GDP. The new regime that emerges from the ongoing crisis, then, is likely to include attempts to revise the role of the third pillar by expanding the mandate of central banks, and ensuring they give more weight to asset prices. Since the interest rate is a very blunt instrument, central bankers and regulators will have to rely on an expanded set of prudential measures. Examples would include a requirement for new financial products to obtain regulatory approval, to ensure that their risk characteristics can be readily determined by a third party; or a demand that any organization that can expect a public safety net—and especially public deposit insurance—should submit to controls of its loan portfolio, so as to reduce credit to "overheating" sectors.[6]

DEMISE OF THE CONSENSUS?

Neoliberal economics has powerful antibodies against evidence contrary to its way of seeing things. However, the current crisis may be severe enough to awaken economists from the "deep slumber of a decided opinion," and render them more receptive to proof that the post-Cold War globalization consensus has strikingly weak empirical foundations. According to the conventional view, in the decades after 1945, governments routinely "intervened" in the economy, especially in developing countries where import-substituting industrialization was the norm. While the developed world liberalized, the global South kept to ISI and, consequently, its relative economic performance lagged. But as of around 1980, under encouragement from the World Bank, IMF and the American and British govern-ments, developing countries increasingly adopted the prescriptions of the global-ization consensus and switched to a strategy of market-friendly, export-led growth and supply-side development. As a result, their performance improved relative not only to the past but also to that of the developed countries; they finally began to catch up. This empirical evidence in turn validated World Bank and IMF pressure on their borrowers to adopt neoliberal policies.

The trouble with this story is that it is largely wrong. Figure 1, overleaf, shows the average income of a number of regions relative to that of the North, expressed in purchasing power parity dollars (PPP$), from 1950 to 2001. Latin America and Africa display a relative decline both before and after 1980; Eastern Europe, not shown, tracks the Latin America line. China, at the bottom of the graph for most of the period, starts to rise in the 1980s and continues thereafter, reaching the aver-age for the South by 2001; the Asia line rises a little, too, after a lag—but this also includes China, which accounts for a large part of its ascent.

Figure 2, opposite, shows the average income of the developing world, excluding the "transitional economies" of the former Soviet bloc, as a proportion of that of the North, expressed in market exchange rates. The top line represents the whole of the global South, the bottom line the global South excluding China. In both cases, the trend from 1960 to 2008 is very different from that postulated by the globalization narrative. The ratio was higher in the period before 1980, fell steeply during the 1980s, flattened out at a low level during the 1990s, and had a small uptick after 2004 because of the commodity boom induced by rapid growth in the PRC. With incomes expressed in terms of PPP, the trend line is consistent with the globalization narrative, turning upwards in the early 1980s

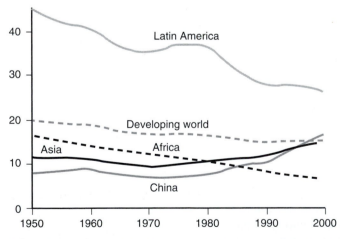

FIGURE 1 ■ Income of World Regions as a Proportion of Northern Incomes
Percentage of income per capita expressed in PPP$. Source: John Ravenhill, ed., Global Political Economy, Oxford 2008, box 12.1.

FIGURE 2 ■ Global South GDP per Capita as % of That of Advanced Countries
Calculated using current prices at market exchange rates. Source: Alan Freeman, "The Poverty of Statistics and the Statistics of Poverty," Third World Quarterly, forthcoming, based on IMF, World Economic Outlook.

and continuing to ascend thereafter; but exclude China and the trend is much the same as in Figure 2.

The notion that globalization generates catch-up growth, then, rests principally on the rise of China. Yet the policies Beijing has pursued are far from identical to those endorsed by the Washington Consensus; it has followed the precepts of Friedrich List and of American policy-makers of the nineteenth century, during the U.S.'s catch-up growth, more than those of Adam Smith or latter-day neoliberals. The state has been an integral promoter of development, and has adopted targeted protection measures as part of a wider strategy for nurturing new industries and technologies; it is now investing heavily in information systems to help Chinese firms engineer their way around Western patents. . . .

RETHINKING THE MODEL

In times of crisis, arguments that had previously been on the margins can gain greater currency. If the disappearance of three out of five big investment banks indicates the seriousness of the present turmoil, it also provides an opportunity to broaden the range of possibilities for an overhaul of the way global finance operates; the fall in pension funds and declining house prices should also enlarge the constituency for major reform. Scholars today face the challenge of rethinking some of the basic intellectual models that have legitimized policy over the past three decades. The fallout from complex, opaque financial products may persuade many of the benefits of a substantially smaller financial sector relative to the real one, and perhaps of a "mixed economy" in finance, where some firms would combine public and private purposes—operating more like utilities than profit maximizers.

But more fundamentally, the globalization model itself needs to be rethought. It over-emphasized capital accumulation or the supply side of the economy, to the detriment of the demand side (since the stress on export-led growth implied that demand was unlimited). The failure of catch-up growth, seen in Figures 1 and 2, stems in part from neoliberalism's lack of attention to domestic demand, reflecting the dominance of neoclassical economics and the marginalization of Keynesian approaches. Developing domestic and regional demand would involve greater efforts towards achieving equality in the distribution of income—and hence a larger role for labour standards, trade unions, the minimum wage and systems of social protection. It would also necessitate strategic management of trade, so as to curb the race-to-the-bottom effects of export-led growth, and foster domestic industry and services that would provide better livelihoods and incomes for the middle and working classes. Controls on cross-border flows of capital, so as to curb speculative surges, would be another key instrument of a demand-led development process, since they would give governments greater autonomy with regard to the exchange rate and in setting interest rates.

The recent strengthening of regional integration processes, meanwhile, should direct attention away from global standards and arrangements which, because of their maximal scope, are necessarily coarse-grained at best. Regional trade agreements between developing countries have distinct advantages over multilateral trade deals, whose terms often serve to break open economies of the global South while preserving intact protections for industry and agriculture in the North. Regional currencies—such as the Asian Currency Unit being discussed by East Asian states, based on a weighted average of key local currencies—could act as a benchmark independent of the us dollar, reducing vulnerability to market turbulence on Wall Street.

Global economic regimes need above all to be rethought to allow a diversity of rules and standards, instead of imposing ever more uniformity. Rather than seeking . . . to make the whole world attain the degree of economic integration found within the federal structure of the U.S., such that nation-states would have no more influence over cross-border flows than U.S. states have over domestic transactions, we might draw inspiration from an analogy with "middleware." Designed to enable different families of software to communicate with each other, middleware offers large organizations an alternative to making one program span their entire structure; it allows more scope for a decentralized choice of programs. If the second leg of the present "double movement" turns out to be a period from which consensus is largely absent, it may also provide space for a wider array of standards and institutions—economic and financial alternatives to the system-wide prescriptions of neoliberalism. This may give the new regime that emerges from the current upheavals greater stability than its predecessor. Whether it provides the basis for a more equitable world, however, will remain an open question—and an urgent challenge—for some time to come.

ENDNOTES

1. The term "Washington Consensus," devised in 1989 by John Williamson to refer to a set of ten policy recommendations, came to be used in a much broader sense, encompassing financial deregulation, free capital mobility, unrestricted purchase of local companies by foreign companies, and unrestricted establishment of subsidiaries.
2. Dean Baker, *The Conservative Nanny State: How the Wealthy Use the Government to Stay Rich and Get Richer,* Washington, DC, 2006.
3. Karl Polanyi, *The Great Transformation,* Boston, 2001 [1944].
4. Nicolas Véron, Matthieu Autret and Alfred Galichon, *Smoke & Mirrors, Inc.: Accounting for Capitalism,* Ithaca, NY, 2006.
5. Jean-Marc Figuet and Delphine Lahet, "Les Accords de Bâle II: quelles conséquences pour le financement bancaire extérieur des pays émergents,?" *Revue d'Economie du Développement,* no. I (March 2007), pp. 47–67.
6. Stephen Bell and John Quiggin, "Asset Price Instability and Policy Responses: The Legacy of Liberalization," *Journal of Economic Issues,* vol. 40, no. 3 (September 2006), pp. 629–49.

 Exercises for Critics of Globalization

Apply what you learned in this chapter by using the online resources on MyPoliSciKit (www.mypoliscikit.com).

 Practice Tests

 Videos:
- "Anti-Globalization Protests"
- "Fair Trade Coffee"

 Simulation: "The North-South Gap: You Are a Coffee Farmer"

Reading Guides:
- Dani Rodrik, "Trading in Illusions"
- John Micklethwait and Adrain Wooldridge, "Why the Globalization Backlash is Stupid"
- Robert Wade, "Financial Regime Change?"

Contemporary Issues in World Politics

With the Cold War having ended almost 30 years ago, we have entered a new era of international politics. In Part 4 we have picked seven features of this era that we believe are the most important for understanding its major contours and that constitute challenges for more systematic analysis. They are: the future of interstate war and terrorism; the causes of, and ways of dealing with, domestic collapse and civil wars; the international community's more activist commitment to the protection of human rights and the rule of international law; the effects on world politics wrought by the rise of nonstate and transnational actors; the necessity of, and difficulties in, dealing with global commons problems, especially global warming; the search for new modes of global governance to mitigate the adverse effects of anarchy; and, finally, future developments that might give us clues to the shape of international politics two decades out.

INTERSTATE WAR AND TERRORISM

War is as old as the time when human beings first organized themselves into groups. It has been the great powers that have fought most, and that have always conducted their policies with the possibility of war in mind. Will the world be as ravaged by war in the decades to come as it has been since the dawn of civilization? Or are we now entering a new era when interstate war will disappear or be transformed? If war continues, will it still be waged between the kinds of actors who were most prominent in the past? Finally, will terrorism at its current magnitude and frequency remain with us for the indefinite future? How does terrorism end?

Robert Jervis, Robert J. Art, and Audrey Kurth Cronin address these questions. Jervis argues that war among the rich democracies of North America, Western Europe, and Japan is not only a thing of the past but is no longer even contemplated. War among the leading powers has been the motor of traditional international politics, and so the coming era will be radically different. The rest of the world is not likely to remain at peace, however, and the United States may continue to intervene abroad. In much of the Third World, conflicts between, but especially within, states rage and disputes over borders and natural resources provide proximate reasons for conflict. Art argues that the future of U.S.–China relations is not as bleak as many would have us believe. Compared to other conflicts between a dominant great power and a rapidly rising challenger, the Sino-American relationship has several factors that should make us more optimistic that a great power war will not result between the two. Cronin surveys the demise of terrorist groups and demonstrates that there are six distinct paths through which terrorist groups die.

CIVIL WARS AND INTERVENTION

Although civil strife and domestic collapse are as old as history, they have become more prominent after the Cold War and have become even more important recently through the perceived links to terrorism. State failures and civil wars are fed by both internal and external causes, which make them particularly hard to understand and deal with. Because of the growth in the number of states—and the heightened consequences of disturbance in one area for regions, if not for the entire world—these subjects are now high on the agenda of both scholars and policymakers. Because we live in a well-established country with a high degree of public order, most of us forget that this situation is not a natural one, but rather the hard-won result of a broad concentration of political, economic, and social forces. Under some circumstances, central authority can be subject not only to violent dispute, but also can be so torn apart that it simply disappears, resulting in the national government being replaced by local warlords, roving bands of thugs, and chaos.

Alan J. Kuperman examines the evolution of humanitarian intervention since World War II and argues that international intervention into societies experiencing violent conflict, however well intentioned, can sometimes exacerbate and prolong the conflict, arguing therefore that all the consequences of such interventions have to be carefully considered before being undertaken. Chaim Kaufmann analyzes the nature of ethnic civil wars, shows why they are so intractable, and surveys the various methods of intervening in them. He concludes that when the conflict has reached a point of no return the physical separation of the warring ethnic groups, either by creating safe areas within a state or by partitioning the state, offers the best long-term hope to stop the killing. Most current discussion focuses not on dividing countries but on rebuilding them. James L. Payne remains pessimistic about the ability of outsiders to rebuild and democratize nations. Of course, the results from several recent attempts, most obviously in Iraq and Afghanistan, are not yet in, but it is clear that beliefs about whether interventions can produce stability and democracy will strongly influence the future course of American policy and the international community.

HUMAN RIGHTS AND INTERNATIONAL LAW

Many NGOs are deeply concerned about human rights, and at bottom, the most fundamental units in the world are not states but individuals. Rhoda E. Howard and Jack Donnelly argue that, although cultures and systems differ, each individual has a set of rights by virtue of being human. In the absence of effective international government, there is no choice but to rely on states for the enforcement of human rights. Increasingly, it has been outside states that have acted, and when he was Secretary General of the UN, Kofi Annan argued that states not only have the right but the duty to intervene in extreme and limited conditions to protect human rights. Steven R. Ratner argues that international law is having a greater effect on state action, and by implication, that international politics are becoming more regulated and domestic-like. More international law is being written, and enforcement is being improved.

TRANSNATIONAL ACTORS

The state system we live in today dates roughly from the Peace of Westphalia, which ended the Thirty Years' War, one of the bloodiest in human history. Consequently, the modern international system of states has just celebrated its 362nd anniversary. Will the state system itself continue? That is, will the state remain the *most* important, although not the only important, actor in world politics?

Part of the answer to these questions lies in assessing how strong nonstate and transnational actors have become vis-à-vis the state. Clearly, these actors have become increasingly important. Margaret E. Keck and Kathryn Sikkink provide a more systematic analysis of NGOs and show how transnational networks operate and affect state action. Sebastian Mallaby takes the unconventional if not perverse position that although NGOs often do great good in the world, we must not forget that they have their own interests and their own views of the interests of those they speak for, and these may not correspond to what is best for those populations. Finally, Phil Williams looks at the role of transnational crime. Overlooked by many scholars, these criminal networks and actors in fact play a large role, especially in countries torn by civil strife.

THE GLOBAL COMMONS

Protection of the global environment is not a new issue, but its political salience has greatly increased over the last 15 years because of factors such as the depletion of the world's fisheries, the degradation of the ozone layer, and the threats to the quality of human life posed by global warming and climate change. The United Nations Conference on the Environment held in Rio in 1992 marked a watershed in international awareness of the increasing threat to the global environment.

Truly global environmental threats, as opposed to strictly national ones, are especially difficult to deal with because they are a "commons" problem. In such cases, concertation of state action does not come easily because the situation looks as follows: No single state owns the resource being consumed (or abused), but all use it (or abuse it), and none can be prevented from using and abusing it. A commons (or public) good is therefore one that no single individual or entity owns, but that all need and can use. For such goods, no individual or state has an incentive to minimize its exploitation unless it is persuaded that all others will act in a similar fashion. This represents a collective action problem: Uncoordinated individual action produces collective disaster. This is the "tragedy of the commons" and the message of Garrett Hardin's article. Solving commons problems is therefore not easy. Drawing on recent findings from psychology, Barry Schwartz suggests several approaches: the problem should be broken up into manageable packages, issues should be presented in terms of avoiding losses rather than making gains, and in addition to offering the usual incentives for good and bad behavior, we should try appealing to people's sense of justice.

Climate change is the biggest and most challenging commons problem of them all. Widespread and growing use of fossil fuels to develop and sustain modern economies has added enough carbon dioxide to the world's atmosphere to cause the average global temperature to increase by approximately .75 degrees centigrade since the onset of the Industrial Revolution in 1750. This may sound insignificant, but it is not. The overall change in global temperature from the depths of the last Ice Age until now can be measured within the range of four to nine degrees centigrade. The best estimates of climatologists are that at present rates of fossil fuel burning, the likely range of average global temperature increase will be 1.1 to 6.4 degrees centigrade. At the high end of this estimate, we will be within the range in which severe climate change occurred in the past. Climate change raises dangers not only of widespread dislocations but also of catastrophic climate change if warming feeds on itself—a situation climatologists call "positive feedback" in which warming produces more warming.

The nations of the world have been wrestling with this extremely complex problem for almost 20 years, with not a great deal of success. The world's poorer developing states have consistently refused to make any binding commitments to reduce their emissions, arguing that the developed states created the problem and therefore should solve it, first by reducing their own emissions and then by giving the developing states the financial resources and technology to build environmentally safe industries. It would be unfair to make them sacrifice their economic development, which is a priority not only for them but for the world as a whole, so they argue. The United States has until recently contributed to the problem by refusing even to make its own binding commitments to reduce carbon emissions. There are complex schemes proposed to combat global warming. David G. Victor offers a politically savvy one: more progress could be made if a smaller group of countries that produce most of the emissions work together to conclude an agreement, rather than seeking a global accord among all states.

GLOBAL GOVERNANCE

Old modes of global government may no longer be appropriate for the new and complex world. The uncoordinated decisions of individual states cannot provide the sort of order that is needed. Too many issues spill over national borders; too many problems require joint efforts by a range of actors; in too many cases, one state's policies will have adverse impacts around the globe. The need for states to come together led to the formation of the League of Nations after World War I and to a stronger United Nations after World War II. As Adam Roberts shows, its role has expanded after the cold war. But unless the Secretary General or parts of the Secretariat develop autonomous powers, the centers of decision will remain with the individual states. This leads Kenneth N. Waltz to argue that international organizations, globalization, and transnational forces have not removed states from their central role: if there is to be world governance, it will come through the decisions and actions of states. Under certain circumstances, the array of international organizations has been strongly influenced by the leading role of the United States. A central question is how this order will accommodate rising powers, especially China. G. John Ikenberry argues that these arrangements are open and flexible enough to accommodate newcomers, thereby greatly contributing to prospects for world peace. Moses Naim's solution to global governance problems is simple: take a multilateral approach but do so by bringing together the smallest number of states that will have the greatest impact on solving a particular problem; hence "minilateralism." Finally, Anne-Marie Slaughter moves away from the state-centric approach all together by suggesting that what is striking about current governance arrangements is the role of networks among units within governments. These horizontal linkages facilitate the cooperation and flexibility that are needed to cope with the current and future conditions.

FUTURE DEVELOPMENTS

Whether the new forces and actors described above will eventually subvert the state system or instead remain subservient to it, whether some new patterns now difficult to imagine will emerge, and whether current and future modes of international governance will be adequate for the challenges ahead is something we will be able to answer definitively only several decades from now. Although these factors will significantly influence what the future of international politics looks like, so, too, will the power distribution among states, the frequency of war, both civil and international, and the effects wrought by demographic factors that have now been set in motion.

This last section provides four selections that touch upon these additional factors. The National Intelligence Council, the arm of the U.S. government responsible for preparing national intelligence estimates, predicts a world in 2025 that will see a decline in America's relative strength and so be more multipolar than it is today, that will see increasing competition among states for strategic natural resources, and that will see the adverse effects of climate change looming ever larger. Barry Posen argues that diffusion of power will not necessarily produce instability. Robert Kagan predicts what he calls "the return to history." By that he means the return of conflict among the great powers over the great ideological divide of democracy versus autocracy, but also a world in which the United States continues to remain the dominant power. Finally, Richard Jackson and Neil Howe portray a world that will experience the "great demographic transformation." This is a world in which the current rich great powers will experience a relative decline in their share of the world's population and gross domestic product, with a corresponding increase in both for the developing world. Today's developed world will have an older population to support and its economy will grow more slowly; today's developing world will get richer but more unstable due to huge population growth. The nation whose future looks the best is the United States: its share of the developed world's population and gross domestic product will expand due largely to its higher rates of fertility and immigration.

Most likely, the world will develop in ways that surprise us. Almost never have people been able to foresee the future; indeed if they could they might act in ways that would make events turn out differently. In 1800 it appeared that the coming century would be a very grim one; in 1900 the future of humankind looked bright. For better or for worse—or perhaps for better and for worse—human beings move in odd ways, collective outcomes diverge from individual preferences, and technological and ideological changes appear unbidden. But for students and scholars as well as for policy-makers, thinking about the future can sharpen ideas and raise questions as well as induce an appropriate sense of humility.

INTERSTATE WAR AND TERRORISM

The Era of Leading Power Peace

ROBERT JERVIS

War and the possibility of war among the great powers has been the motor of international politics, not only strongly influencing the boundaries and distribution of values among them, but deeply affecting their internal arrangements and shaping the fates of the smaller ones. Being seen as an ever-present possibility produced by deeply-rooted factors such as human nature and the lack of world government, this force was expected to continue indefinitely. But I would argue that war among the leading great powers—the most developed states of the United States, West Europe, and Japan—will not occur in the future, and indeed is no longer a source of concern for them (Mueller 1989).

Now, however, the leading states form what Karl Deutsch called a pluralistic security community, a group among whom war is literally unthinkable—i.e., neither the publics nor the political elites nor even the military establishments expect war with each other (Deutsch et al. 1957). No official in the Community would advocate a policy on the grounds that it would improve the state's position in the event of war with other members or allow the state to more effectively threaten them.

Although no one state can move away from the reliance on war by itself lest it become a victim, they can collectively do so if each forsakes the resort to force. This development challenges many of our theories and raises the question of what international politics will be like in the future.

Security communities are not unprecedented. But what is unprecedented is that the states that constitute this one are the leading members of the international

From Robert Jervis, "Theories of War in an Era of Leading-Power Peace: Presidential Address, American Political Science Association, 2001," *American Political Science Review,* Vol. 96, No. 1 (March 2002), pp. 1–14. Copyright © 2002 by The American Political Science Association. Reprinted with the permission of Cambridge University Press. Portions of the text and some footnotes have been omitted.

system and so are natural rivals who in the past were central to the violent struggle for security, power, and contested values. Winston Churchill exaggerated only slightly when he declared that "people talked a lot of nonsense when they said nothing was ever settled by war. Nothing in history was ever settled *except* by wars" (quoted in Gilbert 1983, 860–61). Even cases of major change without war, such as Britain yielding hegemony in the Western hemisphere to the United States at the turn of the twentieth century, were strongly influenced by security calculations. Threatening war, preparing for it, and trying to avoid it have permeated all aspects of politics, and so a world in which war among the most developed states is unthinkable will be very different from the history with which we are familiar. To paraphrase and extend a claim made by Evan Luard (1986, 77), given the scale and frequency of war among the great powers in the preceding millennia, this is a change of spectacular proportions, perhaps the single most striking discontinuity that the history of international politics has anywhere provided.

Two major states, Russia and China, might fight each other or a member of the Community. But, as I will discuss below, such a conflict would be different from traditional wars between great powers. Furthermore, these countries lack many of the attributes of great powers: their internal regimes are shaky, they are not at the forefront of any advanced forms of technology or economic organization, they can pose challenges only regionally, and they have no attraction as models for others. They are not among the most developed states and I think it would be fair to put them outside the ranks of the great powers as well. But their military potential, their status as nuclear powers, and the size of their economies renders that judgment easily debatable and so I will not press it but rather will argue that the set of states that form the Community are not all the great powers, but all the most developed ones.

CENTRAL QUESTIONS

Five questions arise. First, does the existence of the Community mean the end of security threats to its members, and more specifically to the United States? Second, will the Community endure? Third, what are the causes of its construction and maintenance? Fourth, what are the implications for this transformation for the conduct of international affairs? Finally, what does this say about theories of the causes of war?

CONTINUED THREATS

The fact that the United States is not menaced by the most developed countries does not mean that it does not face any military threats at all. Indeed, some see the United States as no more secure than it was during the Cold War, being imperiled by terrorists and "rogue" states, in addition to Russia and China. But even if I am wrong to believe that these claims are greatly exaggerated, these conflicts do not have the potential to drive world politics the way that clashes among the leading powers did in the past. They do not permeate all facets of international politics and structure state–society relations; they do not represent a struggle for dominance in the international system or a direct challenge to American vital interests.

Recent terrorist attacks are of unprecedented magnitude and will have a significant impact on domestic and international politics, but I do not think they have the potential to be a functional substitute for great power war—i.e., to be the driving force of politics. Despite rhetoric to the contrary, there is little chance that all the countries will unite to combat terrorism; the forms of this scourge are too varied and indeed often are a useful tool for states, and states have many other interests that are at least as important as combating terrorism. Similarly, although the events of September 11 have triggered significant changes in American foreign policy and international alignments, I believe that in a fairly short period of time previous outlooks and conflicts of interest will reassert themselves. Even if this is not the case and if combating terrorism becomes the most important goal for most or all states, the move away from leading power war is still both important and puzzling.

WILL THE SECURITY COMMUNITY LAST?

Predictions about the maintenance of the Community are obviously disputable (indeed, limitations on people's ability to predict could undermine it), but nothing in the short period since the end of the Cold War points to an unraveling. We could make a long list of disputes, but there were at least as many in the earlier period. The Europeans' effort to establish an independent security force is aimed at permitting them to intervene when the United States chooses not to (or perhaps by threatening such action, to trigger American intervention), not at fighting the United States. Even if Europe were to unite either to balance against the United States or because of its own internal dynamics and the world were to become bipolar again, it is very unlikely that suspicions, fears for the future, and conflicts of interest would be severe enough to break the Community.

A greater threat would be the failure of Europe to unite coupled with an American withdrawal of forces, which could lead to "security competition" within Europe (Art 1996; Mearsheimer 2001, 385–96). Partly general, the fears would focus on Germany. Their magnitude is hard to gauge and it is difficult to estimate what external shocks or kinds of German behavior would activate them. The fact that Thatcher and Mitterrand opposed German unification is surely not forgotten in Germany and is an indication that concerns remain. But this danger is likely to constitute a self-denying prophecy in two ways. First, many Germans are aware of the need not only to reassure others by tying themselves closely to Europe, but also to seek to make it unlikely that future generations of Germans would want to break these bonds even if they could. Second, Americans who worry about the residual danger will favor keeping some troops in Europe as the ultimate intra-European security guarantee.

Expectations of peace close off important routes to war. The main reason for Japanese aggression in the 1930s was the desire for a self-sufficient sphere that would permit Japan to fight the war with the Western powers that was seen as inevitable, not because of particular conflicts, but because it was believed that great powers always fight each other. By contrast, if states believe that a security community will last they will not be hypersensitive to threats from within it and will not feel the need to undertake precautionary measures that could undermine the security of other members. Thus the United States is not disturbed that British and French nuclear missiles could destroy American cities and while those two countries object to American plans for missile defense, they do not feel the need to increase their forces in response. As long as peace is believed to be very likely, the chance of inadvertent spirals of tension and threat is low.

Nevertheless, the point with which I began this section is unavoidable. World politics can change rapidly and saying that nothing foreseeable will dissolve the Community is not the same as saying that it will not dissolve (Betts 1992). To the extent that it rests on democracy and prosperity (see below), anything that would undermine these would also undermine the Community. Drastic climate change could also shake the foundations of much that we have come to take for granted. But it is hard to see how dynamics at the international level (i.e., the normal trajectory of fears, disputes, and rivalries) could produce war among the leading states. In other words, the Community does not have within it the seeds of its own destruction.

Our faith in the continuation of this peace is increased to the extent that we think we understand its causes and have reason to believe that they will continue. This is our next topic.

EXPLANATIONS FOR THE SECURITY COMMUNITY

There are social constructivist, liberal, and realist explanations for the Community which, although proceeding from different assumptions and often using different terms, invoke overlapping factors.

Social Constructivism

Social constructivist accounts stress the role of norms of non-violence and shared identities that, through an interactive process of reciprocal behaviors and expectations, have led the advanced democracies to assume the role of each other's friend. In contradistinction to the liberal and realist explanations, this downplays the importance of material factors and elevates ideas, images of oneself and others, and conceptions of appropriate conduct. The roots of the changes that have produced this enormous shift in international politics among some countries but not others is not specified in detail, but the process is a self-reinforcing one—a benign cycle of behavior, beliefs, and expectations.

People become socialized into attitudes, beliefs, and values that are conducive to peace. Individuals in the Community may see their own country as strong and good—and even better than others—but they rarely espouse the virulent national-ism that was common in the past. Before World War I, one German figure could pro-claim that the Germans were "the greatest civilized people known to history" while another declared that the Germans were "the chosen people of this century," which explains "why other people hate us. They do not understand us but they fear our tremendous spiritual superiority." Thomas Macaulay similarly wrote that the British were "the greatest and most highly civilized people that ever the world saw" and were "the acknowledged leaders of the human race in the causes of political improvement," while Senator Albert Beveridge proclaimed that "God has made us the master organ-izers of the world" (quoted in Van Evera 1984, 27). These sentiments are shocking today because they are so at variance from what we have been taught to think about others and ourselves. We could not adopt these views without rejecting a broad set of beliefs and values. An understanding of the effects of such conceptions led the Euro-peans, and to an unfortunately lesser extent the Japanese, to de-nationalize and har-monize their textbooks after World War II and has similarly led countries with remaining enemies to follow a different path: The goals for the education of a 12-year-old child in Pakistan include the "ability to know all about India's evil designs about Pakistan; acknowledge and identify forces that may be working against Pakistan; understand the Kashmir problem" (quoted in Kumar 2001, 29).

The central objection to constructionism is that it mistakes effect for cause: its description is correct, but the identities, images, and self-images are superstruc-ture, being the product of peace and of the material incentives discussed below. What is crucial is not people's thinking, but the factors that drive it. The validity of this claim is beyond the reach of current evidence, but it points to a critique of the constructivist argument that the Community will last, which places great faith in the power of socialization and the ability of ideas to replicate and sustain them-selves. This conception may betray an excessive faith in the validity of ideas that seem self-evident today, but that our successors might reject. Constructivism may present us with actors who are "over-socialized" (Wrong 1976, ch. 2) and leave too little role for agency in the form of people who think differently, perhaps because their material conditions are different.

Liberalism

The liberal explanation has received most attention. Although it comes in several variants, the central strands are the pacifying effects of democracy and economic interdependence.

Democracy

The members of the Community are democracies, and many scholars argue that democracies rarely if ever fight each other. Although the statistical evidence is, as usual, subject to debate, Jack Levy is correct to claim that it is "as close as anything we have to an empirical law in international politics" (Levy 1989, 88).

Less secure, however, is our understanding of why this is the case. We have numerous explanations, which can be seen as competing or complementary.

Democracies are systems of dispersed power, and dispersed power means multiple veto points and groups that could block war. (This seems true almost by definition, but if the accounts of former Soviet leaders are to be trusted, Brezhnev was more constrained by his colleagues than was Nixon, at least where arms control was concerned.) Related are the norms of these regimes: democracies function through compromise, non-violence, and respect for law. To the extent that these values and habits govern foreign policy, they are conducive to peace, especially in relations with other democracies who reciprocate.

Other scholars have argued that the key element lies in the realm of information. By having a relatively free flow of intelligence and encouraging debate, democracies are less likely to make egregious errors in estimating what courses of action will maintain the peace. The other side of the informational coin is that democracies can more effectively telegraph their own intentions, and so avoid both unnecessary spirals of conflict and wars that stem from others' incorrect beliefs that the democracy is bluffing (although an obvious cost is an inability to bluff).

Finally, in a recasting of the traditional argument that democracies are less likely to go to war because those who hold ultimate authority (i.e., the general public) will pay the price for conflict, some argue that the institutional and coalitional nature of democratic regimes requires their leaders to pursue successful policies if they are to stay in office. Thus democracies will put greater efforts into winning wars and be careful to choose to fight only wars they can win. Autocracies have a much narrower base and so can stay in power by buying off their supporters even if their foreign policies are unnecessarily costly. These arguments, while highly suggestive, share with earlier liberal thinking quite stylized assumptions about the preferences of societal actors and pay little attention to how each country anticipates the behavior of others and assesses how others expect it to behave.

These explanations for the democratic peace are thoughtful and often ingenious, but not conclusive. Many of them lead us to expect not only dyadic effects, but monadic ones as well—i.e., democracies should be generally peaceful, not only peaceful toward each other, a finding that most scholars deny. They would also lead us to expect that one democracy would not seek to overthrow another, a proposition that is contradicted by American behavior during the Cold War. Furthermore, most of the arguments are built around dyads but it is not entirely clear that the posited causes would apply as well to multilateral groupings like the Community.

The causal role of democracy is hard to establish because these regimes have been relatively rare until recently, much of the democratic peace can be explained by the Soviet threat, and the same factors that lead countries to become democratic (e.g., being relatively rich and secure) are conducive to peace between them. It is particularly important and difficult to control for the role of common interest, which loomed so large during the Cold War. But interests are not objective and may be strongly influenced by the country's internal regime. Thus the democracies may have made common cause during the Cold War in part because they were democracies; common interest may be a mechanism by which the democratic peace is sustained as much as it is a competing explanation for it (for this and related issues, see Farber and Gowa 1995, 1997; Gartzke 1998, 2000; Maoz 1997;

Oneal and Russett 1999; Schweller 2000). Moreover, if democracies are more likely to become economically interdependent with one another, additional common interest will be created. But to bring up the importance of interest is to highlight an ambiguity and raise a question. The ambiguity is whether the theory leads us to expect democracies *never* to fight each other or "merely" to fight *less* than do other dyads. (Most scholars take the latter view, but this does not mean that this is what most versions of the theory actually imply.) The related hypothetical question is: Is it impossible for two democracies to have a conflict of interest so severe that it leads to war? This troubles the stronger version of the argument because it is hard to answer in the affirmative.

But would democracies let such a potent conflict of interest develop? At least as striking as the statistical data is the fact—or rather, the judgment—that the regimes that most disturbed the international order in the twentieth century also devastated their own peoples—the USSR, Germany under the Nazis and, perhaps, under Kaiser Wilhelm. One reason for this connection may be the desire to remake the world (but because the international order was established by countries that were advanced democracies, it may not be surprising that those who opposed it were not). Not all murderous regimes are as ambitious (e.g., Idi Amin's Uganda), and others with both power and grand designs may remain restrained (e.g., Mao's China), but it is hard to understand the disruptive German and Soviet foreign policy without reference to their domestic regimes.

Interdependence

The second leg of the liberal explanation for the Community is the high level of economic interdependence. The basic argument was developed by Cobden, Bright, and the other nineteenth-century British liberals. As the former put it: "Free Trade is God's diplomacy and there is no other certain way of uniting people in bonds of peace." (Quoted in Bourne 1970, 85. For a general treatment of Cobden's views, see Cain 1979. For the most recent evidence, see McMillan 1997; Russett and Oneal 2001, ch. 4; for arguments that interdependence has been exaggerated and misunderstood, see Waltz 1970, 1979 ch. 7, 1999. Most traditional liberal thinking and the rest of my brief discussion assumes symmetry; as Hirschman 1945 showed, asymmetric dependence can provide the basis for exploitative bargaining.) Although the evidence for this proposition remains in dispute, the causal argument is relatively straightforward. "If goods cannot cross borders, armies will" is the central claim, in the words of the nineteenth-century French economist Frederick Bastiat which were often repeated by Secretary of State Cordell Hull (perhaps excessively influenced by the experience of the 1930s). Extensive economic intercourse allows states to gain by trade the wealth that they would otherwise seek through fighting. Relatedly, individuals and groups who conduct these economic relations develop a powerful stake in keeping the peace and maintaining good relations. Thus it is particularly significant that in the contemporary world many firms have important ties abroad and that direct foreign investment holds the fates of important actors hostage to continued good relations. There can be a benign cycle here as increasing levels of trade strengthen the political power of actors who have a stake in deepening these ties.

The liberal view assumes that actors place a high priority on wealth, that trade is a better route to it than conquest, and that actors who gain economically from the exchange are politically powerful. These assumptions are often true, especially in the modern world, but are not without their vulnerabilities. At times honor and glory, in addition to more traditional forms of individual and national interest, can be more salient than economic gain. Thus as the Moroccan crisis of 1911 came to its climax, General von Moltke wrote to his wife: "If we again slip away from this affair with our tail between our legs . . . I shall despair of the future of the German Empire. I shall then retire. But before handing in my resignation I shall move to abolish the Army and to place ourselves under Japanese protectorate; we shall then be in a position to make money without interference and to develop into ninnies" (quoted in Berghahn 1973, 97). Traditional liberal thought understood this well and stressed that economic activity was so potent not only because it gave people an interest in maintaining peace, but because it reconstructed social values to downgrade status and glory and elevate material well-being. It follows that the stability of the Community rests in part upon people giving priority to consumption. Critics decry modern society's embodiment of individualistic, material values, but one can easily imagine that others could generate greater international conflict.

There are four general arguments against the pacific influence of interdependence. First, if it is hard to go from the magnitude of economic flows to the costs that would be incurred if they were disrupted, it is even more difficult to estimate how much political impact these costs will have, which depends on the other considerations in play and the political context. This means that we do not have a theory that tells us the expected magnitude of the effect. Second, even the sign of the effect can be disputed: interdependence can increase conflict as states gain bargaining leverage over each other, fear that others will exploit them, and face additional sources of disputes. These effects might not arise if states expect to remain at peace with each other, however. Third, it is clear that interdependence does not guarantee peace. High levels of economic integration did not prevent World War I, and nations that were much more unified than any security community have peacefully dissolved or fought civil wars. But this does not mean that interdependence is not conducive to peace. Fourth, interdependence may be more an effect than a cause, more the product than a generator of expectations of peace and cooperation.

Realist Explanations

The crudest realist explanation for the Community would focus on the rise of the common threat from Russia and China. While not entirely implausible, this argument does not fit the views espoused by most elites in Japan and Europe, who are relatively unconcerned about these countries and believe that whatever dangers emanate from them would be magnified rather than decreased by a confrontational policy.

American Hegemony

Two other realist accounts are stronger. The first argues that the Community is largely caused by the other enormous change in world politics—the American dominance of world politics. U.S. defense spending, to take the most easily quantifiable indicator, is now greater than that of the next 8 countries combined (O'Hanlon 2001, 4–5). Furthermore, thanks to the Japanese constitution and the integration of armed forces within NATO, America's allies do not have to fear attacks from each other: their militaries (especially Germany's) are so truncated that they could not fight a major war without American assistance or attack each other without undertaking a military buildup that would give others a great deal of warning. American dominance also leads us to expect that key outcomes, from the expansion of NATO, to the American-led wars in Kosovo and the Persian Gulf, to the IMF bailouts of Turkey and Argentina in the spring of 2001, will conform to American preferences.

But closer examination reveals differences between current and past hegemonies. The United States usually gives considerable weight to its partners' views and indeed its own preferences are often influenced by theirs, as was true in Kosovo. For their parts, the other members of the Community seek to harness and constrain American power, not displace it. The American hegemony will surely eventually decay but increased European and Japanese strength need not lead to war, contrary to the expectations of standard theories of hegemony and great power rivalry. Unlike previous eras of hegemony, the current peace seems uncoerced and accepted by most states, which does not fit entirely well with realism.

Nuclear Weapons

The second realist argument was familiar during the Cold War but receives less attention now. This is the pacifying effect of nuclear weapons, which, if possessed in sufficient numbers and invulnerable configurations, make victory impossible and war a feckless option. An immediate objection is that not all the major states in the Community have nuclear weapons. But this is only technically correct: Germany and Japan could produce nuclear weapons if a threat loomed, as their partners fully understand. The other factors discussed in the previous pages may or may not be important; nuclear weapons by themselves would be sufficient to keep the great powers at peace.

While there is a great deal to this argument, it is not without its problems. First, because this kind of deterrence rests on the perceived possibility of war, it may explain peace, but not a security community. Second, mutual deterrence can be used as a platform for hostility, coercion, and even limited wars. In what Glenn Snyder (1965; also see Jervis 1989, 19–23, 74–106) calls the stability-instability paradox, the common realization that all-out war would be irrational provides a license for threats and the use of lower levels of violence. Under some circumstances a state could use the shared fear of nuclear war to exploit others. If the state thinks that the other is preoccupied with the possibility of war and does not anticipate that the state will make the concessions needed to reduce this danger, it will expect the other to retreat and so can stand firm. In other words, the fact that war would be the worst possible outcome for both sides does not automatically lead to uncoerced peace, let alone to a security community.

A Synthetic Interactive Explanation

I think the development and maintenance of the Community is best explained by a combination and reformulation of several factors discussed previously. Even with the qualifications just discussed, a necessary condition is the belief that conquest is difficult and war is terribly costly. When conquest is easy, aggression is encouraged and the security dilemma operates with particular viciousness as even defensive states need to prepare to attack (Van Evera 1999). But when states have modern armies with extensive firepower and, even more, nuclear weapons, it is hard for anyone to believe that war could make sense.

Statesmen must consider the gains that war might bring as well as the costs. Were they to be very high, they might outweigh great expected costs. But, if anything, the expected benefits of war within the Community have declined, in part because the developed countries, including those that lost World War II, are generally satisfied with the status quo. Even in the case that shows the greatest strain—U.S.–Japanese relations—no one has explained how a war could provide either side much gross, let alone net, benefit. It is then hard to locate a problem for which war among the Community members would provide a solution. Furthermore, as liberals have stressed, peace within the Community brings many gains, especially economic.

Of course costs and benefits are subjective, depending as they do on what the actors value, and changes in values are the third leg of my explanation. Most political analysis takes the actors' values for granted because they tend to be widely shared and to change slowly. Their importance and variability becomes clear only when we confront a case like Nazi Germany which, contrary to standard realist conceptions of national interest and security, put everything at risk in order to seek the domination of the Aryan race.

The changes over the last 50–75 years in what the leaders and publics in the developed states value drive some of the calculations of costs and benefits. To start with, war is no longer seen as good in itself; no great power leader today would agree with Theodore Roosevelt that "no triumph of peace is quite so great as the supreme triumph of war" (quoted in Harbaugh 1961, 99). In earlier eras it was commonly believed that war brought out the best in individuals and nations and that the virtues of discipline, risk-taking, and self-sacrifice that war required were central to civilization. Relatedly, honor and glory used to be central values. In a world so constituted, the material benefits of peace would be much less important; high levels of trade, the difficulty of making conquest pay, and even nuclear weapons might not produce peace.

Democracy and identity also operate through what actors value, and may in part be responsible for the decline in militarism just noted. Compromise, consideration for the interests of others, respect for law, and a shunning of violence outside this context all are values that underpin democracy and are reciprocally cultivated by it. The Community also is relatively homogeneous in that its members are all democracies and have values that are compatibly similar. One impulse to war is the desire to change the other country, and this disappears if values are shared. The

United States could conquer Canada, for example, but what would be the point when so much of what it wants to see there is already in place?

Central to the rise of the Community is the decline in territorial disputes among its members. Territory has been the most common cause and object of conflicts in the past, and we have become so accustomed to their absence that it is easy to lose sight of how drastic and consequential this change is. Germans no longer care that Alsace and Lorraine are French; the French are not disturbed by the high level of German presence in these provinces. The French furthermore permitted the Saar to return to Germany and are not bothered by this loss, and indeed do not feel it as a loss at all. Although for years the Germans refused to renounce their claims to the "lost territories" to the east, they did so upon unification and few voices were raised in protest.

The causes of these changes in values in general and nationalism and concern with territory in particular are subject to dispute, as are the developments that could reverse them. In particular, it is unclear how much they are rooted in material changes, most obviously the increased destructiveness of war and the unprecedented prosperity that is seen as linked to good political relations, and to what extent they are more autonomous, following out perhaps a natural progression and building on each other. They may be linked (inextricably?) to high levels of consumption, faith in rationality, and the expectation of progress, although it is not unreasonable to argue that this describes Europe in 1914 as well. The decreased salience of territory and decline of territorial disputes is almost surely produced in part by the decoupling of territorial control and national prosperity, and most of the other relationships between material structures and ideational patterns are complex and reciprocal. Just as capitalism is built and sustained by pre-capitalist values and post-materialism may grow from prosperity so the values that sustain the Community can neither be separated nor simply deduced from changes in the means and levels of production and potential destruction.

The increased destructiveness of war, the benefits of peace, and the changes in values interact and reinforce each other. If war were not so dreadful, it could be considered as an instrument for national enrichment; if peace did not seem to bring prosperity and national well-being, violence would at least be contemplated; that military victory is no longer seen as a positive value both contributes to and is in part explained by the high perceived costs of war. Similarly, expectations of peace allow states to value each other's economic and political successes. Although these may incite envy, they no longer produce strong security fears, as they did in the past. The Community may then contain within it the seeds of its own growth through the feedbacks among its elements.

Another dynamic element is crucial as well: the progress of the Community is path-dependent in that without the Cold War it is unlikely that the factors we have discussed could have overcome prevalent fears and rivalries. The conflict with the Soviet Union produced American security guarantees and an unprecedented sense of common purpose among the states that now form the Community. Since the coalition could be undermined by social unrest or political instability, each country sought to see that the others were well off and resisted the temptation to solve its own problems by exporting them to its neighbors. Since the coalition would have been disrupted had any country developed strong grievances against other members, each had reason to moderate its demands and mediate when conflicts developed between others. To cultivate better relations in the future, leaders consciously portrayed the others as partners and sponsored the socialization practices discussed above. The American willingness to engage in extensive cooperation abroad, the European willingness to go far down the road of integration, the Japanese willingness to tie itself closely to the United States were improbable without the Cold War. But having been established, these forms of cooperation set off positive feedback and are now self-sustaining.

IMPLICATIONS

What are the implications of the existence of the security community for how these states will carry out relations among themselves and for general theories of war and peace?

International Politics Within the Community

In previous eras, no aspect of international politics and few aspects of domestic politics were untouched by the anticipation of future wars among the leading powers. Much will then change in the Community. In the absence of these states amalgamating—a development that is out of the question outside of Europe and unlikely within it—they will neither consider using force against one another nor lose their sovereignty. There will then be significant conflicts of interest without clear means of resolving them. They will continue to be rivals in some respects, and to bargain with each other. Indeed, the stability-instability paradox implies that the shared expectation that disputes will remain peaceful will remove some restraints on vituperation and competitive tactics. The dense network of institutions within the Community should serve to provide multiple means for resolving conflicts, but will also provide multiple ways for a dissatisfied country to show its displeasure and threaten disruption.

The fact that the situation is a new one poses challenges and opportunities for states. What goals will have highest priority? How important will considerations of status be? Will non-military alliances form? Bargaining will continue, and this means that varieties of power, including the ability to help and hurt others, will remain relevant. Threats, bluffs, warnings, the mobilization of resources for future conflicts, intense diplomatic negotiations, and shifting patterns of working with and against others all will remain. But the content of these forms will differ from those of traditional international politics.

Politics within the Community may come to resemble the relations between the United States and Canada and Australia that Keohane and Nye (1977) described as complex interdependence: extensive transnational and transgovernmental relations, bargains carried out across different issue areas, and bargaining power gained through asymmetric dependence but limited by overall common interests. Despite this path-breaking study, however, we know little about how this kind of politics will be conducted. As numerous commentators have noted, economic issues and economic resources will play large roles, but the changed context will matter. Relative economic advantage was sought in the past in part because it contributed to military security. This no longer being the case, the possibilities for cooperation are increased.

Even though force will not be threatened within the Community, it will remain important in relations among its members. During the Cold War the protection the United States afforded to its allies gave it an important moral claim and significant bargaining leverage. Despite the decreased level of threat, this will be true for the indefinite future because militarily Japan and Europe need the United States much more than the United States needs them. While the unique American ability to lead military operations like those in the Persian Gulf and Kosovo causes resentments and frictions with its allies, it also gives it a resource that is potent even—or especially—if it is never explicitly brought to the table.

Four Possible Futures

Even within the contours of a Community, there is a significant range of patterns of relations that are possible, four of which can be briefly sketched.

The greatest change would be a world in which national autonomy would be further diminished and the distinctions between domestic and foreign policy would continue to erode. Medieval Europe, with its overlapping forms of sovereignty rather than compartmentalized nation-states, which might dissolve because they are no longer needed to provide security and can no longer control their economies, is one model here. Although most scholars see the reduction of sovereignty and the growth of the power of non-governmental organizations as conducive to peace and harmony, one can readily imagine sharp conflicts, for example among business interests, labor, and environmentalists (many Marxists see class conflicts as increasingly important); between those with different views of the good life; between those calling for greater centralization to solve common problems and those advocating increased local control. But state power and interest would in any case be greatly decreased. The notion of "national interest," always contested, would become even more problematic.

A second world, not completely incompatible with the first, would be one in which states in the Community play a large role, but with more extensive and intensive cooperation. Relations would be increasingly governed by principles and laws, a change that could benignly spill over into relations outside the Community. Although bargaining would not disappear, there would be more joint efforts to solve common problems and the line between "high" and "low" politics would become even more blurred.

In this world, the United States would share more power and responsibility with the rest of the Community than is true today. While popular with scholars at least as likely is a continuation of the present trajectory in which the United

States maintains hegemony and rejects significant limitations on its freedom of action. National interests would remain distinct and the United States would follow the familiar pattern in which ambitions and perceived interests expand as power does. Both conflicts of interest and the belief that hegemony best produces collective goods would lead the United States to oppose the efforts of others to become a counterweight if not a rival to it. In effect, the United States would lead an empire, but probably a relatively benign one. Doing so would be rendered more difficult by the fact that the American self-image precludes seeing its role for what it is, in part because of the popularity of values of equality and supranationalism. Other members of the Community would resent seeing their interests overridden by the United States on some occasions, but the exploitation would be limited by their bargaining power and the American realization that excessive discontent would have serious long-term consequences. Others might accept these costs in return for the U.S. security guarantee and the ability to keep their own defense spending very low, especially because the alternative to American-dominated stability might be worse.

The fourth model also starts with the American attempt to maintain hegemony, but this time the costs and dangers of American unilateralism become sufficient to lead others to form a counter-balancing coalition, one that might include Russia and China as well. Europe and Japan might also become more assertive because they fear that the United States will eventually withdraw its security guarantee, thereby accelerating if not creating a rift within the Community. Much that realism stresses—the clash of national interests, the weakness of international institutions, maneuvering for advantage, and the use of power and threats—would come to the fore, but with the vital difference that force would not be contemplated and the military balance would enter in only indirectly, as discussed above. This would be a strange mixture of the new and the familiar, and the central question is what *ultima ratio* will replace cannons. What will be the final arbiter of disputes? What kinds of threats will be most potent? How fungible will the relevant forms of power be?

Outlining these possibilities raises two broad questions that I cannot answer. First, is the future essentially determined, as many structural theories would imply, or does it depend on national choices strongly influenced by variable domestic politics, leaders, and accidents? Second, if the future is not determined, how much depends on choices the United States has yet to make, and what will most influence these choices?

IMPLICATIONS FOR THEORIES OF THE CAUSES OF WAR

Whatever its explanation, the very existence of a security community among the leading powers refutes many theories of the causes of war, or at least indicates they are not universally valid. Thus human nature and the drive for dominance, honor, and glory may exist and contribute to a wide variety of human behaviors but they are not fated to lead to war.

The obvious rebuttal is that war still exists outside the Community and that civil wars continue unabated. But only wars fought by members of the Community have the potential to undermine the argument that, under some conditions, attributes of humans and societies that were seen as inevitably producing wars in fact do not do so. The cases that could be marshalled are the Gulf War and the operation in Kosovo, but they do not help these theories. These wars were provoked by others, gained little honor and glory for the Community, and were fought in a manner that minimized the loss of life on the other side. It would be hard to portray them as manifestations of brutal or evil human nature. Indeed, it is more plausible to see the Community's behavior as consistent with a general trend toward its becoming less violent generally: the abolition of official torture and the decreased appeal of capital punishment, to take the most salient examples (Mueller 1989).

The existence of the Community also casts doubt on theories that argue that the leading powers always struggle for dominance for gain, status, or security, and are willing to use force to this end. Traditional Marxist theories claim that capitalists could never cooperate; proponents of the law of uneven growth see changes in the relative power of major states as producing cycles of domination, stability, challenge, and war. Similarly, "power transitions" in which rising powers catch up with dominant ones are seen to be very difficult to manage peacefully. These theories, like the version of hegemonic stability discussed above, have yet to be tested because the United States has not yet declined. But if the arguments made here are correct, transitions will not have the same violent outcome that they had in the past, leading us to pay greater attention to the conditions under which these theories do and do not hold.

For most scholars, the fundamental cause of war is international anarchy, compounded by the security dilemma. These forces press hardest on the leading powers because while they may be able to guarantee the security of others, no one can provide this escape from the state of nature for them. As we have seen, different schools of thought propose different explanations for the rise of the Community and so lead to somewhat different propositions about the conditions under which anarchy can be compatible with peace. Constructivism stresses the importance of identities and ideas; liberalism argues for the power of material incentives for peace; realism looks at the costs of war and the details of the payoff structure; my composite explanation stresses the interaction among several factors of costs, benefits, values, and path-dependence. But what is most important is that the Community constitutes a proof by existence of uncoerced peace without central authority. Because these countries are the most powerful ones and particularly war-prone, the Community poses a fundamental challenge to our understanding of world politics and our expectations of future possibilities.

REFERENCES

Art, Robert J. 1996. "Why Western Europe Needs the United States and NATO." *Political Science Quarterly* 111 (Spring): 1–39.

Berghahn, V. R. 1973. *Germany and the Approach of War in 1914.* New York: St. Martin's Press.

Betts, Richard. 1992. "Systems of Peace or Causes of War? Collective Security, Arms Control, and the New Europe." *International Security* 17 (Summer): 5–43.

Bourne, Kenneth. 1970. *The Foreign Policy of Victorian England: 1830–1902.* Oxford: Clarendon Press.

Cain, Peter. 1979. "Capitalism, War and Internationalism in the Thought of Richard Cobden." *British Journal of International Studies* 5 (October): 229–47.

Deutsch, Karl W., et al. 1957. *Political Community and the North Atlantic Area: International Organizations in the Light of Historical Experience.* Princeton, NJ: Princeton University Press.

Farber, Henry, and Joanne Gowa. 1995. "Polities and Peace." *International Security* 20 (Fall): 123–46.

Farber, Henry and Joanne Gowa. 1997. "Common Interests or Common Polities?" *Journal of Politics* 59 (May): 123–46.

Gartzke, Erik. 1998. "Kant We All Get Along? Motive, Opportunity, and the Origins of the Democratic Peace." *American Journal of Political Science* 42 (1): 1–27.

Gartzke, Erik. 2000. "Preferences and Democratic Peace." *International Studies Quarterly* 44 (June): 191–212.

Gilbert, Martin. 1983. *Winston S. Churchill,* Volume VI, *Finest Hour 1939–1941.* London: Heinemann.

Harbaugh, William Henry. 1961. *The Life and Times of Theodore Roosevelt.* New York: Collier Books.

Hirschman, Albert O. 1945. *National Power and the Structure of Foreign Trade.* Berkeley and Los Angeles: University of California Press.

Jervis, Robert. 1989. *The Meaning of Nuclear Revolution: Statecraft and the Prospect of Armageddon.* Ithaca, NY: Cornell University Press.

Keohane, Robert O., and Joseph Nye, eds. 1977. *Power and Interdependence: World Politics in Transition.* Boston, MA: Little Brown.

Kumar, Amitava. 2001. "Bristling on the Subcontinent." *The Nation.* April 23, 2001, 29–30.

Levy, Jack S. 1989. "Domestic Politics and War." In *The Origins and Prevention of Major Wars,* eds. Robert I. Rotberg and Theodore K. Rabb. Cambridge: Cambridge University Press. pp. 79–100.

Luard, Evan. 1986. *War in International Society: A Study in International Sociology.* London: I.B. Tauris.

Maoz, Zeev. 1997. "The Controversy Over the Democratic Peace: Rearguard Action or Cracks in the Wall?" *International Security* 22 (Summer): 162–98.

McMillan, Susan M. 1997. "Interdependence and Conflict." *Mershon International Studies Review* 41, supplement 1 (May): 33–58.

Mearsheimer, John J. 2001. *The Tragedy of Great Power Politics.* New York: Norton.

Mueller, John. 1989. *Retreat from Doomsday: The Obsolescence of Major War.* New York: Basic Books.

O'Hanlon, Michael E. 2001. *Defense Policy Choices for the Bush Administration.* Washington, DC: Brookings Institution Press.

Oneal, John R., and Bruce Russett. 1999. "Is the Liberal Peace Just an Artifact of Cold War Interests? Assessing Recent Critiques." *International Interactions* 25 (3): 213–41.

Russett, Bruce, and John R. Oneal. 2001. *Triangulating Peace: Democracy, Interdependence, and International Organizations.* New York: Norton.

Schweller, Randall L. 2000. "Democracy and the Post–Cold War Era." In *The New World Order*, eds. Birthe Hansen and Bertel Heurlin. New York: St. Martin's Press. pp. 46–80.

Snyder, Glenn. 1965. "The Balance of Power and the Balance of Terror." In *The Balance of Power*, ed. Paul Seabury. San Francisco: Chandler. pp. 184–201.

Van Evera, Stephen. 1984. "The Cult of the Offensive and the Origins of the First World War." *International Security* 9 (Summer): 58–107.

Van Evera, Stephen. 1999. *Causes of War: Power and the Roots of Conflict*. Ithaca, NY: Cornell University Press.

Waltz, Kenneth N. 1970. "The Myth of National Interdependence." In *The International Corporation*, ed. Charles P. Kindleberger. Cambridge, MA: MIT Press. pp. 205–23.

Waltz, Kenneth N. 1979. *Theory of International Politics*. Reading, MA: Addison-Wesley Publishing.

Waltz, Kenneth N. 1999. "Globalization and Governance." *PS: Political Science & Politics* 32 (December): 693–700.

Wrong, Dennis H. 1976. *Skeptical Sociology*. New York: Columbia University Press.

The United States and the Rise of China

ROBERT J. ART

Today, the United States stands at the pinnacle of its power when power is measured in terms of hard economic and military assets. Although its economy will continue to grow and although it will remain the most powerful military nation on earth for some time to come, America's economic and military edge *relative* to the world's other great powers will inevitably diminish over the next several decades.

The country best positioned to challenge America's preeminence, first in East Asia, and then perhaps later globally, is China. If China's economy continues to grow for two more decades at anything close to the rate of the last two decades, then it will eventually rival and even surpass the United States in the size of its gross domestic product (measured in purchasing power parity terms, not in constant dollar terms), although not in per capital GDP.[1] Even if its economy never catches up to America's, China's remarkable economic growth has already given it significant political influence in East Asia, and that influence will only grow as China's economy continues to grow. Moreover, having emerged as the low-cost manufacturing platform of the world, China's economic influence extends well beyond East Asia and affects not only the rich great powers but also the struggling smaller developing ones, because of both its competitive prices for low cost goods and its voracious appetite for raw materials. China is already the dominant military land power on the East Asian mainland, and it has made significant strides in creating pockets of excellence in its armed forces. If it continues to channel a healthy portion of its GDP into its military forces over several more decades and if it makes a determined naval and air power projection effort, China might be able to deploy a maritime force that could contest America's supremacy at sea in East Asia, much as the German fleet built by Tirpitz in the decade before World War I posed a severe threat to the British fleet in the North Sea.

Historically, the rise of one great power at the expense of the dominant one has nearly always led to conflictual relations between the two, and, more often than not, eventually to a war between them that has dragged in other great powers.[2] Is the history of dominant-rising great power dyads the future for U.S.-China relations?

Clearly, there will be political and economic conflicts and friction between the United States and China as its economic and military power in East Asia, and its global economic and political reach, continue to expand. Clearly, there will also be some arms racing between China and the United States as each jockeys for advantage over the other, and as each is driven by their respective military necessities of intimidating and defending Taiwan, and as the United States responds to China's growing power projection capabilities. Historically, dominant powers have not readily given up their position of number one to rising challengers, and rising challengers have always demanded the fruits that they believe their growing power entitles them to. There is no reason to expect that things will be different in this regard with China and the United States. Thus, they will not be able to avoid a certain level of conflictual relations and political friction over the next several decades.

Are mostly political friction and conflictual relations, and even war, the main things that these two powers have to look forward to, or are there also some significant shared interests and hence bases for cooperation in both the medium and the longer term such that the peace-inducing aspects of the U.S.-China relationship could come to overshadow the conflict-producing ones? No one can say for certain which is the case. However, if we believe that there are distinct elements in the Sino-American relationship that differ from past dominant power-rising power dyads, then the dismal history of such dyads need not be the future of this one. If this is so, then the right policy choices by both countries can keep the two on a path that has more cooperative than conflictual elements to it, thereby avoiding the doom-and-gloom scenario that too many of today's analysts portray.

POWER TRANSITIONS AND SECURITY DILEMMA DYNAMICS

A third benchmark for U.S. policy toward a rising China is this: do not assume that Sino-American relations will follow the course of recent cases where a rising power has challenged a dominant one. There are too many significant differences between these cases and the current one to draw such a firm conclusion.

To defend this assertion, in Table 1 I compare the current Sino-American competition with the three most important rising-power-versus-dominant-power competitions of the last one hundred years—those that resulted in either a great power hegemonic war or a sustained and intense political-military competition for hegemonic dominance between two great powers. (Hegemonic wars and hegemonic political-military competitions are conducted to determine which power will be number one and be able to set the rules of the international system.) The first two competitions—Britain versus Germany in the decade before World War I and Britain versus Germany from 1933–1939—resulted in war; the third—the United States versus the Soviet Union during the Cold War—resulted in an uneasy peace between the two powers, punctuated by numerous proxy wars.[3]

TABLE 1 ■ DOMINANT POWER VERSUS RISING POWER COMPETITIONS

Dominant-Rising Power Dyad	Security Enjoyed by Both Powers Vis-à-Vis One Another	Level of Economic Interdependence	Ideological Competition	Outcome
United Kingdom-Germany pre 1914	In 1914 security thought to be low for the future if corrective action (war) not taken	High	Low	War
United Kingdom-Germany pre 1939	Low in the 1930s due to presumed airpower threat	Low to medium	Medium to high	War
U.S.-Soviet Union during the Cold War	Initially believed to be low; turned out later to be high	Low	High and intense	Cold War; serious crises at first; then an uneasy peace
U.S.-China Today	High for U.S., but problematical for China because Chinese nuclear forces at present are potentially vulnerable to a U.S. first strike	High	As yet, low to nonexistent	To be determined

I focus on three variables in order to explain the outcome of these cases: the level of security that both powers enjoyed, or believed they enjoyed, in general and vis-à-vis one another, with security defined as protection of the state's homeland from physical attack and its political sovereignty from severe infringement; the extent of economic interdependence between them, with interdependence defined in terms of the level of economic interactions—especially trade—between the two states; and the degree and intensity of ideological competition that they experienced. I do not present these three variables as a full-blown deductive theory about war and peace between rising and dominant great powers; such theories have been presented by others, although with somewhat contradictory results.[4] Instead, I argue that these three factors—and especially the first, as made clear below—are the most important ones to look at in order to determine the level and intensity of hostility and conflict, and hence the likelihood of war, between two great powers that believe they are experiencing, or may soon experience, a fundamental power shift between them.

All other things being equal, the intensity of competition and the likelihood of war between a dominant power and a rising challenger should vary as follows. First, the lower the level of security each enjoys or believes it enjoys vis-à-vis the other or in general, the more likely are serious security dilemma dynamics, intense arms racing, and war between the two. Conversely, if these states feel that they are relatively secure from attack and that their political sovereignty is not being compromised (or will not be compromised) by the actions of the other, then they can experience a greater level of hostility that may arise from conflicts over nonsecurity issues without war being the result. There are many reasons why two states can wage war with one another; however, if each believes it is relatively safe from attack by the other, then one of the most powerful historic incentives for war—security—is removed.

Second, under the right conditions, the higher the level of economic interdependence between two states, the less likely will security competitions and war between them take place. The three conditions under which high levels of economic interdependence can be peace-inducing are: (1) when two states believe that they can more profitably resort to economic rather than military means in order to prosper; (2) when they believe that the economic vulnerabilities that result from economic interdependence cannot be quickly and easily turned to their military disadvantage; and (3) when they believe that should the first two conditions change, they can readily protect themselves or find allies who will.[5]

Finally, the greater the ideological differences between the two states, the more intense will be their competition and the more likely they are to experience arms races, intense security dilemmas, and war. Security concerns have been powerful factors for war, but they are not the only factors. Ideological hostilities—conflicts over how social power should be organized within states—have also contributed to hostility and war between states. The Cold War, for example, was not simply about U.S.-Soviet Security, it was also about values—democratic market capitalism versus communism—and which would prevail globally.

Close inspection of Table 1 reveals that neither economic interdependence nor ideological competition is a good predictor of whether a dominant and rising power will go to war or remain at peace. In 1914, for example, Germany was England's second best customer for its exports, and England was Germany's best customer for its exports.[6] Before the war, they did not experience intense ideological competition, and in fact shared many political similarities. Yet, the two ended up at war. Throughout the 1930s, England and Germany did not have as high a level of economic interdependence with one another as they had before World War I, and they did experience some ideological competition.[7] At the outset of, and during the course of, the Cold War, the United States and the Soviet Union experienced a low level of economic interdependence with one another, and their ideological competition was high and intense.[8] Yet they remained in an uneasy peace, although one that was much more fragile during the first part of the Cold War than during the second. Thus, the relationship between levels of economic interdependence and intensity of ideological competition, on the one hand, and war or peace, on the other, is indeterminate. High and low levels of interdependence are correlated with war, and high and low levels of ideological competition are correlated with both war and peace.

Therefore, it is the degree of security enjoyed by these pairs of states vis-à-vis one another, and especially the severity of the threat to its security that the dominant state perceives emanating from the rising state, that constitutes the most important variable to predict whether a hegemonic struggle will result in war.[9] When security was low or believed to be low, intense crises and war were more likely; when security was high or believed to be high, better relations and peace tended to prevail. Economic interdependence and ideological competition are not irrelevant to producing peace and war, but they are only "helper variables." They can reinforce peaceful trends when the security enjoyed by both states vis-à-vis one another is high, but they cannot override the deleterious effects produced when the security enjoyed by both states vis-à-vis one another is low.

In 1914, Germany needed England to stand aside so that it could shore up its failing great power ally Austria-Hungary and deal with the growing power of Russia. Diplomatic isolation for Germany (the dissolution of Austria-Hungary) meant the political encirclement and eventual strangulation of Germany in the eyes of Germany's leaders. If Britain stood aside while Germany attained continental hegemony, however, then Britain's security would be at risk if a hegemonic Germany deployed the resources of the European continent against it. So, in classic security dilemma terms, Britain's security would be at risk by the continental hegemony that Germany believed it needed for its security, and, similarly, Germany's leaders believed that Germany's security would be at risk if Britain denied it continental hegemony. The same logic applies to the British-German struggle during the 1930s. A Nazi Germany that had defeated Russia and vanquished the continent could aggregate its resources and turn them into an invasion force to crush England's defenses. The threat that German hegemony posed to Britain brought on the two World Wars.

Security factors were also central in explaining why the Cold War stayed "cold." The United States and the Soviet Union experienced an intense ideological competition for most of the Cold War, but that competition never turned into a direct war between the two primarily because of the restraining effects of nuclear deterrence. True, the stability-instability paradox did not work to prevent all serious crises between the two, and true, two of these crises—the Berlin Blockade crisis of 1948 and the Cuban Missile crisis of 1962—brought the United States and the Soviet Union closer to war than either would have liked.[10] However, the workings of the stability/instability paradox were ultimately beneficial: it worked to prevent those crises that did occur from escalating to war, and it worked, ultimately, to reduce dramatically the frequency and the severity of crises after the Cuban Missile Crisis. In fact, one could make a strong argument that with one exception serious security crises between the United States and the Soviet Union disappeared after 1973.[11]

China does not present the type of security threat to the United States that Germany did to Britain, or Britain to Germany. America's nuclear forces make it secure from any Chinese attack on the homeland. Moreover, China clearly presents a potentially different type of threat to the United States than the Soviet Union did during the Cold War because the geopolitics of the two situations are different. The Soviet geopolitical (as opposed to the nuclear) threat was twofold: to conquer and dominate the economic-industrial resources of western Eurasia and to control the oil reserves of the Persian Gulf. Europe and the Persian Gulf constituted two of the five power centers of the world during the Cold War—Japan, the Soviet Union, and the United States being the other three. If the Soviets had succeeded in dominating Europe and the Persian Gulf through either conquest or political-military intimidation, then it would have controlled three of the five power centers of the world. That would have been a significant power transition.

China's rise does not constitute the same type of geopolitical threat to the United States that the Soviet Union did. If China ends up dominating the Korean peninsula and a significant part of continental Southeast Asia, so what? As long as Japan remains outside the Chinese sphere of influence and allied with the United States, and as long as the United States retains some naval footholds in Southeast Asia, such as in Singapore, the Philippines, or Indonesia, China's domination of these two areas would not present the same type of geopolitical threat that the Soviet Union did. As long as Europe, the Persian Gulf, Japan, India, and Russia (once it reconstitutes itself as a serious great power) remain either as independent power centers or under U.S. influence, Chinese hegemony on land in East and Southeast Asia will not tip the world balance of power. The vast size and central position of the Soviet Union in Eurasia constituted a geopolitical threat to American influence that China cannot hope to emulate.

If judged by the standards of the last three dominant power-rising power competitions of the last one hundred years, then, the U.S.-China competition appears well placed to be much safer. Certainly, war between the two is not impossible because either or both governments could make a serious misstep over the Taiwan issue. War by miscalculation is always possible, but the possession of nuclear weapons by both sides has to have a restraining effect on both by dramatically raising the costs of miscalculation, thereby increasing the incentives not to miscalculate. Nuclear deterrence should work to lower dramatically the possibility of war by either miscalculation or deliberate decision (or if somehow such a war broke out, then nuclear deterrence should work against its escalation into a large and fearsome one). Apart from the Taiwan issue, it is hard to figure out how to start a war between the United States and China. There are no other territorial disputes of any significance between the two, and there are no foreseeable economic contingencies that could bring on a war between them. Finally, the high economic interdependence and the lack of intense ideological competition between them help to reinforce the pacific effects induced by the condition of mutual assured destruction.

The workings of these three factors should make us cautiously optimistic about keeping Sino-American relations on the peaceful rather than the warlike track. The peaceful track does not, by any means, imply the absence of political and economic conflicts in Sino-American relations, nor does it foreclose coercive diplomatic gambits by each against the other. What it does mean is that the conditions are in place for war to be a low probability event, if policymakers are smart in both states (see below), and that an all-out war is nearly impossible to imagine. By the historical standards of recent dominant-rising state dyads, this is no mean feat.

In sum, there will be some security dilemma dynamics at work in the U.S.-China relationship, both over Taiwan and over maritime supremacy in East Asia should China decide eventually to contest America's maritime hegemony, and there will certainly be economic and political conflicts, but nuclear weapons should work to mute their severity because the security of each state's homeland will never be in doubt as long as each maintains a second-strike capability vis-à-vis the other. If two states cannot conquer one another, then the character of their relation and their competition changes dramatically than would be the case if they could.

NOTES

1. For a skeptical view of this happening anytime soon, see Lester Thurow, "A Chinese Century: Maybe It's the Next One," *New York Times*, August 19, 2007, p. 4 (business section).

2. See Dale C. Copeland, *The Origins of Major War* (Ithaca, NY: Cornell University Press, 2000); and Robert Gilpin, *War and Change in International Politics* (Cambridge: Cambridge University Press, 1981).

3. These three cases do not include all the great power cases of rising-versus-dominant power dyads of the last one hundred years. Most prominently and deliberately excluded is the U.S.-British case of the late nineteenth/early twentieth centuries. In this table, I am focusing on two types of competitions: those that resulted in a great power hegemonic war or those that entailed a hostile, intense, and sustained political competition for hegemony and that involved heavy reliance on military force to fight proxy wars or to engage in arms races so as to achieve political hegemony. The U.S.-British case does not fall into either category, although the United States did threaten the British with a naval arms race after World War I if they did not renounce the Anglo-Japanese Treaty of 1902. By focusing on the three cases I have chosen, I have selected on the dependent variable—on those cases in which the outcome is either war or a sustained political-military rivalry rather than peace or peaceful accommodation, with the result that the conclusions of this analysis are to a degree biased. Nonetheless, there is still analytical merit in focusing on these two types of hegemonic competitions to see what conclusions we can draw. For a slightly different list of important power transitions, see Jacek Kugler and A. F. K. Organski, *The War Ledger* (Chicago: University of Chicago Press, 1980), p. 49. For an analysis of why the U.S.-British case ended in peace, not war, see Stephen R. Rock, *When Peace Breaks Out: Great Power Historical Rapprochement in Historical Perspective* (Chapel Hill: The University of North Carolina Press, 1989), chap. 2. For a more general treatment of the strategies that dominant powers employ to cope with rising powers, see Randell L. Schweller, "Managing the Rise of Great Powers: History and Theory," in Robert S. Ross and Alastair Iain Johnston, eds., *Engaging China: The Management of an Emerging Power* (London: Routledge, 1999), pp. 1–32.

4. There are four distinct theories as to why wars occur between rising and dominant great powers, but in one way or another, all four revolve around perceptions of, or actual manifestations of, fundamental power shifts between the two states. The first three theories argue that the dominant power launches the hegemonic war; the fourth, that the rising power launches the hegemonic war. Dale Copeland argues that the dominant power will launch a preventive war against a rising power when it believes that its own decline is both inevitable and steep and at a time when it believes it is still more powerful than the rising challenger. (See Dale C. Copeland, *The Origins of Major Wars*, chap. 2.) Robert Gilpin argues that hegemonic wars occur between a dominant and rising power when the governance of the system and its power distribution are in disequilibrium, in other words, when the rising power does not benefit from the system as much as its power entitles or enables it to, and although he is a little vague about which state starts the war, it is generally the declining but still dominant power that does. (See Robert Gilpin, *War and Change in World Politics*, chap. 5.) Stephen Van Evera argues that windows of vulnerability and opportunity produce war between a declining dominant and a rising power when the former attacks the latter. (See Stephen Van Evera, *The Causes of War: Power and the Roots of Conflict* [Ithaca, NY: Cornell University Press, 1999], chap. 4.) Finally,

the power transition school, founded by A.F.K. Organski, argues that peace obtains when the dominant state has a huge preponderance of power over any potential challenger, but that wars occur as the power disparity between the dominant and rising power narrows and occurs just before the rising power achieves parity with the dominant power, or at the moment when it has achieved parity, or just after it has overtaken the dominant power—the time when war is initiated depending on which version of the power transition theory is used. (See A.F. K. Organski, *World Politics*, 1st ed. [New York: Alfred A. Knopf, 1958] chap. 12, esp. p. 333; Jacek Kugler and A.F.K. Organski, *The War Ledger*, pp. 19–22 and 49–61; Jacek Kugler and Douglas Lemke, eds., *Parity and War: Evaluations and Extensions of the War Ledger* (Ann Arbor: University of Michigan Press, 1996), chap. 1; and Ronald L. Tammen et al., *Power Transitions: Strategies for the 21st Century* [New York: Chatham House Publishers, 2000], chap. 1.)

5. See Robert J. Art, *A Grand Strategy for America*, pp. 66–67.

6. In 1913, 10 percent of Britain's total trade (imports and exports) was with Germany, and 12 percent of Germany's total trade was with Britain. These percentages are derived from the Correlates of War data. The data was prepared by Katherine Barbieri for her doctoral dissertation *Economic Interdependence and Militarized Interstate Conflict, 1870–1985* (Binghamton University, Binghamton, NY, 1996). The dataset is at http://cow2.la.psu.edu/. I am indebted to Loren Cass for arranging the data for easy use.

7. In 1938, 4 percent of Britain's total trade (imports and exports) was with Germany, and 6 percent of Germany's total trade was with Britain.

8. In 1977, for example, during the height of détente between the United States and the Soviet Union, when one would expect trade to be the highest, the United States sent 1.4 percent of its total exports to the Soviet Union and received 0.3 percent of its total imports from the Soviet Union. By 1983, when détente had ended and U.S.-Soviet relations were hostile, the United States sent 0.1 percent of its exports to, and received 0.1 percent of its imports from, the Soviet Union. In 1977, the Soviets exported 2.5 percent of its exports to the United States and took 8 percent of its imports from the United States. By 1983, these Soviet figures had fallen to 1 percent and 5.7 percent, respectively. See International Monetary Fund, *Direction of Trade Statistics Yearbook, 1984* (Washington, DC: International Monetary Fund, 1984), pp. 378 and 385.

9. This is close to the argument that Dale Copeland makes about the causes of hegemonic great power wars. See Dale C. Copeland, *The Origins of Major War*, chaps. 1 and 2.

10. The stability-instabilty paradox says either that two nuclear-armed and hostile states will start a conventional war with each other because they feel confident that it will not escalate to all-out nuclear war, or that they will not start such a war because they fear that it might escalate to all-out nuclear war. During the Cold War, the paradox produced the second, not the first, effect. Glenn Snyder was the first to formulate the paradox. See Glenn H. Snyder, "The Balance of Power and the Balance of Terror," in Paul Seabury, ed., *The Balance of Power* (San Francisco: Chandler, 1965), pp. 198–199. Also see Robert Jervis, *The Illogic of American Nuclear Strategy* (Ithaca, NY: Cornell University Press, 1984), pp. 31–33 and 148–157.

11. The exception came in November 1983 with the NATO exercise "Able Archer." This was a serious crisis from the Soviets' point of view, and they briefly believed a nuclear from the West was imminent. At the time, however, neither the United States nor NATO was aware of the Soviet concerns, making this crisis hard to classify. See John Lewis Gaddis, *The Cold War: A New History* (New York: Penguin Press, 2005), pp. 227–228.

Ending Terrorism

AUDREY KURTH CRONIN

EXAMINING HOW TERRORIST CAMPAIGNS HAVE ENDED

Although there are natural variations in the way specific [terrorist] groups end, demise generally follows six pathways, usually characterised by watershed events that lead to a diminution in the rate or lethality of attacks. . . . Historical cases are remarkably consistent in demonstrating a relationship between one of these six common pathways and the ending of a group, not least because each of the processes described engages with all three of terrorism's crucial elements: the state, the group and the audience. Some of the processes of decline are set in motion by the state, some by the group itself and some mainly by the audience. . . .

Catching or Killing the Leaders

First among the range of actions a government may take in pushing a group towards its end is to capture or kill its leader. Terrorist groups do sometimes meet their demise as a result of decapitation. The "propagandist-in-chief" is more important for groups that use terrorism than it is for other types of violent political or criminal groups, even if he or she is not operationally directing the group's activities. The mouthpiece's primary purpose is to mobilise followers. If a group is well mobilised, then it is unlikely to rely heavily on terrorist attacks against noncombatants, which can be risky, controversial and counterproductive. Terrorist groups often feature an individual who exploits a sense of hope and a feeling of grievance or frustration, thereby streamlining the frustrating complexities of life and presenting terrorist attacks as a way of nudging history forwards to a new, more desirable future. Little wonder that governments like to target the top.

The effects of decapitation have varied, especially according to whether a group was hierarchically organised and oriented towards a charismatic leader. Cases of groups that were badly damaged by the capture of their leader include Shining Path in Peru, the Real IRA and Aum Shinrikyo. . . . There is considerable evidence to indicate that capturing leaders has been more effective than killing them in ending a group. . . . That said, it is important how leaders are handled after they are apprehended. High-profile arrests sometimes backfire if jailed leaders are allowed to communicate with followers from prison, or when group members still on the

Audrey Kurth Cronin, *Ending Terrorism: Lessons for Defeating al-Qaeda.* Adelphi Series, Vol. 47, Issue 394 (2007), pp. 28–49. Reprinted by permission of the author and the publisher (Taylor & Francis Ltd, http://www.informaworld.com). Portions of the text and some footnotes have been omitted.

outside attempt to free them. Examples include Sheikh Omar Abd al-Rahman (the so-called Blind Sheikh). Convicted for conspiracy in the bombing of the World Trade Center in 1993, he continued to communicate and radicalise followers from his cell. . . . Capturing a group's leader may be effective. The leader is often the source of inspiration for a group and thus its intellectual engine; their incarceration is an implicit answer to the illegitimacy of terrorism, and demonstrates the authority of the rule of law. But it is no guarantee that terrorism will end. . . .

Cases where a group has ended following the *killing* of the leader are less common. The two states most active in carrying out assassinations of terrorist leaders (apart from the United States in its campaign against al-Qaeda) are Israel and Russia. The Israeli government's campaign of targeted killings of Palestinian operatives in groups such as Hamas began openly in October 2000. Killings target not just the top leadership but also mid-level military and political leaders who are believed to be involved in planning operations. According to B'Tselem, an Israeli human-rights organisation, the Israelis have purposely targeted and killed about 202 Palestinians, and 121 people have unintentionally died in operations.[1] The question of whether or not the policy is justified is highly contentious. Many point to evidence of a drop-off in the frequency and lethality of terrorist attacks against Israeli civilians, although determining the degree to which this outcome reflects "targeted killings" as opposed to other factors (such as the security fence) is impossible.[2] Others argue that targeted killings have attracted recruits to terrorist organisations, undercut Palestinian moderates and indirectly led to the election of a Hamas government in 2006. This debate is beyond the scope of this paper: whatever the benefits or drawbacks of targeted killings, they have not ended terrorism.

The other major campaign of killings of terrorist leaders concerns Russian targeting of Chechen leaders. . . . The cost to the Chechen civilian population of the assassination campaign has been enormous. Human-rights abuses in Chechnya persist, and the cycle of retaliatory killings has spread the violence to the broader Caucasus, especially Dagestan, Ingushetia and North Ossetia.[3] Indeed, the Chechen situation is no longer distinct from broader violence and instability in the North Caucasus. Especially when considered beyond the borders of Chechnya, this campaign of assassination, like its Israeli counterpart, has not ended terrorism.

Even in the short term, state targeting of a leader has sometimes backfired, especially in nonhierarchical groups where a ready successor is found or where the leader is killed in the operation and becomes a martyr. Determining whether or not a group will be ended by decapitation means thinking through the second- and third-order effects of removing the leader. Killing or capturing leaders often results in a struggle for succession. This reduces a group's short-term operational effectiveness, but it may also push it to adapt into a more effective, flatter, less hierarchically organised organisation that is harder to destroy. And as a new leader tries to demonstrate his credentials to other members of the group, levels of violence may actually increase.

Before targeting a leader, it is best to think through the question of who the successor is likely to be. In 1973, Israeli agents killed Mohamed Boudia, an Algerian who had orchestrated Palestinian terrorist operations in Western Europe. He was replaced by Carlos ("the jackal"), an even more ruthless and cunning man. It cannot be assumed that the leader waiting in the wings will be less effective or brutal than his predecessor. And the effect on the overall ability of a group to thrive is not foreordained. Will the killing of a leader result in martyrdom and the inspiring of more recruits? Measuring something that has not yet occurred is impossible, of course—assumptions about the so-called "terror stock" are notoriously speculative. . . . Here, governments again have the advantage of being able to learn from trial and error: when a decapitation strategy results in a stronger movement overall, it is time to rethink the policy. The important strategic question for government policy is not just whether attacks are foiled, vengeance is exacted or a group is damaged, but also whether or not a policy of decapitation is helping to bring about the termination of a group in the longer term.

Crushing Terrorism with Force

The second way that states often try to end terrorism is through the use of brute force. This approach may involve aggressive military campaigns abroad (as with Israel's intervention in Lebanon in 1982) or domestic crackdowns at home (as with Turkey and the PKK), or some combination of the two (as in Colombia). Law enforcement is vital to any counter-terrorism strategy. Steady, law-abiding police work, particularly surveillance and prevention, can hold domestic campaigns in check and reassure the populace that legal norms persist; however, normal police work rarely *ends* campaigns, especially when they cross borders. Most governments faced by major terrorist campaigns have been compelled to institute some type of emergency measures to answer the threat.[4] Repression is a natural response to terrorism for most states. . . .it is as common a reaction on the part of democracies as it is for autocratic regimes, especially initially. In a sense, what could be a more natural and legitimate use of force than to avenge the very civilians whose suffrage is at the heart of state power? Whether held to be desirable or regrettable, there is nothing historically *unusual* in the exertion of overwhelming state force, which is after all nothing more than the modern nation-state responding to a threat in exactly the way it is designed to do. But does it work in ending terrorism? At times, domestic and international repression has indeed been effective in pushing groups towards their decline and demise. Historical cases include the Russian government's campaign against Narodnaya Volya, the Peruvian government's repression of Shining Path between 1980 and 1992 and the Turkish government's crushing of the PKK between 1984 and 1999. If the only goal is to end violence against noncombatants for a time within a given territory, then the use of force can be said to have achieved this repeatedly throughout history.

Repression seems particularly prominent in times of state transition: states that are insecure about their domestic or international standing seem especially inclined to use brute force. Post-colonial regimes, keen to establish their legitimacy, have used repression to put down challengers, as in Algeria, Sri Lanka, Egypt and India. Post-Soviet Russia under Putin used overwhelming force in the wake of a series of bombings of civilian apartment blocks in Moscow and Volo-godonsk, blamed on Chechen terrorists. . . .

Yet the overall historical record of efforts to end terrorist campaigns through repression is chequered, for both democratic and nondemocratic states. The use of force exacts a high cost. According to the Turkish government, during the crackdown on the PKK approximately 30,000 people died.[5] The Peruvian government had the worst record of human-rights abuses in the world in the late 1980s: over the course of the campaign against Shining Path, there were more than 7,300 cases of extrajudicial executions by government forces, over 45 percent of them in just two years (1983 and 1985).[6] The brutality of both the Shining Path and the government response set off a cycle of violence. The 2003 report by the Peruvian Truth and Reconciliation Commission claims that approximately 69,000 people died or "disappeared" as a result of the Shining Path's campaign, half of them killed by the group, about a third at the hands of the military and the remainder either unaccounted for or killed by smaller militia forces.

Repression also regularly proves to be only a temporary solution, resulting in the export of the problem to another country or region, as in the spreading of violence from Chechnya to other parts of the Caucasus. It is especially difficult for democracies to engage successfully in repression over time, since such measures require distinguishing targets from the rest of the population, often undermine civil liberties and change the very nature of the state. Keeping a domestic population anxious about the threat of further terrorist attacks and uninformed of the costs of repression appears to be crucial. . . . The use of repression against terrorism can undermine liberal or liberalising regimes, as with Uruguay's crackdown on the Tupamaros and its takeover by a military government in 1973. Massive state repression often kills many more people than the initial terrorist attacks. . . .

States have the power to obliterate entire populations, slaughtering thousands of civilians along with the actors responsible for terrorist attacks. In this sense, the overwhelming use of force by a state cannot *but* work, eventually. But short of that, whether or not repression ends terrorism depends upon how mobilised a population is for a cause, and how despised a regime makes itself in the course of its response.

Achieving the Strategic Objective

Although in the current climate it may be anathema to say so, the third way in which terrorism has ended has been as a result of success. A few terrorist groups have triumphed—that is, they have achieved their long-term strategic or "outcome" goals and then either disbanded or adopted a more legitimate political form and stopped engaging in attacks against non-combatants. Given the nature of the tactic used, it is difficult to discuss this kind of ending dispassionately. And the fact that "success" might be defined by the al-Qaeda movement's more grandiose aims of a united Caliphate is truly antithetical to Western interests. But recognizing that terrorism sometimes succeeds does not legitimise the tactic, and may even be a necessary prerequisite to reducing and eliminating it.

Instances of success are rare, especially when judged against a group's stated strategic aims. The effectiveness of terrorism as a tactic has been overstated in recent years, prejudiced by the dramatic spectacle of the September 11 attacks and the vigorous military response. Overawed by the threat, it seems, many analysts (especially in the United States) have drawn inappropriate parallels between group behaviour and state behaviour when assessing the strategies of terrorism, and have confused terrorism's short-term process and long-term outcome goals. There is a crucial distinction between achievements that perpetuate violence and those that lead to its end.

For groups that use terrorism, tactical or process goals are innumerable and are associated with either gaining relative advantage from a position of weakness, or perpetuating the group itself. . . . Some argue that terrorists engage in attacks as a costly means of signalling resolve to a state; while that is sometimes true, it is just as often the case that such signals are not aimed at governments, but rather at other observers in a wide range of other audiences.[7] Terrorist activities may not be aimed at affecting a state's behaviour at all, or the behaviour of actors related to or sympathetic to the state. Attacks are just as frequently directed at other, more proximate audiences, including competitors for a cause, current members of a group, potential recruits, active supporters, passive supporters or even neutral bystanders. Succeeding in the eyes of these beholders may enable the continuation of a campaign, and has nothing to do with ending terrorism.

Countless short-term objectives can be sought in the bounded reality of a terrorist campaign, all of which may be fruitful in perpetuating a conflict. Terrorist attacks can serve internal organisational goals, such as enhancing one individual's status at the expense of another, or external organizational goals, such as enhancing the position of one group at the expense of another. Suicide attacks against Israeli citizens have at times been used in a macabre competitive process between Palestinian factions.[8] Attacks may be launched simply to ensure the continued survival of a group, by showing ruthlessness or lionising a leader. . . .

Outcome goals, on the other hand, have typically related either to the nature of the state or the governance of its population. Groups may wish to bring down a specific government in order to replace it with a more "just" form of governance. Maoist groups, such as Shining Path in Peru, the Naxalites in India and the New People's Army (NPA) in the Philippines, all seek a new society, where power resides with the peasants. The Russian social revolutionaries and their descendants, including the Italian Red Brigades and Action Directe in France, the Red Army Faction in Germany and the Weather Underground in the United States, sought to overthrow the capitalist system and replace it with a communist society. Fascist groups have sought to wipe out a race and ensure the dominance of the white majority. . . .

As we have seen, national self-determination was the most important goal of terrorism in the twentieth century. In other cases, groups such as the Tamil Tigers, the PKK and the Basque separatists have sought independence or autonomy within an established state. Groups also sometimes aim to bring about a new social organisation as a successor to the nation-state. The Russian anarchists fit this description, although their specific aims evolved and are not easy to summarise. Indeed, long-term aims may be difficult to visualise: the goal may be to bring on the apocalypse (as with Aum Shinrikyo) or to merely act as a catalyst to the forces of history (as with the Russian social revolutionaries).

Very few terror groups achieve their stated strategic aims. According to statistical research conducted for a broader book-length study, the overwhelming majority have failed, with only about 6 percent of groups that rely on terrorism showing full or substantial achievement of their aims.[9] In killing noncombatants, terrorism can attract people's attention, provoke tactical responses, lead a state to undermine itself and create a *cause célèbre*, but it almost never installs new rulers, inspires ideological change, takes over territory or constructs new institutions of governance (as terrorist leaders typically claim). Historically, by virtually any standard of measurement, terrorist successes, by which is meant campaigns that achieve long-term objectives and are then ended, are the rare exceptions.

There are, however, some well-known, even legendary, examples of groups that succeeded in achieving major political change and then either disbanded or moved on to more legitimate political behaviour. These are regularly cited, rightly or wrongly, by successors who hope to duplicate the outcome. The best known is Irgun Zvai Leumi, the Jewish organization that fought to protect Jews in the Palestinian Mandate and to advance the cause of an independent Jewish state. Irgun attacks such as the 1946 bombing of the King David Hotel in Jerusalem hastened Britain's withdrawal from Palestine. Irgun was never a strong organization, lacking both widespread popular support and resources; at no point did it pose a serious military threat to the British. But at the heart of its power was a sophisticated propaganda war, what one prominent member labelled its "campaign of enlightenment," directed especially toward a sympathetic international audience in the wake of horrifying evidence of the plight of the Jewish people during the Second World War. The British were economically crippled in the early postwar years and withdrawing from other commitments elsewhere. The decision to quit Palestine was ripe for implementation and, within the highly politicised international context, Irgun's attacks were an effective catalyst. The group disbanded with the creation of the state of Israel in 1948.

The African National Congress (ANC) is another example of a successful group that used terror tactics. The ANC created a military wing, Umkhonto (MK), and, after nearly five decades of nonviolent resistance, turned to terrorist attacks in 1961. It fought to end apartheid and establish a multiracial state in South Africa. The MK's last attack occurred in 1989, and the ANC became a legitimate political party in 1990, with its leader, Nelson Mandela, elected first president of post-apartheid South Africa. But the question of cause and effect in these two examples (as in others) is complex: there is a great deal of evidence to indicate that both strategic outcomes were achieved at least as much *despite* the use of terrorism as because of it. In the ANC case, for example, the extensive pressures that led to the end of apartheid, including economic, cultural and sporting sanctions by the international community, a revolt among white English- and Afrikaner-speaking youth, a political revolt among members of the South African National Party and widespread, grassroots frustration and organisation on the part of the black community all undermined the legitimacy of the policy of apartheid and were more important than terrorist attacks in ending it.

These and other oft-cited cases lead to the conclusion that the keys to strategic success for terrorist groups are fourfold. Firstly (and most obviously), groups must have well-defined and realizable aims; i.e., it is impossible to succeed if no one knows what your aims are. This is one reason why the most successful groups in the twentieth century were those whose objectives related to territory and the governance of the nation-state, both of which are tangible concepts, widely understood and at the heart of the modern international system. Secondly, groups are best able to succeed when they can convince major powers of the legitimacy of their cause and gain their backing, morally or materially or both. As is the case with insurgencies, terrorist campaigns benefit tremendously from outside support. Thirdly, groups that use terrorism can only succeed when their actions comport with broader historical, economic and political changes that are occurring anyway in the international system. It is no coincidence that the most successful cases in the twentieth century are those where a colonial power found itself unable to hold onto its territories—as in Vietnam, Cyprus, Algeria and Ireland. To determine whether or not a cause is likely to succeed over the long term, therefore, the best "intelligence" is an objective awareness of the changing international political context. Finally, terrorism succeeds best when it is part of a broader campaign and the tactic is replaced by more legitimate means, especially popular uprisings, guerrilla warfare and insurgency. A weak and illegitimate tactic, terrorism *alone* has never succeeded in achieving strategic ends.

Moving Toward a Legitimate Political Process

The fourth means by which terrorism can be said to have ended revolves around the concept of a negotiated settlement. Groups that entered into negotiations with the state have included the Provisional IRA (the 1998 Good Friday accords), the Palestine Liberation Organisation (PLO) (progress in the peace process during the 1990s) and the LTTE (which engaged in talks with the Sri Lankan government between 2002 and 2007). As these cases indicate, however, a process of negotiation is by no means a panacea. . . . Clichés about talking to terrorists do not hold up: after groups survive past the five- or six-year mark, it is not at all clear that refusing to negotiate with them shortens their violent campaigns any more than entering into negotiations prolongs them. Negotiations can facilitate a process of decline, but they have rarely been the single factor driving an outcome.

Looking at the recent history of terrorist campaigns, there are a number of interesting patterns with respect to negotiations. Firstly, there is a direct correlation between the age of the group and the probability of talks. The longer a group exists, the greater the likelihood that a peace process will begin, as groups become desperate for a resolution and governments come to realise that these non-state actors cannot be avoided or crushed. But this does not mean that most groups that engage in terrorist attacks negotiate: only about one in five groups of *any* age have entered into talks on strategic issues. Talks with groups that use terrorism are the exception, not the rule. Secondly, the vast majority of negotiations that do occur yield neither a clear resolution nor a cessation of the conflict. A common scenario has been for negotiations to drag on, occupying an uncertain middle ground between a stable ceasefire and high levels of violence. About half of the groups that have negotiated in recent years have continued violent actions as the talks have unfolded, usually at a lower level of intensity and frequency. Negotiations seem to be more effective in gradually driving a group towards decline than single-handedly occasioning its abrupt end.

Negotiations with terrorist groups have occurred most easily in situations where the group perceives itself to be losing ground. This may transpire for a number of reasons: it may reflect competition with other groups (as with the PLO, with the rise of competitors in the intifada); infiltration by government agents (as with the Provisional IRA); an undercutting of support (as with the LTTE immediately after the September 11 attacks); or a backlash by the group's own constituency (most often due to targeting errors). Indeed, increasing civilian casualties directly caused by a group within its constituency are a common impetus for talks.

A wide range of variables can determine the efficacy of negotiations, including the nature of the organisation (hierarchical groups have an advantage over groups that cannot control their members' actions), the nature of the leadership (groups with a strong leader have an advantage over those that are decentralised), and the nature of public support for the cause (groups with constituencies who have tired of violence are more likely to compromise). There must also be negotiable aims, which is more likely with territorially based groups than with those that primarily espouse left-wing, right-wing or religious/spiritual ideologies—although experience indicates that, whatever their claims, groups' goals typically evolve. The most important condition is that both sides sense that they have achieved a situation where additional violence is counterproductive. . . . Generally, groups are more likely to compromise if their popular support is waning. Since terrorism is a means of political mobilization, it is crucial to determine the degree of popular support for a group when deciding whether negotiations are likely to yield results. Likewise, if a group perceives that the domestic constituency of a state is shifting in ways that serve its interests, it will wait before entering into negotiations. The degree of mobilization for a cause, especially the ways in which popular support and interest are changing, is a crucial variable in determining whether or not negotiations will be promising.

Negotiations instantly change the "narrative" of the terrorist group's violence, affecting its ability to attract or maintain supporters. The direction in which this change proceeds may not be obvious; the relationship between talks and terrorism is not straightforward. States may wish to avoid the appearance of legitimising a non-state group, thereby enraging their own citizens. But avoiding talks may in turn enhance a group's position with its constituents, strengthening the argument that the only way to get the attention of the state is to commit increasingly violent acts. States should assess the likely effects on a group's cohesion and viability. By refusing to talk about the issue that is of concern to a group (if there is one) a government yields the agenda to that group just as surely as if it entered into discussion of the issue, since either position represents the manipulation of state behaviour through the killing of its civilians. While it is important to concentrate on ending attacks in the short term, the story that is being put forth by a group in order to justify its violence may be more central than any physical actions to its long-term viability, and may be more vulnerable to counterattack.

Groups often splinter as a result of talks, and this can be either a good or a bad thing depending on the circumstances. Examples of this pattern include the Provisional IRA and the PLO. Dividing terrorist groups into factions has either isolated the most radical elements, which has the advantage of making them easier to target, or increased the violence against civilians in the short term, as radical factions try to demonstrate their viability by carrying out new attacks. But because negotiations in the wake of terrorist acts are always controversial, splintering has sometimes occurred on the status quo side instead: this was the case, for example, in South Africa (with the Afrikaner white-power group Farmers' Force, or Boeremag) and in Northern Ireland (with the Ulster Volunteer Force (UVF)). . . .

Indeed, there is no guarantee that the military situation will be improved by negotiations, especially in the short term. Groups sometimes enter into talks disingenuously, to ease the pressure of counterterrorist measures and to rearm. Some IRA groups or members (probably of the Provisional IRA) continued to procure weapons following the 1998 Good Friday agreement, buying guns in the United States and attempting to import AN-94 rifles from Russia. The Basque group ETA announced a ceasefire in 1998, following a public backlash against the killing of a popular young councillor, and then renounced it in 1999, claiming that it had wanted a reprieve from government pressure in order to rearm. . . .

Other factors have also been important to the success or failure of negotiations. These include the presence or absence of suicide campaigns: the use of suicide attacks makes resolution especially problematical, as it reduces the willingness or ability of factions to live alongside each other. The presence of strong leaders on both sides of the talks increases the likelihood of success. Although it may be desirable for other reasons, forcing a leadership change often complicates talks, since it may result in a more diffuse organisation that is more difficult to parley with. Finally, the presence or absence of third-party states is important, as are mediators, outside guarantors and other external actors willing to push along or support the negotiations. . . .

Spoilers receive a great deal of attention in the context of negotiations, as terrorist attacks by splinter groups or disgruntled factions aim to derail or destroy talks. Clearly, talks that are not marred by spoiler attacks promise better outcomes. One study examining 14 peace agreements signed between parties to civil wars from 1988 to 1998 concluded that, if terrorist attacks occurred in association with the talks, only one in four treaties were put into effect. If they did not occur, 60 percent took effect[10] Campaigns that rely primarily on terrorist attacks may be even harder than civil wars to resolve. But the cause and effect of spoiler attacks is hard to determine. Spoiler violence is often directed at gaining power within a movement at a time of change or opportunity, rather than seeking to undermine the talks themselves.

Even when they are clearly directed at disrupting talks, spoilers may not have the desired effect. If a foundation of popular support for talks exists, there are strong outside guarantors and the negotiators are identified with the process itself, terrorist "spoiler" attacks can actually strengthen the commitment to negotiations, rather than undermine it. The Northern Ireland peace process comes to mind.

Terrorist incidents were frequently timed to coincide with developments in the talks, but effective public-relations efforts by all parties meant that public anger was directed against the spoilers, making the negotiations more resilient, not less. When spoiler violence occurs, therefore, whether or not interested parties inside and outside the talks label it illegitimate appears to make a difference, especially when the response is outrage at the attackers themselves and renewed support for the talks.

Negotiations have many benefits, and are a common element in the gradual ending of terrorist groups. Given the small number of operatives needed to continue terrorist attacks, however, violence almost never ends instantaneously. Judging the efficacy of negotiations is thus not simply a matter of whether or not they result in the end of violence in the short term. The most likely result for a government that chooses to negotiate and can withstand domestic pressure is long-term management of the threat over a lengthy period of gradual decline. Unlike civil wars and inter-state conflicts, where fighting normally stops while talks proceed, negotiations during terrorist campaigns redirect the contest into a less violent channel as the campaign winds down for other reasons. Talks carry risks and can pose a serious challenge for a democratic state that enters into them without a firm domestic mandate to do so, managed expectations and a back-up plan for when terrorism recurs. From the state's perspective, while negotiations are not a promising tactical means to end terrorist campaigns by themselves, if well handled they are nonetheless a wise and durable strategic tool for managing violence, splintering the opposition and facilitating its longer-term decline.

Implosion and Loss of Popular Support

The fifth way terrorist groups die is because they become cut off from their source of sustenance, or implode. Firstly, and arguably most importantly, groups regularly fail to move beyond the first generation, for reasons that are both internal and external to them. . . .

The generational phases of terrorist campaigns are . . . related to demographic patterns and the growth of radical ideologies internationally. Some grievances have been easier to translate from one generation to another; in the twentieth century, those connected either to territory or to the identity of a group's supporters or constituents conveyed well. Left-wing ideologies have had less staying power than ethno-nationalist causes. The left-wing groups of 1970s Europe were notorious for their inability to articulate a clear vision of their goals, which could be handed down to successors after the first generation of leaders had been captured or eliminated. As the leftist/anarchist philosophies of groups such as the Red Brigades, the Second of June Movement, the Japanese Red Army and the Weather Underground became bankrupt or unintelligible, they found it increasingly difficult to attract new recruits, especially after the dissolution of the Soviet Union.

Right-wing groups have also had difficulty lasting over generations. This is probably a reflection of their peripatetic nature and their decentralized cell structures—though it should also be borne in mind that these characteristics themselves mean that tracking groups' evolution from generation to generation presents prodigious challenges, which may have the effect of limiting our knowledge of their lifespans. . . .

A second cause of self-destruction is infighting and factionalization. The pressures of continuing a campaign have regularly led to counterproductive and dysfunctional behaviour among a group's members, including struggles over doctrine, operations, leadership and tactics. Individuals may struggle for predominance within a group (as with the GIA in Algeria in 1994–95) or over the nature or pace of operations (as with the Provisional IRA or the Red Army Faction). When groups break up into factions, internecine competition may make them more concerned with stamping out competitors than furthering a common cause. Clashes between Palestinian groups in the second intifada come to mind here.

Another common source of internal dispute stems from the nature of the group's ideology or doctrine. Because of their impermanence and relative weakness, and the blatant illegitimacy of their attacks on noncombatants, terrorist groups are almost uniquely dependent on the "story" that justifies their actions and existence. Members who argue over the nature of that crucial narrative often turn against one another. . . .

Sometimes, the story becomes unconvincing even to members, who burn out or come to the conclusion that their aims are not being advanced by terrorist tactics. Some may accept an exit offered by the state. In Italy, "repentance" laws passed in 1980 and 1986 famously contributed to the ending of the Red Brigades and numerous smaller rivals. In Colombia, the April 19 Movement (M-19), under pressure from the government and paramilitary groups, agreed to an amnesty before transforming itself into a political party, Democratic Alliance M-19, to pursue a reform agenda and advocate on behalf of the poor. Most groups are unable to overcome these centrifugal forces, and this is an important reason why the vast majority of groups that rely on terrorist attacks soon self-destruct.

A third reason for self-destruction is the tendency of terrorist groups to lose control over operations. This is a classic problem, especially when groups are faced with police or military pressure that makes it difficult to maintain both personal security and operational efficiency. Groups seeking to evade detection often adopt more horizontal structures so as to limit the damage to a hierarchy if a member is caught. Dating at least to the late nineteenth century, networked terrorist organisations are not new. They can compartmentalise information and keep themselves from detection by the state, and may even be better able to carry out attacks, especially small operations launched against soft targets. However, the sum of these tactical networked operations may not necessarily add up to a logical strategy that advances the purposes of the broader organization. . . . Uncoordinated, poorly planned or badly targeted operations increase the likelihood of a popular backlash against a group.

Without some level of popular support, a group quickly dies. Popular support has dissipated in recent history for a number of reasons, including intimidation (as in Chechnya), the offer of a better alternative (reform movements, employment programmes and amnesties, as in Italy) or the bankruptcy of the group's ideology (as with many of the Marxist groups supported by the Soviet Union and its Eastern European allies). A key source of marginalisation, however, is the organisation's own errors, especially miscalculations in targeting. Terrorist attacks, although shocking and tragic, are designed to mobilise support among a target constituency by demonstrating strength, exploiting hatred of the target or providing an avenue for public retribution. Sometimes, however, the intended effect is not achieved. Misguided, poorly timed, overly brutal or mistakenly targeted attacks can lead to revulsion among a group's actual or potential political constituency and lead to its decline and demise. . . .

Moving to Other Malignant Forms

The sixth and final way terrorism can "end" is when the violence continues, but assumes another form. Groups that use terrorism at times reorient their behaviour, moving away from politically motivated attacks on civilians or noncombatants towards criminality (as with Abu Sayyaf or the Revolutionary Armed Forces of Colombia (FARC)) or toward full insurgency and even conventional war (as with the Algerian FLN or the Kashmiri groups Lashkar-e-Tayiba and Jaish-e-Mohammed). . . .

Terrorism and criminality reflect the two dominions of authority of the modern nation-state: the internal legal dimension and the external strategic dimension. They are intertwined. Nonetheless, there is a distinction between groups that engage primarily in attacks on noncombatants to achieve a political objective, and those that engage primarily in criminal activities to enrich themselves. Both can be brutal, and both may engage in the same types of behaviour, including kidnapping, assassinations and bombings, but their purposes are different. Terrorist groups are revisionist actors who want to alter the national or international political system in some way. Criminal syndicates aim to keep their activities out of view, and seek the perpetuation of the current political order so as to continue their illicit acts. Thus, criminal groups are status-quo actors, content to operate within the current system, which is the source of their riches, even as they distort it and transgress its laws and norms. Criminal behaviour is by no means good news, but when a group moves away from terrorism and towards criminality the challenge it presents can at least potentially be managed within existing legal frameworks. Moreover, criminal activities often harm the reputation of a revolutionary group within its actual or potential constituency, making its commitment to an ideology or cause seem shallow.

Terrorist campaigns may also develop in the direction of more conventional types of violence. Terrorism and insurgency overlap and are cousins, and the same organisations can use both methods, but they are different phenomena. Reviewing the twentieth-century record, the success rate for insurgencies (which attack military targets and typically shore up a constituency's support) has been higher than the success rate for terrorist organisations (which attack civilian or noncombatant targets and often undermine their own support). Terrorism is the *weak* tactic of the weak: used alone it rarely proves to be a winning approach over the long term.

Being seen as an insurgency gives a campaign a degree of legitimacy: "terrorist" is a pejorative term in a way that "insurgent" is not. From the perspective of strategic counter-terrorism, a group gaining enough strength to move into an insurgency is a bad outcome. . . .

IMPLICATIONS FOR COUNTERTERRORISM

The relevant question for policymakers in the midst of the current campaign is not "how are we doing?" but rather "how will it end?" Believing that a conflict never ends is psychologically self-defeating: war is prolonged because we have no firm idea how to avoid classic mistakes and bring it to a close, and thus we do not put in place policies that are designed with an end in mind. But there is a great deal of experience with terrorist campaigns ending, either because of actions taken against them or because of dynamics of their own, frequently related to the vulnerable connection between groups and their constituents or audiences.

Concentrating on the six patterns discussed here, and determining which is most relevant to the current threat, is the best way to confound the short-term strategies of terrorism. While this cannot guarantee an outcome, knowledge of these long-standing patterns can enable leaders to see beyond the time-honored and persistent tactics of terrorism. Above all else is the imperative to think beyond the passions of those who are hurt, frightened or angry. Policymakers who become caught up in the short-term goals and spectacle of terrorist attacks relinquish the broader historical perspective and phlegmatic approach that is crucial to the reassertion of state power. Their goal must be to think strategically and avoid falling into the trap of reacting narrowly and directly to the violent initiatives taken by these groups. Consciously driving a terrorist campaign toward its end is preferable to answering the tactical elements of a movement as it unfolds, and is also far more likely to result in success.

NOTES

1. The number of Palestinians killed through targeted killings is tallied by B'Tselem at http://www.btselem.org/english/Statistics/Casualties_Data.asp?Category=19.
2. The rate began to drop off before the "fence" was erected, and the targeted killing policy is widely considered to be a success in Israel. Cause and effect appears to be much more complicated, however. Edward Kaplan et al. present careful data indicating that the killing of terrorist suspects stimulated recruitment to the terror stock, arguing that preventive arrests, not targeted killings, were mainly responsible for the reduction in suicide bombings. Edward H. Kaplan, Alex Mintz, Shaul Mishal, and Claudio Samban, "What Happened to Suicide Bombings in Israel?: Insights from a Terror Stock Model," *Studies in Conflict and Terrorism,* vol. 28, no. 3, May-June 2005, pp. 225–35.
3. "Attacks Reported in Ingushetia, Stavropol and North Ossetia," *Chechnya Weekly,* vol. 8, no. 48, The Jamestown Foundation, 13 December 2007, http://jamestown.org/chechnya_weekly/article.php?articleid=2373851.

4. See Oren Gross and Fionnuala Ni Aoláin, *Law in Times of Crisis: Emergency Powers in Theory and Practice* (Cambridge: Cambridge University Press, 2006).
5. The 30,000 deaths involved PKK members, civilians and members of the security forces. See Henri J. Barkey, "Turkey and the PKK: A Pyrrhic Victory," in Art and Richardson (eds), *Democracy and Counterterrorism: Lessons from the Past* (Washington, DC: U.S. Institute of Peace Press, 2007), p. 344.
6. The Truth and Reconciliation Commission, Final Report, Volume 6, *The Periods of Violence,* p. 53.
7. Ivan Arreguin-Toft, "How the Weak Win Wars: A Theory of Asymmetric Conflict," *International Security,* vol. 26, no. 1, Summer 2001, pp. 93–128.
8. Mia Bloom, "Palestinian Suicide Bombing: Public Support, Market Share and Outbidding," *Political Science Quarterly,* vol. 119, no. 1, Summer 2004, pp. 61–88.
9. This conclusion is drawn from careful study of 450 durable terrorist organisations listed by the MIPT's Terrorism Knowledge Base. Only organisations that met the requirement of sustained (repeated) attacks harming civilians through physical injury or death were included in this analysis. . . .
10. Andrew Kydd and Barbara F. Walter, "Sabotaging the Peace: The Politics of Extremist Violence," *International Organization,* vol. 56, no. 2, Spring 2002, p. 264, using data from the International Policy Institute for Counter-Terrorism database, the Interdisciplinary Center, Herzliya; and Barbara F. Walter, *Committing to Peace: The Successful Settlement of Civil Wars* (Princeton, NJ: Princeton University Press, 2002).

mypoliscikit Exercises for Interstate War and Terrorism

Apply what you learned in this chapter by using the online resources on MyPoliSciKit (www.mypoliscikit.com).

 Practice Tests

 Videos:
- "The South Ossetia Crisis"
- "Winning the Global War on Terror"

 Simulation: "Military Force: You Are a Military Commander"

 Reading Guides:
- Robert Jervis, "The Era of Leading Power Peace"
- Robert J. Art, "The United States and the Rise of China"
- Audrey Cronin, "Ending Terrorism"

CIVIL WARS
AND INTERVENTION

Humanitarian Intervention

ALAN J. KUPERMAN

INTRODUCTION

Humanitarian intervention is not identical to the promotion of human rights but is related to it—in ways that sometimes are obvious but also can be quite counterintuitive. Strictly speaking, humanitarian intervention is the use of diplomatic, economic, and military resources by one or more states or international organizations intended primarily to protect civilians who are endangered in another state. These civilians may be at risk either from natural disaster or from political violence (including war) in which they are targeted deliberately or suffer from the resulting social disruption.

Because civil war may be both the cause and consequence of human rights violations, there is an intimate relationship between humanitarian intervention and the promotion of human rights. Persistent violations of a group's human rights may cause members of that group to feel so aggrieved and frustrated that they eventually take up arms and rebel, triggering a civil war. During the course of war, civilians may suffer both humanitarian deprivation—inadequate food, water, shelter, and medical care—and blatant violation of their human rights, including arbitrary detention, forced displacement, or summary violence. International action that is able to end the war may alleviate both problems, so that humanitarian intervention sometimes also promotes human rights.

But at other times, the two goals are contradictory. Efforts to promote human rights may exacerbate humanitarian suffering. Or humanitarian intervention may exacerbate violations of human rights. In such cases, advocates may have to decide which of these two worthy causes is their higher priority, and temporarily sacrifice

From Alan J. Kuperman, "Humanitarian Intervention," in *Human Rights: Politics & Practice* edited by Michael Goodhart (2009), excerpts from pp. 335–343, 350–351, 352 by permission of Oxford University Press.

the other. Philosophers and social scientists label this the dilemma, or trade-off, between 'peace and justice'. . . .

EVOLVING CONCEPTS

Humanitarian intervention was originally defined narrowly as the provision of vital materials to at-risk civilians, expressly avoiding any action or even commentary related to the possible political causes of civilian suffering. The prototypical humanitarian organization in this tradition is the International Committee of the Red Cross (ICRC), which originated in 1863 at the international conference that also gave rise the following year to the original version of the Geneva Convention and Protocols that assure wartime protection of medical care for civilians and soldiers. The ICRC philosophy is to eschew any political criticism of the states where it intervenes, in order to facilitate its humanitarian mandate. For example, if the ICRC were to criticize a government for intentionally harming its civilians, that government might bar the organization from entering the country to provide humanitarian aid, resulting in greater harm to the civilians. Thus, traditional humanitarian organizations, such as the ICRC, explicitly subordinate concern over human rights violations in order to facilitate their humanitarian objective. On several occasions, the ICRC has been harshly criticized for this strictly neutral stance—notably during the Holocaust, when it witnessed but did not report or condemn Nazi crimes.

A broader definition of humanitarian intervention has emerged over the last four decades. A key turning point was Nigeria's 1967–1970 secessionist war in its Biafra region, when some ICRC employees rejected their organization's political neutrality. They believed that the government of Nigeria was intentionally inflicting humanitarian deprivation on the Biafra region in a ruthless attempt to compel the secessionists to abandon their aspirations of self-determination and independence. In their opinion, merely providing humanitarian aid to the victims, as ICRC was doing, did not address the root cause of the suffering. Accordingly, these frustrated humanitarians split from the ICRC and formed their own organization in 1971, namely, *Médecins Sans Frontières* (MSF; Doctors Without Borders), which would not only provide aid but also condemn state policies that they believed created suffering in the first place. MSF abandoned the ICRC's principle of political neutrality on grounds that naming and shaming human rights violations was the best way to reduce humanitarian suffering in the long run, even if it might interfere with their ability to provide aid in the short run.

Impartial and Neutral

Humanitarians often claim to be both impartial and neutral in their interventions, but in practice it may be impossible to attain both goals simultaneously during a civil war. Impartiality denotes that aid is delivered solely on the basis of need, without consideration of the political or military allegiance of the recipient. Neutrality means that the intervention strives not to affect the balance of power between the contending parties. The incompatibility of impartiality and neutrality stems from two facts: civil wars are usually lopsided rather than symmetric, and humanitarian intervention also conveys strategic benefits. At any point in a civil war, one of the sides is usually winning in the sense of suffering less. Accordingly, when interveners deliver humanitarian aid impartially, they provide it mainly to the weaker party and often require the stronger party to halt hostilities to facilitate delivery. Both of these actions alter the balance of power in the conflict, strengthening the weaker party relative to the stronger, so that the intervention is not neutral. If interveners strive to be neutral, then they must provide equal aid to the side that is not suffering as much, which would violate the principle of impartiality.

In the 1990s, the concept of humanitarian intervention was expanded again to include the use of military force, not merely to protect delivery of aid, but in some cases to deter or defeat actors perceived as aggressors endangering civilians. The end of the Cold War broke the U.S.-Soviet deadlock in the United Nations Security Council, enabling the authorization, on a case-by-case basis, of intervention using all necessary means, including military force, to protect civilians. Examples are discussed in the next section.

In 2001, following several such interventions, the *ad hoc* International Commission on Intervention and State Sovereignty (ICISS, 2001) concluded that there was a Responsibility to Protect—that is, a generalized obligation of states to intervene through a variety of means to protect civilians on humanitarian grounds. . . .

MILITARY INTERVENTION

During most of modern history, the norm of sovereignty prohibited states from intervening in the internal affairs of other recognized states. . . . The norm was adopted to reduce the incidence of war and to promote international stability. It arose in response to the horribly bloody "religious wars" between Catholics and Protestants in Europe during the sixteenth and seventeenth centuries that culminated in the 'Thirty Years War' of 1618–1648. Such wars were fought largely over the internal behaviour of states—specifically, their religion—rather than their external behaviour. Wise statesmen and jurists realized that war could be frequent and particularly savage if it were permitted to be fought over such internal differences, in light of the inherent diversity of states and the intense passions aroused by disputes over ostensibly universal values.

Accordingly, a norm of sovereignty was established in 1648 by the Treaty of Westphalia, ending the Thirty Years War. Henceforth, war could legally be fought only over the external, not internal, behaviour of states. States would enjoy total sovereignty over their internal affairs, and no other state could intervene with force or otherwise. Although the norm was sometimes violated, it stood as a pillar of international law for over 300 years. The principle was reiterated in the UN Charter of 1945, which in its first chapter (Articles 2.4 and 2.7) prohibits intervention by either the United Nations or its members in the internal affairs of states: "All Members shall refrain in their international relations from the threat or use of force against the territorial integrity or political independence of any state. . . .Nothing contained in the present Charter shall authorize the United Nations to intervene in matters which are essentially within the domestic jurisdiction of any state or shall require the Members to submit such matters to settlement under the present Charter." These prohibitions hold unless the Security Council approves a resolution in a specific case under Chapter VII of the Charter, authorizing intervention in response to a threat to *international* peace and security, or unless a state is acting in self-defence against aggression under Article 51 of the Charter.

Eroding the Norm of Sovereignty

The first modern, legal intrusion on the norm of sovereignty was the UN's 1948 Convention on the Prevention and Punishment of the Crime of Genocide, adopted in the wake of the Holocaust. In the convention, signers "undertake to prevent and to punish" the crime of genocide. Given that genocide may be committed by a state against its own citizens, the convention thus commits signers to intervene in another state based solely on the internal behaviour of that state. The responsibility to protect further erodes the norm of sovereignty, endorsing intervention to prevent not only genocide but other massive violations of human rights that occur within a state, including war crimes, ethnic cleansing, and crimes against humanity. To remain consistent with the UN Charter, advocates maintain that the widespread violation of human rights is no longer "essentially within the domestic jurisdiction of any state." In this way, the norm is gradually evolving to privilege some individual human rights over state sovereignty, although the ultimate extent of that evolution is still to be determined.

Even prior to the formal erosion of the sovereignty norm, states occasionally intervened in the internal affairs of other states on humanitarian or human rights grounds. In the late nineteenth century, for example, some European states intervened with diplomatic pressure and threats against the Ottoman Empire over treatment of its Christian peoples, including Armenians, who were seeking greater rights. In the late 1960s, several states intervened in Nigeria on behalf of ethnic Ibos, who were suffering from the government's response to the armed secession of their Biafra region.

Military Force

The widespread advent of humanitarian intervention, especially with military force, emerged after the Cold War. The model was established in 1991, following the Gulf War that expelled Iraqi troops from Kuwait. In March of that year, in northern Iraq, ethnic Kurd separatists launched a rebellion against the Baghdad regime of Saddam Hussein. The Iraqi army responded with brutal suppression, compelling ethnic Kurds to flee northward toward the mountains bordering Turkey, creating a humanitarian emergency. In April 1991, the United States launched Operation Provide Comfort, a military intervention justified on humanitarian grounds. The United Nations (in Security Council Resolution 688) quickly urged its members to contribute to the humanitarian effort, and a coalition of states then helped the United States to protect the Kurds, establish refugee camps, provide humanitarian aid, and assist with resettlement. The United States also spearheaded a no-fly zone over the Kurdish area of Iraq, conducting missions from bases in Turkey to patrol and shoot down any Iraqi aircraft operating in that airspace. The intervention thus provided not merely emergency humanitarian aid, but long-term military assistance that shifted the balance of power within Iraq, effectively rewarding the Kurds with political autonomy that also promoted their human rights.

The use of military force in humanitarian intervention has since become widespread. Such action is sometimes carried out with the consent of the target state, typically authorized under Chapter VI of the UN Charter. In other cases it is nonconsensual, authorized either under Chapter VII of the UN Charter or outside the legal bounds of that charter, as in Kosovo where intervention controversially was authorized by NATO rather than the UN. Interveners have deployed troops to protect civilians in at least twenty countries: Afghanistan, Albania, Bosnia, Burundi, Central African Republic, Croatia, Democratic Republic of Congo, East Timor, Georgia, Haiti, Iraq, Ivory Coast, Kosovo, Liberia, Macedonia, Rwanda, Sierra Leone, Somalia, Sudan, and Tajikistan—some on multiple occasions. In addition, interveners have deployed troops or monitors to support peace processes in another 16 countries: Cambodia, Chad, Comoros, El Salvador, Eritrea, Ethiopia, Guatemala, Guinea Bissau, Kuwait, Libya, Moldova, Mozambique, Papua New Guinea, Peru, Solomon Islands, and Western Sahara. Although the latter missions are not explicitly authorized to protect civilians, they are motivated heavily by the desire to shield civilians from renewed violence. In some cases, such as Sudan's long-standing north–south civil war, the international community has also applied sanctions against states or provided covert aid to rebels in an attempt to coerce a halt to violence.

The increased frequency and extent of humanitarian intervention has spurred rapid growth in both government spending and the number of non-governmental organizations (NGOs) devoted to this mission. . . .

Major Interventions

Over the last two decades, several cases of humanitarian military intervention have been especially prominent (see Box 1). In 1992, the United Nations and the United States deployed troops to Somalia to facilitate the delivery of humanitarian aid to civilians who had been cut off, sometimes deliberately, by a long-running civil war. Although impartial, the intervention was not neutral in that it diminished the power of a Somali warlord, Mohammad Farrah Aideed, who retaliated by killing UN troops from Pakistan. The United States responded by targeting the warlord, who again retaliated by killing eighteen US troops in a single battle in October 1993, an engagement immortalized in the film "Blackhawk Down." The interveners withdrew during the next 18 months, after alleviating the immediate humanitarian emergency but failing to address the root causes of instability that still produce civilian suffering in Somalia.

From 1992 to 1995, the United Nations and NATO—a U.S.-European military alliance—conducted a complex humanitarian military intervention in Bosnia, as detailed later in this chapter.

Soon after, in neighbouring Serbia's Kosovo province, ethnic Albanian militants of the Kosovo Liberation Army responded to government oppression by

BOX 1 ■ MAJOR HUMANITARIAN MILITARY INTERVENTIONS

(Chronologically, by country and initial year of intervention)

Iraq, 1991

U.S.-led coalition delivers aid to ethnic Kurds and enforces no-fly zone to prevent attacks by Iraqi air forces.

Somalia, 1992

UN and U.S. interventions protect aid deliveries and unsuccessfully attempt nation-building, leading to the killing of peacekeepers.

Bosnia, 1992

UN, NATO, and U.S. protect aid deliveries, bomb Serb forces for attacking civilians, and facilitate military aid to opposing ethnic groups, eventually leading to peace.

Kosovo, 1999

NATO bombs Serbia for attacking civilians, leading initially to increased violence against ethnic Albanians, then withdrawal of Serb forces, and finally revenge attacks against Serbs.

East Timor, 1999

Australia-led force establishes peace and facilitates the return of refugees in the wake of the independence referendum that triggered militia violence.

Sierra Leone, 2000

UK deploys troops to reinforce UN peacekeepers, enabling the defeat of rebels who had mutilated and killed civilians and violated peace accords.

DR Congo, 2003

French-led deployment reinforces UN peacekeepers, reducing the tribal fighting in eastern DR Congo that had displaced and killed thousands of civilians.

Darfur, 2004

African Union deploys monitors and peacekeepers who protect some civilians in refugee camps but fail to end the violence.

---

launching a secessionist rebellion. Serbian leader Slobodan Milosevic retaliated with a harsh counter-insurgency that targeted the rebels but also killed several hundred civilians and displaced hundreds of thousands during 1998. The United States first intervened to protect these civilians by threatening to bomb Serbia with NATO air strikes, which compelled Milosevic in October 1998 to withdraw many Serbian forces and permit international monitors. But the ethnic Albanian rebels renewed attacks, reigniting war that again displaced civilians. The United States then drafted a peace agreement that promised Kosovo an independence referendum after three years, and demanded in February 1999 that Milosevic sign it or face NATO attack. This time, Milosevic refused, so NATO commenced bombing in late March 1999. Serbian forces responded by quickly expelling some 850,000 ethnic Albanians from Kosovo, approximately half their population in the province, and killing about 10,000. After 11 weeks of NATO bombing, Milosevic relented, signing a peace agreement to remove all his forces from Kosovo and to permit international peacekeepers. As the ethnic Albanian refugees returned, they forcibly displaced some 100,000 Serbs, approximately half their population in the province, and killed hundreds more, despite the presence of peacekeepers. Proponents of the intervention argue that it prevented even more Serb violence against Albanian civilians, while critics respond that it backfired, amplifying such violence and failing to prevent vengeance against Serb civilians.

Failure to Intervene

The failure to intervene has been harshly criticized in several recent cases of large-scale violence against civilians. In Rwanda, ethnic Tutsi rebels invaded in 1990 and fought for three years against a government controlled by members of the ethnic Hutu majority. In 1993, a peace agreement permitted the deployment of 2,500 UN peacekeepers. But in April 1994, the Hutu president was assassinated, and Hutu extremists immediately launched a genocidal campaign that killed half a million Tutsi (three-quarters of their population in the country) in just three months. Tens of thousands of Hutu were also killed. Most UN peacekeepers were withdrawn upon the renewal of violence, although 500 remained and protected several thousand civilians. The UN authorized a humanitarian military intervention one month later, in May 1994, but international reinforcements did not arrive in Rwanda until late June 1994, by which time the genocide was virtually over. In retrospect, many advocates of intervention have claimed that a quick UN deployment could have prevented the genocide, although this is disputed. . . .

In Sudan's northwest region of Darfur, militant members of African tribes launched a rebellion in 2003, complaining of neglect and discrimination by the Arab-dominated regime in Khartoum. Sudan's government retaliated with army deployments, indiscriminate air strikes, and the arming of local Arab militias, who conducted a scorched earth counter-insurgency against African villages. These attacks displaced two million civilians, resulting in tens of thousands of deaths. In 2004, the *African Union* (AU) authorized a small military intervention to monitor the situation and to facilitate humanitarian aid—a force that grew to 7,000 troops over the next three years. Violence diminished, but most of the affected civilians remained displaced, vulnerable, and dependent on humanitarian aid. In 2007, the United Nations authorized a larger, hybrid UN–AU force of 26,000 troops and police, but, as of late 2008, less than a quarter of the extra personnel had deployed, owing to the reluctance of potential troop contributors and the opposition of Sudan to certain contingents. Advocates of intervention urged the international community to deploy forces even without Sudan's permission, but sceptics feared that this could exacerbate the violence.

OBSTACLES TO EFFECTIVENESS

Several factors can impede timely humanitarian intervention in civil conflicts. Perhaps most obvious is the lack of *political will* by potential interveners, as discussed by Samantha Power (2002) in her book *A Problem from Hell*. She argues that powerful states could intervene fairly easily, including with military force, to prevent genocide but do not because they give low priority to humanitarian concerns in comparison to their traditional national interests of security and prosperity. Undoubtedly, states do relegate humanitarian concerns to a lower priority and this is one reason why they sometimes fail to intervene, or do so belatedly and inadequately, as in Rwanda and Darfur.

But there also are practical obstacles to a timely response, as discussed in my book, *The Limits of Humanitarian Intervention: Genocide in Rwanda* (Kuperman, 2001). This work identifies three common obstacles to effective intervention: the rapid pace of violence against civilians; the delay in accurate information reaching potential interveners; and the logistical hurdles to deploying an adequate force. In Rwanda, for example, I found that most of the Tutsi victims were killed in the first three weeks, but even regional experts did not realize what was happening for two weeks, while it would have required more than a month to deploy forces urgently by air to stop the genocide. Thus, even if potential interveners had possessed the political will, they could not have intervened quickly enough to prevent most of the genocide.

These obstacles to timely intervention are not universal but are common in man-made humanitarian crises. For example, violence against civilians has often been very quick: Croatia in 1995, where more than 100,000 ethnic Serbs were expelled from the Krajina region in less than a week; Kosovo in 1999, where most of the targeted ethnic Albanians were expelled in less than two weeks; and East Timor in 1999, where most of the infrastructure was destroyed and most of the population displaced in less than a week. In Darfur, the period of peak violence against civilians lasted considerably longer, perhaps a year, but it was not widely reported in Western media until spring 2004, by which time most of the potential displacement and killing had already taken place.

The deployment of intervention forces also confronts certain physical limitations that cannot be overcome by political will. Transporting forces by sea from Western military bases to conflict zones typically requires at least a month to load, travel, and unload. Air transport is quicker for transporting initial intervention forces, but another month or more is required to deploy essential weapons, equipment, and supplies by air because of logistical obstacles such as the small payload of transport aircraft, the limited throughput capacity of regional airfields, and the considerable mass of modern military forces. Therefore, even if humanitarian advocates could generate sufficient political will for military intervention, the forces would often arrive too late to protect most at-risk civilians. If humanitarians actually want to avert civilian suffering, they need to contemplate other, less forceful strategies.

UNINTENDED CONSEQUENCES

Humanitarian intervention can have a wide range of unintended consequences contrary to its intent of protecting civilians. These perverse consequences sometimes arise simply from the delivery of subsistence commodities, as documented by John Prendergast (1996), Alex de Waal (1998), Mary Anderson (1999), and Fiona Terry (2002). Since militants often intermingle with civilians in places such as refugee camps, humanitarian aid may provide sustenance to rebels, enabling them to fight longer. The camps may inhibit reintegration too, thereby perpetuating grievance and mobilization that prolong or renew war. Combatants may also intercept aid and resell it, or charge a tax for its safe delivery, acquiring funds for their war effort. In some cases, combatants may even fight each other to control the delivery of aid, so humanitarian assistance unintentionally creates extra incentive for war.

Humanitarian aid can also undermine local economies and governance in several ways. First, the provision of free assistance may make it impossible for local farmers and businessmen to sell their goods, hindering economic development and potentially compelling them to turn to war to make a living. International aid organizations also siphon off local talent by employing skilled individuals as translators, drivers, and office workers, diminishing the human capital necessary for domestic entrepreneurship and good government. Moreover, so long as essential social services are provided by external actors, local government may be deprived of the legitimacy that is essential for successful peace-building. Finally, because humanitarian NGOs engage in fierce competition to win government contracts, they may concentrate more on the rapid delivery of aid than on preventing such unintended consequences.

Military force on humanitarian grounds may also backfire. Richard Betts (1994) observes that military intervention can vary in two ways—being either biased or impartial, and either limited or overwhelming—which yields four potential combinations. One effective combination is limited-biased intervention on behalf of the stronger party, enabling it to attain victory and thereby end the violence. Two other effective combinations are overwhelming intervention in either a biased or impartial manner, so that a powerful intervener simply imposes a settlement. But, unfortunately, the typical combination in humanitarian military intervention is limited-impartial, says Betts, which assists the weaker party just enough to prolong the fighting but not to end it (see Table 1). Similarly, Edward Luttwak (1999) has noted that well-intentioned intervention backfires by prolonging war and the resulting humanitarian suffering. The better way to promote stability and humanitarianism, he argues, is not to intervene but instead to let the war burn out more quickly by permitting the victory of the stronger side.

Moral Hazard

My own research warns of a systemic *moral hazard* problem whereby the responsibility to protect may perversely increase the human suffering that it intends to alleviate (Crawford and Kuperman, 2006; Kuperman, 2008). The root of the problem is that such civilian suffering often stems from state retaliation against a substate group for rebellion (such as armed secession) by some of its members. Humanitarian intervention not only protects at-risk civilians but often facilitates, intentionally or not, the political objectives of the rebels. The expectation of intervention can therefore encourage rebellion by lowering its anticipated cost and increasing its likelihood of success. Some militants even deliberately provoke state retaliation against civilians in order to attract intervention. Although humanitarian

TABLE 1 ■ FOUR STRATEGIES FOR HUMANITARIAN MILITARY INTERVENTION

	Limited Force	Overwhelming Force
Impartial	Most common. Saves lives in short-term, but may prolong war and resultant humanitarian suffering. **(Bosnia: UN peacekeepers, 1992–1995)**	Rare. Can end violence quickly, but at cost of major military commitment and entanglement in renewed violence if perceived as non-neutral. **(Somalia: US peacekeepers, 1992–1995)**
Biased	Less common. Works faster if biased towards stronger party. Or can end violence gradually by helping weaker side to win, but at risk of short-term backlash against civilians. **(Kosovo: NATO bombing of Yugoslavia, 1999)**	Rare. Can end violence by quickly helping one side to win, but at costs of major military commitment and loss of neutrality. **(Iraq: U.S. led intervention and no-fly zone in Kurd region, 1991–2003)**

Adapted from Betts (1994).

intervention may help rebels attain their political goals, it usually is too late or inadequate to avert retaliation against civilians. Thus, the responsibility to protect resembles an imperfect insurance policy against genocidal violence. It creates moral hazard that encourages the excessively risky or fraudulent behaviour of rebellion by members of groups that are vulnerable to retaliation, but it cannot fully protect the group's civilians against the violent backlash. As a result, the emerging norm of humanitarian intervention may cause some civilian suffering that otherwise would not occur. The most commonly cited examples of the moral hazard of humanitarian intervention are Kosovo, Darfur, and Bosnia—the last of which is detailed in the following section.

The moral hazard problem can arise from any international action that is primarily motivated by the humanitarian desire to protect civilian targets of state violence but which also helps rebels. The spectrum of such action is wide, ranging from low-cost measures that respect traditional state sovereignty to high-cost ones that impinge on it, including: rhetorical condemnation, threats or imposition of economic sanctions, recognizing the independence of secessionist entities, air strikes on military or economic assets, military assistance to or coordination with rebels perceived as defending at-risk civilians, consensual deployment of peacekeepers, and nonconsensual deployment of troops for peace enforcement. . . .

CONCLUSION

Some advocates of forceful intervention claim that it can simultaneously promote humanitarian and human rights objectives. In reality, there often is a trade-off between the two. This is most obvious for military intervention in support of "freedom fighters"—those militants who claim to be fighting for their group's human rights, as in Bosnia. Such intervention unfortunately encourages the launching and perpetuation of rebellion or armed secession, which often provokes states to retaliate in a manner that inflicts suffering on the group's civilians. Forceful intervention to promote human rights thus often exacerbates humanitarian suffering. In theory, a timely and robust military intervention might achieve both objectives, but it is typically impossible to overcome the political and practical obstacles to such action.

Fortunately, this dilemma can be overcome through less forceful and more precise intervention methods. Relief aid should be delivered in ways that benefit mainly civilians—for example, by distributing it at refugee camps that are policed to exclude rebels, or at least their weapons. Human rights can be supported by intervening diplomatically and economically on behalf of nonviolent protest groups—for example, by offering trade and aid to states that address the legitimate grievances of such resistance movements. Threats of forceful intervention should be reserved for cases in which states either attack nonviolent groups or respond disproportionately to rebellion by deliberately targeting civilians. Such an enlightened approach, discouraging substate groups from rebelling while raising the incentives for states to liberalize, has the potential to promote both humanitarian and human rights objectives.

These lessons are illustrated by further investigation into the case of Kosovo (Kuperman, 2008). Starting in 1989, Serbia revoked the autonomy of this province, disenfranchised the local ethnic Albanian majority, banned public education in the Albanian language, dismissed most ethnic Albanian professionals from their jobs, and instituted repressive police patrols—a wide spread and systematic violation of human rights. For the next eight years, the ethnic Albanians resisted by nonviolent means, which provided an ideal opportunity for the international community to use diplomatic sticks and carrots to persuade Serbia to restore human rights, without risking a genocidal backlash because Serbia faced no violent opposition in the province. Analogous nonviolent movements, typically benefiting from international support, have succeeded in promoting human rights in many countries, including India, the United States, South Africa, the Philippines, Indonesia, Serbia, Ukraine, and Lebanon.

Unfortunately, the international community devoted insufficient support to Kosovo's nonviolent, human rights movement. As a result, this pacifist resistance eventually gave way in 1997 to a rebellion by militant ethnic Albanians, which provoked a violent counter-insurgency by Serbian forces that also endangered Albanian civilians. Interveners still might have mitigated violence if they had targeted humanitarian aid mainly to the affected civilians. Instead, the United States coordinated with the rebels and threatened to attack Serbia, and then NATO followed through on that threat—which only fuelled the Albanian rebellion, exacerbated Serbian retaliation, and magnified several-fold the humanitarian suffering.

This case demonstrates that, in order to promote both human rights and humanitarianism, the international community should focus its leverage to persuade oppressive states to meet the legitimate demands of nonviolent groups.

Failing that, if a rebellion breaks out, intervention should be aimed at helping civilians, not rebels, to avoid exacerbating rebellion and the resulting backlash against civilians.

The good news is that it is possible to simultaneously promote human rights and humanitarianism. The cautionary note is that, unless intervention is properly designed to avoid rewarding rebels, the promotion of one of these admirable goals could well undermine the other.

Possible and Impossible Solutions to Ethnic Civil Wars

CHAIM KAUFMANN

. . . This paper offers a theory of how ethnic wars end, and proposes an intervention strategy based on it.[1] The theory rests on two insights: First, in ethnic wars both hypernationalist mobilization rhetoric and real atrocities harden ethnic identities to the point that cross-ethnic political appeals are unlikely to be made and even less likely to be heard. Second, intermingled population settlement patterns create real security dilemmas that intensify violence, motivate ethnic "cleansing," and prevent de-escalation unless the groups are separated. As a result, restoring civil politics in multi-ethnic states shattered by war is impossible because the war itself destroys the possibilities for ethnic cooperation.

Stable resolutions of ethnic civil wars are possible, but only when the opposing groups are demographically separated into defensible enclaves. Separation reduces both incentives and opportunity for further combat, and largely eliminates both reasons and chances for ethnic cleansing of civilians. While ethnic fighting can be stopped by other means, such as peace enforcement by international forces or by a conquering empire, such peaces last only as long as the enforcers remain.

This means that to save lives threatened by genocide, the international community must abandon attempts to restore war-torn multi-ethnic states. Instead, it must facilitate and protect population movements to create true national homelands. Sovereignty is secondary: Defensible ethnic enclaves reduce violence with or without independent sovereignty, while partition without separation does nothing to stop mass killing. Once massacres have taken place, ethnic cleansing will occur. The alternative is to let the *interahamwe* and the Chetniks "cleanse" their enemies in their own way.

The remainder of this paper has three parts. The next part develops a theory of how ethnic wars end. Then, I present a strategy for international military intervention to stop ethnic wars and dampen future violence and rebut possible objections to this strategy. The conclusion addresses the moral and political stakes in humanitarian intervention in ethnic conflicts.

From Chaim Kaufmann, "Possible and Impossible Solutions to Ethnic Civil Wars," *International Security*, Vol. 20, No. 4 (Spring 1996), pp. 136–175. © 1996 by the President and Fellows of Harvard College and the Massachusetts Institute of Technology. Reprinted by permission of MIT Press Journals. Portions of the text and some footnotes have been omitted.

HOW ETHNIC CIVIL WARS END

Civil wars are not all alike. Ethnic conflicts are disputes between communities which see themselves as having distinct heritages over the power relationship between the communities, while ideological civil wars are contests between factions within the same community over how that community should be governed.[2] The key difference is the flexibility of individual loyalties, which are quite fluid in ideological conflicts, but almost completely rigid in ethnic wars.[3]

The possible and impossible solutions to ethnic civil wars follow from this fact. War hardens ethnic identities to the point that cross-ethnic political appeals become futile, which means that victory can be assured only by physical control over the territory in dispute. Ethnic wars also generate intense security dilemmas, both because the escalation of each side's mobilization rhetoric presents a real threat to the other, and even more because intermingled population settlement patterns create defensive vulnerabilities and offensive opportunities.

Once this occurs, the war cannot end until the security dilemma is reduced by physical separation of the rival groups. Solutions that aim at restoring multi-ethnic civil politics and at avoiding population transfers—such as power-sharing, state rebuilding, or identity reconstruction—cannot work because they do nothing to dampen the security dilemma, and because ethnic fears and hatreds hardened by war are extremely resistant to change.

The result is that ethnic wars can end in only three ways: with complete victory of one side; by temporary suppression of the conflict by third party military occupation; or by self-governance of separate communities. The record of the ethnic wars of the last half century bears this out.

The Dynamics of Ethnic War

It is useful to compare characteristics of ethnic conflicts with those of ideological conflicts. The latter are competitions between the government and the rebels for the loyalties of the people. The critical features of these conflicts are that ideological loyalties are changeable and difficult to assess, and the same population serves as the shared mobilization base for both sides. As a result, winning the "hearts and minds" of the population is both possible and necessary for victory. The most important instruments are political, economic, and social reforms that redress popular grievances such as poverty, inequality, corruption, and physical insecurity. Control of access to population is also important, both to allow recruitment and implementation of reform promises, and to block the enemy from these tasks. Population control, however, cannot be guaranteed solely by physical control over territory, but depends on careful intelligence, persuasion, and coercion. Purely military successes are often indecisive as long as the enemy's base of political support is undamaged.

Ethnic wars, however, have nearly the opposite properties. Individual loyalties are both rigid and transparent, while each side's mobilization base is limited to members of its own group in friendly-controlled territory. The result is that ethnic conflicts are primarily military struggles in which victory depends on physical control over the disputed territory, not on appeals to members of the other group.

Identity in Ethnic Wars

Competition to sway individual loyalties does not play an important role in ethnic civil wars, because ethnic identities are fixed by birth. While not everyone may be mobilized as an active fighter for his or her own group, hardly anyone ever fights for the opposing ethnic group.

Different identity categories imply their own membership rules. Ideological identity is relatively soft, as it is a matter of individual belief, or sometimes of political behavior. Religious identities are harder, because while they also depend on belief, change generally requires formal acceptance by the new faith, which may be denied. Ethnic identities are hardest, since they depend on language, culture, and religion, which are hard to change, as well as parentage, which no one can change.

Ethnic identities are hardened further by intense conflict, so that leaders cannot broaden their appeals to include members of opposing groups. As ethnic conflicts escalate, populations come increasingly to hold enemy images of the other groups either because of deliberate efforts by elites to create such images or because of increasing real threats. . . .

Once the conflict reaches the level of large-scale violence, tales of atrocities—true or invented—perpetuated or planned against members of the group by the ethnic enemy provide hard-liners with an unanswerable argument. In March 1992 a Serb woman in Foca in Eastern Bosnia was convinced that "there were lists of Serbs who were marked for death. My two sons were down on the list to be slaughtered like pigs. I was listed under rape." The fact that neither she nor other townspeople had seen any such lists did not prevent them from believing such tales without question.[4] The Croatian Ustasha in World War II went further, terrorizing Serbs in order to provoke a backlash that could then be used to mobilize Croats for defense against Serb retaliation.

In this environment, cross-ethnic appeals are not likely to attract members of the other group. The Yugoslav Partisans in World War II are often credited with transcending the ethnic conflict between the Croatian Ustasha and the Serbian Chetniks with an anti-German, pan-Yugoslav program. In fact it did not work. Tito was a Croat, but Partisan officers as well as the rank and file were virtually all Serbs and Montenegrins. Only in 1944, when German withdrawal made Partisan victory certain, did Croats begin to join the Partisans in numbers, not because they preferred a multi-ethnic Yugoslavia to a Greater Croatia, but because they preferred a multi-ethnic Yugoslavia to a Yugoslavia cleansed of Croatians. . . .

Ethnic war also shrinks scope for individual identity choice. Even those who put little value on their ethnic identity are pressed towards ethnic mobilization for two reasons. First, extremists within each community are likely to impose sanctions on those who do not contribute to the cause. In 1992 the leader of the Croatian Democratic Union in Bosnia was dismissed on the ground that he "was too much Bosnian, too little Croat." Conciliation is easy to denounce as dangerous to group security or as actually traitorous. Such arguments drove nationalist extremists to overthrow President Makarios of Cyprus in 1974, to assassinate Mahatma Gandhi in 1948, to massacre nearly the whole government of Rwanda in 1994, and to kill Yitzhak Rabin in 1995.

Second and more important, identity is often imposed by the opposing group, specifically by its most murderous members. Assimilation or political passivity did no good for German Jews, Rwandan Tutsis, or Azerbaijanis in Nagorno-Karabakh. A Bosnian Muslim schoolteacher recently lamented:

> We never, until the war, thought of ourselves as Muslims. We were Yugoslavs. But when we began to be murdered, because we are Muslims, things changed. The definition of who we are today has been determined by our killers.[5]

Choice contracts further the longer the conflict continues. Multi-ethnic towns as yet untouched by war are swamped by radicalized refugees, undermining moderate leaders who preach tolerance. For example, while a portion of the pre-war Serb population remained in Bosnian government-controlled Sarajevo when the fighting started, their numbers have declined as the government has taken on a more narrowly Muslim religious character over years of war, and pressure on Serbs has increased. Where 80,000 remained in July 1993, only 30,000 were left in August 1995. The Tutsi Rwandan Patriotic Front (RPF) showed remarkable restraint during the 1994 civil war, but since then the RPF has imprisoned tens of thousands of genocide suspects in appalling conditions, failed to prevent massacres of thousands of Hutu civilians in several incidents, and allowed Tutsi squatters to seize the property of many absent Hutus.

What can finally eliminate identity choice altogether is fear of genocide. The hypernationalist rhetoric used for group mobilization often includes images of the enemy group as a threat to the physical existence of the nation, in turn justifying unlimited violence against the ethnic enemy; this threatening discourse can usually be observed by members of the target group. Even worse are actual massacres of civilians, especially when condoned by leaders of the perpetrating group, which are virtually certain to convince the members of the targeted group that group defense is their only option. . . .

Identifying Loyalties

A consequence of the hardness of ethnic identities is that in ethnic wars assessing individual loyalties is much easier than in ideological conflicts. Even if some members of both groups remain unmobilized, as long as virtually none actively support the other group, each side can treat all co-ethnics as friends without risk of coddling an enemy agent and can treat all members of the other group as enemies without risk of losing a recruit.

Although it often requires effort, each side can almost always identify members of its own and the other group in any territory it controls. Ethnicity can be identified by outward appearance, public or private records, and local social knowledge. In societies where ethnicity is important, it is often officially recorded in personal identity documents or in censuses. In 1994 Rwandan death squads used neighborhood target lists prepared in advance, as well as roadblocks that checked identity cards. In the 1983 riots in Sri Lanka, Sinhalese mobs went through mixed neighborhoods selecting Tamil dwellings for destruction with the help of Buddhist monks carrying electoral lists. While it might not have been possible to predict the Yugoslav civil war thirty years in advance, one could have identified the members of each of the warring groups from the 1961 census, which identified the nationality of all but 1.8 percent of the population.

Where public records are not adequate, private ones can be used instead. Pre–World War II Yugoslav censuses relied on church records. Absent any records at all, reliable demographic intelligence can often be obtained from local co-ethnics. . . .

Finally, in unprepared encounters ethnicity can often be gauged by outward appearance: Tutsis are generally tall and thin, while Hutus are relatively short and stocky; Russians are generally fairer than Kazakhs. When physiognomy is ambiguous, other signs such as language or accent, surname, dress, posture, ritual mutilation, diet, habits, occupation, region or neighborhood within urban areas, or certain possessions may give clues. Residents of Zagreb, for example, are marked as Serbs by certain names, attendance at an Orthodox church, or possession of books printed in Cyrillic.

Perhaps the strongest evidence of intelligence reliability in ethnic conflicts is that—in dramatic contrast to ideological insurgencies—history records almost no instances of mistaken "cleansing" of co-ethnics.

The Decisiveness of Territory

Another consequence of the hardness of ethnic identities is that population control depends wholly on territorial control. Since each side can recruit only from its own community and only in friendly-controlled territory, incentives to seize areas populated by co-ethnics are strong, as is the pressure to cleanse friendly-controlled territory of enemy ethnics by relocation to *de facto* concentration camps, expulsion, or massacre.

Because of the decisiveness of territorial control, military strategy in ethnic wars is very different than in ideological conflicts. Unlike ideological insurgents, who often evade rather than risk battle, or a counter-insurgent government, which might forbear to attack rather than risk bombarding civilians, ethnic combatants must fight for every piece of land. By contrast, combatants in ethnic wars are much less free to decline unfavorable battles because they cannot afford to abandon any settlement to an enemy who is likely to "cleanse" it by massacre, expulsion, destruction of homes, and possibly colonization. By the time a town can be retaken, its value will have been lost.

In ethnic civil wars, military operations are decisive. Attrition matters because the side's mobilization pools are separate and can be depleted. Most important, since each side's mobilization base is limited to members of its own community, in friendly-controlled territory, conquering the enemy's population centers reduces its mobilization base, while loss of friendly settlements reduces one's own. Military control of the entire territory at issue is tantamount to total victory.

Security Dilemmas in Ethnic Wars

The second problem that must be overcome by any remedy for severe ethnic conflict is the security dilemma. Regardless of the origins of ethnic strife, once violence (or abuse of state power by one group that controls it) reaches the point that ethnic communities cannot rely on the state to protect them, each community must mobilize to take responsibility for its own security.

Under conditions of anarchy, each group's mobilization constitutes a real threat to the security of others for two reasons. First, the nationalist rhetoric that accompanies mobilization often seems to and often does indicate offensive intent. Under these conditions, group identity itself can be seen by other groups as a threat to their safety.

Second, military capability acquired for defense can usually also be used for offense. Further, offense often has an advantage over defense in inter-community conflict, especially when settlement patterns are inter-mingled, because isolated pockets are harder to hold than to take.

The reality of the mutual security threats means that solutions to ethnic conflicts must do more than undo the causes; until or unless the security dilemma can be reduced or eliminated, neither side can afford to demobilize.

Demography and Security Dilemmas

The severity of ethnic security dilemmas is greatest when demography is most intermixed, weakest when community settlements are most separate. The more mixed the opposing groups, the stronger the offense in relation to the defense; the more separated they are, the stronger the defense in relation to offense.[6] When settlement patterns are extremely mixed, both sides are vulnerable to attack not only by organized military forces but also by local militias or gangs from adjacent towns or neighborhoods. Since well-defined fronts are impossible, there is no effective means of defense against such raids. Accordingly, each side has a strong incentive—at both national and local levels—to kill or drive out enemy populations before the enemy does the same to it, as well as to create homogeneous enclaves more practical to defend.

Better, but still bad, are well-defined enclaves with islands of one or both sides' populations behind the other's front. Each side then has an incentive to attack to rescue its surrounded co-ethnics before they are destroyed by the enemy, as well as incentives to wipe out enemy islands behind its own lines, both to pre-empt rescue attempts and to eliminate possible bases for fifth columnists or guerrillas.

The safest pattern is a well-defined demographic front that separates nearly homogeneous regions. Such a front can be defended by organized military forces, so populations are not at risk unless defenses are breached. At the same time the strongest motive for attack disappears, since there are few or no endangered co-ethnics behind enemy lines.

Further, offensive and defensive mobilization measures are more distinguishable when populations are separated than when they are mixed. Although hypernationalist political rhetoric, as well as conventional military forces, have both offensive and defensive uses regardless of population settlement patterns, some other forms of ethnic mobilization do not. Local militias and ethnically based local self-governing authorities have both offensive and defensive capabilities when populations are mixed: Ethnic militias can become death squads, while local governments dominated by one group can disenfranchise minorities. When populations are separated, however, such local organizations have defensive value only.

War and Ethnic Unmixing

Because of the security dilemma, ethnic war causes ethnic unmixing. The war between Greece and Turkey, the partition of India, the 1948–49 Arab-Israeli war, and the recent war between Armenia and Azerbaijan were all followed by emigration or expulsion of most of the minority populations on each side. More than one million Ibo left northern Nigeria during the Nigerian Civil War. Following 1983 pogroms, three-fourths of the Tamil population of Colombo fled to the predominantly Tamil north and east of the island. By the end of 1994, only about 70,000 non-Serbs remained in Serb-controlled areas of Bosnia, with less than 40,000 Serbs still in Muslim- and Croat-controlled regions. Of 600,000 Serbs in pre-war Croatia, probably no more than 100,000 remain outside of Serb-controlled eastern Slavonia.

Collapse of multi-ethnic states often causes some ethnic unmixing even without war. The retreat of the Ottoman Empire from the Balkans sparked movement of Muslims southward and eastward as well as some unmixing of different Christian peoples in the southern Balkans. Twelve million Germans left Eastern Europe after World War II, one and a half million between 1950 and 1987, and another one and a half million since 1989, essentially dissolving the German diaspora. Of 25 million Russians outside Russia in 1989, as many as three to four million had gone to Russia by the end of 1992. From 1990 to 1993, 200,000 Hungarians left Vojvodina, replaced by 400,000 Serb refugees from other parts of ex-Yugoslavia.

Ethnic Separation and Peace

Once ethnic groups are mobilized for war, the war cannot end until the populations are separated into defensible, mostly homogeneous regions. Even if an international force or an imperial conqueror were to impose peace, the conflict would resume as soon as it left. Even if a national government were to somehow re-create, despite mutual suspicions, neither group could safely entrust its security to it. Continuing mutual threat also ensures perpetuation of hypernationalist propaganda, both for mobilization and because the plausibility of the threat posed by the enemy gives radical nationalists an unanswerable advantage over moderates in intra-group debates.

Ethnic separation does not guarantee peace, but it allows it. Once populations are separated, both cleansing and rescue imperatives disappear; war is no longer mandatory. At the same time, any attempt to seize more territory requires a major conventional military offensive. Thus the conflict changes from one of mutual preemptive ethnic cleansing to something approaching conventional interstate war, in which normal deterrence dynamics apply. Mutual deterrence does not guarantee that there will be no further violence, but it reduces the probability of outbreaks, as well as the likely aims and intensity of those that do occur.

There have been no wars among Bulgaria, Greece, and Turkey since their population exchanges of the 1920s. Ethnic violence on Cyprus, which reached crisis on several occasions between 1960 and 1974, has been zero since the partition and population exchange which followed Turkish invasion. The Armenian-Azeri ethnic conflict, sparked by independence demands of the mostly Armenian Nagorno-Karabakh Autonomous Oblast, escalated to full-scale war by 1992. Armenian conquest of all of Karabakh together with the land which formerly separated it from Armenia proper, along with displacement of nearly all members of each group from enemy-controlled territories, created a defensible separation with no minorities to fight over, leading to a cease-fire in April 1994.

THEORIES OF ETHNIC PEACE

Those considering humanitarian intervention to end ethnic civil wars should set as their goal lasting safety, rather than perfect peace. Given the persistence of ethnic rivalries, "safety" is best defined as freedom from threats of ethnic murder, expropriation, or expulsion for the overwhelming majority of civilians of all groups. Absence of formal peace, even occasional terrorism or border skirmishes, would not undermine this, provided that the great majority of civilians are not at risk. "Lasting" must mean that the situation remains stable indefinitely after the intervention forces leave. Truces of weeks, months, or even years do not qualify as lasting safety if ethnic cleansing eventually resumes with full force.

Alternatives to Separation

Besides demographic separation, the literature on possible solutions to ethnic conflicts contains four main alternatives: suppression, reconstruction of ethnic identities, power-sharing, and state-building.

Suppression
Many ethnic civil wars lead to the complete victory of one side and the forcible suppression of the other. This may reduce violence in some cases, but will never be an aim of outsiders considering humanitarian intervention. Further, remission of violence may be only temporary, as the defeated group usually rebels again at any opportunity. Even the fact that certain conquerors, such as the English in Scotland or the Dutch in Friesland, eventually permitted genuine political assimilation after decades of suppression, does not recommend this as a remedy for endangered peoples today.

Reconstruction of Ethnic Identities
The most ambitious program to end ethnic violence would be to reconstruct ethnic identities according to the "Constructivist Model" of nationalism. Constructivists

argue that individual and group identities are fluid, continually being made and re-made in social discourse. Further, these identities are manipulable by political entrepreneurs. Violent ethnic conflicts are the result of pernicious group identities created by hypernationalist myth-making; many inter-group conflicts are quite recent, as are the ethnic identities themselves.

The key is elite rivalries within communities, in which aggressive leaders use hypernationalist propaganda to gain and hold power. History does not matter; whether past inter-community relations have in fact been peaceful or conflictual, leaders can redefine, reinterpret, and invent facts to suit their arguments, including alleged atrocities and exaggerated or imagined threats. This process can feed on itself, as nationalists use the self-fulfilling nature of their arguments both to escalate the conflict and to justify their own power, so that intra-community politics becomes a competition in hypernationalist extremism, and inter-community relations enter a descending spiral of violence.

It follows that ethnic conflicts generated by the promotion of pernicious, exclusive identities should be reversible by encouraging individuals and groups to adopt more benign, inclusive identities. Leaders can choose to mobilize support on the basis of broader identities that transcend the ethnic division, such as ideology, class, or civic loyalty to the nation-state. If members of the opposing groups can be persuaded to adopt a larger identity, ethnic antagonisms should fade away. . . .

However, even if ethnic hostility can be "constructed," there are strong reasons to believe that violent conflicts cannot be "reconstructed" back to ethnic harmony. Identity reconstruction under conditions of intense conflict is probably impossible because once ethnic groups are mobilized for war, they will have already produced, and will continue reproducing, social institutions and discourses that reinforce their group identity and shut out or shout down competing identities.

Replacement of ethnicity by some other basis for political identification requires that political parties have cross-ethnic appeal, but examples of this in the midst of ethnic violence are virtually impossible to find. . . . In fact, even ethnic tension far short of war often undermines not just political appeals across ethnic lines but also appeals within a single group for cooperation with other groups. In Yugoslavia in the 1920s, Malaya in the 1940s, Ceylon in the 1950s, and in Nigeria in the 1950s and 1960, parties that advocated cooperation across ethnic lines proved unable to compete with strictly nationalist parties.

Even if constructivists are right that the ancient past does not matter, recent history does. Intense violence creates personal experiences of fear, misery, and loss which lock people into their group identity and their enemy relationship with the other group. Elite as well as mass opinions are affected; more than 5,000 deaths in the 1946 Calcutta riots convinced many previously optimistic Hindu and Muslim leaders that the groups could not live together. The Tutsi-controlled government in Burundi, which had witnessed the partial genocide against Tutsis in Rwanda in 1962–63 and survived Hutu-led coup attempts in 1965 and 1969, regarded the 1972 rebellion as another attempt at genocide, and responded by murdering between 100,000 and 200,000 Hutus. Fresh rounds of violence in 1988 and 1993–94 have reinforced the apocalyptic fears of both sides.

Finally, literacy preserves atrocity memories and enhances their use for political mobilization.[7] The result is that atrocity histories cannot be reconstructed; victims can sometimes be persuaded to accept exaggerated atrocity tales, but cannot be talked out of real ones. The result is that the bounds of debate are permanently altered; the leaders who used World War II Croatian atrocities to whip up Serbian nationalism in the 1980s were making use of a resource which, since then, remains always available in Serbian political discourse.

If direct action to transform exclusive ethnic identities into inclusive civic order is infeasible, outside powers or international institutions could enforce peace temporarily in the hope that reduced security threats would permit moderate leaders within each group to promote the reconstruction of more benign identities. While persuading ethnic war survivors to adopt an overarching identity may be impossible, a sufficiently prolonged period of guaranteed safety might allow moderate leaders to temper some of the most extreme hypernationalism back toward more benign, albeit still separate nationalisms. However, this still leaves both sides vulnerable to later revival of hypernationalism by radical political entrepreneurs, especially after the peacekeepers have left and security threats once again appear more realistic.

Power-Sharing

The best-developed blueprint for civic peace in multi-ethnic states is power-sharing or "consociational democracy," proposed by Arend Lijphart. This approach assumes that ethnicity is somewhat manipulable, but not so freely as constructivists say. Ethnic division, however, need not result in conflict; even if political mobilization is organized on ethnic lines, civil politics can be maintained if ethnic elites adhere to a power-sharing bargain that equitably protects all groups. The key components are: 1) joint exercise of governmental power; 2) proportional distribution of government funds and jobs; 3) autonomy on ethnic issues (which, if groups are concentrated territorially, may be achieved by regional federation); and 4) a minority veto on issues of vital importance to each group. Even if power-sharing can avert potential ethnic conflicts or dampen mild ones, our concern here is whether it can bring peace under the conditions of intense violence and extreme ethnic mobilization that are likely to motivate intervention.

The answer is no. The indispensable component of any power-sharing deal is a plausible minority veto, one which the strongest side will accept and which the weaker side believes that the stronger will respect. Traditions of stronger loyalties to the state than to parochial groups and histories of inter-ethnic compromise could provide reason for confidence, but in a civil war these will have been destroyed, if they were ever present, by the fighting itself and accompanying ethnic mobilization.

Only a balance of power among the competing groups can provide a "hard" veto—one which the majority must respect. Regional concentration of populations could partially substitute for balanced power if the minority group can credibly threaten to secede if its veto is overridden. In any situation where humanitarian intervention might be considered, however, these conditions too are unlikely to be met. Interventions are likely to be aimed at saving a weak group that cannot defend itself; balanced sides do not need defense. Demographic separation is also unlikely, because if the populations were already separated, the ethnic cleansing and related atrocities which are most likely to provoke intervention would not be occurring.

The core reason why power-sharing cannot resolve ethnic civil wars is that it is inherently voluntaristic; it requires conscious decisions by elites to cooperate to avoid ethnic strife. Under conditions of hypernationalist mobilization and real security threats, group leaders are unlikely to be receptive to compromise, and even if they are, they cannot act without being discredited and replaced by harder-line rivals.

Could outside intervention make power-sharing work? One approach would be to adjust the balance of power between the warring sides to a "hurting stalemate" by arming the weaker side, blockading the stronger, or partially disarming the stronger by direct military intervention. When both sides realize that further fighting will bring them costs but no profit, they will negotiate an agreement. This can balance power, although if populations are still intermingled it may actually worsen security dilemmas and increase violence—especially against civilians—as both sides eliminate the threats posed by pockets of the opposing group in their midst.

Further, once there has been heavy fighting, the sides are likely to distrust each other far too much to entrust any authority to a central government that could potentially be used against them. . . .

The final approach is international imposition of power-sharing, which requires occupying the country to coerce both sides into accepting the agreement and to prevent inter-ethnic violence until it can be implemented. The interveners, however, cannot bind the stronger side to uphold the agreement after the intervention forces leave. . . . The British did impose power-sharing as a condition for Cypriot independence, but it broke down almost immediately. The Greek Cypriots, incensed by what they saw as Turkish Cypriot abuse of their minority veto, simply overrode the veto and operated the government in violation of the constitution. Similarly, while at independence in 1948 the Sri Lankan constitution banned religious or communal discrimination, the Sinhalese majority promptly disenfranchised half of the Tamils on the grounds that they were actually Indians, and increasingly discriminated against Tamils in education, government employment, and other areas.

State-Building

Gerald Helman and Steven Ratner argue that states in which government breaks down, economic failure, and internal violence imperil their own citizens and threaten neighboring states can be rescued by international "conservatorship" to administer critical government functions until the country can govern itself following a free and fair election. Ideally, the failed state would voluntarily delegate specified functions to an international executor, although in extreme cases involving massive violations of human rights or the prospect of large-scale warfare, the international community could act even without an invitation.

As with imposing power-sharing, this requires occupying the country (and may require conquering it), coercing all sides to accept a democratic constitution, enforcing peace until elections can be held, and administering the economy and the elections. Conservatorship thus requires even more finesse than enforced power-sharing, and probably more military risks.

Helman and Ratner cite the UN intervention in Cambodia in 1992–93 to create a safe environment for free elections as conservatorship's best success. However, this was an ideological war over the governance of Cambodia, not an ethnic conflict over disempowering minorities or dismembering the country. By contrast, the growth of the U.S.-UN mission in Somalia from famine relief to state-rebuilding was a failure, and no one has been so bold as to propose conservatorship for Bosnia or Rwanda.

Even if conservatorship could rapidly, effectively, and cheaply stop an ethnic civil war, rebuild institutions, and ensure free elections, nothing would be gained unless the electoral outcome protected all parties' interests and safety; that is, power-sharing would still be necessary. Thus, in serious ethnic conflicts, conservatorship would only be a more expensive way to reach the same impasse.

Ethnic Separation

Regardless of the causes of a particular conflict, once communities are mobilized for violence, the reality of mutual security threats prevents both demobilization and de-escalation of hypernationalist discourse. Thus, lasting peace requires removal of the security dilemma. The most effective and in many cases the only way to do this is to separate the ethnic groups. The more intense the violence, the more likely it is that separation will be the only option.

The exact threshold remains an open question. The deductive logic of the problem suggests that the critical variable is fear for survival. Once a majority of either group comes to believe that the killing of noncombatants of their own group is not considered a crime by the other, they cannot accept any governing arrangement that could be captured by the enemy group and used against them.

The most persuasive source of such beliefs is the massacre of civilians, but it is not clear that there is a specific number of incidents or total deaths beyond which ethnic reconciliation becomes impossible. More important is the extent to which wide sections of the attacking group seem to condone the killings, and can be observed doing so by members of the target group. In this situation the attacks are likely to be seen as reflecting not just the bloodthirstiness of a particular regime or terrorist faction, but the preference of the opposing group as a whole, which means that no promise of non-repetition can be believed.

Testing this proposition directly requires better data on the attitudes of threatened populations during and after ethnic wars than we now have. Next best is aggregate analysis of the patterns of ends of ethnic wars, supplemented by investigation of individual cases as deeply as the data permits. I make a start at such an analysis below.

How Ethnic Wars Have Ended

At least 46 significant ethnic civil wars have ended since 1944.[8] Of the total, nineteen were ended by the military victory of one side, sixteen by *de jure* or *de facto* partition, and two have been suppressed by military occupation by a third party. Only nine ethnic civil wars have been ended by a negotiated agreement that did not partition the country. (See Table 1.)

TABLE 1 ■ ETHNIC CIVIL WARS RESOLVED 1944–1997

Combatants	Dates	Deaths (000s)	Outcome
A. Military victory (19):			
Kurds vs. Iran	45–80s	40	Suppressed
Karens, others vs. Myanmar	45–	400	Largely suppressed; sporadic violence
Chinese vs. Malaya	48–60	15	Suppressed
Tibetans vs. China	51–89	100	Suppressed
Hmong vs. Laos	59–72	50	Suppressed
Katangans vs. Congo	60–64	100	Suppressed
Papuans vs. Indonesia	64–86	19	Suppressed
Blacks vs. Rhodesia	65–80	50	Rebels victorious
Ibos vs. Nigeria	67–70	2000	Suppressed
Hmong vs. Thailand	67–80	.30	Suppressed
Palestinians vs. Jordan	70	15	Suppressed
Timorese vs. Indonesia	74–82	200	Suppressed
Aceh vs. Indonesia	75–80s	15	Suppressed
Tigreans, others vs. Ethiopia	75–91	600	Rebels victorious
Uighurs etc. vs. China	80	2	Suppressed
Sikhs vs. India	84	25	Suppressed
Bouganvilleans vs. Papua	88	1	Suppressed
Tutsis vs. Rwanda	90–94	750	Rebels victorious
Shiites vs. Iraq	91	35	Suppressed
B. *De facto* or *de jure* partition (16):			
Ukrainians vs. USSR	44–50s	150	Suppressed; later independent 1991
Lithuanians vs. USSR	45–52	40	Suppressed; later independent 1991
Muslims vs. Sikhs, Hindus (India)	46–47	.500	Partition 1947
Jews vs. Arabs (Palestine)	47–49	20	Partition 1948
Eritreans vs. Ethiopia	61–91	250	Independent 1993
Turks vs. Cyprus	63–74	.10	*De facto* partition
Bengalis vs. Pakistan	71	1000	Independent 1971
Armenians vs. Azerbaijan	88–	15	*De facto* partition
Somali clans	88–	350	*De facto* partition in N.; ongoing in
South Ossetians	90–92	1	*De facto* partition
Russians vs. Moldova	92–	2	*De facto* partition
Slovenia vs. Yugoslavia	91	1	Independent 1991
Croatia vs. Yugoslavia	91–95	30	Independent 1991
Serbs vs. Bosnia	92–95	150	*De facto* partition
Abkhazians vs. Georgia	92–	15	*De facto* partition; sporadic violence
Chechnyans vs. Russia	94–97	.20	*De facto* partition
C. Conflict suppressed by ongoing 3rd party military occupation (2):			
Kurds vs. Iraq	60–	215	*De facto* partition

Lebanese Civil War	75–90	120	Nominal power sharing; *de facto* partition.

D. Regional Autonomy Agreements (8):

Nagas vs. India	52–75	13	Autonomy 1972
Basques vs. Spain	59–80s	1	Autonomy 1980
Tripuras vs. India	67–89	13	Autonomy 1972
Moros vs. Philippines	72–87	50	Limited autonomy 1990
Baluchis vs. Pakistan	73–77	.5	Limited autonomy
Chittagong hill peoples vs. Bangladesh	75–89	24	Limited autonomy 1989
Miskitos vs. Nicaragua	81–88	1	Autonomy 1990
Mayas vs. Guatemala	61–97	166	Limited autonomy 1997

E. Power-sharing Agreements (1):

The data support the argument that separation of groups is the key to ending ethnic civil wars. Every case in which the state was preserved by agreement involved a regionally concentrated minority, and in every case but one the solution reinforced the ethnic role in politics by allowing regionally concentrated minorities to control their own destinies through autonomy for the regions where they form a majority of the population. South Africa is a partial exception, since the main element of the agreement was majority rule, although even in this case the powers reserved to the provinces offer some autonomy to whites, coloreds, and Zulus. There is not a single case where non-ethnic civil politics were created or restored by reconstruction of ethnic identities, power-sharing coalitions, or state-building.

Further, deaths in these cases average roughly five times lower than in the wars which ended in either suppression or partition: slightly more than 30,000, compared to about 175,000. This lends support to the proposition that the more extreme the violence, the less the chances for any form of reconciliation. Finally, it should be noted that all eight of the cases resolved through autonomy involve groups that were largely demographically separated even at the beginning of the conflict, which may help explain why there were fewer deaths.

INTERVENTION TO RESOLVE ETHNIC CIVIL WARS

International interventions that seek to ensure lasting safety for populations endangered by ethnic war—whether by the United Nations, by major powers with global reach, or by regional powers—must be guided by two principles. First, settlements must aim at physically separating the warring communities and establishing a balance of relative strength that makes it unprofitable for either side to attempt to revise the territorial settlement. Second, although economic or military assistance may suffice in some cases, direct military intervention will be necessary when aid to the weaker side would create a window of opportunity for the stronger, or when there is an immediate need to stop ongoing genocide.

Designing Settlements

Unless outsiders are willing to provide permanent security guarantees, stable resolution of an ethnic civil war requires separation of the groups into defensible regions. The critical variable is demography, not sovereignty. Political partition without ethnic separation leaves incentives for ethnic cleansing unchanged; it actually increases them if it creates new minorities. Conversely, demographic separation dampens ethnic conflicts even without separate sovereignty, although the more intense the previous fighting, the smaller the prospects for preserving a single state, even if loosely federated.

Partition without ethnic separation increases conflict because, while boundaries of sovereign successor states may provide defensible fronts that reduce the vulnerability of the majority group in each state, stay-behind minorities are completely exposed. Significant irredenta are both a call to their ethnic homeland and a danger to their hosts. They create incentives to mount rescue or ethnic cleansing operations before the situation solidifies. Greece's 1920 invasion of Turkey was justified in this way, while the 1947 decision to partition Palestine generated a civil war in advance of implementation, and the inclusion of Muslim-majority Kashmir within India has helped cause three wars. International recognition of Croatian and Bosnian independence did more to cause than to stop Serbian invasion. The war between Armenia and Azerbaijan has the same source, as do concerns over the international security risks of the several Russian diasporas.

Inter-ethnic security dilemmas can be nearly or wholly eliminated without partition if three conditions are met: First, there must be enough demographic separation that ethnic regions do not themselves contain militarily significant minorities. Second, there must be enough regional self-defense capability that abrogating the autonomy of any region would be more costly than any possible motive for doing so. Third, local autonomy must be so complete that minority groups can protect their key interests even lacking any influence at the national level. Even after an ethnic war, a single state could offer some advantages, not least of which are the economic benefits of a common market. However, potential interveners should recognize that groups that control distinct territories can insist on the *de facto* partition, and often will.

While peace requires separation of groups into distinct regions, it does not require total ethnic purity. Rather, remaining minorities must be small enough that the host group does not fear them as either a potential military threat or a possible target for irredentist rescue operations. Before the Krajina offensive, for example, President Franjo Tudjman of Croatia is said to have thought that the 12 percent Serb minority in Croatia was too large, but that half as many would be tolerable. The 173,000 Arabs remaining in Israel by 1951 were too few and too disorganized to be seen as a serious threat.

Geographic distribution of minorities is also important; in particular, concentrations near disputed borders or astride strategic communications constitute both a military vulnerability and an irredentist opportunity, and so are likely to spark conflict. It is not surprising that India's portion of Kashmir, with its Muslim majority, has been at the center of three interstate wars and an ongoing insurgency which continues today, while there has been no international conflict over the hundred million Muslims who live dispersed throughout most of the rest of India, and relatively little violence.

Where possible, inter-group boundaries should be drawn along the best defensive terrain, such as rivers and mountain ranges. Lines should also be as short as possible, to allow the heaviest possible manning of defensive fronts. . . . Access to the sea or to a friendly neighbor is also important, both for trade and for possible military assistance. Successor state arsenals should be encouraged, by aid to the weaker or sanctions on the stronger, to focus on defensive armaments such as forward artillery and antiaircraft missiles and rockets, while avoiding instruments that could make blitzkrieg attacks possible, such as tanks, fighter-bombers, and mobile artillery. These conditions would make subsequent offensives exceedingly expensive and likely to fail.

Intervention Strategy

The level of international action required to resolve an ethnic war will depend on the military situation on the ground. If there is an existing stalemate along defensible lines, the international community should simply recognize and strengthen it, providing transportation, protection, and resettlement assistance for refugees. However, where one side has the capacity to go on the offensive against the other, intervention will be necessary.

Interventions should therefore almost always be on behalf of the weaker side; the stronger needs no defense. Moreover, unless the international community can agree on a clear aggressor and a clear victim, there is no moral or political case for intervention. If both sides have behaved so badly that there is little to choose between them, intervention should not and probably will not be undertaken.[9] Almost no one in the West, for instance, has advocated assisting either side in the Croatian-Serb conflict.[10] While the intervention itself could be carried out by any willing actors, UN sponsorship is highly desirable, most of all to head off possible external aid to the group identified as the aggressor. . . .

OBJECTIONS TO ETHNIC SEPARATION AND PARTITION

There are five important objections to ethnic separation as policy for resolving ethnic conflicts: that it encourages splintering of states, that population exchanges cause human suffering, that it simply transforms civil wars into international ones, that rump states will not be viable, and that, in the end, it does nothing to resolve ethnic antagonisms.

Among most international organizations, western leaders, and scholars, population exchanges and partition are anathema. They contradict cherished western values of social integration, trample on the international legal norm of state sovereignty, and suggest particular policies that have been condemned by most of the world (e.g., Turkey's unilateral partition of Cyprus). The integrity of states and their borders is usually seen as a paramount principle, while self-determination takes second place. In ethnic wars, however, saving lives may require ignoring state-centered legal norms. The legal costs of ethnic separation must be compared to the human consequences, both immediate and long term, if the warring groups are not separated. To paraphrase Winston Churchill: separation is the worst solution, except for all the others.

Partition Encourages Splintering of States

If international interventions for ethnic separation encourage secession attempts elsewhere, they could increase rather than decrease global ethnic violence. However, this is unlikely, because government use of force to suppress them makes almost all secession attempts extremely costly; only groups that see no viable alternative try. What intervention can do is reduce loss of life where states are breaking up anyway. An expectation that the international community will never intervene, however, encourages repression of minorities, as in Turkey or the Sudan, and wars of ethnic conquest, as by Serbia.

Population Transfers Cause Suffering

Separation of intermingled ethnic groups necessarily involves significant refugee flows, usually in both directions. Population transfers during ethnic conflicts have often led to much suffering, so an obvious question is whether foreign intervention to relocate populations would only increase suffering. In fact, however, the biggest cause of suffering in population exchanges is spontaneous refugee movement. Planned population transfers are much safer. When ethnic conflicts turn violent, they generate spontaneous refugee movements as people flee from intense fighting or are kicked out by neighbors, marauding gangs, or a conquering army. Spontaneous refugees frequently suffer direct attack by hostile civilians or armed forces. They often leave precipitately, with inadequate money, transport, or food supplies, and before relief can be organized. They make vulnerable targets for banditry and plunder, and are often so needy as to be likely perpetrators also. Planned population exchanges can address all of these risks by preparing refugee relief and security operations in advance.

In the 1947 India-Pakistan exchange, nearly the entire movement of between 12 and 16 million people took place in a few months. The British were surprised by the speed with which this movement took place, and were not ready to control, support, and protect the refugees. Estimates of deaths go as high as one million. In the first stages of the population exchanges among Greece, Bulgaria, and Turkey in the 1920s, hundreds of thousands of refugees moved spontaneously and many died due to banditry and exposure. When after 1925 the League of Nations deployed capable relief services, the remaining transfers—one million, over 60 percent of the total—were carried out in an organized and planned way, with virtually no losses.

A related criticism is that transfers require the intervenors to operate *de facto* concentration camps for civilians of the opposing ethnic groups until transfers can be carried out. However, this is safer than the alternatives of administration by the local ally or allowing the war to run its course. As with transfers, the risks to the internees depend on planning and resources.

Separation Merely Substitutes International for Civil Wars

Post-separation wars are possible, motivated either by revanchism or by security fears if one side suspects the other of revisionist plans. The frequency and human cost of such wars, however, must be compared to the likely consequences of not separating. When the alternative is intercommunal slaughter, separation is the only defensible choice.

In fact the record of twentieth-century ethnic partitions is fairly good. The partition of Ireland has produced no interstate violence, although intercommunal violence continues in demographically mixed Northern Ireland. India and Pakistan have fought two wars since partition, one in 1965 over ethnically mixed Kashmir while the second in 1971 resulted not from Indo-Pakistani state rivalry or Hindu-Muslim religious conflict but from ethnic conflict between (West) Pakistanis and Bengalis. Indian intervention resolved the conflict by enabling the independence of Bangladesh. These wars have been much less dangerous, especially to civilians, than the political and possible physical extinction that Muslims feared if the subcontinent were not divided. The worst post-partition history is probably that of the Arab-Israeli conflict. Even here, civilian deaths would almost certainly have been higher without partition. It is difficult even to imagine any alternative; the British could not and would not stay, and neither side would share power or submit to rule by the other.

Rump States Will Not be Viable

Many analysts of ethnic conflict question the economic and military viability of partitioned states. History, however, records no examples of ethnic partitions which failed for economic reasons. In any case, intervenors have substantial influence over economic outcomes: They can determine partition lines, guarantee trade access and, if necessary, provide significant aid in relation to the economic sizes of likely candidates. Peace itself also enhances recovery prospects.

Thus the more important issue is military viability, particularly since intervention will most often be in favor of the weaker side. If the client has economic strength comparable to the opponent, it can provide for its own defense. If it does not, the intervenors will have to provide military aid and possibly a security guarantee.

Ensuring the client's security will be made easier by the opponent's scarcity of options for revision. First, any large-scale conventional attack is likely to fail because the intervenors will have drawn the borders for maximum defensibility and ensured that the client is better armed. If necessary, they can lend further assistance through air strikes. Breaking up conventional offensives is what high-technology air power does best.

Second, infiltration of small guerrilla parties, if successful over a period of time, could cause boundaries to become "fuzzy," and eventually to break down. This has been a major concern of some observers of Bosnia, but it should not be. Infiltration can only work where at least some civilians will support, house, feed, and hide the guerrillas. After ethnic separation, however, any infiltrators would be entering a completely hostile region where no one will help them; instead, all will inform on them and cooperate fully with authorities against them. The worst case is probably Israel, where terrorist infiltration has cost lives, but never comes close to threatening the state's territorial integrity. Retaliatory capabilities could also allow the client to dampen, even stop, such behavior.

Partition Does not Resolve Ethnic Hatreds

It is not clear that it is in anyone's power to resolve ethnic hatreds once there has been large-scale violence, especially murders of civilians. In the long run, however, separation may help reduce inter-ethnic antagonism; once real security threats are reduced, the plausibility of hypernationalist appeals may eventually decline. Certainly ethnic hostility cannot be reduced without separation. As long as either side fears, even intermittently, that it will be attacked by the other, past atrocities and old hatreds can easily be aroused. If, however, it becomes and remains implausible that the other group could ever seriously endanger the nation, hypernationalist drum-beating may fall on deafer and deafer ears.

The only stronger measure would be to attempt a thorough re-engineering of the involved groups' political and social systems, comparable to the rehabilitation of Germany after World War II. The costs would be steep, since this would require conquering the country and occupying it for a long time, possibly for decades. The apparent benignification of Germany suggests that, if the international community is prepared to go this far, this approach could succeed.

CONCLUSION

Humanitarian intervention to establish lasting safety for peoples endangered by ethnic civil wars is feasible, but only if the international community is prepared to recognize that some shattered states cannot be restored, and that population transfers are sometimes necessary. . . .

Ultimately we have a responsibility to be honest with ourselves as well as with the victims of ethnic wars all over the world. The world's major powers must decide whether they will be willing to spend any of their own soldiers' lives to save strangers, or whether they will continue to offer false hopes to endangered peoples.

NOTES

1. Ethnic wars involve organized large-scale violence, whether by regular forces (Turkish or Iraqi operations against the Kurds) or highly mobilized civilian populations (the *interahamwe* in Rwanda or the Palestinian *intifada*). A frequent aspect is "ethnic cleansing": efforts by members of one ethnic group to eliminate the population of another from a certain area by means such as discrimination, expropriation, terror, expulsion, and massacre. For proposals on managing ethnic rivalries involving lower levels of ethnic mobilization and violence, see Stephen Van Evera, "Managing the Eastern Crisis: Preventing War in the Former Soviet Empire," *Security Studies* 3 (Spring 1992), 361–382; Ted Hopf, "Managing Soviet Disintegration: A Demand for Behavioral Regimes," *International Security* 17, 1 (Summer 1992), 44–75.

2. An ethnic group (or nation) is commonly defined as a body of individuals who purportedly share cultural or racial characteristics, especially common ancestry or territorial origin, which distinguish them from members of other groups. See Max Weber (Guenther Roth, and Claus Wittich, eds.), *Economy and Society: An Outline of Interpretive Sociology,* Vol. 1 (Berkeley, Calif.: University of California Press, 1968), pp. 389–395; Anthony D. Smith, *National Identity* (Reno: University of Nevada Press, 1991), pp. 14, 21. Opposing communities in ethnic civil conflicts hold irreconcilable visions of the identity, borders, and citizenship of the state. They do not seek to control a state whose identity all sides accept, but rather to redefine or divide the state itself. By contrast, ideological conflicts may be defined as those in which all sides share a common vision of community membership, a common preference for political organization of the community as a single state, and a common sense of the legitimate boundaries of that state. The opposing sides seek control of the state, not its division or destruction. It follows that some religious conflicts—those between confessions which see themselves as separate communities, as between Catholics and Protestants in Northern Ireland—are best categorized with ethnic conflicts, while others—over interpretation of a shared religion, e.g., disputes over the social roles of Islam in Iran, Algeria, and Egypt—should be considered ideological contests. On religious differences as ethnic divisions, see Arent Lijphart, "The Power-Sharing Approach," in Joseph V. Montville, ed., *Conflict and Peacemaking in Multiethnic Societies* (Lexington, Mass.: Lexington Books, 1990), pp. 491–509, at 491.

3. While the discussion below delineates ideal types, mixed cases occur. The key distinction is the extent to which mobilization appeals are based on race or confession (ethnic rather than on political, economic, or social ideals (ideological). During the Cold War a number of Third World ethnic conflicts were misidentified by the superpowers as ideological struggles because local groups stressed ideology to gain outside support. In Angola the MPLA drew their support from the coastal Kimbundu tribe, the FNLA from the Bankongo in the north (and across the border in Zaire), and UNITA from Ovimbundu, Chokwe, and Ngangela in the interior of the south. The former were aided by the Soviets and the latter two, at various times, by both the United States and China. . . .

4. Reported by Andrej Gustinčić of *Reuters,* cited in Misha Glenny, *The Fall of Yugoslavia* (New York: Penguin, 1992), p. 166. Another tactic used by extremists to radicalize

co-ethnics is to accuse the other side of crimes similar to their own. In July 1992, amid large-scale rape of Bosnian Muslim women by Serb forces, Bosnian Serbs accused Muslims of impregnating kidnapped Serb women in order to create a new race of Janissary soldiers. Roy Gutman, *A Witness to Genocide* (New York: Macmillan, 1993), p. x.

5. Mikica Babić quoted in Chris Hedges, "War Turns Sarajevo Away from Europe," *New York Times* (July 28, 1995).

6. Increased geographic intermixing of ethnic groups often intensifies conflict, particularly if the state is too weak or too biased to assure the security of all groups. Increasing numbers of Jewish settlers in the West Bank had this effect on Israeli-Palestinian relations. A major reason for the failure of the negotiations that preceded the Nigerian civil war was the inability of northern leaders to guarantee the safety of Ibo living in the northern region. Harold D. Nelson, ed., *Nigeria: A Country Study* (Washington, D.C.: U.S. GPO, 1982), p. 55.

7. Ethnic combatants have noticed this. In World War II, the Croatian Ustasha refused to accept educated Serbs as converts because they were assumed to have a national consciousness independent of religion, whereas illiterate peasants were expected to forget their Serbian identity once converted. In 1992 Bosnian Serb ethnic cleansers annihilated the most educated Muslims. . . . Tutsi massacres of Hutus in Burundi in 1972 concentrated on educated people who were seen as potential ethnic leaders and afterwards the government restricted admission of Hutus to secondary schools. . . .

8. This total does not include civil wars which stopped temporarily but in which the same combatants later resumed fighting over the same issues (e.g., Burundi or Sudan) or cases in which peace agreements have been signed but not fully implemented as of this writing (e.g., Palestinians vs. Israel, Ovimbundu vs. Angola).

9. This is why the strongest advocates of intervention in Bosnia have emphasized Serb crimes, while those opposed to intervention insist on the moral equivalence of the two sides. Anthony Lewis, "Crimes of War," *New York Times* (April 25, 1994); Charles G. Boyd, "Making Peace with the Guilty," *Foreign Affairs*, 74, 5 (September/October 1995), pp. 22–38.

10. Further, attempts at even-handed intervention rarely achieve their goals, leading either to nearly complete passivity, as in the case of UNPROFOR in Bosnia, or eventually to open combat against one or all sides. At worst, peace-keeping efforts may actually prolong fighting. . . .

Deconstructing Nation Building

JAMES L. PAYNE

When plunging into war, hope generally triumphs over experience. The past—the quiet statistical tabulation of what happened when this was tried before—tends to be ignored in the heat of angry oratory and the thump of military boots. At the outset, it is easy to believe that force will be successful in upholding virtue and that history has no relevance.

Lately, this confidence in the force of arms has centered on nation building, that is, the idea of invading and occupying a land afflicted by dictatorship or civil war and turning it into a democracy. Alas, in their enthusiasm for nation building by force of arms, neither the theorists nor the practitioners have seriously looked at the historical experience with this kind of policy. If, after the troops leave, another dictatorship or another civil war ensues, then one has ploughed the sea. One has suffered the costs of the invasion—Americans killed, local inhabitants killed, destruction of property, tax money squandered, loss of international support, and so on—to no lasting purpose.

To see how nation building in general works out, I have compiled a list of all the cases since 1850 in which the United States and Great Britain employed military forces in a foreign land to cultivate democracy. I included only those cases where ground troops were deployed and clearly intervened in local politics. I have left aside the cases involving lesser types of involvement such as sending aid or military advisors or limited peace-keeping efforts or simply having military bases in the country.

In order to constitute a complete case of attempted nation building, troops have to have left the country (or be uninvolved politically if based in the country) so that we may see whether, in the absence of military support, a stable democracy continued to exist. For this reason we cannot use ongoing involvements such as Bosnia, Kosovo, Afghanistan, and Iraq. The application of this definition identifies 51 instances of attempted nation building by Britain and the United States. The question is, how often did they succeed?

The meaning of success involves more than holding an election and setting up a government. Nation building implies building, that is, constructing a lasting edifice. The nation builders concur in this notion of durability. Their idea isn't just to hold elections, get out, and have the country revert to anarchy or dictatorship. As President Bush has said, the aim in Iraq is to create lasting institutions of freedom. To call a

James L. Payne, "Deconstructing Nation Building," *The American Conservative*, October 24, 2005, pp. 13–15. Reprinted by permission of the publisher.

nation-building effort a success, therefore, we need to see that the military occupation of the target country was followed by the establishment of an enduring democracy.

To identify results in these terms, I inspected the political history of each country after the troop withdrawal. I looked for events betokening the collapse of democratic rule, including the suppression of opposition leaders or parties, major infringements of freedoms of speech, press, and assembly, violent transfers of power, murder of political leaders by other leaders, and significant civil war. I required large and multiple failures along these lines as evidence of democratic failure. A few arrests of opposition leaders were not enough to disqualify the country as a democracy nor a few assassinations of ambiguous meaning nor a simple military coup nor the resignation of an executive in the face of massive street demonstrations. If numerous free and fair elections were held, this was taken as strong evidence that democracy survived. Elections that were one-sided and to some degree rigged by the incumbents were taken as a negative sign, but they did not, in themselves, disqualify the country as democratic.

The results of applying these principles to the political outcomes in the 51 cases of intervention are shown in the following table. Overall, the results indicate that military intervention succeeded in leaving behind democracies in 14 cases—27 percent of the time. The conclusion, then, is that nation building by force is generally unsuccessful. A president who went around the world invading countries to make them democratic would fail most of the time. One group of countries that seem especially resistant to democracy-building efforts are the Arab lands. There have been nine interventions in Arab countries in the past century. In no case did stable democracy follow the military occupation.

In assessing the effectiveness of nation-building efforts, we should be careful not to confuse conjunction with cause. Just because some military interventions have been followed by democracy, this does not mean that the interventions caused the democracy. There is a worldwide movement against the use of force, and this trend promotes democratic development. Rulers are becoming less disposed to use violence to repress oppositions, and oppositions are less inclined to use force against incumbents. As a result, countries are becoming democracies on their own, without any outside help.

For example, we might be tempted to praise the British occupation of Malaysia as bringing democracy. But in the same period, the neighboring Asian country of Thailand, not occupied, also joined the camp of democratic nations. In fact, in Freedom House's survey of political rights and civil liberties, Thailand ranks ahead of Malaysia. It is quite possible, then, that Malaysia would have become a democracy without British intervention.

South Korea presents an interesting lesson in the effectiveness of nation building. Beginning in 1945, when U.S. troops landed, the United States was heavily involved in guiding political decisions in South Korea. This political involvement essentially ceased after 1961, and the South Koreans were allowed to go their own way politically. This way proved to be a military dictatorship under General Park Chung-Hee, which lasted until his murder in 1979. Thereupon followed two coups, a violent uprising in Kwangju, and many bloody street demonstrations. In 1985, however, the suppression of civil liberties had been greatly relaxed and competitive elections were held. Since that time, South Korea can be called a democracy (albeit a noisy one with plenty of corruption). So here is a case where 16 years of American tutelage brought failure in terms of democratic nation building, where the country evolved to democracy on its own 25 years after American involvement in local politics ceased.

Nations around the world are gradually becoming democratic on their own. Therefore, the 14 cases of nation-building "success" cannot be attributed to military intervention. These countries might well have become democracies without it.

The nation-building idea has a critical, generally overlooked, gap: who knows how to do it? Pundits and presidents talk about nation building as if it were a settled technology, like building bridges or removing gall bladders. Huge amounts of government and foundation money have been poured into the topic of democracy building, and academics and bureaucrats have produced reams of verbose commentary. But still there is no concrete, useable body of knowledge.

And, being a non-specialty, there cannot be any experts in it. The people who end up doing the so-called nation building are simply ordinary government employees who happen to wind up at the scene of the military occupation. Many

NATION-BUILDING MILITARY OCCUPATIONS BY THE UNITED STATES AND GREAT BRITAIN, 1850–2000

U.S. Occupations		British Occupations	
Austria 1945–1955	success	Botswana 1886–1966	success
Cuba 1898–1902	failure	Brunei 1888–1984	failure
Cuba 1906–1909	failure	Burma (Myanmar) 1885–1948	failure
Cuba 1917–1922	failure	Cyprus 1914–1960	failure
Dominican Republic 1911–1924	failure	Egypt 1882–1922	failure
Dominican Republic 1965–1967	success	Fiji 1874–1970	success
Grenada 1983–1985	success	Ghana 1886–1957	failure
Haiti 1915–1934	failure	Iraq 1917–1932	failure
Haiti 1994–1996	failure	Iraq 1941–1947	failure
Honduras 1924	failure	Jordan 1921–1956	failure
Italy 1943–1945	success	Kenya 1894–1963	failure
Japan 1945–1952	success	Lesotho 1884–1966	failure
Lebanon 1958	failure	Malawi (Nyasaland) 1891–1964	failure
Lebanon 1982–1984	failure	Malaysia 1909–1957	success
Mexico 1914–1917	failure	Maldives 1887–1976	success
Nicaragua 1909–1910	failure	Nigeria 1861–1960	failure
Nicaragua 1912–1925	failure	Palestine 1917–1948	failure
Nicaragua 1926–1933	failure	Sierra Leone 1885–1961	failure
Panama 1903–1933	failure	Solomon Islands 1893–1978	success
Panama 1989–1995	success	South Yemen (Aden) 1934–1967	failure
Philippines 1898–1946	success	Sudan 1899–1956	failure
Somalia 1992–1994	failure	Swaziland 1903–1968	failure
South Korea 1945–1961	failure	Tanzania 1920– 1963	failure
West Germany 1945–1952	success	Tonga 1900–1970	success
		Uganda 1894–1962	failure
		Zambia (N. Rhodesia) 1891–1964	failure
		Zimbabwe (S. Rhodesia) 1888–1980	failure

times they are military officers with no background in politics, sociology, or social psychology—not that it would help them. For the most part, these government employees see their mission as getting themselves and the U.S. out of the country without too much egg on their faces. They have no clearer idea of how to "instill democratic culture" than the readers of this page.

A look at some specific examples of nation building illustrates the intellectual vacuum. The 1989 U.S. invasion of Panama is credited in our tabulation as a nation-building success. Was this positive outcome the result of the expert application of political science? One of the nation builders, Lt. Col. John T. Fishel, has written a book on the Panama experience that gives quite a different picture. Fishel was Chief of Policy and Strategy for U.S. forces in Panama, and it was his job to figure out how to implement the mission statement. The orders looked simple on paper: "Conduct nation building operations to ensure democracy." But Fishel quickly discovered that the instruction was meaningless because democracy was an "undefined goal." It seemed to him that it wasn't the job of military officers to figure out how to implement this undefined objective, but, as he observes with a touch of irritation, "there are no U.S. civilian strategists clearly articulating strategies to achieve democracy."

> The fact that there was no clear definition of the conditions that constitute democracy meant that the Military Support Group and the other U.S. government agencies that were attempting to assist the Endara government had only the vaguest concept of what actions and programs would lead the country toward democracy. . . .

In practice, what the goal of "ensuring democracy" boiled down to was installing Guillermo Endara, the winner of a previous election, as president, supporting him as he became increasingly highhanded and unpopular, and then stepping away after his opponent was elected in 1994. . . .

Austria presents an instructive example of what nation building has actually amounted to on the ground. In our tabulation, Austria is classified as a case of successful nation building, but a close look reveals that the U.S. role was irrelevant, if not harmful.

After the war, Austria was jointly occupied by Russia as well as the Western powers. The Soviets brought Karl Renner, the elderly and respected Austrian Socialist leader, to Vienna to be the head of a provisional government. Renner's provisional government declared the establishment of the Democratic Austrian Republic on April 27, 1945. For six months, the United States refused to recognize this government (fearing that the Russians were up to no good in supporting it). Finally, when it could not be denied that the provisional government was popular and functioning, the United States recognized it.

Austria thus presents a doubly ironic lesson in how nation building unfolds. The United States—the democratic power—stood in the way of local leaders who were attempting to establish a democratic regime, and the Soviet Union—the world's leading dictatorship—unintentionally acted as midwife for the first democratic administration. Obviously, in Austria, no democracy needed to be "built." The democratic forces in Austria were strong enough to establish a democracy of their own, and they did it in spite of the "nation builders."

The advocates of nation building need to go back and take a close look at what really happened in the postwar political evolution of the defeated powers. In the lore of nation building, it is supposed that American experts applied sophisticated social engineering that forced these countries to become democracies against their will. It wasn't that way at all. These countries became democracies on their own, and the bumptious generals and paper-shuffling bureaucrats of the military occupation were generally more of a hindrance than a help.

The recent intervention in Iraq further illustrates how haphazard and unfocused nation building is in practice. While the military campaign was a success, the occupation and administration has been characterized by naïveté and improvisation. The U.S. had no policy to check looting after victory, nor the forces to do it, and the result was a ravaging of local infrastructure, the rapid formation of gangs of thugs and paramilitary fighters, and a loss of local support for the U.S. effort. The civilian administration was first put in the hands of retired Lt. Gen. Jay Garner, who was two weeks late getting to Baghdad, and who naively expected to find a functioning government in the country. After a month, the hapless Garner was fired, replaced by Paul Bremer as chief administrator. Two months after the invasion, Lt. Gen. William Wallace, the V Corps commander, described the nation-building "technique" U.S. officials were applying in Iraq: "We're making this up here as we go along."

Nation building by military force is not a coherent, defensible policy. It is based on no theory, it has no proven technique or methodology, and there are no experts who know how to do it. The record shows that it usually fails, and even when it appears to succeed, the positive result owes more to historical evolution and local political culture than anything nation builders might have done.

 Exercises for Civil Wars and Intervention

Apply what you learned in this chapter by using the online resources on MyPoliSciKit (www.mypoliscikit.com).

  Practice Tests

  Videos:
- "Building Peace in the Middle East"
- "The Crisis in Darfur"

Reading Guides:
- Alan J. Kuperman, "Humanitarian Intervention"
- Chaim Kaufmann, "Possible and Impossible Solutions to Ethnic Civil Wars"
- James L. Payne, "Deconstructing Nation Building"

HUMAN RIGHTS
AND INTERNATIONAL LAW

Human Rights in World Politics

RHODA E. HOWARD AND JACK DONNELLY

The International Human Rights Covenants[1] note that human rights "derive from the inherent dignity of the human person." But while the struggle to assure a life of dignity is probably as old as human society itself, reliance on human rights as a mechanism to realize that dignity is a relatively recent development.

Human rights are, by definition, the rights one has simply because one is a human being. This simple and relatively uncontroversial definition, though, is more complicated than it may appear on the surface. It identifies human rights as *rights*, in the strict and strong sense of that term, and it establishes that they are held simply by virtue of being human. . . .

WHAT RIGHTS DO WE HAVE?

The definition of human or natural rights as the rights of each person simply as a human being specifies their character; they are rights. The definition also specifies their source: (human) nature. . . .

What is it in human nature that gives rise to human rights? There are two basic answers to this question. On the one hand, many people argue that human rights arise from human needs, from the naturally given requisites for physical and mental health and well-being. On the other hand, many argue that human rights reflect the minimum requirements for human dignity or *moral* personality. These latter arguments derive from essentially philosophical theories of human "nature," dignity, or moral personality.

Needs theories of human rights run into the problem of empirical confirmations; the simple fact is that there is sound scientific evidence only for a very narrow list of human needs. But if we use "needs" in a broader, in part nonscientific, sense, then the two theories overlap. We can thus say that people have human rights to those things "needed" for a life of dignity, for the full development of their moral personality. The "nature" that gives rise to human rights is thus *moral* nature.

This moral nature is, in part, a social creation. Human nature, in the relevant sense, is an amalgam consisting both of psycho-biological facts (constraints and possibilities) and of the social structures and experiences that are no less a part of the essential nature of men and women. Human beings are not isolated individuals, but rather individuals who are essentially social creatures, in part even social creations. Therefore, a theory of human rights must recognize both the essential universality of human nature and the no less essential particularity arising from cultural and socioeconomic traditions and institutions.

Human rights are, by their nature, universal; it is not coincidental that we have a *Universal* Declaration of Human Rights, for human rights are the rights of all men and women. Therefore, in its basic outlines a list of human rights must apply at least more or less "across the board." But the nature of human beings is also shaped by the particular societies in which they live. Thus the universality of human rights must be qualified in at least two important ways.

First, the forms in which universal rights are institutionalized are subject to some legitimate cultural and political variation. For example, what counts as popular participation in government may vary, within a certain range, from society to society. Both multiparty and single-party regimes may reflect legitimate notions of political participation. Although the ruling party cannot be removed from power, in some one-party states individual representatives can be changed and electoral pressure may result in significant policy changes.

Second, and no less important, the universality (in principle) of human rights is qualified by the obvious fact that any particular list, no matter how broad its cross-cultural and international acceptance, reflects the necessarily contingent understandings of a particular era. For example, in the seventeenth and eighteenth centuries, the rights of man were indeed the rights of men, not women, and social and economic rights (other than the right to private property) were unheard of. Thus we must expect a gradual evolution of even a consensual list of human rights, as collective understandings of the essential elements of human dignity, the conditions of moral personality, evolve in response to changing ideas and material circumstances.

In other words, human rights are by their essential nature universal in form. They are, by definition, the rights held by each (and every) person simply as a human being. But any universal list of human rights is subject to a variety of justifiable implementations.

In our time, the Universal Declaration of Human Rights (1948) is a minimum list that is nearly universally accepted, although additional rights have been added (e.g., self-determination) and further new rights (e.g., the right to nondiscrimination on the grounds of sexual orientation or the right to peace) may be added in the future. We are in no position to offer a philosophical defense of the list of rights in the Universal Declaration. To do so would require an account of the source of human rights—human nature—that would certainly exceed the space available to us. Nonetheless, the Universal Declaration is nearly universally accepted by states. For practical political purposes we can treat it as authoritative. . . .

INTERNATIONAL HUMAN RIGHTS INSTITUTIONS

The international context of national practices deserves some attention. There are, as we have already noted, international human rights standards that are widely accepted—in principle at least—by states. Thus the discussion and evaluation of national practices take place within an overarching set of international standards to which virtually all states have explicitly committed themselves. Whatever the force of claims of national sovereignty, with its attendant legal immunity from international action, the evaluation of national human rights practices from the perspective of the international standards of the Universal Declaration thus is certainly appropriate, even if one is uncomfortable with the moral claim sketched above that such universalistic scrutiny is demanded by the very idea of human rights.

In the literature on international relations it has recently become fashionable to talk of "international regimes," that is, norms and decision-making procedures accepted by states in a given issue area. National human rights practices do take place within the broader context of an international human rights regime centered on the United Nations.

We have already sketched the principal norms of this regime—the list of rights in the Universal Declaration. These norms/rights are further elaborated in two major treaties, the International Covenant on Economic, Social and Cultural Rights and the International Covenant on Civil and Political Rights, which were opened for signature and ratification in 1966 and came into force in 1976. Almost all of the countries studied in this volume have ratified (become a party to) both the Covenant on Civil and Political Rights and the Covenant on Economic, Social and Cultural Rights. . . . Even the countries that are not parties to the Covenants often accept the principles of the Universal Declaration. In addition, there are a variety of single-issue treaties that have been formulated under UN auspices on topics such as racial discrimination, the rights of women, and torture. These later Covenants and Conventions go into much greater detail than the Universal Declaration and include a few important changes. For example, the Covenants prominently include a right to national self-determination, which is absent in the Universal Declaration, but do not include a right to private property. Nevertheless, for the most part they can be seen simply as elaborations on the Universal Declaration, which remains the central normative document in the international human rights regime.

What is the legal and political force of these norms? The Universal Declaration of Human Rights was proclaimed in 1948 by the United Nations General Assembly.

As such, it has no force of law. Resolutions of the General Assembly, even solemn declarations, are merely recommendations to states; the General Assembly has no international legislative powers. Over the years, however, the Universal Declaration has come to be something more than a mere recommendation.

There are two principal sources of international law, namely, treaty and custom. Although today we tend to think first of treaty, historically custom is at least as important. A rule or principle attains the force of customary international law when it can meet two tests. First, the principle or rule must reflect the general practice of the overwhelming majority of states. Second, what lawyers call *opinio juris*, the sense of obligation, must be taken into account. Is the customary practice seen by states as an obligation, rather than a mere convenience or courtesy? Today it is a common view of international lawyers that the Universal Declaration has attained something of the status of customary international law, so that the rights it contains are in some important sense binding on states.

Furthermore, the International Human Rights Covenants are treaties and as such do have the force of international law, but only for the parties to the treaties, that is, those states that have (voluntarily) ratified or acceded to the treaties. The same is true of the single-issue treaties that round out the regime's norms. It is perhaps possible that the norms of the Covenants are coming to acquire the force of customary international law even for states that are not parties. But in either case, the fundamental weakness of international law is underscored: Virtually all international legal obligations are voluntarily accepted.

This is obviously the case for treaties: states are free to become parties or not entirely as they choose. It is no less true, though, of custom, where the tests of state practice and *opinio juris* likewise assure that international legal obligation is only voluntarily acquired. In fact, a state that explicitly rejects a practice during the process of custom formation is exempt even from customary international legal obligations. For example, Saudi Arabia's objection to the provisions on the equal rights of women during the drafting of the Universal Declaration might be held to exempt it from such a norm, even if the norm is accepted internationally as customarily binding. Such considerations are particularly important when we ask what force there is to international law and what mechanisms exist to implement and enforce the rights specified in the Universal Declaration and the Covenants.

Acceptance of an obligation by states does not carry with it acceptance of any method of international enforcement. Quite the contrary. Unless there is an explicit enforcement mechanism attached to the obligation, its enforcement rests simply on the good faith of the parties. The Universal Declaration contains no enforcement mechanisms of any sort. Even if we accept it as having the force of international law, its implementation is left entirely in the hands of individual states. The Covenants do have some implementation machinery, but the machinery's practical weakness is perhaps its most striking feature. . . .

The one other major locus of activity in the international human rights regime is the UN Commission on Human Rights. In addition to being the body that played the principal role in the formulation of the Universal Declaration, the Covenants and most of the major single-issue human rights treaties, it has some weak implementation powers. Its public discussion of human rights situations in various countries can help to mobilize international public opinion, which is not always utterly useless in helping to reform national practice. For example, in the 1970s the Commission played a major role in publicizing the human rights conditions in Chile, Israel, and South Africa. Furthermore, it is empowered by ECOSOC resolution 1503 (1970) to investigate communications (complaints) from individuals and groups that "appear to reveal a consistent pattern of gross and reliably attested violations of human rights."

The 1503 procedure, however, is at least as thoroughly hemmed in by constraints as are the other enforcement mechanisms that we have considered. Although individuals may communicate grievances, the 1503 procedure deals only with "*situations*" of gross and systematic violations, not the particular cases of individuals. Individuals cannot even obtain an international judgment in their particular case, let alone international enforcement of the human rights obligations of their government. Furthermore, the entire procedure remains confidential until a case is concluded, although the Commission does publicly announce a "blacklist" of countries being studied. In only four cases (Equatorial Guinea, Haiti, Malawi, and Uruguay) has the Commission gone public with a 1503 case. Its most forceful conclusion was a 1980 resolution provoked by the plight of Jehovah's Witnesses in Malawi, which merely expressed the hope that all human rights were being respected in Malawi.

In addition to this global human rights regime, there are regional regimes. The 1981 African Charter of Human and Peoples' Rights, drawn up by the Organization of African Unity, provides for a Human Rights Commission, but it is not yet functioning. In Europe and the Americas there are highly developed systems involving both commissions with very strong investigatory powers and regional human rights courts with the authority to make legally binding decisions on complaints by individuals (although only eight states have accepted the jurisdiction of the Inter-American Court of Human Rights).

Even in Europe and the Americas, however, implementation and enforcement remain primarily national. In nearly thirty years the European Commission of Human Rights has considered only about 350 cases, while the European Court of Human Rights has handled only one-fifth that number. Such regional powers certainly should not be ignored or denigrated. They provide authoritative interpretations in cases of genuine disagreements and a powerful check on backsliding and occasional deviations by states. But the real force of even the European regime lies in the voluntary acceptance of human rights by the states in question, which has infinitely more to do with domestic politics than with international procedures.

In sum, at the international level there are comprehensive, authoritative human rights norms that are widely accepted as binding on all states. Implementation and enforcement of these norms, however, both in theory and in practice, are left to states. The international context of national human rights practices certainly cannot be ignored. Furthermore, international norms may have an important socializing effect on national leaders and be useful to national advocates of improved domestic human rights practices. But the real work of implementing and enforcing human rights takes place at the national level. . . . Before the level of the nation-state is discussed, however, one final element of the international context needs to be considered, namely, human rights as an issue in national foreign policies.

HUMAN RIGHTS AND FOREIGN POLICY

Beyond the human rights related activities of states in international institutions such as those discussed in the preceding section, many states have chosen to make human rights a concern in their bilateral foreign relations.[3] In fact, much of the surge of interest in human rights in the last decade can be traced to the catalyzing effect of President Jimmy Carter's (1977–1981) efforts to make international human rights an objective of U.S. foreign policy.

In a discussion of human rights as an issue in national foreign policy, at least three problems need to be considered. First, a nation must select a particular set of rights to pursue. Second, the legal and moral issues raised by intervention on behalf of human rights abroad need to be explored. Third, human rights concerns must be integrated into the nation's broader foreign policy, since human rights are at best only one of several foreign policy objectives.

The international normative consensus on human rights noted above largely solves the problem of the choice of a set of rights to pursue, for unless a state chooses a list very similar to that of the Universal Declaration, its efforts are almost certain to be dismissed as fatally flawed by partisan or ideological bias. Thus, for example, claims by officials of the Reagan administration that economic and social rights are not really true human rights are almost universally denounced. By the same token, the Carter administration's serious attention to economic and social rights, even if it was ultimately subordinate to a concern for civil and political rights, greatly contributed to the international perception of its policy as genuinely concerned with human rights, not just a new rhetoric for the Cold War or neo-colonialism. Such an international perception is almost a necessary condition—although by no means a sufficient condition—for an effective international human rights policy.

A state is, of course, free to pursue any objectives it wishes in its foreign policy. If it wishes its human rights policy to be taken seriously, however, the policy must at least be enunciated in terms consistent with the international consensus that has been forged around the Universal Declaration. In practice, some rights must be given particular prominence in a nation's foreign policy, given the limited material resources and international political capital of even the most powerful state, but the basic contours of policy must be set by the Universal Declaration.

After the rights to be pursued have been selected, the second problem, that of intervention on behalf of human rights, arises. When state A pursues human rights in its relations with state B, A usually will be seeking to alter the way that B treats its own citizens. This is, by definition, a matter essentially within the domestic jurisdiction of B and thus outside the legitimate jurisdiction of A. A's action, therefore, is vulnerable to the charge of intervention, a charge that carries considerable legal, moral, and political force in a world, such as ours, that is structured at the international level around sovereign nation-states.

The legal problems raised by foreign policy action on behalf of human rights abroad are probably the most troubling. Sovereignty entails the principle of nonintervention; to say that A has sovereign jurisdiction over X is essentially equivalent to saying that no one else may intervene in A with respect to X. Because sovereignty is the foundation of international law, any foreign policy action that amounts to intervention is prohibited by international law. On the face of it at least, this prohibition applies to action on behalf of human rights as much as any other activity.

It might be suggested that we can circumvent the legal proscription of intervention in the case of human rights by reference to particular treaties or even the general international normative consensus discussed above. International norms per se, however, do not authorize even international organizations, let alone individual states acting independently, to enforce those norms. Even if all states are legally bound to implement the rights enumerated in the Universal Declaration, it simply does not follow, in logic or in law, that any particular state or group of states is entitled to enforce that obligation. States are perfectly free to accept international legal obligations that have no enforcement mechanisms attached.

Scrupulously avoiding intervention (coercive interference) thus still leaves considerable room for international action at improving the human rights performance of a foreign country. Quiet diplomacy, public protests or condemnations, downgrading or breaking diplomatic relations, reducing or halting foreign aid, and selective or comprehensive restrictions of trade and other forms of interaction are all actions that fall short of intervention. Thus in most circumstances they will be legally permissible actions on behalf of human rights abroad.

An international legal perspective on humanitarian intervention, however, does not exhaust the subject. Recently, several authors have argued, strongly and we believe convincingly, that moral considerations in at least some circumstances justify humanitarian intervention on behalf of human rights.[4] Michael Walzer, whose book *Just and Unjust Wars* has provoked much of the recent moral discussion of humanitarian intervention, can be taken as illustrative of such arguments.

Walzer presents a strong defense of the morality of the general international principle of nonintervention, arguing that it gives force to the basic right of peoples to self-determination, which in turn rests on the rights of individuals, acting in concert as a community, to choose their own government. Walzer has been criticized for interpreting this principle in a way that is excessively favorable to states by arguing that the presumption of legitimacy (and thus against intervention) should hold in all but the most extreme circumstances. Nonetheless, even Walzer allows that intervention must be permitted "when the violation of human rights is so terrible that it makes talk of community or self-determination. . .seem cynical and irrelevant,"[5] when gross, persistent, and systematic violations of human rights shock the moral conscience of mankind.

The idea underlying such arguments is that human rights are of such paramount moral importance that gross and systematic violations present a moral justification for remedial international action. If the international community as a whole cannot or will not act—and above we have shown that an effective collective international response will usually be impossible—then one or more states may be morally justified in acting ad hoc on behalf of the international community.

International law and morality thus lead to different and conflicting conclusions in at least some cases. One of the functions of international politics is to help to resolve such a conflict; political considerations will play a substantial role in determining how a state will respond in its foreign policy to the competing moral and legal demands placed on it. But the political dimensions of such decisions point to the practical dangers by moral arguments in favor of humanitarian intervention. . . .

Human rights may be moral concerns, but often they are not *merely* moral concerns. Morality and realism are not necessarily incompatible, and to treat them as if they always were can harm not only a state's human rights policy but its broader foreign policy as well.

Sometimes a country can afford to act on its human rights concerns; other times it cannot. Politics involves compromise, as a result of multiple and not always compatible goals that are pursued and the resistance of a world that more often than not is unsupportive of the particular objectives being sought. Human rights, like other goals of foreign policy, must at times be compromised. In some instances there is little that a country can afford to do even in the face of major human rights violations. . . .

If such variations in the treatment of human rights violators are to be part of a consistent policy, human rights concerns need to be explicitly and coherently integrated into the broader framework of foreign policy. A human rights policy must be an integral part of, not just something tacked on to, a country's overall foreign policy.

Difficult decisions have to be made about the relative weights to be given to human rights, as well as other foreign policy goals, and at least rough rules for making trade-offs need to be formulated. Furthermore, such decisions need to be made early in the process of working out a policy, and as a matter of principle. Ad hoc responses to immediate problems and crises, which have been the rule in the human rights policies of countries such as Canada and the United States, are almost sure to lead to inconsistencies and incoherence, both in appearance and in fact. Without such efforts to integrate human rights into the structure of national foreign policy, any trade-offs that are made will remain, literally, unprincipled.

Standards will be undeniably difficult to formulate, and their application will raise no less severe problems. Hard cases and exceptions are unavoidable. So are gray areas and fuzzy boundaries. Unless such efforts are seriously undertaken, however, the resulting policy is likely to appear baseless or inconsistent, and probably will be so in fact as well.

There are many opportunities for foreign policy action on behalf of human rights in foreign countries, but effective action requires the same sort of care and attention required for success in any area of foreign policy. . . .

CULTURE AND HUMAN RIGHTS

This view of the creation of the individual, with individual needs for human rights is criticized by many advocates of the "cultural relativist" school of human rights. They present the argument that human rights are a "Western construct with limited [universal] applicability."[6] But cultural relativism, as applied to human rights, fails to grasp the nature of culture. A number of erroneous assumptions underlies this viewpoint.

Criticism of the universality of human rights often stems from erroneous perceptions of the persistence of traditional societies, societies in which principles of social justice are based not on rights but on status and on the intermixture of privilege and responsibility. Often anthropologically anachronistic pictures are presented of premodern societies, taking no account whatsoever of the social change we have described above. It is assumed that culture is a static entity. But culture—like the individual—is adaptive. One can accept the principle that customs, values, and norms do indeed glue society together, and that they will endure, without assuming cultural stasis. Even though elements of culture have a strong hold of people's individual psyches, cultures can and do change. Individuals are actors who can influence their own fate, even if their range of choice is circumscribed by the prevalent social structure, culture, or ideology.

Cultural relativist arguments also often assume that culture is a unitary and unique whole; that is, that one is born into, and will always be, a part of a distinctive, comprehensive, and integrated set of cultural values and institutions that cannot be changed incrementally or only in part. Since in each culture the social norms and roles vary, so, it is argued, human rights must vary. The norms of each society are held to be both valuable in and of their own right, and so firmly rooted as to be impervious to challenge. Therefore, such arguments are applicable only to certain Western societies; to impose them on other societies from which they did not originally arise would do serious and irreparable damage to those cultures. In fact, though, people are quite adept cultural accommodationists; they are able to choose which aspects of a "new" culture they wish to adopt and which aspects of the "old" they wish to retain. For example, the marabouts (priests), who lead Senegal's traditional Muslim brotherhoods, have become leading political figures and have acquired considerable wealth and power through the peanut trade.

Still another assumption of the cultural relativism school is that culture is unaffected by social structure. But structure does affect culture. To a significant extent cultures and values reflect the basic economic and political organization of a society. For example, a society such as Tokugawa Japan that moves from a feudal structure to an organized bureaucratic state is bound to experience changes in values. Or the amalgamation of many different ethnic groups into one nation-state inevitably changes the way that individuals view themselves: For example, state-sponsored retention of ethnic customs, as under Canada's multicultural policy of preserving ethnic communities, cannot mask the fact that most of those communities are merging into the larger Canadian society.

A final assumption of the cultural relativist view of human rights is that cultural practices are neutral in their impact on different individuals and groups. Yet very few social practices, whether cultural or otherwise, distribute the same benefits to each member of a group. In considering any cultural practice it is useful to ask, who benefits from its retention? Those who speak for the group are usually those most capable of articulating the group's values to the outside world. But such spokesmen are likely to stress, in their articulation of "group" values, those particular values that are most to their own advantage. Both those who choose to adopt "new" ideals, such as political democracy or atheism, and those who choose to retain "old" ideals, such as a God-fearing political consensus, may be doing so in their own interests. Culture is both influenced by, and an instrument of, conflict among individuals or social groups. Just as those who attempt to modify or change customs may have personal interests in so doing, so also do those who attempt to preserve them. Quite often, relativist arguments are adopted principally to protect the interests of those in power.

Thus the notion that human rights cannot be applied across cultures violates both the principle of human rights and its practice. Human rights mean precisely that: rights held by virtue of being human. Human rights do not mean human dignity, nor do they represent the sum of personal resources (material, moral, or spiritual) that an individual might hold. Cultural variances that do not violate basic human rights undoubtedly enrich the world. But to permit the interests of the powerful to masquerade behind spurious defenses of cultural relativity is merely to lessen the chance that the victims of their policies will be able to complain. In the modern world, concepts such as cultural relativity, which deny to individuals the moral right to make comparisons and to insist on universal standards of right and wrong, are happily adopted by those who control the state.

THIRD WORLD CRITICISMS

In recent years a number of commentators from the Third World have criticized the concept of universal human rights. Frequently, the intention of the criticisms appears to be to exempt some Third World governments from the standard of judgment generated by the concept of universal human rights. Much of the criticism in fact serves to cover abuses of human rights by state corporatist, developmental dictatorship, or allegedly "socialist" regimes.

A common criticism of the concept of universal human rights is that since it is Western in origin, it must be limited in its applicability to the Western world. Both logically and empirically, this criticism is invalid. Knowledge is not limited in its applicability to its place or people of origin—one does not assume, for example, that medicines discovered in the developed Western world will cure only people of European origin. Nor is it reasonable to state that knowledge or thought of a certain kind—about social arrangements instead of about human biology or natural science—is limited to its place of origin. Those same Third World critics who reject universal concepts of human rights often happily accept Marxist socialism, which also originated in the Western world, in the mind of a German Jew.

The fact that human rights is originally a liberal notion, rooted in the rise of a class of bourgeois citizens in Europe who demanded individual rights against the power of kings and nobility, does not make human rights inapplicable to the rest of the world. As we argue above, all over the world there are now formal states, whose citizens are increasingly individualized. All over the world, therefore, there are people who need protections against the depradations of class-ruled governments.

Moreover, whatever the liberal origins of human rights, the list now accepted as universal includes a wide range of economic and social rights that were first advocated by socialist and social-democratic critics of liberalism. Although eighteenth-century liberals stressed the right to private property, the 1966 International Human Rights Covenants do not mention it, substituting instead the right to sovereignty over national resources. . . . To attribute the idea of universal human rights to an outdated liberalism, unaffected by later notions of welfare democracy and uninfluenced by socialist concerns with economic rights, is simply incorrect.

The absence of a right to private property in the Covenants indicates a sensitivity to the legitimate preoccupations of socialist and postcolonial Third World governments. Conservative critics of recent trends in international human rights in fact deplore the right to national sovereignty over resources, as some of them also deplore any attention to the economic rights of the individual. We certainly do not share this view of rights; we believe that the economic rights of the individual are as important as civil and political rights. But it is the individual we are concerned with. We would like to see a world in which *every individual* has enough to eat, not merely a world in which every *state* has the right to economic sovereignty.

We are skeptical, therefore, of the radical Third Worldist assertion that "group" rights ought to be more important than individual rights. Too often, the "group" in question proves to be the state. Why allocate rights to a social institution that is already the chief violator of individuals' rights? Similarly, we fear the expression "peoples' rights." The communal rights of individuals to practice their own religion, speak their own language, and indulge in their own ancestral customs are protected in the Covenant on Civil and Political Rights. Individuals are free to come together in groups to engage in those cultural practices which are meaningful to them. On the other hand, often a "group" right can simply mean that the individual is subordinate to the group—for example, that the individual Christian fundamentalist in the Soviet Union risks arrest because of the desire of the larger "group" to enforce official atheism.

The one compelling use that we can envisage for the term "group rights" is in protection of native peoples, usually hunter-gatherers, pastoralists, or subsistence agriculturalists, whose property rights as collectivities are being violated by the larger state societies that encroach upon them. Such groups are fighting a battle against the forces of modernization and the state's accumulative tendencies. For example, native peoples in Canada began in the 1970s to object to state development projects, such as the James Bay Hydroelectric project in Quebec, which deprived them of their traditional lands. At the moment, there is no international human rights protection for such groups or their "way of life."

One way to protect such group rights would be to incorporate the group as a legal entity in order to preserve their land claims. However, even if the law protects such group rights, individual members of the group may prefer to move into the larger society in response to the processes of modernization discussed above. Both opinions must be protected.

If the purpose of group rights is to protect large, established groups of people who share the same territory, customs, language, religion, and ancestry, then such protection could only occur at the expense of states' rights. These groups, under international human rights law, do not have the right to withdraw from the states that enfold them. Moreover, it is clearly not the intention of Third World defenders of group rights to allow such a right to secession. A first principle of the Organization of African Unity, for example, is to preserve the sovereignty of all its member states not only against outside attack but also against internal attempts at secession. Group rights appear to mean, in practice, states' rights. But the rights of states are the rights of the individuals and classes who control the state.

Many Third World and socialist regimes also argue that rights ought to be tied to duties. A citizen's rights, it is argued, ought to be contingent upon his duties toward the society at large—privilege is contingent on responsibility. Such a view of rights made sense in nonstate societies in which each "person" fulfilled his roles along with others, all of the roles together creating a close-knit, tradition-bound group. But in modern state societies, to tie rights to duties is to risk the former's complete disappearance. All duties will be aimed toward the preservation of the state and of the interests of those who control it.

It is true that no human rights are absolute; even in societies that adhere in principle to the liberal ethos, individuals are frequently deprived of rights, especially in wartime or if they are convicted of criminal acts. However, such deprivations can legitimately be made only after the most scrupulous protection of civil and political rights under the rule of law. The difficulty with tying rights to duties without the intermediate step of scrutiny by a genuinely independent judiciary is the likelihood of wholesale cancellation of rights by the ruling class. But if one has rights merely because one is human, and for no other reason, then it is much more difficult, in principle, for the state to cancel them. It cannot legitimate the denial of rights by saying that only certain types of human beings, exhibiting certain kinds of behavior, are entitled to them.

One final criticism of the view of universal human rights embedded in the International Covenants is that an undue stress is laid on civil and political rights, whereas the overriding rights priority in the Third World is economic rights. In this view, the state as the agent of economic development—and hence, presumably, of eventual distribution of economic goods or "rights" to the masses—should not be bothered with problems of guaranteeing political participation in decision making, or of protecting people's basic civil rights. These rights, it is argued, come "after" development is completed. The empirical basis for this argument is weak. . . . Economic development per se will not guarantee future human rights, whether of an economic or any other kind. Often, development means economic growth, but without equitable distributive measures. Moreover, development strategies often fail because of insufficient attention to citizens' needs and views. Finally, development plans are often a cover for the continued violations of citizens' rights by the ruling class.

Thus we return to where we started: the rights of all men and women against all governments to treatment as free, equal, materially and physically secure persons. This is what human dignity means and requires in our era. And the individual human rights of the Universal Declaration and the Covenants are the means by which individuals today carry out the struggle to achieve their dignity. . . .

NOTES

1. The International Bill of Human Rights includes the Universal Declaration of Human Rights (1948), the International Covenant on Economic, Social and Cultural Rights (1966), the International Covenant on Civil and Political Rights (1966), and the Optional Protocol to the latter Covenant.
2. Howard Tolley, "The Concealed Crack in the Citadel: The United Nations Commission on Human Rights' Response to Confidential Communications," *Human Rights Quarterly* 6 (November 1984): 420–62.
3. This section draws heavily on Jack Donnelly, "Human Rights and Foreign Policy," *World Politics* 34 (July 1982): 574–95, and "Human Rights, Humanitarian Intervention and American Foreign Policy: Law, Morality and Politics," *Journal of International Affairs* 37 (Winter 1984): 311–28.
4. See, for example, Jerome Slater and Terry Nardin, "Nonintervention and Human Rights," *Journal of Politics* 48 (February 1986): 86–96; Charles R. Beitz, "Nonintervention and Communal Integrity," *Philosophy and Public Affairs* 9 (Summer 1980): 385–91; and Robert Matthews and Cranford Pratt, "Human Rights and Foreign Policy: Principles and Canadian Practice," *Human Rights Quarterly* 7 (May 1985): 159–88.
5. Michael Walzer, *Just and Unjust Wars* (New York: Basic Books, 1977), p. 90. For criticisms of Walzer see Slater and Nardin, "Nonintervention"; Beitz, "Nonintervention"; and David Luban, "The Romance of the Nation State," *Philosophy and Public Affairs* 9 (Summer 1980): 392–97.
6. Adamantia Pollis and Peter Schwab, "Human Rights: A Western Concept with Limited Applicability," in *Human Rights: Cultural and Ideological Perspectives,* Pollis and Schwab, ed. (New York: Praeger, 1979), pp. 1–18.

Reflections on Intervention

KOFI ANNAN

The United Nations is . . . an association of sovereign States, and sovereign States do tend to be extremely jealous of their sovereignty. Small States, especially, are fearful of intervention in their affairs by great Powers. And indeed, our century has seen many examples of the strong "intervening"—or interfering—in the affairs of the weak, from the Allied intervention in the Russian civil war in 1918 to the Soviet "interventions" in Hungary, Czechoslovakia and Afghanistan. Others might refer to the American intervention in Viet Nam, or even the Turkish intervention in Cyprus in 1974. The motives, and the legal justification, may be better in some cases than others, but the word "intervention" has come to be used almost as a synonym for "invasion."

The Charter of the United Nations gives great responsibilities to great Powers, in their capacity as permanent members of the Security Council. But as a safeguard against abuse of those powers, Article 2.7 of the Charter protects national sovereignty even from intervention by the United Nations itself. I'm sure everyone in this audience knows it by heart. But, let me remind you—just in case—that Article forbids the United Nations to intervene "in matters which are essentially within the domestic jurisdiction of any State."

That prohibition is just as relevant today as it was in 1945: violations of sovereignty remain violations of the global order. Yet, in other contexts the word "intervention" has a more benign meaning. We all applaud the policeman who intervenes to stop a fight, or the teacher who prevents big boys from bullying a smaller one. And medicine uses the word "intervention" to describe the act of the surgeon, who saves life by "intervening" to remove malignant growth, or to repair damaged organs. Of course, the most intrusive methods of treatment are not always to be recommended. A wise doctor knows when to let nature take its course. But a doctor who never intervened would have few admirers, and probably even fewer patients.

So it is in international affairs. Why was the United Nations established, if not to act as a benign policeman or doctor? Our job is to intervene: to prevent conflict where we can, to put a stop to it when it has broken out, or—when neither of those things is possible—at least to contain it and prevent it from spreading. That is what the world expects of us, even though—alas—the United Nations by no means always lives up to such expectations. It is also what the Charter requires of us, particularly in Chapter VI, which deals with the peaceful settlement of disputes, and Chapter VII, which describes the action the United Nations must take when peace comes under threat, or is actually broken.

The purpose of Article 2.7, which I quoted just now, was to confine such interventions to cases where the international peace is threatened or broken, and to keep the United Nations from interfering in purely domestic disputes. Yet even that article carries the important rider that "this principle shall not prejudice the application of enforcement measures under Chapter VII." In other words, even national sovereignty can be set aside if it stands in the way of the Security Council's overriding duty to preserve international peace and security. On the face of it, there is a simple distinction between international conflict, which is clearly the United Nations business, and domestic disputes, which are not. The very phrase "domestic dispute" sounds reassuring. It suggests a little local difficulty which the State in question can easily settle, if only it is left alone to do so.

We all know that in recent years it has not been like that. Most wars nowadays are civil wars. Or at least that is how they start. And these civil wars are anything but benign. In fact they are "civil" only in the sense that civilians—that is, non-combatants—have become the main victims.

In the First World War, roughly 90 per cent of those killed were soldiers, and only 10 per cent civilians. In the Second World War, even if we count all the victims of Nazi death camps as war casualties, civilians made up only half, or just over half, of all those killed. But in many of today's conflicts, civilians have become the main targets of violence. It is now conventional to put the proportion of civilian casualties somewhere in the region of 75 per cent.

I say "conventional" because the truth is that no one really knows. Relief agencies such as the Office of the United Nations High Commissioner for Refugees (UNHCR) and the Red Cross rightly devote their resources to helping the living rather than counting the dead. Armies count their own losses, and sometimes make boasts about the number of enemies they have killed. But there is no agency whose job is to keep a tally of civilians killed. The victims of today's brutal conflicts are not merely anonymous, but literally countless.

Yet so long as the conflict rages within the borders of a single State, the old orthodoxy would require us to let it rage. We should leave it to "burn itself out," or perhaps to "fester." (You can choose your own euphemism.) We should leave it even to escalate, regardless of human consequences, at least until the point when its effects begin to spill over into neighbouring States so that it becomes, in the words of so many Security Council resolutions, "a threat to international peace and security."

In reality, this "old orthodoxy" was never absolute. The Charter, after all, was issued in the name of "the peoples," not the governments, of the United Nations. Its aim is not only to preserve international peace—vitally important though that is—but also "to reaffirm faith in fundamental human rights, in the dignity and worth of the human person." The Charter protects the sovereignty of peoples. It was never meant as a licence for governments to trample on human rights and human dignity. Sovereignty implies responsibility, not just power.

This year we celebrate the fiftieth anniversary of the Universal Declaration of Human Rights. That declaration was not meant as a purely rhetorical statement. The General Assembly which adopted it also decided, in the same month, that it had the right to express its concern about the apartheid system in South Africa. The principle of international concern for human rights took precedence over the claim of non-interference in internal affairs.

And the day before it adopted the Universal Declaration, the General Assembly had adopted the Convention on the Prevention and Punishment of the Crime of Genocide, which puts all States under an obligation to "prevent and punish" this most heinous of crimes. It also allows them to "call upon the competent organs of the United Nations" to take action for this purpose.

Since genocide is almost always committed with the connivance, if not the direct participation, of the State authorities, it is hard to see how the United Nations could prevent it without intervening in a State's internal affairs. . . .

State frontiers, ladies and gentlemen, should no longer be seen as a watertight protection for war criminals or mass murderers. The fact that a conflict is "internal" does not give the parties any right to disregard the most basic rules of human conduct. Besides, most "internal" conflicts do not stay internal for very long. They soon "spill over" into neighbouring countries.

The most obvious and tragic way this happens is through the flow of refugees. But there are others, one of which is the spread of knowledge. News today travels around the world more rapidly than we could imagine even a few years ago. Human suffering on a large scale has become impossible to keep quiet. People in far-off countries not only hear about it, but often see it on their TV screens.

That in turn leads to public outrage, and pressure on governments to "do something," in other words, to intervene. Moreover, today's conflicts do not only spread across existing frontiers. Sometimes they actually give birth to new States, which of course means new frontiers. In such cases, what started as an internal conflict becomes an international one. That happens when peoples who formerly lived together in one State find each other's behaviour so threatening, or so offensive, that they can no longer do so. Such separations are seldom as smooth and trouble-free as the famous "velvet divorce" between Czechs and Slovaks. All too often they happen in the midst of, or at the end of, a long and bitter conflict, as was the case with Pakistan and Bangladesh, with the former Yugoslav republics, and with Ethiopia and Eritrea. In other cases, such as the former Soviet Union, the initial separation may be largely non-violent, and yet it soon gives rise to new conflicts, which pose new problems to the international community. In many cases, the conflict eventually becomes so dangerous that the international community finds itself obliged to intervene. By then it can only do so in the most intrusive and expensive way, which is military intervention.

And yet the most effective interventions are not military. It is much better, from every point of view, if action can be taken to resolve or manage a conflict before it reaches the military stage.

Sometimes this action may take the form of economic advice and assistance. In so many cases, ethnic tensions are exacerbated by poverty and famine, or by uneven economic development which brings wealth to one section of a community while destroying the homes and livelihood of another. If outsiders can help avert this by suitably targeted aid and investment, by giving information and training to local entrepreneurs, or by suggesting more appropriate State policies, their "intervention" should surely be welcomed by all concerned. That is why I see the work of the United Nations Development Programme, and of our sister Bretton Woods institutions in Washington, as organically linked to the United Nations work on peace and security.

In other cases what is most needed is skillful and timely diplomacy. . . .[but] if diplomacy is to succeed, it must be backed both by force and by fairness. The agreement was also a reminder to the entire world of why this Organization was established in the first place: to prevent the outbreak of unnecessary conflict; to seek to find international solutions to international problems; to obtain respect for international law and agreements from a recalcitrant party without destroying forever that party's dignity and willingness to cooperate. . . .

We must assume . . . that there will always be some tragic cases where peaceful means have failed: where extreme violence is being used, and only forceful intervention can stop it. Even during the cold war, when the United Nations' own enforcement capacity was largely paralysed by divisions in the Security Council, there were cases where extreme violations of human rights in one country led to military intervention by one of its neighbours. In 1971 Indian intervention ended the civil war in East Pakistan, allowing Bangladesh to achieve independence. In 1978 Viet Nam intervened in Cambodia, putting an end to the genocidal rule of the Khmer Rouge. In 1979 Tanzania intervened to overthrow Idi Amin's erratic dictatorship in Uganda.

In all three of those cases the intervening States gave refugee flows across the border as the reason why they had to act. But what justified their action in the eyes of the world was the internal character of the regimes they acted against. And history has by and large ratified that verdict. Few would now deny that in those cases intervention was a lesser evil than allowing massacre and extreme oppression to continue. Yet at the time, in all three cases, the international community was divided and disturbed. Why? Because these interventions were unilateral. The States in question had no mandate from anyone else to act as they did. And that sets an uncomfortable precedent.

Can we really afford to let each State be the judge of its own right, or duty, to intervene in another State's internal conflict? If we do, will we not be forced to legitimize Hitler's championship of the Sudeten Germans, or Soviet intervention in Afghanistan?

Most of us would prefer, I think—especially now that the cold war is over—to see such decisions taken collectively, by an international institution whose authority is generally respected. And surely the only institution competent to assume that role is the Security Council of the United Nations. The Charter clearly assigns responsibility to the Council for maintaining international peace and security.

I would argue, therefore, that only the Council has the authority to decide that the internal situation in any State is so grave as to justify forceful intervention.

As you know, many Member States feel that the Council's authority now needs to be strengthened by an increase in its membership, bringing in new permanent members or possibly adding a new category of member. Unfortunately a consensus on the details of such a reform has yet to be reached.

This is a matter for the Member States. As Secretary-General I would make only three points. First, the Security Council must become more representative in order to reflect current realities, rather than the realities of 1945. Secondly, the Council's authority depends not only on the representative character of its membership but also on the quality and speed of its decisions. Humanity is ill served when the Council is unable to react quickly and decisively in a crisis. Thirdly, the delay in reaching agreement on reform, however regrettable, must not be allowed to detract from the Council's authority and responsibility in the meanwhile.

The Council in its present form derives its authority from the Charter. That gives it a unique legitimacy as the linch-pin of world order, which all Member States should value and respect. It also places a unique responsibility on Council members, both permanent and non-permanent—a responsibility of which their governments and indeed their citizens should be fully conscious.

Of course the fact that the Council has this unique responsibility does not mean that the intervention itself should always be undertaken directly by the United Nations, in the sense of forces wearing blue helmets and controlled by the United Nations Secretariat. No one knows better than I do, as a former Under-Secretary-General in charge of peacekeeping, that the United Nations lacks the capacity for directing large-scale military enforcement operations.

At least for the foreseeable future, such operations will have to be undertaken by Member States, or by regional organizations. But they need to have the authority of the Security Council behind them, expressed in an authorizing resolution. That formula, developed in 1990 to deal with the Iraqi aggression against Kuwait, has proved its usefulness and will no doubt be used again in future crises.

But we should not assume that intervention always needs to be on a massive scale. There are cases where the speed of the action may be far more crucial than the size of the force. Personally, I am haunted by the experience of Rwanda in 1994: a terrible demonstration of what can happen when there is no intervention, or at least none in the crucial early weeks of a crisis. General Dallaire, the commander of the United Nations mission, has indicated that with a force of even modest size and means he could have prevented much of the killing. Indeed he has said that 5,000 peacekeepers could have saved 500,000 lives. How tragic it is that at the crucial moment the opposite course was chosen, and the size of the force reduced.

Surely things would have been different if the Security Council had at its disposal a small rapid reaction force, ready to move at a few days' notice. I believe that if we are to avert further such disasters in the future we need such a capacity; that Member States must have appropriately trained stand-by forces immediately available, and must be willing to send them quickly when the Security Council requests it. . . .

In any case, let me stress that I am not asking for a standing army at the beck and call of the Secretary-General. The decision to intervene, I repeat, can only be taken by the Security Council. But at present the Council's authority is diminished, because it lacks the means to intervene effectively even when it wishes to do so.

Let me conclude by coming back to where I started. The United Nations is an association of sovereign States, but the rights it exists to uphold belong to peoples, not governments. By the same token, it is wrong to think the obligations of United Nations membership fall only on States. Each one of us—whether as workers in government, in intergovernmental or non-governmental organizations, in business, in the media, or simply as human beings—has an obligation to do whatever he or she can to correct injustice. Each of us has a duty to halt—or, better, to prevent—the infliction of suffering. . . .

When People are in danger, everyone has a duty to speak out. No one has a right to pass by on the other side. If we are tempted to do so, we should call to mind the unforgettable warning of Martin Niemöller, the German Protestant theologian who lived through the Nazi persecution:

"In Germany they came first for the Communists. And I did not speak up because I was not a Communist. Then they came for the Jews. And I did not speak up, because I was not a Jew. Then they came for the trade unionists. And I did not speak up, because I was not a trade unionist. Then they came for the Catholics. And I did not speak up, because I was a Protestant. Then they came for me. And by that time there was no one left to speak up."

International Law: The Trials of Global Norms

STEVEN R. RATNER

The move from describing the world to prescribing for it forms the core of international law. Can those committing human rights atrocities—war criminals from Bosnia or political leaders from Cambodia—be tried in foreign courts or before international tribunals? How can members of the United Nations ensure respect for the decisions of its Security Council? What is the best way to regulate transnational environmental hazards such as greenhouse gas emissions or ocean dumping? Can the United States allow its citizens to sue European companies for their use of land and factories confiscated by the Cuban government from Americans more than a generation ago?

All these questions turn on political decisions by states—but what international lawyers see and seek in such scenarios is a process whose actions are informed and influenced by principles of law, not just raw power. For international lawyers, devising and enforcing universal rules of conduct for states means overcoming two cardinal challenges: how to make such precepts legitimate in a diverse community of nations; and how to make them stick in the absence of any one sovereign authority or supranational enforcement mechanism. . . .

Today, the end of the Cold War has loosened many of the blockages to international lawmaking and implementation. Although legal scholars still ask what states can do on their own—pass extraterritorial laws, use force, or prosecute war criminals—they do so assuming that coordinated action is now more feasible than in the past. Global and regional treaties such as the Chemical Weapons Convention, the Convention on the Prohibition of Anti-Personnel Mines, the Maastrict Treaty, and the North American Free Trade Agreement now serve as the starting point for scrutinizing state behavior according to some objective standard.

The ground seems ready then for an acceleration of this century's great trend in international law: the increasing international regulation of more and more issues once typically seen as part of state domestic jurisdiction. But any attempt to create the lofty, supranational legal edifice idealized by some of the field's practitioners and scholars promises to be problematic at best. Once paralyzed by the

From Stephen R. Ratner, "International Law: The Trials of Global Norms," *Foreign Policy,* issue #110 (Spring 1998), pp. 65–75. © 1998 by the Carnegie Endowment for International Peace. Reprinted with permission. www.foreignpolicy.com.

deadlock between East and West, and between North and South, the international legal system must now contend not just with the challenge of persuading new states such as Belarus or Croatia to comply with established norms but of coping with Somalia and other failed states, whose circumstances make a mockery of international rules. International law must seek to embrace a growing range of forms, topics, and technologies, as well as a host of new actors. And as it moves further away from strictly "foreign" concerns—the treatment of diplomats or ships on the seas—to traditionally domestic areas—environmental or labor standards—its proponents must increasingly confront new obstacles head-on.

NEW REALITIES, NEW IDEAS

This new global context surrounding the field has led to at least four fundamental shifts in the kinds of issues that legal scholars now talk about and study.

New Forms, New Players

Traditionally, most rules of international law could be found in one of two places: treaties—binding, written agreements between states; or customary law—uncodified, but equally binding rules based on longstanding behavior that states accept as compulsory. The strategic arms reduction treaties requiring the United States and Russia to cut their nuclear weapons arsenals offer examples of the former; the rule that governments cannot be sued in the courts of another state for most of their public acts provides an example of the latter. Historically, treaties have gradually displaced much customary law, as international rules have become increasingly codified.

But as new domains from the environment to the Internet come to be seen as appropriate for international regulation, states are sometimes reluctant to embrace any sort of binding rule. In the past, many legal scholars and international courts simply accepted the notion that no law governed a particular subject until a new treaty was concluded or states signaled their consent to a new customary-law rule (witness the reluctance with which human rights norms were considered law prior to the UN's two key treaties in 1966) or, alternatively, struggled to find customary law where none existed. However, today all but the most doctrinaire of scholars see a role for so-called soft law—precepts emanating from international bodies that conform in some sense to expectations of required behavior but that are not binding on states.

For example, in 1992 the World Bank completed a set of Guidelines on the Treatment of Foreign Direct Investment. Though these are not binding on any bank member, states and corporations invoke them as the standard for how developing nations should treat foreign capital to encourage investment. This soft law enables states to adjust to the regulation of many new areas of international concern without fearing a violation (and possible legal countermeasures) if they fail to comply. Normative expectations are built more quickly than they would through the evolution of a customary-law rule, and more gently than if a new treaty rule were foisted on states. Soft law principles also represent a starting point for new hard law, which attaches a penalty to noncompliance. In this case, the bank's guidelines have served as the basis for the negotiation of a new treaty—the Multilateral Agreement on Investment (MAI)—by the Organization for Economic Cooperation and Development (OECD). The MAI gives foreign investors the right to take any government to international arbitration for compensation when a law or state practice limits their freedom to invest or divest.

Whether in the case of hard or soft law, new participants are making increased demands for representation in international bodies, conferences, and other legal groupings and processes. They include substate entities, both those recognized in some way by the international community (Chechnya, Hong Kong) and those not (Tibet, Kashmir); nongovernmental organizations (NGOs); and corporations. Claiming that the states to which they belong do not always adequately represent their interests, these nonstate actors demand a say in the content of new norms. Some have faced staunch opposition to their participation in decision making: In 1995, China's government relegated NGOs to a distant venue during the UN's Fourth World Conference on Women in Beijing.

But other groups may succeed even as far as effectively taking over an official delegation. For example, U.S. telecommunications companies such as Motorola have seemed almost to dictate U.S. positions in the International Telecommunication Union (ITU), the UN agency responsible for setting global telecommunications standards. At the ITU's 1992 conference on allocating the radio spectrum for new technologies, Motorola's stake in protecting its plans for new satellites became a paramount U.S. interest, resulting in a sizeable Motorola team attending as part of the U.S. delegation. Other corporations have acted outside government channels entirely by promulgating private codes: In response to public pressure, Nike issued a set of self-imposed rules to protect worker rights in the developing world. It is not that states are no longer the primary makers of international law. But . . . these other actors have independent views—and the resources to push them—that do not fit neatly into traditional theories of how law is made and enforced.

New Enforcement Strategies

Most states comply with much, even most, international law almost continually—whether the law of the sea, diplomatic immunity, or civil aviation rules. But without mechanisms to bring transgressors into line, international law will be "law" in name only. This state of affairs, when it occurs, is ignored by too many lawyers, who delight in large bodies of rules but often discount patterns of noncompliance. For example, Western governments, and many scholars, insisted throughout the 1960s and 1970s that when nationalizing foreign property, developing states were legally bound to compensate former owners for the full economic value, despite those states' repeated refusals to pay such huge sums.

The traditional toolbox to secure compliance with the law of nations consists of negotiations, mediation, countermeasures (reciprocal action against the violator), or, in rare cases, recourse to supranational judicial bodies such as the International Court of Justice. (The last of these was the linchpin of the world of law that Americans such as Andrew Carnegie and Elihu Root sought to bring into being.) For many years, these tools have been supplemented by the work of international institutions, whose reports and resolutions often help "mobilize shame" against violators. But today, states, NGOs, and private entities, aided by their lawyers, have striven for sanctions with more teeth. They have galvanized the UN Security Council to issue economic sanctions against Iraq, Haiti, Libya, Serbia, Sudan, and other nations refusing to comply with UN resolutions.

On the free-trade front, the dispute settlement panels in the World Trade Organization (WTO) now have the legal authority to issue binding rulings that allow the victor in a trade dispute to impose specific tariffs on the loser. . . . And the UN's ad hoc criminal tribunals for the former Yugoslavia and Rwanda show that it is at least possible to devise institutions to punish individuals for human rights atrocities. Nonetheless, as the impunity to date of former Bosnian Serb president Radovan Karadzic and General Ratko Mladic reveals, the success of these enforcement mechanisms depends on the willingness of states to support them: legalism meets realism. . . .

Increasingly, domestic courts provide an additional venue to enforce international law. In Spain, for example, Judge Manuel García Castellóni of the National Court has agreed to hear a controversial human rights case involving charges against Chile's former dictator, General Augusto Pinochet. Meanwhile, Castellóni's colleague, Judge Baltasar Garzón, hears testimony against those responsible for the "Dirty War" of the 1970s in Argentina. (Spain is asserting jurisdiction in both cases because its nationals were among the thousands of victims tortured and killed.) And though Karadzic remains at large, he has been sued in U.S. federal court under the Alien Tort Claims Act, which allows foreign nationals recovery against Karadzic for the rape and torture of civilians during his "ethnic cleansing" campaign in the former Yugoslavia. At a minimum, this provides a symbolic measure of solace for his victims.

The Legitimacy Problem

Even as scholars seek to devise better enforcement mechanisms, a serious debate is brewing about the legitimacy of such measures. As international organizations are freed up to take more actions by the end of the East-West conflict and the tempering of North-South tensions, the United States and its like-minded allies seem well positioned to impose their agenda on all. Legal scholars question whether Western dominance of the Organization for Security and Cooperation in Europe, UN, WTO, and other international institutions is not merely raw power asserting its muscle again, albeit through multilateral bodies, to the detriment of a genuine rule of law. That this debate is more than academic can be seen vividly in the ongoing discussion about reforming the Security Council. Many Americans may laud the council's new muscle—during the last five years, it has slapped a debilitating embargo and weapons inspection regime on Iraq, prohibited air traffic with Libya due to its sanctuary for those accused of the Pan Am 103 bombing, and approved a U.S.-led occupation of Haiti. But smaller states feel threatened by a Security Council in which the West is often able to convince enough states to approve such council actions, and only a Chinese veto (which was used only once in the last 25 years) seems to protect them. . . .

Focusing on enforcement and legitimacy also provides a useful lens through which to evaluate U.S. reactions to international norms: Even as the United States seeks to strengthen the enforcement of international law for its own ends, it has often recoiled at the prospect that these norms might be enforced against it. In the WTO, the very dispute resolution panels that the United States hopes to use to force open closed markets could order it to choose between environmental protection laws (such as those banning imports of tuna caught in nets that kill dolphins) and the prospects of retaliatory sanctions if those laws have incidental discriminatory effects on trade. In such a scenario, international law, as interpreted by the WTO, becomes the friend of business and bugaboo of environmentalists. But when the UN seeks to promulgate environmental law, as it has with the proposed greenhouse gas convention just concluded at Kyoto, then the tables are turned.

Similarly, the United States wants to use the Security Council to keep in place a comprehensive sanctions regime on Iraq that has the diplomatic appeal of being "international" rather than "U.S.-imposed," all the while holding back on paying its dues because not all UN programs conform to Washington's wishes. As the world's sole superpower, the United States can defy international standards with little fear of immediate sanction; but other states will begin to question its motives in trying to strengthen important legal regimes such as those covering nuclear and chemical nonproliferation.

New Linkages

The notion of hermetically sealed areas of international law—each a nice chapter in a treatise—is increasingly anachronistic. Environmental and trade law can no longer be discussed separately as the tuna–dolphin example shows; and when private investors have to reckon with serious abuses by local governments, foreign investment law cannot be examined without some consideration of human rights and labor law. The result is a new breed of scholarship linking previously distinct subjects and the realization among some practitioners that overspecialization leads to myopic lawyering.

Moreover, beyond the legal field, international lawyers must address the two-way interaction between international law and broader sociological and cultural trends in society. In one notable example, the debate on a clash of cultures involving so-called Asian values has forced students of human rights to stand back and consider whether rights granted in human rights treaties mean the same thing in all states. Can Singapore suppress free speech for the goal of national unity and development, especially if it claims that its culture sees uninhibited political speech as less than a birthright? Of course, cultural assertions tend to be overly broad, and many human rights activists interpret these claims as excuses for authoritarianism; the arguments, however, can no longer be ignored, and black and white rules of treaty interpretation will not help much.

In the other direction, the proliferation of new norms has direct effects on debates over globalization—the "Jihad versus McWorld" controversy. A global treaty on ozone or greenhouse gases, for instance, will clearly accommodate different perspectives on the priority of environmental protection versus development, but once adopted it cannot tolerate violations in the name of "diversity." Indeed, almost by definition, the decision by states to subject a once strictly domestic conceit to international regulation means that cultural, value-based, or "sovereignty" arguments no longer enjoy the upper hand. If a state elects not to sign a major treaty, or ignores one it has assigned—as with the United States and the agreement on the elimination of landmines or Iraq and the one on nuclear nonproliferation—it is more likely to be condemned as a pariah than admired for its rugged individualism.

mypoliscikit Exercises for Human Rights and International Law

Apply what you learned in this chapter by using the online resources on MyPoliSciKit (www.mypoliscikit.com).

 Practice Tests

 Videos:
- "Ken Saro-Wiwa"
- "The Crisis in Darfur"

 Simulation: "Human Rights: You Are a Refugee"

 Reading Guides:
- Rhoda E. Howard and Jack Donnelly, "Human Rights in World Politics"
- Kofi Annan, "Reflections on Intervention"
- Stephen R. Ratner, "International Law: The Trials of Global Norms"

TRANSNATIONAL ACTORS

Transnational Activist Networks

MARGARET E. KECK AND KATHRYN SIKKINK

Networks are forms of organization characterized by voluntary, reciprocal, and horizontal patterns of communication and exchange. . . . Major actors in advocacy networks may include the following: (1) international and domestic nongovernmental research and advocacy organizations; (2) local social movements; (3) foundations; (4) the media; (5) churches, trade unions, consumer organizations, and intellectuals; (6) parts of regional and international intergovernmental organizations; and (7) parts of the executive and/or parliamentary branches of governments. Not all these will be present in each advocacy network. Initial research suggests, however, that international and domestic NGOs [non-governmental organizations] play a central role in all advocacy networks, usually initiating actions and pressuring more powerful actors to take positions. NGOs introduce new ideas, provide information, and lobby for policy changes.

Groups in a network share values and frequently exchange information and services. The flow of information among actors in the network reveals a dense web of connections among these groups, both formal and informal. The movement of funds and services is especially notable between foundations and NGOs, and some NGOs provide services such as training for other NGOs in the same and sometimes other advocacy networks. Personnel also circulate within and among networks, as relevant players move from one to another in a version of the "revolving door.". . .

Advocacy networks are not new. We can find examples as far back as the nineteenth-century campaign for the abolition of slavery. But their number, size, and professionalism, and the speed, density, and complexity of international linkages among them has grown dramatically in the last three decades. . . .

Transnational advocacy networks appear most likely to emerge around those issues where (1) channels between domestic groups and their governments are blocked or hampered or where such channels are ineffective for resolving a conflict, setting into motion the "boomerang" pattern of influence characteristic of these networks; (2) activists or "political entrepreneurs" believe that networking will further their missions and campaigns, and actively promote networks; and (3) conferences and other forms of international contact create arenas for forming and strengthening networks. Where channels of participation are blocked, the international arena may be the only means that domestic activists have to gain attention to their issues. Boomerang strategies are most common in campaigns where the target is a state's domestic policies or behavior; where a campaign seeks broad procedural change involving dispersed actors, strategies are more diffuse.

It is no accident that so many advocacy networks address claims about rights in their campaigns. Governments are the primary "guarantors" of rights, but also their primary violators. When a government violates or refuses to recognize rights, individuals and domestic groups often have no recourse within domestic political or judicial arenas. They may seek international connections finally to express their concerns and even to protect their lives.

When channels between the state and its domestic actors are blocked, the boomerang pattern of influence characteristic of transnational networks may occur: Domestic NGOs bypass their state and directly search out international allies to try to bring pressure on their states from outside. This is most obviously the case in human rights campaigns. Similarly, indigenous rights campaigns and environmental campaigns that support the demands of local peoples for participation in development projects that would affect them frequently involve this kind of triangulation. Linkages are important for both sides: For the less powerful Third World actors, networks provide access, leverage, and information (and often money) they could not expect to have on their own; for northern groups, they make credible the assertion that they are struggling with, and not only for, their southern partners. Not surprisingly, such relationships can produce considerable tensions. . . .

Just as oppression and injustice do not themselves produce movements or revolutions, claims around issues amenable to international action do not produce transnational networks. Activists—"people who care enough about some issue that they are prepared to incur significant costs and act to achieve their goals"[1]—do. They create them when they believe that transnational networking will further their organizational missions—by sharing information, attaining greater visibility, gaining access to wider publics, multiplying channels of institutional access, and so forth. For example, in the campaign to stop the promotion of infant formula to poor women in developing countries, organizers settled on a boycott of Nestlé, the largest producer, as its main tactic. Because Nestlé was a transnational actor, activists believed a transnational network was necessary to bring pressure on corporations and governments.[2] Over time, in such issue areas, participation in transnational networks has become an essential component of the collective identities of the activists involved, and networking a part of their common repertoire. The political entrepreneurs who become the core networkers for a new campaign have often gained experience in earlier ones.

Opportunities for network activities have increased over the last two decades. In addition to the efforts of pioneers, a proliferation of international organizations and conferences has provided foci for connections. Cheaper air travel and new electronic communication technologies speed information flows and simplify personal contact among activists. Underlying these trends is a broader cultural shift. The new networks have depended on the creation of a new kind of global public (or civil society), which grew as a cultural legacy of the 1960s. . . .

HOW DO TRANSNATIONAL ADVOCACY NETWORKS WORK?

Transnational advocacy networks seek influence in many of the same ways that other political groups or social movements do. Since they are not powerful in a traditional sense of the word, they must use the power of their information, ideas, and strategies to alter the information and value contexts within which states make policies. The bulk of what networks do might be termed persuasion or socialization, but neither process is devoid of conflict. Persuasion and socialization often involve not just reasoning with opponents, but also bringing pressure, arm-twisting, encouraging sanctions, and shaming. . . .

Our typology of tactics that networks use in their efforts at persuasion, socialization, and pressure includes (1) *information politics,* or the ability to quickly and credibly generate politically usable information and move it to where it will have the most impact; (2) *symbolic politics,* or the ability to call upon symbols, actions, or stories that make sense of a situation for an audience that is frequently far away; (3) *leverage politics,* or the ability to call upon powerful actors to affect a situation where weaker members of a network are unlikely to have influence; and (4) *accountability politics,* or the effort to hold powerful actors to their previously stated policies or principles. . . .

Network members actively seek ways to bring issues to the public agenda by framing them in innovative ways and by seeking hospitable venues. Sometimes they create issues by framing old problems in new ways; occasionally they help transform other actors' understanding of their identities and their interests. Land use rights in the Amazon, for example, took on an entirely different character and gained quite different allies viewed in a deforestation frame than they did in either social justice or regional development frames. In the 1970s and 1980s many states decided for the first time that promotion of human rights in other countries was a legitimate foreign policy goal and an authentic expression of national interest. This decision came in part from interaction with an emerging global human rights network. We argue that this represents not the victory of morality over self-interest, but a transformed understanding of national interest, possible in part because of structured interactions between state components and networks. This changed understanding cannot be derived solely from changing global and economic conditions, although these are relevant. . . .

Information Politics

Information binds network members together and is essential for network effectiveness. Many information exchanges are informal—telephone calls, e-mail and fax communications, and the circulation of newsletters, pamphlets, and bulletins.

They provide information that would not otherwise be available, from sources that might not otherwise be heard, and they must make this information comprehensible and useful to activists and publics who may be geographically and/or socially distant.

Nonstate actors gain influence by serving as alternate sources of information. Information flows in advocacy networks provide not only facts but testimony— stories told by people whose lives have been affected. Moreover, activists interpret facts and testimony, usually framing issues simply, in terms of right and wrong, because their purpose is to persuade people and stimulate them to act. How does this process of persuasion occur? An effective frame must show that a given state of affairs is neither natural nor accidental, identify the responsible party or parties, and propose credible solutions. These aims require clear, powerful messages that appeal to shared principles, which often have more impact on state policy than advice of technical experts. An important part of the political struggle over information is precisely whether an issue is defined primarily as technical—and thus subject to consideration by "qualified" experts—or as something that concerns a broader global constituency. . . .

Networks strive to uncover and investigate problems, and alert the press and policymakers. One activist described this as the "human rights methodology"— "promoting change by reporting facts."[3] To be credible, the information produced by networks must be reliable and well documented. To gain attention, the information must be timely and dramatic. Sometimes these multiple goals of information politics conflict, but both credibility and drama seem to be essential components of a strategy aimed at persuading publics and policymakers to change their minds.

The notion of "reporting facts" does not fully express the way networks strategically use information to frame issues. Networks call attention to issues, or even create issues by using language that dramatizes and draws attention to their concerns. A good example is the recent campaign against the practice of female genital mutilation. Before 1976 the widespread practice of female circumcision in many African and a few Asian and Middle Eastern countries was known outside these regions mainly among medical experts and anthropologists.[4] A controversial campaign, initiated in 1974 by a network of women's and human rights organizations, began to draw wider attention to the issues by renaming the problem. Previously the practice was referred to by technically "neutral" terms such as female circumcision, clitoridectomy, or infibulation. The campaign around female genital "mutilation" raised its salience, literally creating the issue as a matter of public international concern. By renaming the practice the network broke the linkage with male circumcision (seen as a personal medical or cultural decision), implied a linkage with the more feared procedure of castration, and reframed the issue as one of violence against women. It thus resituated the practice as a human rights violation. . . .

Human rights activists, baby food campaigners, and women's groups . . . dramatize the situations of the victims and turn the cold facts into human stories, intended to move people to action. The baby food campaign, for example, relied heavily on public health studies that proved that improper bottle feeding contributed to infant malnutrition and mortality, and that corporate sales promotion was leading to a decline in breast feeding. Network activists repackaged and interpreted this information in dramatic ways designed to promote action: The British development organization War on Want published a pamphlet entitled "The Baby Killers," which the Swiss Third World Action Group translated into German and retitled "Nestlé Kills Babies." Nestlé inadvertently gave activists a prominent public forum when it sued the Third World Action Group for defamation and libel. . . .

A dense web of north-south exchange, aided by computer and fax communication, means that governments can no longer monopolize information flows as they could a mere half-decade ago. These technologies have had an enormous impact on moving information to and from Third World countries, where mail service has often been slow and precarious; they also give special advantages, of course, to organizations that have access to them. A good example of the new informational role of networks occurred when U.S. environmentalists pressured President George Bush to raise the issue of gold miners' ongoing invasions of the Yanomami indigenous reserve when Brazilian president Fernando Collor de Mello was in Washington in 1991. Collor believed that he had squelched protest over the Yanomami question by creating major media events out of the dynamiting of airstrips used by gold miners, but network members had current information faxed from Brazil, and they countered his claims with evidence that miners had rebuilt the airstrips and were still invading the Yanomami area. . . .

The media is an essential partner in network information politics. To reach a broader audience, networks strive to attract press attention. Sympathetic journalists may become part of the network, but more often network activists cultivate a reputation for credibility with the press, and package their information in a timely and dramatic way to draw press attention.

Symbolic Politics

Activists frame issues by identifying and providing convincing explanations for powerful symbolic events, which in turn become catalysts for the growth of networks. Symbolic interpretation is part of the process of persuasion by which networks create awareness and expand their constituencies. Awarding the 1992 Nobel Peace Prize to Maya activist Rigoberta Menchú and the UN's designation of 1993 as the Year of Indigenous Peoples heightened public awareness of the situation of indigenous peoples in the Americas. Indigenous peoples' use of 1992, the 500th anniversary of the voyage of Columbus to the Americas, to raise a host of issues well illustrates the use of symbolic events to reshape understandings. . . .

Leverage Politics

Activists in advocacy networks are concerned with political effectiveness. Their definition of effectiveness often includes some policy change by "target actors" such as governments, international financial institutions like the World Bank, or private actors like transnational corporations. In order to bring about policy change, networks need to pressure and persuade more powerful actors. To gain influence the networks seek leverage (the word appears often in the discourse of advocacy organizations) over more powerful actors. By leveraging more powerful institutions, weak groups gain influence far beyond their ability to influence state practices directly. The identification of material or moral leverage is a crucial strategic step in network campaigns.

Material leverage usually links the issue to money or goods (but potentially also to votes in international organizations, prestigious offices, or other benefits). The human rights issue became negotiable because governments or financial institutions connected human rights practices to military and economic aid, or to bilateral diplomatic relations. In the United States, human rights groups got leverage by providing policy-makers with information that convinced them to cut off military and economic aid. To make the issue negotiable, NGOs first had to raise its profile or salience, using information and symbolic politics. Then more powerful members of the network had to link cooperation to something else of value: money, trade, or prestige. Similarly, in the environmentalists' multilateral development bank campaign, linkage of environmental protection with access to loans was very powerful.

Although NGO influence often depends on securing powerful allies, their credibility still depends in part on their ability to mobilize their own members and affect public opinion via the media. In democracies the potential to influence votes gives large membership organizations an advantage over nonmembership organizations in lobbying for policy change; environmental organizations, several of whose memberships number in the millions, are more likely to have this added clout than are human rights organizations.

Moral leverage involves what some commentators have called the "*mobilization of shame,*" where the behavior of target actors is held up to the light of international scrutiny. Network activists exert moral leverage on the assumption that governments value the good opinion of others; insofar as networks can demonstrate that a state is violating international obligations or is not living up to its own claims, they hope to jeopardize its credit enough to motivate a change in policy or behavior. The degree to which states are vulnerable to this kind of pressure varies, and will be discussed further below.

Accountability Politics

Networks devote considerable energy to convincing governments and other actors to publicly change their positions on issues. This is often dismissed as inconsequential change, since talk is cheap and governments sometimes change discursive positions hoping to divert network and public attention. Network activists, however, try to make such statements into opportunities for accountability politics. Once a government has publicly committed itself to a principle—for example, in favor of human rights or democracy—networks can use those positions, and their command of information, to expose the distance between discourse and practice. This is embarrassing to many governments, which may try to save face by closing that distance.

Perhaps the best example of network accountability politics was the ability of the human rights network to use the human rights provisions of the 1975 Helsinki Accords to pressure the Soviet Union and the governments of Eastern Europe for change. The Helsinki Accords helped revive the human rights movement in the Soviet Union, spawned new organizations like the Moscow Helsinki Group and the Helsinki Watch Committee in the United States, and helped protect activists from repression.[5] The human rights network referred to Moscow's obligations under the Helsinki Final Act and juxtaposed these with examples of abuses. . . .

NOTES

1. Pamela E. Oliver and Gerald Marwell, "Mobilizing Technologies for Collective Action," in *Frontiers in Social Movement Theory*, ed. Aldon D. Morris and Carol McClurg Mueller (New Haven: Yale University Press, 1992), p. 252.
2. See Kathryn Sikkink, "Codes of Conduct for Transnational Corporations: The Case of the WHO/UNICEF Code," *International Organization* 40 (Autumn 1986): 815–40.
3. Dorothy Q. Thomas, "Holding Governments Accountable by Public Pressure," in *Ours by Right: Women's Rights as Human Rights*, ed. Joanna Kerr (London: Zed Books, 1993), p. 83.
4. Female genital mutilation is most widely practiced in Africa, where it is reported to occur in at least twenty-six countries. Between 85 and 114 million women in the world today are estimated to have experienced genital mutilation. *World Bank Development Report 1993: Investing in Health* (New York: Oxford University Press, 1993), p. 50.
5. Discussion of the Helsinki Accords is based on Daniel Thomas, "Norms and Change in World Politics: Human Rights, the Helsinki Accords, and the Demise of Communism, 1975–1990," Ph.D. diss., Cornell University, 1997.

NGOs: Fighting Poverty, Hurting the Poor

SEBASTIAN MALLABY

Last year, I visited Uganda. I wanted to understand how a showcase of African hopelessness turned around, cutting the number of people living below the national poverty line by almost 40 percent during the 1990s. But I wanted to get to the bottom of another issue, too. The World Bank was promoting a dam near the source of the river Nile, at a beautiful spot called Bujagali. Western nongovernmental organizations (NGOs) were in revolt: The International Rivers Network, based in Berkeley, California, maintained that the Ugandan environmental movement was outraged at the likely damage to waterfalls at the site, and that the poor who lived there would be uprooted from their land for the sake of electricity they couldn't afford. It was surely a clash that went to the heart of the globalization struggle. Was the NGO movement acting as a civilized check on industrialization, standing up for millions of poor people whose views the World Bank ignored? Or was it retarding the battle against poverty by withholding electricity that would fuel economic growth, ultimately benefiting poor citizens?

I called the Berkeley activists and asked for some advice. Who ran this Ugandan environmental movement they claimed was so outraged? Where were the villagers who would be cruelly dislocated by the dam project? NGOs such as the International Rivers Network usually love helping Western journalists, and because these journalists are generally far from the scene of the disputed development project, they sometimes simply report what they are told. But now that I was in Uganda, a few hours' drive from the proposed dam, I got a warier response. Lori Pottinger, the International Rivers activist who led the Bujagali campaign, explained that her Ugandan counterparts were preoccupied just then, and that snooping around the villages at the Bujagali site would get me into trouble with the authorities.

Not wanting to give up right away, I tracked down Pottinger's Ugandan counterparts by other means and telephoned their office. A friendly voice invited me to come over straightaway. When I arrived, the group's young director sat me down and plied me with leaflets and reports that gratefully acknowledged the sponsorship of a group called the Swedish Society for Nature Conservation. After half an hour of conversation, I asked the question that really concerned me: What kind of organization was this?

"This is a membership organization," I was told.

"How many members?" I asked. My host kindly stood up and rummaged about in his desk, returning with a blue notebook.

"Here is the list," he said triumphantly. Uganda's National Association of Professional Environmentalists had all of 25 members—not exactly a broad platform from which to oppose electricity for millions.

My next move was to visit Bujagali. I met up with a Ugandan sociologist who knew the region well and promised to translate for me. She stopped at a cluster of buildings on the edge of the dam site to check in with the local government representative who, far from threatening to call the cops, greeted us cheerfully. For the next three hours, we interviewed villager after villager and found the same story: The "dam people" had come and promised generous financial terms, and the villagers were happy to accept them and relocate. My sociologist companion said we might have sample bias because we were interviewing men, who might value cash more than the land that women tended. So we interviewed some women, who offered the same pro-project line. The only people who objected to the dam were those living just outside its perimeter. They were angry because the project would not affect them, meaning no generous payout.

This story is a tragedy for Uganda. Clinics and factories are being deprived of electricity by Californians whose idea of an electricity crisis is a handful of summer blackouts. But it is also a tragedy for the fight against poverty worldwide, because projects in dozens of countries are similarly held up for fear of activist resistance. Time after time, feisty Internet-enabled groups make scary claims about the iniquities of development projects. Time after time, Western publics raised on stories of World Bank white elephants believe them. Lawmakers in European parliaments and the U.S. Congress accept NGO arguments at face value, and the government officials who sit on the World Bank's board respond by blocking funding for deserving projects.

The consequences can be preposterously ironic. NGOs claim to campaign on behalf of poor people, yet many of their campaigns harm the poor. They claim to protect the environment, but by forcing the World Bank to pull out of sensitive projects, they cause these schemes to go ahead without the environmental safeguards that the bank would have imposed on them. Likewise, NGOs purport to hold the World Bank accountable, yet the bank is answerable to the governments who are its shareholders; it is the NGOs' accountability that is murky. Furthermore, the offensives mounted by activist groups sometimes have no basis in fact whatsoever. If you think this an exaggeration, consider the story of an anti-poverty effort in China's western province of Qinghai.

OUT, DAM SPOT

There was nothing apparently controversial when, in April 1999, the World Bank concluded negotiations on a project in Qinghai. China was the bank's star client at the time, having lifted around 200 million people out of poverty during the previous decade. The Qinghai project was designed to move 58,000 farmers from a hopelessly parched hillside to another part of the province irrigated by a small dam. Farmers' incomes would rise from around 20 cents a day to a level at which they could actually subsist. China had carried out some 30 such relocation projects in the past. All had reduced poverty.

The day the Qinghai loan negotiations concluded, the bank's project manager, Petros Aklilu, got a call from the Tibet Information Network in London. Qinghai borders on the Chinese administrative division known as the Tibet Autonomous Region. Because the region covers part of historical Tibet and 1 million of Qinghai's 5 million inhabitants are Tibetan, the interest of Tibet-watchers was not surprising. Aklilu explained that the scheme would benefit the 3,500 Tibetans who would move to newly irrigated land, and that Tibetans who stayed behind would benefit from reduced population pressure in their area. In sum, although China's Tibet policy was abominable, the bank's project would actually help Tibetans. Aklilu put down the phone and forgot about the conversation.

He soon had cause to remember it. Within a few days, the Tibet Information Network published a story in its newsletter about a "controversial" World Bank project that would "dramatically affect the demography" of Qinghai by moving ethnic Chinese into a culturally Tibetan area. This was a strange claim. First, no Tibetans lived in the immediate settlement area: The nearest were 276 nomadic herders (the bank had counted them carefully) who wintered 37 miles south of the project. Second, Qinghai had been part of China for as long as the United States had been independent. It was no more Tibetan than Texas is Mexican. But the Tibet Information Network was not deterred. "Population transfer of Chinese into traditional Tibetan areas has become a major concern for Tibetans," the group's newsletter said ominously.

Within a few weeks, the London activists had forged an international coalition. It drew from the various legions of the anti-World Bank army: environmental groups opposed to dams; human rights groups opposed to relocation; other groups opposing cooperation with China. Representatives of 59 organizations—an astonishing worldwide network stretching from Mexico to Thailand—dispatched a long letter to World Bank President Jim Wolfensohn protesting the transfer of "Chinese farmers into a traditionally Tibetan area." Campaigners deluged the bank with e-mails and faxes, anti-bank posters appeared around Washington, and Tibet activists set up camp outside the bank's headquarters. A rap star from the Beastie Boys declared that the bank's loan would lead to the "destruction of the Tibetan peoples."

Despite the inaccuracy of this claim, the activists quickly won allies in Hollywood and the U.S. Congress, most notably the actor Richard Gere, who had recently narrated a documentary film about Tibet, and Democratic Rep. Nancy Pelosi of California. On June 15, 1999, a press release announcing a joint appearance by Pelosi and a pro-Tibet musician stated that the bank planned to move "60,000 ethnic Chinese" into Qinghai, even though Han Chinese constituted only 40 percent of the 58,000 settlers, and even though these Han Chinese were not moving into Qinghai, just relocating within the province. Sixty members of congress fired off a complaint to Wolfensohn, and Sen. Jesse Helms, a far-right Republican politician from North Carolina, leapt at the chance to condemn China and the World Bank in a single breath. When a World Bank delegation went to Capitol Hill to mollify the law-makers, it was confronted with a map that did not even show Qinghai. The entire province had been labeled Tibet, never mind that Tibetans accounted for only one in five people there.

The bank was totally encircled. It was simultaneously up against student protestors and the right wing of the Republican Party, and although the bank's assailants were flat wrong on the facts, nobody was willing to stick up for the institution. In June 1999, the Clinton administration announced that it would vote against the Qinghai project when it came before the World Bank's board. The Lilliputian activists had taken on the bank, and they had won the first round.

APPEASEMENT DENIED

The most common reaction to this sort of story is that the bank must communicate better with its critics and learn how to compromise with them. Unfortunately, this prescription is naive. It presumes the critics are open to compromise. But campaigning NGOs, as distinct from those with real development programs in the field, almost have to be radical. If they stop denouncing big organizations, nobody will send them cash or quote them in the newspapers. Partly for this reason, and partly out of a likeable conviction that the status quo is never good enough, most NGOs do not have an off switch. You can do everything possible to meet them halfway, but they will still demonstrate outside your building. Of course, there will be grown-up groups like Oxfam, World Vision, or the World Wildlife Fund that may accept your olive branch. But they will be the exceptions, and they may cooperate only cautiously. They don't want to be the next target for the radicals.

The second round of the Qinghai battle illustrated this problem. Confronted with the news that the Clinton administration would block the project, Wolfensohn flew into a rage. He worried about threats by the U.S. Congress to cut contributions to the bank's subsidized lending program if the project went ahead, undermining the bank's ability to help its poorest clients. He fretted that the adverse publicity might cost him a chance at winning a Nobel Peace Prize and that his Hollywood connections would turn on him. And he feared that one of his central achievements would be jeopardized: Since taking the helm of the bank in 1995, Wolfensohn had done more than any of his predecessors to reach out to NGOs. He welcomed the bank's most ardent critics to private dinners at his home, made a point of meeting with them wherever he traveled, and even created commissions to solicit their advice on World Bank policy.

When the Qinghai battle came to a head, Wolfensohn did everything possible to defuse it. He went out of his way to hear the arguments of the NGOs, treating his own staff with much less deference. He summoned the project team to his office and demanded to know whose arse he should kick first. After much raging and fuming, he hit upon a scheme that would meet the NGOs part way. The project would be referred to the bank's Inspection Panel, a tribunal staffed by eminent persons who investigate projects' compliance with the bank's environmental and social safeguards.

The activists alleged several instances of non-compliance. They claimed, for example, that one guideline requiring "special action" to protect ethnic minorities was breached, along with another requiring that resettlement be voluntary. The critics focused particularly on the bank's environmental safeguards. The bank had classified Qinghai as a "Category B" project (posing medium risk to the environment), rather than a high-risk "Category A," and therefore commissioned an arguably skimpy environmental impact study. By referring these claims to the Inspection Panel, Wolfensohn calculated that a political fight over Tibet would now become a technical inquiry into the bank's operational guidelines.

In a sane world, this strategy would have bought some peace with the activists. But the day after the bank decided to convene an Inspection Panel, a pair of students climbed up the face of the bank's headquarters and unfurled a banner proclaiming, "World Bank Approves China's Genocide in Tibet." Privately, other Tibet groups disapproved of these tactics—after all, there was no evidence of genocide—but they were unwilling to speak out publicly against their fellow activists. Meanwhile, members of congress continued to toe the NGO line. Republican Sens. Connie Mack of Florida and Benjamin Gilman of New York accused the bank of "cultural genocide." A House of Representatives subcommittee voted in 1999 to cut contributions to the bank's soft-loan window by $220 million.

When the Inspection Panel inquiry got under way, it only succeeded in bringing the activist attack inside the World Bank's building. The head of the Inspection Panel, Canadian environmentalist Jim MacNeill, clearly favored activists over bank staff, whom he treated with prosecutorial vigor. He seemed more interested in finding technical infringements of the bank's safeguard policies than in asking the big questions: Would the Qinghai project reduce poverty? The answer was yes, but the panel seemed indifferent. Would it cause environmental damage? The bottom line was no, and yet the panel insisted on poking holes in the bank's procedures.

The panel's final report, delivered in April 2000, was a 160-page indictment of the Qinghai project. It insisted that the scheme should have been rated Category A for environmental riskiness, that insufficient attention had been paid to the impact on Mongolian and Tibetan nomads, and that the recruitment of volunteers for resettlement was compromised because interviews were not confidential. The panel's report did not worry too much about whether a Category A environmental assessment would have found reasons to oppose the project or whether nomads might actually benefit from clinics or other facilities created by the project. It did not dwell on the fact that, whatever the circumstances of the interviews, the farmers' desire to relocate was beyond doubt. Indeed, many more people wanted to move than the project could accommodate.

In June 2000, the bank's management made a last-ditch attempt to placate the NGOs by proposing another year's worth of studies and project preparation the bank estimated would cost $2 million. Yet the NGOs continued their calls for canceling the project. In July, the bank board rejected the managers' proposal, and the second round of the Qinghai battle came to a close: China informed the bank that it would withdraw its request for financing.

Not long after the World Bank pulled out of Qinghai, a delegation of Tibet activists went to visit Wolfensohn. They had heard that the Chinese government was pressing ahead with the resettlement project by itself. It later became apparent that China planned to ignore the bank's environmental conditions and move more people to the new area. The NGOs were having a hard time discovering the details of the Chinese plans, so they asked Wolfensohn what was going on.

"How the fuck do I know what they're doing?" Wolfensohn shot back. "You just got us out of there!"

THE SLEEPING BANK AWAKENS

Versions of this story play out all over the world. The bank designs a reasonable project, which inevitably has flaws. NGOs seize on these flaws and add a large sprinkling of inflammatory rhetoric. The World Bank pulls out, but the project goes ahead anyway, minus the bank's social and environmental safeguards. Because of the fear of NGO assault, the bank is obliged to follow its precautionary guidelines to the letter, adding many months and dollars to project preparation. According to a bank study carried out in 2001, safeguard policies of one kind or another inflate total project preparation costs by somewhere between $200 million and $300 million annually. This money comes out of the hides of the world's poor, and the associated delays mean further months without the electricity or clean water that a bank project might bring—harming the poor a second time over.

The bank's expense and delays do not even benefit the environmental and human rights agendas that NGOs hold so dear. Because of the high cost of doing business with the bank, countries with the option of borrowing on private capital markets increasingly do so. For example, China, which borrowed $1.7 billion from the World Bank in 2000, accepted only half as much in 2001 and 2002—and the infrastructure that China built without the bank's financing was subjected to less scrutiny. Some level of conditionality is essential, but after waves of punishing assault by NGOs, the World Bank has come to reflect the agenda of activists who insist upon perfectionist safeguards. In sum, the world's premier development institution has come perilously close to losing touch with the needs and realities of developing countries.

The good news is that many within the bank have come to understand this dilemma. After experiences like Qinghai and a decade of Wolfensohn's efforts to woo the NGOs, they have rightly realized that you can't win over every critic. For example, the bank invited several NGOs to participate in a commission tasked with setting standards for future dams; the commission responded with a list of standards so onerous as to make most dams unviable. In late 2001, a group within the bank pushed back, persuading the bank's board that the institution should not feel bound by the commission's excessive recommendations. This year, a bank-appointed commission on extractive industries followed the NGOs' lead, calling on the World Bank to pull out of all oil and coal projects because of the pollution they create. But this demand overlooks the developing world's need for energy, which has to be satisfied somehow. And it fails to acknowledge that 2.3 billion people currently depend on wood and other biomass fuels that cause even more deforestation and air pollution. Thankfully, the bank's management rejected the commission's recommendation.

This nascent counterattack must go broader than one institution, however. The lesson of the Qinghai battle is that the bank cannot fight the NGOs alone. Commentators, politicians, and Hollywood celebrities must resist the temptation to side uncritically with feisty activists.

The World Bank's predicament is part of a larger conundrum that bedevils globalization. In many of the world's rich capitals, and especially in Washington, public policy is decided by a bewildering array of interest groups campaigning single-mindedly for narrow goals. A similar army of advocates pounds upon big international institutions like the bank, demanding they bend to particular concerns: no damage to indigenous peoples, no harm to rain forests, nothing that might threaten human rights, or Tibet, or democratic values. However noble many of the activists' motives, and however flawed the big institutions' record, this constant campaigning threatens to disable not just the World Bank but regional development banks and governmental aid organizations such as the U.S. Agency for International Development. If this takes place, the world may lose the potential for good that big organizations offer: to rise above the single-issue advocacy that small groups tend to pursue and to square off against humanity's grandest problems in all their hideous complexity.

Transnational Organized Crime and the State

PHIL WILLIAMS

One of the most important characteristics of global politics at the beginning of the twenty-first century is the multiplicity of actors. An environment that, for a long time, was regarded as the domain of states is now seen by most commentators as much more complex: states share the stage with a wide variety of non-state or "sovereignty-free actors," ranging from transnational and multinational companies with global markets to non-governmental organizations concerned with good causes such as peace and disarmament, preventing further environmental degradation, famine and disaster relief, poverty alleviation, and the like.[1] There is also a new breed of criminal actor—transnational criminal organizations—that is interested not in the pursuit of good, but in the pursuit of wealth, and the use of criminal means to obtain it. Transnational criminal organizations are not new; they have been around as long as there has been a demand for the smuggling of goods across borders. The difference today, however, is that there are more of them, they are more varied, and they possess greater wealth and power than ever before. Furthermore, whereas most states in the past seemed to have the capacity to keep organized crime under control, this is no longer so obviously the case. Indeed, transnational organized crime has emerged as a major challenger to individual states—especially those in transition and those that are still developing economically—and to international governance. . . .

TRANSNATIONAL ORGANIZED CRIME AND STATES

Organized crime both threatens states and exploits states. In terms of the threats to states, there are several aspects of transnational organized crime that need to be taken into account:

> organized crime structures. These embody a concentration of illegal power in society that can significantly influence political, economic, and social life. In some countries organized crime is little more than a marginal problem,

From Phil Williams, "Transnational Organized Crime and the State," from *The Emergence of Private Authority in Global Governance*, Rodney Bruce Hall and Thomas J. Biersteker, eds., pp. 161–181. © Rodney Bruce Hall and Thomas J. Biersteker 2002. Reprinted with the permission of Cambridge University Press. Portions of the text and some footnotes have been omitted.

existing on the fringes of society and having little impact on the way that the society functions or is governed. In others, however, organized crime has succeeded in embedding itself not only in the social fabric and the economy but also in the political system. In some cases, organized crime and the state apparatus develop a deeply symbiotic and collusive relationship.

organized crime activities that provide the profits and that can range from drug trafficking and arms trafficking, to extortion and infiltration of licit business. These activities are generally against the law in most states. The irony, of course, is that prohibition or even regulation of some products that are in demand increases their price and encourages the development of criminal markets.

organized crime strategies and processes designed to manage the risks posed by governments and law enforcement agencies. Most transnational criminal organizations adopt some kind of risk management strategy that is designed to protect the organization and its activities. One of its most potent risk management tools is corruption, which is intended to neutralize the control powers of states but can also undermine their power and authority. Indeed, organized crime—corruption networks can be understood as the HIV virus of the modern state, circumventing and breaking down the natural defenses of the body politic.

It is clear from this that organized crime is a challenge to states, irrespective of whichever dimension or meaning is attributed to states. This is evident in Table 1, which looks at how the three major aspects of organized crime impinge on the four dimensions of states elucidated above.

Transnational organized crime activities, for example, fundamentally challenge the territorial sovereignty of states and, in particular, any notion that states can determine who or what comes across their border, and what activities are permissible in the territory under their jurisdiction. Transnational criminal organizations typically circumvent border controls and, rather than negotiating with the government for access to legal markets (as transnational corporations do), operate clandestinely. Insofar as there is negotiation, it occurs with domestic organized crime groups that have ready-made distribution networks for illegal goods and services. Indeed, alliances among criminal organizations are becoming increasingly important in allowing foreign groups to enter new domestic markets, compensating for their weaknesses and lack of local knowledge, and overcoming border restrictions. Ironically, although transnational criminal organizations violate national borders as a matter of routine, they also exploit these borders in several ways. In the first place, national borders often bring with them highly significant price differentials. A kilo of cocaine, for example, increases in value approximately sixfold once it has crossed the Mexican–United States border. Second, organized crime uses borders defensively. During one period when they were fighting extradition to the United States, for example, the leaders of the Medellin and Cali cartels became major champions of Colombian nationalism and sovereignty. Their arguments were resonant with the symbolism of sovereignty and reveal that, although drug trafficking groups and other transnational criminal organizations represent both private power and private authority, they are not averse to appealing to more traditional state authority when the need presents itself.

TABLE 1 ■ ORGANIZED CRIME AND THE STATE

Aspects of Organized Crime	Sovereign Entity	System of Rules	Institutions and People	Functions
Activities such as various forms of trafficking	Smuggling work with illegal power structure	Undermine and exploit prohibition of goods and services	Challenge and justification for resources for social control and criminal justice	Challenge to law and order
Power manifested in use of violence	Challenge state monopoly of coercive power and create nogo zones	Replace rule of law with rule of violence	Intimidate judiciary and law enforcement and ensure low penalties or acquittals for organized crime figures	Extortion threatens business and property supposedly protected by the state
Risk management strategies, especially corruption	Operational corruption to protect trafficking activities	Organized crime buys immunity from system of rules through corruption of law enforcement and judiciary	Corrosion of institutions such as police, judiciary, and the military as well as financial institutions	Corruption undermines good governance and democratic procedures

The hypocrisy of this, of course, is very striking given the routine way in which criminal organizations violate national borders and national laws. Indeed, in some cases, their challenge to state authority goes even further and the state has to accept that there are "no-go zones" in which it has no authority and little, if any, presence. Criminal activities also challenge the system of rules that states attempt to impose. There is another deep irony here: criminal organizations operate in criminal markets that are particularly lucrative because they are a direct product of state policies on prohibition and regulation of certain goods and services. The challenge to state institutions and functions from criminal activities is more tangential but still significant—to the extent that law enforcement institutions fail to stem these activities and provide order and safety for citizens, then questions about the efficacy of the state apparatus come to the fore. At the same time, criminal activities provide a rationale for strengthening state institutions and devoting more resources to the functions of social control and border control.

The power of criminal organizations is a threat to the state as sovereign entity in that the state claims a monopoly of coercive power; criminal organizations also exercise such power and use violence to remove competitors and obstacles to their businesses. In a few cases, criminal organizations have launched major assaults on the state, using terror tactics in an effort to intimidate the authorities. Criminal violence is a frontal attack on the notion of the state as a system of rules and its concomitant, the rule of law. This violence is sometimes directed at particular state institutions such as the judiciary or law enforcement agencies. . . . Violence and the threat of violence by criminal organizations are also often directed against large and small businesses as part of extortion. To the extent that this succeeds, the state has failed in one of its major functions, securing the safety and prosperity of its citizens.

If violence is the most dramatic manifestation of the power of organized crime, the wealth that criminal organizations often have available is another form of power—and is used as the basis for risk management strategies by criminal organizations. The wealth of criminal organizations is used for corruption, in ways that undermine the very foundations of good governance. Although corruption is often treated as a condition, in this context it has to be seen as a very powerful instrument used by criminal organizations to ensure that the risks to them and to their activities are minimized. Corruption is used to undermine border control efforts, to ensure that organized crime, in effect, can operate outside the system of rules that apply to other citizens, to neutralize state institutions and people combating organized crime, and to inhibit the proper functioning of the criminal justice system. The targets and objectives of corruption are examined more fully below.

If transnational criminal organizations, in some respects, pose major challenges to the functioning of states, in other ways their activities and behavior acknowledge the continued importance of the state. Indeed, transnational criminal organizations in effect accept and use states in several ways. In the first place a state—particularly one that has been neutralized by the power of organized crime—can provide a safe haven, i.e., protection from other states and a base from which the criminal organizations can operate with impunity. The capacity to provide safe havens or sanctuaries actually makes states very important to criminal organizations. Another attraction is that states have access to all sorts of resources that criminal organizations might want to obtain or export. In such cases, criminal organizations will seek access to institutions and people who formally control these resources. Indeed, from the perspective of criminal organizations, states can be understood in terms of four categories: home, host, transshipment, and service. Home states are in some respects the most important—they provide the location from which criminal organizations operate their transnational businesses. Consequently, a congenial, low-risk environment is critical.

This is less true of host or market states which are the destination for many of the illegal products of criminal organizations that are shipped across borders. Host or market states generally have lucrative markets or other targets for their criminal activity—with the result that criminal organizations are sometimes willing to incur a significant level of risk in order to operate within them. Moreover, there are some things that give transnational criminal organizations an advantage in host states, compensating for the difficulties of establishing corruption networks of the kind that are so potent in the home state. Among these are the capacity to operate within ethnic enclaves, which provide cover and recruitment and which are difficult for law enforcement to penetrate because of language and cultural barriers. States that act as hosts or markets for organized crime rarely face fundamental challenges in the way that home states do—partly because ethnic-based criminal organizations are not rooted in local or national power structures.

Before illegal products reach their final destination in the market states, they generally have to pass through one or more transshipment states. These states are located on major transit routes for certain kinds of illicit commodities such as drugs, arms, or illegal aliens, and become the transshipment states because of their access to the target (i.e., the market or final destination for the illicit products) and the ease of transit, which is largely a function of state capacity for interdiction. Such states suffer from the violation of their sovereignty and are particularly vulnerable to operational corruption (i.e., corruption designed to facilitate the movements of illicit goods through the state).

The other kind of state, from the perspective of criminal organizations, is what might be termed a service state. Service states generally have particular sectors of activity—usually the financial sector—that can be exploited by criminal organizations to move, hide, and protect the proceeds of their illegal activities. Those states which make up the offshore banking world—a world that incorporates many Caribbean states and European states such as Luxembourg, Austria, Monaco, Switzerland, and Cyprus, and that extends to minuscule South Pacific jurisdictions such as Vanuatu, Niue, and Nauru—offer bank secrecy and pose few problems for criminal organizations seeking to hide and protect their money. The biggest challenge to the small service states is corruption, which is used to resist any efforts to clean up their activities and develop banking safeguards such as know-your-customer rules. The irony here—as with the notion of home states as sanctuaries—is that transnational criminal organizations are fully exploiting the sovereignty of some states for defensive purposes even as their trafficking activities are grossly violating the sovereignty of others. . . .

TRANSNATIONAL ORGANIZED CRIME AND WEAK STATES

It became increasingly clear throughout the 1980s and the 1990s that the rise of transnational organized crime was inextricably connected with the weakness of many states in the international system. Yet state weakness is not a new phenomenon. Nor is the link between weak states and organized crime particularly novel. The weakness of the Italian state in the nineteenth century facilitated the rise of the mafia in Sicily: with the state incapable of providing protection and arbitration for business, the mafia developed to fill the vacuum.[3] Similarly, but of more recent vintage, during the 1970s and 1980s, the weakness of the Colombian state and its lack of control over territory nominally under its jurisdiction was a major factor in explaining the rise of Colombia as the corporate headquarters of the South American cocaine industry. State weakness gave Colombian drug trafficking organizations a comparative advantage over their counterparts in Peru and Bolivia.[4] . . .

As well as being the result of a sudden collapse of an old regime, state weakness can also reflect a more long-term failure to develop viable, legitimate, and effective state institutions. Whatever the short- or long-term causes of weakness, however, weak states tend to share certain characteristics: there is a low level of state legitimacy; border controls are weak; rules are ineffective; the institutions and people who represent the state put other goals above the public interest; there is little economic or social provision for the citizenry; business is not legally regulated or protected;

social control through a fair and efficient criminal justice system is lacking; and other typical state functions are not carried out with either efficiency or effectiveness. Not surprisingly, these weaknesses provide a greenhouse effect for organized crime. . . . weak states suffer from capacity gaps, and . . . capacity gaps lead to functional holes (i.e., a failure of the state to fulfill certain basic functions that are normally associated with states and that are expected by the citizenry). Capacity gaps and functional holes are exploited by criminal organizations in one of two ways—either by filling them and, in effect, substituting or compensating for the state, or by exploiting the room for maneuver that they provide. In effect, functional holes provide space that can either be filled by organized crime or in which organized crime can operate virtually unhindered. The ways in which capacity gaps and the resulting functional holes are exploited by criminal organizations is summarized in Table 2.

Organized crime tends to develop in response to a particular combination of opportunities on the one side and pressures and incentives on the other. Capacity gaps and functional holes feed all aspects of this equation, offering multiple opportunities for—and few constraints on—organized criminal activity.

One aspect of state weakness with particular relevance to the development of organized crime has been the inadequate development of effective criminal justice systems that are efficient, effective, fair, and equitable and that incorporate measures specifically designed to prevent and control various forms of racketeering and money laundering. . . . The resulting functional holes mean that organized crime can operate with a high level of impunity or, at the very least, a minimum of risk. The prospects that major organized crime figures will be caught and incarcerated are minimal. Although rank-and-file members of criminal enterprises might be arrested, the organ-

TABLE 2 ■ CAPACITY GAPS, FUNCTIONAL HOLES, AND TRANSNATIONAL ORGANIZED CRIME

Capacity gaps	Functional holes	Implications for organized crime
Social control	Ineffective criminal justice system	Organized crime operates with impunity
Social welfare	Lack of provision for citizens	– Migration to illegal economy – Organized crime recruitment – Paternalism substitute for state
Business regulation	Lack of regulatory framework	– Organized crime as arbitrator, protector, and debt collector
Oversight and accountability	Lack of control and transparency	– Opportunity for extensive use of corruption – Hijacking of privatization processes
Border control	Weak interdiction capability	– Use state for transshipment of various illegal products
Legitimacy	Lack of authority and affiliation	– Build on patron–client links and other relationships that are more important than loyalty to the state
Electoral norms and patterns	Campaign financing	– Opportunity to influence election outcomes and cut deals with politicians

izers and leaders are often able to operate with remarkable freedom. And even when they are arrested, they are often able to buy acquittals or remarkably light sentences.

The legal capacity gaps are not confined to criminal law. The failure of some states to provide adequate and appropriate regulatory frameworks for business can have profound implications for organized crime, offering opportunities either to fill or to exploit the resulting functional hole. In Russia, for example, the lack of an appropriate regulatory framework for business providing recourse for debt collection and effective and peaceful arbitration of disputes has been a huge problem during the move toward a free market economy. In the absence of such a framework, there is neither protection nor contract enforcement, a condition that allows organized crime to become a surrogate for government. The change in the principles on which the economy is based preceded the development of appropriate regulatory and legal provisions and led some businessmen to turn to criminal organizations to collect outstanding debts or to settle disputes. Recourse to these unorthodox methods had two consequences: it gave criminal organizations an *entrée* into the business world, thereby creating a seamless web between the licit and the illicit, and it encouraged legitimate businesses to resort to increasingly ruthless methods against their competitors. . . .

A variant on this theme of regulatory gaps can be found in several African states where the lack of regulations in key economic sectors, including those involved in the extraction of minerals and other natural resources, fuels criminal activity by leaders, by domestic and transnational criminal organizations, and by rebel armies and warlords. While a well-defined regulatory framework might not be a sufficient condition for stopping criminal looting of state resources, it is almost certainly a necessary one. Moreover, the absence of such a framework gives the problem a self-perpetuating quality: political or territorial control of certain regions not only yields rich rewards to criminals (or rebel groups) but also deprives governments of resources that could help to fuel economic growth, infrastructure improvements, and the like. The result is a lack of resources to reduce the capacity gap and fill the functional hole and which in turn contributes to its continued exploitation.

Another capacity gap that is often overlooked concerns economic management and social welfare. The resulting functional hole is a lack of provision for the welfare of the citizens. While other dimensions of weakness offer opportunities for criminal behavior, this type of weakness creates pressures and incentives for citizens to engage in criminal activities. . . . Amidst conditions of economic hardship caused by unemployment and hyperinflation, there is a tendency to turn to extra-legal means of obtaining basic needs. Illicit means of advancement offer opportunities that are simply not available in the licit economy. During the 1990s this took a unique form in Russia as a result of the decline in status of some of the central institutions of the state, such as the military and the intelligence agencies. Not surprisingly, therefore, corruption in the Russian military has become pervasive, with all ranks engaging in their own entrepreneurial activities and selling both light and heavy weapons to anyone with the money to pay. Equally if not more striking was the migration into organized crime of specialists in violence—former special forces and KGB operatives—who were trained and then discarded by the state. Many contract killings in Russia have the hallmark of former KGB agents and, for important victims at least, reap relatively high rewards.

Another variant on the social welfare hole is that some criminal organizations and criminal leaders engage in a form of paternalism that earns them considerable gratitude and at least tacit support from members of the populace. In Colombia during the 1980s, for example, Pablo Escobar initiated a program called Medellin Without Slums that provided new houses for poor people. Very visible, and sometimes even ostentatious, support for charities is another aspect of the same tendency. In effect, organized crime becomes a surrogate for the state. Although the functional hole is filled to only a very modest extent by organized crime, the benefits from this are considerable—and the contrast between criminal provision and the apparent ineptitude or indifference of the state could hardly be more marked.

Another capacity gap in weak states is the inability to control borders. In states-in-transition this is often a major shift from the state of affairs in the old regime when the state was isolated from the world. Not only do such states generally display a greater degree of openness to the outside world, but they also encourage external trade and investment. The difficulty is that, when borders are opened, controlling who and what enters and distinguishing between licit and illegitimate business activity become much more difficult. Criminal organizations take advantage of this and states that have holes in their border control are prime candidates for transshipment of illegal goods. . . .

TRANSNATIONAL ORGANIZED CRIME AND CORRUPTION

One of the problems with many discussions of corruption is that it is treated simply as a condition or pathology that needs to be corrected. In the present context, it makes much more sense to treat corruption as an instrument. The key then becomes a matter of determining who is corrupting whom for what purposes and using what means. Although much corruption stems from officials intent on using public office for private gain, organized crime groups use corruption as a major instrument to ensure both a congenial environment and the success of their activities. As suggested above, corruption is one of the most important instruments used by criminal organizations as part of their risk management strategies. Not surprisingly, they have some very specific targets for corruption. Some of these are identified in Table 3 which provides a generic overview of potential targets of corruption along with the benefits that can be obtained by criminal groups.

Among the specific objectives of criminal organizations in using corruption is the neutralization of border control authorities in the home state, in transshipment states, and in destination or market states. This involves what might be termed operational corruption and is designed to ensure that the trafficking process itself is subjected to as little interference, interdiction, and damage as possible. More serious is the use of "systemic" corruption to neutralize the punitive powers of the state. Criminal organizations essentially want a congenial low-risk environment from which they can operate with impunity. Consequently, they have many targets for corruption, including the police and the military, the judiciary (to ensure favorable verdicts or, at the very least, lenient penalties), the legislature (to inhibit the

TABLE 3 ■ TARGETS AND OBJECTIVES OF CORRUPTION

Target of corruption	Objective of corruption
Executive branch	– Create a safe haven
	– Obtain protection and support
	– Obtain information
Legislature	– Obtain favorable legislation
	– Block unfavorable initiatives
	– Obtain informal support group
Political parties	– Ensure tacit support through funding
	– Receive favors in return for votes
	– Create obligations for new government members
Judiciary	– Obtain dismissal of cases
	– Obtain light sentences
	– Overturn guilty verdicts
Police	– Obtain information and advance warning
	– Obtain time for countermeasures
	– Create capacity for sabotage
	– Persuade police to act against rivals
Customs	– Neutralize inspections
	– Protect shipments of drugs
	– Obtain information on standard search procedures
Banks	– *Obtain approval for money laundering*
	– *Meet "know-your-customer" requirements*
	– *Avoid filing of suspicious activity reports*
Businesses	– *Obtain opportunities for money laundering through legitimate companies*
	– *Develop opportunities for false invoicing*
	– Develop legitimate cover for trafficking
Civil society	– Develop reputation for paternalism
	– Obtain legitimacy
	– Obtain public support
	– Acquire information
Media outlets	– Influence public debate
	– Develop lobbying capacity
	– Enhance legitimacy

passage of effective and stringent laws), and the executive branch (to obtain protection and support). The best of all positions for criminal organizations is to have political protection at very high levels. This, in effect, offers not simply a risk management approach but risk prevention. To the extent that this approach succeeds, there is less need for the criminals to initiate countermeasures to offset law enforcement and the like. It is also particularly corrosive of the state.

Corruption, of course, is not confined to state structures. It can also extend to the private sector where criminal organizations seek to infiltrate, corrupt, and control companies that can provide an apparently legitimate cover for their activities. In addition, criminal organizations often seek to corrupt and coopt financial institutions to ensure that they can be used to move and hide the proceeds of drug trafficking and other criminal activities. In effect, corrupting bank officials is a means of circumventing the impact of regulations relating to suspicious transactions and due diligence. The Russian banking system, for example, has been heavily infiltrated by organized crime, which has used a mixture of violence and corruption to obtain control of a significant number of banks—some of which have developed correspondent banking relationships with many Western banks.

Whatever the target, however, corruption invariably involves exchange relationships and mechanisms. In some cases this will simply be money for favors—payoffs that allow the recipients a lifestyle that is far more lavish than their income can support. For those being corrupted, the obligation is to provide tacit support for criminal organizations, to provide these organizations with critical information, and to ensure that there is little interference with their activities. For the criminal organizations, although this might require a substantial portion of the proceeds of their crimes, the investment can be understood simply as one of the necessary costs of illegal enterprise. As suggested above, in some cases politicians will sell their covert protection and support in return for mobilization of voters in elections or financial support for electoral campaigns. In this connection, it is worth emphasizing that some of the trends of the 1990s, particularly those toward democratization and decentralization, provided new opportunities for corruption. In many countries where democratization is moving ahead, for example, politicians need campaign finance and a capacity to mobilize voters. This offers organized crime a major opportunity to play a major role in the political system.

In some cases, the use of corruption goes beyond neutralization and, in effect, enables organized crime to capture the state through the development of what Roy Godson has termed a "political–criminal nexus."[5] In captured states there is a symbiosis between politicians and criminals: the criminals provide money and help to mobilize political support for the politicians; the politicians provide protection, information, and support for the criminals. In some cases, the state apparatus is gradually enmeshed in a fully symbiotic relationship with criminal organizations, becoming a real partner in these activities rather than merely a relatively passive beneficiary. In a collusive relationship of this kind, high-level representatives of the state go beyond protecting the organization to working closely with it in the furtherance of its criminal enterprise. There are some collusive relationships, however, in which the collusion is relatively low-key and covert and others in which it is more overt. Japan during the Cold War provided an example of low-key collusion between state authorities and home state criminal organizations. Italy under successive Christian Democrat governments from the 1950s through to the 1980s offered a classic example of a protection-for-votes deal, although one that fell apart in the 1980s. Another classic example of high-level political support for criminal organizations occurred in Mexico where Raul Salinas, brother of President Salinas, became the protector of drug trafficking organizations, and in return was able to deposit well over US $100 million in Swiss bank accounts. . . .

One of the key issues in these collusive or highly symbiotic relationships that is insufficiently understood—and rarely even discussed—concerns the distribution of power. Since it is the weaknesses of the state, however, that lead to the dynamic growth of organized crime, it would not be surprising if the criminals—with their capacity for violence—were not, in some respects at least, the dominant element in the relationship. In effect this reverses the relationship in strong states such as the USSR, where organized crime operated, but within parameters determined by the state and its officials. . . .

CONCLUSIONS

Charles Tilly in an oft-quoted comment once noted that the state was simply the most efficient and effective form of organized crime.[6] In effect, the state legitimized organized crime by transforming extortion into taxation, brute force into authority, and rule by fear into rule by consent of the governed. The implication of the preceding analysis, however, is that in the last decade or so there have been signs that organized crime has been fighting back and that the state is not as successful as it was in the period of state-building so trenchantly dissected by Tilly. The issue remains, however, as to whether transnational organized crime is appropriately understood as an example of private authority or is simply a case of private power that seeks to masquerade as public authority.

The answer to this question has to go beyond a simple dichotomy, to recognize that organized crime combines elements of power and authority in ways that are very distinctive. On the one side, it is clear that organized crime relies heavily on power and has actually turned the capacity for coercion into a highly lucrative art form through its strategies for extorting business. Moreover, organized crime very clearly challenges the government monopoly of violence. In the two cases where this has been particularly overt and brutal—Italy and Colombia—organized crime lost much of its popular support and the state was ultimately able to mobilize even greater power and beat back the challenge. It is also clear that organized crime, whether operating domestically or transnationally, has distinctive features that set it apart from other private actors. It lacks accountability, and for the most part operates covertly. Moreover, unlike other private authorities, it seeks to undermine or circumvent international norms, rules, and regulations. Furthermore, the clandestine activities that are an essential part of organized crime, by their very nature, do nothing to build authority or legitimacy.

Yet there are dimensions of organized crime that suggest authority rather than power. The wealth that organized crime accrues through its operations in some cases is used to create a base from which it is sometimes possible to develop a degree of legitimacy that can be parlayed into authority structures. Similarly, the exploitation of functional holes in ways that substitute for the state, for example, gives organized crime some degree of legitimacy and, at the domestic level at least, provides a crude form of governance in certain areas where it would otherwise be absent. Similarly, the occasional use of paternalism to build domestic support can be understood as an attempt to transform power based on fear into more legitimate notions of authority and approval, if not actually consent. It is also clear that organized crime flourishes in societies where family, kinship, clan relations, and patron–client relationships are the primary points of reference and loyalty. In this sense, organized crime can be understood as an alternative forum to the state for allegiance and affiliation. This is also true in diaspora communities. Ethnic migrants are often marginalized in their new home, and as a result develop little loyalty for the political authorities and little trust in law enforcement. Instead, they develop coping mechanisms that include organized crime, black market activities, and, in the Chinese case, their own underground banking system sometimes referred to as "flying money." The underground banking system is particularly interesting in that it is based on trust and ostracism for those who betray it. Moreover, in some immigrant communities, organized crime figures are likely to have considerable authority and influence at least within the confines of the community. Insofar as authority involves allegiance that is given voluntarily rather than coerced, then it is clear that, in some communities, organized crime can be understood in terms of private authority. In other words, when public authority is weak, and state legitimacy is low, other less formal, often illicit forms of authority will thrive. Organized crime can be understood as one of these. In sum, there are some grounds for treating organized crime as private illicit authority.

In some ways, however, the most intriguing aspect of transnational organized crime is the tendency of at least some criminal organizations to cloak their power in the mantle of state authority. This is not to suggest that the criminal symbiosis will determine all aspects of state behavior. In instances in which the state is captured by organized crime, the state will still carry out many of its traditional functions in international relations in the normal way. At the same time, the state authorities will take measures to ensure that organized crime functions unhindered and uninhibited in its pursuit of wealth. In domestic terms this will mean doing little to close the capacity gaps or fill the functional holes; organized crime must be allowed to continue to function unhindered and in a low-risk environment. The implication is that there will continue to be states that provide sanctuaries or safe havens for criminal organizations. Indeed, their number could well increase as transnational criminal organizations continue to entrench themselves in weak states in the former Soviet Union, Africa, Latin America, and parts of Asia.

Because of differing degrees of vulnerability, however, some states are not only strong enough to resist transnational organized crime but also willing to confront criminal organizations, seeking to reduce their power, to stem their activities, and to dismantle their organizational structures. Not surprisingly, those states that adopt a confrontational strategy toward transnational criminal organizations are usually both strong and legitimate. In effect, this suggests a differentiated state approach that acknowledges that some states are in retreat but that others are not. . . . If some states are fighting back against transnational organized crime, the task will not be easy—not least because weak and captured states will seriously hinder multilateral efforts to combat transnational organized crime. Efforts to provide global regimes or multilateral attacks on organized crime will suffer from the problem of defecting states. The defections themselves will take various forms. In the case of weak states there will be tacit defections, as nominal adherence to global regimes and multilateral efforts is not accompanied by substantive actions. There will also be overt defections by captured and criminal states. Such defections will have serious consequences, ensuring that regimes aimed at combating transnational organized crime will be seriously incomplete, and that criminal organizations will continue to enjoy geographic and jurisdictional loopholes. The result will be not the containment of criminal activity but its displacement—geographical and methodological. In short, multilateral efforts by states to combat transnational organized crime will continue to exhibit serious deficiencies. Sanctuary or safe-haven states will continue to put transnational criminal organizations out of the reach of those states whose laws they have violated and whose populations provide customers for their illicit products and services.

There is another possible consequence that is even more disturbing: it is not inconceivable that the major global divide will be caused not by competing ideologies, the struggle for power, or Huntington's "clash of civilizations," but by clashes between states that uphold law and order and those that are dominated by criminal interests and criminal authorities.

NOTES

1. James Rosenau, *Turbulence in World Politics* (Princeton, N.J.: Princeton University Press, 1990).
2. Fenton Bressler, *Interpol* (London: Mandarin, 1993).
3. Diego Gambetta, *The Sicilian Mafia: The Business of Private Protection* (Cambridge, Mass.: Harvard University Press, 1993).
4. Francisco E. Thoumi, *Political Economy and Illegal Drugs in Colombia* (Boulder, Colo.: Lynne Rienner, 1995), pp. 172–73.
5. Roy Godson, "Political–Criminal Nexus: Overview," *Trends in Organized Crime*, 3 (1) (Fall 1997), 4–7.
6. Charles Tilly, "War Making and State Making as Organized Crime," in Peter B. Evans, Dietrich Rueschemeyer, and Theda Skocpol (eds.), *Bringing the State Back In* (Cambridge: Cambridge University Press, 1985), pp. 169–91.

mypoliscikit   Exercises for Transnational Actors

Apply what you learned in this chapter by using the online resources on MyPoliSciKit (www.mypoliscikit.com).

 Practice Tests

 Videos:
- "Deforestation in the Brazilian Amazon"
- "Conflict Diamonds and the Kimberly Process"

 Reading Guides:
- Margeret E. Keck and Kathryn Sikkink, "Transnational Activist Networks"
- Sebastian Mallaby, "NGOs: Fighting Poverty, Hurting the Poor"
- Phil Williams, "Transnational Organized Crime and the State"

THE GLOBAL COMMONS

The Tragedy of the Commons

GARRETT HARDIN

We can make little progress in working toward optimum population size until we explicitly exorcize the spirit of Adam Smith in the field of practical demography. In economic affairs, *The Wealth of Nations* (1776) popularized the "invisible hand," the idea that an individual who "intends only his own gain," is, as it were, "led by an invisible hand to promote . . . the public interest."[1] Adam Smith did not assert that this was invariably true, and perhaps neither did any of his followers. But he contributed to a dominant tendency of thought that has ever since interfered with positive action based on rational analysis, namely, the tendency to assume that decisions reached individually will, in fact, be the best decisions for an entire society. If this assumption is correct it justifies the continuance of our present policy of laissez-faire in reproduction. If it is correct we can assume that men will control their individual fecundity so as to produce the optimum population. If the assumption is not correct, we need to reexamine our individual freedoms to see which ones are defensible.

TRAGEDY OF FREEDOM IN A COMMONS

The rebuttal to the invisible hand in population control is to be found in a scenario first sketched in a little-known pamphlet in 1833 by a mathematical amateur named William Foster Lloyd (1794–1852).[2] We may well call it "the tragedy of the commons," using the word "tragedy" as the philosopher Whitehead used it: "The essence of dramatic tragedy is not unhappiness. It resides in the solemnity of the remorseless working of things."[3] He then goes on to say, "This inevitableness of destiny can only be illustrated in terms of human life by incidents which in fact

From Garrett Hardin, "The Tragedy of the Commons," *Science*, Vol. 162 (13 December 1968), pp. 1243–1248. Reprinted with permission from AAAS. Portions of the text and some footnotes have been omitted.

involve unhappiness. For it is only by them that the futility of escape can be made evident in the drama."

The tragedy of the commons develops in this way. Picture a pasture open to all. It is to be expected that each herdsman will try to keep as many cattle as possible on the commons. Such an arrangement may work reasonably satisfactorily for centuries because tribal wars, poaching, and disease keep the numbers of both man and beast well below the carrying capacity of the land. Finally, however, comes the day of reckoning, that is, the day when the long-desired goal of social stability becomes a reality. At this point, the inherent logic of the commons remorselessly generates tragedy.

As a rational being, each herdsman seeks to maximize his gain. Explicitly or implicitly, more or less consciously, he asks, "What is the utility *to me* of adding one more animal to my herd?" This utility has one negative and one positive component.

The positive component is a function of the increment of one animal. Since the herdsman receives all the proceeds from the sale of the additional animal, the positive utility is nearly $+1$.

The negative component is a function of the additional overgrazing created by one more animal. Since, however, the effects of overgrazing are shared by all the herdsmen, the negative utility for any particular decision-making herdsman is only a fraction of -1.

Adding together the component partial utilities, the rational herdsman concludes that the only sensible course for him to pursue is to add another animal to his herd. And another; and another. . . . But this is the conclusion reached by each and every rational herdsman sharing a commons. Therein is the tragedy. Each man is locked into a system that compels him to increase his herd without limit—in a world that is limited. Ruin is the destination toward which all men rush, each pursuing his own best interest in a society that believes in the freedom of the commons. Freedom in a commons brings ruin to all. . . .

In an approximate way, the logic of the commons has been understood for a long time, perhaps since the discovery of agriculture or the invention of private property in real estate. But it is understood mostly only in special cases which are not sufficiently generalized. Even at this late date, cattlemen leasing national land on the western ranges demonstrate no more than an ambivalent understanding, in constantly pressuring federal authorities to increase the head count to the point where overgrazing produces erosion and weed-dominance. Likewise, the oceans of the world continue to suffer from the survival of the philosophy of the commons. Maritime nations will respond automatically to the shibboleth of the "freedom of the seas." Professing to believe in the "inexhaustible resources of the oceans," they bring species after species of fish and whales closer to extinction. . . .

POLLUTION

In a reverse way, the tragedy of the commons reappears in problems of pollution. Here it is not a question of taking something out of the commons, but of putting something in—sewage, or chemical, radioactive, and heat wastes into water; noxious and dangerous fumes into the air; and distracting and unpleasant advertising signs into the line of sight. The calculations of utility are much the same as before. The rational man finds that his share of the cost of the wastes he discharges into the commons is less than the cost of purifying his wastes before releasing them. Since this is true for everyone, we are locked into a system of "fouling our own nest," so long as we behave only as independent, rational, free-enterprisers.

The tragedy of the commons as a food basket is averted by private property, or something formally like it. But the air and waters surrounding us cannot readily be fenced, and so the tragedy of the commons as a cesspool must be prevented by different means, by coercive laws or taxing devices that make it cheaper for the polluter to treat his pollutant than to discharge them untreated. We have not progressed as far with the solution of this problem as we have with the first. Indeed, our particular concept of private property, which deters us from exhausting the positive resources of the earth, favors pollution. The owner of a factory on the bank of a stream—whose property extends to the middle of the stream—often has difficulty seeing why it is not his natural right to muddy the waters flowing past his door. The law, always behind the times, requires elaborate stitching and fitting to adapt to it this newly perceived aspect of the commons.

The pollution problem is a consequence of populations. It did not much matter how a lonely American frontiersman disposed of his waste. "Flowing water purifies itself every 10 miles," my grandfather used to say, and the myth was near enough to the truth when he was a boy, for there were not too many people. But as population became denser, the natural chemical and biological recycling processes became overloaded, calling for a redefinition of property rights.

HOW TO LEGISLATE TEMPERANCE?

Analysis of the pollution problem as a function of population density uncovers a not generally recognized principle of morality, namely: *The morality of an act is a function of the state of the system at the time it is performed.*[4] Using the commons as a cesspool does not harm the general public under frontier conditions, because there is no public; the same behavior in a metropolis is unbearable. A hundred and fifty years ago a plainsman could kill an American bison, cut out only the tongue for his dinner, and discard the rest of the animal. He was not in any important sense being wasteful. Today, with only a few thousand bison left, we would be appalled by such behavior. . . .

That morality is system-sensitive escaped the attention of most codifiers of ethics in the past. "Thou shalt not . . . " is the form of traditional ethical directives which make no allowance for particular circumstances. The laws of our society follow the pattern of ancient ethics, and therefore are poorly suited to governing a complex, crowded, changeable world. Our epicyclic solution is to augment statutory law with administrative law. Since it is practically impossible to spell out all the conditions under which it is safe to burn trash in the backyard or to run an automobile without smog-control, by law we delegate the details to bureaus. The result is administrative law, which is rightly feared for an ancient reason—*Quis custodiet ipsos custodes?*—" Who shall watch the watchers themselves?" John Adams said that we must have "a government of laws and not men." Bureau administrators, trying to evaluate the morality of acts in the total system, are singularly liable to corruption, producing a government by men, not laws.

Prohibition is easy to legislate (though not necessarily to enforce); but how do we legislate temperance? Experience indicates that it can be accomplished best through the mediation of administrative law. We limit possibilities unnecessarily if we suppose that the sentiment of *Quis custodiet* denies us the use of administrative law. We should rather retain the phrase as a perpetual reminder of fearful dangers we cannot avoid. The great challenge facing us now is to invent the corrective feedbacks that are needed to keep custodians honest. We must find ways to legitimate the needed authority of both the custodians and the corrective feedbacks.

FREEDOM TO BREED IS INTOLERABLE

The tragedy of the commons is involved in population problems in another way. In a world governed solely by the principle of "dog eat dog"—if indeed there ever was such a world—how many children a family had would not be a matter of public concern. Parents who bred too exuberantly would leave fewer descendants, not more, because they would be unable to care adequately for their children. . . .

If each human family were dependent only on its own resources; *if* the children of improvident parents starved to death; *if*, thus, overbreeding brought its own "punishment" to the germ line—*then* there would be no public interest in controlling the breeding of families. But our society is deeply committed to the welfare state and hence is confronted with another aspect of the tragedy of the commons.

In a welfare state, how shall we deal with the family, the religion, the race, or the class (or indeed any distinguishable and cohesive group) that adopts overbreeding as a policy to secure its own aggrandizement? To couple the concept of freedom to breed with the belief that everyone born has an equal right to the commons is to lock the world into a tragic course of action. . . .

CONSCIENCE IS SELF-ELIMINATING

It is a mistake to think that we can control the breeding of mankind in the long run by an appeal to conscience. Charles Galton Darwin made this point when he spoke on the centennial of the publication of his grandfather's great book. The argument is straightforward and Darwinian.

People vary. Confronted with appeals to limit breeding, some people will undoubtedly respond to the plea more than others. Those who have more children will produce a larger fraction of the next generation than those with more susceptible consciences. The difference will be accentuated, generation by generation.

In C. G. Darwin's words: "It may well be that it would take hundreds' of generations for the progenitive instinct to develop in this way, but if it should do so, nature would have taken her revenge, and the variety *Homo contracipiens* would become extinct and would be replaced by the variety *Homo progenitivus.*"[5]

The argument assumes that conscience or the desire for children (no matter which) is hereditary—but hereditary only in the most general formal sense. The result will be the same whether the attitude is transmitted through germ cells, or exosomatically. . . . The argument has here been stated in the context of the population problem, but it applies equally well to any instance in which society appeals to an individual exploiting a commons to restrain himself for the general good—by means of his conscience. To make such an appeal is to set up a selective system that works toward the elimination of conscience from the race. . . .

MUTUAL COERCION MUTUALLY AGREED UPON

The social arrangements that produce responsibility are arrangements that created coercion, of some sort. Consider bank-robbing. The man who takes money from a bank acts as if the bank were a commons. How do we prevent such action? Certainly not by trying to control his behavior solely by a verbal appeal to his sense of responsibility. Rather than rely on propaganda we follow Frankel's lead and insist that a bank is not a commons; we seek the definite social arrangements that will keep it from becoming a commons. That we thereby infringe on the freedom of would-be robbers we neither deny nor regret.

The morality of bank-robbing is particularly easy to understand because we accept complete prohibition of this activity. We are willing to say "Thou shalt not rob banks," without providing for exceptions. But temperance also can be created by coercion. Taxing is a good coercive device. To keep downtown shoppers temperate in their use of parking space we introduce parking meters for short periods, and traffic fines for longer ones. We need not actually forbid a citizen to park as long as he wants to; we need merely make it increasingly expensive for him to do so. Not prohibition, but carefully biased options are what we offer him. A Madison Avenue man might call this persuasion; I prefer the greater candor of the word coercion. . . .

To many, the word coercion implies arbitrary decisions of distant and irresponsible bureaucrats; but this is not a necessary part of its meaning. The only kind of coercion I recommend is mutual coercion, mutually agreed upon by the majority of the people affected.

To say that we mutually agree to coercion is not to say that we are required to enjoy it, or even to pretend we enjoy it. Who enjoys taxes? We all grumble about them. But we accept compulsory taxes because we recognize that voluntary taxes would favor the conscienceless. We institute and (grumblingly) support taxes and other coercive devices to escape the horror of the commons. . . .

RECOGNITION OF NECESSITY

Perhaps the simplest summary of this analysis of man's population problems is this: The commons, if justifiable at all, is justifiable only under conditions of low population density. As the human population has increased, the commons has had to be abandoned in one aspect after another.

First we abandoned the commons in food gathering, enclosing farm land and restricting pastures and hunting and fishing areas. These restrictions are still not complete throughout the world.

Somewhat later we saw that the commons as a place for waste disposal would also have to be abandoned. Restrictions on the disposal of domestic sewage are widely accepted in the Western world; we are still struggling to close the commons to pollution by automobiles, factories, insecticide sprayers, fertilizing operations, and atomic energy installations. . . .

Every new enclosure of the commons involves the infringement of somebody's personal liberty. Infringements made in the distant past are accepted because no contemporary complains of a loss. It is the newly proposed infringements that we vigorously oppose; cries of "rights" and "freedom" fill the air. But what does "freedom" mean? When men mutually agreed to pass laws against robbing, mankind became more free, not less so. Individuals locked into the logic of the commons are free only to bring on universal ruin; once they see the necessity of mutual coercion, they become free to pursue other goals. I believe it was Hegel who said, "Freedom is the recognition of necessity."

The most important aspect of necessity that we must now recognize is the necessity of abandoning the commons in breeding. No technical solution can rescue us from the misery of overpopulation. Freedom to breed will bring ruin to all. At the moment, to avoid hard decisions many of us are tempted to propagandize for conscience and responsible parenthood. The temptation must be resisted, because an appeal to independently acting consciences selects for the disappearance of all conscience in the long run, and an increase in anxiety in the short.

The only way we can preserve and nurture other and more precious freedoms is by relinquishing the freedom to breed, and that very soon. "Freedom is the recognition of necessity"—and it is the role of education to reveal to all the necessity of abandoning the freedom to breed. Only so can we put an end to this aspect of the tragedy of the commons.

NOTES

1. Adam Smith, *The Wealth of Nations* (New York: Modern Library, 1937), p. 423.
2. William Foster Lloyd, *Two Lectures on the Checks to Population* (Oxford: Oxford University Press, 1853), reprinted in part in *Population, Evolution, and Birth Control,* A. Harding, ed. (San Francisco: Freeman, 1964), p. 37.
3. A. N. Whitehead, *Science and the Modern World* (New York: Mentor, 1948), p. 17.
4. J. Fletcher, *Situation Ethics* (Philadelphia: Westminster, 1966).
5. S. Tax, ed., *Evolution after Darwin,* Vol. 2 (Chicago: University of Chicago Press, 1960), p. 469.

Tyranny for the Commons Man

BARRY SCHWARTZ

How does one escape a dilemma in which multiple individuals acting in their own rational self-interest can ultimately destroy a shared limited resource—even when it is clear this serves no one in the long run?

In 1968, Science published Garrett Hardin's landmark article "The Tragedy of the Commons." °Hardin relied on the metaphor of a small English village in the eighteenth century. Each family has a house with a small plot of land for growing vegetables. In addition, there is a large, common area used by all the villagers to graze their livestock. Each villager has a cow or two that provide the family with its milk. The common area is large enough to support the entire village. Then the village begins to grow. Families get larger, and procure an extra cow. New families move in. Suddenly, the common is threatened; it is being overgrazed. Grass is consumed so fast that there is not enough time for it to replenish itself before rains erode the topsoil. Each cow no longer has quite enough to eat, and thus yields less milk than it did before. If the overuse of the common continues, there will be a slow but sure decrease in the number of animals it can support until, finally, it becomes useless for grazing.

We are now dealing with a tragedy of the global commons. There is one earth, one atmosphere and one water supply, and 6 billion people are sharing it. Badly. The wealthy are overgrazing, and the poor can't wait to join them. Examples are plentiful: the overharvesting of trees by lumber companies; the overplanting of land by farmers; the overdevelopment of suburban communities; the extraction of petroleum from a common pool by oil companies; and the overcrowding of highways and other public facilities. These behaviors make whatever benefits users derive from those resources vanishingly small. The issues are as far ranging as contamination of water by toxic wastes, pollution of the atmosphere by carbon dioxide and various particulates, and profligate use of water and energy. Now we must tackle the global-commons problem before the line on Al Gore's global-warming graph reaches the moon.

From the point of view of an individual villager, since he needs the milk from his two or three cows even if they produce less than before, less is better than nothing. Besides, how much difference will it make if he alone shows restraint in his use

<hr>

°*Editors Note:* Hardin's essay is printed in Part 4.

From Barry Schwartz, "Tyranny for the Commons Man," *The National Interest*, Number 102 (July/August 2009), pp. 64–75. Copyright © 2009 The National Interest. Reprinted with permission. Portions of the text have been omitted.

of the common? Indeed, his temptation might be to add still another cow to make up for this setback. The slow decrease in overall dairy-product yield in the village has little impact on him, especially in comparison to how he would be affected if he stopped using the common altogether. What would be best for this villager is if everyone else in the village showed restraint. Then he could continue to use the common as before, with plenty of grass to take care of his cows. He could, in this way, be a free rider on the moderation shown by others. But of course, everyone would like to be a free rider. The result is that none of the villagers modify their behavior, and the common is destroyed.

Rational individuals (and states) will always benefit by being free riders in the short term. If you do the right thing, you lose; you're a sucker. Doing the wrong thing at least keeps you even. In the long term, when you decide to keep yourself even with others, you (and everyone else) still end up worse-off than before. As the common erodes, it becomes less able to sustain those who depend on it.

There is an important and quite general feature to the commons problem—what economist Thomas Schelling called "the tyranny of small decisions." When deciding whether to add another cow to your herd, you are not choosing to destroy a common resource in order to get a little more milk. Faced with that choice, you might refrain. The choice you see is a little more milk in exchange for a little less grass. Good deal. So, commons problems are marked by conflicts between individual and collective interests and between short-term and long-term interests. It is from this tragic dilemma that we must escape.

One approach to the commons problem appeals to the moral side of people and states. It suggests that we should educate the populace about the dangers and social costs of pollution, wanton use of energy and public lands, and the like, and exhort them to exercise moderation as citizens of the world. In theory, if we tell people the right thing to do—and show that if they all adhere to a set of behaviors, the world will be better-off—we can count on them to act morally. But such appeals are unlikely to have a broad-enough influence to do the job. Some people will do the right thing simply because it's the right thing, but many others will not curb their habits, desires, and need for more and better. This is true even within a society that shares at least some values. Globally, a strictly moral appeal is close to a nonstarter (though, as I will suggest at the end of this article, finding a way to moralize the global commons effectively could be quite powerful).

A second approach appeals to our self-interested side, offering incentives for good behavior and punishments for bad. It amounts to using various economic tools to privatize the commons. So nonpolluters and energy conservers get tax breaks. And polluters pay fees for the privilege. President Obama's cap-and-trade plan for reducing greenhouse-gas emissions is a ready example. And we already see this logic in effect domestically on a small scale. Purchasers of inefficient automobiles pay a luxury tax. Tobacco and alcohol are taxed to help defray the social (medical) costs of their use. Permits are sold to regulate the use of parks and beaches. Fees (tolls) are charged for highway use, and they can be scaled so it is almost prohibitively expensive to drive during rush hour. A tax is added to downtown parking to defray costs and improve the quality of mass transit.

Policies like these are designed to reframe the incentives in the relevant situations, making individual interest line up with collective interest. We can choose not to exercise restraint, but only at a price. And the price will be high enough either to induce compliance or to compensate society for profligacy.

This approach is promising. Yet there are better and worse ways to use incentives and restraints to save the global commons. Psychologists have developed insights in recent years about how people make decisions; efforts to change behavior can be made more effective. Some of psychology's lessons can be applied to interactions between states, thereby helping governments better approach negotiations. Others target individuals. Inherent to the global-commons problem is the need not only for behavioral change by states but also by their citizens. Also inherent to the global-commons problem is a need for perhaps-unprecedented international cooperation. Free riders will make addressing global warming extremely difficult. And the developed world already has myriad incentives to continue its excesses. Maintaining GDP growth, securing better resources for their populations, increasing market competitiveness and even controlling national-security-dominating sea-lanes can be extremely important to states—just as important in the short run, perhaps, as conserving resources is in the long run. The developing world will be fast on the developed world's heels, hoping to employ the same abuses to impel its societies onward. The key to success lies in overcoming the tyranny of small decisions.

The commons problem starts at its base as a more sophisticated version of the prisoner's dilemma, an exercise that has been used to model everything from littering to nuclear proliferation. As we know from these exercises in which convicts stay mum or rat out their partners to cut a deal on their sentence, both inmates do better collectively over the long term by cooperating with each other and staying silent. But in any one-shot game, there will be no trust between the two of them and so they will both rat out one another. People often think negotiations about the global commons aren't dominated by the nasty and brutish forces one normally associates with international power politics (or our nation's prisons). After all, goes the argument, the commons involves "softer" security issues and sits so low on the foreign-policy-priority food chain that different tools and techniques are required. But this is not the case. Every one of the psychological strategies for approaching international talks is built on the idea of "cooperating" or "defecting." And whether one is dealing with hard or soft stakes, iterative and cooperative negotiations with clear costs and incentives are the most successful. At all levels of the international-negotiating spectrum, there are situations in which cooperation is possible even though people are vulnerable in the short run to exploitation. . . .

Chances of success are . . . increased if you "start out nice." That is, cooperating. True, cooperators are vulnerable to exploitation, but they open the possibility of a virtuous cycle of mutual cooperation. Defectors are doomed to a vicious cycle of defection. Political scientist Robert Axelrod showed some years ago that the simple strategy of "tit-for-tat"—start out cooperating and from then on, do whatever your partner did on the previous turn—bested all comers in a prisoner's dilemma "tournament." (Actually, it bested all comers but "tit-for-two-tats," an even nicer, more forgiving strategy.) And this was in a situation in which the aim was to win, not to cooperate. The point is that cooperation does work and can be incentivized so it becomes the preferable strategy.

This is not a blindly optimistic set of recommendations, simply relying on all states' better natures. As key in negotiations is the need to punish defection. What Axelrod found is that overly cooperative strategies were vulnerable to exploitation by defectors. And once a defection in tit-for-tat reciprocation begins, it is hard to avoid a vicious cycle.

It is difficult enough to get cooperation from largely law-abiding citizens within a state. In the international sphere with no supranational governing body, the task is almost insurmountable. All the climate-change treaties will continue to be useless without real costs for defections and real incentives for cooperation.

As states enter these negotiating processes, leaders must also beware of "naive realism" and "reactive devaluation." Parties to a conflict tend to think that while they see the issue "objectively," the other side is biased. Stanford psychology professor Lee Ross dubs this psychological characteristic naive realism, and it's not hard to see how it can lead to a negotiating impasse ("We're being so reasonable; why are they so intransigent?"). It is hard to get into a virtuous cycle of cooperation if the parties cannot see the negotiations from the other side's perspective. Because not only do states suffer from naive realism but they tend also to devalue what the other party offers. Suppose, for example, limits on fishing rights in international waters and standards for smokestack emissions are on the table. "We'll pollute less if we can fish more," you offer. "No deal," says your negotiating partner, "you're getting more than you're giving." "OK, then," you say, "we'll fish less if we can pollute more." "No deal," says your negotiating partner, "you're getting more than you're giving." And you, of course, would say the same thing if your partner made either of those offers. We seem to assume that if someone is willing to give something up, it must be worth less than we think it is.

Both naive realism and reactive devaluation are real obstacles to reaching negotiated agreements, and I don't see how we can effectively save the global commons without brokering international accords. Nor do I see a way to eliminate naive realism and reactive devaluation. My hope is that if negotiating partners know about these processes, they will stifle their first impulse to reject offers, understanding that these offers are probably more reasonable than they appear. It would likely help to assume the best rather than the worst at the start of a negotiation, again affirming the need to "start out nice." That way, the other party's offers won't automatically arouse suspicion. And it would help to have colleagues role-play the other side's arguments in advance. If you live with those arguments for a while, you may come to see that the other side of the story is just as reasonable as is yours. Just as perspective-taking is essential in a good friend, a good parent, a good lover, a good teacher or a good doctor, so it is in a good negotiator.

And again, as we're creating these iterative processes not only multi-play but also multi-option games are necessary. It is a truism of negotiation that the more things on the table, the better the parties can do. With more of what you want at stake and what you don't want on offer, the effects of reactive devaluation can be minimized. The way to make a negotiation into a non-zero-sum game is to include items that the parties don't care about equally. If I give in on A–D, he'll give in on E–H. Since I don't care so much about A–D, I'll end up in a better position than that in which I started. Since he doesn't care so much about E–H, so will he. The way to reach a mutually beneficial agreement is for each party to give in on the things that matter more to the other party than they do to him. The more things on the table, the more likely it is that some of them will be valued differently by the various parties. And what is true logically is also true empirically. In MBA-program negotiating exercises, students get higher scores when there are, say, eight items in play than when there are only four. The negotiators—both sides—do better.

But, alas, this recommendation comes with a caveat: what is true logically and empirically is not true psychologically. The participants may do better, but they feel worse, because they leave the negotiation thinking about all the things they gave up. As psychologists Daniel Kahneman and Amos Tversky have captured with "prospect theory" (for which Kahneman was awarded a Nobel Prize in economics), losses hurt more than wins help. "Sure, I gained on items A–D, but I lost on items E–H. Four losses. Disaster!" If each thing you give up hurts more than each thing you acquire, the feeling of loss multiplies more than the feeling of gain does. So you conduct a successful, complex deal and you feel like a failure. All you can think about is what you left on the table.

Why should this matter if, objectively, you actually did better in the complex negotiation than you would have in a simpler one? It matters because whether you participate in further talks depends on how good you feel about the one you just completed. As we know, iterative processes make for better outcomes. If you feel that you failed or were out-negotiated or were exploited, you won't come back for more. So, paradoxically perhaps, the research suggests that you will be more likely to have sustained negotiations if you keep the agendas simple than if you make them complex and multidimensional, so that everyone can "win" something.

Thus we're left at something of an impasse. Complexity means everyone can win, which is good. But it also means that everyone can lose, which, for psychological reasons, is bad. Perhaps the thing to do is not worry so much about the future attitude of negotiators who are stung by what they gave up in the last round. You can always bring in fresh negotiators, who are not carrying that psychological baggage, to the next one. . . .

Without change on the domestic level, international agreements will mean little. And for change to occur at home, people within states must be willing to make sacrifices . . . [which] must be shared in a way that is publicly verifiable because people, like states, care about fairness. They care enough to punish those who exploit power, even at a cost to themselves, as the much-studied "ultimatum game" has shown. In the ultimatum game, one player is given a resource—say $10—to share with another player. The second player can either accept the offer, with each player getting the designated share, or reject it, with each player getting nothing. Of course, a "rational" player in control of the $10 will make a small offer, knowing that the other "rational" player will accept it, since something is better than nothing. But, as we've come to learn, recipients routinely reject small offers even though it makes them worse-off. And the proposers, who know that recipients will reject small offers, in fact make large ones. The most common offer is a fifty-fifty split. So evidence of shared sacrifice is important to satisfy people's sense of justice.

This sacrifice is not impossible to imagine. People are adaptable. They get used to things. If you make them pay more for gas, or make them keep their houses colder in winter and warmer in summer, they'll be angry, but they'll get over it. So the time to demand sacrifice is early in an official's term in office. By the time the official is up for reelection, people will have taken 78-degree thermostat settings in the summer as the new normal.

To ease such behavioral change, much as in international negotiations, tasks should be scaled down to manageable pieces. Nobody is going to save the global commons alone. But each of us can forgo meat a few times a week, fly one less time a year, carry cloth tote bags and so on. These bite-size chunks will make it easier for people to feel like they are doing their part. Though these sorts of small efforts probably cannot be legislated, they make wonderful topics for bully pulpits and examples for opinion leaders to set. The Obama vegetable garden by itself isn't going to change how Americans eat. But many social phenomena are susceptible to what Duke economics and political science professor Timur Kuran describes as "informational cascades." Someone out there who won't take the lead in using cloth bags is almost ready to do so. Just one example will tip that person's behavior. And once there are two adherents, other people, whose "tipping threshold" is a bit higher, will come on board. This will make it easier for others, and so on. Before you know it, plastic grocery bags will have gone the way of the rotary phone.

And in yet another bit of psychological tweaking, we can focus on what will be lost, not what will be gained. Remember prospect theory. Losing $100 makes people feel more than twice as bad as winning $100 makes people feel good. Kahneman and Tversky also showed that it is relatively easy to induce people to think of the same decision as involving gains or losses by manipulating the way in which the decision is framed: we aren't gaining clean drinking water by conserving, we're losing it by polluting; we aren't saving lives by ridding the air we breathe of contaminants, we're killing people by not doing so. . . .

We can see that in all of these cases, it is in some part about reframing these dilemmas to play to people's sense of right and wrong. There is good evidence that moral motives have a stronger hold on people than purely instrumental, economic ones. University of Pennsylvania psychologist Paul Rozin has shown that people who are vegetarians for moral reasons (treatment of animals, profligate use of natural resources) are disgusted, not tempted, by the thought of eating meat. In contrast, those we might call "health vegetarians" remain tempted by those juicy burgers, whether or not they succumb. Similarly, the public attitude toward cigarettes turned on a dime once the effects of secondhand smoke on innocent victims cast smoking in moral terms. No longer were we hesitant to ask someone in a restaurant if he minded blowing his smoke in another direction. We piped right up, full of righteous indignation. Now, we don't even have to venture forth; more and more, smoking in indoor public places is against the law.

I know that moralizing the preservation of the global commons is easier said than done. There is plenty of preaching about the environment already, and it doesn't seem to be doing a good-enough job. Whether it will eventually create a new, widely shared moral norm remains to be seen. My experience with college students leaves me hopeful; for many of them, "steward the earth" has become the eleventh commandment, or replaced one of the original ten. The guiding idea of many students I talk to is roughly that the earth is a treasure, to be protected and nurtured and sustained, and not a "resource" to be used and discarded. If you have an attitude like that, conservation entails no sacrifice; it becomes part of the pleasure of being alive.

Above all, if we're going to save the global commons, as individuals and as a nation, we have to give up the doctrine of American exceptionalism. Ninety percent of people think they are above-average drivers. Ninety-nine percent of newlyweds think they will not be in the 50 percent of married couples who divorce. Eighty-five percent of college professors think they're better than the average teacher. And in international negotiations, the United States always thinks it is better than everyone else—more reasonable, more generous, more concerned with justice. We have to acknowledge that there really is no justification for having an ecological footprint that is three or four times the per capita footprint of other developed countries, and more than ten times the footprint of developing countries. We have to get over ourselves, at least a little bit. . . .

International Cooperation on Climate Change: Numbers, Interests and Institutions

DAVID G. VICTOR

Arild Underdal's exposition on the problems of international cooperation is marked by sparseness and clarity. . . . Underdal's "law of the least ambitious program" [is] a seminal model that explains why so many formal international agreements did little more than codify the interests of laggards.[1] Arild Underdal's "law of the least ambitious program" holds that the effectiveness of an international agreement is limited by the commitment level of the agreement's least interested party. Cooperation schemes ("trade-offs") can be used in theory to entice reluctant parties; in practice, however, these schemes are likely to be difficult to construct and monitor and are thus under-utilized. Actual levels of cooperation will deviate little from the least ambitious. . . .

In this essay I'd like to revisit Underdal's law . . . to suggest ways to improve international cooperation on climate change. The time for new thinking is opportune. The Kyoto Protocol is set to run through 2012, yet negotiations on the form and substance of international commitments for 2013 and beyond have just begun. Although the diplomatic community is talented at painting stiff smiles on their client instruments, the situation with Kyoto does not portend well for the planet. The world's largest emitter, the US, is not a member of the treaty. The second largest emitter, the EU, has joined Kyoto and is making some significant efforts toward compliance, but these barely alter the global trajectory of CO_2 emissions. The third largest emitter, China, is a member but faces no limit on its emissions (which will soon surpass those of the EU).[*] The fourth largest emitter, Russia, is a member only because the treaty condones inaction and offers the prospect of profit from selling surplus emission credits. The fifth largest emitter is Japan, whose interests are similar to those of the EU, but who is struggling to find ways to adjust greenhouse gas emissions. The sixth is India which, like China, has vehemently protested limits on its emissions. . . .

---

[*]Editors' note: As of 2007, China passed the United States as the largest emitter of CO_2.

From David G. Victor, "Toward Effective International Cooperation on Climate Change: Numbers, Interests, and Institutions," *Global Environmental Politics*, 6:3 (August 2006), pp. 90–103. © 2006 by the Massachusetts Institute of Technology. Reprinted by permission of MIT Press Journals. Portions of the text and some footnotes have been omitted.

According to Underdal's law, a treaty negotiated by these emitters (and a host of other countries whose interests are not dissimilar to those of the "big six") will be nearly devoid of substance. That's because the interests of these different countries diverge—some, such as China and Russia have little ambition for effective cooperation. This prediction accurately describes Kyoto's fate; the "commitments" being implemented under Kyoto are, in effect, a non-cooperative outcome. Governments have promised to do what they would have done anyway. The European Union's efforts reflect that some European governments (especially in the Northern countries with active Green parties and publics who are animated by the dangers of a changing climate) are under intense pressure to address the issue even as other Europeans (notably the ten new entrants as well as most of the poorer nations in the south) are not. The developing countries and Russia are focused on development, not controlling emissions, and thus they have consented to participate in an agreement that requires no efforts whose cost is not compensated. And in a few cases (notably Australia and the US), governments misunderstood or misrepresented what they could deliver and made erroneous promises in Kyoto. Those nations realized their false promises in painful ways and have since withdrawn. The United States, under the Bush administration, has withdrawn in a particularly aggressive and unconstructive fashion.

Crafting a more effective climate change response requires returning to fundamentals, and here I briefly address three: the demand for international cooperation; the numbers of countries participating and their interests; and the design of the institutions that aim to promote cooperation. For each a wooly conventional wisdom has arisen, but a closer analysis suggests policy choices that vary considerably. And for each we can look to Arild Underdal in part, to chart a path toward more effective international institutions.

1. THE DEMAND FOR COOPERATION

Every analysis of international cooperation must begin with the question: who wants to cooperate, and why? The conventional wisdom is that global cooperation arises out of the interests shared by all countries, to varying degrees to address the problem of changing climate. Failures to cooperate, therefore, are the result of some "market failure"—for example, the failure of countries to understand their interests, or the transactional difficulties associated with assembling many nations into a cooperative solution. International institutions—such as treaties, organizations, and behavioral norms—aid cooperation by reducing those transaction costs, focusing efforts on particular solutions, creating reputational risks for failure and the like.

The demand for cooperative climate policy, like any matter for international collaboration, should not be conceived in general terms but through the eyes of particular societies and the governments who serve as their agents. This is the standard rationalist assumption that usually holds. The following four aspects of climate damages will affect whether and how nations are likely to mobilize to address the dangers of changing climate.

One aspect of this issue is the increasing capacity of societies to "climate proof" themselves. An ever-smaller fraction of economic activity depends directly on the weather and climate; human capacity to adapt to changing weather, such as by building dikes and irrigation systems, has risen sharply in the last century and shows no sign of exhaustion.[2] The countries that have the greatest capabilities to respond to changing climate and which are also, in general, the largest emitters (at least on a per-capita basis) are also those most proofed against vagaries in the climate.

A second important aspect of what is known about climate effects is that their time horizons are long. Thus the calculation of reluctant developing countries is, perhaps, entirely rational. Combating global warming would require them to incur possibly a substantial cost in controlling emissions today for quite uncertain benefits in the future. By contrast, they could invest the same resources today in development, which automatically will improve their future capacity to adapt if climate should change (while also achieving many other benefits from development). This line of logic is rooted in Wildavsky's famous dictum that "richer is safer."[3]

A third aspect of climate science is that in fact some societies might welcome a dose of new climate—up to a point. The most famous of these is Russia (and more generally the former Soviet Union), where agriculture and forestry—which are the most climate-sensitive of economic activities—probably stand to gain from the longer growing seasons that accompany warmer weather.

The fourth aspect of climate damages is that there is one scenario for changing climate that all countries have an unequivocal interest in avoiding: abrupt (or so-called "catastrophic") climate change, such as would be caused if any of the following were to occur: the sea level were to rise a meter or more over just a few decades; the world's climate were to "flip" to a different regime; warming destabilized large amounts of methane currently locked in the permafrost (which would trigger still more warming, as methane is a strong greenhouse gas); or the ecological integrity of the Amazon or some other huge swath of the world's ecosystems were undermined. Even the most "climate proofed" societies will have a hard time responding to such abrupt change. Natural ecosystems, which societies tend to value even more as they become wealthier, will be particularly vulnerable to extinctions and other catastrophic consequences if the climate changes abruptly. Paleoclimatologists have uncovered evidence for incidents of abrupt climate changes in the past and some models point to such dangers over the next century. This is one of the few ways that risks of climate change could become evaluated in ways that are akin to traditional security threats, and nearly every society has shown that it is willing to spend something (often much) to avert even low probability threats that could have large catastrophic consequences.

These four attributes of the climate problem make it possible to venture some predictions. It seems likely that all societies will be willing to contribute at least marginally to the effort to avoid extreme dangers. However, nobody knows how to chart the thresholds, and societies are likely to vary in their tolerance of risk. For example, as with Russia, Canadian agriculture stands to benefit from a longer growing season. But some Canadians are much more concerned about the risks of unchecked climate change—such as on the country's permafrost region—and thus the country as a whole is now making some effort to control emissions. Political entrepreneurs are discovering that extreme events make for a more compelling political logic for controlling the emissions that cause climate change, and with time and learning an ever-larger amount of political activity on climate change will focus on these scenarios.

For the same reasons, efforts to build an international regime to control climate change on a shared "objective" are likely to fail because countries, in fact, do not have shared assessments of the danger and opportunity. Article 2 of the UNFCCC [United Nations Framework Convention on Climate Change] lays out exactly that objective (it calls for avoiding "dangerous anthropogenic interference in the climate system"), and considerable diplomatic and scientific effort have focused on putting Article 2 into practice. Those efforts are built on an unrealistic vision of politics. In fact, there is a whole range of interests and objectives; the only area where they are likely to coincide is in avoiding obviously extreme scenarios. But those obvious extremes are so distinct in time that they have no meaningful impact on the debate today.

Underdal's pessimistic logic is particularly applicable here because the dispersion of interests partly explains the difficulty of collective action. If some key emitters are unconcerned with all but an extreme change in climate then even those who are more risk-averse will be reluctant to invest in emission controls that could be undone by others whose efforts lag.

2. THE SUPPLY OF COOPERATION: NUMBERS

A second area of misrule by conventional wisdom concerns the architecture of cooperation. Analysts and diplomats have arrived at the conclusion that climate change is best addressed through cooperative processes that are broad in membership. Part of this conventional wisdom rests on the observation that climate change is a global problem and thus requires a global solution. Part rests on the notion that cooperative regimes are best established in broad, nondiscriminatory terms and then deepened with experience. Here, too, the conventional wisdom is incomplete or wrong.

All else equal, cooperative regimes with broad membership are better for global problems than are narrow systems. But the choice of a broad regime carries costs that are so severe that "all else" is never equal. These costs include, notably, the complexity of negotiating package deals among countries whose interests are highly diverse. Complexity probably rises exponentially with membership because each new member creates new nodes in a network of relationships (and thus complications). And leverage over the problem—measured by emissions—saturates quickly as numbers rise. The top six emitters (counting the EU as a single emitter) account for 64% of world emissions of CO_2 from burning fossil fuels; the top dozen are responsible for about 74%. Gaining another ten percent of emissions requires adding another 10 countries. Political scientists haven't worked out a tight, empirically grounded theory to suggest the optimal number of countries to engage. But we do have some theoretical tools that point to the minimum number of countries (or units) that must participate to make collective action rational—the so-called "k group."[4] My hunch is that it is about a dozen—the top ten emitters from burning fossil fuels, plus Brazil and Indonesia (two of the top emitters of CO_2 from changes in land use). At numbers greater than a dozen negotiating complexity will overwhelm the advantages of additional leverage. If engaging fewer than a dozen members, the club will be too exclusive to gain leverage and too exclusive to allow concerns about the disadvantages to competitors. Even with a relatively small group it will be extremely difficult to negotiate a viable package deal—interests vary enormously and so do the starting points. (China's per-capita emissions, for example, are one-tenth that of the US.)

Advocates for broad membership claim that larger numbers are needed, nonetheless, to confer legitimacy on the enterprise, promote shared understanding, and set standards. The legitimacy claim is hardest to test, but the accumulated evidence in other areas of international cooperation suggests it is wrong. The World Trade Organization, notably, has emerged to be the most effective example of global cooperation by focusing, through the original General Agreement on Tariffs and Trade (GATT), on a limited number of countries whose interests (and capabilities) were sufficiently aligned to allow cooperation. Over time, experience and success have allowed deeper and wider cooperation (and also led to negotiations that extend over much longer time periods because they are more complex). Widening and deepening occurred at the same time, rather than in sequential order. The GATT round that ended in the early 1990s with the creation of the WTO has included much more than simply the tariff bindings that were the core of the first GATT agreement. Similarly, the EU emerged from a more focused cooperation (on infrastructures and key commodities such as coal and steel) among a limited number of countries. With experience and the confidence of success the EU has expanded and deepened. The recent expansion to include 10 new countries, and the agenda for talks with Turkey, may test the limits of EU expansion.

In these cases, along with most instances of deep cooperation, the role of "legitimacy" is probably a lot less important than the practical benefits that arise from crafting agreements around the core interests of a smaller number of countries. Avoiding the distraction of peripheral or contrary interests is especially important for the case of climate change because many of the countries that have been centrally involved in the "broad then deep" approach to regime building would be harmed by successful efforts to control emissions—these include major hydrocarbon exporters (e.g., OPEC members, most of whom are members of the UNFCCC and Kyoto), countries wary that successful efforts to control emissions might inspire obligations for them to do the same (e.g., most developing countries), and economies worried that any harm to major consuming markets will hurt their exports (again, notably developing countries). It is possible to craft agreements to accommodate these diverging interests, but such arrangements are complicated and costly to design—as are most diplomatic efforts that deviate from obvious common interest. . . .

3. ORGANIZING COOPERATION: THE ROLE OF INSTITUTIONS

A third area of erroneous conventional wisdom concerns the design of institutions. Here, the common assumption is that legally binding instruments, negotiated within the universal framework of the United Nations, are the best keystones for international cooperation. Much of that conventional wisdom is based on practice: every high profile global environmental problem has been the subject of a global binding treaty and thus, by assumption, treaty instruments must be best.

The evidence for this proposition is scant. . . . Nonbinding agreements are more flexible and less prone to raise concerns about noncompliance, and thus they allow governments to adopt ambitious targets and far-ranging commitments. In contrast, binding agreements are usually crafted through processes dominated by lawyers who are particularly focused on assuring compliance. A binding commitment might be useful for codifying an effort that is already in hand (or which requires actions that are easy for governments to deliver). But uncertain, strenuous efforts at cooperation are easier to organize when the commitments are not formally binding. Non-binding commitments, alone, can be as ineffective as much binding law (or even more so). However, the nonbinding instrument allows for a process through which governments commit to (and implement) more ambitious courses of action. This liberating role for nonbinding instruments usually requires high-level political engagement and special institutions that review and focus on national performance. . . .

Environmental cooperation has been focused on problems that are easy to solve—games of harmony or simple coordination. Environmental cooperation has rarely tackled problems of real collaboration, where self-interested parties defect from the solution that is best for their collective interest, unless they face strong penalties (enforcement) or inducements (compensation) to implement costly measures and sustain the collective effort. Every environmental issue has within it a universe of cooperation games—from harmony cases where interests align, to coordination games where there is a self-enforcing agreement but initial dispute over the best design, to collaboration games where each member cooperates only if it thinks others will as well, to instances of deadlock where no meaningful agreement is possible. For example, the effort to protect wetlands spans from a game of harmony (e.g., governments agree to declare their intention to protect wetlands) to coordination (e.g., governments agree to focus wetland protection efforts on wetlands along bird migration corridors) to deep collaboration (e.g., every government agrees to specific costly measures that, collectively, ensure protection of bird migration routes) to deadlock (e.g., governments agree not to alter wetlands from their natural state and to forfeit one billion dollars in escrow if they don't comply). The global 1971 Ramsar Convention, which is the focus of international legal efforts to protect wetlands, is at the harmony end of the scale. Other regional agreements that affect wetlands, notably in Europe, are examples a bit further along the scale to coordination. Thus for the purposes of political analysis, there isn't a "wetlands" problem but rather many different wetlands problems.

The multiplicity of problem types may explain why treaty registers are filled with so many environmental treaties. As soon as an issue appears on the international agenda, almost immediately an effort is launched to negotiate an agreement. If the treaty-making process were focused on reaching agreements to *solve* the environmental problem at hand then treaty registers would be practically empty. Instead, the negotiation process is a diplomatic effort to identify the problem type that can earn agreement. Since the willingness to pay is often low when negotiations begin and failure to reach agreement yields symbolic costs, the negotiation process usually discovers a way to frame the issue at hand so that the agreement is marked by harmony or simple coordination. Most issues that arrive on the environmental agenda can quickly yield a stable, shallow agreement. My sense is that over the last three decades—from the 1972 Stockholm Conference to the present—the efficiency of this search for shallowness has increased as participants and institutions have learned how to play the game. It has become easier to agree on formats and language because models can be adopted from the scores of precedents. Extant organizations can serve new agreements. Institutionalization has facilitated further institutionalization. This process may also explain why nearly every effort at environmental cooperation now begins with a "framework convention" that is long on vision and procedure but short on commitments. No other area of international cooperation has adopted this kind of process because, perhaps, no other area of cooperation is so focused on ensuring the delivery of symbolic benefits.

It is no surprise, therefore, that many agreements result, participation in those agreements is high, and compliance is nearly perfect. That outcome is a reflection of binding design.

Binding instruments still play an important role—not so much as leaders of action but as codifiers. That, indeed, is one of the ways that binding instruments contributed to the overall effectiveness of the North Sea, Baltic Sea and European acid rain regimes. By this theory, international cooperation emerges through ambitious commitments, efforts, and experiments that are undertaken more readily when agreements are nonbinding. Through those experiments governments gain confidence in what they can deliver and then become more willing to embrace binding commitments. Applied to the case of climate change, the strictest elements of cooperation will emerge from the "bottom up," rooted in experience, rather than being imposed "top down" through commitments whose ambition is realized through binding enforcement. . . .

4. TOWARD A NEW SYNTHESIS

On each of these three fronts—the demand for international cooperation, the numbers of essential countries, and the choice of instruments—conventional wisdom is not well rooted in the actual practice of effective international cooperation. With an eye to conventional wisdom, the advocates who care most about devising effective solutions to the climate problem have, ironically, sent policy astray into schemes and institutions that are neither sustainable nor likely to exert much leverage.

A full solution to this problem . . . will include large-scale research and demonstration of new technologies, since efforts to cut the cost of controlling carbon will make everything else politically easier. It will include some new strategies for engaging developing countries. And it will include some new approaches to international cooperation that draw on the influence of Arild Underdal.

In the area of international cooperation the solutions lie in efforts to create a club of a small number of important countries and craft the elements of serious cooperation. Those efforts probably can't emerge within the UNFCCC process because it is too large and inclusive. Nor can it easily arise from other available forums, such as the G8, because their membership is too skewed to include the core dozen or so countries that must be part of an effective solution. The most interesting idea for a new institution is outgoing Canadian Prime Minister Paul Martin's concept for a forum of leaders from the twenty key countries (L20). Martin has offered a general vision; a series of meetings have applied the concept to major issues in world affairs, including climate change and energy (www.l20.org). Whether by creation of a new institution such as the L20 or reform of an existing forum such as the G8, such a standing body would offer a way to craft deals among the smaller number of countries that matters most. (Even then, 20 may be too large.)

Success with this institution will require careful attention to underlying interests and to the institutions needed for follow-up. A deal that simultaneously involves the advanced industrialized countries and key developing countries must find a way to engage the latter without requiring the politically impossible task of getting them to agree to cap their emissions. My colleagues Tom Heller and P.R. Shukla have offered one solution to the problem—to identify development paths that coincide with the developing countries' interests while also reducing emissions that cause climate change. . . . (Examples include clean natural gas infrastructures in China, which would help the Chinese address local air pollution problems while also cutting by half the emissions of CO_2 when compared with coal.) Success with those schemes should help to change interests and make the wariest nations more willing to control their emissions.

The variable geometry of the L20 (or a reformed G8) can play a large role in overcoming the pessimism of Underdal's law. At the same time, a concerted effort to focus on more effective ways to slow climate change can offer a model that is useful for many other troubling issues in international cooperation.

NOTES

1. Arild Underdal, *The Politics of International Fisheries Management: The Case of the Northeast Atlantic* (New York: Columbia University Press, 1980).
2. J. H. Ausubel, "Does Climate Still Matter?" *Nature*, Vol. 350 (1991), pp. 649–652.
3. Aaron Wildavsky, *Searching for Safety* (New Brunswick, New Jersey: Transaction Books, 1988).
4. Thomas Schelling, *Micromotives and Macrobehavior* (New York: Norton, 1978), Chapter 7.

Exercises for The Global Commons

Apply what you learned in this chapter by using the online resources on MyPoliSciKit (www.mypoliscikit.com).

 Practice Tests

 Videos:
- "Carteret's Climate Refugees"
- "Establishing Carbon Markets"

 Simulation: "Transnational Issues: You Are an Environmental Consultant"

Reading Guides:
- Garrett Hardin, "The Tragedy of the Commons"
- Barry Schwartz, "Tyranny for the Commons Man"
- David G. Victor, "International Cooperation on Climate Change: Numbers, Interests, and Institutions"

GLOBAL GOVERNANCE

The United Nations and International Security

ADAM ROBERTS

In recent years, there has been a remarkable growth in demands for the services of the United Nations (UN) in the field of international security. The 1991 authorized action in Iraq was quickly followed in 1992 by a fivefold increase in the numbers of troops deployed in UN peace-keeping activities and by an increase in the types of roles they perform. At long last, the United Nations seemed to offer the prospect of moving decisively away from the anarchic reliance on force, largely on a unilateral basis, by individual sovereign states. The United Nations has, and will probably continue to have, a far more central role in security issues than it did during the Cold War.

However, the United Nations' multifaceted role in the security field faces a huge array of problems. Almost every difficulty connected with the preparation, deployment, and use of force has re-emerged in a UN context and does not appear to be any easier to address. Excessive demands have been placed on the United Nations, which has been asked to pour the oil of peace-keeping on the troubled waters of a huge number of conflicts, to develop its role in preventing breaches of the peace, and to play a central part in defeating aggression and tackling the after-effects of war. Arms control, too, is embroiled in controversy, with various states—Iraq and North Korea being the clearest examples—challenging what they see as a discriminatory non-proliferation regime. Above all, the increasing role of the United Nations in international security raises two central questions: First, is there a real coherence in the vast array of security activities undertaken by the United Nations? Second, is there a danger that the elemental force of ethnic conflict could defeat the United Nations' efforts? . . .

From Adam Roberts, "The United Nations and International Security," *Survival: The IISS Quarterly,* Vol. 35, No. 2 (Summer 1993), pp. 3–30, copyright © The International Institute for Strategic Studies, reprinted by permission of the author and Taylor & Francis Ltd, (http://www.tandf.co.uk/journals) on behalf of The International Institute for Strategic Studies. Portions of the text have been omitted.

This article advances the following propositions about the United Nations' post–Cold War role in the field of international security:

1. The United Nations has become seriously overloaded with security issues, for good and enduring reasons. The extent to which it can transfer these responsibilities to regional organizations is debatable.
2. Most conflicts in the contemporary world involve an element of civil war or inter-ethnic struggle. They are different in character from those conflicts, essentially interstate, that the United Nations was established to tackle.
3. There is only limited agreement among the major powers about the basis of international security and only a limited shared interest in ensuring that international norms are effectively implemented.
4. The structure of the Security Council, including the system of five veto-wielding permanent members, is in danger of losing its legitimacy. Although a formal change of membership or powers will be very hard to achieve, changes in the Council's procedures and practices may be both desirable and possible.
5. There are some advantages in the practice whereby enforcement has taken the form of authorized military action by groups of states, rather than coming under direct UN command as a literal reading of the UN Charter would suggest. . . .
6. Although the United Nations' role is increasing, basic questions about collective security remain. There is no prospect of a general system of collective security supplanting existing strategic arrangements.

These propositions . . . are in no way intended as criticism of the increased emphasis given to the United Nations and its role in the foreign policies of many states. Rather, they constitute a plea for the sober assessment of both the merits and defects of an increased role, as well as for constructive thinking about some of the difficult issues it poses, and a caution against the hasty abandonment of some still-valuable aspects of traditional approaches to international relations.

THE OVERLOAD PROBLEM

. . . Reasons for such a heavy demand to deal with wars, civil strife, and other crises are numerous and persuasive. Whatever difficulties the United Nations may face in the coming years, these reasons will not suddenly disappear. Three stand out. First, the impressive record of the United Nations in the years 1987–92 has raised expectations. The United Nations has contributed to the settlement of numerous regional conflicts, including the Iran–Iraq War, the South African presence in Namibia, the Soviet presence in Afghanistan, and the Vietnamese presence in Cambodia. It provided a framework for the expulsion of Iraq from Kuwait. Second, given a choice, states contemplating the use of force beyond their borders often prefer to do it in a multilateral, especially UN, context. A multilateral approach helps neutralize domestic political opposition, increases the opportunity that operations have limited and legitimate goals, and reduces the risk of large-scale force being used by adversaries or rival powers. Third, the United Nations has some notable advantages over regional organizations in tackling security problems: It is universal; it has a reputation, even if it is now under threat, for impartiality; and it has a more clear set of arrangements for making decisions on security issues than do most regional organizations, including even the North Atlantic Treaty Organization (NATO). . . .

Recognizing that the United Nations is seriously overloaded, much thought has been given to the question of cooperation with regional security organizations. . . . The idea that the United Nations and regional institutions could share responsibility for security seems to be emerging, albeit hesitantly, in Europe. The proliferation of European bodies with responsibilities in the security field is notorious: The Conference on Security and Cooperation in Europe (CSCE), NATO, the European Community (EC), the Western European Union (WEU), and the North Atlantic Cooperation Council (NACC) all play roles of varying importance. . . . Despite such developments, enlarging the international security role of regional organizations is easier said than done. These organizations have a bewildering variety of purposes and memberships, and they often have great difficulty in reaching decisions and in taking action. Many regional bodies are seen as too partial to one side. Moreover, it is often far from self-evident which regional body should have the principal role in addressing a given problem. The United Nations has often encouraged regional bodies to handle crises only to find that important aspects of the problems remained within its own domain.

THE CHANGING CHARACTER OF CONFLICT

Many of the conflicts in the contemporary world have a very different character from those that the United Nations was designed to address. Above all, those who framed the UN Charter had in mind the problem of international war, waged by well-organized states. This reflected the view, still common today, that aggression and international war constitute the supreme problem of international relations. Although the problem of interstate war has by no means disappeared, for many, civil war—whether internationalized or not—has always represented the deadlier threat. Some of the twentieth century's principal political philosophies have underestimated the significance of ethnicity, however defined, as a powerful political force and source of conflict; this is now changing through the pressure of events. . . .

In the overwhelming majority of UN Security Council operations today, there is a strong element of civil war and communal conflict. For the United Nations, involvement in such a conflict is hardly new, as the long-standing and continuing problems of Palestine/Israel and Cyprus bear witness. The collapse of large multinational states and empires almost always causes severe dislocations, including the emergence or re-emergence of ethnic, religious, regional, and other animosities. The absence of fully legitimate political systems, traditions, regimes, and state frontiers all increase the likelihood that a narrowly ethnic definition of "nations" prevails. These difficulties are compounded by the fact that, for the most part, the geographical distribution of populations is so messy that the harmonious realization of national self-determination is impossible. Conflict-ridden parts of the former Yugoslavia and the former Soviet Union are merely the two most conspicuous contemporary examples of imperial collapse leading to inter-ethnic war. In both cases, the taboo against changing old "colonial" frontiers has been undermined much more quickly and seriously than occurred in post-colonial states in Africa and elsewhere in the decades following European decolonization. . . . It is by no means impossible that internal conflicts could drag the United Nations down; its inability to prevent a resumption of war in Angola following the September 1992 elections is an ominous indicator of this type of hazard.

Internal conflicts, especially those with a communal or ethnic dimension, present special risks for international engagement, whether in the form of mediation, peace-keeping, or forceful military intervention. First, internal conflicts tend to be "nasty, brutish, and long," and they leave communities with deep and enduring mutual suspicions based on traumatic experiences and continuing proximity. Intervention requires a willingness to stay what may be a very long course. Second, internal conflicts are typically conducted under the leadership of non-governmental or semi-governmental entities, which may see great advantages in the degree of recognition involved in negotiating with UN representatives and yet be unwilling or unable to carry out the terms of agreements. Third, internal conflicts typically involve the use of force directed against the civilian populations, thus becoming especially bitter and posing difficult problems related to the protection of dispersed and vulnerable civilians. Fourth, internal conflicts are often conducted with small weapons: rifles, knives and the arsonist's match. It is very difficult to control the use of such weaponry by bombing, arms embargoes, or formal methods of arms control. Finally, in cases such as these, there is frequently no territorial *status quo ante* to which to return. Cease-fires and other agreements are vulnerable to the charge that they legitimize the use of force and that they create impossibly complicated "leopard-spot" territorial arrangements, based on ethnic territorial units that are small and separated and, thus, difficult to defend. . . .

Communal and ethnic conflicts raise awkward issues about the criteria used in recognizing political entities as states and in favoring their admission to the United Nations. When the United Nations admits member-states, it is in fact conferring a particularly important form of recognition, and it is also implicitly underwriting the inviolability of their frontiers. Yet, the United Nations does not appear to be taking sufficient account of traditional criteria for recognition, which include careful consideration of whether a state really exists and coheres as a political and social entity. Many European states also forgot these traditional criteria in some of their recent acts of recognition, many of which did not involve setting up diplomatic missions. If the results of recognition are risky security commitments to purported states that never really attained internal cohesion, public support for UN action may be weakened.

Such conflicts also raise issues about the appropriateness of certain principles derived from interstate relations, including the principle that changing frontiers by force can never be accepted. This principle, which is very important in contemporary international relations, has been frequently reiterated by the international community in connection with the Yugoslav crisis. A successful armed grab for territory on largely ethnic grounds would indeed set a deeply worrying precedent. Yet, it must be asked whether it is wise to express this legal principle so forcefully in circumstances in which existing "frontiers" have no physical existence, in which they lack both logic and legitimacy, in which there are such deep-seated ethnic problems, and in which almost any imaginable outcome will involve recognition of the consequences of frontier violations.

LIMITED HARMONY AMONG THE MAJOR POWERS

. . . It is undeniable, and very welcome, that there is more agreement among states about international security issues now than there was during the Cold War. However, there remain fundamental differences of both interest and perception. These may not be enough to prevent the Security Council from reaching decisions on key issues, but they can frustrate efforts to turn decisions into actions in fast-changing situations. . . .

Differences of interest amongst states are complemented by differences in perceptions about the fundamental nature of world politics. Depending largely on their different historical experiences, some states view colonial domination and imperialism as the most serious problems in international relations; others see civil war as the most dangerous threat to international security; yet others view aggressive conquest and international war as the central problems.

Such serious differences of perception and interest are, of course, reflected in the proceedings of the UN Security Council. One should not necessarily expect relations among major powers to be good, and there may be perfectly valid reasons why countries perceive major security problems differently. [For example,] China's world-view, although undergoing important changes, retains distinctive elements—including a fear of foreign subversion, a strong belief in state sovereignty, and some identification with developing states—which could set it against other Security Council members.

THE PROBLEMATIC STRUCTURE OF THE SECURITY COUNCIL

. . . If the United Nations is indeed to have an enlarged role in security affairs, its system of decision-making must be seen to be legitimate.

The powers of the Security Council are, in theory, very extensive: "The Members of the United Nations agree to accept and carry out the decisions of the Security Council in accordance with the present Charter." In practice, the Security Council cannot impose its will on the membership in the way this statement implies and, despite the absence of any system of formal constitutional challenge, there is no sign of the emergence of a doctrine even hinting at the infallibility of UN Security Council pronouncements. However, these limitations on the power of the Security Council do not mean that states, having successfully retained considerable sovereign powers in security matters, see the existing arrangements as satisfactory.

The criticisms of the composition of the Security Council involve several elements: doubt about preserving unaltered, half a century later, the special position of those countries that were allies in the Second World War; concern that three of those powers—France, Britain, and the United States—make most of the agenda-setting decisions in running the Security Council; irritation, especially on the part of Germany and Japan, about "taxation without representation," and frustration that the views of the non-permanent members of the Security Council, and indeed of the great majority of the 181-strong General Assembly, count for little. These criticisms could become much more serious if events take such a turn that they coincide with a perception that the Security Council has made serious misjudgments on central issues. . . .

In the history of the United Nations, much more has been achieved by changes in practice, rather than Charter revision. More thought will have to be given to how the Security Council might develop its procedures and practices: for example, by strengthening the selection of non-permanent members to reflect their contributions to the United Nations' work and developing more regular Security Council consultation with major states and interested parties. Such changes, although difficult to implement, might go at least some way towards meeting the strong concerns of certain states about being left out of decisions that affect them vitally.

THE PROBLEM OF ORGANIZING ENFORCEMENT ACTIONS

The issue of organizing enforcement actions is central to almost every discussion of the United Nations' future role. It brings out the conflict between "Charter fundamentalists," who would like such actions to be organized precisely in accord with the UN Charter, and those with a "common law" approach, who believe the most important guide is UN practice.

Three times in the UN era, major military action authorized by the United Nations has been under US, not UN, command: in Korea in 1950–53, Iraq in 1990–91, and Somalia in 1992–93. These episodes suggest the emergence of a system in which the United Nations authorizes military actions, which are then placed under the control of a state or group of states. There are important advantages to such an arrangement. First, it reflects the reality that not all states feel equally involved in every enforcement action. Moreover, military actions require extremely close coordination between intelligence-gathering and operations, a smoothly functioning decision-making machine, and forces with some experience of working together to perform dangerous and complex tasks. These things are more likely to be achieved through existing national armed forces, alliances, and military relationships, than they are within the structure of a UN command. As habits of cooperation between armed forces develop, and as the United Nations itself grows, the scope for action under direct UN command may increase, but this will inevitably be a slow process. . . .

Experience seems to show that mobilizing for collective security only works when one power takes the lead. However, as a result of the effort, that same power may be reluctant to continue assuming the entire burden of collective security. After the Korean War, the United States tried to set up regional alliances to reduce its direct military obligation. After the 1991 Gulf War, the United States was manifestly reluctant to get entangled in Iraq and to underwrite all security arrangements in the area. . . . The issue of UN versus authorized national command arises in non-enforcement connections as well. As UN-controlled peace-keeping forces become involved in more complex missions, in which neat distinctions between peace-keeping and enforcement are eroded, the adequacy of the United Nations' existing machinery for controlling complex operations in distant countries is increasingly called into question. . . .

PROSPECTS FOR COLLECTIVE SECURITY

Is it possible to say that out of the rubble of the Cold War a system of collective security is emerging? . . . The term "collective security" normally refers to a system in which each state in the system accepts that the security of one is the concern of all and agrees to join in a collective response to aggression. In this sense, it is distinct from collective defense or alliance systems, in which groups of states ally with each other, principally against possible external threats.

"Collective security" proposals have been in circulation since the beginning of the modern states system and were indeed aired at the negotiations that led to the 1648 Peace of Westphalia. The attractive theory of collective security, when tested against some basic questions, often reveals some fundamental flaws.

Whose collective security? There is always a risk that a collective security system will be seen as protecting only certain countries or interests or as privileging certain principles at the expense of others. Some countries may, for whatever reason, feel excluded from its benefits or threatened by it. The anxieties expressed by some countries in the developing world regarding the concept of the "New World Order," while they have not yet crystallized into definite opposition to any specific UN action, are evidence of concern on this point.

Can there be consistent responses to security problems? Although the UN system is the first truly global international system and although it involves the subscription of virtually all countries in the world to a common set of principles, it is not yet evident that the same principles and practices could or should be applied consistently to different problems, countries, and regions. Difficulties can arise both from the consistent application of principles to situations that are fundamentally different and from the inconsistent application of principles. It is also not yet apparent that collective security can operate as effectively for East Timor or Tibet as for Kuwait. The widespread perception that Israel has successfully defied UN Security Council resolutions while other states have not, although arguably facile in certain respects, illustrates the explosiveness of emerging accusations of "double standards" at the United Nations. The political price of apparent inconsistency could be high.

Against which types of threat is a system of collective security intended to operate? There is no agreement that collective security should apply equally to the following: massive aggression and annexation; cross-border incursions; environmental despoliation; acts of terrorism; human rights violations within a state; communal and ethnic conflict; and the collapse of state structures under assault from internal opposition. In 1990–91, many people argued that it was the particularly flagrant nature of the Iraqi invasion, occupation, and annexation of Kuwait that justified the coalition's response; even then, the international military response was far from unanimous. The fact that this argument was so widely used underlines the point that in cases in which aggression is not so blatant, it might be much harder to secure an international military response; a state caught up in such a conflict might have to look after its own interests. Since 1991, inspired partly by the establishment of "safe havens" in northern Iraq and partly by a trend of opinion, admittedly far from universal, in favor of democracy, there has been some increased advocacy, not least in France and the United States, of a right of intervention in states even in the absence of a formal invitation. This remains a deeply contentious issue and serves as a useful reminder that the ends towards which collective security efforts might be directed are not fixed.

How collective does enforcement have to be? Is complete unanimity impossible to attain, especially in the case of military action? Is there still space for some states to be neutral? In practice, there has never been, on the global level, a truly "collective" case (let alone system) of collective security. In the Gulf crisis of 1990–91, the key UN Security Council resolution avoided the call for all states to take military action. Instead, it merely authorized "member-states co-operating with the Government of Kuwait" to use "all necessary means" to implement relevant UN resolutions. This implied that it was still legitimate for a state to have a status of neutrality or non-belligerency in this conflict. It marked an interesting and realistic interpretation of some optimistic provisions in Chapter VII of the UN Charter.

How can a system of collective security actively deter a particular threat to a particular country? In the wake of the 1991 Gulf War, there was much discussion as to possible means by which, in the future, invasions could be deterred before disaster struck. . . . Following a unanimous Security Council decision of 11 December 1992, the idea was implemented by the United Nations for the first time in Macedonia. Ironically, a state that until April 1993 remained a non-member was thus receiving protection from a state, Yugoslavia, that was still, for most practical purposes, a UN member. Despite remarkable progress, the idea of "preventive deployment" is fraught with difficulty. There is the risk that large numbers of states would request it, that it would be insufficient to discourage aggression, and that it might be used by a government as an alternative to providing for its own defense. It should not, however, be taken for granted that military deployments are absolutely essential. There may also be some residual deterrent value in the lessons of Korea (1950–53) and Kuwait (1990–91); twice, under UN auspices, the United States has led coalitions that have gone to the defense of invaded states to which the United States was not bound by formal alliance commitments and in which it had no troops deployed at the time. This curious fact may not be entirely lost on would-be aggressors. Yet, there are bound to be cases in which some kinds of preventive UN deployments, of which Macedonia is a harbinger, are considered necessary.

Who pays for collective security? The question of burden-sharing in international security matters is notoriously complex, as shown by the experience of NATO, of UN peace-keeping, and of the US-led operations in the 1990–91 Gulf crisis. In 1992, the annual cost of UN peace-keeping activities was the highest ever—about $2.8 billion. Unpaid contributions towards UN peace-keeping operations in September 1992 stood at $844 million, but by the beginning of 1993, this figure was reduced to about $670 million. States have responded well to the increased costs of peace-keeping. However, if more UN peace-keeping (or other) operations go badly, there could be added difficulty in securing payment. Even if they do not, there are problems to be addressed. During the US presidential campaign, Bill Clinton, while indicating that he would act on payment of the US debt to the United Nations, repeatedly called for new agreements for sharing the costs of maintaining peace and suggested that the US apportionment of UN peace-keeping costs be reduced from 30.4% to 25%. The extraordinary paradox of the country most deeply involved in military support for an international organization being simultaneously its major (though steadily repaying) defaulter is yet one more illustration of the gulf between the theory of collective security and its practice.

Globalization and Governance

KENNETH N. WALTZ

In 1979 I described the interdependence of states as low but increasing. It has increased, but only to about the 1910 level if measured by trade or capital flows as a percentage of GNP; lower if measured by the mobility of labor, and lower still if measured by the mutual military dependence of states. Yet one feels that the world has become a smaller one. International travel has become faster, easier, and cheaper; music, art, cuisines, and cinema have all become cosmopolitan in the world's major centers and beyond. The *Peony Pavilion* was produced in its entirety for the first time in 400 years, and it was presented not in Shanghai or Beijing, but in New York. Communication is almost instantaneous, and more than words can be transmitted, which makes the reduced mobility of labor of less consequence. High-technology jobs can be brought to the workers instead of the workers to the jobs; foreigners can become part of American design teams without leaving their homelands. Before World War I, the close interdependence of states was thought of as heralding an era of peace among nations and democracy and prosperity within them. Associating interdependence, peace, democracy, and prosperity is nothing new. In his much translated and widely read book, *The Great Illusion* (1933), Norman Angell summed up the texts of generations of classical and neoclassical economists and drew from them the dramatic conclusion that wars would no longer be fought because they would not pay. World War I instead produced the great disillusion, which reduced political optimism to a level that remained low almost until the end of the Cold War. I say "almost" because beginning in the 1970s a new optimism, strikingly similar in content to the old, began to resurface. Interdependence was again associated with peace and peace increasingly with democracy, which began to spread wonderfully to Latin America, to Asia, and with the Soviet Union's collapse, to Eastern Europe. Francis Fukuyama (1992) foresaw a time when all states would be liberal democracies and, more recently, Michael Doyle (1997) projected the year for it to happen as lying between 2050 and 2100. John Mueller (1989), heralding the disappearance of war among the world's advanced countries, argued that Norman Angell's premises were right all along, but that he had published his book prematurely.

Robert Keohane and Joseph Nye in their 1977 book, *Power and Interdependence,* strengthened the notion that interdependence promotes peace and limits the use of force by arguing that simple interdependence had become complex interdependence, binding the economic and hence the political interests of states ever more tightly together. Now, we hear from many sides that interdependence has reached yet another height, transcending states and making *The Borderless World*, which is the title and theme of Kenichi Ohmae's 1990 book. People, firms, markets matter more; states matter less. Each tightening of the economic screw raises the benefits of economic exchange and makes war among the more advanced states increasingly costly. The simple and plausible propositions are that as the benefits of peace rise, so do the costs of war. When states perceive wars to be immensely costly, they will be disinclined to fight them. War becomes rare, but is not abolished because even the strongest economic forces cannot conquer fear or eliminate concern for national honor (Friedman 1999, 196–97).

Economic interests become so strong that markets begin to replace politics at home and abroad. That economics depresses politics and limits its significance is taken to be a happy thought. The first section of this paper examines its application domestically; the second, internationally.

THE STATE OF THE STATE

Globalization is the fad of the 1990s, and globalization is made in America. Thomas Friedman's *The Lexus and the Olive Tree* is a celebration of the American way, of market capitalism and liberal democracy. Free markets, transparency, and flexibility are the watchwords. The "electronic herd" moves vast amounts of capital in and out of countries according to their political and economic merits. Capital moves almost instantaneously into countries with stable governments, progressive economies, open accounting, and honest dealing, and out of countries lacking those qualities. States can defy the "herd," but they will pay a price, usually a steep one, as did Thailand, Malaysia, Indonesia, and South Korea in the 1990s. Some countries may defy the herd inadvertently (the countries just mentioned); others, out of ideological conviction (Cuba and North Korea); some, because they can afford to (oil-rich countries); others, because history has passed them by (many African countries).

Countries wishing to attract capital and to gain the benefits of today's and tomorrow's technology have to don the "golden straitjacket," a package of policies including balanced budgets, economic deregulation, openness to investment and trade, and a stable currency. The herd decides which countries to reward and which to punish, and nothing can be done about its decisions. In September 1997, at a World Bank meeting, Malaysia's prime minister, Dr. Mahathir Mohammad, complained bitterly that great powers and international speculators had forced Asian countries to open their markets and had manipulated their currencies in order to destroy them. Friedman (1999, 93) wonders what Robert Rubin, then-U.S. treasury secretary, might have said in response. He imagines it would have been something like this: "What planet are you living on? . . . Globalization isn't a choice, it's a reality, . . . and the only way you can grow at the speed that your people want to grow is by tapping into the global stock and bond markets, by seeking out multinationals to invest in your country, and by selling into the global trading system what your factories produce. And the most basic truth about globalization is this: *No one is in charge.*"

The herd has no telephone number. When the herd decides to withdraw capital from a country, there is no one to complain to or to petition for relief. Decisions of the herd are collective ones. They are not made; they happen, and they happen because many investors individually make decisions simultaneously and on similar grounds to invest or to withdraw their funds. Do what displeases the herd, and it will trample you into the ground. Globalization is shaped by markets, not by governments.

Globalization means homogenization. Prices, products, wages, wealth, and rates of interest and profit tend to become the same all over the world. Like any powerful movement for change, globalization encounters resistance—in America, from religious fundamentalists; abroad, from anti-Americanists; everywhere from cultural traditionalists. And the resisters become bitter because consciously or not they know they are doomed. Driven by technology, international finance sweeps all before it. Under the protection of American military power, globalization proceeds relentlessly. As Friedman proclaims: "America truly is the ultimate benign hegemony" (375).

The "end of the Cold War and the collapse of communism have discredited all models other than liberal democracy." The statement is by Larry Diamond, and Friedman repeats it with approval. There is one best way, and America has found it. "It's a post-industrial world, and America today is good at everything that is post-industrial" (145, 303). The herd does not care about forms of government as such, but it values and rewards "stability, predictability, transparency, and the ability to transfer and protect its private property." Liberal democracies represent the one best way. The message to all governments is clear: Conform or suffer.

There is much in what Friedman says, and he says it very well. But how much? And, specifically, what is the effect of closer interdependence on the conduct of the internal and external affairs of nations?

First, we should ask how far globalization has proceeded? As everyone knows, much of the world has been left aside: most of Africa and Latin America, Russia, all of the Middle East except Israel, and large parts of Asia. Moreover, for many countries, the degree of participation in the global economy varies by region. Northern Italy, for example, is in; southern Italy is out. In fact, globalization is not global but is mainly limited to northern latitudes. Linda Weiss points out that, as of 1991, 81% of the world stock of foreign direct investment was in high-wage countries of the north: mainly the United States, followed by the United Kingdom, Germany, and Canada. She adds that the extent of concentration has grown by 12 points since 1967 (Weiss 1998; cf., Hirst and Thompson 1996, 72).

Second, we should compare the interdependence of nations now with interdependence earlier. The first paragraph of this paper suggests that in most ways we have not exceeded levels reached in 1910. The rapid growth of international trade and investment from the middle 1850s into the 1910s preceded a prolonged period of war, internal revolution, and national insularity. After World War II, protection-ist policies lingered as the United States opened its borders to trade while taking a relaxed attitude toward countries that protected their markets during the years of recovery from war's devastation. One might say that from 1914 into the 1960s an interdependence deficit developed, which helps to explain the steady growth of interdependence thereafter. Among the richest 24 industrial economies (the OECD countries), exports grew at about twice the rate of GDP after 1960. In 1960, exports were 9.5% of their GDPs; in 1900, 20.5% (Wade 1996, 62; cf., Weiss 1998, 171). Finding that 1999 approximately equals 1910 in extent of interdepend-ence is hardly surprising. What is true of trade also holds for capital flows, again as a percentage of GDP (Hirst and Thompson 1996, 36).

Third, money markets may be the only economic sector one can say has become truly global. Finance capital moves freely across the frontiers of OECD countries and quite freely elsewhere (Weiss 1998, xii). Robert Wade notes that real interest rates within northern countries and between northern and southern coun-tries vary by no more than 5%. This seems quite large until one notices variations across countries of 10 to 50 times in real wages, years of schooling, and numbers of working scientists. Still, with the movement of financial assets as with commodi-ties, the present remains like the past. Despite today's ease of communication, financial markets at the turn of the previous century were at least as integrated as they are now (Wade 1996, 73–75).

Obviously, the world is not one. Sadly, the disparities of the North and South remain wide. Perhaps surprisingly, among the countries that are thought of as being in the zone of globalization, differences are considerable and persistent. To take just one example, financial patterns differ markedly across countries. The United States depends on capital imports, Western Europe does not, and Japan is a major capital exporter. The more closely one looks, the more one finds varia-tions. That is hardly surprising. What looks smooth, uniform, and simple from a distance, on closer inspection proves to be pockmarked, variegated, and complex. Yet here, the variations are large enough to sustain the conclusion that globaliza-tion, even within its zone, is not a statement about the present, but a prediction about the future.

Many globalizers underestimate the extent to which the new looks like the old. In any competitive system the winners are imitated by the losers, or they continue to lose. In political as in economic development, latecomers imitate the practices and adopt the institution of the countries who have shown the way. Occasionally, someone finds a way to outflank, to invent a new way, or to ingeniously modify an old way to gain an advantage; and then the process of imitation begins anew. That competitors begin to look like one another if the competition is close and continu-ous is a familiar story. Competition among states has always led some of them to imitate others politically, militarily, and economically; but the apostles of globaliza-tion argue that the process has now sped up immensely and that the straitjacket allows little room to wiggle. In the old political era, the strong vanquished the weak; in the new economic era, "the fast eat the slow" (Klaus Schwab quoted in Friedman 1999, 171). No longer is it "Do what the strong party says or risk physical punishment"; but instead "Do what the electronic herd requires or remain impoverished." But then, in a competitive system there are always winners and losers. A few do exceptionally well, some get along, and many bring up the rear.

States have to conform to the ways of the more successful among them or pay a stiff price for not doing so. We then have to ask what is the state of the state? What becomes of politics within the coils of encompassing economic processes? The message of globalizers is that economic and technological forces impose near uniformity of political and economic forms and functions on states. They do so because the herd is attracted only to countries with reliable, stable, and open governments—that is, to liberal democratic ones.

Yet a glance at just the past 75 years reveals that a variety of political-economic systems have produced impressive results and were admired in their day for doing so. In the 1930s and again in the 1950s, the Soviet Union's economic growth rates were among the world's highest, so impressive in the '50s that America feared being overtaken and passed by. In the 1960s President Kennedy got "the country moving again," and America's radically different system gained world respect. In the '70s, Western European welfare states with managed and directed economics were highly regarded. In the late '70s and through much of the '80s, the Japanese brand of neomercantilism was thought to be the wave of the future; and Western Europe and the United States worried about being able to keep up. Imitate or perish was the counsel of some; pry the Japanese economy open and make it compete on our grounds was the message of others. America did not succeed in doing much of either. Yet in the 1990s, its economy has flourished. Globalizers offer it as the ultimate political-economic model—and so history again comes to an end. Yet it is odd to conclude from a decade's experience that the one best model has at last appeared. Globalization, if it were realized, would mean a near uniformity of conditions across countries. Even in the 1990s, one finds little evidence of globalization. The advanced countries of the world have enjoyed or suffered quite different fates. Major Western European countries were plagued by high and persistent unemployment; Northeast and Southeast Asian countries experienced economic stagnation or collapse while China continued to do quite well; and we know about the United States.

Variation in the fortunes of nations underlines the point: The country that has done best, at least lately, is the United States. Those who have fared poorly have supposedly done so because they have failed to conform to the American Way. Globalizers do not claim that globalization is complete, but only that it is in process and that the process is irreversible. Some evidence supports the conclusion; some does not. Looking at the big picture, one notices that nations whose economies have faltered or failed have been more fully controlled, directed, and supported governmentally than the American economy. Soviet-style economies failed miserably; in China, only the free-market sector flourishes; the once much-favored Swedish model has proved wanting. One can easily add more examples. From them it is tempting to leap to the conclusion that America has indeed found, or stumbled onto, the one best way.

Obviously, Thomas Friedman thinks so. Tip O'Neill, when he was a congressman from Massachusetts, declared that all politics are local. Wrong, Friedman says, all politics have become global. "The electronic herd," he writes, "turns the whole world into a parliamentary system, in which every government lives under the fear of a no-confidence vote from the herd" (1999, 62, 115).

I find it hard to believe that economic processes direct or determine a nation's policies, that spontaneously arrived-at decisions about where to place resources reward or punish a national economy so strongly that a government either does what pleases the "herd" or its economy fails to prosper or even risks collapse. We all recall recent cases, some of them mentioned above, that seem to support Friedman's thesis. Mentioning them both makes a point and raises doubts.

First, within advanced countries at similar levels of development that are closely interrelated, one expects uniformities of form and function to be most fully displayed. Yet Stephen Woolcock, looking at forms of corporate governance within the European community, finds a "spectrum of approaches" and expects it to persist for the foreseeable future (1996, 196). Since the 1950s, the economies of Germany and France have grown more closely together as each became the principal trading partner of the other. Yet a study of the two countries concludes that France has copied German policies but has been unwilling or unable to copy institutions (Boltho 1996). GDP per work hour among seven of the most prosperous countries came close together between the 1950s and the 1980s (Boyer 1996, 37). Countries at a high level of development do tend to converge in productivity, but that is something of a tautology.

Second, even if all politics have become global, economies remain local perhaps to a surprising extent. Countries with large economies continue to do most of their business at home. Americans produce 88% of the goods they buy. Sectors that are scarcely involved in international trade, such as government, construction, nonprofit organizations, utilities, and wholesale and retail trade employ 82% of Americans (Lawrence 1997, 21). As Paul Krugman says, "The United States is still almost 90% an economy that produces goods and services for its own use" (1997, 166). For the world's three largest economies—the United States, Japan, and the European Union—taken as a unit, exports are 12% or less of GDP (Weiss 1998, 176). What I found to be true in 1970 remains true today: The world is less interdependent than is usually supposed (Waltz 1970). Moreover, developed countries, oil imports aside, do the bulk of their external business with one another, and that means that the extent of their dependence on commodities that they could not produce for themselves is further reduced.

Reinforcing the parochial pattern of productivity, the famous footloose corporations in fact turn out to be firmly anchored in their home bases. One study of the world's 100 largest corporations concludes that not one of them could be called truly "global" or "footloose." Another study found one multinational corporation that seemed to be leaving its home base: Britain's chemical company, ICI (Weiss 1998, 18, 22; cf., Hirst and Thompson 1996, 82–93, 90, 95ff.). On all the important counts—location of most assets, site of research and development, ownership, and management—the importance of a corporation's home base is marked. And the technological prowess of corporations corresponds closely to that of the countries in which they are located.

Third, the *"transformative capacity"* of states, as Linda Weiss emphasizes, is the key to their success in the world economy (Weiss 1998, xii). Because technological innovation is rapid, and because economic conditions at home and abroad change often, states that adapt easily have considerable advantages. International politics remains inter-national. As the title of a review by William H. McNeill (1997) puts it, "Territorial States Buried Too Soon." Global or world politics has not taken over from national politics. The twentieth century was the century of the nation-state. The twenty-first will be too. Trade and technology do not determine a single best way to organize a polity and its economy. National systems display a great deal of resilience. States still have a wide range of choice. Most states survive, and the units that survive in competitive systems are those with the ability to adapt. Some do it well, and they grow and prosper. Others just manage to get along. That's the way it is in competitive systems. In this spirit, Ezra Taft Benson, when he was President Eisenhower's secretary of agriculture, gave this kindly advice to America's small farmers: "Get big or get out." Success in competitive systems requires the units of the system to adopt ways they would prefer to avoid.

States adapt to their environment. Some are light afoot, and others are heavy. The United States looked to be heavy afoot in the 1980s when Japan's economy was booming. Sometimes it seemed that MITI (Ministry of International Trade and Industry) was manned by geniuses who guided Japan's economy effortlessly to its impressive accomplishments. Now it is the United States that appears light afoot, lighter than any other country. Its government is open: Accurate financial information flows freely, most economic decisions are made by private firms. These are the characteristics that make for flexibility and for quick adaptation to changing conditions.

Competitive systems select for success. Over time, the qualities that make for success vary. Students of American government point out that one of the advantages of a federal system is that the separate states can act as laboratories for social-economic experimentation. When some states succeed, others may imitate them. The same thought applies to nations. One must wonder who the next winner will be.

States adapt; they also protect themselves. Different nations, with distinct institutions and traditions, protect themselves in different ways. Japan fosters industries, defends them, and manages its trade. The United States uses its political, economic, and military leverage to protect itself and manipulate international events to promote its interests. Thus, as David E. Spiro elaborately shows, international markets and institutions did not recycle petrodollars after 1974. The United States did. Despite many statements to the contrary, the United States worked effectively through different administrations and under different cabinet secretaries to undermine markets and thwart international institutions. Its leverage enabled it to manipulate the oil crisis to serve its own interests (1999, chap. 6).

Many of the interdependers of the 1970s expected the state to wither and fade away. Charles Kindleberger wrote in 1969 that "the nation-state is just about through as an economic unit" (207). Globalizers of the 1990s believe that this time it really is happening. The state has lost its "monopoly over internal sovereignty," Wolfgang H. Reinecke writes, and as "an externally sovereign actor" it "will become a thing of the past" (1997, 137; cf., Thurow 1999). Internally, the state's monopoly has never been complete, but it seems more nearly so now than earlier, at least in well-established states. The range of governmental functions and the extent of state control over society and economy has seldom been fuller than it is now. In many parts of the world the concern has been not with the state's diminished internal powers but with their increase. And although state control has lessened somewhat recently, does anyone believe that the United States and Britain, for example, are back to a 1930s level, let alone to a nineteenth-century level of governmental regulation?

States perform essential political social-economic functions, and no other organization appears as a possible competitor to them. They foster the institutions that make internal peace and prosperity possible. In the state of nature, as Kant put it, there is "no mine and thine." States turn possession into property and thus make saving, production, and prosperity possible. The sovereign state with fixed borders has proved to be the best organization for keeping peace and fostering the conditions for economic well being. We do not have to wonder what happens to society and economy when a state begins to fade away. We have all too many examples. A few obvious ones are China in the 1920s and '30s and again in the 1960s and '70s, post-Soviet Russia, and many African states since their independence. The less competent a state, the likelier it is to dissolve into component parts or to be unable to adapt to transnational developments. Challenges at home and abroad test the mettle of states. Some states fail, and other states pass the tests nicely. In modern times, enough states always make it to keep the international system going as a system of states. The challenges vary; states endure. They have proved to be hardy survivors.

Having asked how international conditions affect states, I now reverse the question and ask how states affect the conduct of international political affairs.

THE STATE IN INTERNATIONAL POLITICS

Economic globalization would mean that the world economy, or at least the globalized portion of it, would be integrated and not merely interdependent. The difference between an interdependent and an integrated world is a qualitative one and not a mere matter of proportionately more trade and a greater and more rapid flow of capital. With integration, the world would look like one big state. Economic markets and economic interests cannot perform the functions of government. Integration requires or presumes a government to protect, direct, and control. Interdependence, in contrast to integration, is "the mere mutualism" of states, as Émile Durkheim put it. It is not only less close than usually thought but also politically less consequential. Interdependence did not produce the world-shaking events of 1989–91. A political event, the failure of one of the world's two great powers, did that. Had the configuration of international politics not fundamentally changed, neither the unification of Germany nor the war against Saddam Hussein would have been possible. The most important events in international politics are explained by differences in the capabilities of states, not by economic forces operating across states or transcending them. Interdependers, and globalizers even more so, argue that the international economic interests of states work against their going to war. True, they do. Yet if one asks whether economic interests or nuclear weapons inhibit war more strongly, the answer obviously is nuclear weapons. European great powers prior to World War I were tightly tied together economically. They nevertheless fought a long and bloody war. The United States and the Soviet Union were not even loosely connected economically. They co-existed peacefully through the four-and-a-half decades of the Cold War. The most important causes of peace, as of war, are found in international-political conditions, including the weaponry available to states. Events following the Cold War dramatically demonstrate the political weakness of economic forces. The integration (not just the interdependence) of the parts of the Soviet Union and of Yugoslavia, with all of their entangling economic interests, did not prevent their disintegration. Governments and people sacrifice welfare and even security to nationalism, ethnicity, and religion.

Political explanations weigh heavily in accounting for international-political events. National *politics*, not international markets, account for many international *economic* developments. A number of students of politics and of economics believe that blocs are becoming more common internationally. Economic interests and market forces do not create blocs; governments do. Without governmental decisions, the Coal and Steel Community, the European Economic Community, and the European Union would not have emerged. The representatives of states negotiate regulations in the European Commission. The Single-Market Act of 1985 provided that some types of directives would require less than a unanimous vote in the Council of Ministers. This political act cleared the way for passage of most of the harmonization standards for Europe (Dumez and Jeunemaître 1996, 229). American governments forged NAFTA; Japan fashioned an East and Southeast Asian producing and trading area. The decisions and acts of a country, or a set of countries arriving at political agreements, shape international political and economic institutions. Governments now intervene much more in international economic matters than they did in the earlier era of interdependence. Before World War I, foreign-ministry officials were famed for their lack of knowledge of, or interest in, economic affairs. Because governments have become much more active in economic affairs at home and abroad, interdependence has become less of an autonomous force in international politics.

The many commentators who exaggerate the closeness of interdependence, and even more so those who write of globalization, think in unit rather than in systemic terms. Many small states import and export large shares of their gross domestic products. States with large GDPs do not. They are little dependent on others, while a number of other states heavily depend on them. The terms of political, economic, and military competition are set by the larger units of the international-political system. Through centuries of multipolarity, with five or so great powers of comparable size competing with one another, the international system was quite closely interdependent. Under bi- and unipolarity the degree of interdependence declined markedly.

States are differentiated from one another not by function but primarily by capability. For two reasons, inequalities across states have greater political impact than inequalities across income groups within states. First, the inequalities of states are larger and have been growing more rapidly. Rich countries have become richer while poor countries have remained poor. Second, in a system without central governance, the influence of the units of greater capability is disproportionately large because there are no effective laws and institutions to direct and constrain them. They are able to work the system to their advantage, as the petrodollar example showed. I argued in 1970 that what counts are states' capacity to adjust to external conditions and their ability to use their economic leverage for political advantage. The United States was then and is still doubly blessed. It remains highly important in the international economy, serving as a principal market for a number of countries and as a major supplier of goods and services, yet its dependence on others is quite low. Precisely because the United States is relatively little dependent on others, it has a wide range of policy choices and the ability both to bring pressure on others and to assist them. The "herd" with its capital may flee from countries when it collectively decides that they are politically and economically unworthy, but some countries abroad, like some firms at home, are so important that they cannot be allowed to fail. National governments and international agencies then come to the rescue. The United States is the country that most often has the ability and the will to step in. The agency that most often acts is the IMF, and most countries think of the IMF as the enforcement arm of the U.S. Treasury (Strange 1996, 192). Thomas Friedman believes that when the "herd" makes its decisions, there is no appeal; but often there is an appeal, and it is for a bail out organized by the United States.

The international economy, like national economies, operates within a set of rules and institutions. Rules and institutions have to be made and sustained. Britain, to a large extent, provided this service prior to World War I; no one did between the wars, and the United States has done so since. More than any other state, the United States makes the rules and maintains the institutions that shape the international political economy.

Economically, the United States is the world's most important country; militarily, it is not only the most important country, it is the decisive one. Thomas Friedman puts the point simply: The world is sustained by "the presence of American power and America's willingness to use that power against those who would threaten the system of globalization. . . . The hidden hand of the market will never work without a hidden fist" (1999, 373). But the hidden fist is in full view. On its military forces, the United States outspends the next six or seven big spenders combined. When force is needed to keep or to restore the peace, either the United States leads the way or the peace is not kept. The Cold War militarized international politics. Relations between the United States and the Soviet Union, and among some other countries as well, came to be defined largely in a single dimension, the military one. As the German sociologist Erich Weede has remarked, "National security decision making in some . . . democracies (most notably in West Germany) is actually penetrated by the United States" (1989, 225). . . .

Many globalizers believe that the world is increasingly ruled by markets. Looking at the state among states leads to a different conclusion. The main difference between international politics now and earlier is not found in the increased interdependence of states but in their growing inequality. With the end of bipolarity, the distribution of capabilities across states has become extremely lopsided. Rather than elevating economic forces and depressing political ones, the inequalities of international politics enhance the political role of one country. Politics, as usual, prevails over economics.[1]

NOTE

1. The picture of the purpose and the performance of states is especially clear in Thomson and Krasner (1989).

REFERENCES

Angell, Norman. 1933. *The Great Illusion.* New York: G.P. Putnam's Sons.

Boltho, Andrea. 1996. "Has France Converged on Germany?" In *National Diversity and Global Capitalism,* ed. Suzanne Berger and Ronald Dore. Ithaca: Cornell University Press.

Boyer, Robert. 1996. "The Convergence Hypothesis Revisited: Globalization But Still the Century of Nations." In *National Diversity and Global Capitalism,* ed. Suzanne Berger and Ronald Dore. Ithaca: Cornell University Press.

Carter, Ashton B., and William J. Perry. 1999. *Preventive Defense: A New Security Strategy for America.* Washington, DC: The Brookings Institution.

———, and John D. Steinbruner. 1992. *A New Concept of Cooperative Security.* Washington, DC: The Brookings Institution.

Doyle, Michael W. 1997. *Ways of War and Peace: Realism, Liberalism, and Socialism.* New York: W.W. Norton.

Dumez, Hervé, and Alain Jeunemaître. 1996. "The Convergence of Competition Policies in Europe: Internal Dynamics and External Imposition." In *National Diversity and Global Capitalism,* ed. Suzanne Berger and Ronald Dore. Ithaca: Cornell University Press.

Fukuyama, Francis. 1992. *The End of History and the Last Man.* New York: Free Press.

Friedman, Thomas L. 1999. *The Lexus and the Olive Tree.* New York: Farrar, Straus, Giroux.

Gardner, Lloyd. 1995. *Pay Any Price: Lyndon Johnson and the Wars for Vietnam.* Chicago: I.R. Dee.

Hirst, Paul, and Grahame Thompson. 1996. *Globalization in Question: The International Economy and the Possibilities of Governance.* Cambridge, UK: Polity Press.

Huntington, Samuel P. 1999. "The Lonely Superpower." *Foreign Affairs* 78 (March/April).

Ikenberry, John. 1998/99. "Institutions, Strategic Restraint, and the Persistence of American Postwar Order." *International Security* 23 (Winter): 77–78.

Keohane, Robert O., and Joseph S. Nye. 1977. *Power and Interdependence: World Politics in Transition.* Boston: Little, Brown.

Kindleberger, Charles P. 1969. *American Business Abroad.* New Haven: Yale University Press.

Krugman, Paul. 1997. "Competitiveness: A Dangerous Obsession." In *The New Shape of World Politics*. New York: W.W. Norton and *Foreign Affairs*.

Lawrence, Robert Z. 1997. "Workers and Economists II: Resist the Binge." In *The New Shape of Politics*. New York: W.W. Norton and *Foreign Affairs*.

Mueller, John. 1989. *Retreat from Doomsday: The Obsolescence of Major War.* New York: Basic Books.

McNeill, William H. 1997. "Territorial States Buried Too Soon." *Mershon International Studies Review*.

Nye, Joseph Jr. 1999. "Redefining the National Interest." *Foreign Affairs* 78 (July/August).

Ohmae, Kenichi. 1990. *The Borderless World: Power and Strategy in the Interlinked Economy.* New York: HarperBusiness.

Reinecke, Wolfgang H. 1997. "Global Public Policy." *Foreign Affairs* 76 (November/December).

Spiro, David E. 1999. *The Hidden Hand of American Hegemony: Petrodollar Recycling and International Markets.* Ithaca: Cornell University Press.

Strange, Susan. 1996. *The Retreat of the State: The Diffusion of Power in the World Economy.* Cambridge: Cambridge University Press.

Thomson, Janice E., and Stephen D. Krasner. 1989. "Global Transactions and the Consolidation of Sovereignty." In *Global Changes and Theoretical Challenges: Approaches to World Politics for the 1990s*, ed. Ernst-Otto Czempiel and James N. Rosenau. Lexington, MA: Lexington Books.

Thurow, Lester C. 1999. *Building Wealth: The New Rules for Individuals, Companies, and Nations in a Knowledge-Based Economy.* New York: HarperCollins.

Wade, Robert. 1996. "Globalization and Its Limits: Reports of the Death of the National Economy Are Grossly Exaggerated." In *National Diversity and Global Capitalism*, ed. Suzanne Berger and Ronald Dore. Ithaca: Cornell University Press.

Waltz, Kenneth N. 1970. "The Myth of National Interdependence." In *The International Corporation*, ed. Charles P. Kindleberger. Cambridge, MA: MIT Press.

———. "Structural Realism after the Cold War." Presented at the Annual Meeting of the American Political Science Association, Boston.

Weede, Erich. 1989. "Collective Goods in an Interdependent World: Authority and Order as Determinants of Peace and Prosperity." In *Global Changes and Theoretical Challenges: Approaches to World Politics for the 1990s*, ed. Ernst-Otto Czempiel and James N. Rosenau. Lexington, MA: Lexington Books.

Weiss, Linda. 1998. *The Myth of the Powerless State: Governing the Economy in a Global Era.* Cambridge, UK: Polity Press.

Woolcock, Stephen. 1996. "Competition among Forms of Corporate Governance in the European Community: The Case of Britain." In *National Diversity and Global Capitalism*, ed. Suzanne Berger and Ronald Dore. Ithaca: Cornell University Press.

Rising Powers and Global Institutions

G. JOHN IKENBERRY

For over half a century, the United States has dominated world politics—and today's global institutions reflect this reality. America emerged preeminent after World War II and built postwar international order around a remarkable array of governance institutions, most notably the UN, IMF, World Bank, GATT, and regional security alliances. The end of the Cold War consolidated this American-led global institutional order. Throughout this period, Western Europe has been America's willing partner. Together, their economies and military capacities over-shadowed the rest of the world, even as the West liquidated its colonial empires. The Atlantic world that they inhabit has been the geopolitical center of gravity and the modernizing vanguard of the global system. In a very real sense, America and the West have laid down the rules and institutions of the postwar world. They have been its creators, owners, managers, and chief beneficiaries.

But this is changing. Today, a group of fast growing developing countries—led by China and India—are rising up and in the next several decades will have economies that will rival the United States and Europe. For the first time in the modern era, economic growth is bringing non-Western developing countries into the top ranks of the world system. This dramatic observation was made in a 2003 Goldman Sachs study, which noted that if present economic trends continue, by 2050 the countries of Brazil, Russia, India and China—the BRICs—could have economies that together would be larger than the old G-6 advanced countries—the United States, Japan, Great Britain, Germany, France and Italy.[1] According to these economic projections, China will pass the Europeans and Japan by 2020 and the United States by 2045.

These fast growing developing countries are already becoming an international economic force. According to *The Economist*, developing countries now produce half of the global GDP. They hold most of the world's financial reserves and are placing huge new demands on energy and raw materials.

These are remarkable developments with potentially far-reaching implications for power and governance in world politics.[2] The non-Western, middle-tier developing

---

Introduction by G. John Ikenberry, adapted from G. John Ikenberry and Thomas Wright, "Rising Powers and Global Institutions," © 2008 by The Century Foundation, Inc. Reprinted by permission.

countries are rising up and forcing change in the global system. Their collective size and impact on trade, finance, energy, and the environment will make them important players. Their economic development will create opportunities—but they will also create pressures, shortages, and other negative externalities. They will be harder to ignore or leave outside the doors of power. At the 2006 annual meeting of the IMF and World Bank in Singapore, representatives from several of these rising countries noted that their economies were stronger than several of the advanced economies—and they insisted on gaining greater voice over the setting of policies.

Indeed, lurking among these developments are questions about the implications for the postwar institutions of governance. How will these rising states impact the existing system of international institutions? Will they seek to integrate and operate within existing institutions or seek to transform or work around them? To what extent will these institutions need to be reformed so as to accommodate these rising developing countries? To what extent will these countries seek to develop their own institutions or build new alliances among themselves in pursuit of their economic and political goals? What are the implications for the political direction and issue agendas of global institutions like the United Nations and Bretton Woods institutions? How should the United States and Europe respond to these new institutional challenges?

Behind these developments are deeper historical and theoretical questions about the rise and decline of great powers and transitions in global order. The rise of newly powerful states is one of the classic "problems" of international relations, and historically it has been a source of conflict and violence. Established great powers that have organized and presided over the international system—and put in place the prevailing rules and institutions—face rising states with their own interests and, increasingly, the power to assert those interests. Powerful but declining states, struggling to stay in control of the global system, face challenger states bent on change. It is this grand historical drama that has repeatedly played itself out over the centuries—and generated upheaval and war.

But the current international order—the order that the rising developing states face—is different than past international orders. It is a much more institutionalized order than previous orders—with denser and more complex and multilayered governance rules and institutions. The rising states themselves are different than past challengers. With the exception of China and perhaps Russia, none of the current rising states are potential military challengers to Western powers. They each have specific niches and comparative advantages that are propelling their economic advance. But for all of them, their economic growth is deeply dependent on trade and investment within the existing world economy. . . .

First, unlike the past, there are a wide array of channels and mechanisms that allow the new rising states to integrate and join the governance arrangements of the old order. The big point here is that seen in historical perspective, the existing U.S.-led institutionalized order is easier to join and harder to overturn. The specific character of today's rising states (other than perhaps China, they are not fully functional "great powers") and the interests, incentives, and constraints that they manifest and face make integration and accommodation more likely than radical transformation.

Second, the specific character of existing global institutions provides opportunities for membership and voice. Three points are important. One is that the existing institutional order provides some protections for rising economic powers. For example, China may have growing interest in working within the WTO because that institution provides protections against discriminatory treatment which a rising economic power like China is likely to face. Second, several of these institutions also are relatively easy to operate within and rise up through their hierarchies. The World Bank and IMF are institutions where governance leadership is based on economic shares which growing countries can leverage into greater institutional voice. The UN Security Council is more resistant to this sort of incremental shift in role and leadership. Finally, existing institutions do have incentives to integrate and accommodate rising states in various ways. For example, the IMF has a crisis of mission and its existing shareholders see the expansion of a role for countries such as India and China as part of a strategy for renewing the institution and preserving its mission.

Third, each institution has its own specific array of constraints and opportunities for rising states. . . . As noted, each institution—with its existing shareholders—has a distinct capacity and willingness to accommodate new powers and redistribute voice and authority. We will survey the institutions and the variations.

Fourth, each country has its own assets and problems as it faces existing global institutions. All of these countries have a dominant interest in the maintenance of stable and open order—and therefore have incentives to support rules and institutions that support stability and openness. Their ability to push for change in institutions varies with their assets and geopolitical position. . . .

Finally, we . . . [t]he American-led postwar institutions are generally formal-based global multilateral institutions. These institutions will not disappear. But two alternative forms of governance are likely to grow in importance. One is informal "steering committees"—such as the G-8 and G-20. These institutions have advantages for rising states. They are easier to join (particularly in contrast with the UN) and they do not entail direct diminishment of sovereignty. Another is regional governance institutions. These also provide advantages for rising states. They give these states greater authority than they might have within global institutions. Regional institutions also allow for cooperation on specific problems that are particularly pressing for these states. So, overall, the balance of governance institutions will be redrawn. . . .

RISING STATES AND INTERNATIONAL ORDER

The rise and decline of states is one of the enduring dramas of international relations, frequently generating security competition and conflict that shapes and reshapes the global landscape. We can begin by situating the current version of this classic drama in wider historical and comparative perspective, identifying both recurring dynamics and novel features. These moments—what are often called "power transitions"—are fraught with danger. But distinctive features of the current international order suggest that this particular power transition—or the set of power transitions that are unfolding simultaneously—will not be entirely like those in the past. The current international order is harder to overturn and easier to join.

First, it is useful to see the international order as a hierarchical political system that more-or-less reflects the interests of the dominant states. Change occurs as great powers rise and decline and as they struggle over the rules and institutions of order. Robert Gilpin provides a classic account of international relations in these terms. The history of world politics is marked by a succession of powerful—or hegemonic—states that rise up to organize the international system. The hierarchical international order is maintained as long as the leading state remains powerful enough to enforce the rules and institutions of order. When this state declines, the existing order begins to unravel and break apart. As Gilpin contends, "a precondition for political change lies in a disjuncture between the existing social system and the redistribution of power toward those actors who would benefit most from a change in the system."[3] Steady and inevitable shifts in the distribution of power among states give rise to new challenger states that eventually engage in geopolitical struggle over the terms of order. Ultimately, the result is the overturning of the old order and the triumph of new dominant states that reorganize the rules and institutions of the international order to fit their interests.[4]

Second, these power transitions historically have often generated conflict and even war. E.H. Carr argues that the "problem of peaceful change" is a central dilemma of international relations.[5] The rise of post-Bismarck Germany in the late nineteenth century—and the ensuing great power rivalry, arms races, instabilities, realignments, and a thirty-year war between England and Germany—is the classic case. Germany's ascent began with its unification under Bismarck in 1870 and the rapid growth of its economy. By the 1880s and 1890s it was acquiring overseas territories and building a modern navy. In 1870, Britain had a 3 to 1 advantage in economic power over Germany but by 1903 Germany had pulled ahead of Britain in overall economic and military power.[6] The rise of German power triggered the classic dynamics of a power transition: as Germany unified and grew, so too did its dissatisfactions, demands and ambitions; and as it grew more powerful, security dilemmas emerged and Germany increasingly appeared as a threat to other great powers in Europe. The result, of course, was a European war.

Third, not all power transitions generate war or overturn the old order. Britain ceded power to a rapidly growing America in the early decades of the 20th century without great conflict or a rupture in relations. Japan grew from 5 percent of the American GNP in the late 1940s to over 60 percent of its size in the early 1990s without challenging existing international order. Power has been redistributed within Western Europe since the end of World War II with negligible impact upon the security community of member states of the European Economic Community, later to become the European Union. Clearly there are different types of power ascents and power transitions. Some states have grown rapidly in economic or geopolitical power and, in the end, accommodated themselves in the existing international order (Japan). Other great powers have risen up and indeed sought to challenge the existing great power order (post-Bismarck Germany). Some power transition moments led to the breakdown of the old order and the establishment of a new global hierarchy of order (Britain after 1815 and America after 1945). Other power transitions do not result in a transformed international order but to more limited adjustments in the regional and global system (Japan and Germany in the postwar era).

Fourth, a variety of factors shape the way in which power transitions unfold. Clearly, the character of rising power "dissatisfaction" can vary. This is true in regard to subjective judgments of leaders about their interests and desires for a greater governance role. But there is also variation in the ability of rising states to in fact advance their expanding economic and political goals within an existing international order. Moreover, the actual ability of rising states to launch or experience gains from challenging and overturning the existing international order will vary. In the current age where China, the United States, and other great powers possess nuclear weapons, the costs and benefits—indeed the rationality—of hegemonic war are reduced to essentially zero. Likewise, the power transition dynamic is typically seen to play out between the world's dominant state and a rising state. It is seen as a dyadic drama between two states. But the actual power of the leading state is much greater if its power is effectively aggregated with other great powers allied with it. In this sense, a rising state faces not just a lead state but—at least potentially—a wider coalition of status quo great powers arrayed around the hegemonic state. Finally, the character of the international order—and the degree to which it is based on coercion or consent—will matter. It will influence how a rising state calculates its interests and the choices it makes to either integrate or challenge the order. It will influence the ability of the leading state to aggregate power and enforce the rules and maintain a stable international hierarchy.

Indeed, the actual character of hierarchy and rule within an international order can vary widely. (a) The international order can be dominated by a single state or it can be dominated by a group of states that together are bound together and govern the system. (b) The international order can be rigidly hierarchical and governed by coercive domination exercised by the leading state in the system or it can be relatively open and benevolent, organized around reciprocal, consensual, and rule-based relations. (c) The international order can be organized so that the material benefits that are generated accrue disproportionately to the lead state or the material benefits of participation within the order can be more widely shared.[7] The point of these observations is to suggest a general proposition, namely, that the more the international order is dominated by a group of states that are bound together in deeply-rooted institutions, the more the international order is open, consensual and rule-based, and the more the benefits of the order are spread widely—the more likely that rising powers can secure their interests through integrating into rather than challenging the order and the greater the incentives will exist for rising states to accommodate themselves to that order.

Fifth, the existing international order is substantially different from past international orders along the dimensions indicated above. In general terms, it is more open, institutionalized, consensual, and rule-based than past international orders. The United States emerged as the world's preeminent power after World War II amidst sharp and dramatic shifts in the global distribution of power. More so than Britain in the 19th century or other hegemonic states in earlier eras, the United States built its order around institutionalized relationships. This is order built around multilateralism, alliance partnership, strategic restraint, cooperative security, and institutional and rule-based relationships. The UN, IMF, World Bank, NATO, GATT, and other institutions that emerged provided the most rule-based structure for political and economic relations in history. The institutional underpinning of this order made America's power position both more durable and less threatening to other states—rising, declining, or otherwise. It is the order that came to dominate the global system for half a century—surviving the end of the Cold War and other upheavals.[8]

This array of multilateral institutions and security pacts are not simply functional mechanisms that generate collective action. They are also elements of political architecture that allow states within the order to do business with each other. The liberal character of the international order provides access points and opportunities for political communication and reciprocal influence. In effect, the political architecture has given the postwar order its distinctive liberal hegemonic character. Rules, institutions, networks, and political relationships are embedded in this order giving it its overall character: an open and expandable liberal order, one in which the powerful capitalist democracies are tied together through alliances and governance institutions; an order that, more so than the past, it built around agreed upon universal rules that allow access and participation of a wide and growing array of states; and an order where the material benefits of the open system flow in all directions.

Sixth, these characteristics of the existing international order have implications for the rise of new states. Generally speaking, it is an order that is harder to overturn and easier to join. It is harder to overturn for several reasons. The removal of great power war as a source of change in the international system means that it is harder for rising states to wield power in pursuit of a radically new set of rules and organizational principles of order. Change, by necessity, becomes more incremental. Moments do not open up where declining states are defeated and the old order rests in ruins—moments that in the past have given rising states incredible opportunities to recast rules and arrangements of the international system. It is harder to push old and declining states off the international stage. At the same time, the existing international order is one in which the postwar advanced democracies are tied together in a cooperative and durable complex political system. Rising states confront not just the United States but a dense and expansive system of economic, political and security relationships. Past rising states confronted individual great powers. Today's rising states confront an entire global social formation. It is one thing to struggle against a specific, powerful state. It is another thing to struggle against an entire global way of life.

At the same time, the existing international order is easier to join. The complexity and multifaceted features of this open and institutionalized system provide multiple access points and pathways for integration. It is hard to shut out new states that meet the requirements for participation, particularly in economic and political governance areas. WTO membership, for example, has specific criteria for membership. The universalistic features of these rules reduce the biases and exclusions that might otherwise present blockages on the integration of rising states. The rules and principles of the existing system also provide attractive tools for these rising states. They are a source of rule-based protection to discrimination and exclusion. The same logic applies for the older—and declining—members of the system. The liberal and rule-based character of the international system turns the integration of new states into an incremental process of adjustment. The challenges to the existing order are not fundamental but turn on less monumental questions of rules and membership.

It is worth remembering that the postwar international order that newly rising states confront is an international order that absorbed both Japan and Germany after the war—the states which integrated and rose up to be the second and third most powerful economies in the world. Mechanisms for dealing with power transitions exist. When the United States faced a rising Japan in the 1980s, it pushed Tokyo to open up and liberalize its economy. The United States and Europe together invited Japan into intergovernmental groupings such as the OECD and the G-7 process. Private sector groups—such as the Trilateral Commission and other business councils—also sought to integrate Japan into the Western economic order. Germany also has followed a postwar path of growth and normalization as a great power by renewing its commitments to European and Atlantic institutions. The leading states within this order—Great Britain, France, Germany, Japan, and the United States—have all experienced rising and declining economic growth rates and military expenditures, but never have these relative gains and losses in power triggered security competition or power transition conflict.

So the upshot is that rising states today face both opportunities and constraints. The process of institutional adjustment to these newly powerful countries will necessarily be incremental. These power transitions are likely to be more peaceful and incremental than in past episodes. . . .

NOTES

1. "Dreaming with BRICs: The Path to 2050," *Global Economics Paper No. 99*, Goldman Sachs, 1 October 2003.
2. For examples of articles and studies that address this issue see Daniel Drezner, "The New New World Order," *Foreign Affairs*, March/April 2007; National Intelligence Council, *Mapping the Global Future; The World in 2020*, Washington DC: GPO, 2004.
3. Robert Gilpin, *War and Change in World Politics* (New York: Cambridge University Press, 1981), p. 9.
4. Gilpin, *War and Change in World Politics*.
5. E.H. Carr, *The Twenty Years Crisis, 1919–1939: An Introduction to the Study of International Relations* (New York: Harper and Row, 1964), pp. 208–23.
6. Britain remained economically more advanced but Germany's population was a third larger than Britain and its advancing industrial economy allowed it to engage in a sustained military arms build up. See Paul Kennedy, *The Rise and Fall of the Great Powers* (New York: Random House, 1987).
7. For a discussion of types of international order, see G. John Ikenberry, *After Victory: Institutions, Strategic Restraint, and the Rebuilding of Order After Major War* (Princeton: Princeton University Press, 2001).
8. See Ikenberry, *After Victory*; Geir Lundestad, *The American 'Empire'* (New York: Oxford University Press, 1990); and Charles S. Maier, *Among Empires: American Ascendancy and Its Predecessors* (Cambridge: Harvard University Press, 2006).

Minilateralism

MOISÉS NAÍM

Never say never. Because of the global economic crisis, habits that seemed unalterable are suddenly being altered. Americans are now saving more and consuming less. Financial institutions are no longer betting the house on risky investments they do not understand. Wealthy oil-exporting countries are tightening their belts. At least some emerging markets long prone to financial accidents are behaving with uncharacteristic prudence. Everywhere, change is in the air.

Everywhere, that is, except in the way humanity responds to its most menacing threats. You know the list: climate change, nuclear proliferation, terrorism, pandemics, trade protectionism, and more. Not one can be solved, or even effectively contained, without more successful international collaboration. And that is not happening.

When was the last time you heard that a large number of countries agreed to a major international accord on a pressing issue? Not in more than a decade. The last successful multilateral trade agreement dates back to 1994, when 123 countries gathered to negotiate the creation of the World Trade Organization and agreed on a new set of rules for international trade. Since then, all other attempts to reach a global trade deal have crashed. The same is true with multilateral efforts to curb nuclear proliferation; the last significant international nonproliferation agreement was in 1995, when 185 countries agreed to extend an existing nonproliferation treaty. In the decade and a half since, multilateral initiatives have not only failed, but India, Pakistan, and North Korea have demonstrated their certain status as nuclear powers. On the environment, the Kyoto Protocol, a global deal aimed at reducing greenhouse gas emissions, has been ratified by 184 countries since it was adopted in 1997, but the United States, the world's second-largest air polluter after China, has not done so, and many of the signatories have missed their targets.

The most recent multilateral initiative successfully endorsed by a large number of countries was in 2000, when 192 nations signed the United Nations Millennium Declaration, an ambitious set of eight goals ranging from halving the world's extreme poverty to halting the spread of HIV/AIDS and providing universal primary education—all by 2015. Although some progress toward achieving these

Moisés Naím, "Minilateralism," *Foreign Policy*, issue #173 (July/August 2009), pp. 135–136. Copyright 2009 by WashingtonPost.Newsweek Interactive, LLC. Reproduced with permission of Foreign Policy in the format Textbook via Copyright Clearance Center. www.foreignpolicy.com

goals has been made—mostly thanks to Asia's spectacular economic performance—the failure of rich countries to fully fund these efforts, execution problems in poor countries, and the global economic downturn make the achievement of the goals by 2015 unlikely.

The pattern is clear: Since the early 1990s, the need for effective multicountry collaboration has soared, but at the same time multilateral talks have inevitably failed; deadlines have been missed; financial commitments and promises have not been honored; execution has stalled; and international collective action has fallen far short of what was offered and, more importantly, needed. These failures represent not only the perpetual lack of international consensus, but also a flawed obsession with multilateralism as the panacea for all the world's ills.

So what is to be done? To start, let's forget about trying to get the planet's nearly 200 countries to agree. We need to abandon that fool's errand in favor of a new idea: minilateralism.

By minilateralism, I mean a smarter, more targeted approach: We should bring to the table the smallest possible number of countries needed to have the largest possible impact on solving a particular problem. Think of this as minilateralism's magic number.

The magic number, of course, will vary greatly depending on the problem. Take trade, for example. The Group of Twenty (G-20), which includes both rich and poor countries from six continents, accounts for 85 percent of the world's economy. The members of the G-20 could reach a major trade deal among themselves and make it of even greater significance by allowing any other country to join if it wishes to do so. Presumably, many would. Same with climate change. There, too, the magic number is about 20: The world's 20 top polluters account for 75 percent of the planet's greenhouse gas emissions. The number for nuclear proliferation is 21—enough to include both recognized and de facto nuclear countries, and several other powers who care about them. African poverty? About a dozen, including all the major donor countries and the sub-Saharan countries most in need. As for HIV/AIDS, 19 countries account for nearly two thirds of the world's AIDS-related deaths.

Of course, countries not invited to the table will denounce this approach as undemocratic and exclusionary. But the magic number will break the world's untenable gridlock, and agreements reached by the small number of countries whose actions are needed to generate real solutions can provide the foundation on which more-inclusive deals can be subsequently built. Minilateral deals can and should be open to any other country willing to play by the rules agreed upon by the original group.

The defects of minilateralism pale in comparison with the stalemate that characterizes twenty-first-century multilateralism. It has become far too dangerous to continue to rely on large-scale multilateral negotiations that stopped yielding results almost two decades ago. The minilateralism of magic numbers is not a magic solution. But it's a far better bet at this point than the multilateralism of wishful thinking.

Government Networks and Global Governance

ANNE-MARIE SLAUGHTER

There can, of course, be no one blueprint for world order. The proposal advanced here is part of an active and ongoing debate. In the spirit of such debate, it is important to acknowledge that the model of world order I put forward rests on a combination of descriptive and predictive empirical claims, which can be summarized in basic terms:

- The state is not the only actor in the international system, but it is still the most important actor.
- The state is not disappearing, but it is disaggregating into its component institutions, which are increasingly interacting principally with their foreign counterparts across borders.
- These institutions still represent distinct national or state interests, even as they also recognize common professional identities and substantive experience as judges, regulators, ministers, and legislators.
- Different states have evolved and will continue to evolve mechanisms for reaggregating the interests of their distinct institutions when necessary. In many circumstances, therefore, states will still interact with one another as unitary actors in more traditional ways.
- Government networks exist alongside and sometimes within more traditional international organizations. . . .

I am not arguing that a new world order of government networks will replace the existing infrastructure of international institutions, but rather complement and strengthen it. States can be disaggregated for many purposes and in many contexts and still be completely unitary actors when necessary, such as in decisions to go to war. And even their component parts still represent national interests in various ways.

HORIZONTAL NETWORKS

The structural core of a disaggregated world order is a set of horizontal networks among national government officials in their respective issue areas, ranging from

From Slaughter, Anne-Marie, *A New World Order*, pp. 18–23, 261–271. © 2004 by Princeton University Press. Reprinted by permission of Princeton University Press. Portions of the text and some footnotes have been omitted.

central banking through antitrust regulation and environmental protection to law enforcement and human rights protection. These networks operate both between high-level officials directly responsive to the national political process—the ministerial level—as well as between lower level national regulators. They may be surprisingly spontaneous—informal, flexible, and of varying membership—or institutionalized within official international organizations. For instance, national finance ministers meet regularly under the auspices of the G-7 and the G-20, but also as members of the IMF [International Monetary Fund] Board of Governors. The extent and the kind of power they may exercise within these two forums differ in significant ways, but the basic structure of governance and the identity of the governors remains the same.

Horizontal information networks, as the name suggests, bring together regulators, judges, or legislators to exchange information and to collect and distill best practices. This information exchange can also take place through technical assistance and training programs provided by one country's officials to another. The direction of such training is not always developed country to developing country, either; it can also be from developed country to developed country, as when U.S. antitrust officials spent six months training their New Zealand counterparts.

Enforcement networks typically spring up due to the inability of government officials in one country to enforce that country's laws, either by means of a regulatory agency or through a court. But enforcement cooperation must also inevitably involve a great deal of information exchange and can also involve assistance programs of various types. Legislators can also collaborate on how to draft complementary legislation so as to avoid enforcement loopholes.

Finally, harmonization networks, which are typically authorized by treaty or executive agreement, bring regulators together to ensure that their rules in a particular substantive area conform to a common regulatory standard. Judges can also engage in the equivalent activity, but in a much more ad hoc manner. Harmonization is often politically very controversial, with critics charging that the "technical" process of achieving convergence ignores the many winners and losers in domestic publics, most of whom do not have any input into the process.

VERTICAL NETWORKS

In a disaggregated world order, horizontal government networks would be more numerous than vertical networks, but vertical networks would have a crucial role to play. Although a core principle of such an order is the importance of keeping global governance functions primarily in the hands of domestic government officials, in some circumstances states do come together the way citizens might and choose to delegate their individual governing authority to a "higher" organization—a "supranational" organization that does exist, at least conceptually, above the state. The officials of these organizations do in fact replicate the governing functions that states exercise regarding their citizens. Thus, for instance, states can truly decide that the only way to reduce tariffs or subsidies is to adopt a body of rules prohibiting them and allow an independent court or tribunal to enforce those rules. Alternatively, states can come together and give an international court the power to try war criminals—the same function that national courts perform—in circumstances in which national courts are unwilling or unable to do so.

These supranational organizations can be far more effective in performing the functions states charge them to perform if they can link up directly with national government institutions. Absent a world government, it is impossible to grant supranational officials genuine coercive power: judges on supranational tribunals cannot call in the global equivalent of federal marshals if their judgments are not obeyed; global regulators cannot impose fines and enforce them through global courts. NAFTA is a supranational institution charged with gathering information on environmental enforcement policies and compiling a record of complaints of nonenforcement by private actors. This is an attempt to enhance enforcement through the provision of information. Similarly, the European Union is beginning to create Europe-level "information agencies," designed to collect and disseminate information needed by networks of national regulators. Such agencies can also provide benchmarks of progress for their national counterparts against accepted global or regional standards.

DISAGGREGATED INTERNATIONAL ORGANIZATIONS

Thinking about world order in terms of both horizontal and vertical government networks challenges our current concept of an "international organization." Many international organizations are primarily convening structures for horizontal networks of national officials. Others are genuinely "supranational," in the sense that they constitute an entity distinct from national governments that has a separate identity and loyalty and which exercises some measure of genuine autonomous power. For example, the Ministerial Conference of the WTO [World Trade Organization] is a gathering of national trade ministers, who can only exercise power by consensus. Dispute-resolution panels of the WTO, by contrast, are composed of three independent experts charged with interpreting and enforcing the rules of the WTO against national governments.

Both of these types of international/supranational organizations differ from traditional international organizations—most notably the United Nations itself—that are composed of formal delegations from each of the member states, typically headed by an ambassador serving in the capacity of permanent representative. . . .

In a world of disaggregated states that nevertheless still act as unitary actors under some circumstances, it is important to be able to distinguish between different types of international organizations in terms both of the relevant government officials who represent their states within them and the degree and type of autonomous power they can exercise. Where international organizations have become sufficiently specialized to develop the equivalent of an executive, judicial, and even legislative branch, vertical government networks become possible. Where they are specialized in a specific issue area but exercise little or no autonomous power, they can be hosts for horizontal government networks. But when they are regional or global organizations charged with assuring peace and security, or similar very general functions, they represent an older and much more formal model of international cooperation, conducted by diplomats more than domestic government officials.

Here, then, is the structural blueprint of a new world order of government networks, complete with a set of assumptions about the nature of states and the types of international organizations those states have and will continue to create. But order must be backed by power. How can these various networks actually influence political, economic, and social outcomes to achieve substantive results? Any conception of world order must assume some set of such results. It takes structures, power, and norms to achieve them. . . .

CONCLUSION

Global governance through government networks is good public policy for the world and good national foreign policy for the United States, the European Union, APEC [Asia-Pacific Economic Cooperation] members, and all developing countries seeking to participate in global regulatory processes and needing to strengthen their capacity for domestic governance. Even in their current form, government networks promote convergence, compliance with international agreements, and improved cooperation among nations on a wide range of regulatory and judicial issues. A world order self-consciously created out of horizontal and vertical government networks could go much further. It could create a genuine global rule of law without centralized global institutions and could engage, socialize, support, and constrain government officials of every type in every nation. In this future, we could see disaggregated government institutions—the members of government networks—as actual bearers of a measure of sovereignty, strengthening them still further, but also subjecting them to specific legal obligations. This would be a genuinely different world, with its own challenges and its own promise.

Government Networks and Global Public Policy

Wolfgang Reinecke, like many others, argues that national governments are losing their ability to formulate and implement national public policy within territorial borders rendered increasingly porous by the forces of globalization, immigration, and the information revolution. He proposes that they "delegate tasks to other actors and institutions that are in a better position to implement global public policies—not only to public sector agencies like the World Bank and the IMF, but also business, labor, and nongovernmental organizations."[1] He offers this strategy as an alternative to "[f]orming a global government," which "would require states to abdicate their sovereignty not only in daily affairs but in a formal sense as well."[2] In other words, national governments have already lost their sovereignty, but they should compensate for that loss by delegating their responsibilities to a host of nonstate actors—international organizations, corporations, and NGOs.

This is precisely the globalization tri-lemma. National governments are losing power. They can only recreate this power at the global level by creating a global government, but that is "unrealistic,"[3] so the alternative is a hodgepodge of private sector and public international organizations, for profit and not for profit. It is exactly this hodgepodge that Reinecke calls governance instead of government, and it is exactly why another group of critics fear that the formulation of global public policy is being left to experts, enthusiasts, international bureaucrats, and transnational businesspeople—everyone, that is, but politically accountable government officials.

A self-conscious world order of government networks could address these problems. National government officials would retain primary power over public policy, but work together to formulate and implement it globally. They would delegate some power to supranational officials, but then work closely with those officials through vertical networks. And they would interact intensively with existing international organizations, corporations, NGOs, and other actors in transnational society, but in a way that makes it clear that government networks are the accountable core of these larger policy networks.

This conception of a networked world order rests on fundamentally different assumptions about both the international system and international law. The old model of the international system assumes unitary states that negotiate formal legal agreements with one another and implement them from the top down, with a great emphasis on verification and enforcement. The new model advanced here assumes disaggregated states in which national government officials interact intensively with one another and adopt codes of best practices and agree on coordinated solutions to common problems—agreements that have no legal force but that can be directly implemented by the officials who negotiated them. At the same time, in this new model, states still acting as unitary actors will realize that some problems cannot be effectively addressed without delegating actual sovereign power to a limited number of supranational government officials, such as judges and arbitrators in the WTO, NAFTA, and the ICC. In such cases, the international agreements negotiated will be more immediately and automatically effective than the majority of agreements negotiated in the old system because they will be directly enforced through vertical government networks.

In practice, of course, these two models of the international system will coexist. Government networks, both horizontal and vertical, will operate alongside and even within traditional international organizations. . . .

What transgovernmental networks can do that traditional international organizations cannot, however, is to counter and engage transnational corporate, civic, and criminal networks. They permit a loose, flexible structure that can bring in national officials from a wide range of different countries as needed to address specific problems. They can target problems at their roots, plug loopholes in national jurisdictions, and respond to goods, people, and ideas streaming across borders. Their members can educate, bolster, and regulate one another in essentially the same ways that make private transnational networks so effective. They are indeed the "institutions of globalization," and far better suited to global governance in an age of globalization and information.

National Support for Government Networks

The European Union is pioneering governance through government networks in its internal affairs. As . . . multiple examples . . . emphasize—from the relations between national courts and the ECJ [European Court of Justice] to the creation of European information agencies to help the networks of regulators across the European Union—the European Union is a vibrant laboratory for how to establish the necessary degree of collective cooperation among a diverse group of states while retaining the dominant locus of political power at the national level. It has limited supranational institutions, and though they are more powerful than any that currently exist at the global level, they cannot function without the active cooperation and participation of national government officials. Beyond the Court and the commission, the power in the European Union rests with networks of national ministers and lower-level officials, who make decisions at the European level and implement them at the national level.

The European Union has many features that make its distinctive form of government by network exportable to other regions and to the world at large. It remains a collection of distinct nations, even as it works to create the governing power and institutions at the supranational level necessary to solve common problems and advance common interests for all its members. We might thus expect the European Union to support the creation of global government networks. In fact, however, it is the United States that has led the way in supporting these networks at the global level. . . .

Over the longer term, government networks can tackle the domestic roots of international problems and can do so both multilaterally and in a way that empowers domestic government officials in countries around the world to help themselves. The exchange of information, development of collective standards, provision of training and technical assistance, ongoing monitoring and support, and active engagement in enforcement cooperation that does and can take place in government networks can give government officials in weak, poor, and transitional countries the boost they need. Their counterparts in more powerful countries, meanwhile, can reach beyond their borders to try to address problems that have an impact within their borders.

For maximum impact and effectiveness, however, the work of government networks cannot be done in the shadows. Existing networks breed suspicion and opposition in many quarters, leading to charges of technocracy, distortion of global and national political processes, elitism and inequality. The United States and other countries should champion them openly as mechanisms of global governance and be prepared to reform and improve them as necessary. They will almost certainly have to become more visible and engage more systematically with corporate and civic networks. They should include more and more effective networks of legislators as well as of regulators and judges. And their members are likely to be subject to more national oversight and regulation specifically aimed at integrating the national and international dimensions of their jobs.

To maximize the accountability of the participants in government networks, it would be possible to take a step further and give them a measure of individual, or rather institutional, sovereignty. In a world of disaggregated states, the sovereignty that has traditionally attached to unitary states should arguably also be disaggregated. Taking this step, however, requires a different conception of the very nature of sovereignty. As described in the next section, sovereignty understood as capacity rather than autonomy can easily attach to the component parts of states and includes responsibilities as well as rights.

Disaggregated Sovereignty

Theorists, pundits, and policymakers all recognize that traditional conceptions of sovereignty are inadequate to capture the complexity of contemporary international relations. The result is a seemingly endless debate about the changing nature of sovereignty: What does it mean? Does it still exist? Is it useful? Everyone in this debate still assumes that sovereignty is an attribute borne by an entire state, acting as a unit. Yet if states are acting in the international system through their component government institutions—regulatory agencies, ministries, courts, legislatures—why shouldn't each of these institutions exercise a measure of sovereignty as specifically defined and tailored to their functions and capabilities?

This proposal may seem fanciful, or even frightening, if we think about sovereignty the old way—as the power to be left alone, to exclude, to counter any external meddling or interference. Consider, however, the "new sovereignty," defined by Abram and Antonia Chayes as the capacity to participate in international institutions of all types—in collective efforts to steer the international system and address global and regional problems together with their national and supranational counterparts.[6] This is a conception of sovereignty that would accord status and recognition to states in the international system to the extent that they are willing and able to engage with other states, and thus necessarily accept mutual obligations.

Chayes and Chayes, like Reinecke, begin from the proposition that the world has moved beyond interdependence. Interdependence refers to a general condition in which states are mutually dependent on and vulnerable to what other states do, but interdependence still assumes a baseline of separation, autonomy, and defined boundaries. States may be deeply dependent on each other's choices and decisions, but those choices and decisions still drive and shape the international system. For Chayes and Chayes, by contrast, the international system itself has become a "tightly woven fabric of international agreements, organizations and institutions that shape [states'] relations with one another and penetrate deeply into their internal economics and politics."[7]

If the background conditions for the international system are connection rather than separation, interaction rather than isolation, and institutions rather than free space, then sovereignty-as-autonomy makes no sense. The new sovereignty is status, membership, "connection to the rest of the world and the political ability to be an actor within it."[8] However paradoxical it sounds, the measure of a state's capacity to act as an independent unit within the international system—the condition that "sovereignty" purports both to grant and describe—depends on the breadth and depth of its links to other states.

This conception of sovereignty fits neatly with a conception of a disaggregated world order. If the principal moving parts of that order are the agencies, institutions, and the officials within them who are collectively responsible for the legislative, executive, and judicial functions of government, then they must be able to exercise legislative, executive, and judicial sovereignty. They must be able to exercise at least some independent rights and be subject to some independent, or at least distinct, obligations. These rights and obligations may devolve from more unitary rights and obligations applicable to the unitary state, or they may evolve from the functional requirements of meaningful and effective transgovernmental relations. Nonetheless the sovereignty of "states" must become a more flexible and practical attribute.

If sovereignty is relational rather than insular, in the sense that it describes a capacity to engage rather than a right to resist, then its devolution onto ministers, legislators, and judges is not so difficult to imagine. The concept of judicial comity . . . rests on judges' respect for each other's competence as members of the same profession and institutional enterprise across borders. It assumes that a fully "sovereign" court is entitled to its fair share of disputes when conflicts arise, can negotiate cooperative solutions in transnational disputes, and can participate in a transnational judicial dialogue about issues of common concern. Regulators would be similarly empowered to interact with their fellow regulators to engage in the full range of activities. . . . And legislators would be directly empowered to catch up.

If, however, disaggregated state institutions are already engaged in these activities . . . what difference does it make if they are granted formal capacity to do what they are already doing? The principal advantage is that subjecting government institutions directly to international obligations could buttress clean institutions against corrupt ones and rights-respecting institutions against their more oppressive counterparts. Each government institution would have an independent obligation to interpret and implement international legal obligations, much as each branch of the U.S. government has an independent obligation to ensure that its actions conform to the Constitution. As in the domestic context, either the courts or the legislature would have the last word in case of disputed interpretations of international law so as to ensure the possibility of national unity where necessary. In many cases, however, international legal obligations concerning trade, the environment, judicial independence, human rights, arms control, and other areas would devolve directly on government institutions charged with responsibility for the issue area in question.

By becoming enrolled and enmeshed in global government networks, individual government institutions would affirm their judicial, legislative, or regulatory sovereignty. They would participate in the formulation and implementation of professional norms and the development of best practices on substantive issues. And they would be aware that they are performing before their constituents, their peers, and the global community at large, as bearers of rights and status in that community. . . .

At first glance, disaggregating the state and granting at least a measure of sovereignty to its component parts might appear to weaken the state. On the contrary, it will bolster the power of the state as the primary actor in the international system. Giving each government institution a measure of legitimate authority under international law, with accompanying duties, marks government officials as distinctive in larger policy networks and allows the state to extend its reach. If sovereignty were still understood as exclusive and impermeable rather than relational, strengthening the state would mean building higher walls to protect its domestic autonomy. Yet in a world in which sovereignty means the capacity to participate in cooperative regimes in the collective interest of all states, expanding the formal capacity of different state institutions to interact with their counterparts around the world means expanding state power.

In conclusion, consider the following thought experiment. Imagine beginning with a world of sovereign states and trying to design a feasible, effective, and just system of global governance. Imagine that the governments of many of those states are seeking to fight crime, collect taxes, guarantee civil rights and civil liberties, protect the environment, regulate financial markets, provide a measure of social security, ensure the safety of consumer products, and represent their citizens fairly and accurately. Now assume that for a host of reasons, national government officials cannot do their jobs solely within their borders. Assume further that some of the problems they seek to address have global dimensions, and that the creators and vectors of those problems are acting through transnational networks. At the same time, individuals, groups, and organizations that can help address those problems are also acting through transnational networks. Finally, assume that one of the things the citizens of all these countries want is a safer, fairer, cleaner world.

These national government officials would never cede power to a world government, although they would certainly recognize that, with respect to some specific problems, only genuinely powerful supranational institutions could overcome the collective action problems inherent in formulating and implementing global solutions. In most cases, however, they would seek to work together in a variety of ways, recognizing that they could only do their jobs properly at the national level by interacting—whether in cooperation and conflict—at the global level. Their ordinary government jobs—regulating, judging, legislating—would thus come to include both domestic and international activity. Over time, they would also come to recognize responsibilities not only to their national constituents but to broader global constituencies. If granted a measure of sovereignty to participate in collective decision making with one another, they would also have to live up to obligations to those broader constituencies.

In short, they would create a world order. It would encompass many of the elements of the present international system and build on the trends I have described, but would overlay and surround them with government networks of all kinds. It would be a world order created by, and composed of, disaggregated state institutions, allowing nation-states to evolve in ways that keep up with changes in the private sector and that expand state power. It would be an effective world order, in the sense of being able to translate paper principles into individual and organizational action. To be truly effective, however, it would also have to be a just world order, as inclusive, respectful, tolerant, and equal as possible. . . .

NOTES

1. Wolfgang H. Reinecke, "Global Public Policy," *Foreign Affairs* Vol. 76 (1997), p. 132.
2. Ibid.
3. Ibid.
4. Ibid., p. 133, p. 127.
5. Ibid.
6. Chayes and Chayes, *The New Sovereignty*, p. 4.
7. Abram Chayes and Antonia Handler Chayes, *The New Sovereignty: Compliance with International Regulatory Agreements* (Cambridge: Harward University Press, 1995), p. 4.
8. Ibid.

 Exercises for Global Governance

Apply what you learned in this chapter by using the online resources on MyPoliSciKit (www.mypoliscikit.com).

 Practice Tests

 Videos:
- "Diplomacy and Foreign Policy"
- "Western Arm Sales and the Rwandan Genocide"

Reading Guides:
- Adam Roberts, "The United Nations and International Security"
- Kenneth N. Waltz, "Globalization and Governance"
- John Ikenberry, "Rising Powers and Global Institutions"
- Moisés Naím, "Minilateralism"
- Anne-Marie Slaughter, "Government Networks and Global Governance"

FUTURE DEVELOPMENTS

Global Trends 2025

THE U.S. NATIONAL INTELLIGENCE COUNCIL

EXECUTIVE SUMMARY

The international system—as constructed following the Second World War—will be almost unrecognizable by 2025 owing to the rise of emerging powers, a globalizing economy, an historic transfer of relative wealth and economic power from West to East, and the growing influence of nonstate actors. By 2025, the international system will be a global multipolar one with gaps in national power[1] continuing to narrow between developed and developing countries. Concurrent with the shift in power among nation-states, the relative power of various nonstate actors—including businesses, tribes, religious organizations, and criminal networks—is increasing. The players are changing, but so too are the scope and breadth of transnational issues important for continued global prosperity. Aging populations in the developed world; growing energy, food, and water constraints; and worries about climate change will limit and diminish what will still be an historically unprecedented age of prosperity.

Historically, emerging multipolar systems have been more unstable than bipolar or unipolar ones. Despite the recent financial volatility—which could end up accelerating many ongoing trends—we do not believe that we are headed toward a complete breakdown of the international system, as occurred in 1914–1918 when an earlier phase of globalization came to a halt. However, the next 20 years of transition to a new system are fraught with risks. Strategic rivalries are most likely to revolve around trade, investments, and technological innovation and acquisition, but we cannot rule out a 19th century-like scenario of arms races, territorial expansion, and military rivalries.

This is a story with no clear outcome, as illustrated by a series of vignettes we use to map out divergent futures. Although the United States is likely to remain the single most powerful actor, the United States' relative strength—even in the military realm—will decline and U.S. leverage will become more constrained. At

From "Executive Summary," *Global Trends 2025: A Transformed World* (National Intelligence Council, November 2008), pp. viii–xii.

the same time, the extent to which other actors—both state and nonstate—will be willing or able to shoulder increased burdens is unclear. Policymakers and publics will have to cope with a growing demand for multilateral cooperation when the international system will be stressed by the incomplete transition from the old to a still-forming new order.

Economic Growth Fueling Rise of Emerging Players

In terms of size, speed, and directional flow, the transfer of global wealth and economic power now under way—roughly from West to East—is without precedent in modern history. This shift derives from two sources. First, increases in oil and commodity prices have generated windfall profits for the Gulf states and Russia. Second, lower costs combined with government policies have shifted the locus of manufacturing and some service industries to Asia.

Growth projections for Brazil, Russia, India, and China (the BRICs) indicate they will collectively match the original G-7's share of global GDP by 2040–2050. China is poised to have more impact on the world over the next 20 years than any other country. If current trends persist, by 2025 China will have the world's second largest economy and will be a leading military power. It also could be the largest importer of natural resources and the biggest polluter. India probably will continue to enjoy relatively rapid economic growth and will strive for a multipolar world in which New Delhi is one of the poles. China and India must decide the extent to which they are willing and capable of playing increasing global roles and how each will relate to the other. Russia has the potential to be richer, more powerful, and more self-assured in 2025 if it invests in human capital, expands and diversifies its economy, and integrates with global markets. On the other hand, Russia could experience a significant decline if it fails to take these steps and oil and gas prices remain in the $50–70 per barrel range. No other countries are projected to rise to the level of China, India, or Russia, and none is likely to match their individual global clout. We expect, however, to see the political and economic power of other countries—such as Indonesia, Iran, and Turkey—to increase.

For the most part, China, India, and Russia are not following the Western liberal model for self-development but instead are using a different model, "state capitalism." State capitalism is a loose term used to describe a system of economic management that gives a prominent role to the state. Other rising powers—South Korea, Taiwan, and Singapore—also used state capitalism to develop their economies. However, the impact of Russia, and particularly China, following this path is potentially much greater owing to their size and approach to "democratization." We remain optimistic about the *long-term* prospects for greater democratization, even though advances are likely to be slow and globalization is subjecting many recently democratized countries to increasing social and economic pressures with the potential to undermine liberal institutions.

Many other countries will fall further behind economically. Sub-Saharan Africa will remain the region most vulnerable to economic disruption, population stresses, civil conflict, and political instability. Despite increased global demand for commodities for which Sub-Saharan Africa will be a major supplier, local populations are unlikely to experience significant economic gain. Windfall profits arising from sustained increases in commodity prices might further entrench corrupt or otherwise ill-equipped governments in several regions, diminishing the prospects for democratic and market-based reforms. Although many of Latin America's major countries will have become middle income powers by 2025, others, particularly those such as Venezuela and Bolivia that have embraced populist policies for a protracted period, will lag behind—and some, such as Haiti, will have become even poorer and less governable. Overall, Latin America will continue to lag behind Asia and other fast-growing areas in terms of economic competitiveness.

Asia, Africa, and Latin America will account for virtually all population growth over the next 20 years; less than 3 percent of the growth will occur in the West. Europe and Japan will continue to far outdistance the emerging powers of China and India in per capita wealth, but they will struggle to maintain robust growth rates because the size of their working-age populations will decrease. The U.S. will be a partial exception to the aging of populations in the developed world because it will experience higher birth rates and more immigration. The number of migrants seeking to move from disadvantaged to relatively privileged countries is likely to increase.

The number of countries with youthful age structures in the current "arc of instability" is projected to decline by as much as 40 percent. Three of every four youth-bulge countries that remain will be located in Sub-Saharan Africa; nearly all of the remainder will be located in the core of the Middle East, scattered through southern and central Asia, and in the Pacific Islands.

New Transnational Agenda

Resource issues will gain prominence on the international agenda. Unprecedented global economic growth—positive in so many other regards—will continue to put pressure on a number of highly strategic resources, including energy, food, and water, and demand is projected to outstrip easily available supplies over the next decade or so. For example, non-OPEC liquid hydrocarbon production—crude oil, natural gas liquids, and unconventionals such as tar sands—will not grow commensurate with demand. Oil and gas production of many traditional energy producers already is declining. Elsewhere—in China, India, and Mexico—production has flattened. Countries capable of significantly expanding production will dwindle; oil and gas production will be concentrated in unstable areas. As a result of this and other factors, the world will be in the midst of a fundamental energy transition away from oil toward natural gas, coal and other alternatives.

The World Bank estimates that demand for food will rise by 50 percent by 2030, as a result of growing world population, rising affluence, and the shift to Western dietary preferences by a larger middle class. Lack of access to stable supplies of water is reaching critical proportions, particularly for agricultural purposes, and the problem will worsen because of rapid urbanization worldwide and the roughly 1.2 billion persons to be added over the next 20 years. Today, experts consider 21 countries, with a combined population of about 600 million, to be either cropland or freshwater scarce. Owing to continuing population growth, 36 countries, with about 1.4 billion people, are projected to fall into this category by 2025.

Climate change is expected to exacerbate resource scarcities. Although the impact of climate change will vary by region, a number of regions will begin to suffer harmful effects, particularly water scarcity and loss of agricultural production. Regional differences in agricultural production are likely to become more pronounced over time with declines disproportionately concentrated in developing countries, particularly those in Sub-Saharan Africa. Agricultural losses are expected to mount with substantial impacts forecast by most economists by late this century. For many developing countries, decreased agricultural output will be devastating because agriculture accounts for a large share of their economies and many of their citizens live close to subsistence levels.

New technologies could again provide solutions, such as viable alternatives to fossil fuels or means to overcome food and water constraints. However, all current technologies are inadequate for replacing the traditional energy architecture on the scale needed, and new energy technologies probably will not be commercially viable and widespread by 2025. The pace of technological innovation will be key. Even with a favorable policy and funding environment for biofuels, clean coal, or hydrogen, the transition to new fuels will be slow. Major technologies historically have had an "adoption lag." In the energy sector, a recent study found that it takes an average of 25 years for a new production technology to become widely adopted.

Despite what are seen as long odds now, we cannot rule out the possibility of an energy transition by 2025 that would avoid the costs of an energy infrastructure overhaul. The greatest possibility for a relatively quick and inexpensive transition during the period comes from better renewable generation sources (photovoltaic and wind) and improvements in battery technology. With many of these technologies, the infrastructure cost hurdle for individual projects would be lower, enabling many small economic actors to develop their own energy transformation projects that directly serve their interests—e.g., stationary fuel cells powering homes and offices, recharging plug-in hybrid autos, and selling energy back to the grid. Also, energy conversion schemes—such as plans to generate hydrogen for automotive fuel cells from electricity in the homeowner's garage—could avoid the need to develop complex hydrogen transportation infrastructure.

Prospects for Terrorism, Conflict, and Proliferation

Terrorism, proliferation, and conflict will remain key concerns even as resource issues move up on the international agenda. Terrorism is unlikely to disappear by 2025, but its appeal could diminish if economic growth continues and youth unemployment is mitigated in the Middle East. Economic opportunities for youth and greater political pluralism probably would dissuade some from joining terrorists' ranks, but others—motivated by a variety of factors, such as a desire for revenge or to become "martyrs"—will continue to turn to violence to pursue their objectives.

In the absence of employment opportunities and legal means for political expression, conditions will be ripe for disaffection, growing radicalism, and possible recruitment of youths into terrorist groups. Terrorist groups in 2025 will likely be a combination of descendants of long-established groups—that inherit organizational structures, command and control processes, and training procedures necessary to conduct sophisticated attacks—and newly emergent collections of the angry and disenfranchised that become self-radicalized. For those terrorist groups that are active in 2025, the diffusion of technologies and scientific knowledge will place some of the world's most dangerous capabilities within their reach. One of our greatest concerns continues to be that terrorist or other malevolent groups might acquire and employ biological agents, or less likely, a nuclear device, to create mass casualties.

Although Iran's acquisition of nuclear weapons is not inevitable, other coun-tries' worries about a nuclear-armed Iran could lead states in the region to develop new security arrangements with external powers, acquire additional weapons, and consider pursuing their own nuclear ambitions. It is not clear that the type of stable deterrent relationship that existed between the great powers for most of the Cold War would emerge naturally in the Middle East with a nuclear-weapons capable Iran. Episodes of low-intensity conflict taking place under a nuclear umbrella could lead to an unintended escalation and broader conflict if clear red lines between those states involved are not well established.

We believe ideological conflicts akin to the Cold War are unlikely to take root in a world in which most states will be preoccupied with the pragmatic challenges of globalization and shifting global power alignments. The force of ideology is likely to be strongest in the Muslim world—particularly the Arab core. In those countries that are likely to struggle with youth bulges and weak economic under-pinnings—such as Pakistan, Afghanistan, Nigeria, and Yemen—the radical Salafi trend of Islam is likely to gain traction.

Types of conflict we have not seen for awhile—such as over resources—could reemerge. Perceptions of energy scarcity will drive countries to take actions to assure their future access to energy supplies. In the worst case, this could result in interstate conflicts if government leaders deem assured access to energy resources, for example, to be essential for maintaining domestic stability and the survival of their regimes. However, even actions short of war will have important geopolitical conse-quences. Maritime security concerns are providing a rationale for naval buildups and modernization efforts, such as China's and India's development of blue-water naval capabilities. The buildup of regional naval capabilities could lead to increased ten-sions, rivalries, and counterbalancing moves but it also will create opportunities for multinational cooperation in protecting critical sea lanes. With water becoming more scarce in Asia and the Middle East, cooperation to manage changing water resources is likely to become more difficult within and between states.

The risk of nuclear weapon use over the next 20 years, although remaining very low, is likely to be greater than it is today as a result of several converging trends. The spread of nuclear technologies and expertise is generating concerns about the potential emergence of new nuclear weapon states and the acquisition of nuclear materials by terrorist groups. Ongoing low-intensity clashes between India and Pakistan continue to raise the specter that such events could escalate to a broader conflict between those nuclear powers. The possibility of a future disruptive regime change or collapse occurring in a weak state with nuclear weapons also continues to raise questions regarding the ability of such a state to control and secure its nuclear arsenals.

If nuclear weapons are used in the next 15–20 years, the international system will be shocked as it experiences immediate humanitarian, economic, and political-military repercussions. A future use of nuclear weapons probably would bring about significant geopolitical changes as some states would seek to establish or reinforce security alliances with existing nuclear powers and others would push for global nuclear disarmament.

A More Complex International System

The trend toward greater diffusion of authority and power that has been occurring for a couple decades is likely to accelerate because of the emergence of new global players, the worsening institutional deficit, potential expansion of regional blocs, and enhanced strength of nonstate actors and networks. The multiplicity of actors on the international scene could add strength—in terms of filling gaps left by aging post-World War II institutions—or further fragment the international system and incapacitate international cooperation. The diversity in type of actor raises the likelihood of fragmentation occurring over the next two decades, particularly given the wide array of transnational challenges facing the international community.

The rising BRIC powers are unlikely to challenge the international system as did Germany and Japan in the nineteenth and twentieth centuries, but because of their growing geopolitical and economic clout, they will have a high degree of freedom to customize their political and economic policies rather than fully adopting Western norms. They also are likely to want to preserve their policy freedom to maneuver, allowing others to carry the primary burden for dealing with such issues as terrorism, climate change, proliferation, and energy security.

Existing multilateral institutions—which are large and cumbersome and were designed for a different geopolitical order—will have difficulty adapting quickly to undertake new missions, accommodate changing memberships, and augment their resources.

Nongovernmental organizations (NGOs)—concentrating on specific issues—increasingly will be a part of the landscape, but NGO networks are likely to be limited in their ability to effect change in the absence of concerted efforts by multilateral institutions or governments. Efforts at greater inclusiveness—to reflect the emergence of the newer powers—may make it harder for international organizations to tackle transnational challenges. Respect for the dissenting views of member nations will continue to shape the agenda of organizations and limit the kinds of solutions that can be attempted.

Greater Asian regionalism—possible by 2025—would have global implications, sparking or reinforcing a trend toward three trade and financial clusters that could become quasi-blocs: North America, Europe, and East Asia. Establishment of such quasi-blocs would have implications for the ability to achieve future global

World Trade Organization (WTO) agreements. Regional clusters could compete in setting transregional product standards for information technology, biotechnology, nanotechnology, intellectual property rights, and other aspects of the "new economy." On the other hand, an absence of regional cooperation in Asia could help spur competition among China, India, and Japan over resources such as energy.

Intrinsic to the growing complexity of the overlapping roles of states, institutions, and nonstate actors is the proliferation of political identities, which is leading to establishment of new networks and rediscovered communities. No one political identity is likely to be dominant in most societies by 2025. Religion-based networks may be quintessential issue networks and overall may play a more powerful role on many transnational issues such as the environment and inequalities than secular groupings.

The United States: Less Dominant Power

By 2025 the U.S. will find itself as one of a number of important actors on the world stage, albeit still the most powerful one. Even in the military realm, where the U.S. will continue to possess considerable advantages in 2025, advances by others in science and technology, expanded adoption of irregular warfare tactics by both state and nonstate actors, proliferation of long-range precision weapons, and growing use of cyber warfare attacks increasingly will constrict U.S. freedom of action. A more constrained U.S. role has implications for others and the likelihood of new agenda issues being tackled effectively. Despite the recent rise in anti-Americanism, the U.S. probably will continue to be seen as a much-needed regional balancer in the Middle East and Asia. The U.S. will continue to be expected to play a significant role in using its military power to counter global terrorism. On newer security issues like climate change, U.S. leadership will be widely perceived as critical to leveraging competing and divisive views to find solutions. At the same time, the multiplicity of influential actors and distrust of vast power means less room for the U.S. to call the shots without the support of strong partnerships. Developments in the rest of the world, including internal developments in a number of key states—particularly China and Russia—are also likely to be crucial determinants of U.S. policy.

2025—What Kind of Future?

The above trends suggest major discontinuities, shocks, and surprises, which we highlight throughout the text. Examples include nuclear weapons use or a pandemic. In some cases, the surprise element is only a matter of timing: an energy transition, for example, is inevitable; the only questions are when and how abruptly or smoothly such a transition occurs. An energy transition from one type of fuel (fossil fuels) to another (alternative) is an event that historically has only happened once a century at most with momentous consequences. The transition from wood to coal helped trigger industrialization. In this case, a transition—particularly an abrupt one—out of fossil fuels would have major repercussions for energy producers in the Middle East and Eurasia, potentially causing permanent decline of some states as global and regional powers.

Other discontinuities are less predictable. They are likely to result from an interaction of several trends and depend on the quality of leadership. We put uncertainties such as whether China or Russia becomes a democracy in this category. China's growing middle class increases the chances but does not make such a development inevitable. Political pluralism seems less likely in Russia in the absence of economic diversification. Pressure from below may force the issue, or a leader might begin or enhance the democratization process to sustain the economy or spur economic growth. A sustained plunge in the price of oil and gas would alter the outlook and increase prospects for greater political and economic liberalization in Russia. If either country were to democratize, it would represent another wave of democratization with wide significance for many other developing states.

Also uncertain are the outcomes of demographic challenges facing Europe, Japan, and even Russia. In none of these cases does demography have to spell destiny with less regional and global power an inevitable outcome. Technology, the role of immigration, public health improvements, and laws encouraging greater female participation in the economy are some of the measures that could change the trajectory of current trends pointing toward less economic growth, increased social tensions, and possible decline.

Whether global institutions adapt and revive—another key uncertainty—also is a function of leadership. Current trends suggest a dispersion of power and authority will create a global governance deficit. Reversing those trend lines would require strong leadership in the international community by a number of powers, including the emerging ones. . . .

NOTE

1. National power scores, computed by the International Futures computer model, are the product of an index combining the weighted factors of GDP, defense spending, population, and technology.

Emerging Multipolarity: Why Should We Care?

BARRY R. POSEN

THE MULTIPOLAR MOMENT

Theorists and historians know multipolarity better than they do the other two structures of power, but there are no active statesmen today with experience of a multipolar system. The relatively equal distribution of capabilities in a multipolar world, with three or more consequential powers, produces one basic pattern of behavior: The arithmetic of coalitions influences matters great and small. The overall balance of capabilities, and the military balance in particular, are easily altered in a significant way depending on who sides with whom. Internal efforts cannot accomplish nearly as much change, at such a low cost, in such a short time.

Thus states are slower to react to others' internal military developments, because allies can be had to redress the balance. In a multipolar system, states should lack confidence that significant military buildups can help them much, because other states can combine against them. Autonomous military power does remain important, and states will look to their own military capabilities, but diminishing returns should set in sooner than they would in other structures of power.

Diplomacy becomes a respected career again under multipolarity. Hans Morgenthau, a great admirer of multipolarity, was also a great admirer of diplomacy. Isolation is perhaps the most dangerous situation in multipolarity, so states will pay close and constant attention to the game of coalition building. They will try to find and secure allies for themselves, and will eye warily the efforts of others to do the same. All will try to improve their own coalitions and erode those of others.

If indeed the distribution of capabilities among great powers is slowly evolving toward multipolarity, what behaviors might we predict? As we try to say something about real matters in a real world, a problem quickly emerges: Other facts of the case begin to complicate our analysis, even if we stick largely to security matters. The United States is buffered by oceans from much of the world's traditional security competition and remains well endowed with the human and material resources to go it alone. Indeed, many of the world's consequential powers are buffered by geography from one another. All but two of the consequential powers possess significant nuclear forces, which makes them difficult to conquer or even coerce. Japan and Germany are excluded from the nuclear club, but could enter it quickly.

Arguably, even among great powers, a close examination of conventional capabilities might show an emerging "defense dominant" world. It seems plausible that, among proximate technological, economic, and social equals, an ongoing revolution in military information technology—including surveillance and precision targeting—will make it harder to attack than to defend. It should be more difficult to take ground than to hold it, and more challenging to cross oceans with men and materiel and land them on a hostile shore than to prevent amphibious attack. All of these factors, added to a somewhat more equitable distribution of military power, should tend to mute great power military competition.

Some competition for power is to be expected, however. The experience of the United States as the unipole should be a cautionary one—an extremely secure state nevertheless reached out to expand its power and influence. A great deal of American behavior overseas was elicited by some combination of fear about the future and temptation presented by a power vacuum. We can expect national security establishments to worry about the future: So long as anarchy permits predation, they will ensure against the possibility.

Uncertainty about power relationships also will remain. States in normal times may distill economic power into military power at only a fraction of the level they could achieve under other conditions, and none can truly know the others' possible energy or efficiency to distill in the future. Thus, they will seek some comfort margin in the military capabilities that matter most to them, which will in turn discomfit others.

Moreover, some natural resources will seem scarce. Even if market-oriented states eschew direct control of foreign production, they will wish to maintain privileged influence over these producers, as we have seen in the case of energy supplies. States also will continue to worry about the strategic value of key geographic features, locally and globally. All members of the system likely will continue to compete, therefore, to improve their position and simultaneously undermine that of their brothers and sisters.

THE DIFFUSION OF POWER

The emerging era's great powers, beyond their direct concerns with one another, are likely to face a phenomenon that some are calling "the diffusion of power." This concept remains a bit airy but it encompasses several trends that appear to be real and meaningful. First, despite Western military-technological prowess, the gap appears to be narrowing between the great powers' military capabilities and those of middle powers, small states, and non-state groups that choose to oppose them—at least when it comes to military forces pertinent to conquest and occupation.

One reason for this was the collapse of the Soviet Union and Warsaw Pact, which permitted a vast outflow of infantry weapons. At the same time, some of the former Soviet republics and East European Warsaw Pact states inherited arms production capabilities in search of markets. China will soon begin to produce and export moderately sophisticated military equipment. In addition, some new producers have entered the market, with Iran perhaps the most noteworthy. More states are able to make medium-quality military equipment than has previously been the case. This has the effect of making small states and non-state actors more independent of great power influence than they once were, and more able to inflict costs on great powers that attack them.

Military skill also seems to have diffused. The spread of literacy and the freer flow of people, goods, and information associated with globalization may permit states and non-state groups that are willing to fight larger powers to share lessons and improve their overall military expertise. Moreover, across the developing world, weapons and expertise can be combined with significant numbers of motivated young men. The upshot is that great powers may have to pay a higher premium to push the smaller ones around than has been true in the recent past.

Although comparison is tricky, it is striking that the Americans' effort in Iraq has been about as time-consuming and costly in dollar terms as their effort in Vietnam, and the adversary in Iraq did not have a superpower patron, or even a particularly good cross-border sanctuary. The United States did deploy many fewer people for the Iraq operation than it did in Vietnam, and suffered fewer deaths. A comparison of overall casualties, however, awaits clearer information about the range and duration of less visible physical and psychological injuries that US forces have suffered. The less visible human costs appear to be significant.

The diffusion of power has another meaning. Across much of the developing world, central governments weakened more or less as the cold war ended. Pakistan is only the scariest example. Weakening central governments may find themselves at war with domestic political factions, or as willing or unwilling hosts to violent non-state actors. Even before the Al Qaeda attacks on New York and Washington on September 11, 2001, the great powers were uneasy about these weak or failing states. They loathed the human rights violations that are a hallmark of civil war. And they feared the negative externalities of refugee flows and criminal enterprises. The 9/11 attacks added a concern that these poorly governed spaces would prove hospitable to terrorist groups. Most great power military intervention since the end of the cold war has been driven by the problem of weakened central governments.

Finally, there is particularly great concern about states that are capable enough to build advanced weapons, especially nuclear weapons, but nevertheless weak enough to risk collapse and the loss of control over said weapons. Pakistan is again the most troubling example. The diffusion of power in this case thus creates a strange combination—major threats to the safety of the strong emanating from the weak.

In such an environment, we can expect that the great powers will continue to view the developing world as a source of security threats, meriting intervention. But not all great powers in a multipolar system will agree on any given project, so some will view the "defensive" projects of others as having ulterior motives. Some states will have an incentive to hinder the efforts of their peers to pacify ungoverned spaces. Their direct interest may be engaged, or the intervention may prove a tempting opportunity to "bleed" other great powers. Their capabilities to do so will improve, particularly given the growing military skill of the indigenous peoples they can assist. States organizing interventions will therefore be very concerned about costs. They will seek allies to spread the costs around, and will attempt to dissuade others from helping the locals.

PERSISTENT COMPETITION

What general patterns of great power behavior could emerge in a multipolar environment, based on the situation discussed above? First, the competition for power is likely to persist, though this is more a statement of general realist religious conviction than an inference from the multipolar structure of power. Second, because of "defense dominance," the pattern of competition will look much like an endless series of games played for small stakes. States will want more, but will not wish to court disaster.

Third, and consequently, states will look for ways to "measure power" without war. The diplomacy of making and breaking coalitions, and counting allies, will present itself as an attractive, if complex, alternative. Fourth, competitors likely will believe that the safe way to improve one's relative position is to pursue policies that weaken others. Increasing others' costs when they undertake initiatives will seem wiser than undertaking one's own adventures. John Mearsheimer's "bait and bleed" strategies may become more common.

Fifth, the diffusion of power will continue to seduce great power adventures. Yet the capabilities of local actors, and the potential intervention, even if indirect, of other great powers, will raise the potential costs of those adventures. Therefore, these projects too will increase the importance of other powers. Diplomacy will be required to discourage opposition, encourage alliance, or at least elicit neutrality. Sixth, in general, geography may matter more. If capabilities are more equal, states will have to make harder choices about the kinds of military power they generate. Land powers will be land powers, and sea powers will be sea powers, and thus to tilt with each other they will require allies of the other type.

THE QUESTION OF STABILITY

The transition from bipolarity to unipolarity was marked by dramatic events. Perhaps the intense nature of the bipolar competition naturally led to a stark finish of one kind or another: a preventive war, or a national collapse. Unipolarity seems destined for a different kind of transition. The United States has many attributes that contribute to its power advantage and its security, and that have made the world unipolar. It seems unlikely that all of these advantages would suddenly disappear. Direct competition with the United States will appear daunting for quite some time to come.

The costs of U.S. efforts to make the world over in its image, relative to the benefits of such efforts, will ultimately begin to tell, however. America will gradually be inclined to do less. At the same time, uneven growth will alter the basic balance of capabilities among the principal powers. The American capability advantage in economic power will diminish, and concomitantly its advantage in military power will likely narrow. As this occurs, the other principal powers will find themselves better able to tilt with the United States, but also more dependent on themselves. A multipolar order may gradually creep up on us, rather than emerge with a crash.

Many theorists have debated whether one kind of power structure is more "stable" than another. But definitions of stability are fluid. Some mean peace, others mean only the absence of great war, and still others merely mean persistence. Some believe multipolarity is more stable, while others assert the stability of bipolar worlds.

We have experienced long periods of relative peace in multipolar systems. Some scholars refer to the period between the end of the Napoleonic Wars and the outbreak of the First World War as the "hundred years' peace." In that time crises erupted and major powers fought limited wars, but no truly great war took place. That period was, of course, followed by a bloodbath.

The bipolar era lasted a little less than half a century, and no superpower war occurred. But the cold war was characterized by vast military spending, numerous dangerous crises, horrendous proxy wars, and a nuclear arms race that left tens of thousands of warheads on both sides, an absurd accumulation of destructive power. It also probably exhausted the Soviet Union.

The National Intelligence Council's *Global Trends 2025* report warns that multipolar systems are "more unstable than bipolar or unipolar systems." This sentence is difficult to decode. I find it more accurate to speak simply of the differences among these systems. Bipolarity is a tightly coupled, simple, and intensely competitive system. Opportunities for creative expansionists are few, but life is very tense. Multipolarity is complex, flexible, and full of options, and these very qualities seduce the creative expansionist into a search for opportunities, which occasionally exist.

Unipolarity is still the least understood structure of power. Leadership by a single very great power with an incentive to manage the system limits competition among the others through a combination of deterrence and reassurance, but we do not have a good sense of just how superior that power needs to be to sustain this happy outcome. If multipolarity is indeed on the horizon, all I can suggest is that the pattern of international politics ahead will likely be quite different from that of the past 65 years.

The Return of History

ROBERT KAGAN

The world has become normal again. The years immediately following the end of the Cold War offered a tantalizing glimpse at the possibility of a new kind of international order, with nations growing together or disappearing altogether, ideological conflicts melting away, cultures intermingling, and increasingly free commerce and communications. But that was a mirage, the hopeful anticipation of a liberal, democratic world that wanted to believe the end of the cold war did not just end one strategic and ideological conflict but all strategic and ideological conflict. . . . Today the nations of the West still cling to that vision. Evidence to the contrary—the turn toward autocracy in Russia or the growing military ambitions of China—is either dismissed as temporary aberrations or denied entirely.

The world has not been transformed, however. Nations remain as strong as ever, and so too do the nationalist ambitions, the passions, and the competition among nations that have shaped history. The world is still "unipolar," with the United States remaining the only superpower. But international competition among great powers has returned, with the United States, Russia, China, Europe, Japan, India, Iran, and others vying for regional predominance. Struggles for honor and status and influence in the world have once again become key features of the international scene. Ideologically, it is not a time of convergence but of divergence. The competition between liberalism and absolutism has reemerged, with the nations of the world increasingly lining up, as in the past, along ideological lines. Finally, there is the fault line between modernity and tradition, the violent struggle of Islamic fundamentalists against the powers and the modern secular cultures that, in their view, have penetrated and polluted their Islamic world.

How will the United States deal with such a world? Today there is much discussion of the so-called Bush doctrine and what may follow it. Many believe the world is in turmoil not because it is in turmoil but because George W. Bush made it so by destroying the new hopeful era. . . . The first illusion, however, is that Bush really changed anything. Since the end of World War II, at least, American leaders of both parties have pursued a fairly consistent approach to the world. They have regarded the United States as the "indispensable nation" and the "locomotive at the head of mankind." They have amassed power and influence and deployed them in ever widening arcs around the globe on behalf of interests, ideals, and ambitions, both tangible and intangible. Since 1945 Americans have insisted on acquiring and maintaining military supremacy, a "preponderance of power" in the world rather than a balance of power with other nations. They have operated on the ideological conviction that liberal democracy is the only legitimate form of government and that other forms of government are not only illegitimate but transitory. They have declared their readiness to "support free peoples who are resisting attempted subjugation" by forces of oppression, to "pay any price, bear any burden" to defend freedom, to seek "democratic enlargement" in the world, and to work for the "end of tyranny." They have been impatient with the status quo. They have seen America as a catalyst for change in human affairs and employed the strategies and tactics of "maximalism," seeking revolutionary rather than gradualist solutions to problems. Therefore they have often been at odds with the more cautious approaches of their allies. . . .

These American traditions, together with historical events beyond Americans' control, have catapulted the United States to a position of preeminence in the world. Since the end of the cold war and the emergence of this "unipolar" world, there has been much anticipation of the end of unipolarity and the rise of a multipolar world in which the United States is no longer the predominant power. Yet American predominance in the main categories of power persists as a key feature of the international system. The enormous and productive American economy remains at the center of the international economic system. American democratic principles are shared by over a hundred nations. The American military is not only the largest but the only one capable of projecting force into distant theaters. Chinese strategists see the world not as multipolar but as characterized by "one superpower, many great powers," and this configuration seems likely to persist into the future absent either a catastrophic blow to American power or a decision by the United States to diminish its power and international influence voluntarily.[1]

The anticipated global balancing has for the most part not occurred. Russia and China certainly share a common and openly expressed goal of checking American hegemony. They have created at least one institution, the Shanghai Cooperation Organization, aimed at resisting American influence in Central Asia, and China is the only power in the world, other than the United States, engaged in a long-term military buildup. But Sino-Russian hostility to American predominance has not yet produced a concerted and cooperative effort at balancing. China's buildup is driven at least as much by its own long-term ambitions as by a desire to balance the United States. Russia has been using its vast reserves of oil and natural gas as a lever to compensate for its lack of military power, but it either cannot or does not want to increase its military capability sufficiently to begin counterbalancing the United States. Overall, Russian military power remains in decline. In addition, the two powers do not trust one another. They are traditional rivals, and the rise of China inspires at least as much nervousness in Russia as it does in the

United States. At the moment, moreover, China is less abrasively confrontational with the United States. Its dependence on the American market and foreign investment and its perception that the United States remains a potentially formidable adversary mitigate against an openly confrontational approach.

In any case, China and Russia cannot balance the United States without at least some help from Europe, Japan, India, and at least some of the other advanced democratic nations. But those powerful players are not joining the effort. Europe has rejected the option of making itself a counterweight to American power. This is true even among the older members of the European Union (EU), among whom neither France, Germany, Italy, nor Spain proposes such counterbalancing, despite a public opinion hostile to the Bush administration. Now that the EU has expanded to include the nations of Central and Eastern Europe and the Baltic states, who fear threats from the East, not from the West, the prospect of a unified Europe counterbalancing the United States is practically nil. As for Japan and India, the clear trend in recent years has been toward closer strategic cooperation with the United States.

If anything, the most notable balancing over the past decade has been aimed not at the American superpower but at the two large powers China and Russia. Japan, Australia, and even South Korea and the nations of Southeast Asia have all engaged in "hedging" against a rising China. This has led them to seek closer relations with Washington, especially in the cases of Japan and Australia. India has also drawn closer to the United States and is clearly engaged in balancing against China. Russia's efforts to increase its influence over what it regards as its "near abroad," meanwhile, have produced tensions and negative reactions in the Baltics and Eastern Europe. Because these nations are now members of the EU, this has also complicated EU-Russian relations. On balance, traditional allies of the United States in East Asia and in Europe, although their publics may be more anti-American than they were in the past, nevertheless pursue policies that reflect more concern about the powerful states in their midst than about the United States. . . .[2]

Overall, there is no shortage of other countries willing to host U.S. forces, a good indication that much of the world continues to tolerate and even lend support to American geopolitical primacy, if only as a protection against more worrying foes.

Predominance is not the same thing as omnipotence. The fact that the United States has more power than everyone else does not mean it can impose its will on everyone else. American predominance in the early years after World War II did not prevent the North Korean invasion of the South, a Communist victory in China, the Soviet acquisition of the hydrogen bomb, or the consolidation of the Soviet empire in Eastern Europe—all far greater strategic setbacks than anything the United States has yet suffered or is likely to suffer in Iraq and Afghanistan. Nor does predominance mean the United States will succeed in all its endeavors, any more than it did six decades ago. . . . So long as the United States remains at the center of the international economy and the predominant military power, so long as the American public continues to support American predominance, as it has consistently for six decades, and so long as potential challengers inspire more fear than sympathy among their neighbors, the structure of the international system should remain as the Chinese describe it: one superpower and many great powers.

This is a good thing, and it should continue to be a primary goal of American foreign policy to perpetuate this relatively benign international configuration of power. The unipolar order with the United States as the predominant power is unavoidably riddled with flaws and contradictions. It inspires fears and jealousies. The United States is not immune to error, like all other nations, and because of its size and importance in the international system those errors are magnified and take on greater significance than the errors of less powerful nations. Compared with the ideal Kantian international order, in which all the world's powers would be peace-loving equals, conducting themselves wisely, prudently, and in strict obeisance to international law, the unipolar system is both dangerous and unjust. Compared with any plausible alternative in the real world, however, it is relatively stable and less likely to produce a major war between great powers. It is also comparatively benevolent, from a liberal perspective, for it is more conducive to the principles of economic and political liberalism that Americans and many others value.

American predominance does not stand in the way of progress toward a better world, therefore. It stands in the way of regression toward a more dangerous world. For the choice is not between an American-dominated order and a world that looks like the EU. The future international order will be shaped by those who have the power to shape it. The leaders of a post-American world will not meet in Brussels but in Beijing, Moscow, and Washington.

If the world is marked by the persistence of unipolarity, it is nevertheless also being shaped by the reemergence of competitive national ambitions of the kind that have shaped human affairs from time immemorial. During the cold war, this historical tendency of great powers to jostle with one another for status and influence, as well as for wealth and power, was largely suppressed by the two superpowers and their rigid bipolar order. Since the end of the Cold War, the United States has not been powerful enough, and probably could never be powerful enough, to suppress by itself this normal tendency of nations. This does not mean that the world has returned to multipolarity, as none of the large powers is yet attempting to compete with the superpower for global predominance. Nevertheless, several large powers are now competing for regional predominance, both with the United States and with each other.

National ambition drives China's foreign policy today, and although it is tempered by prudence and the desire to appear as unthreatening as possible to the rest of the world, the Chinese are powerfully motivated to return their nation to what they regard as its traditional position as the preeminent power in East Asia. They do not share a European, postmodern view that power is passé; hence their now two-decades-long military buildup and modernization. Like the Americans, they believe that power, including military power, is a good thing to have and that it is better to have more of it than less. Perhaps more significant is the Chinese perception, also shared by Americans, that status and honor, and not just wealth and security, are important for a nation.

Japan, meanwhile, which in the past could have been counted as an aspiring postmodern power—with its pacifist constitution and low defense spending—now appears embarked on a more traditional national course. Partly this is in reaction to the rising power of China and concerns about North Korea's nuclear weapons. But it is also driven by Japan's own national ambition to be a leader in East Asia or at least not to play second fiddle or "little brother" to China. China and Japan are now in a competitive quest to augment their own status and power and to prevent the other's rise to predominance, and this competition has a military and strategic, as well as an economic and political, component. Their competition is such that a nation such as South Korea, with a long, unhappy history as a pawn between the two powers, is once again worrying about both a "greater China" and the return of Japanese nationalism. . . .

Russian foreign policy, too, looks more like something from the nineteenth century. It is being driven by a typical, and typically Russian, blend of national resentment and ambition. A postmodern Russia simply seeking integration into the new European order . . . would not be troubled by the eastward enlargement of the EU and NATO, would not insist on predominant influence over its "near abroad," and would not use its natural resources as means of gaining geopolitical leverage and enhancing Russia's international status in an attempt to regain the lost glories of the Soviet empire and of Peter the Great. But Russia, like China and Japan, is moved by more traditional great-power considerations, including the pursuit of those valuable if intangible national interests: honor and respect. Although Russian leaders complain about threats to their security from NATO and the United States, the Russian sense of insecurity has more to do with resentment and national identity than with plausible external military threats. But that does not make insecurity less a factor in Russia's relations with the world. Indeed, it makes finding compromise with the Russians all the more difficult.

One could add others to this list of great powers with traditional rather than postmodern aspirations. India's regional ambitions are more muted, or are focused most intently on Pakistan, but it is clearly engaged in competition with China for dominance in the Indian Ocean and sees itself, correctly, as an emerging great power on the world scene. In the Middle East there is Iran, which mingles religious fervor with a historical sense of superiority and leadership in its region. Its nuclear program is as much about the desire for regional hegemony as about defending Iranian territory from attack by the United States.

Even the EU itself, in its way, expresses a pan-European national ambition to play a significant role in the world, and it has become the vehicle for channeling German and French, if not British, ambitions in what Europeans regard as a safe supranational direction. Europeans seek honor and respect, too, but of a postmodern variety. The honor they seek is to occupy the moral high ground in the world, to exercise moral authority, to wield political and economic influence as an antidote to militarism, to be the keeper of the global conscience, and to be recognized and admired by others for playing this role.

Islam is not a nation, but many Muslims express a kind of religious nationalism, and the leaders of radical Islam, including al Qaeda, do seek to establish a theocratic nation or confederation of nations that would encompass a wide swath of the Middle East and beyond. Like national movements elsewhere, Islamists have a yearning for respect, including self-respect, and a desire for honor. Their national identity has been molded in defiance against stronger and often oppressive outside powers and also by memories of ancient superiority over those same powers. China had its "century of humiliation." Islamists have more than a century of humiliation to look back on, a humiliation of which Israel has become the living symbol, which is partly why even Muslims who are neither radical nor fundamentalist proffer their sympathy and even their support to violent extremists who can turn the tables on the dominant liberal West, and particularly on a dominant America which implanted and still feeds the Israeli cancer in their midst.

Finally, there is the United States itself. As a matter of national policy stretching back across numerous administrations, Democratic and Republican, liberal and conservative, Americans have insisted on preserving regional predominance in East Asia, the Middle East, the Western Hemisphere, until recently Europe, and now, increasingly, in Central Asia. Since the end of the Cold War, beginning with the first Bush administration and continuing through the Clinton years, the United States did not retract but expanded its influence eastward across Europe and into the Middle East, Central Asia, and the Caucasus. The United States, too, is more of a traditional than a postmodern power, and though Americans are loath to acknowledge it, they generally prefer their global place as "No. 1" and are equally loath to relinquish it. Once having entered a region, whether for practical or idealistic reasons, they are remarkably slow to withdraw from it until they believe they have substantially transformed it in their own image.

The jostling for status and influence among these ambitious nations and would-be nations is a second defining feature of the new post–Cold War international system. Nationalism in all its forms is back, if it ever went away, and so is international competition for power, influence, honor, and status. If the United States chose to accept a diminished global role, to become one among equals, the world would surely devolve into a more equal multipolar competition. These more equal powers would not be any more committed to international laws and institutions than nations have been throughout history. They would settle disputes as great and lesser powers have done in the past, sometimes through diplomacy and accommodation but often through confrontation and wars of varying scope, intensity, and destructiveness. One novel aspect of such a multipolar world is that most of these powers would possess nuclear weapons. That could make wars between them less likely, or it could simply make them more catastrophic.

People who believe that a multipolar order would be preferable to the present American predominance often succumb to a basic logical fallacy. They believe that the international order the world enjoys today exists independently of American power. They imagine that in a world in which American power was diminished, the aspects of international order that they like would remain in place. But that is not the way it works. International order does not rest on ideas and institutions. It is shaped by configurations of power. The international order we know today reflects the distribution of power in the world since World War II, and especially since the end of the

Cold War. A different configuration of power, a multipolar world, in which the poles were Russia, China, the United States, India, and Europe, would produce its own kind of order, with different rules and norms reflecting the interests of the powerful states that would have a hand in shaping it. Would that international order be an improvement? Perhaps for Beijing and Moscow it would. But it is doubtful that it would suit the tastes of enlightenment liberals in the United States and Europe.

The current order, of course, not only is far from perfect but also offers no guarantee against major conflict among the world's great powers. Even under the umbrella of unipolarity, regional conflicts involving the large powers may erupt. War could erupt between China and Taiwan and draw in both the United States and Japan. . . . Conflict between India and Pakistan remains possible, as does conflict between Iran and Israel or other Middle Eastern states. These, too, could draw in other great powers, including the United States.

Such conflicts may be unavoidable no matter what policies the United States pursues. But they are more likely to erupt if the United States weakens or withdraws from its positions of regional dominance. This is especially true in East Asia, where most nations agree that a reliable American power has a stabilizing and pacific effect on the region. In Europe, too, the departure of the United States from the scene—even if it remained the world's most powerful nation—could be destabilizing. It could tempt Russia to an even more overbearing and potentially forceful approach to unruly nations on its periphery.

In the Middle East, competition for influence among powers both inside and outside the region has raged for at least two centuries. The rise of Islamic fundamentalism does not change this. It only adds a new and more threatening dimension to the competition, which neither a sudden end to the conflict between Israel and the Palestinians nor an immediate American withdrawal from Iraq would change. The region and the states within it remain relatively weak. A diminution of American influence would not be followed by a diminution of other external influences. An American withdrawal from Iraq will not return things to "normal" or to a new kind of stability in the region. It will produce a new instability, one likely to draw the United States back in again. The alternative to American predominance in the region is not balance and peace. It is further competition.

The alternative to American regional predominance, in short, is not a new regional stability. In an era of burgeoning nationalism, the future is likely to be one of intensified competition among nations and nationalist movements. Difficult as it may be to extend American predominance into the future, no one should imagine that a reduction of American power or a retraction of American influence and global involvement will provide an easier path.

Complicating the equation, and adding to the stakes, is that the return to the international competition of ambitious nations has been accompanied by a return to global ideological competition. More precisely, the two-centuries-old struggle between political liberalism and autocracy has reemerged as a defining characteristic of the present era.

The assumption that the death of Communism would bring an end to disagreements about the proper form of government and society seemed more plausible in the 1990s, when both Russia and China were thought to be moving toward political, as well as economic, liberalism. Such a development would have produced a remarkable ideological convergence among all the great powers of the world and heralded a genuinely new era in human development.

But those expectations have proved misplaced. China has not liberalized but shored up its autocratic government. Russia has turned away from imperfect liberalism decisively toward autocracy. Of the world's great powers today, therefore, two of the largest, with over 1½ billion people, have governments committed to autocratic rule and seem to have the ability to sustain themselves in power for the foreseeable future, with evident popular approval.

Many assume that Russian and Chinese leaders do not believe in anything, and therefore they cannot be said to represent an ideology, but that is mistaken. Communism and liberal capitalism are not the only ideologies the world has ever known. The rulers of China and Russia do have a set of beliefs that guide them in both domestic and foreign policy. They believe that autocracy is better for their nations than democracy. They believe it offers order and stability and the possibility of prosperity. They believe that for their large, fractious nations, a strong government is essential to prevent chaos and collapse. They believe that democracy is not the answer and that they are serving the best interests of their peoples by holding and wielding power the way they do. This is not a novel or, from a historical perspective, even a disreputable idea. The European monarchies of the seventeenth, eighteenth, and nineteenth centuries were thoroughly convinced of the superiority of their form of government. Only in the past half-century has liberalism gained widespread popularity around the world, and even today some American thinkers exalt "liberal autocracy" over what they, too, disdain as "illiberal democracy." If two of the world's largest powers share a common commitment to autocratic government, autocracy is not dead as an ideology. . . .

Autocrats can hardly be expected to aid in legitimizing an evolution in the international system toward "limited sovereignty" and "the responsibility to protect." For even if the people and governments pushing this evolution do not believe they are establishing the precedent for international interventions against Russia and China, the leaders of those nations have no choice but to contemplate the possibility and to try to shield themselves. China, after all, has been a victim of international sanctions imposed by the U.S.-led liberal world, and for killing far fewer people than did the governments of Sudan or Zimbabwe. Nor do China's rulers forget that if the liberal world had had its way in 1989, they would now be out of office, probably imprisoned, possibly dead. . . . Neither Russia nor China has any interest in assisting liberal nations in their crusade against autocracies around the world. Moreover, they can see their comparative advantage over the West when it comes to gaining influence with autocratic governments in Africa, Asia, or Latin America, governments that can provide access to oil and other vital natural resources or that, in the case of Burma, are strategically located. Moscow knows that it can have more influence with governments in Kazakhstan and Turkmenistan because, unlike the liberal West, it can unreservedly support their regimes. And it is a simple matter of addition that the more autocracies there are in the world, the less isolated Beijing and Moscow will be in international forums such as the United Nations. The more dictatorships there are, the more global resistance they will offer against the liberal West's efforts to place limits on sovereignty in the interest of advancing liberalism.

The general effect of the rise of these two large autocratic powers, therefore, will be to increase the likelihood that autocracy will spread in some parts of the world. This is not because Russia and China are evangelists for autocracy or want to set off a worldwide autocratic revolution. This is not the cold war redux. It is more like the nineteenth century redux. In the nineteenth century the absolutist rulers of Russia and Austria shored up fellow autocracies, in France, for instance, and used force to suppress liberal rebellions in Germany, Italy, and Spain. China and Russia may not go that far, at least not yet. But Ukraine has already been a battleground between forces supported by the liberal West and forces supported by Russia. The great power autocracies will inevitably offer support and friendship to those who feel besieged by the United States and other liberal nations. Autocrats and would-be autocrats will know that they can again find powerful allies and patrons, something that was not as true in the 1990s. . . .

But through the 1980s and 1990s the autocratic model seemed less attractive, as dictatorships of both right and left fell before the liberal tide. That tide has not yet turned in the other direction, but the future may bring a return to a global competition between different forms of government, with the world's great powers on opposite sides.

This has implications for international institutions and for American foreign policy. It is difficult to speak of an "international community" with any confidence. The term suggests agreement on international norms of behavior, an international morality, even an international conscience. The idea of such a community took hold in the 1990s, at a time when the general assumption was that the movement of Russia and China toward Western liberalism was producing a global commonality of thinking about human affairs. But by the late 1990s it was already clear that the international community lacked a foundation of common understanding. This was exposed most blatantly in the war over Kosovo, which divided the liberal West from both Russia and China and from many other non-European nations. Today, it is apparent on the issue of Sudan and Darfur. In the future, incidents that expose the hollowness of the term *international community* will likely proliferate.

As for the UN Security Council, after a brief awakening from the cold war coma, it is falling back to its former condition of near-paralysis. The agile diplomacy of France and the tactical caution of China have at times obscured the fact that the Security Council on most major issues is clearly divided between the autocracies and the democracies, with the latter systematically pressing for sanctions and other punitive actions against Iran, North Korea, Sudan, and other autocracies and the former just as systematically resisting and attempting to weaken the effect of such actions. This is a rut that is likely to deepen in the coming years.

The problem goes beyond the Security Council. Efforts to achieve any international consensus in any forum are going to be more and more difficult because of the widening gap between the liberal and autocratic governments. The current divisions between the United States and its European allies that have garnered so much attention in recent years are going to be overtaken by the more fundamental ideological divisions, and especially by growing tensions between the democratic transatlantic alliance and Russia.

The divisions will be sharper where ideological fault lines coincide with those caused by competitive national ambitions. It may be largely accidental that two of the world's more nationalistic powers are also the two leading autocracies, but this fact will have immense geopolitical significance.

Under these circumstances, calls for a new "concert" of nations in which Russia, China, the United States, Europe, and other great powers operate under some kind of international condominium are unlikely to succeed. The early-nineteenth-century Concert of Europe operated under the umbrella of a common morality and shared principles of government. It aimed not only at the preservation of a European peace but also, and more important, at the maintenance of a monarchical and aristocratic order against the liberal and radical challenges presented by the French and American revolutions and their echoes in Germany, Italy, and Poland. The Concert gradually broke down under the strains of popular nationalism, fueled in part by the rise of liberalism.

Today there is little sense of shared morality and common political principle among the great powers. Quite the contrary. There is suspicion and growing hostility and the well-grounded view on the part of the autocracies that the democracies, whatever they say, would welcome their overthrow. Any concert among them would be built on a shaky foundation likely to collapse at the first serious test. . . .

The Islamists' struggle against the powerful and often impersonal forces of modernization, capitalism, and globalization is a fact of life in the world today. Much of this fight has been peaceful, but some of it has been violent and now, oddly, poses by far the greatest threat of a catastrophic attack on the mainland of the United States.

It is odd because the struggle between modernization and globalization on the one hand and traditionalism on the other is largely a sideshow on the international stage. The future is more likely to be dominated by the struggle among the great powers and between the great ideologies of liberalism and autocracy than by the effort of some radical Islamists to restore an imagined past of piety. But of course that struggle has taken on a new and frightening dimension. Normally, when old and less technologically advanced civilizations have confronted more advanced civilizations, their inadequate weapons reflected their backwardness. Today, the radical proponents of Islamic traditionalism, though they abhor the modern world, nevertheless not only are using the ancient methods of assassination and suicidal attacks but also are deploying the weapons of the modern world against it. Modernization and globalization inflamed their rebellion and also armed them for the fight.

It is a lonely and ultimately desperate fight, for in the struggle between tradition and modernization, tradition cannot win—though traditional forces armed with modern technology can put up a good fight. All the world's rich and powerful nations have more or less embraced the economic, technological, and even social aspects of modernization and globalization. All have embraced, albeit with varying degrees of complaint and resistance, the free flow of goods, finances, and services and the intermingling of cultures and lifestyles that characterize the modern world. Increasingly, their people watch the same television shows, listen to the same music, and go to the same movies. And, along with this dominant modern culture, they have accepted, even as they may also deplore, the essential characteristics of a modern morality and aesthetics: the sexual, as well as political and economic, liberation of women; the weakening of church authority and the strengthening of secularism; the existence of what used to be called the counterculture; free expression in the arts (if not in politics), which includes the freedom to commit blasphemy and to lampoon symbols of faith, authority, and morality—these and all the countless effects of liberalism and capitalism unleashed and unchecked by the constraining hand of tradition, a powerful church, or a moralistic and domineering government. The Chinese have learned that although it is possible to have capitalism without political liberalization, it is much harder to have capitalism without cultural liberalization.

Today radical Islamists are the last holdout against these powerful forces of globalization and modernization. They seek to carve out a part of the world in which they can be left alone, shielded from what they regard as the soul-destroying licentiousness of unchecked liberalism and capitalism. The tragedy is that their goal is impossible to achieve. Neither the United States nor the other great powers will turn over control of the Middle East to these fundamentalist forces, if only because the region is of such vital strategic importance to the rest of the world. The outside powers have strong internal allies, as well, including the majority of the populations of the Middle East who have been willing and even eager to make peace with modernity. Nor is it conceivable in this modern world that a people can wall themselves off from modernity, even if the majority wanted to. Could the great Islamic theocracy that al Qaeda and others hope to erect ever completely block out the sights and sounds of the rest of the world, and thereby shield its people from the temptations of modernity? The mullahs have not even succeeded at doing that in Iran. The project is fantastic.

The world is thus faced with the prospect of a protracted struggle in which the goals of the extreme Islamists can never be satisfied because neither the United States nor anyone else has the ability to give them what they want. The West is quite simply not capable of retreating as far as the Islamic extremists require. . . .

NOTES

1. Rosalie Chen, "China Perceives America: Perspectives of International Relations Experts," *Journal of Contemporary China* 12, no. 35 (2003).
2. This is what William Wohlforth predicted almost a decade ago. See William C. Wohlforth, "The Stability of a Unipolar World," *International Security* 24, no. 1 (Summer 1999).
3. Hans J. Morgenthau, "The Mainsprings of American Foreign Policy: The National Interest vs. Moral Abstractions," *The American Political Science Review* 44, no. 4 (December 1950): 838.

A Demographic Map
of Our Geopolitical Future

RICHARD JACKSON AND NEIL HOWE

This [article] is about the geopolitical implications of "global aging"—the dramatic transformation in population age structures and growth rates being brought about by falling fertility and rising longevity worldwide. Its viewpoint is that of the United States in particular and of today's developed countries in general. Its timeframe is roughly the next half-century, from today through 2050. . . .

THE DEMOGRAPHIC TRANSFORMATION

■ *The world is entering a demographic transformation of unprecedented dimensions.*

Global aging is not a transitory wave like the baby *boom* that many affluent countries experienced in the 1950s or the baby *bust* that they experienced in the 1930s. It is, instead, a fundamental demographic shift with no parallel in the history of humanity. "When this revolution has run its course," observe aging experts Alan Pifer and Lydia Bronte, "the impact will have been at least as powerful as that of any of the great economic and social movements of the past."[1]

Consider median age. Until the beginning of the twentieth century, a national median age higher than 30 was practically unheard of. As recently as 1950, no nation in the world had a median age higher than 36. Today, 8 of the 16 nations of Western Europe have a median age of 40 or higher. By 2050, 6 will have a median age of 50 or higher. So will Japan, the East Asian Tigers, and 17 of the 24 nations in Eastern Europe and the Russian sphere. (See Figure 1.) Or consider population growth. Throughout history, populations have usually behaved in one of two ways. They have grown steadily, or they have declined fitfully due to disease, starvation, or violence. In the coming decades, we will see something entirely new: large, low-birthrate populations that steadily contract. There are already 18 countries in the

From Richard Jackson and Neil Howe, "A Demographic Map of Our Geopolitical Future" from *The Graying of the Great Powers: Demography and Geopolitics in the 21st Century*. Washington, DC: Center for Strategic and International Studies, 2008, pp. 185–196. Reprinted by permission of the Center for Strategic and International Studies. Portions of the text and some footnotes have been omitted.

Taiwan	56.3	Hong Kong, SAR	54.0	Armenia	52.3
Japan	56.2	Ukraine	54.0	Croatia	52.1
Bulgaria	55.9	Romania	53.9	Cuba	52.0
South Korea	55.5	Slovakia	53.9	Germany	51.8
Slovenia	55.3	Latvia	53.8	Belarus	51.7
Czech Republic	55.0	Italy	53.5	Hungary	51.2
Poland	54.4	Greece	53.3	Portugal	51.1
Singapore	54.3	Lithuania	52.8	Austria	50.9
Spain	54.2	Bosnia and Herzegovina	52.7	Georgia	50.2

FIGURE 1 ■ Countries Whose Median Age Is Projected to Be 50 or Over in 2050*

Source: World Population Prospects (UN, 2007); and Population Projections for Taiwan Area, 2006–2051, Council for Economic Planning and Development, Taiwan, www.cepd.gov.tw/encontent/. For demographic scenario, see The Graying of the Great Powers, appendix 1, section 3.

*Note: *Excludes countries with populations of less than 1 million.*

world with contracting populations. By 2050 there will be 44, the vast majority of them in Europe. (See Figure 2.) As historian Niall Ferguson has written, we are about to witness "the greatest sustained reduction in European population since the Black Death of the fourteenth century."[2]

> ■ *The coming transformation is both certain and lasting. There is almost no chance that it will not happen—or that it will be reversed in our lifetime.*

Alreading Declining		Decline Beginning 2009–2029		Decline Beginning 2030–2050	
Hungary	(1981)	Italy	(2010)	Azerbaijan	(2030)
Bulgaria	(1986)	Slovakia	(2011)	Denmark	(2031)
Estonia	(1990)	Bosnia and	(2011)	Belgium	(2031)
Georgia	(1990)	Herzegovina		Thailand	(2033)
Latvia	(1990)	Greece	(2014)	North Korea	(2035)
Armenia	(1991)	Serbia	(2014)	Singapore	(2035)
Romania	(1991)	Portugal	(2016)	Netherlands	(2037)
Lithuania	(1992)	Cuba	(2018)	Switzerland	(2040)
Ukraine	(1992)	Macedonia	(2018)	UK	(2044)
Moldova	(1993)	Spain	(2019)	Hong Kong, SAR	(2044)
Belarus	(1994)	Taiwan	(2019)	Puerto Rico	(2044)
Russian Federation	(1994)	South Korea	(2020)	Kazakhstan	(2045)
Czech Republic	(1995)	Austria	(2024)		
Poland	(1997)	Finland	(2027)		
Germany	(2006)	China	(2029)		
Japan	(2008)				
Croatia	(2008)				
Slovenia	(2008)				

FIGURE 2 ■ Countries Projected to Have Declining Populations, by Period of the Decline's Onset*

Source: See Figure 1.

*Note: *Excludes countries with populations of less than 1 million.*

The public may suppose that population projections 50 years into the future are highly speculative. But in fact, demographic aging is about as close as social science ever comes to a certain forecast. Every demographer agrees that it is happening and that, absent a global catastrophe—a colliding comet or a deadly super virus—it will continue to gather momentum.

The reason is simple: Anyone over the age of 45 in the year 2050 has already been born and can therefore be counted. And though the number of younger people cannot be projected as precisely, few demographers believe that low fertility rates in the developed world will recover any time soon. Even if they do experience a strong and lasting rebound, the declining share of young (childbearing-age) adults in the population will delay the positive impact on age structure and population growth. Because of demographic momentum, population growth takes a long time to slow down. Once stopped, it also takes a long time to speed up again.

- *The transformation will affect different groups of countries at different times. The regions of the world will become more unalike before they become more alike.*

As the term global aging correctly implies, nearly every country in the world is projected to experience some shift toward slower population growth and an older age structure. This does not mean, however, that the world is demographically converging. Most of today's youngest countries (such as those in sub-Saharan Africa) are projected to experience the least aging. Most of today's oldest countries (such as those in Europe) are projected to experience the most aging. As a result, the world will see an increasing divergence, or "spread," of demographic outcomes over the foreseeable future. . . .

- *In the developed world, the transformation will have sweeping economic, social, and political consequences that could undermine the ability of the United States and its traditional allies to maintain security. The consequences can be divided into three main types:*

Changes in Demographic Size. The growth rates of the service-age population, of the working-age population, and (therefore) of the GDP in the typical developed country will all fall far beneath their historical trend and also beneath growth rates in most of the rest of the world. In many developed countries, workforces will actually shrink from one decade to the next—and GDPs may stagnate or even decline.

Changes in Economic Performance. As populations age and economic growth slows, employees may become less adaptable and mobile, innovation and entrepreneurship may decline, rates of savings and investment may fall, public-sector deficits may rise, and current account balances may turn negative. All of this threatens to impair economic performance.

Changes in Social Mood. Psychologically, older societies will become more conservative in outlook and possibly more risk-averse in electoral and leadership behavior. Elder domination of electorates will tend to lock in current public spending commitments at the expense of new priorities. Smaller family size may make the public less willing to risk scarce youth in war. Meanwhile, the rapid growth in minority populations, due to ongoing immigration and higher-than-average minority fertility, may undermine civic cohesion and foster a new diaspora politics.

■ *In the developing world, the transformation will have more varied consequences—propelling some countries toward greater prosperity and stability, while giving rise to dangerous new security threats in others.*

At the opportunity end of the spectrum, some developing countries will learn to translate the "demographic dividend" created by their declining fertility into higher savings rates, greater human capital development, efficient and open markets, rising incomes and living standards, and stable democratic institutions. Some will follow the meteoric success path of a South Korea or Taiwan, others the slower-but-still-steady success path of an India or Malaysia.

A larger share of the developing world, unfortunately, stands nearer to the challenge end. There are the countries (most notably, in sub-Saharan Africa) least touched by global aging, whose large youth bulges, high poverty rates, weak governments, and chronic civil unrest offer the least prospect of success. There are the countries (most notably, in the Muslim world) where population growth is declining and substantial economic growth is more likely—but where terrorism and destructive revolutions and wars are also more likely. And then there are the countries whose demographic transformation will be so extreme (Russia) or is arriving so rapidly (China) that it could trigger an economic and political crisis. Russia, Ukraine, and the other Christian countries of the Commonwealth of Independent States (CIS), afflicted both by very low fertility and declining life expectancy, are projected to lose an astonishing one-third of their population by 2050. China, having suddenly adopted a one-child policy in the 1970s, will face a developed country's level of old-age dependency with only a developing country's income.

THE GEOPOLITICAL IMPLICATIONS

■ *The population and GDP of the developed world will shrink steadily as a share of the world totals. In tandem, the global influence of the developed world will likely decline.*

During the era of the Industrial Revolution and Western imperial expansion, the population of what we now call the developed world grew faster than the rest of the world's population. From 17 percent in 1820, its share of the world's population rose steadily, peaking at 25 percent in 1930. Since then, its share has declined. By 2005, it stood at just 13 percent—and it is projected to decline still further in the future to below 10 percent by 2050. As a share of the world's economy, the collective GDP of the developed countries will similarly shrink, from 54 percent in 2005 (in purchasing power parity dollars) to 31 percent by 2050.

Driving this decline will be not just the slower growth of the developed world, but also the surging expansion of such large, newly market-oriented economies as China, India, and Brazil. . . .

■ *The population and GDP of the United States will expand steadily as a share of the developed-world totals. In tandem, the influence of the United States within the developed world will likely rise.*

Over the last two centuries, the U.S. share of the developed world's population has risen almost continuously, from a mere 6 percent in 1820 to 34 percent today. With its higher rates of fertility and immigration, the U.S. share will continue to grow in the future—to 43 percent by 2050. By then, 58 percent of the developed world's population will live in English-speaking countries, up from 42 percent in 1950. The relative U.S. economic position will improve even more dramatically. As recently as the early 1980s, the GDPs of Western Europe and the United States (again, in purchasing power parity dollars) were about the same, each at 37 percent of total developed-world GDP. By 2050, the U.S. share will rise to 54 percent and the Western European share will shrink to 23 percent. The Japanese share will meanwhile decline from 14 percent to 8 percent. By the middle of the twenty-first century, the dominant strength of the U.S. economy in the developed world will have only one historical parallel: the immediate aftermath of World War II, exactly 100 years earlier at the birth of the "Pax Americana."

Implications: Many of today's multilateral theorists look forward to a global order in which the U.S. influence diminishes. In fact, any reasonable demographic projection points to a growing U.S. dominance among the developed nations that preside over this global order. . . .

■ *Most nations in sub-Saharan Africa and some nations in the Muslim world will possess large ongoing youth bulges that could render them chronically unstable until at least the 2030s.*

Political demographers generally define a youth bulge as the ratio of youth aged 15 to 24 to all adults aged 15 and over. As the youth bulge rises, so does the likelihood of civil unrest, revolution, and war. In today's sub-Saharan Africa, burdened by the world's highest fertility rates and ravaged by AIDS (which decimates the ranks of older adults), the *average* youth bulge is 36 percent. Several Muslim-majority nations (both Arab and non-Arab) have youth bulges of similar size. These include Afghanistan, Iraq, the Palestinian Territories, Somalia, Sudan, and Yemen. In recent years, most of these nations have amply demonstrated the correlation between extreme youth and violence. If the correlation endures, chronic unrest could persist in much of sub-Saharan Africa and parts of the Muslim world through the 2030s—or even longer if fertility rates do not fall as quickly as projected.

Implications: While many of these nations will likely remain "trouble spots" for decades to come, most of the trouble will not have geopolitical repercussions—

12 LARGEST COUNTRIES RANKED BY POPULATION SIZE*

Ranking	1950	2005	2050
1	China	China	India
2	India	India	China
3	*United States*	*United States*	*United States*
4	Russian Federation	Indonesia	Indonesia
5	*Japan*	Brazil	Pakistan
6	Indonesia	Pakistan	Nigeria
7	*Germany*	Bangladesh	Bangladesh
8	Brazil	Russian Federation	Brazil
9	*UK*	Nigeria	Ethiopia
10	*Italy*	*Japan*	Dem. Rep. Congo
11	Bangladesh	Mexico	Philippines
12	*France*	Viet Nam	Mexico
		(14) *Germany*	(18) *Japan*
	(20) *France*	(26) *Germany*	
	(21) *UK*	(27) *France*	
	(23) *Italy*	(32) *UK*	
		(39) *Italy*	

*Developed countries are in boldface; future rankings for developed countries projected to fall beneath 12th place are indicated in parentheses.
Source: *World Population Prospects* (UN, 2007). For demographic scenario, see *The Graying of the Great Powers*, appendix 1, section 3.

except when it involves terrorism or interferes with the flow of important natural resources. . . .

- *Many nations in North Africa, the Middle East, South and East Asia, and the former Soviet bloc—including China, Russia, Iran, and Pakistan—are now experiencing rapid or extreme demographic change that could push them either toward civil collapse or (in reaction) neo-authoritarianism.*

Some of these nations have buoyantly growing economies, while others do not. Some have a recent history of political upheaval, while others do not. Yet all are rapidly modernizing—and all are encountering mounting social stress from some combination of globalization, urbanization, rising inequality, family breakdown, environmental degradation, ethnic conflict, and religious radicalism. China faces the extra challenge of handling a vast tide of elder dependents come the 2020s, when it will just be becoming a middle-income country. Russia must cope with a rate of population decline that has no historical precedent in the absence of pandemic. Any of these nations could, at some point, suffer upheaval and collapse—with serious regional (and perhaps even global) repercussions. In response to the threat of disorder, many will be tempted to opt for neo-authoritarian regimes (following the current lead of China or Russia).

Implications: Although these fast-transitioning countries may experience less chronic violence than the large youth-bulge countries, the crises they do experience will tend to be more serious. Their economies are more productive, their governments are better financed, their militaries are better armed, and their rival factions are better organized. . . .

- *The threat of ethnic and religious conflict will continue to be a growing security challenge both in the developing and developed worlds.*

Over the last 20 years, ethnic conflict in the developing countries has been on the rise. The causes include widening population growth differentials between higher- and lower-fertility ethnic groups; the reemergence of ethnic loyalties suppressed during the Cold War; the rise of electoral democracies that enable ethnic groups to vie against each other at the ballot box; and globalization, which may also provoke ethnic resentment by enriching some groups at the expense of others. Meanwhile, in many developed countries, ethnic tensions are being inflamed by the rapid growth of immigrant minorities as a share of the population. All of these trends can be expected to continue in the decades to come. Religious conflict is also likely to intensify due to the following fact: Fully nine-tenths of the world's population growth between now and 2050 is projected to occur in exactly those regions—sub-Saharan Africa, the Arab world, non-Arab Muslim Asia, and South Asia—where religious conflict (between and among Muslims, Christians, Jews, and Hindus) is already a serious problem. Within those regions, moreover, the disproportionate fertility of devout families will ensure that younger generations will be, if anything, more committed to their faiths. . . .

- *Throughout the world, the 2020s will likely emerge as a decade of maximum geopolitical danger.*

In the developed world, the 2020s is the decade in which global aging will hit the hardest. Workforces will practically stop growing everywhere except the United States—and will begin to shrink rapidly in much of Western Europe and Japan—with potentially serious economic consequences. The ratio of elderly to working-age adults will surge, with especially large jumps in countries (like the United States) that had large postwar baby booms. Some governments may experience a fiscal crisis. Meanwhile, in the developing world, new demographic stresses will appear. Many Muslim-majority countries (both Arab and non-Arab) along with some Latin American countries will experience a temporary resurgence in the number of young people in the 2020s. This youth echo boom (a 30-percent jump in the number of 15- to 24-year-olds in Iran over just 10 years) may rock regimes. The countries of the Russian sphere and Eastern Europe will enter their decade of fastest workforce decline, even as China, by 2025, finally surpasses the United States in total GDP (in purchasing power parity dollars). Yet China will face its own aging challenge by the 2020s, when its last large generation, born in the 1960s, begins to retire. . . .

■ *The aging developed countries will face chronic shortages of young-adult manpower—posing challenges both for their economies and their security forces.*

As the developed world ages, domestic youth shortages will create powerful economic incentives to encourage immigration and trade and to expand all types of offshoring. Political opposition from aging workforces and older electorates is certain. With the number of service-age youth flat or declining in most countries (especially in the rural subcultures that have traditionally supplied recruits), militaries will be hard-pressed to maintain force levels—especially if smaller families are less willing to put their children at risk in war. Militaries will need to resort to creative expedients. They will outsource all non-vital functions. They will try substituting high-tech capital, such as robotics and unmanned craft, for labor. They may offer citizenship for service, directly hire overseas combatants (in effect, mercenaries), or enter "service alliances" with friendly developing countries.

Implications: Many developed countries will be tempted to abandon military forces altogether, especially forces capable of large-scale combat, which will render them permanent free riders on their allies. Countries retaining major forces, the United States foremost among them, will need to carefully weigh the potential benefits of labor-intensive security missions (such as occupation, nation building, and counterinsurgency) against the high costs. Informal burden-sharing may give way to a more formal assessment of global levies—or to alliance-shattering declarations of neutrality.

■ *An aging developed world may struggle to remain culturally attractive and politically relevant to younger societies.*

Today's liberal and democratic global order owes its durability not only to the developed countries' capacity to defend it against aggressors, but more importantly to the positive global reputation of the developed countries themselves. Their mores and institutions embody this order. This is sometimes called the "soft power" of liberal democracy, and it has widespread support both as a way of life and as a force in global affairs. All of this may change if, as the developed countries age, they are no longer regarded as progressive advocates for the future of all peoples, but rather as mere elder defenders of their own privileged hegemony. . . .

NOTES

1. Alan Pifer and Lydia Bronte, "Introduction: Squaring the Pyramid," in *Our Aging Society: Paradox and Promise,* eds. Alan Pifer and Lydia Bronte (New York, W.W. Norton, 1986), 3.
2. Niall Ferguson, "Eurabia?" *The New York Times Magazine,* April 4, 2004.

Exercises for Future Developments

Apply what you learned in this chapter by using the online resources on MyPoliSciKit (www.mypoliscikit.com).

   Practice Tests

   Video: "The Zapatista Rebellion"

   Simulation: "Integration: You Are a Citizen of Europe"

Reading Guides:
- The U.S. National Intelligence Council, "The World in 2025"
- Barry Posen, "Emerging Multipolarity"
- Robert Kagan, "The Return of History"
- Richard Jackson and Neil Howe, "A Demographic Map of Our Geopolitical Future"